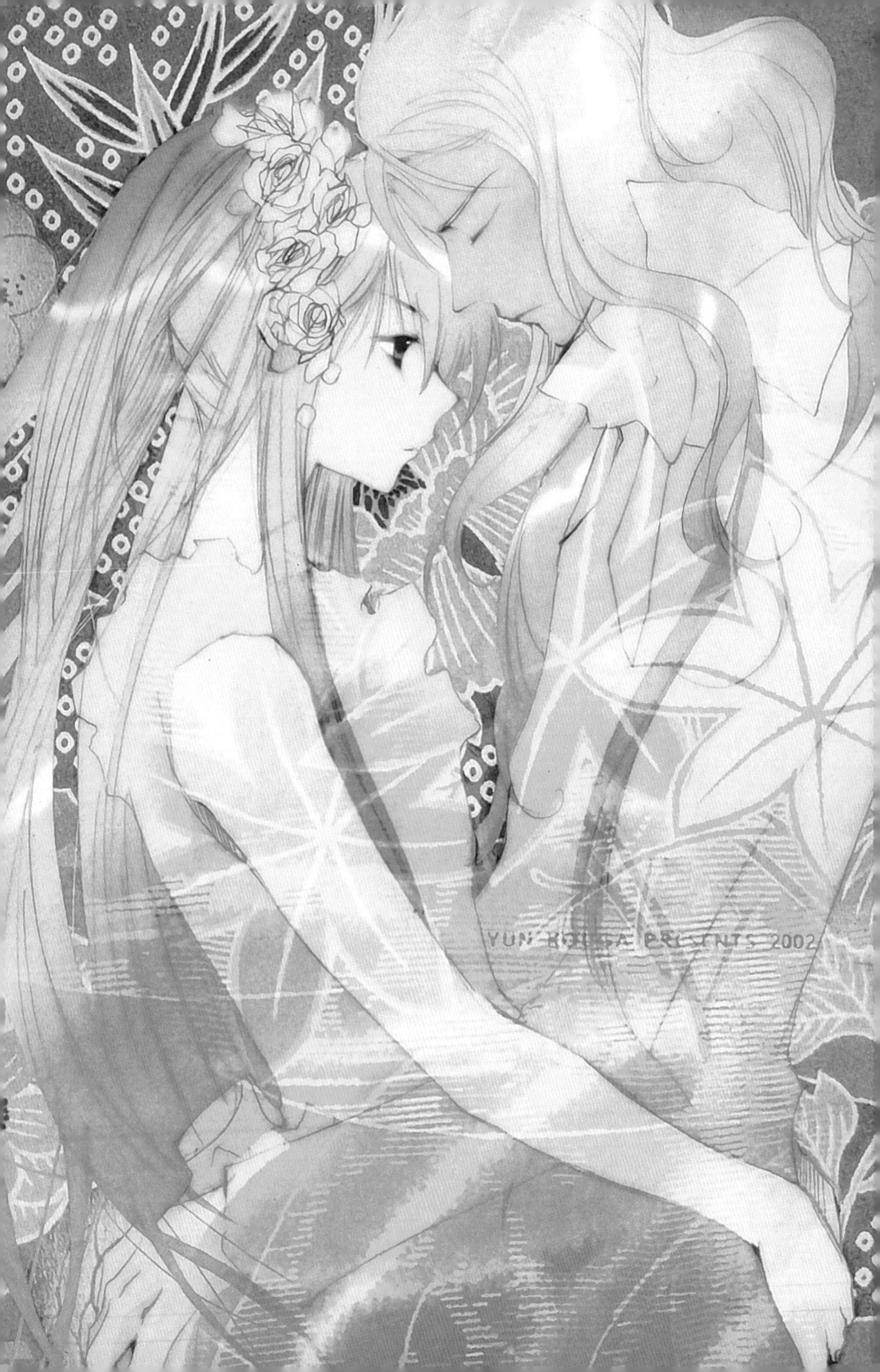
YUN KOUGA PRESENTS 2002

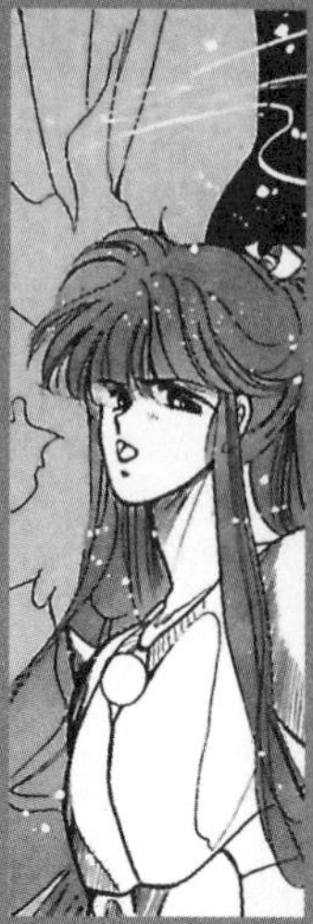

EARTHIAN

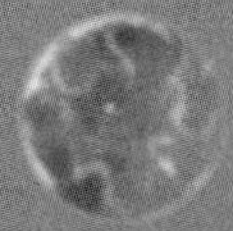

CONTENTS

E A R T H I A N

YUN KOUGA

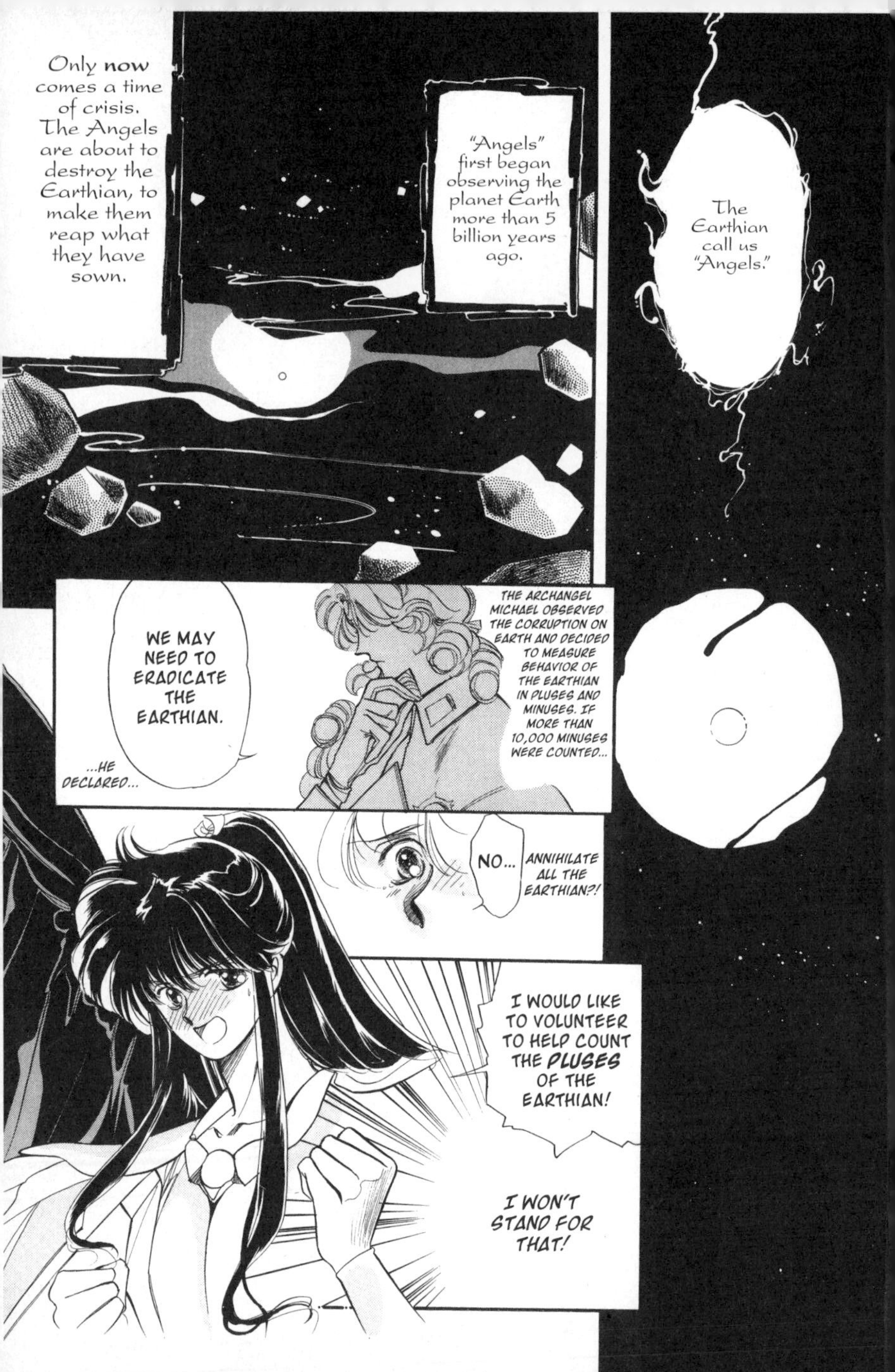

The Earthian call us "Angels."
"Angels" first began observing the planet Earth more than 5 billion years ago.
Only **now** comes a time of crisis. The Angels are about to destroy the Earthian, to make them reap what they have sown.
THE ARCHANGEL MICHAEL OBSERVED THE CORRUPTION ON EARTH AND DECIDED TO MEASURE BEHAVIOR OF THE EARTHIAN IN PLUSES AND MINUSES. IF MORE THAN 10,000 MINUSES WERE COUNTED...
WE MAY NEED TO ERADICATE THE EARTHIAN.
...HE DECLARED...
NO...
ANNIHILATE ALL THE EARTHIAN?!
I WOULD LIKE TO VOLUNTEER TO HELP COUNT THE *PLUSES* OF THE EARTHIAN!
I WON'T STAND FOR THAT!

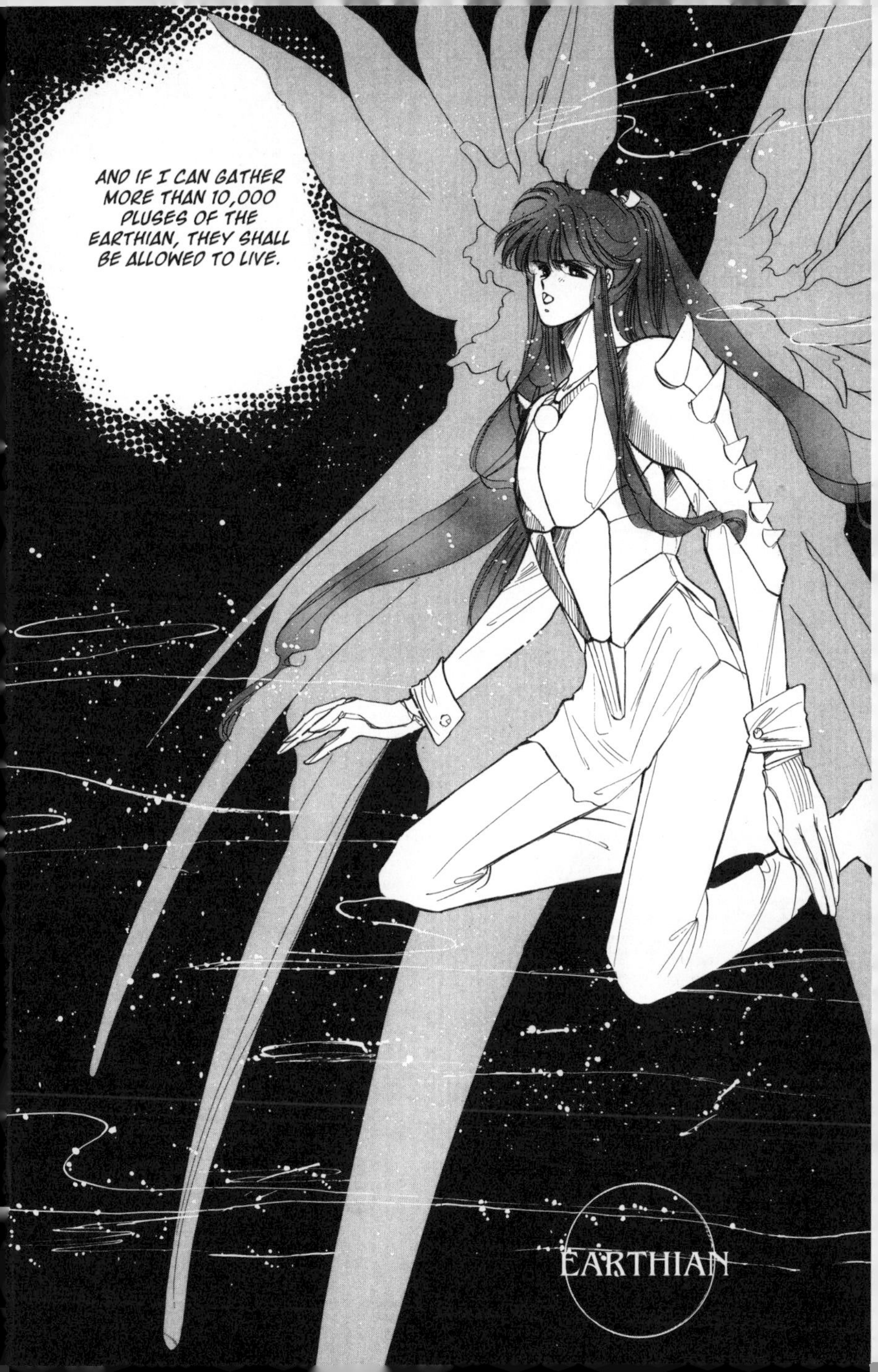
AND IF I CAN GATHER MORE THAN 10,000 PLUSES OF THE EARTHIAN, THEY SHALL BE ALLOWED TO LIVE.
EARTHIAN

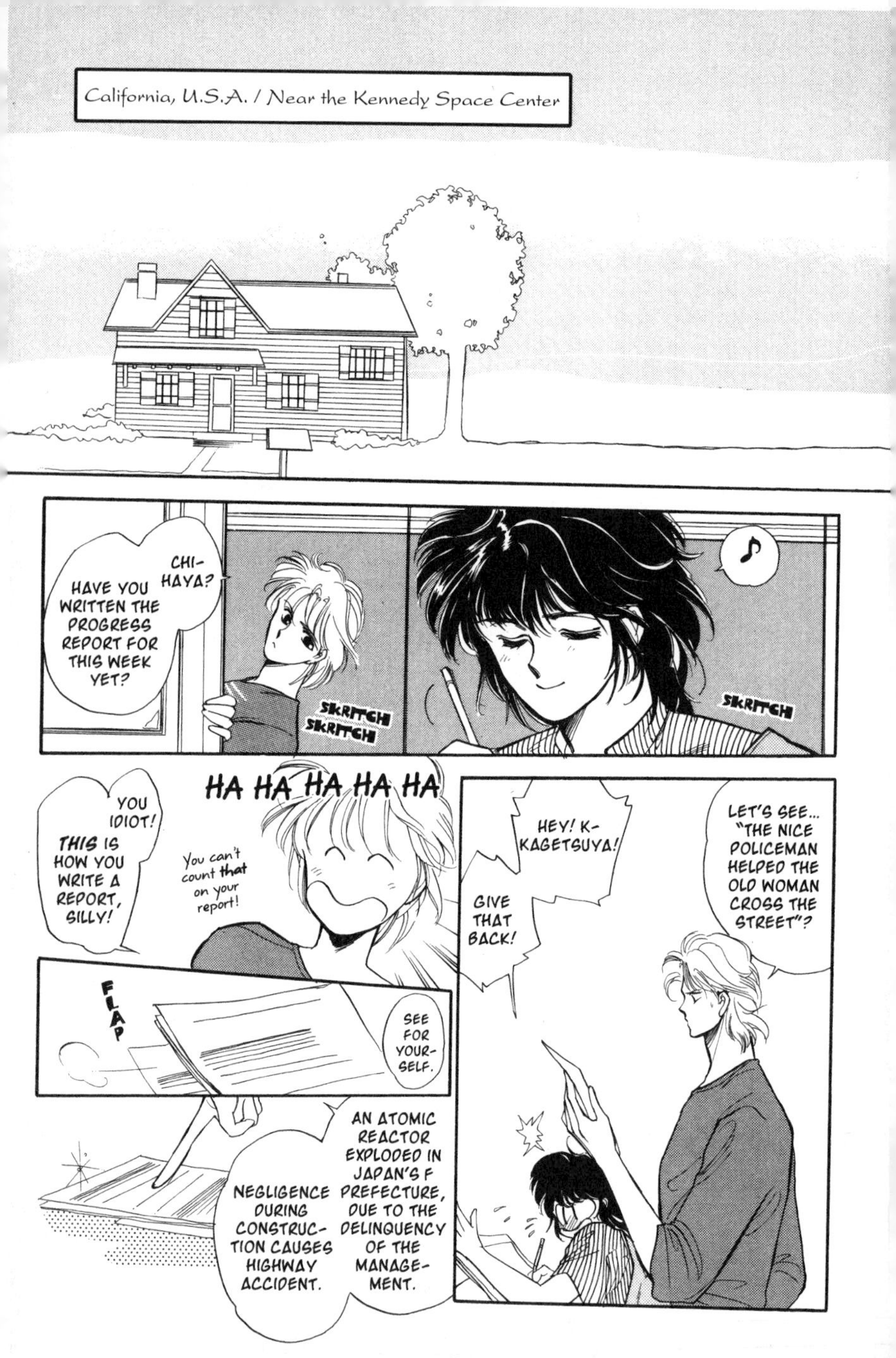
California, U.S.A. / Near the Kennedy Space Center
♪
SKRITCH
CHI-HAYA?
HAVE YOU WRITTEN THE PROGRESS REPORT FOR THIS WEEK YET?
SKRITCH SKRITCH
LET'S SEE... "THE NICE POLICEMAN HELPED THE OLD WOMAN CROSS THE STREET"?
HEY! K-KAGETSUYA!
GIVE THAT BACK!
HA HA HA HA HA
YOU IDIOT! THIS IS HOW YOU WRITE A REPORT, SILLY!
You can't count that on your report!
SEE FOR YOUR-SELF.
FLAP
AN ATOMIC REACTOR EXPLODED IN JAPAN'S F PREFECTURE, DUE TO THE DELINQUENCY OF THE MANAGE-MENT.
NEGLIGENCE DURING CONSTRUC-TION CAUSES HIGHWAY ACCIDENT.

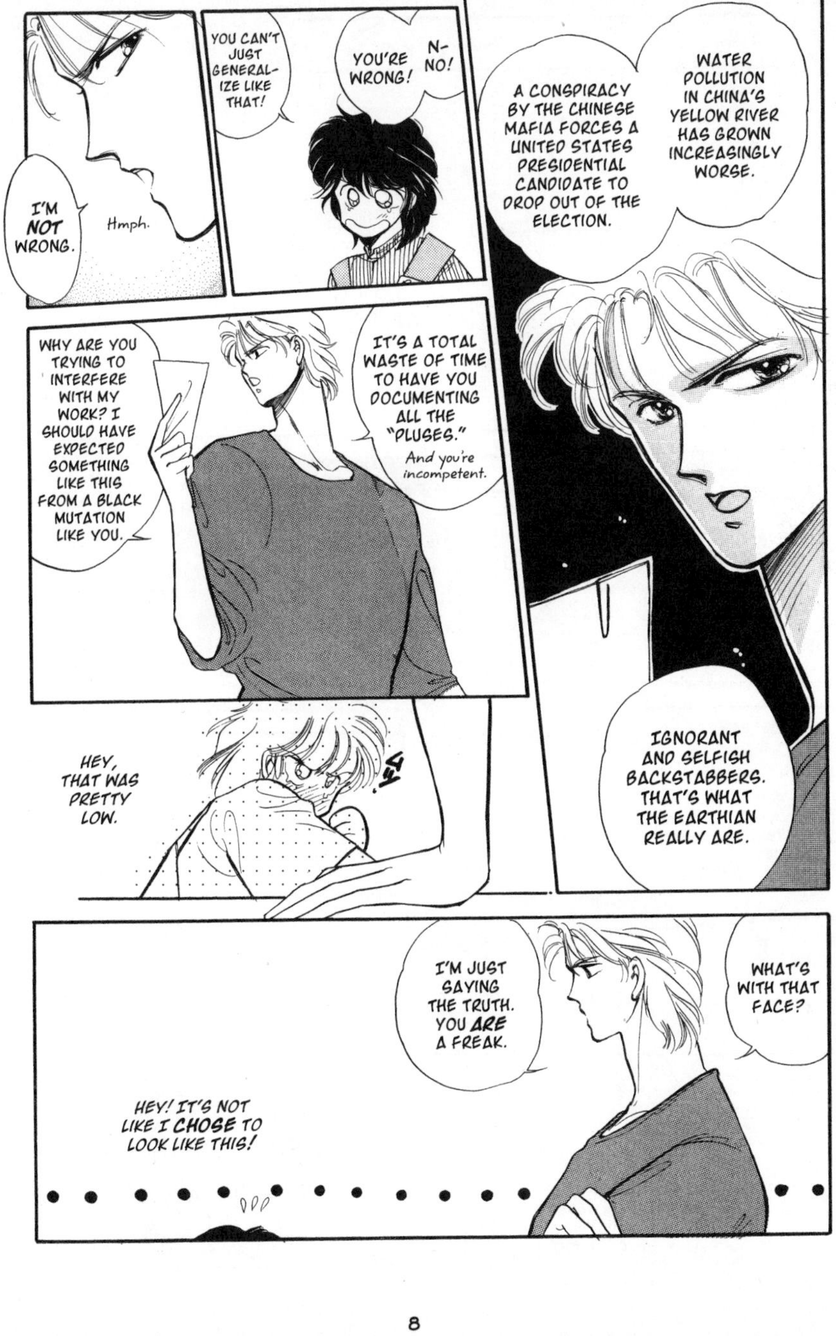
WATER POLLUTION IN CHINA'S YELLOW RIVER HAS GROWN INCREASINGLY WORSE.
A CONSPIRACY BY THE CHINESE MAFIA FORCES A UNITED STATES PRESIDENTIAL CANDIDATE TO DROP OUT OF THE ELECTION.
IGNORANT AND SELFISH BACKSTABBERS. THAT'S WHAT THE EARTHIAN REALLY ARE.
N-NO!
YOU'RE WRONG!
YOU CAN'T JUST GENERAL-IZE LIKE THAT!
Hmph.
I'M **NOT** WRONG.
IT'S A TOTAL WASTE OF TIME TO HAVE YOU DOCUMENTING ALL THE "PLUSES."
And you're incompetent.
WHY ARE YOU TRYING TO INTERFERE WITH MY WORK? I SHOULD HAVE EXPECTED SOMETHING LIKE THIS FROM A BLACK MUTATION LIKE YOU.
HEY, THAT WAS PRETTY LOW.
WHAT'S WITH THAT FACE?
I'M JUST SAYING THE TRUTH. YOU **ARE** A FREAK.
HEY! IT'S NOT LIKE I **CHOSE** TO LOOK LIKE THIS!

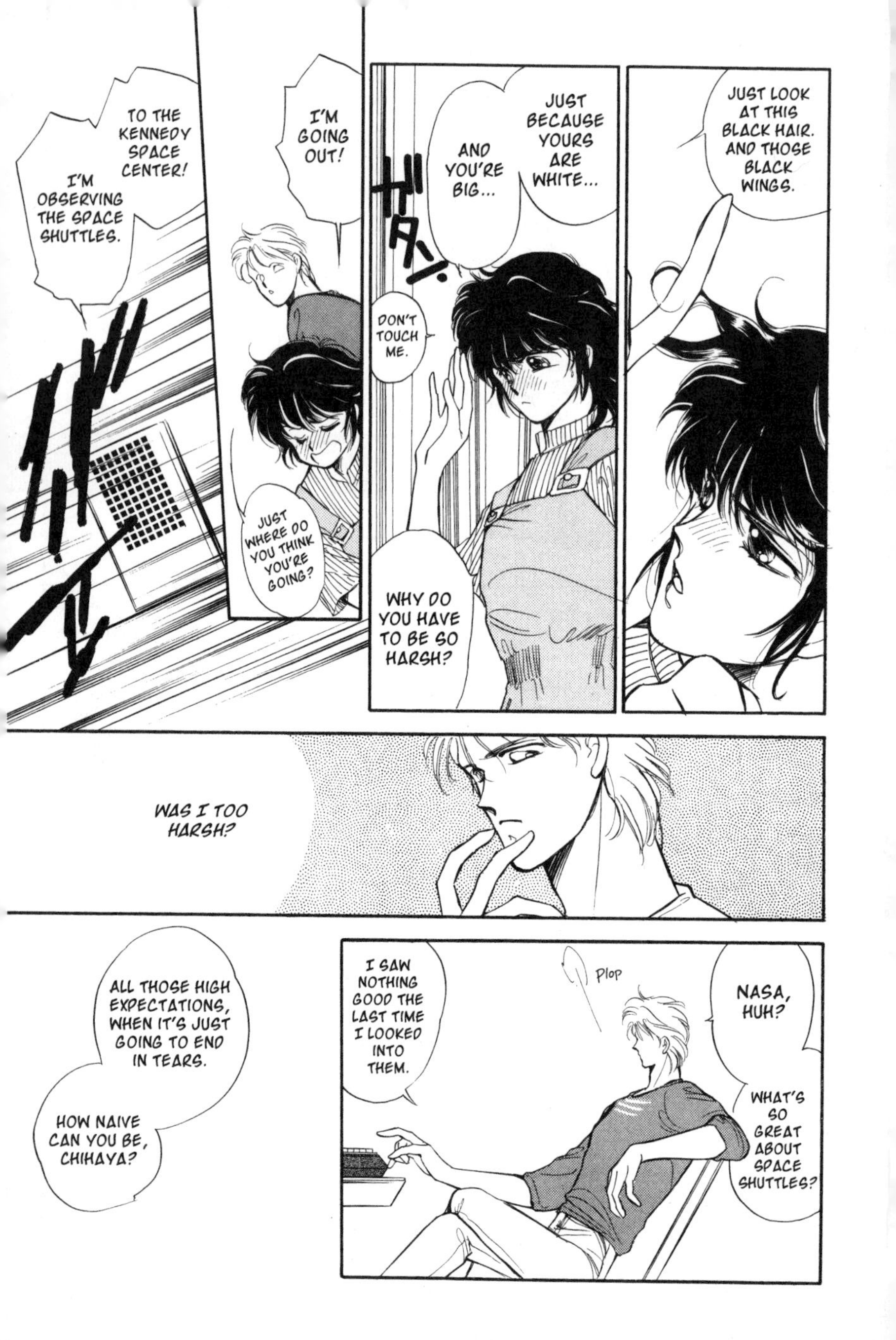
JUST LOOK AT THIS BLACK HAIR. AND THOSE BLACK WINGS.
JUST BECAUSE YOURS ARE WHITE...
AND YOU'RE BIG...
DON'T TOUCH ME.
WHY DO YOU HAVE TO BE SO HARSH?
I'M GOING OUT!
JUST WHERE DO YOU THINK YOU'RE GOING?
TO THE KENNEDY SPACE CENTER!
I'M OBSERVING THE SPACE SHUTTLES.
WAS I TOO HARSH?
NASA, HUH?
Plop
I SAW NOTHING GOOD THE LAST TIME I LOOKED INTO THEM.
WHAT'S SO GREAT ABOUT SPACE SHUTTLES?
ALL THOSE HIGH EXPECTATIONS, WHEN IT'S JUST GOING TO END IN TEARS.
HOW NAIVE CAN YOU BE, CHIHAYA?

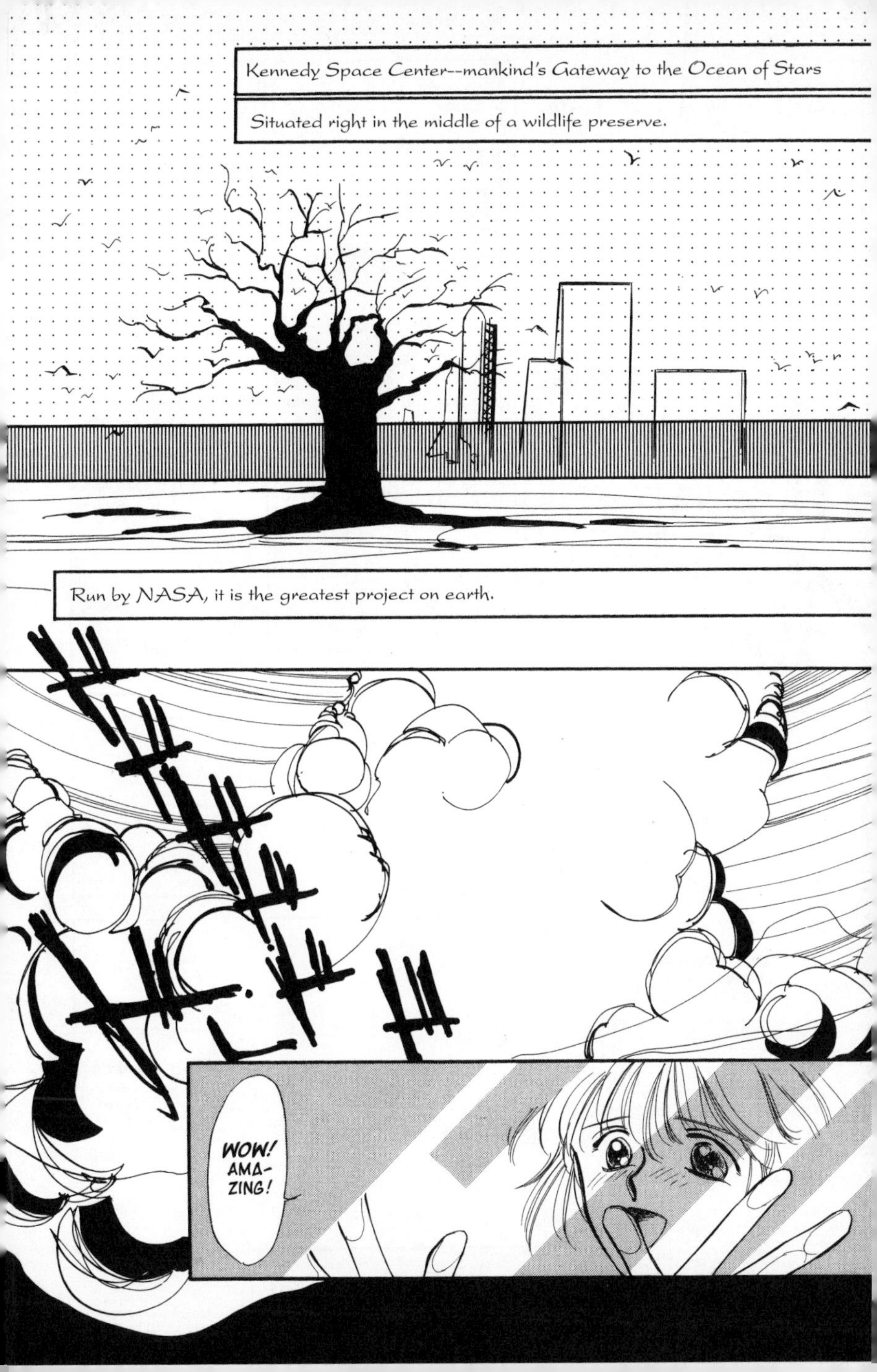
Kennedy Space Center--mankind's Gateway to the Ocean of Stars
Situated right in the middle of a wildlife preserve.
Run by NASA, it is the greatest project on earth.
WOW! AMA-ZING!

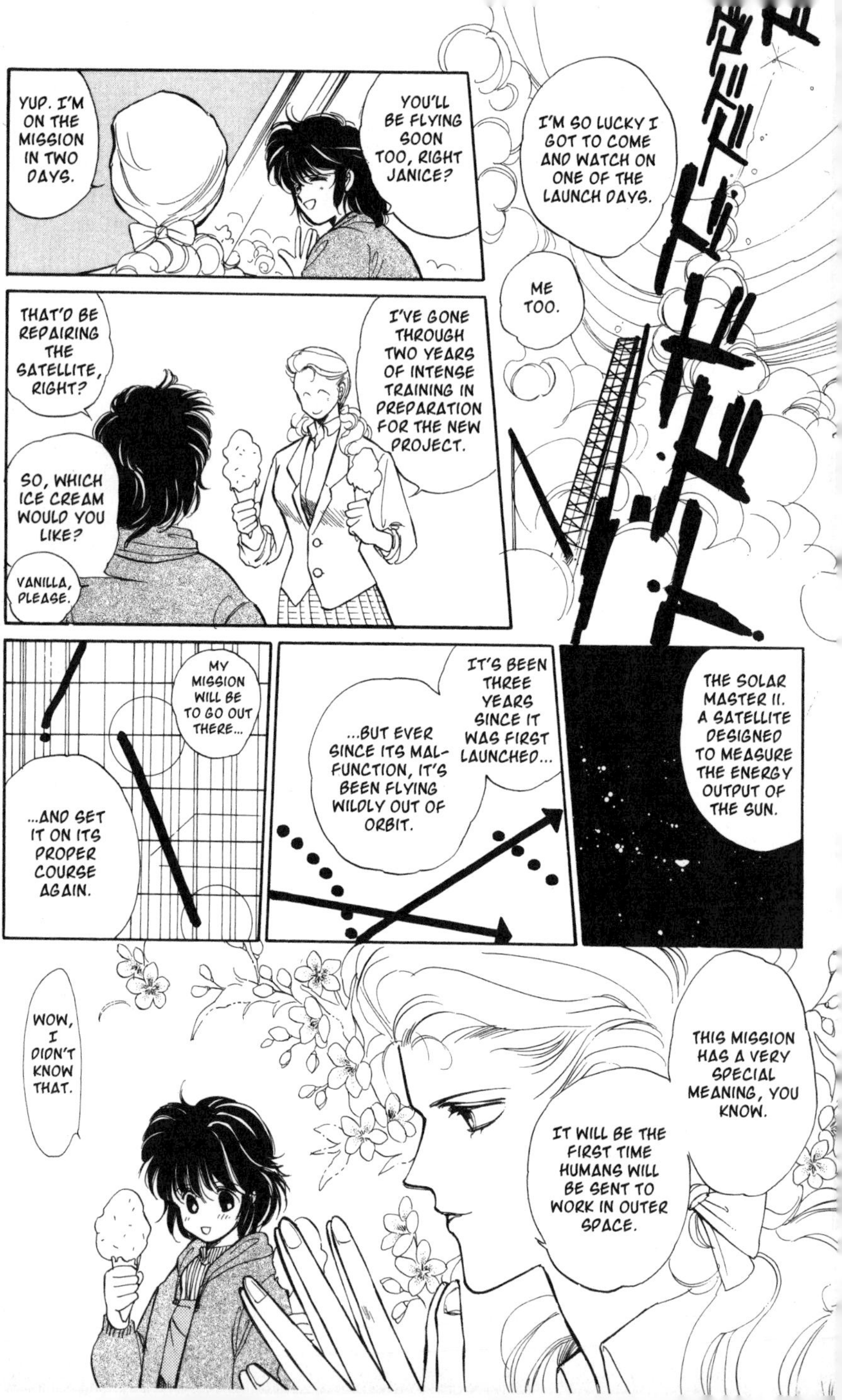

I'M SO LUCKY I GOT TO COME AND WATCH ON ONE OF THE LAUNCH DAYS.
ME TOO.
YOU'LL BE FLYING SOON TOO, RIGHT JANICE?
YUP. I'M ON THE MISSION IN TWO DAYS.
I'VE GONE THROUGH TWO YEARS OF INTENSE TRAINING IN PREPARATION FOR THE NEW PROJECT.
THAT'D BE REPAIRING THE SATELLITE, RIGHT?
SO, WHICH ICE CREAM WOULD YOU LIKE?
VANILLA, PLEASE.
THE SOLAR MASTER II. A SATELLITE DESIGNED TO MEASURE THE ENERGY OUTPUT OF THE SUN.
IT'S BEEN THREE YEARS SINCE IT WAS FIRST LAUNCHED...
...BUT EVER SINCE ITS MAL-FUNCTION, IT'S BEEN FLYING WILDLY OUT OF ORBIT.
MY MISSION WILL BE TO GO OUT THERE...
...AND SET IT ON ITS PROPER COURSE AGAIN.
THIS MISSION HAS A VERY SPECIAL MEANING, YOU KNOW.
IT WILL BE THE FIRST TIME HUMANS WILL BE SENT TO WORK IN OUTER SPACE.
WOW, I DIDN'T KNOW THAT.

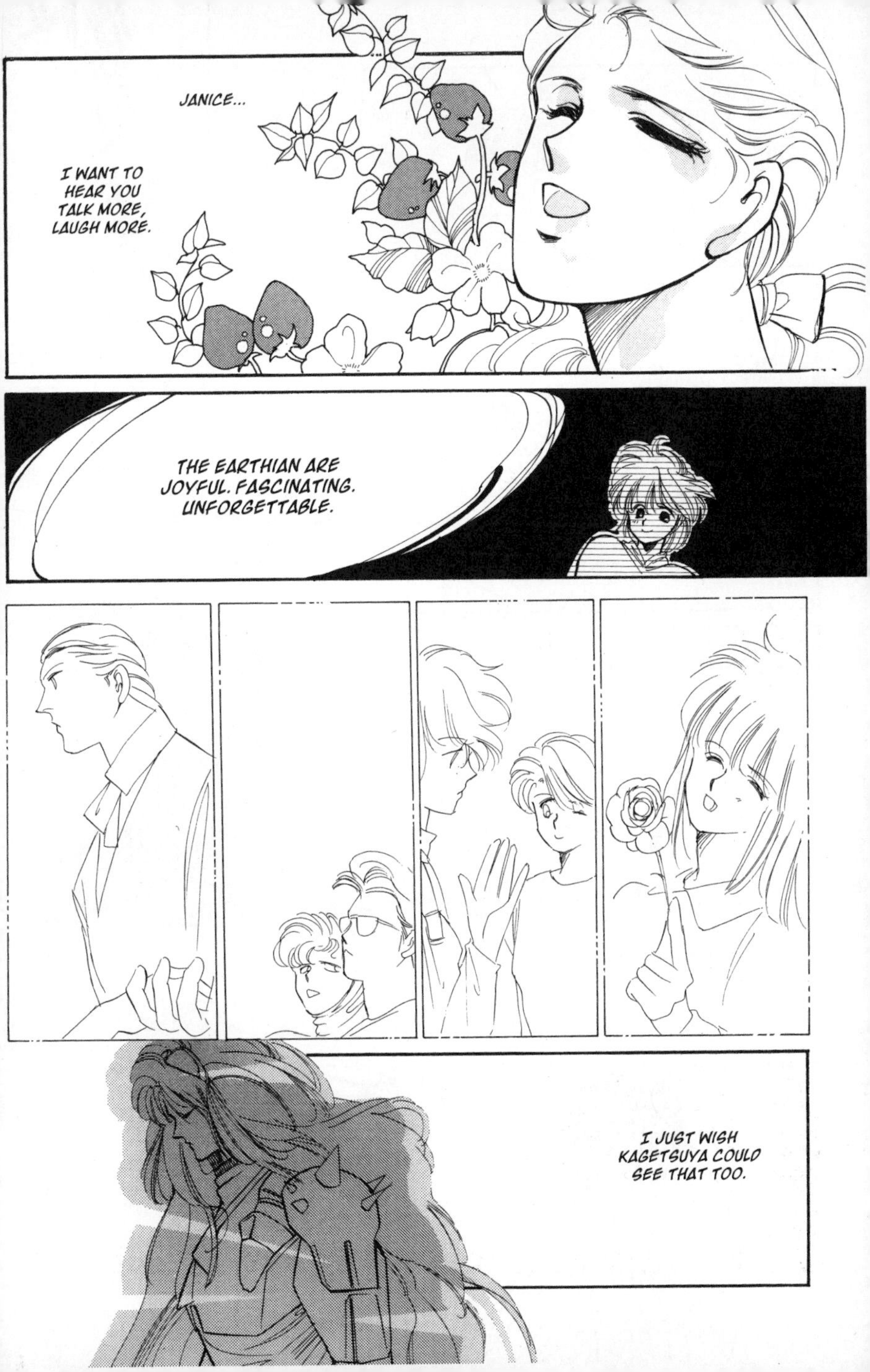
JANICE...
I WANT TO HEAR YOU TALK MORE, LAUGH MORE.
THE EARTHIAN ARE JOYFUL. FASCINATING. UNFORGETTABLE.
I JUST WISH KAGETSUYA COULD SEE THAT TOO.

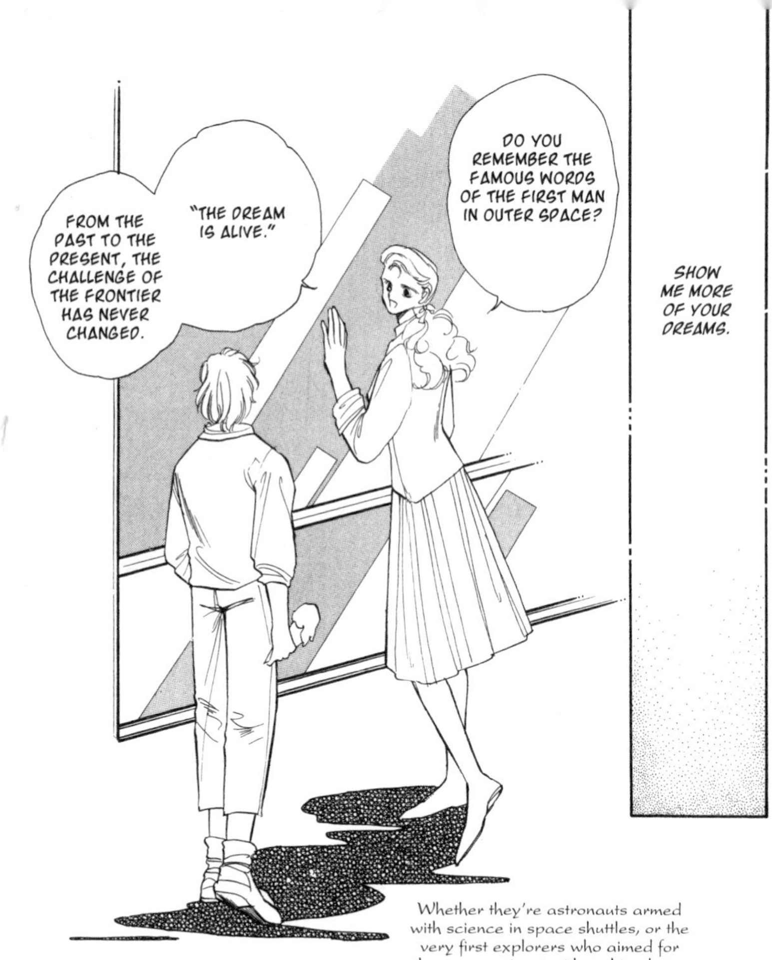
DO YOU REMEMBER THE FAMOUS WORDS OF THE FIRST MAN IN OUTER SPACE?
"THE DREAM IS ALIVE."
FROM THE PAST TO THE PRESENT, THE CHALLENGE OF THE FRONTIER HAS NEVER CHANGED.
SHOW ME MORE OF YOUR DREAMS.

Whether they're astronauts armed with science in space shuttles, or the very first explorers who aimed for the new continent with nothing but a single rifle in hand...

...I'm sure all pioneers were trembling in fear and awe.

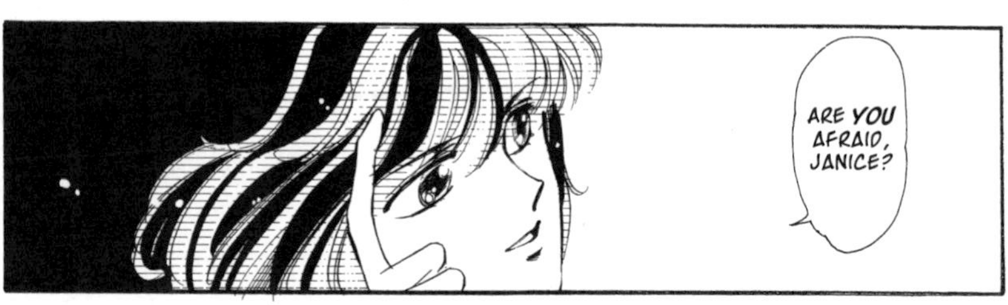
ARE YOU AFRAID, JANICE?

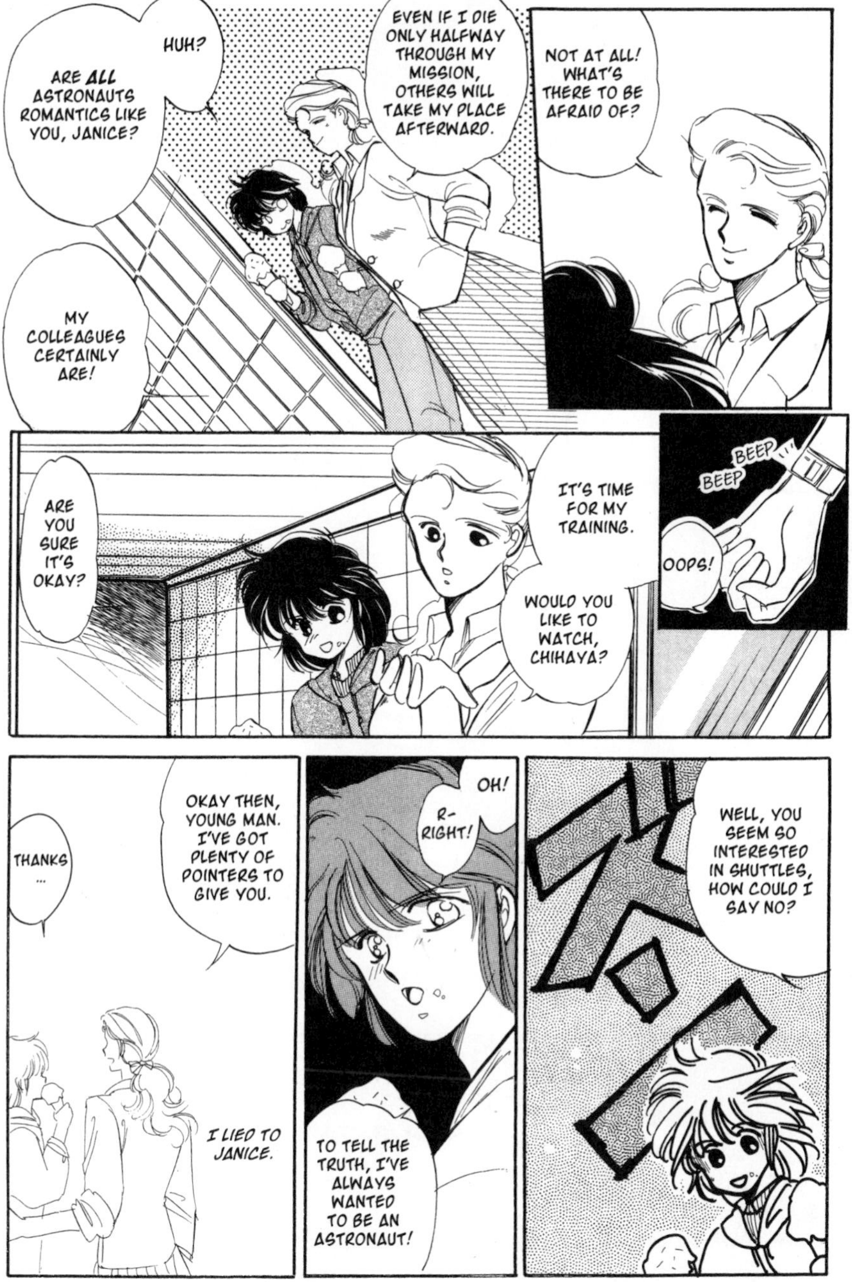
NOT AT ALL! WHAT'S THERE TO BE AFRAID OF?
EVEN IF I DIE ONLY HALFWAY THROUGH MY MISSION, OTHERS WILL TAKE MY PLACE AFTERWARD.
HUH?
ARE **ALL** ASTRONAUTS ROMANTICS LIKE YOU, JANICE?
MY COLLEAGUES CERTAINLY ARE!
BEEP
BEEP
OOPS!
IT'S TIME FOR MY TRAINING.
WOULD YOU LIKE TO WATCH, CHIHAYA?
ARE YOU SURE IT'S OKAY?
WELL, YOU SEEM SO INTERESTED IN SHUTTLES, HOW COULD I SAY NO?
OH!
R-RIGHT!
TO TELL THE TRUTH, I'VE ALWAYS WANTED TO BE AN ASTRONAUT!
OKAY THEN, YOUNG MAN. I'VE GOT PLENTY OF POINTERS TO GIVE YOU.
THANKS ...
I LIED TO JANICE.

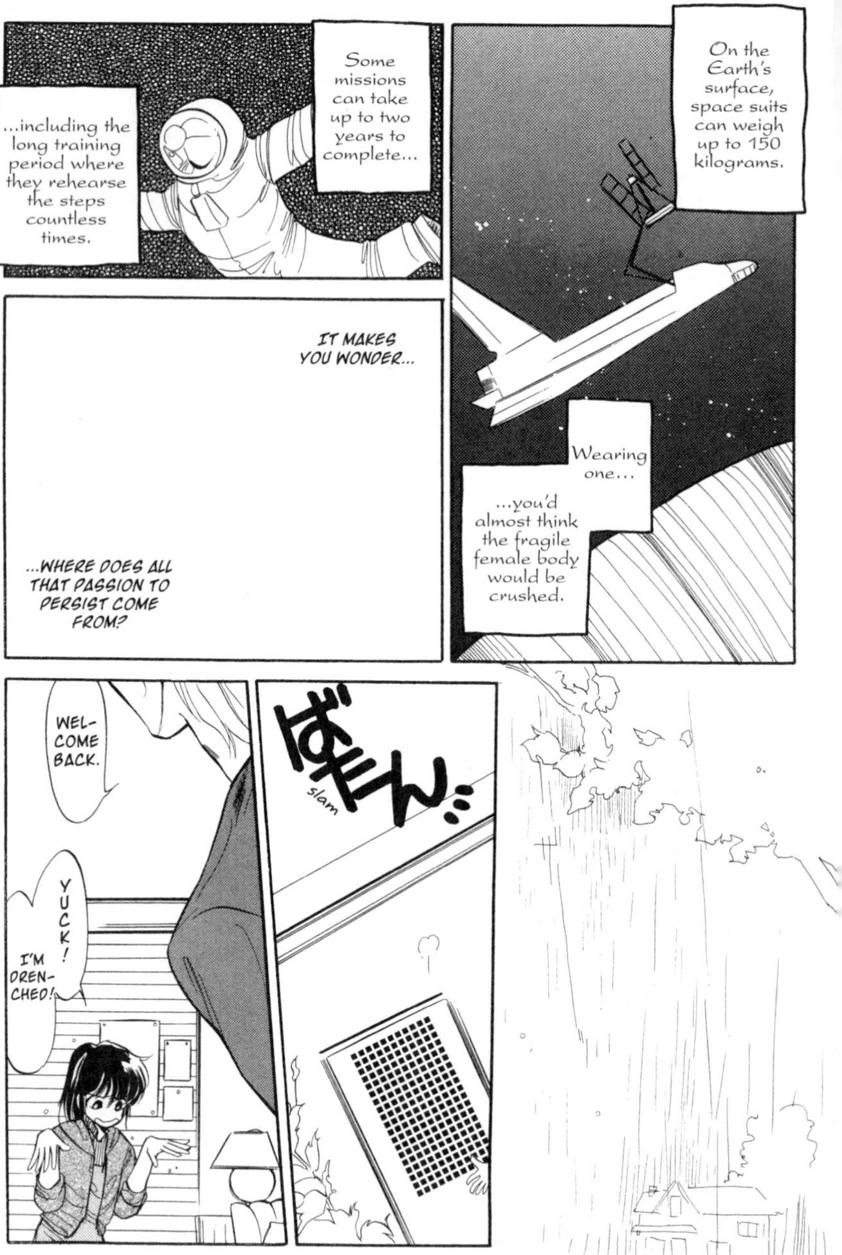
On the Earth's surface, space suits can weigh up to 150 kilograms.
Wearing one...
...you'd almost think the fragile female body would be crushed.
Some missions can take up to two years to complete...
...including the long training period where they rehearse the steps countless times.
IT MAKES YOU WONDER...
...WHERE DOES ALL THAT PASSION TO PERSIST COME FROM?
ばたん
slam
WEL-COME BACK.
YUCK!
I'M DREN-CHED!

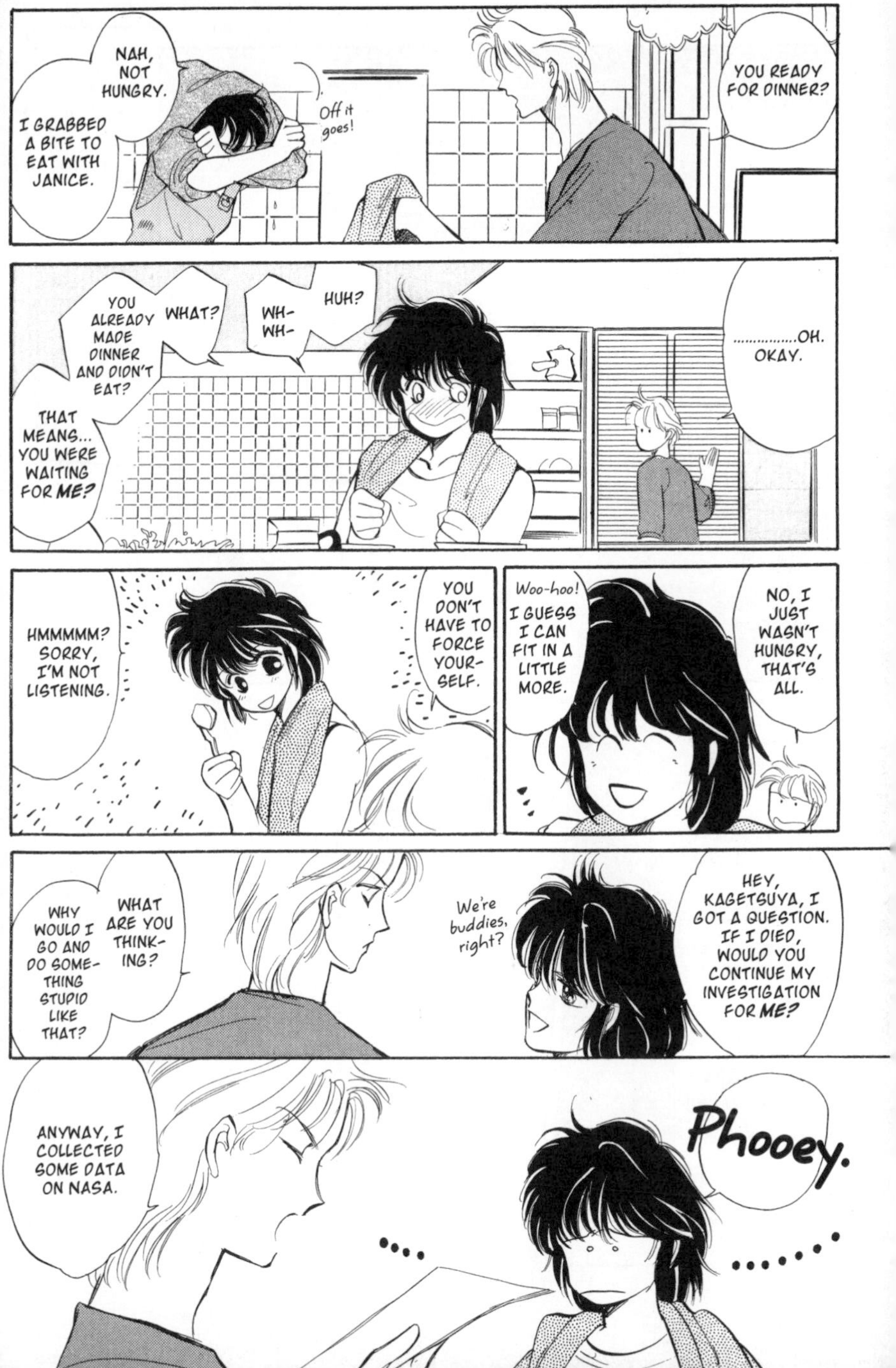
YOU READY FOR DINNER?
Off it goes!
NAH, NOT HUNGRY.
I GRABBED A BITE TO EAT WITH JANICE.
..............OH. OKAY.
HUH?
WH- WH-
WHAT?
YOU ALREADY MADE DINNER AND DIDN'T EAT?
THAT MEANS... YOU WERE WAITING FOR **ME?**
NO, I JUST WASN'T HUNGRY, THAT'S ALL.
Woo-hoo!
I GUESS I CAN FIT IN A LITTLE MORE.
YOU DON'T HAVE TO FORCE YOURSELF.
HMMMMM? SORRY, I'M NOT LISTENING.
HEY, KAGETSUYA, I GOT A QUESTION. IF I DIED, WOULD YOU CONTINUE MY INVESTIGATION FOR **ME?**
We're buddies, right?
WHAT ARE YOU THINKING?
WHY WOULD I GO AND DO SOMETHING STUPID LIKE THAT?
Phooey.
....
...
ANYWAY, I COLLECTED SOME DATA ON NASA.

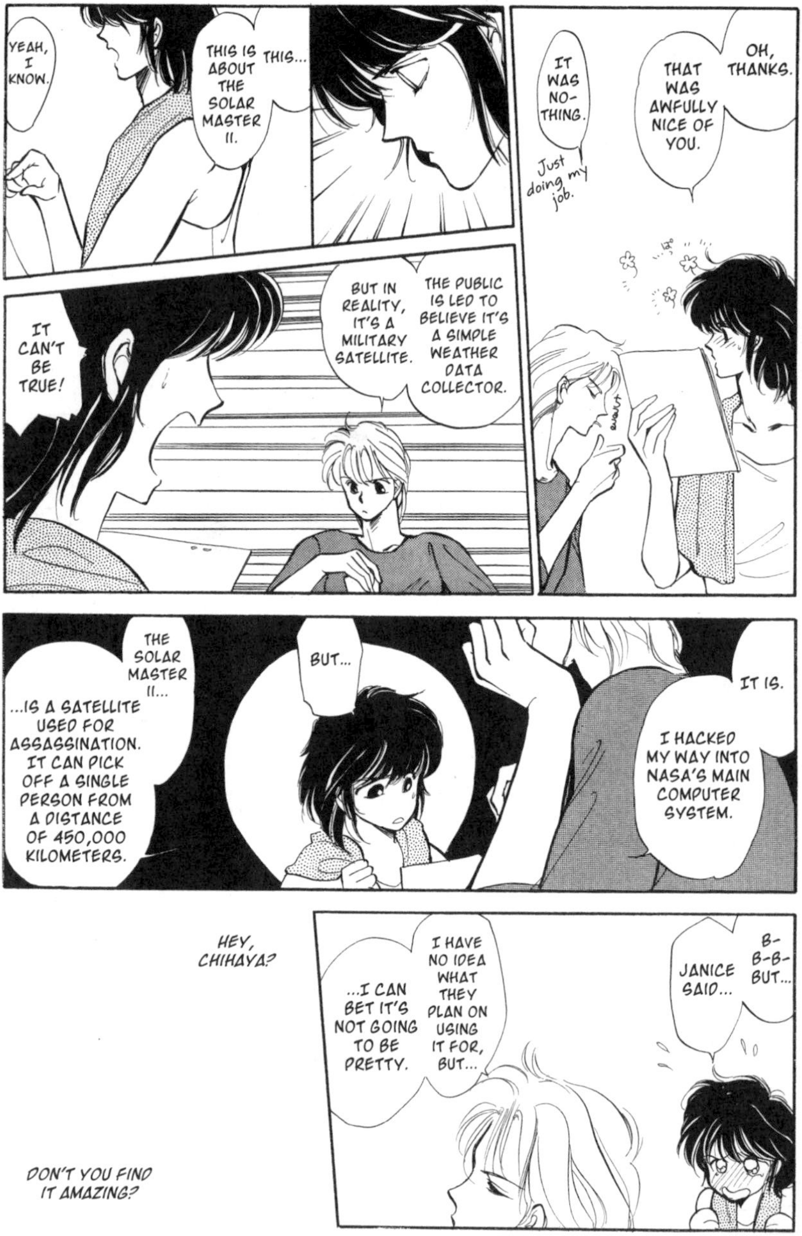
OH, THANKS.
THAT WAS AWFULLY NICE OF YOU.
IT WAS NOTHING.
Just doing my job.
THIS...
THIS IS ABOUT THE SOLAR MASTER II.
YEAH, I KNOW.
THE PUBLIC IS LED TO BELIEVE IT'S A SIMPLE WEATHER DATA COLLECTOR.
BUT IN REALITY, IT'S A MILITARY SATELLITE.
IT CAN'T BE TRUE!
IT IS.
I HACKED MY WAY INTO NASA'S MAIN COMPUTER SYSTEM.
BUT...
THE SOLAR MASTER II...
...IS A SATELLITE USED FOR ASSASSINATION. IT CAN PICK OFF A SINGLE PERSON FROM A DISTANCE OF 450,000 KILOMETERS.
B-B-B-BUT...
JANICE SAID...
I HAVE NO IDEA WHAT THEY PLAN ON USING IT FOR, BUT...
...I CAN BET IT'S NOT GOING TO BE PRETTY.
HEY, CHIHAYA?
DON'T YOU FIND IT AMAZING?

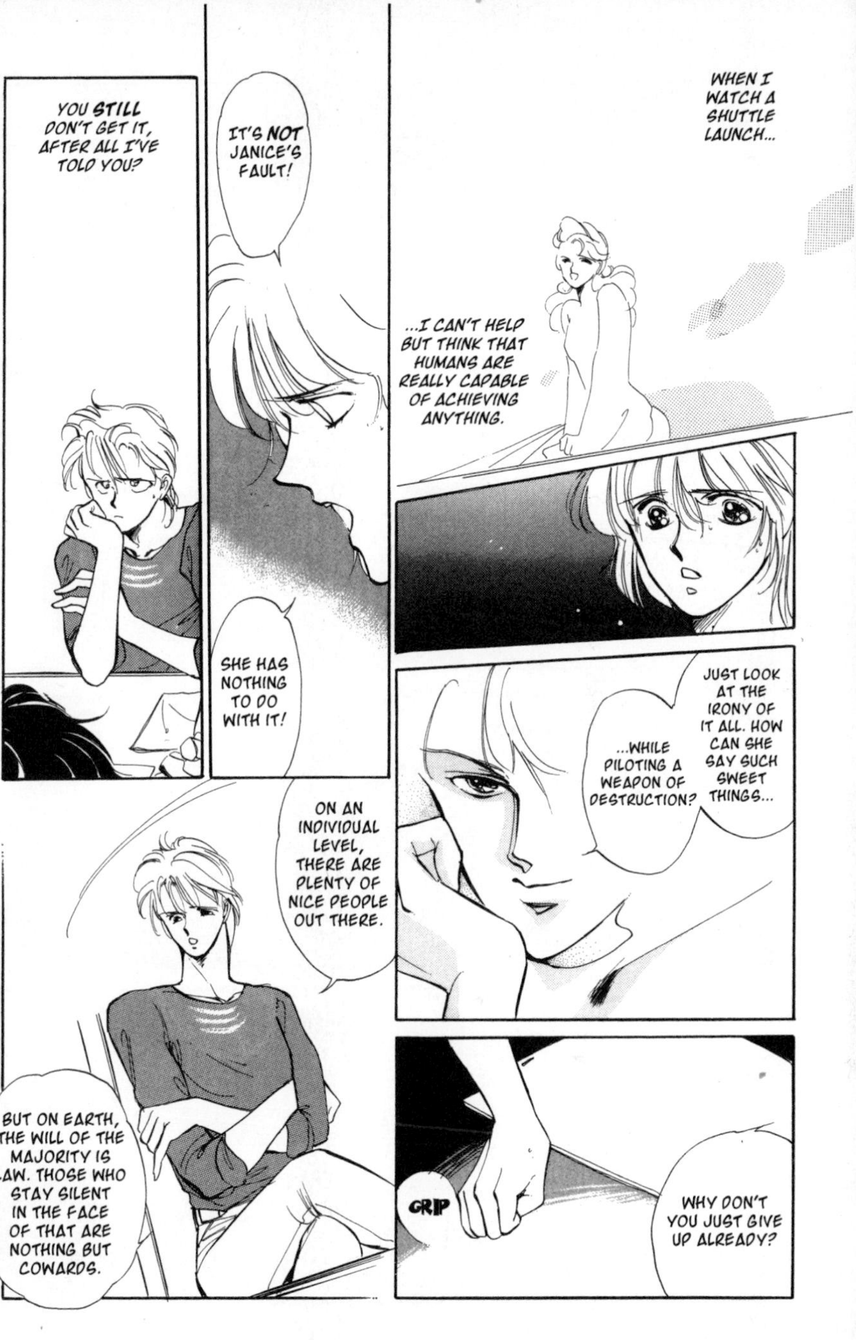
WHEN I WATCH A SHUTTLE LAUNCH...
...I CAN'T HELP BUT THINK THAT HUMANS ARE REALLY CAPABLE OF ACHIEVING ANYTHING.
IT'S **NOT** JANICE'S FAULT!
SHE HAS NOTHING TO DO WITH IT!
YOU **STILL** DON'T GET IT, AFTER ALL I'VE TOLD YOU?
JUST LOOK AT THE IRONY OF IT ALL. HOW CAN SHE SAY SUCH SWEET THINGS...
...WHILE PILOTING A WEAPON OF DESTRUCTION?
ON AN INDIVIDUAL LEVEL, THERE ARE PLENTY OF NICE PEOPLE OUT THERE.
BUT ON EARTH, THE WILL OF THE MAJORITY IS LAW. THOSE WHO STAY SILENT IN THE FACE OF THAT ARE NOTHING BUT COWARDS.
GRIP
WHY DON'T YOU JUST GIVE UP ALREADY?

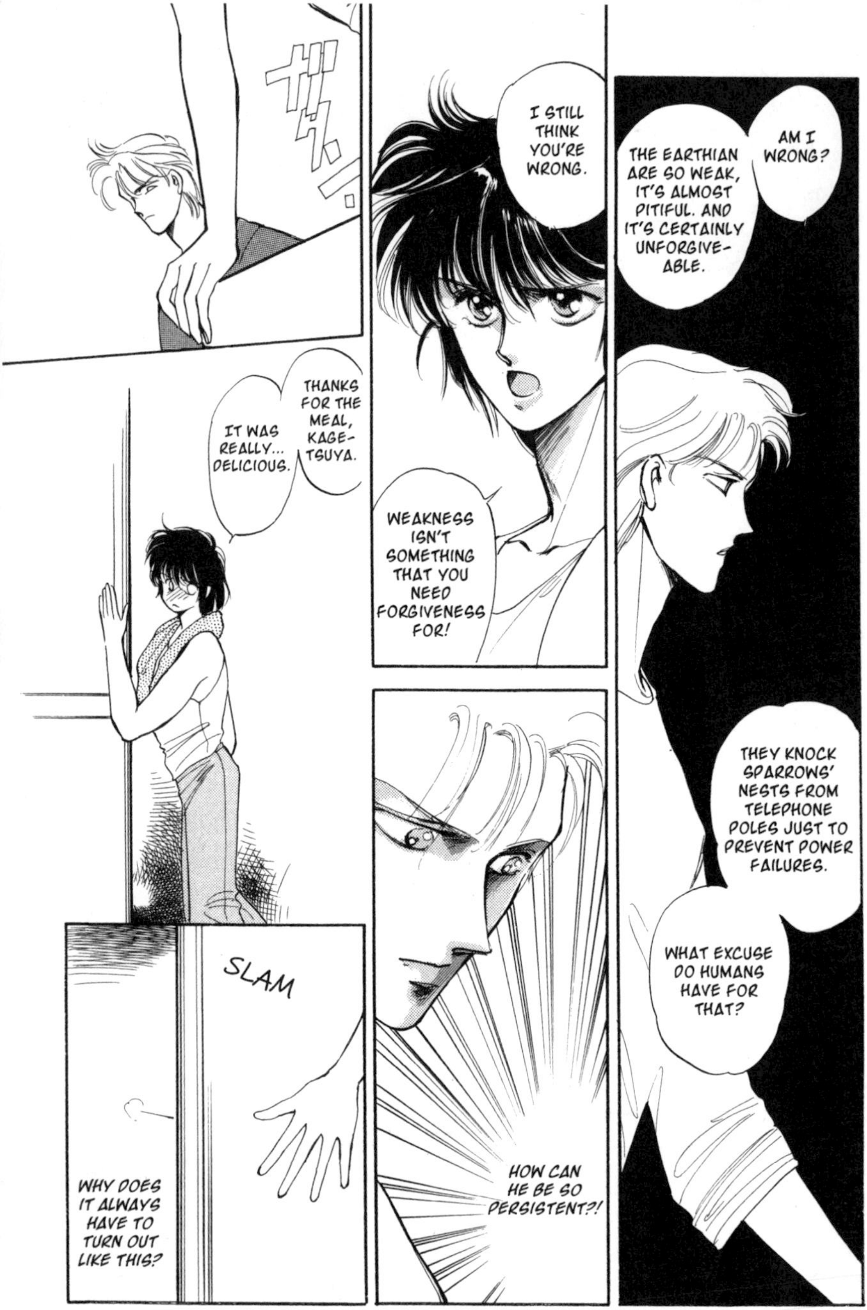
AM I WRONG?
THE EARTHIAN ARE SO WEAK, IT'S ALMOST PITIFUL. AND IT'S CERTAINLY UNFORGIVE-ABLE.
THEY KNOCK SPARROWS' NESTS FROM TELEPHONE POLES JUST TO PREVENT POWER FAILURES.
WHAT EXCUSE DO HUMANS HAVE FOR THAT?
I STILL THINK YOU'RE WRONG.
WEAKNESS ISN'T SOMETHING THAT YOU NEED FORGIVENESS FOR!
HOW CAN HE BE SO PERSISTENT?!
THANKS FOR THE MEAL, KAGE-TSUYA.
IT WAS REALLY... DELICIOUS.
SLAM
WHY DOES IT ALWAYS HAVE TO TURN OUT LIKE THIS?

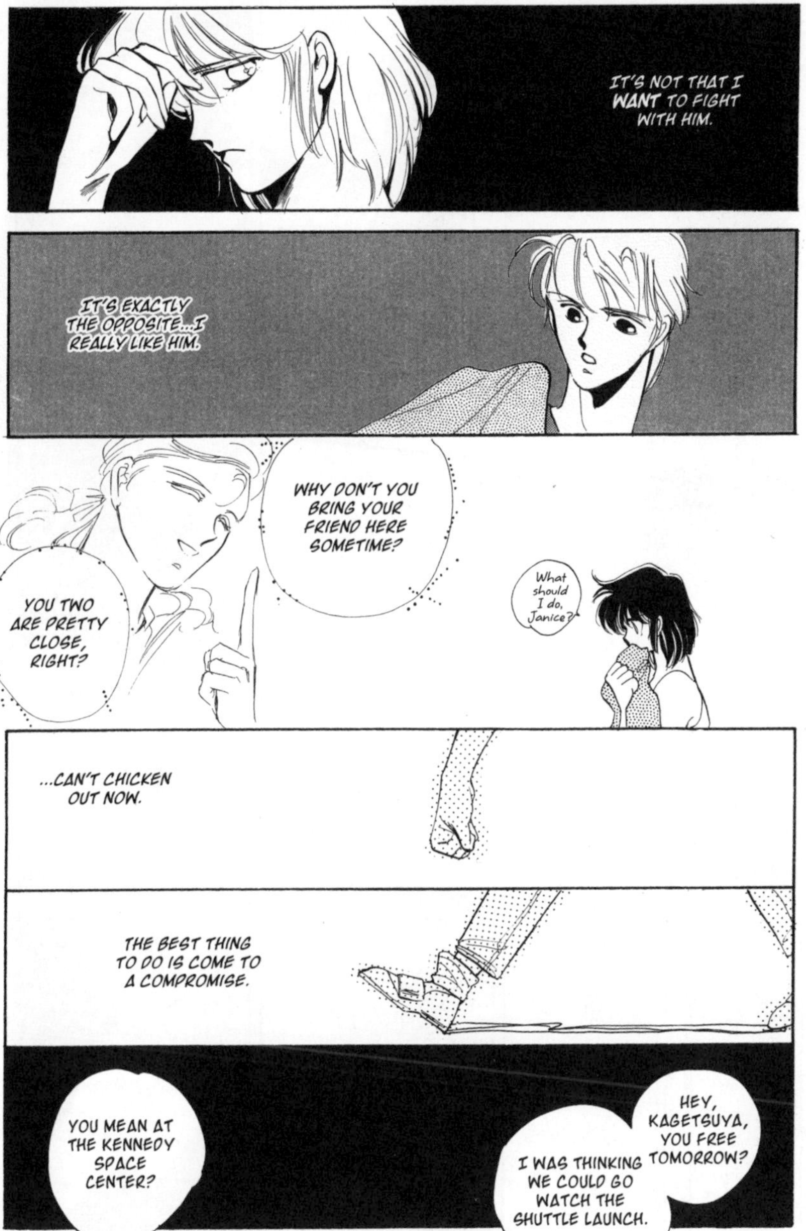
IT'S NOT THAT I WANT TO FIGHT WITH HIM.
IT'S EXACTLY THE OPPOSITE...I REALLY LIKE HIM.
What should I do, Janice?
WHY DON'T YOU BRING YOUR FRIEND HERE SOMETIME?
YOU TWO ARE PRETTY CLOSE, RIGHT?
...CAN'T CHICKEN OUT NOW.
THE BEST THING TO DO IS COME TO A COMPROMISE.
HEY, KAGETSUYA, YOU FREE TOMORROW?
I WAS THINKING WE COULD GO WATCH THE SHUTTLE LAUNCH.
YOU MEAN AT THE KENNEDY SPACE CENTER?

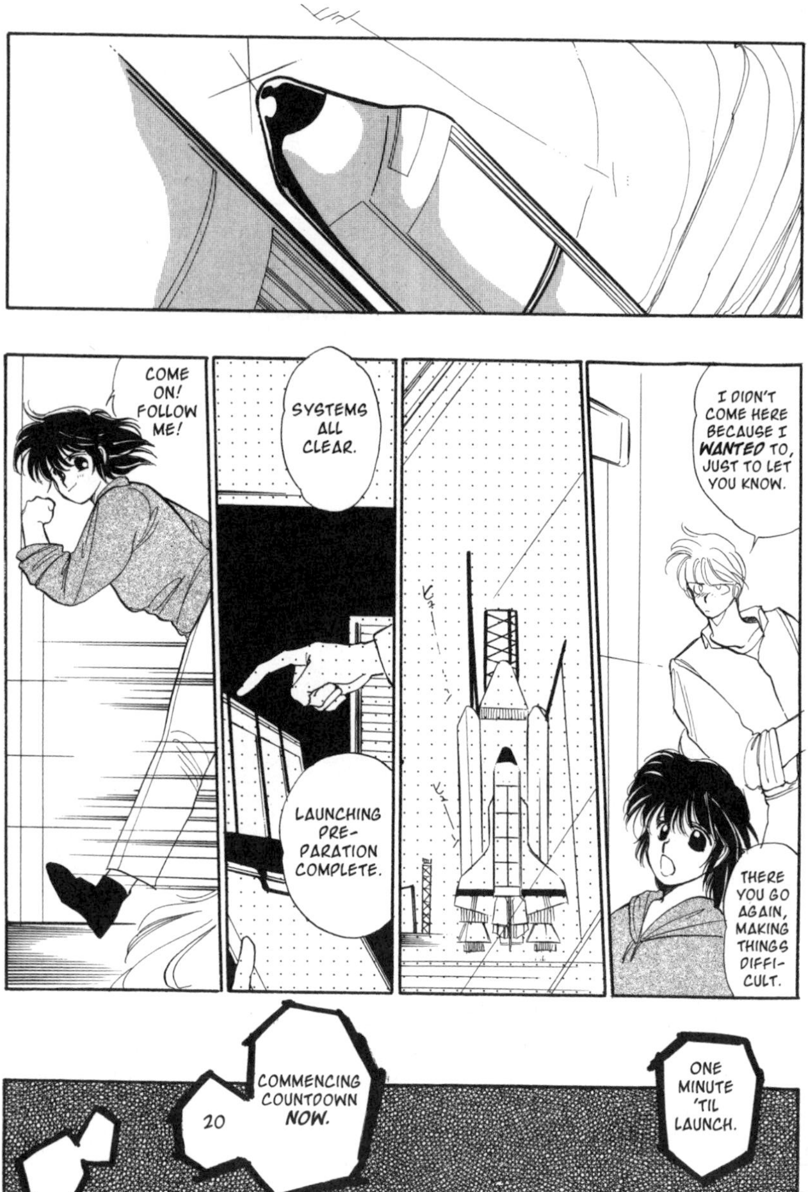
I DIDN'T COME HERE BECAUSE I WANTED TO, JUST TO LET YOU KNOW.
THERE YOU GO AGAIN, MAKING THINGS DIFFI-CULT.
SYSTEMS ALL CLEAR.
LAUNCHING PRE-PARATION COMPLETE.
COME ON! FOLLOW ME!
ONE MINUTE 'TIL LAUNCH.
COMMENCING COUNTDOWN NOW.
20

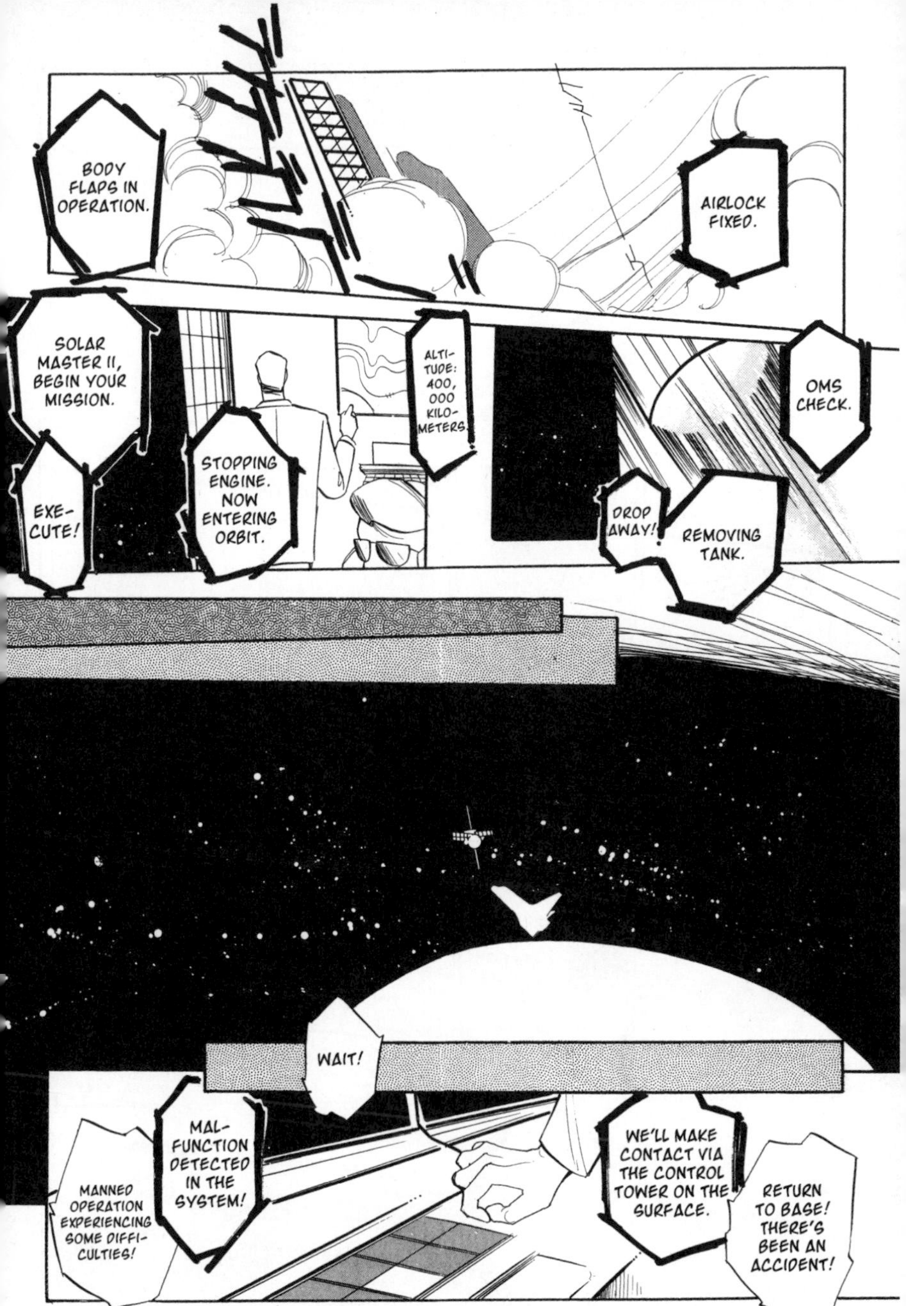
AIRLOCK FIXED.
BODY FLAPS IN OPERATION.
OMS CHECK.
REMOVING TANK.
DROP AWAY!
ALTITUDE: 400,000 KILOMETERS.
SOLAR MASTER II, BEGIN YOUR MISSION.
STOPPING ENGINE. NOW ENTERING ORBIT.
EXECUTE!
WAIT!
RETURN TO BASE! THERE'S BEEN AN ACCIDENT!
WE'LL MAKE CONTACT VIA THE CONTROL TOWER ON THE SURFACE.
MALFUNCTION DETECTED IN THE SYSTEM!
MANNED OPERATION EXPERIENCING SOME DIFFICULTIES!

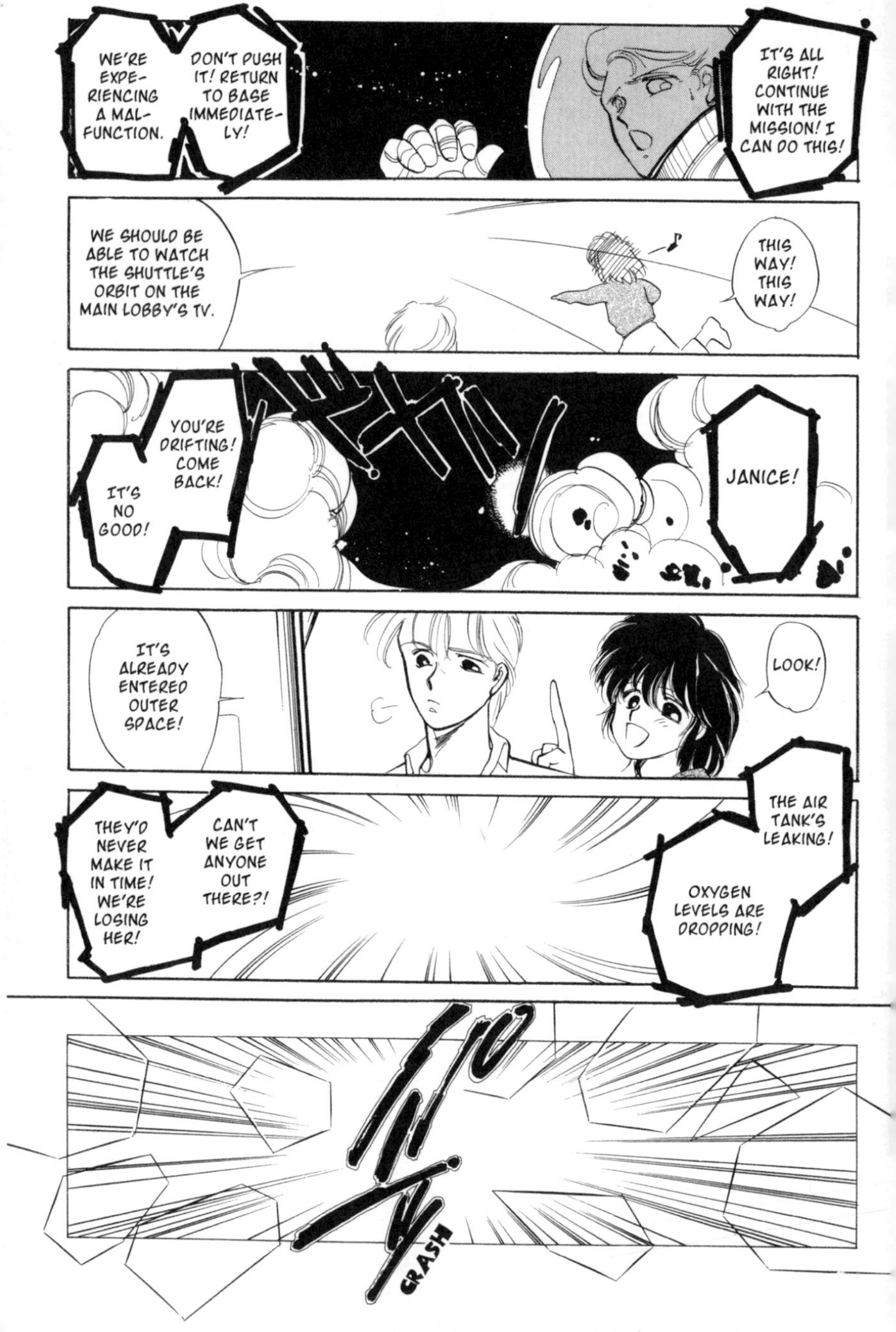
IT'S ALL RIGHT! CONTINUE WITH THE MISSION! I CAN DO THIS!
DON'T PUSH IT! RETURN TO BASE IMMEDIATELY!
WE'RE EXPERIENCING A MALFUNCTION.
THIS WAY! THIS WAY!
WE SHOULD BE ABLE TO WATCH THE SHUTTLE'S ORBIT ON THE MAIN LOBBY'S TV.
JANICE!
YOU'RE DRIFTING! COME BACK!
IT'S NO GOOD!
LOOK!
IT'S ALREADY ENTERED OUTER SPACE!
THE AIR TANK'S LEAKING!
OXYGEN LEVELS ARE DROPPING!
CAN'T WE GET ANYONE OUT THERE?!
THEY'D NEVER MAKE IT IN TIME! WE'RE LOSING HER!
CRASH

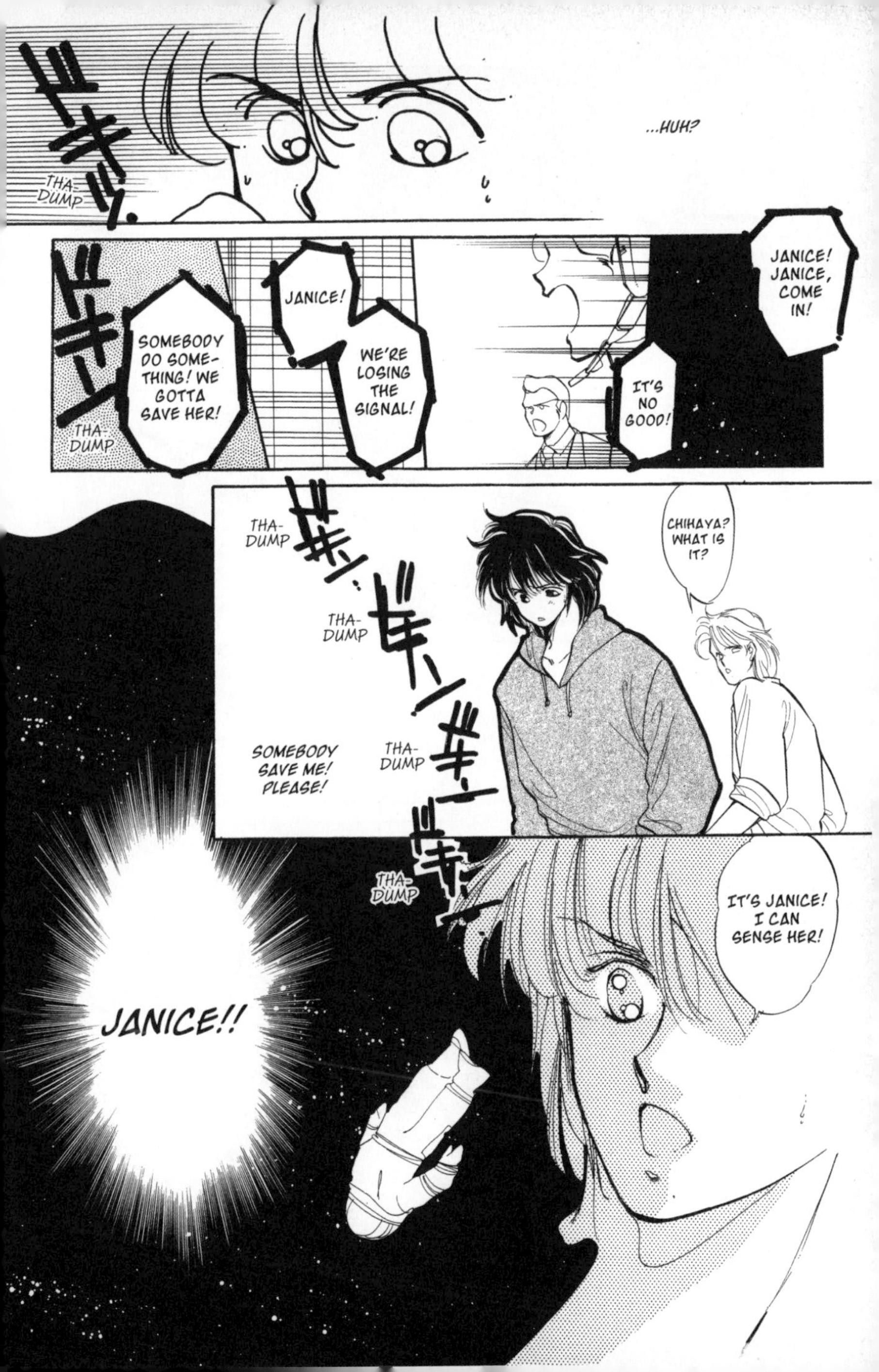
...HUH?
THA-DUMP
JANICE! JANICE, COME IN!
IT'S NO GOOD!
JANICE!
WE'RE LOSING THE SIGNAL!
SOMEBODY DO SOMETHING! WE GOTTA SAVE HER!
THA-DUMP
CHIHAYA? WHAT IS IT?
THA-DUMP
THA-DUMP
THA-DUMP
SOMEBODY SAVE ME! PLEASE!
IT'S JANICE! I CAN SENSE HER!
THA-DUMP
JANICE!!

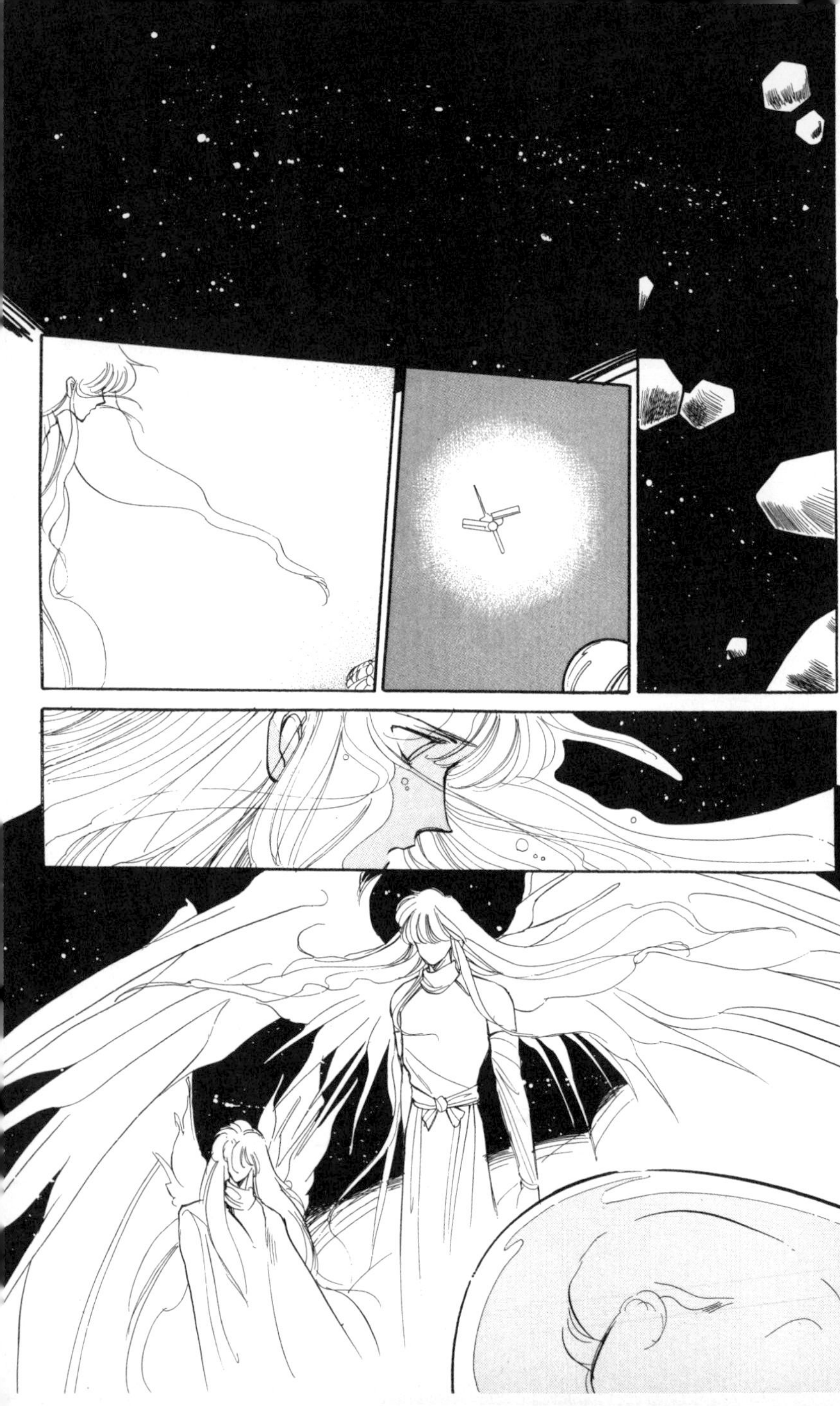

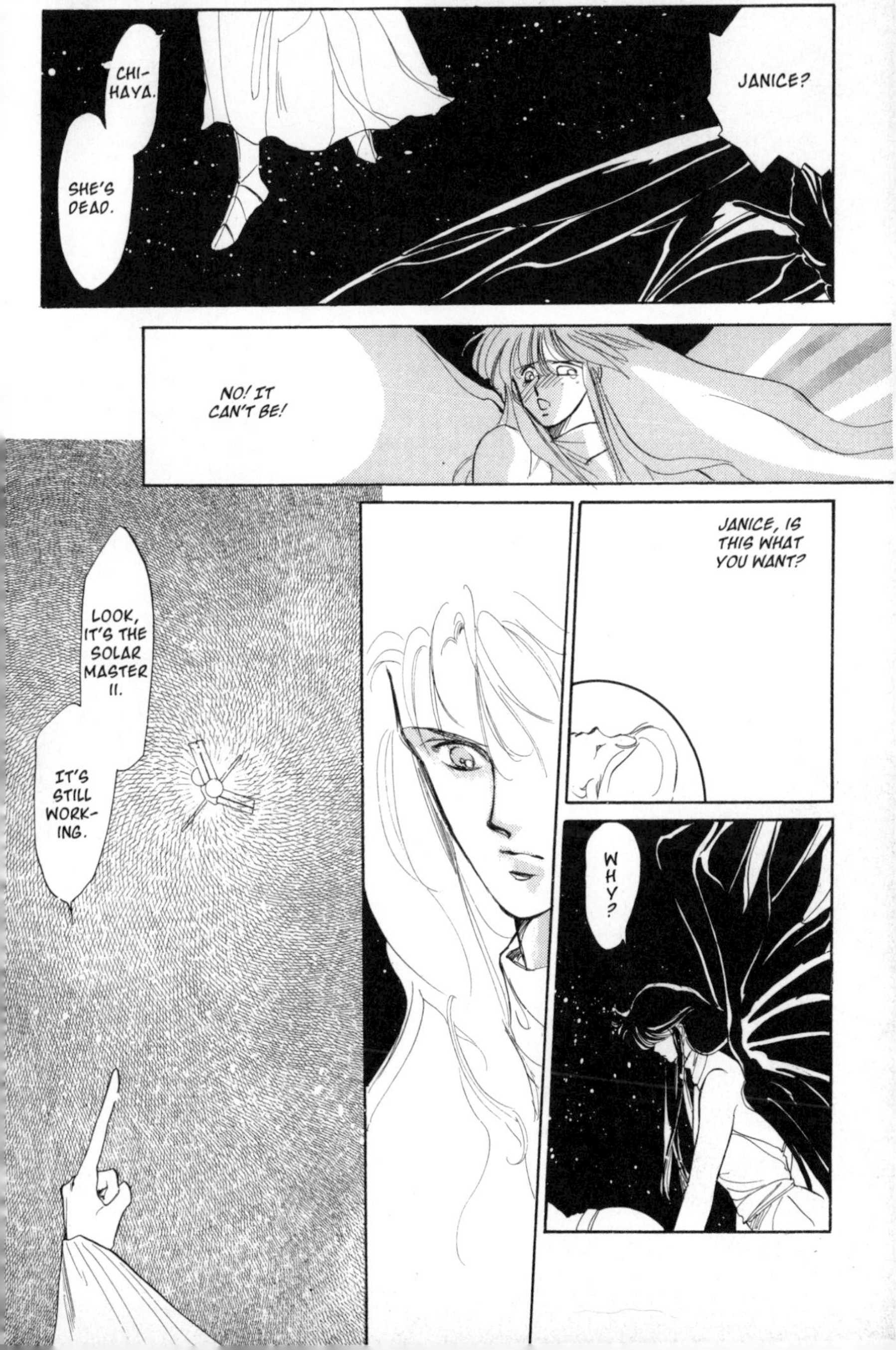
JANICE?
CHI-HAYA.
SHE'S DEAD.
NO! IT CAN'T BE!
JANICE, IS THIS WHAT YOU WANT?
WHY?
LOOK, IT'S THE SOLAR MASTER II.
IT'S STILL WORKING.

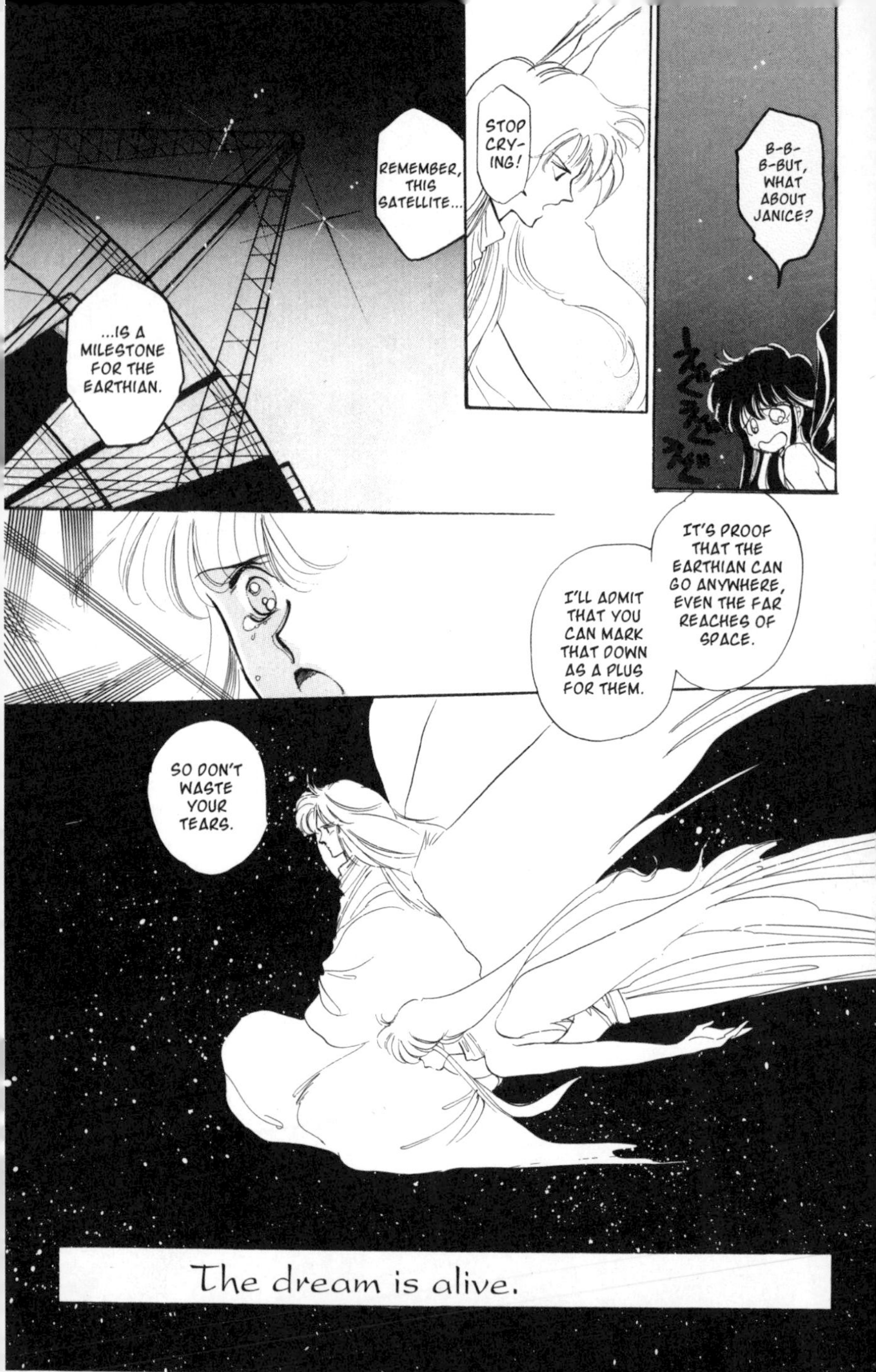
B-B-B-BUT, WHAT ABOUT JANICE?
STOP CRYING!
REMEMBER, THIS SATELLITE...
...IS A MILESTONE FOR THE EARTHIAN.
IT'S PROOF THAT THE EARTHIAN CAN GO ANYWHERE, EVEN THE FAR REACHES OF SPACE.
I'LL ADMIT THAT YOU CAN MARK THAT DOWN AS A PLUS FOR THEM.
SO DON'T WASTE YOUR TEARS.
The dream is alive.

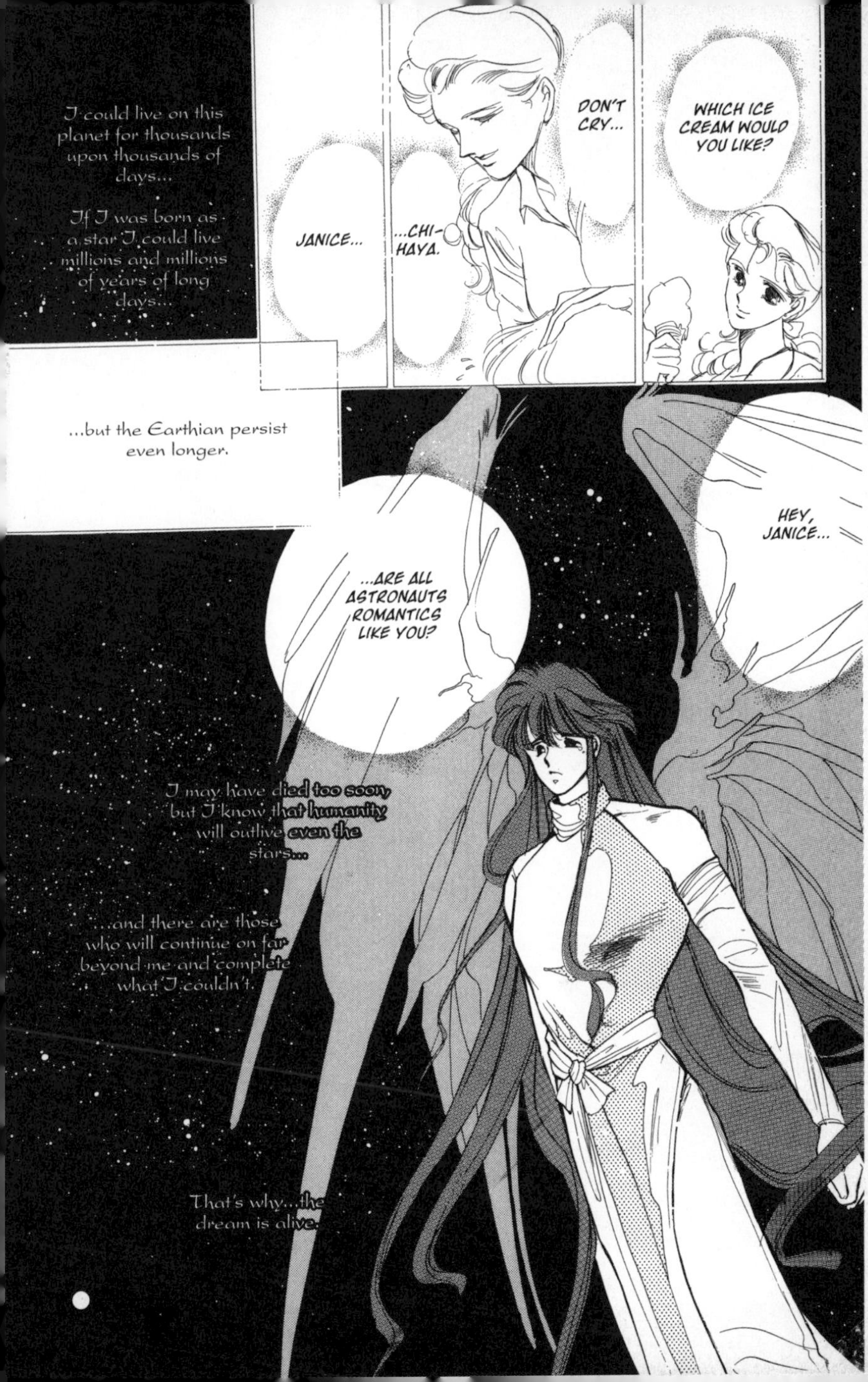
WHICH ICE CREAM WOULD YOU LIKE?
DON'T CRY...
...CHI-HAYA.
JANICE...
I could live on this planet for thousands upon thousands of days...
If I was born as a star I could live millions and millions of years of long days...
...but the Earthian persist even longer.
HEY, JANICE...
...ARE ALL ASTRONAUTS ROMANTICS LIKE YOU?
I may have died too soon, but I know that humanity will outlive even the stars...
...and there are those who will continue on far beyond me and complete what I couldn't.
That's why...the dream is alive.

HONG KONG CHINESE

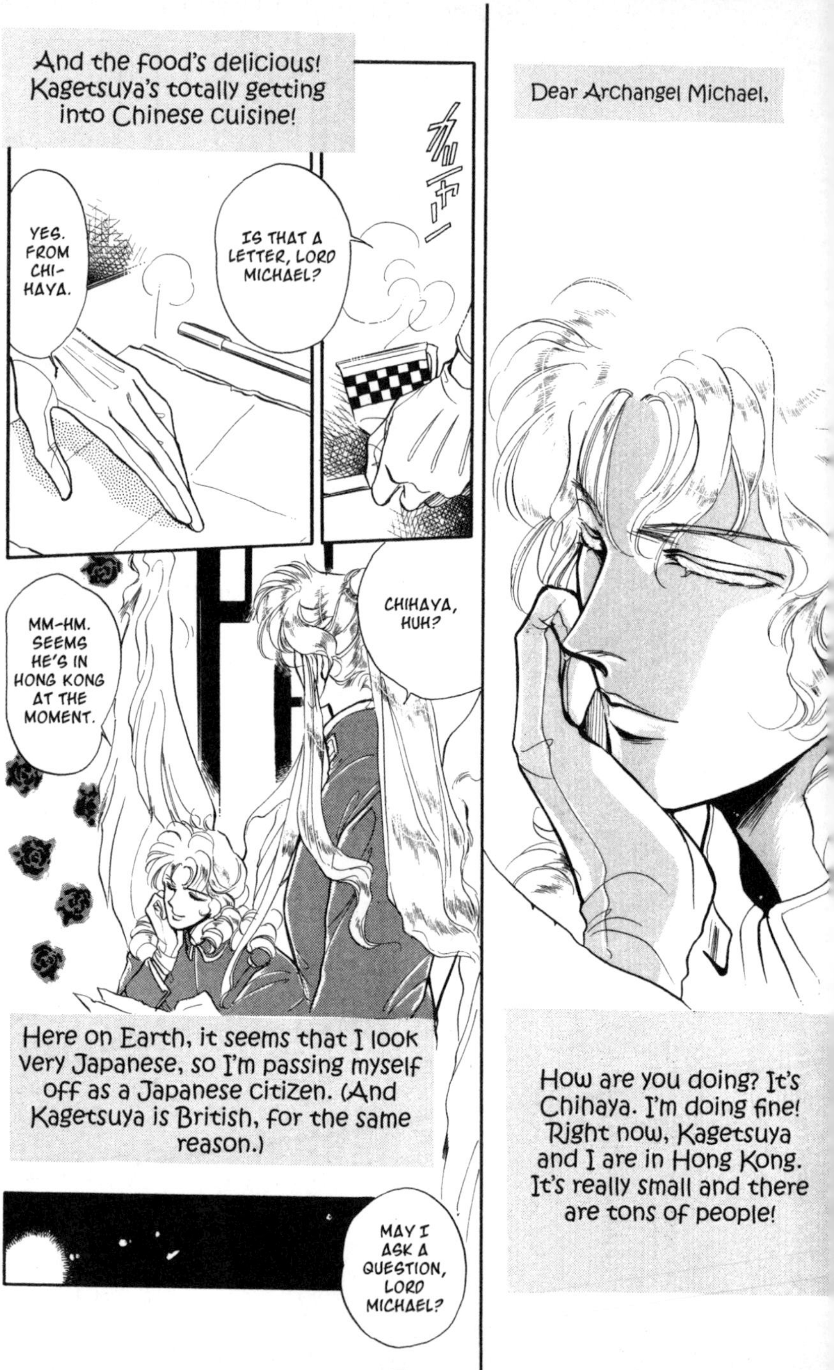
Dear Archangel Michael,
How are you doing? It's Chihaya. I'm doing fine! Right now, Kagetsuya and I are in Hong Kong. It's really small and there are tons of people!
And the food's delicious! Kagetsuya's totally getting into Chinese cuisine!
IS THAT A LETTER, LORD MICHAEL?
YES. FROM CHI-HAYA.
CHIHAYA, HUH?
MM-HM. SEEMS HE'S IN HONG KONG AT THE MOMENT.
Here on Earth, it seems that I look very Japanese, so I'm passing myself off as a Japanese citizen. (And Kagetsuya is British, for the same reason.)
MAY I ASK A QUESTION, LORD MICHAEL?

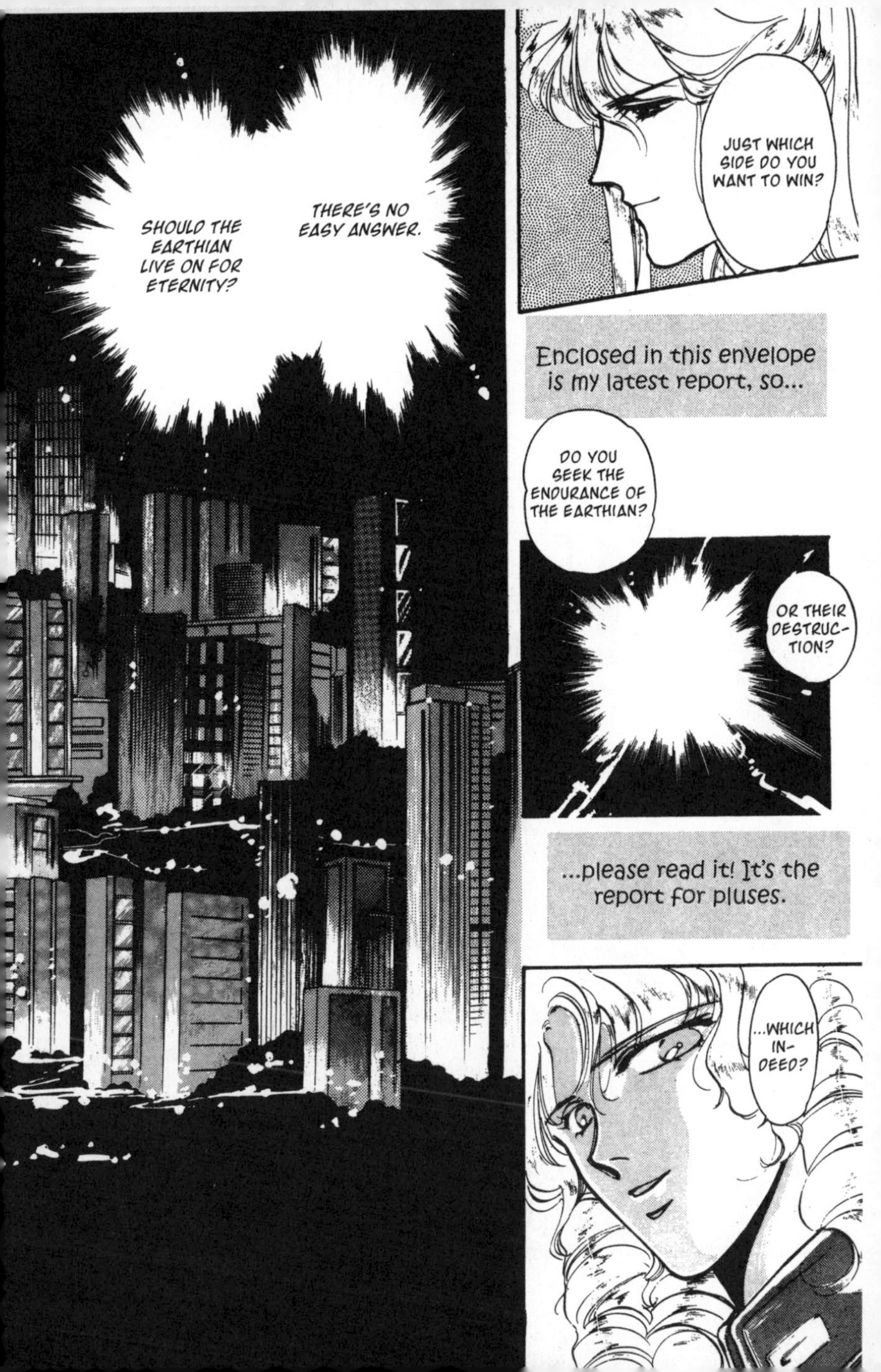
JUST WHICH SIDE DO YOU WANT TO WIN?
Enclosed in this envelope is my latest report, so...
DO YOU SEEK THE ENDURANCE OF THE EARTHIAN?
OR THEIR DESTRUC-TION?
...please read it! It's the report for pluses.
...WHICH IN-DEED?
THERE'S NO EASY ANSWER.
SHOULD THE EARTHIAN LIVE ON FOR ETERNITY?

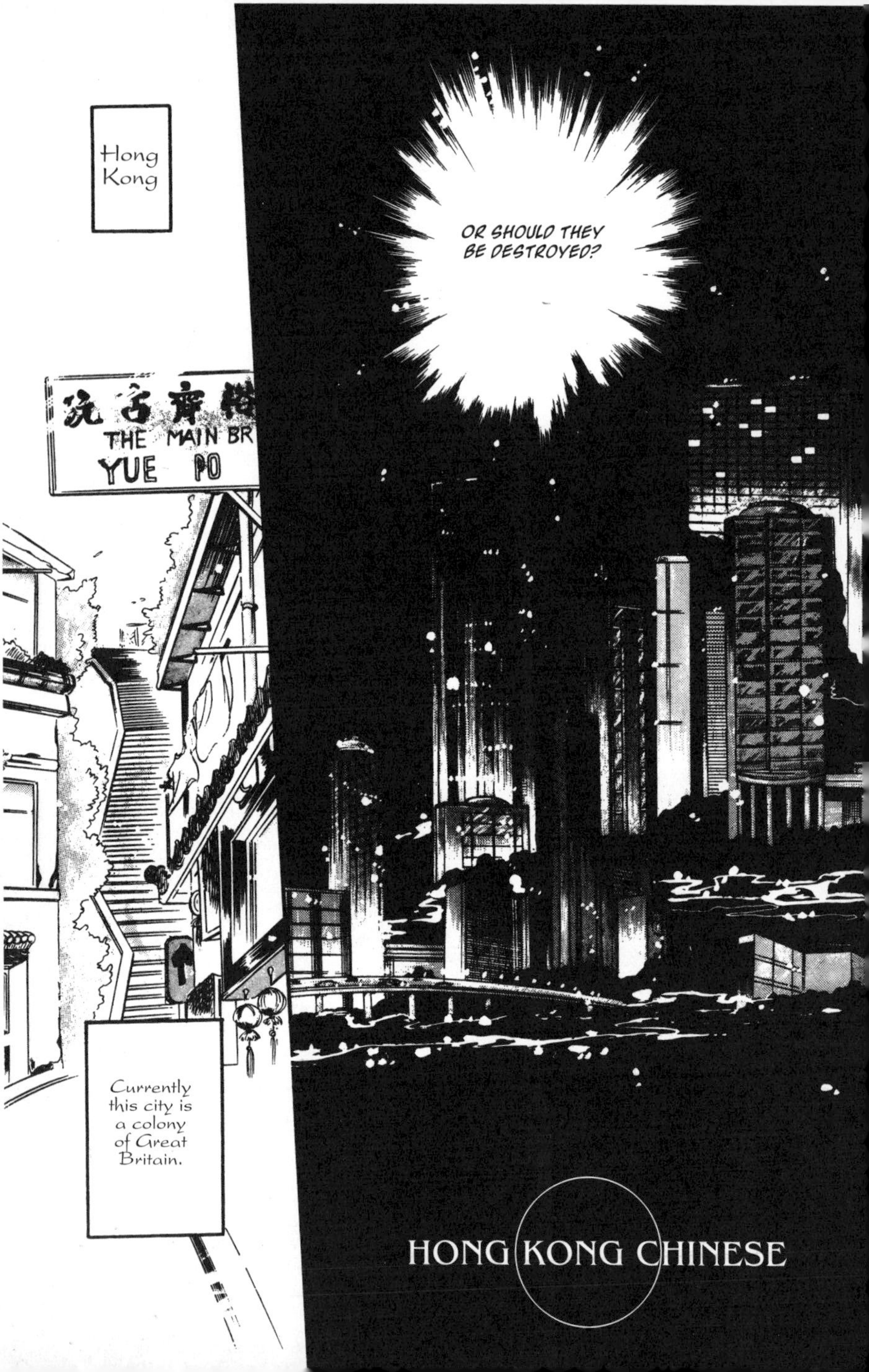
OR SHOULD THEY BE DESTROYED?
HONG KONG CHINESE
Hong Kong
THE MAIN BR
YUE PO
Currently this city is a colony of Great Britain.

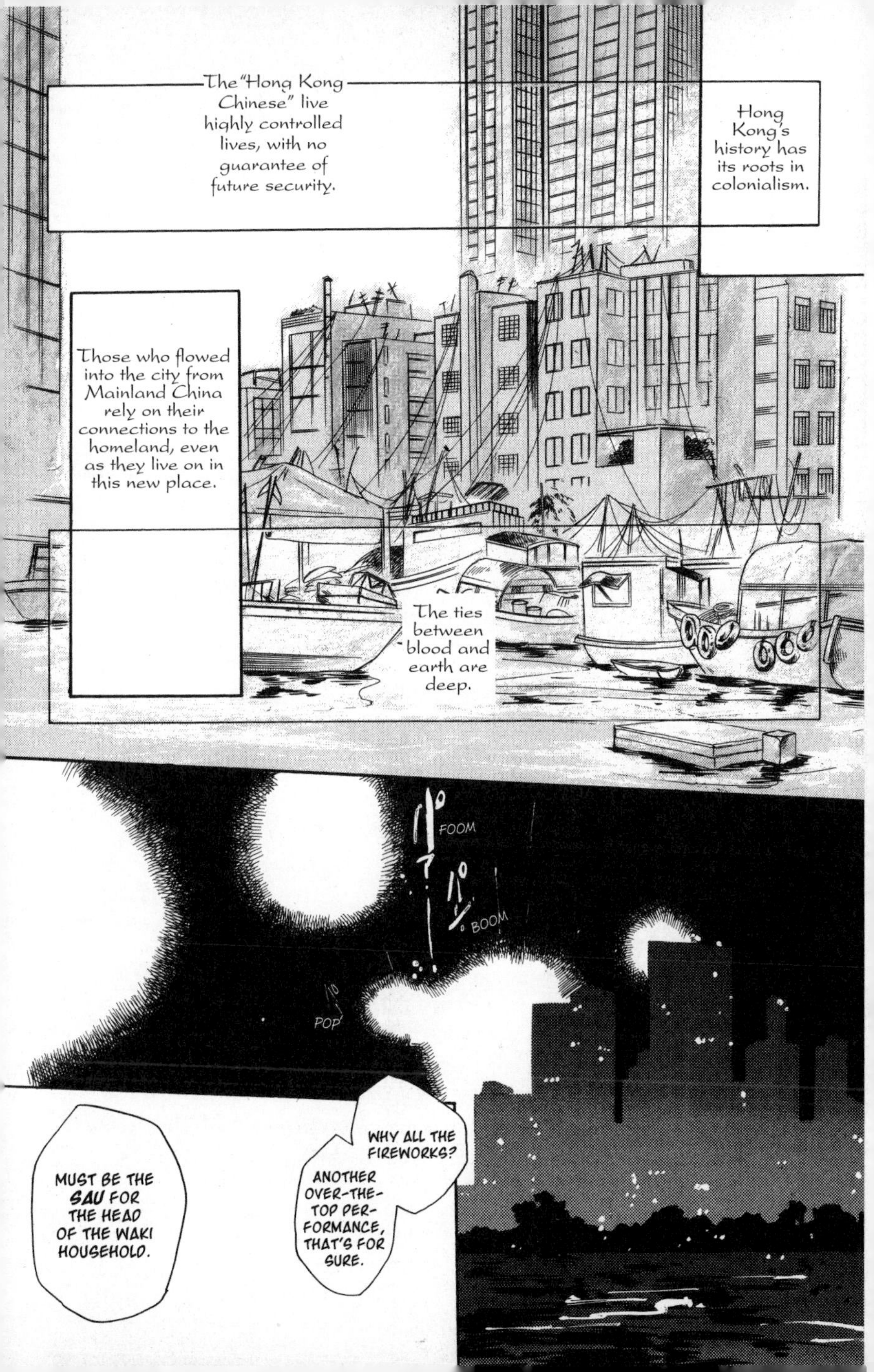
Hong Kong's history has its roots in colonialism.
The "Hong Kong Chinese" live highly controlled lives, with no guarantee of future security.
Those who flowed into the city from Mainland China rely on their connections to the homeland, even as they live on in this new place.
The ties between blood and earth are deep.
FOOM
BOOM
POP
WHY ALL THE FIREWORKS?
ANOTHER OVER-THE-TOP PERFORMANCE, THAT'S FOR SURE.
MUST BE THE SAU FOR THE HEAD OF THE WAKI HOUSEHOLD.

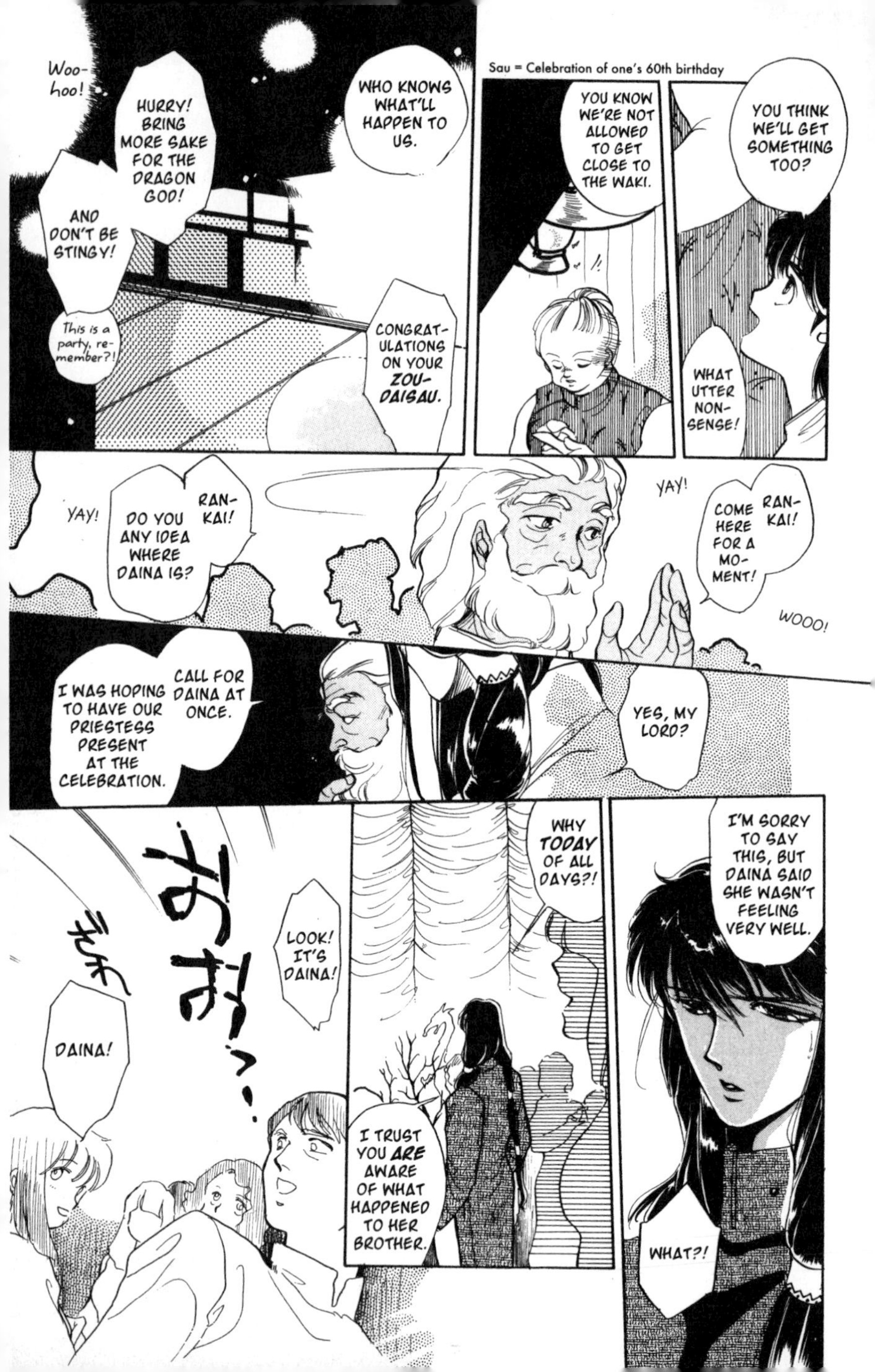
Sau = Celebration of one's 60th birthday
YOU THINK WE'LL GET SOMETHING TOO?
WHAT UTTER NON-SENSE!
YOU KNOW WE'RE NOT ALLOWED TO GET CLOSE TO THE WAKI.
WHO KNOWS WHAT'LL HAPPEN TO US.
HURRY! BRING MORE SAKE FOR THE DRAGON GOD!
Woo-hoo!
CONGRAT-ULATIONS ON YOUR ***ZOU-DAISAU***.
AND DON'T BE STINGY!
This is a party, re-member?!
WOOO!
RAN-KAI! COME HERE FOR A MO-MENT!
YAY!
RAN-KAI! DO YOU ANY IDEA WHERE DAINA IS?
YAY!
YES, MY LORD?
CALL FOR DAINA AT ONCE.
I WAS HOPING TO HAVE OUR PRIESTESS PRESENT AT THE CELEBRATION.
I'M SORRY TO SAY THIS, BUT DAINA SAID SHE WASN'T FEELING VERY WELL.
WHAT?!
WHY ***TODAY*** OF ALL DAYS?!
I TRUST YOU ***ARE*** AWARE OF WHAT HAPPENED TO HER BROTHER.
LOOK! IT'S DAINA!
おおっ…!
DAINA!

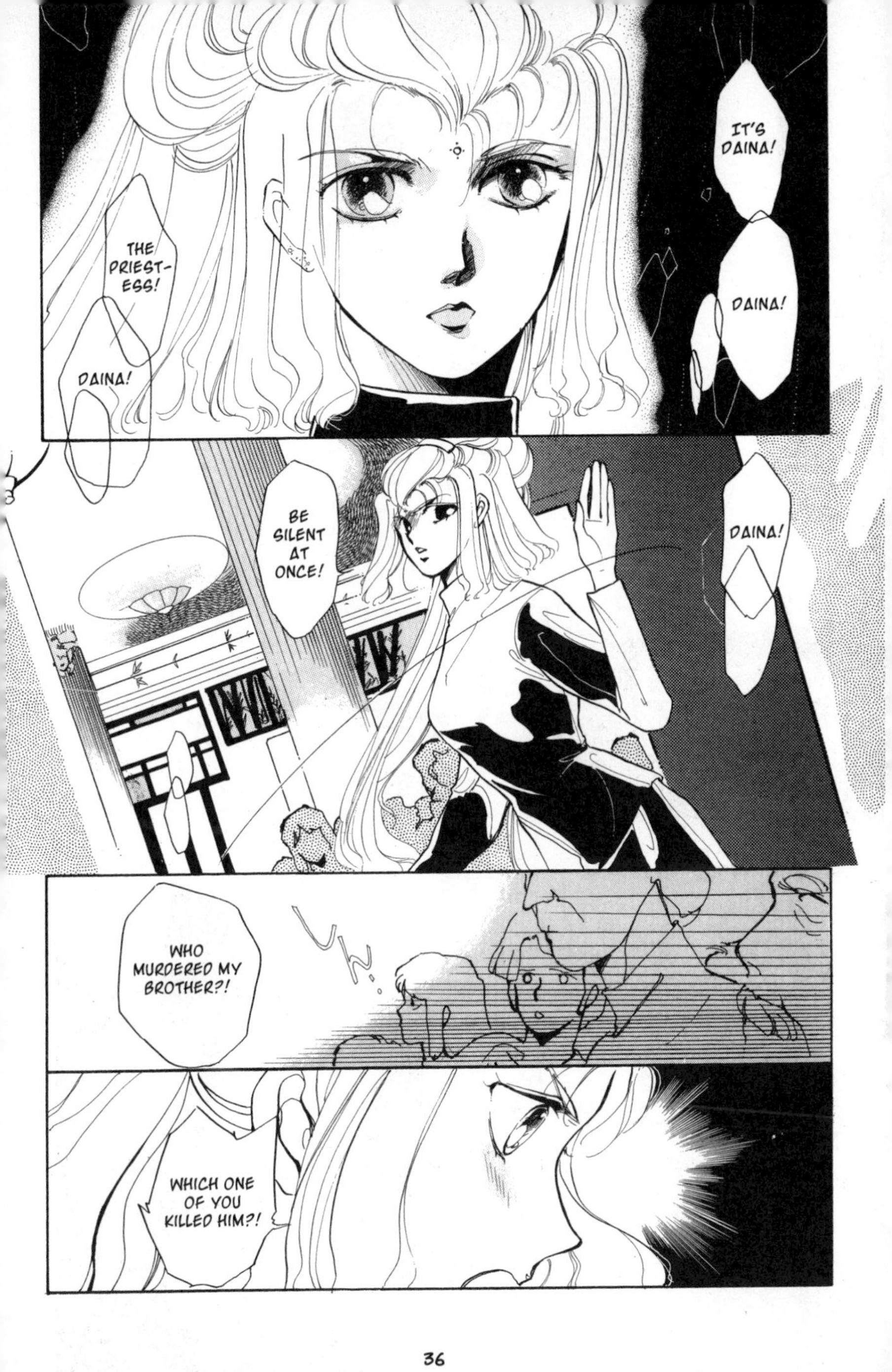
IT'S DAINA!
DAINA!
THE PRIEST-ESS!
DAINA!
DAINA!
BE SILENT AT ONCE!
WHO MURDERED MY BROTHER?!
WHICH ONE OF YOU KILLED HIM?!

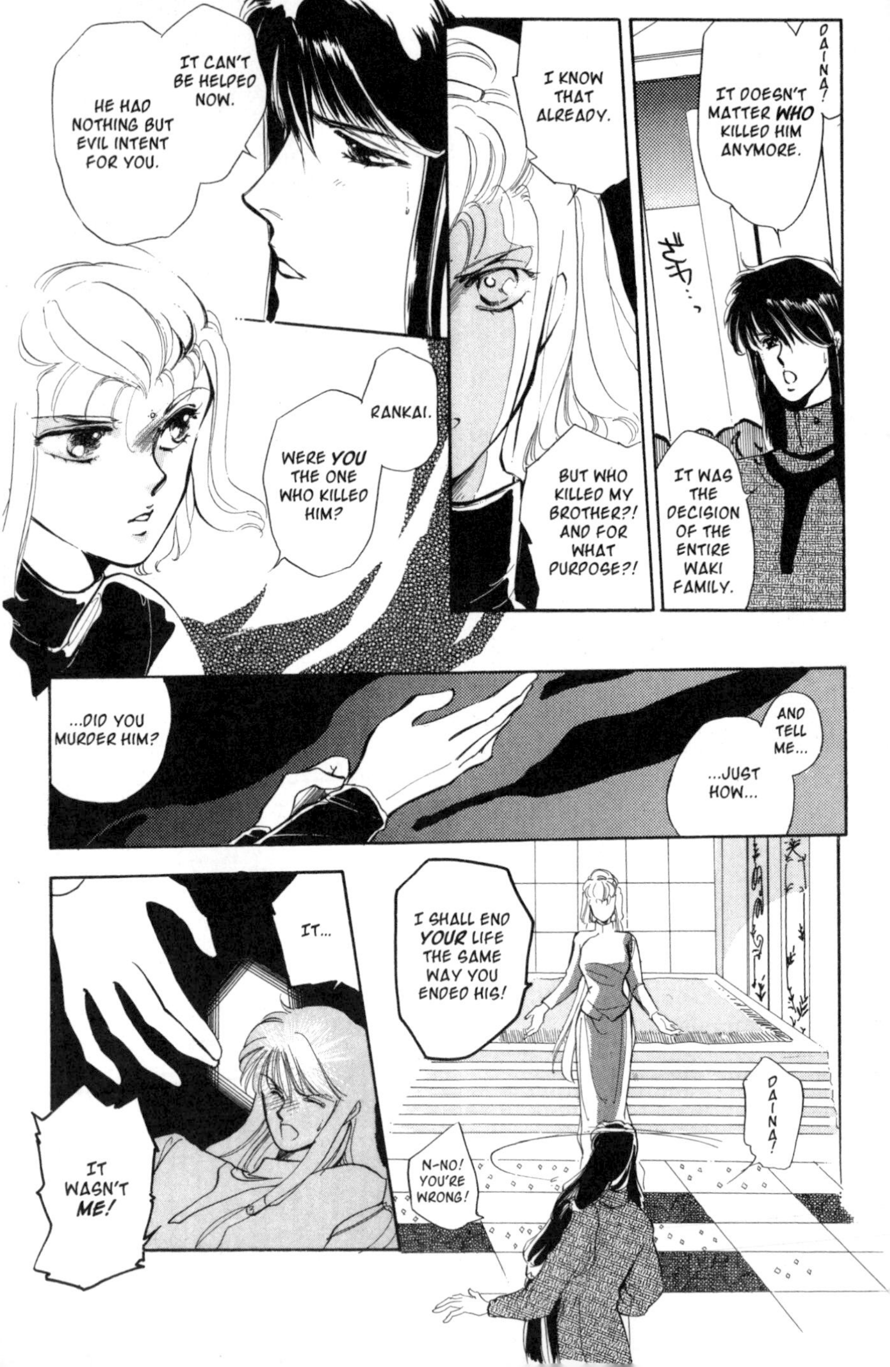
DAINA!
IT DOESN'T MATTER WHO KILLED HIM ANYMORE.
IT WAS THE DECISION OF THE ENTIRE WAKI FAMILY.
I KNOW THAT ALREADY.
BUT WHO KILLED MY BROTHER?! AND FOR WHAT PURPOSE?!
IT CAN'T BE HELPED NOW.
HE HAD NOTHING BUT EVIL INTENT FOR YOU.
RANKAI.
WERE YOU THE ONE WHO KILLED HIM?
AND TELL ME...
...JUST HOW...
...DID YOU MURDER HIM?
I SHALL END YOUR LIFE THE SAME WAY YOU ENDED HIS!
DAINA!
N-NO! YOU'RE WRONG!
IT...
IT WASN'T ME!

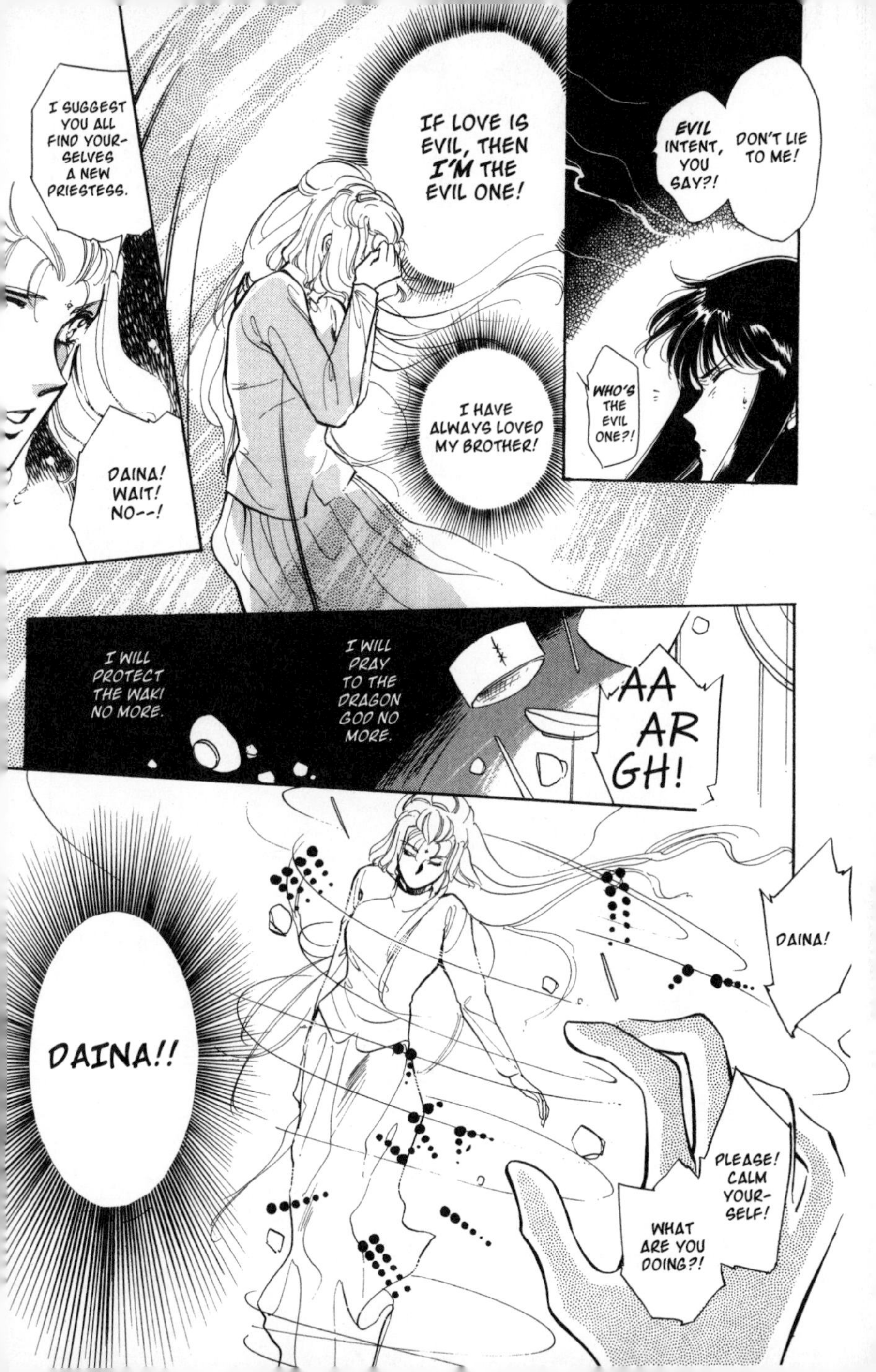
DON'T LIE TO ME!
EVIL INTENT, YOU SAY?!
WHO'S THE EVIL ONE?!
IF LOVE IS EVIL, THEN I'M THE EVIL ONE!
I HAVE ALWAYS LOVED MY BROTHER!
I SUGGEST YOU ALL FIND YOURSELVES A NEW PRIESTESS.
DAINA! WAIT! NO--!
AAARGH!
I WILL PRAY TO THE DRAGON GOD NO MORE.
I WILL PROTECT THE WAKI NO MORE.
DAINA!
PLEASE! CALM YOURSELF!
WHAT ARE YOU DOING?!
DAINA!!

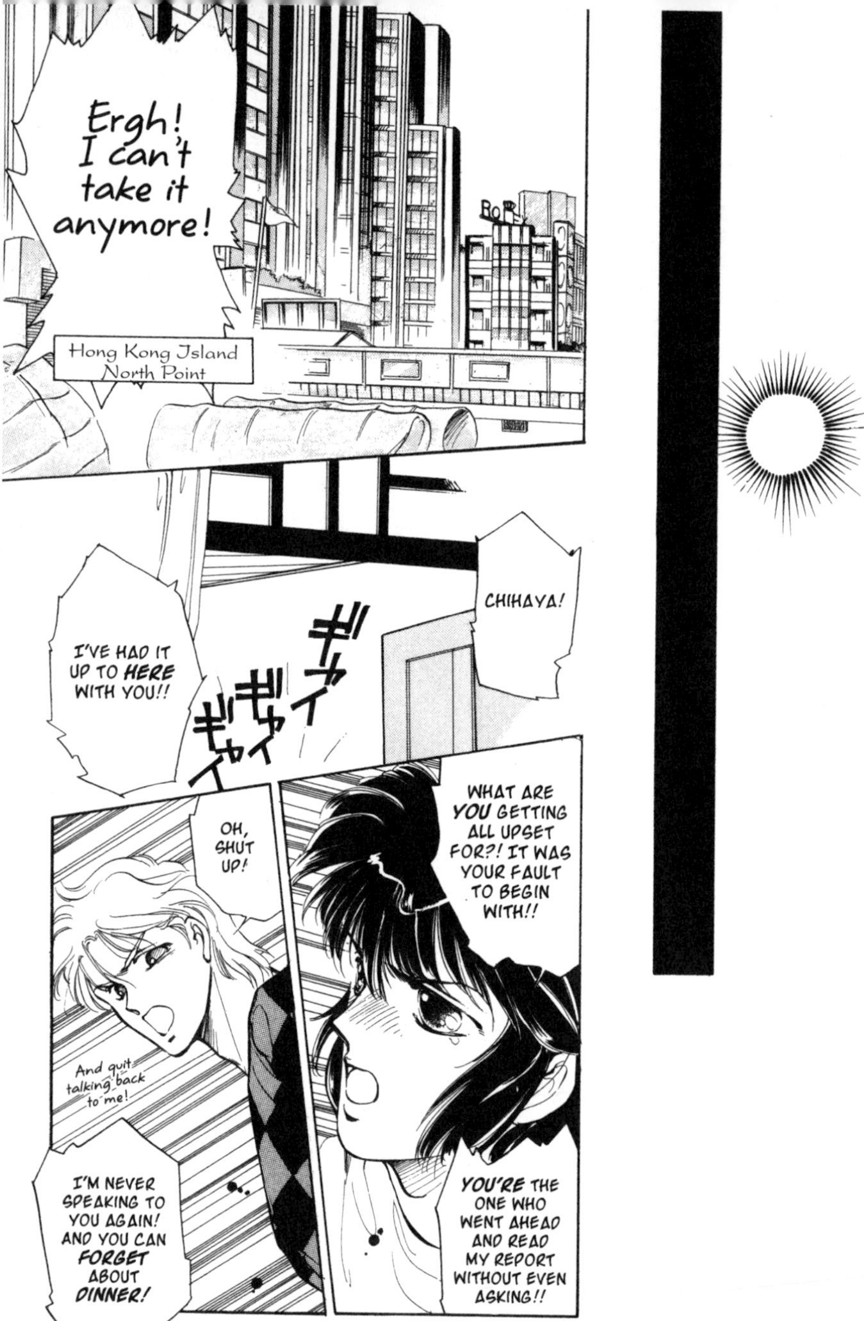
Ergh! I can't take it anymore!
Hong Kong Island North Point
CHIHAYA!
ギャイ ギャイ ギャイ
I'VE HAD IT UP TO HERE WITH YOU!!
WHAT ARE YOU GETTING ALL UPSET FOR?! IT WAS YOUR FAULT TO BEGIN WITH!!
YOU'RE THE ONE WHO WENT AHEAD AND READ MY REPORT WITHOUT EVEN ASKING!!
OH, SHUT UP!
And quit talking back to me!
I'M NEVER SPEAKING TO YOU AGAIN! AND YOU CAN FORGET ABOUT DINNER!

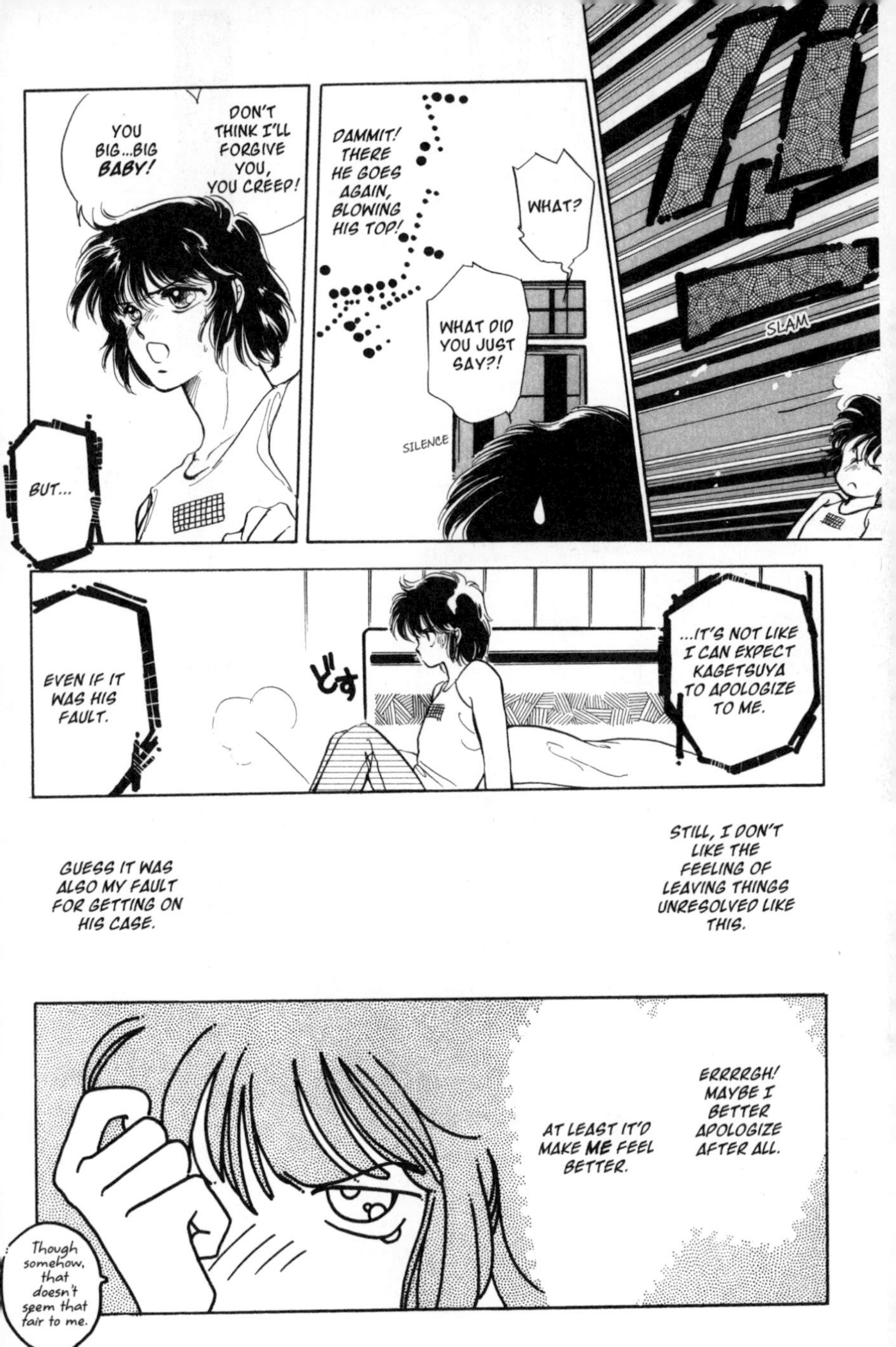
SLAM
WHAT?
DAMMIT! THERE HE GOES AGAIN, BLOWING HIS TOP!
WHAT DID YOU JUST SAY?!
SILENCE
DON'T THINK I'LL FORGIVE YOU, YOU CREEP!
YOU BIG...BIG **BABY!**
BUT...
...IT'S NOT LIKE I CAN EXPECT KAGETSUYA TO APOLOGIZE TO ME.
どす
EVEN IF IT WAS HIS FAULT.
STILL, I DON'T LIKE THE FEELING OF LEAVING THINGS UNRESOLVED LIKE THIS.
GUESS IT WAS ALSO MY FAULT FOR GETTING ON HIS CASE.
ERRRRGH! MAYBE I BETTER APOLOGIZE AFTER ALL.
AT LEAST IT'D MAKE **ME** FEEL BETTER.
Though somehow, that doesn't seem that fair to me.

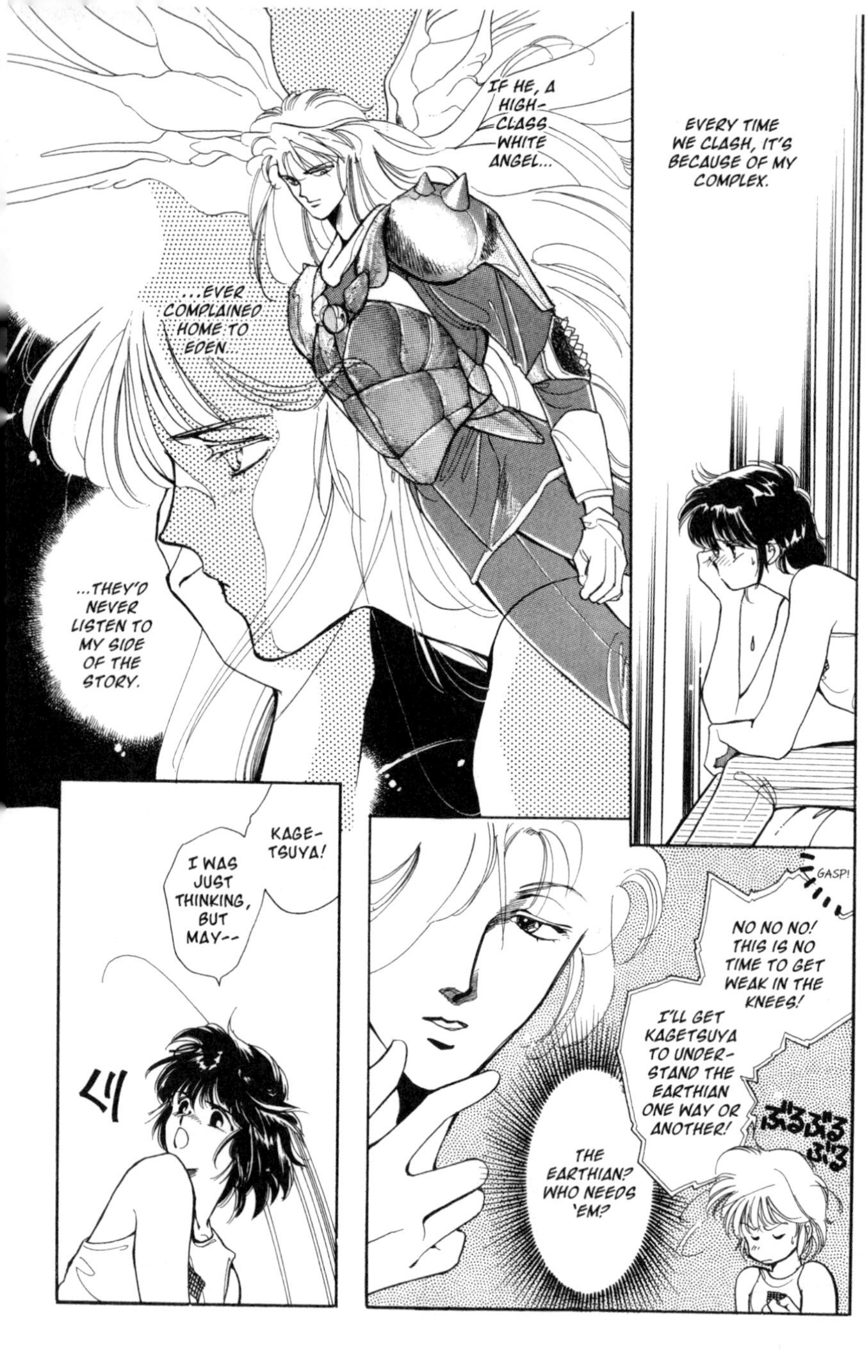
EVERY TIME WE CLASH, IT'S BECAUSE OF MY COMPLEX.
IF HE, A HIGH-CLASS WHITE ANGEL...
...EVER COMPLAINED HOME TO EDEN...
...THEY'D NEVER LISTEN TO MY SIDE OF THE STORY.
GASP!
NO NO NO! THIS IS NO TIME TO GET WEAK IN THE KNEES!
I'LL GET KAGETSUYA TO UNDER-STAND THE EARTHIAN ONE WAY OR ANOTHER!
ぶるぶるぶる
THE EARTHIAN? WHO NEEDS 'EM?
KAGE-TSUYA!
I WAS JUST THINKING, BUT MAY--
くり

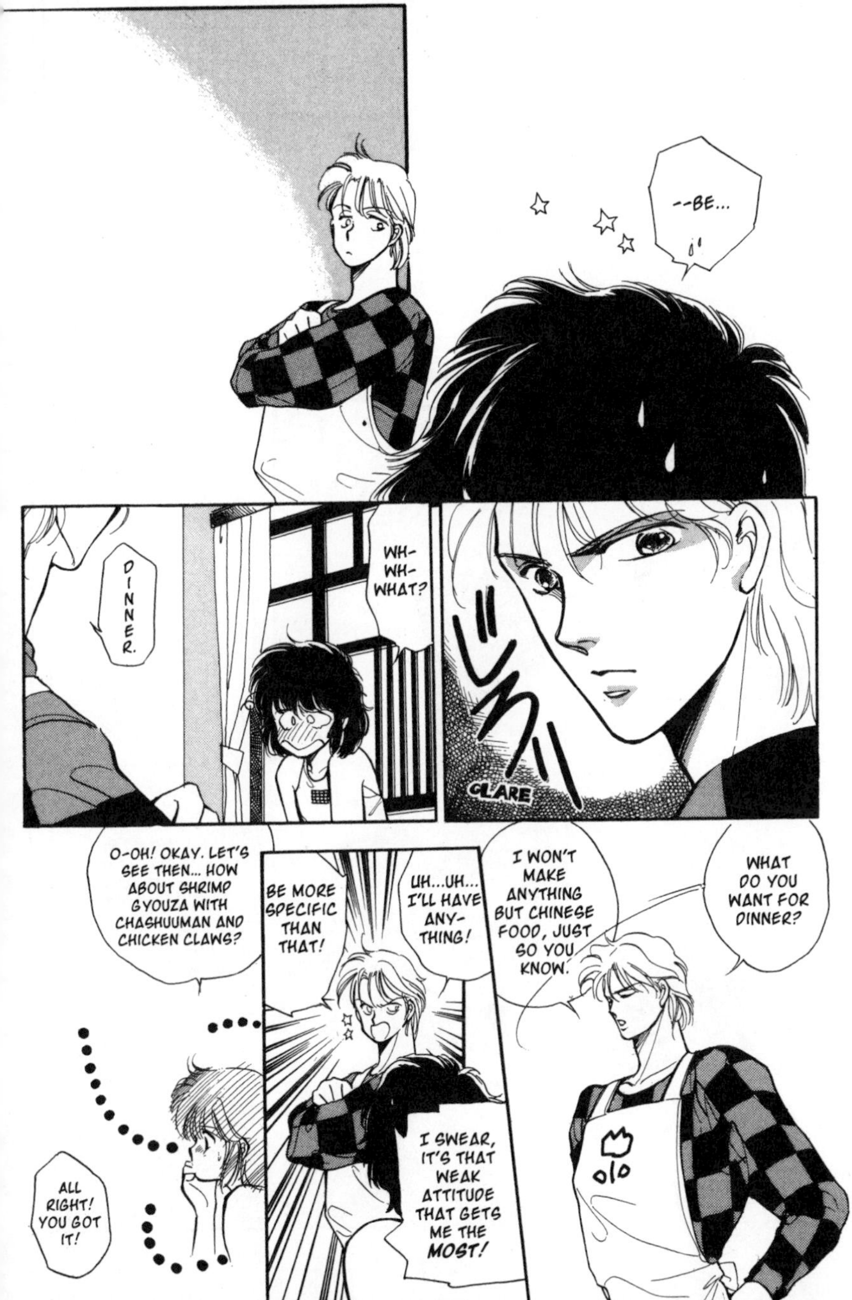
--BE...
GLARE
WH-WH-WHAT?
DINNER.
WHAT DO YOU WANT FOR DINNER?
I WON'T MAKE ANYTHING BUT CHINESE FOOD, JUST SO YOU KNOW.
UH...UH... I'LL HAVE ANY-THING!
BE MORE SPECIFIC THAN THAT!
I SWEAR, IT'S THAT WEAK ATTITUDE THAT GETS ME THE **MOST!**
O-OH! OKAY. LET'S SEE THEN... HOW ABOUT SHRIMP GYOUZA WITH CHASHUUMAN AND CHICKEN CLAWS?
ALL RIGHT! YOU GOT IT!

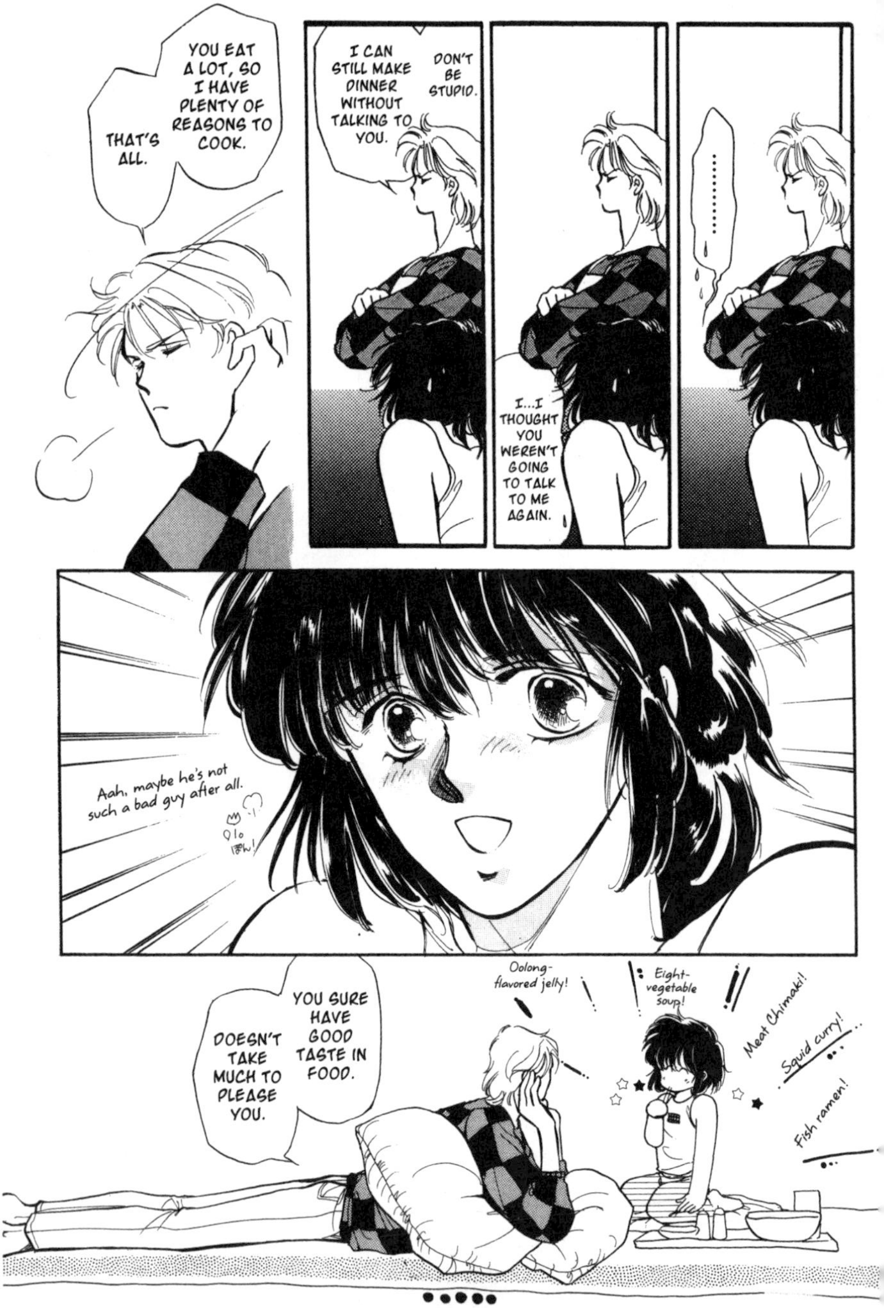
....
I...I THOUGHT YOU WEREN'T GOING TO TALK TO ME AGAIN.
DON'T BE STUPID.
I CAN STILL MAKE DINNER WITHOUT TALKING TO YOU.
YOU EAT A LOT, SO I HAVE PLENTY OF REASONS TO COOK.
THAT'S ALL.
Aah, maybe he's not such a bad guy after all.
ぽん!
Fish ramen!
Squid curry!
Meat Chimaki!
Eight-vegetable soup!
Oolong-flavored jelly!
YOU SURE HAVE GOOD TASTE IN FOOD.
DOESN'T TAKE MUCH TO PLEASE YOU.

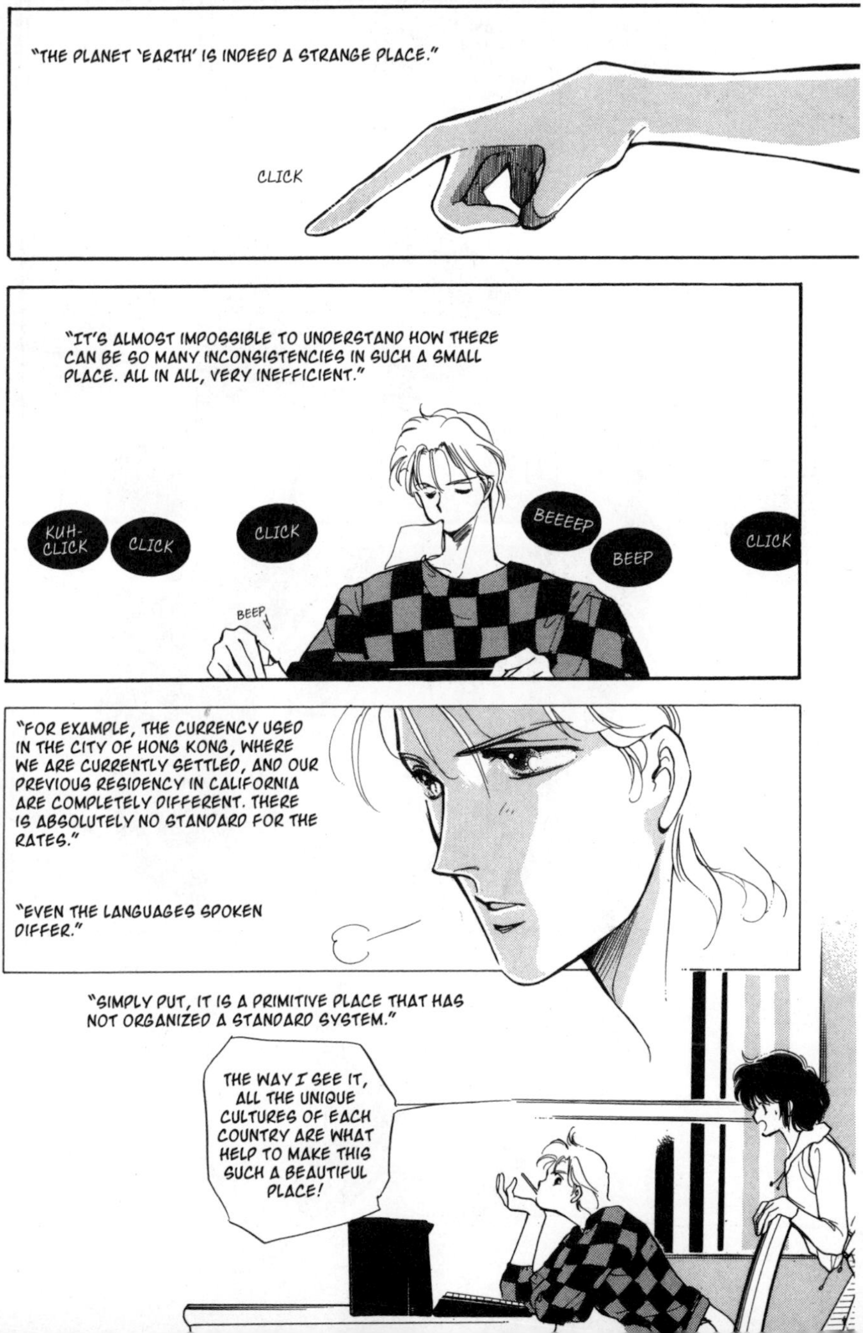
"THE PLANET 'EARTH' IS INDEED A STRANGE PLACE."
CLICK
"IT'S ALMOST IMPOSSIBLE TO UNDERSTAND HOW THERE CAN BE SO MANY INCONSISTENCIES IN SUCH A SMALL PLACE. ALL IN ALL, VERY INEFFICIENT."
CLICK
BEEP
BEEEEP
CLICK
CLICK
KUH-CLICK
BEEP
"FOR EXAMPLE, THE CURRENCY USED IN THE CITY OF HONG KONG, WHERE WE ARE CURRENTLY SETTLED, AND OUR PREVIOUS RESIDENCY IN CALIFORNIA ARE COMPLETELY DIFFERENT. THERE IS ABSOLUTELY NO STANDARD FOR THE RATES."
"EVEN THE LANGUAGES SPOKEN DIFFER."
"SIMPLY PUT, IT IS A PRIMITIVE PLACE THAT HAS NOT ORGANIZED A STANDARD SYSTEM."
THE WAY I SEE IT, ALL THE UNIQUE CULTURES OF EACH COUNTRY ARE WHAT HELP TO MAKE THIS SUCH A BEAUTIFUL PLACE!

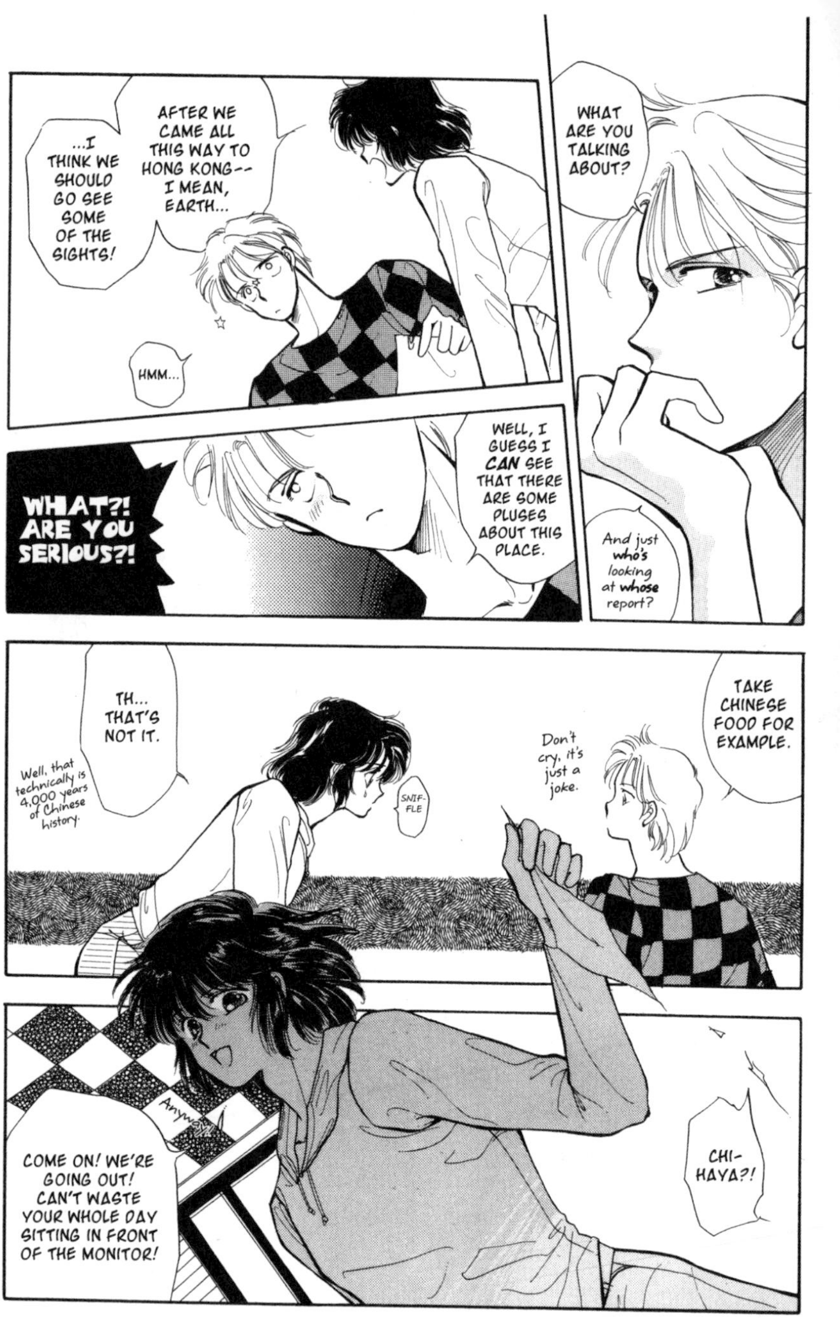
WHAT ARE YOU TALKING ABOUT?
And just who's looking at whose report?
AFTER WE CAME ALL THIS WAY TO HONG KONG-- I MEAN, EARTH...
...I THINK WE SHOULD GO SEE SOME OF THE SIGHTS!
HMM...
WELL, I GUESS I CAN SEE THAT THERE ARE SOME PLUSES ABOUT THIS PLACE.
WHAT?! ARE YOU SERIOUS?!
TAKE CHINESE FOOD FOR EXAMPLE.
Don't cry, it's just a joke.
SNIF-FLE
TH... THAT'S NOT IT.
Well, that technically is 4,000 years of Chinese history.
CHI-HAYA?!
COME ON! WE'RE GOING OUT! CAN'T WASTE YOUR WHOLE DAY SITTING IN FRONT OF THE MONITOR!

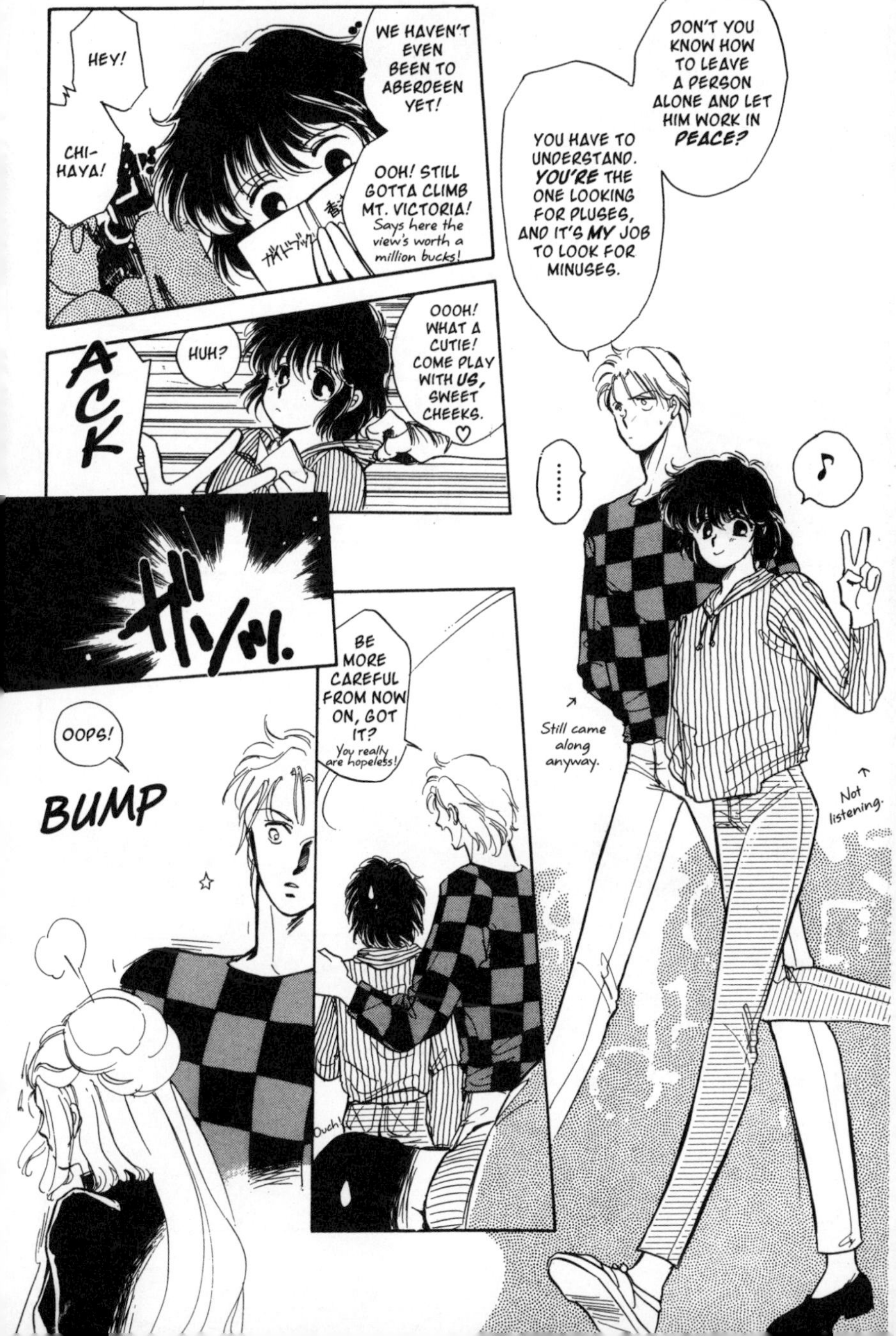
DON'T YOU KNOW HOW TO LEAVE A PERSON ALONE AND LET HIM WORK IN PEACE?
YOU HAVE TO UNDERSTAND. YOU'RE THE ONE LOOKING FOR PLUSES, AND IT'S MY JOB TO LOOK FOR MINUSES.
......
♪
Still came along anyway.
Not listening.
WE HAVEN'T EVEN BEEN TO ABERDEEN YET!
OOH! STILL GOTTA CLIMB MT. VICTORIA! Says here the view's worth a million bucks!
HEY!
CHI-HAYA!
OOOH! WHAT A CUTIE! COME PLAY WITH US, SWEET CHEEKS. ♡
HUH?
ACK
BE MORE CAREFUL FROM NOW ON, GOT IT? You really are hopeless!
Ouch!
OOPS!
BUMP

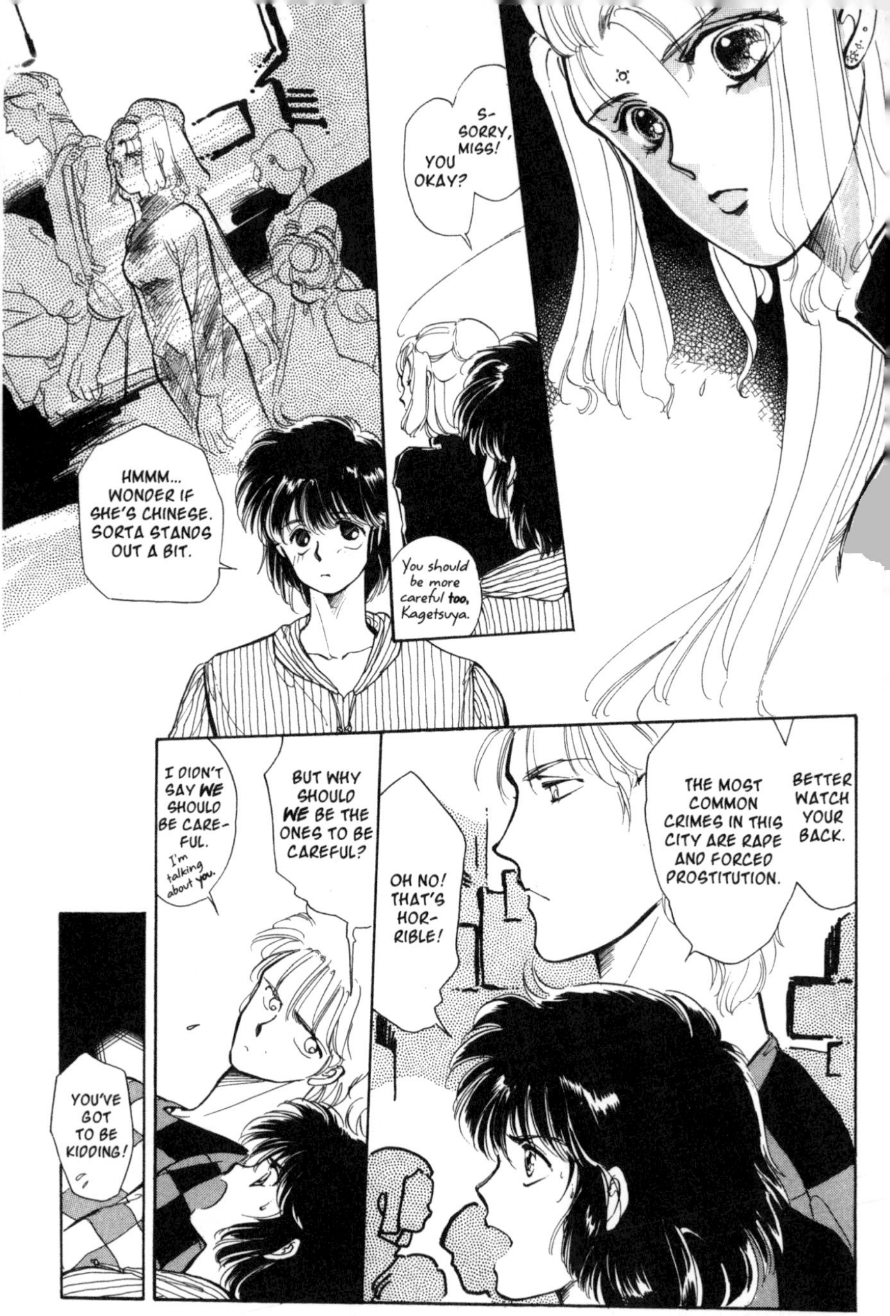
S-SORRY, MISS! YOU OKAY?
You should be more careful **too,** Kagetsuya.
HMMM... WONDER IF SHE'S CHINESE. SORTA STANDS OUT A BIT.
BETTER WATCH YOUR BACK.
THE MOST COMMON CRIMES IN THIS CITY ARE RAPE AND FORCED PROSTITUTION.
OH NO! THAT'S HORRIBLE!
BUT WHY SHOULD **WE** BE THE ONES TO BE CAREFUL?
I DIDN'T SAY **WE** SHOULD BE CAREFUL.
I'm talking about **you.**
YOU'VE GOT TO BE KIDDING!

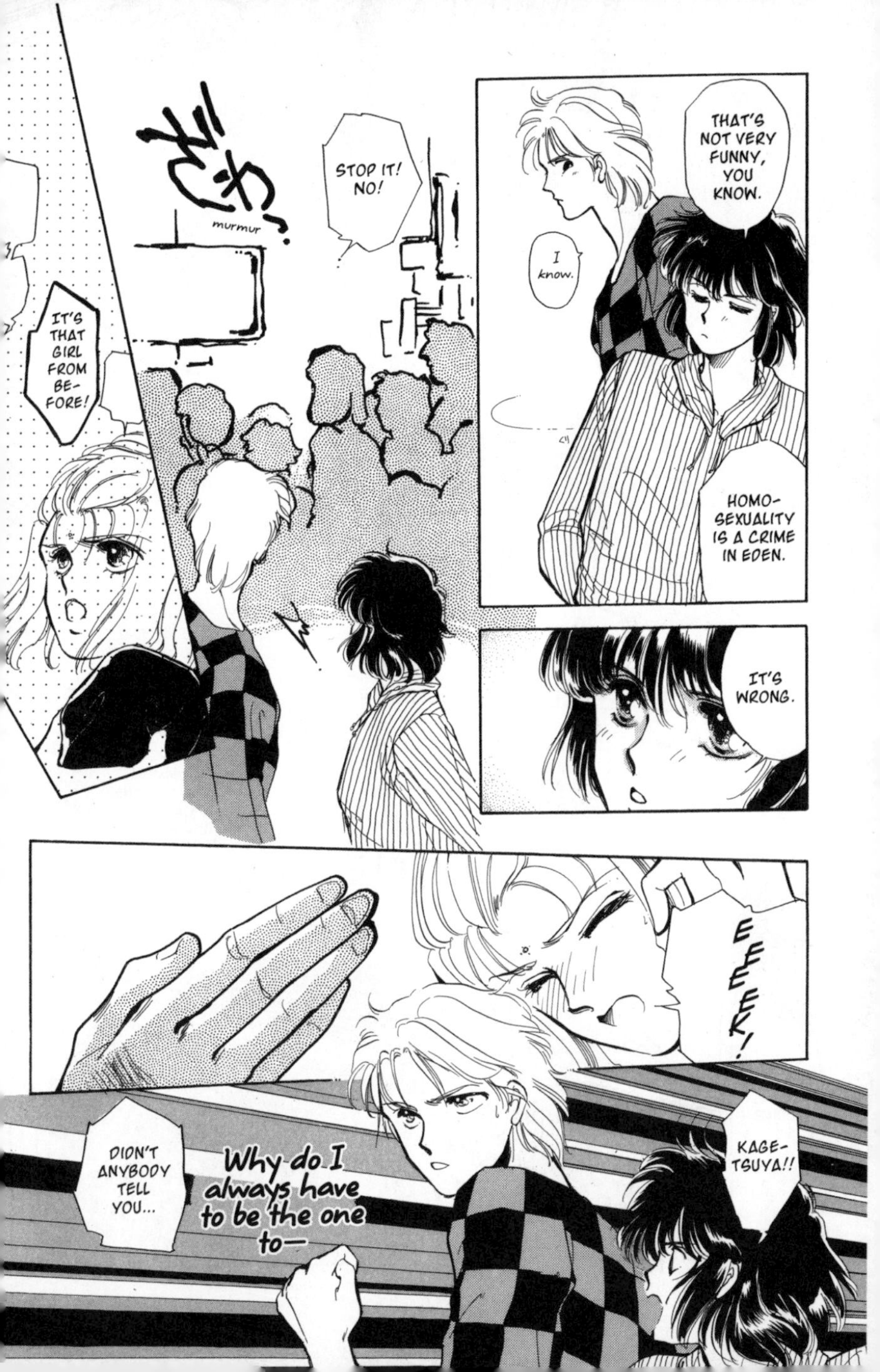
THAT'S NOT VERY FUNNY, YOU KNOW.
I know.
HOMO-SEXUALITY IS A CRIME IN EDEN.
IT'S WRONG.
STOP IT! NO!
murmur
IT'S THAT GIRL FROM BE-FORE!
EEEEK!
KAGE-TSUYA!!
DIDN'T ANYBODY TELL YOU...
Why do I always have to be the one to—

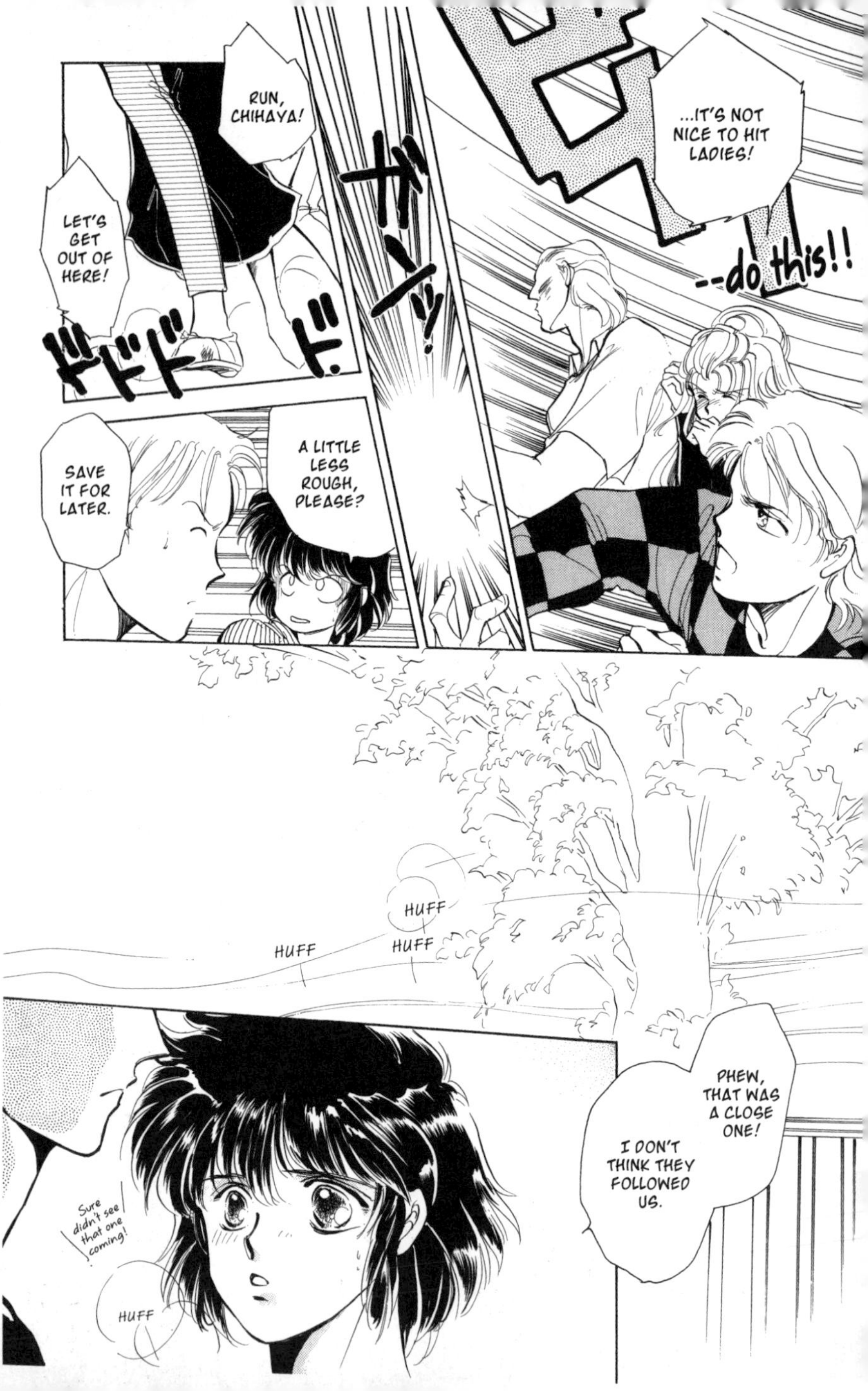
...IT'S NOT NICE TO HIT LADIES!
--do this!!
ガンッ!
RUN, CHIHAYA!
LET'S GET OUT OF HERE!
ドドドド
A LITTLE LESS ROUGH, PLEASE?
SAVE IT FOR LATER.
HUFF
HUFF
HUFF
PHEW, THAT WAS A CLOSE ONE!
I DON'T THINK THEY FOLLOWED US.
Sure didn't see that one coming!
HUFF

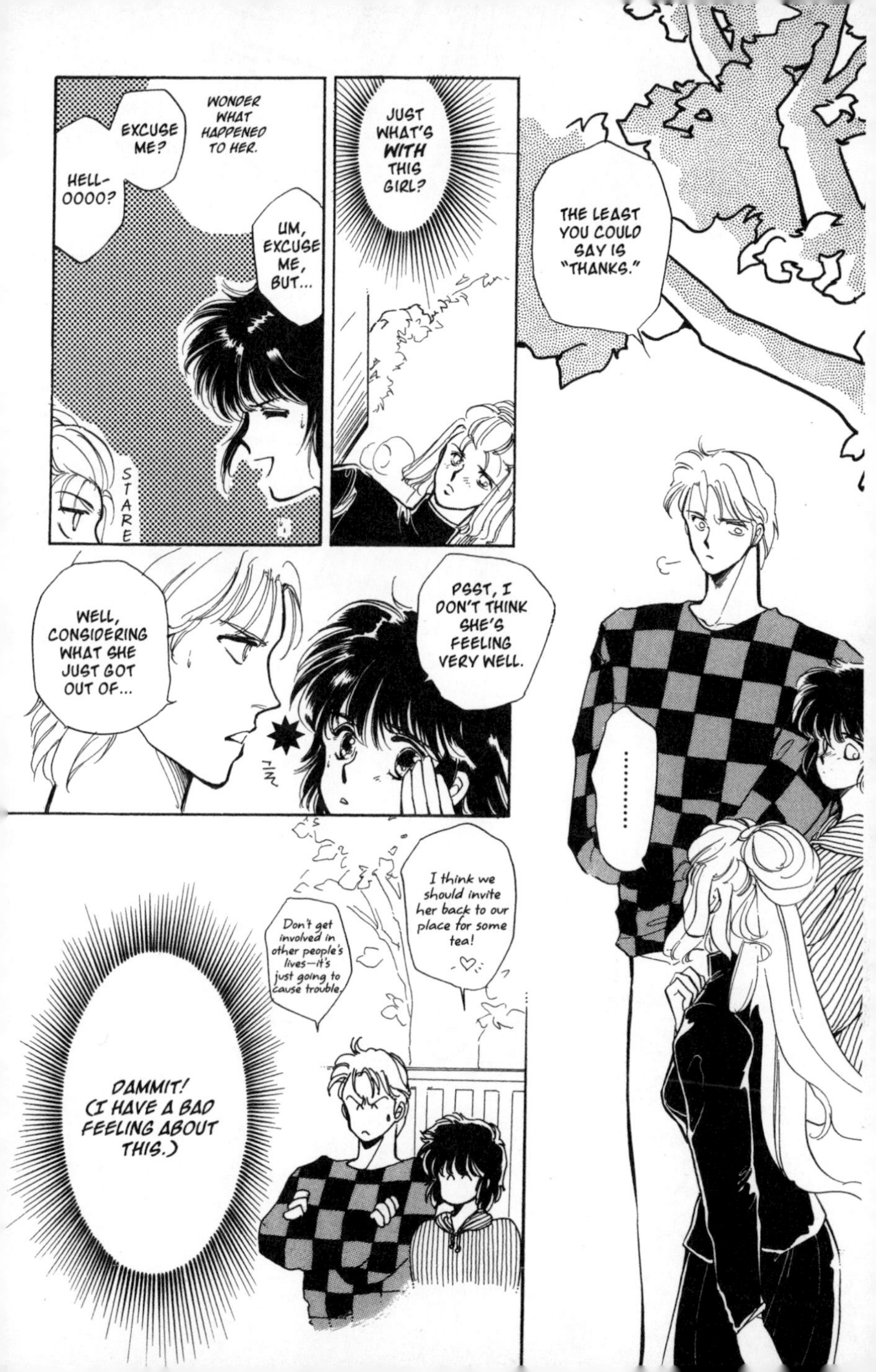
THE LEAST YOU COULD SAY IS "THANKS."
......
JUST WHAT'S **WITH** THIS GIRL?
WONDER WHAT HAPPENED TO HER.
UM, EXCUSE ME, BUT...
EXCUSE ME?
HELL-OOOO?
STARE
PSST, I DON'T THINK SHE'S FEELING VERY WELL.
WELL, CONSIDERING WHAT SHE JUST GOT OUT OF...
I think we should invite her back to our place for some tea!
Don't get involved in other people's lives—it's just going to cause trouble.
DAMMIT! (I HAVE A BAD FEELING ABOUT THIS.)

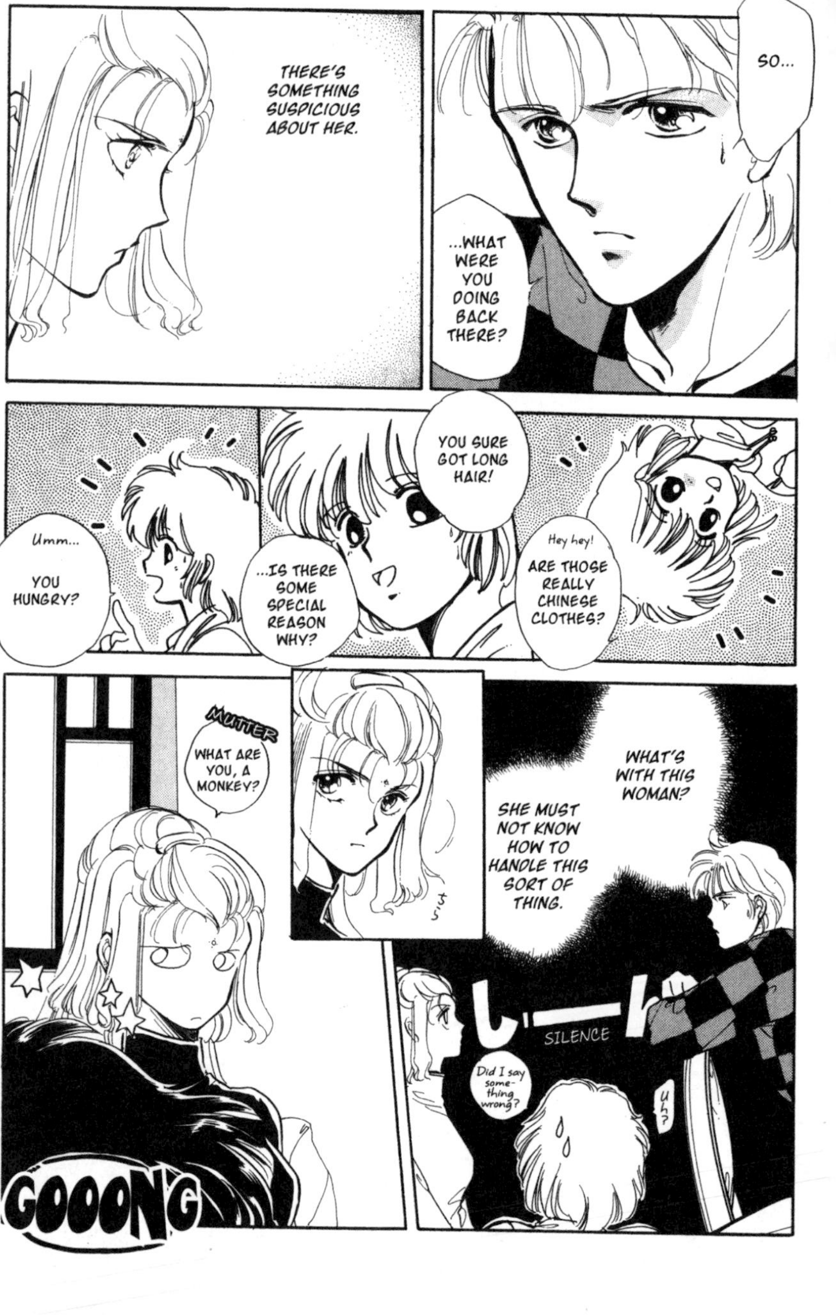
SO...
...WHAT WERE YOU DOING BACK THERE?
THERE'S SOMETHING SUSPICIOUS ABOUT HER.
Hey hey!
ARE THOSE REALLY CHINESE CLOTHES?
YOU SURE GOT LONG HAIR!
...IS THERE SOME SPECIAL REASON WHY?
Umm...
YOU HUNGRY?
WHAT'S WITH THIS WOMAN?
SHE MUST NOT KNOW HOW TO HANDLE THIS SORT OF THING.
SILENCE
Uh?
Did I say something wrong?
MUTTER
WHAT ARE YOU, A MONKEY?
GOOONG

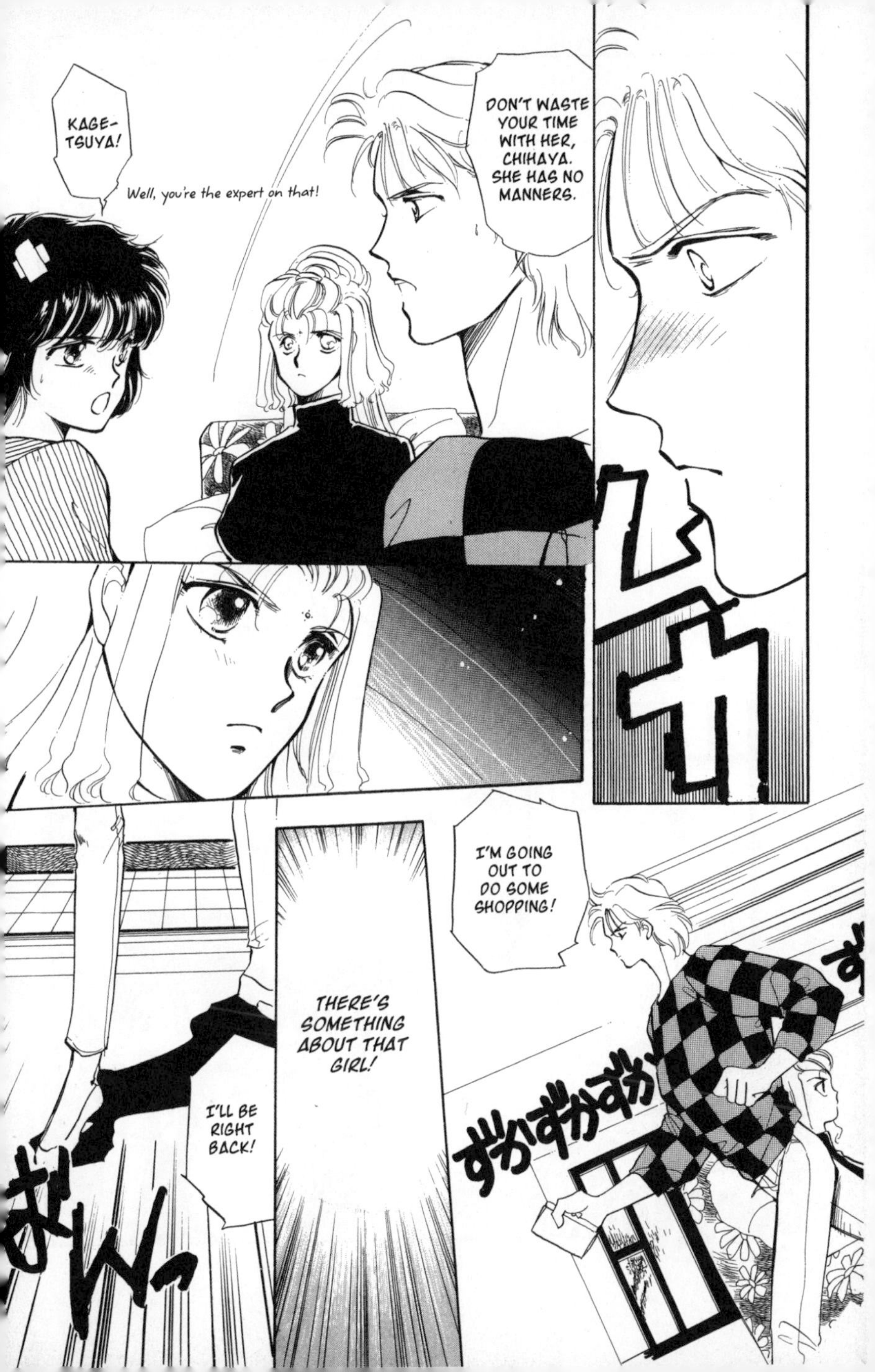
ムカ
DON'T WASTE YOUR TIME WITH HER, CHIHAYA. SHE HAS NO MANNERS.
KAGE-TSUYA!
Well, you're the expert on that!
I'M GOING OUT TO DO SOME SHOPPING!
ず
ずかずかずか
THERE'S SOMETHING ABOUT THAT GIRL!
I'LL BE RIGHT BACK!
ずんっ

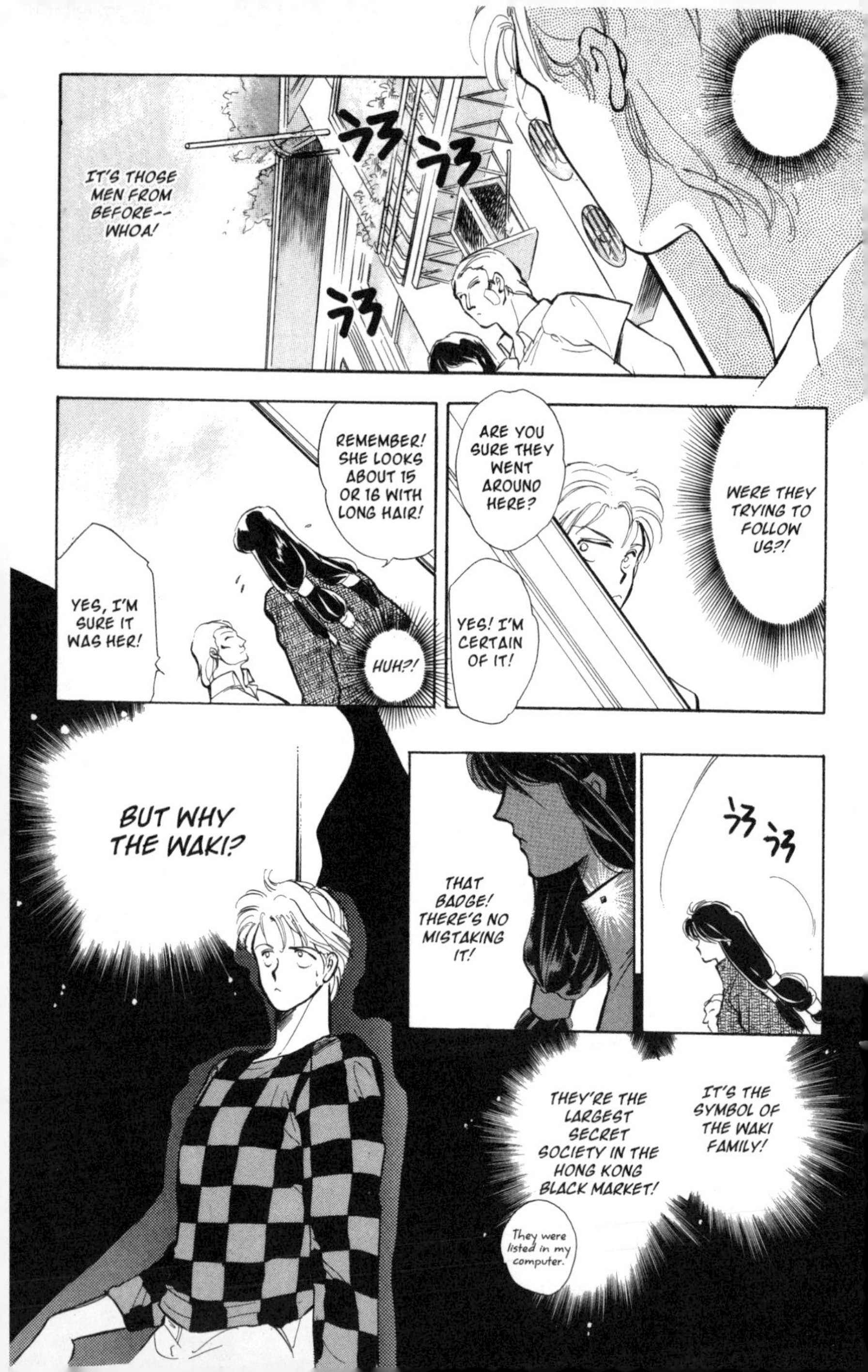

うろ
うろ
うろ
IT'S THOSE MEN FROM BEFORE-- WHOA!
WERE THEY TRYING TO FOLLOW US?!
ARE YOU SURE THEY WENT AROUND HERE?
YES! I'M CERTAIN OF IT!
REMEMBER! SHE LOOKS ABOUT 15 OR 16 WITH LONG HAIR!
YES, I'M SURE IT WAS HER!
HUH?!
うろ うろ
THAT BADGE! THERE'S NO MISTAKING IT!
IT'S THE SYMBOL OF THE WAKI FAMILY!
THEY'RE THE LARGEST SECRET SOCIETY IN THE HONG KONG BLACK MARKET!
They were listed in my computer.
BUT WHY THE WAKI?

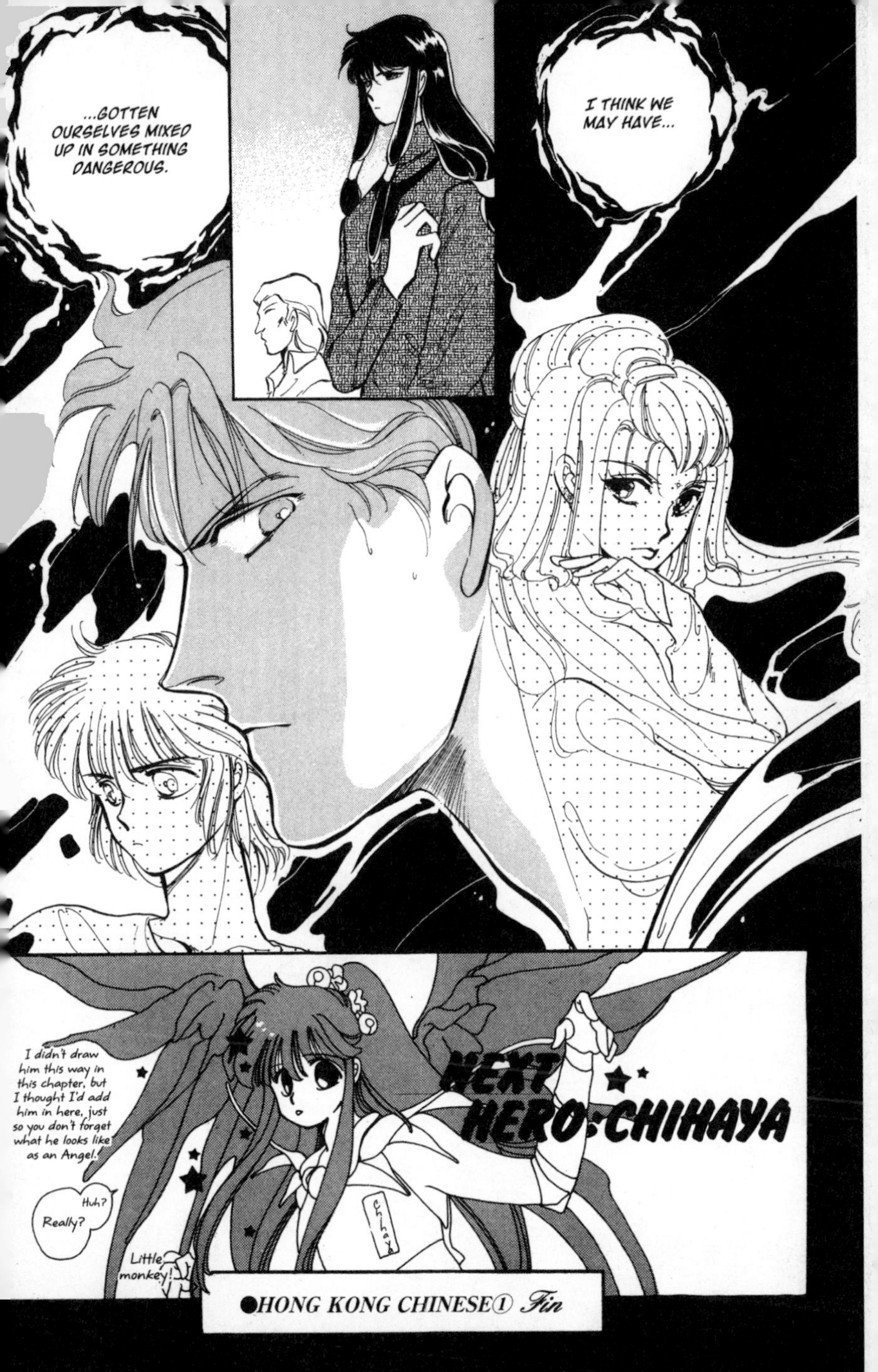

I THINK WE MAY HAVE...
...GOTTEN OURSELVES MIXED UP IN SOMETHING DANGEROUS.
NEXT HERO: CHIHAYA
Chihaya
I didn't draw him this way in this chapter, but I thought I'd add him in here, just so you don't forget what he looks like as an Angel.
Huh? Really?
Little monkey!
●HONG KONG CHINESE① Fin

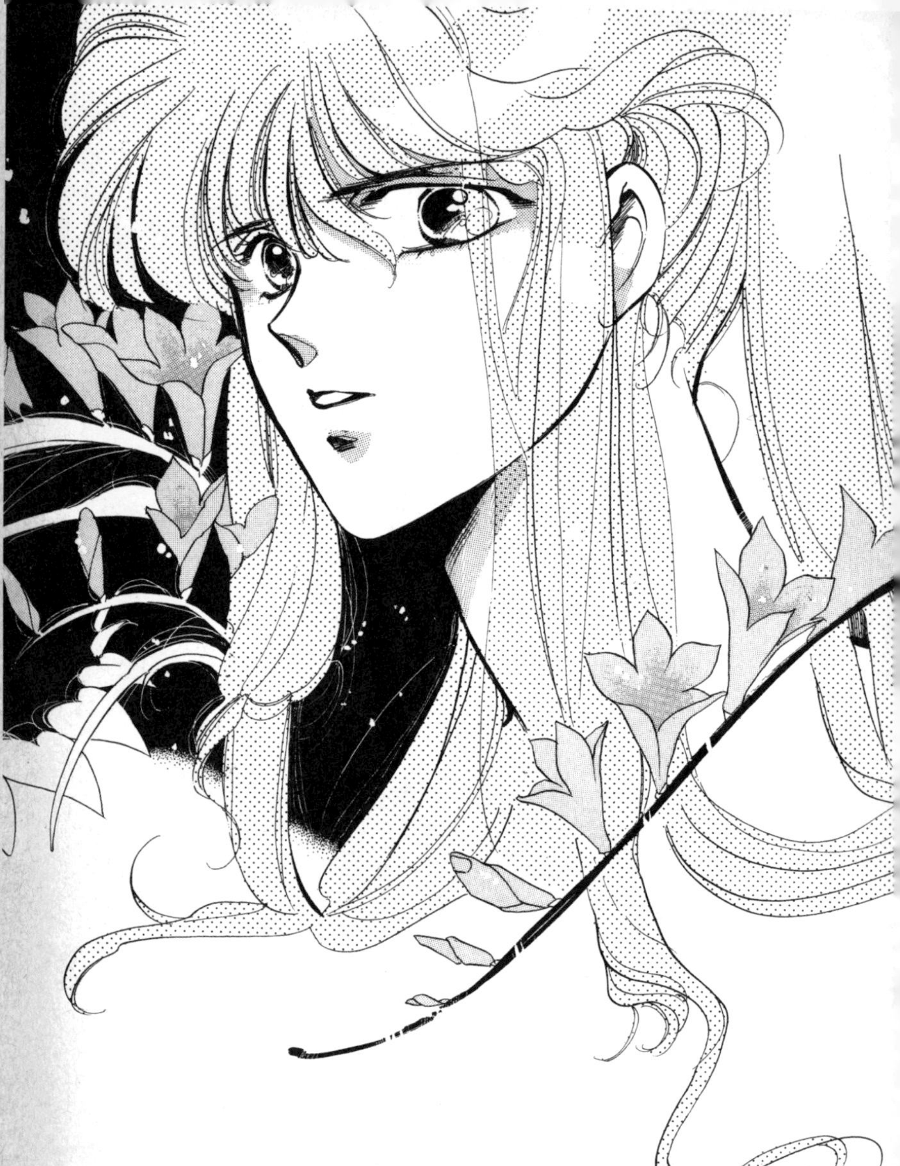

HONG KONG CHINESE PART 2

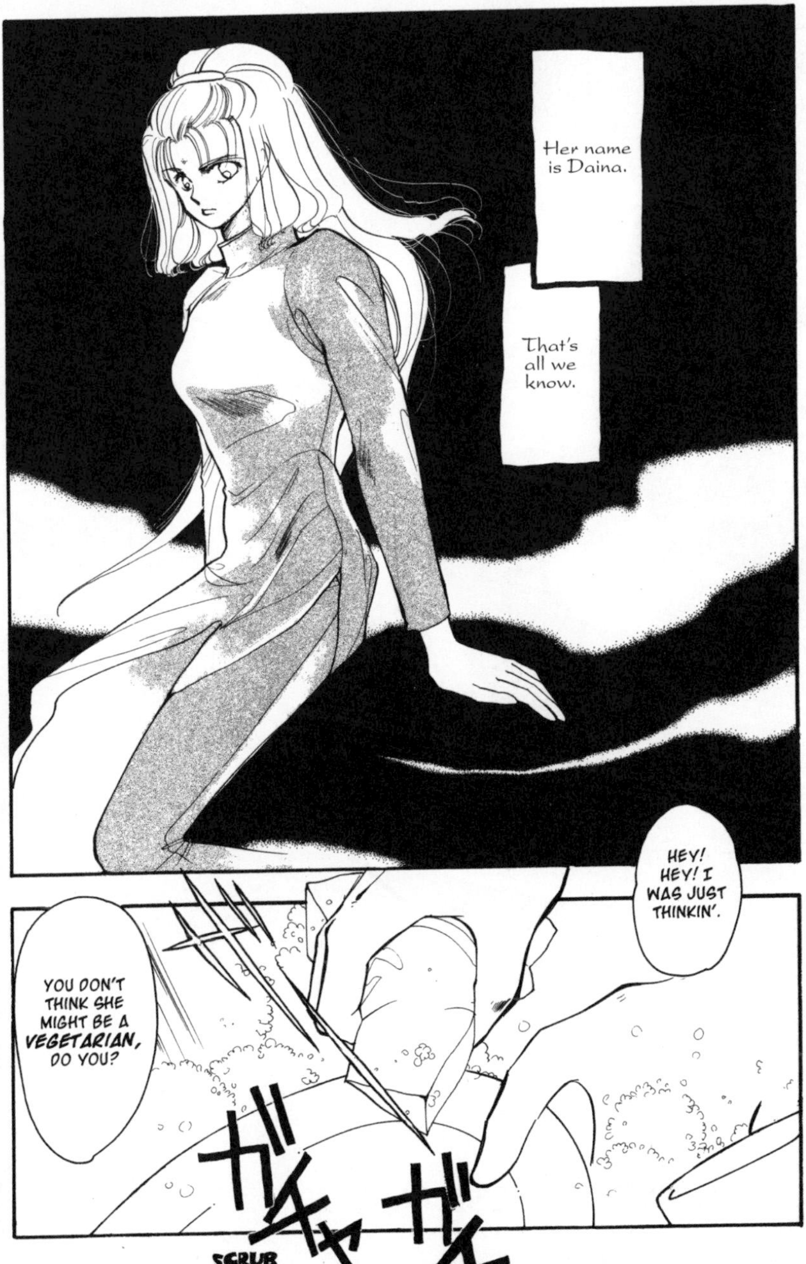
Her name is Daina.
That's all we know.
HEY! HEY! I WAS JUST THINKIN'.
YOU DON'T THINK SHE MIGHT BE A VEGETARIAN, DO YOU?
SCRUB
SCRUB

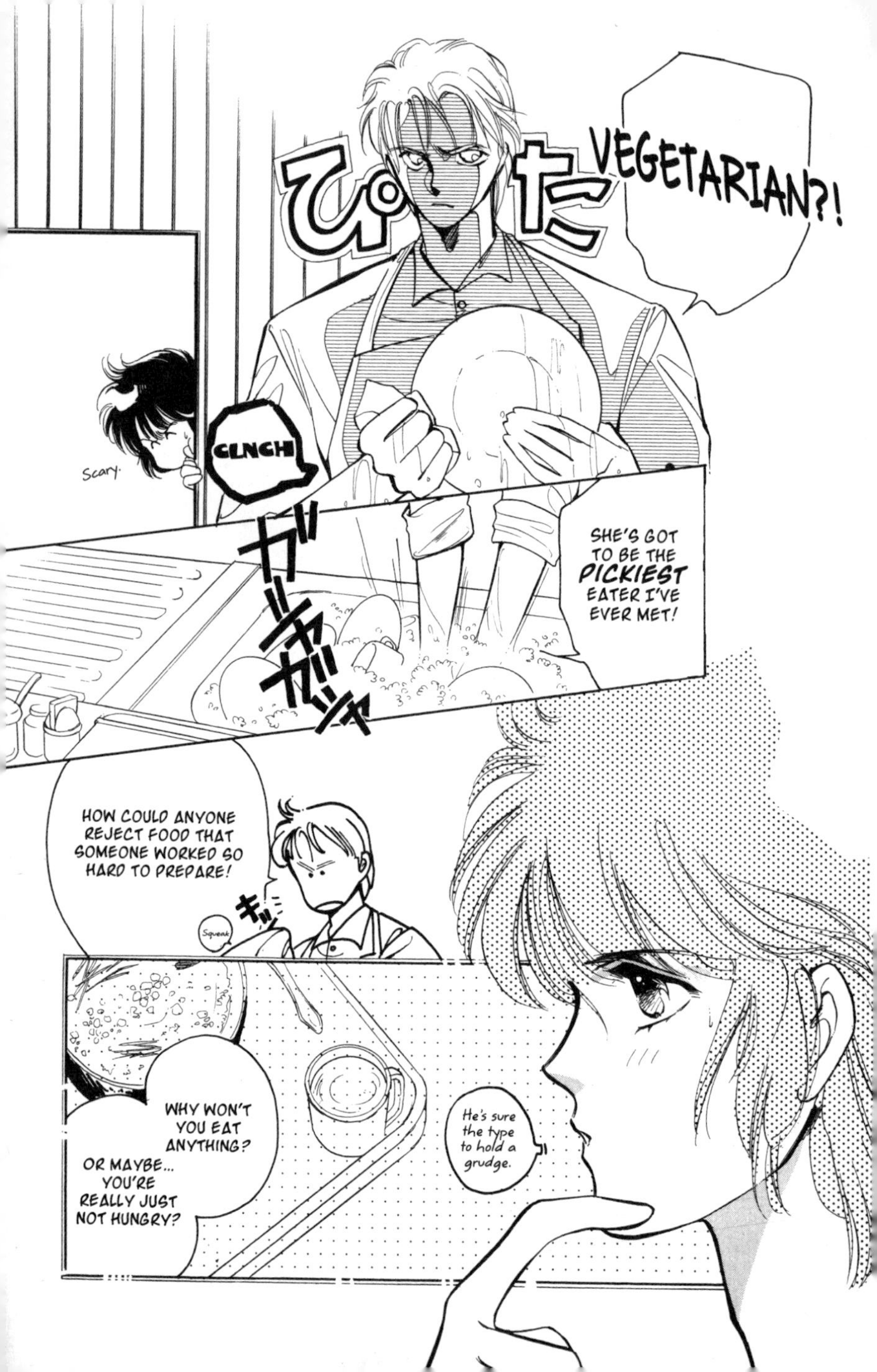
VEGETARIAN?!
GLNCH
Scary.
SHE'S GOT TO BE THE PICKIEST EATER I'VE EVER MET!
HOW COULD ANYONE REJECT FOOD THAT SOMEONE WORKED SO HARD TO PREPARE!
Squeak
He's sure the type to hold a grudge.
WHY WON'T YOU EAT ANYTHING? OR MAYBE... YOU'RE REALLY JUST NOT HUNGRY?

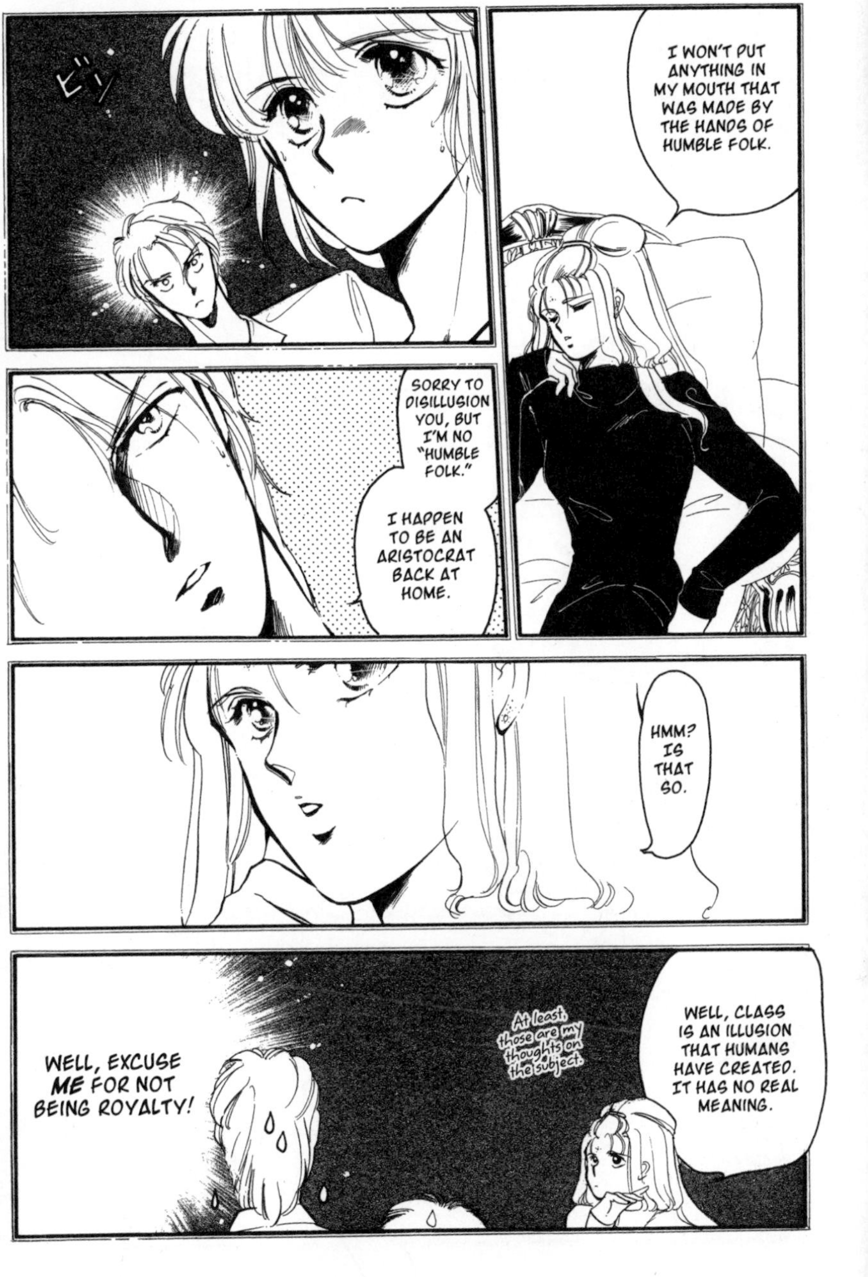

I WON'T PUT ANYTHING IN MY MOUTH THAT WAS MADE BY THE HANDS OF HUMBLE FOLK.
SORRY TO DISILLUSION YOU, BUT I'M NO "HUMBLE FOLK."
I HAPPEN TO BE AN ARISTOCRAT BACK AT HOME.
HMM? IS THAT SO.
WELL, CLASS IS AN ILLUSION THAT HUMANS HAVE CREATED. IT HAS NO REAL MEANING.
At least, those are my thoughts on the subject.
WELL, EXCUSE ***ME*** FOR NOT BEING ROYALTY!

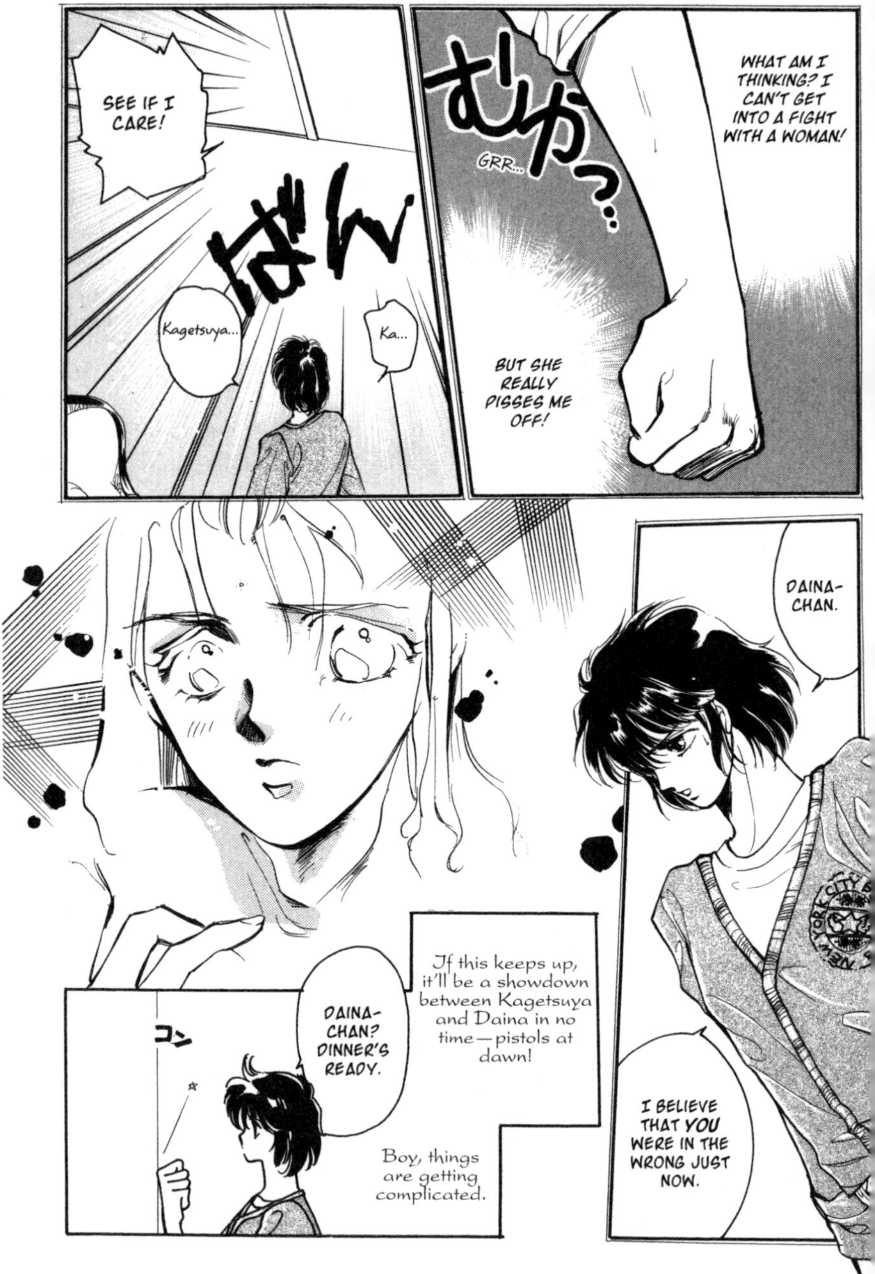
WHAT AM I THINKING? I CAN'T GET INTO A FIGHT WITH A WOMAN!
むかっ…
GRR...
BUT SHE REALLY PISSES ME OFF!
SEE IF I CARE!
ばん
Ka...
Kagetsuya...
DAINA-CHAN.
I BELIEVE THAT YOU WERE IN THE WRONG JUST NOW.
If this keeps up, it'll be a showdown between Kagetsuya and Daina in no time—pistols at dawn!
DAINA-CHAN? DINNER'S READY.
コン
Boy, things are getting complicated.

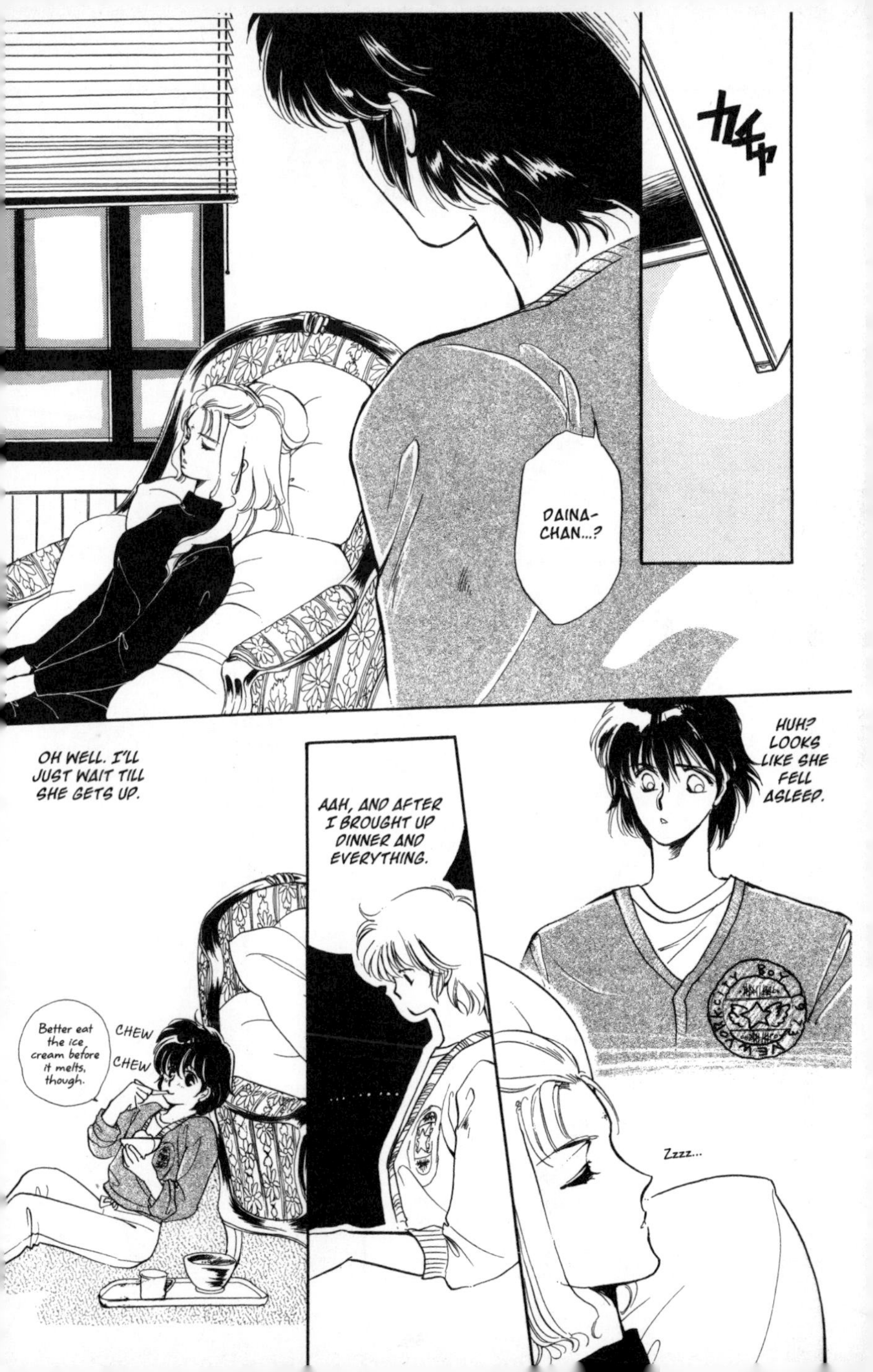
カチャ
DAINA-CHAN...?
HUH? LOOKS LIKE SHE FELL ASLEEP.
Zzzz...
AAH, AND AFTER I BROUGHT UP DINNER AND EVERYTHING.
......
OH WELL. I'LL JUST WAIT TILL SHE GETS UP.
Better eat the ice cream before it melts, though.
CHEW
CHEW

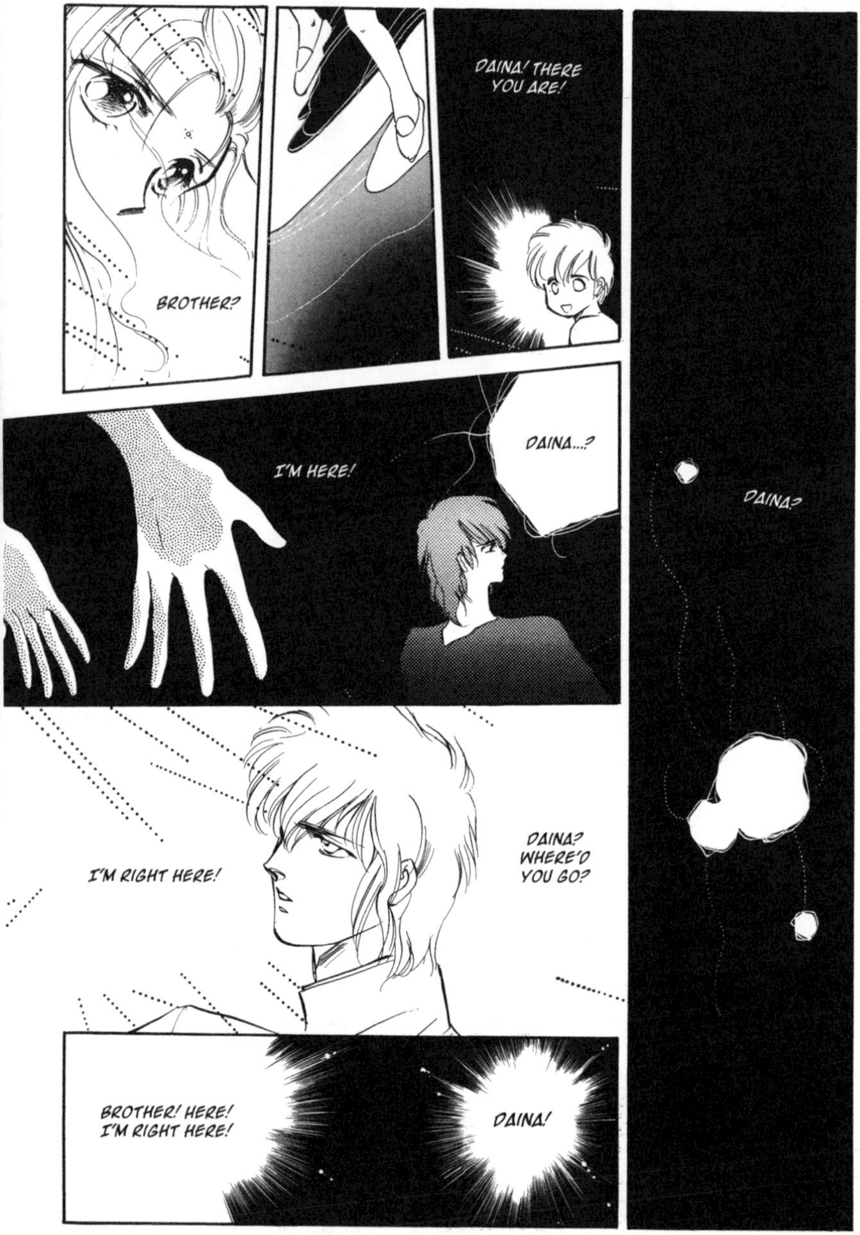
DAINA?
DAINA! THERE YOU ARE!
BROTHER?
DAINA...?
I'M HERE!
DAINA? WHERE'D YOU GO?
I'M RIGHT HERE!
DAINA!
BROTHER! HERE! I'M RIGHT HERE!

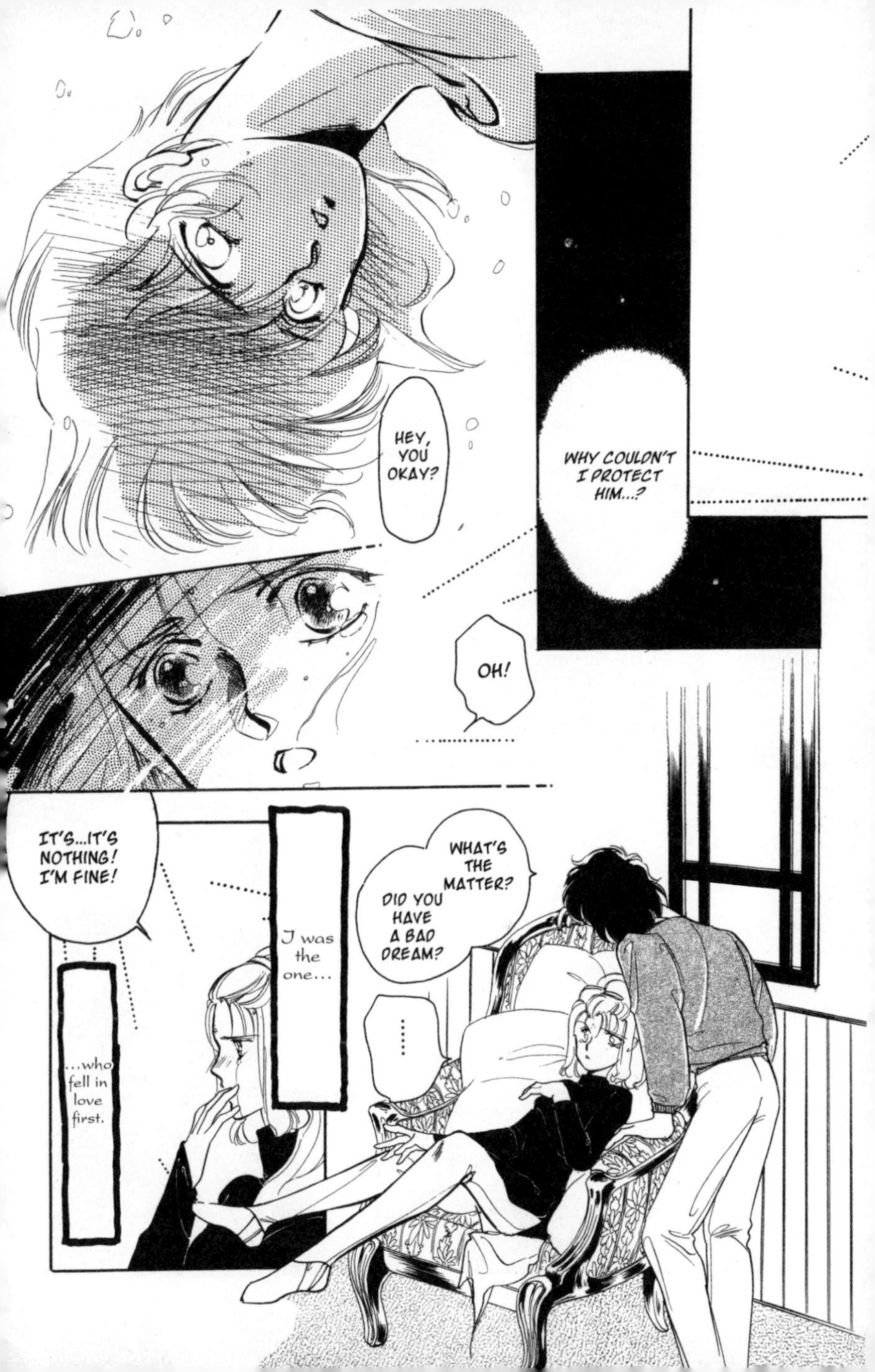
WHY COULDN'T I PROTECT HIM...?
HEY, YOU OKAY?
OH!
WHAT'S THE MATTER?
DID YOU HAVE A BAD DREAM?
...
IT'S...IT'S NOTHING! I'M FINE!
I was the one...
...who fell in love first.

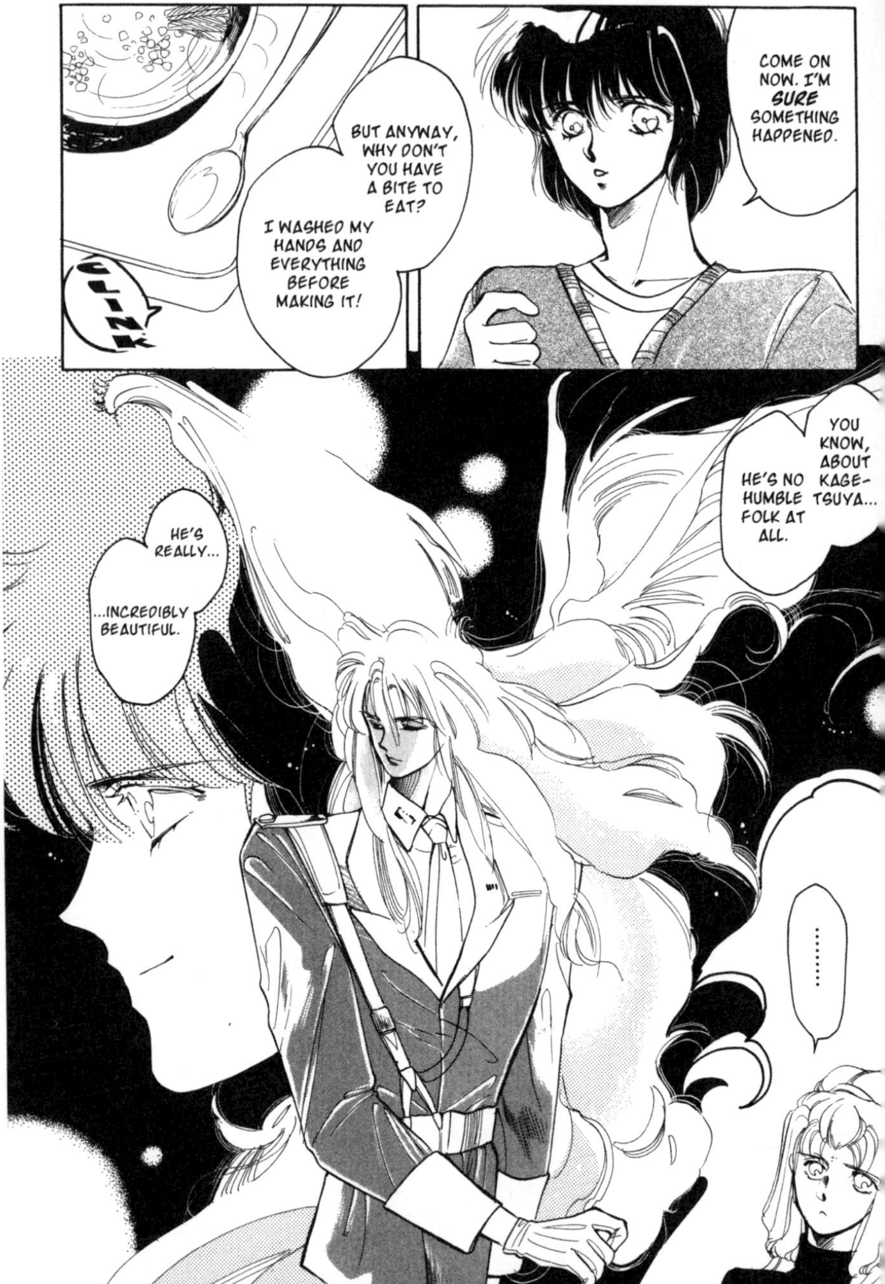
COME ON NOW. I'M SURE SOMETHING HAPPENED.
BUT ANYWAY, WHY DON'T YOU HAVE A BITE TO EAT?
I WASHED MY HANDS AND EVERYTHING BEFORE MAKING IT!
CLINK
YOU KNOW, ABOUT KAGE-TSUYA...
HE'S NO HUMBLE FOLK AT ALL.
HE'S REALLY...
...INCREDIBLY BEAUTIFUL.
......

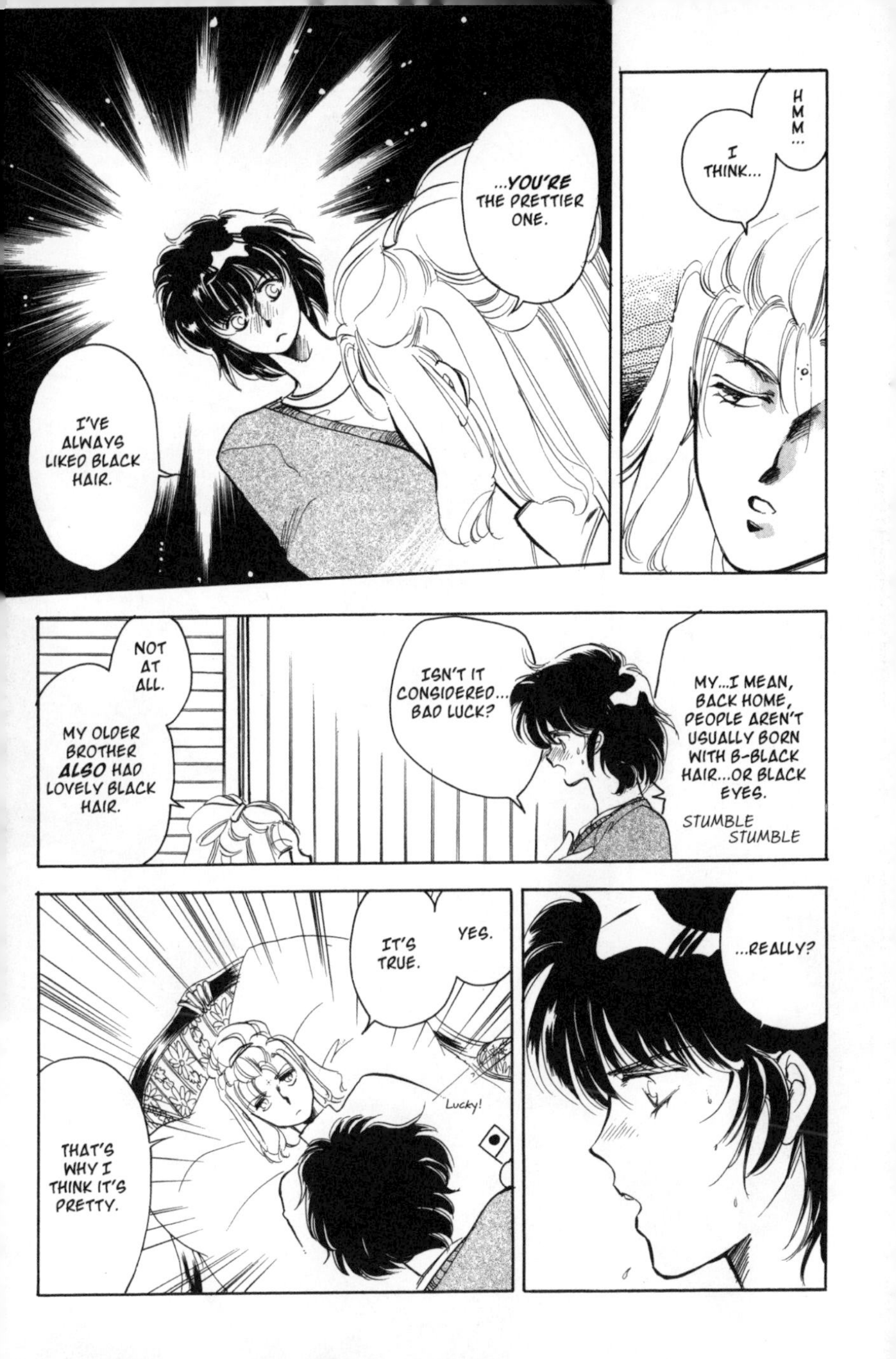
HMM... I THINK...
...YOU'RE THE PRETTIER ONE.
I'VE ALWAYS LIKED BLACK HAIR.
MY...I MEAN, BACK HOME, PEOPLE AREN'T USUALLY BORN WITH B-BLACK HAIR...OR BLACK EYES.
STUMBLE STUMBLE
ISN'T IT CONSIDERED... BAD LUCK?
NOT AT ALL.
MY OLDER BROTHER ALSO HAD LOVELY BLACK HAIR.
...REALLY?
YES.
IT'S TRUE.
Lucky!
THAT'S WHY I THINK IT'S PRETTY.

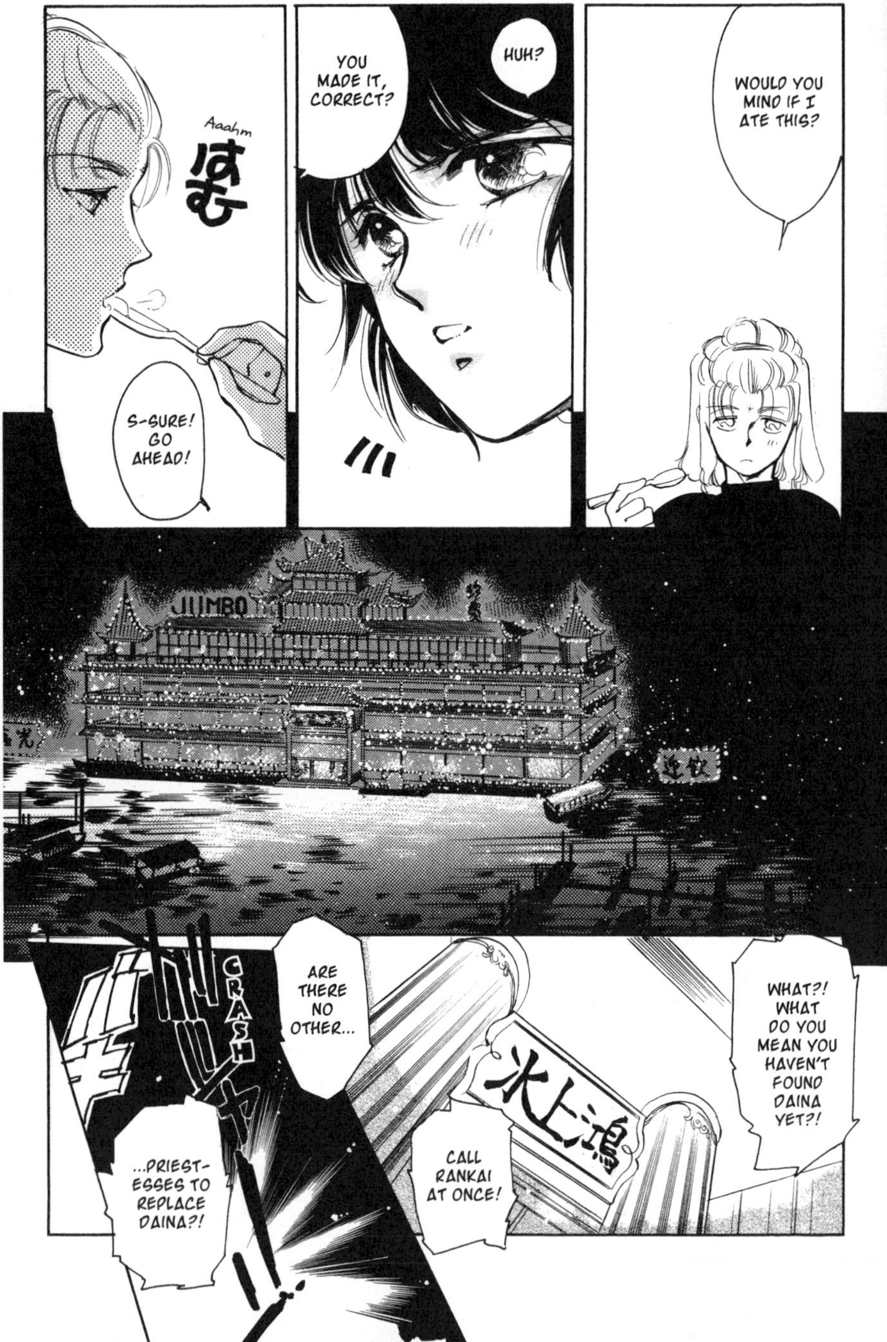
WOULD YOU MIND IF I ATE THIS?
HUH?
YOU MADE IT, CORRECT?
Aaahm
はむ
S-SURE! GO AHEAD!
JUMBO
WHAT?! WHAT DO YOU MEAN YOU HAVEN'T FOUND DAINA YET?!
CALL RANKAI AT ONCE!
氷上鴻
ARE THERE NO OTHER...
...PRIEST-ESSES TO REPLACE DAINA?!
CRASH

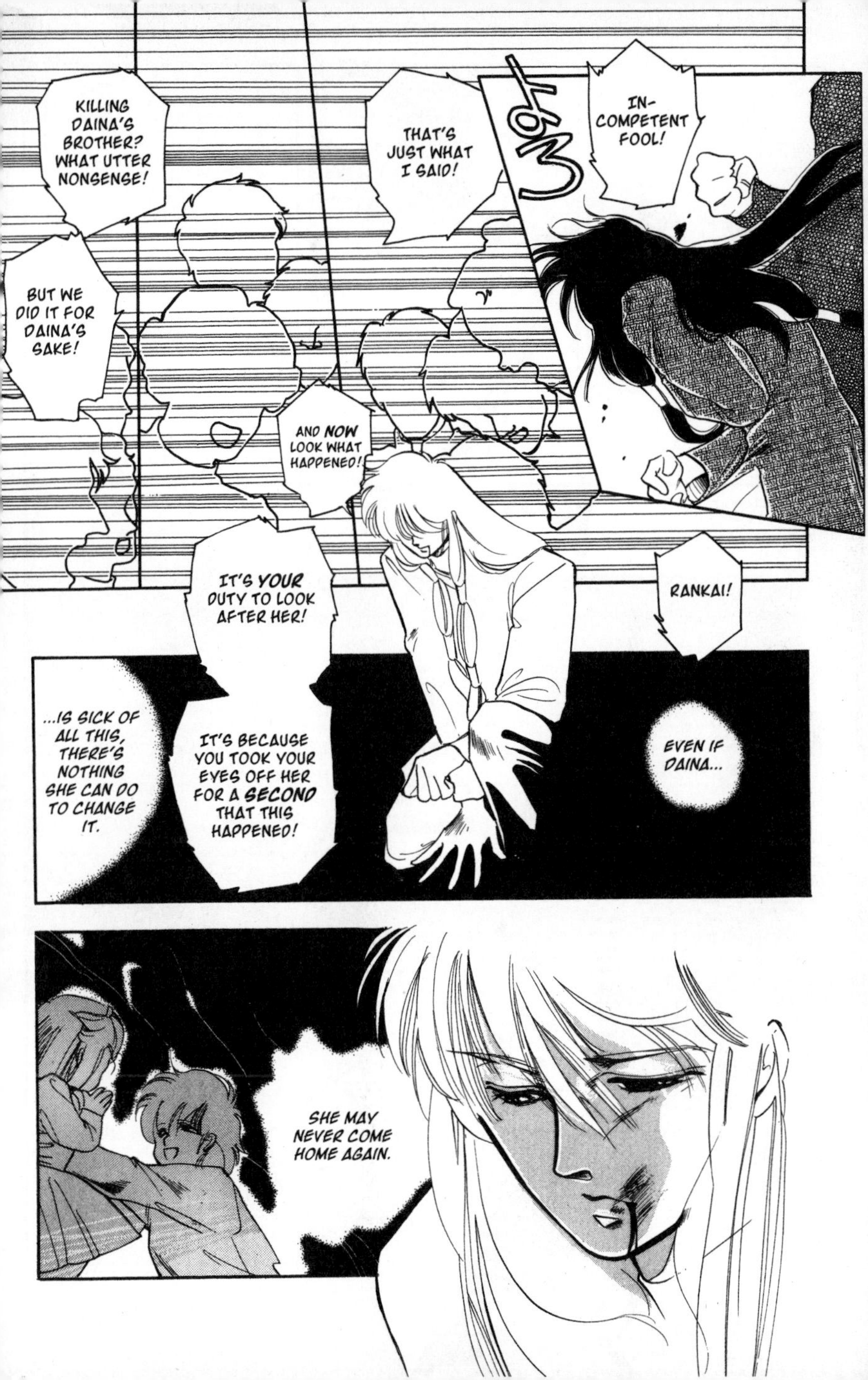
IN-COMPETENT FOOL!
THAT'S JUST WHAT I SAID!
KILLING DAINA'S BROTHER? WHAT UTTER NONSENSE!
BUT WE DID IT FOR DAINA'S SAKE!
AND NOW LOOK WHAT HAPPENED!
IT'S YOUR DUTY TO LOOK AFTER HER!
RANKAI!
EVEN IF DAINA...
IT'S BECAUSE YOU TOOK YOUR EYES OFF HER FOR A SECOND THAT THIS HAPPENED!
...IS SICK OF ALL THIS, THERE'S NOTHING SHE CAN DO TO CHANGE IT.
SHE MAY NEVER COME HOME AGAIN.

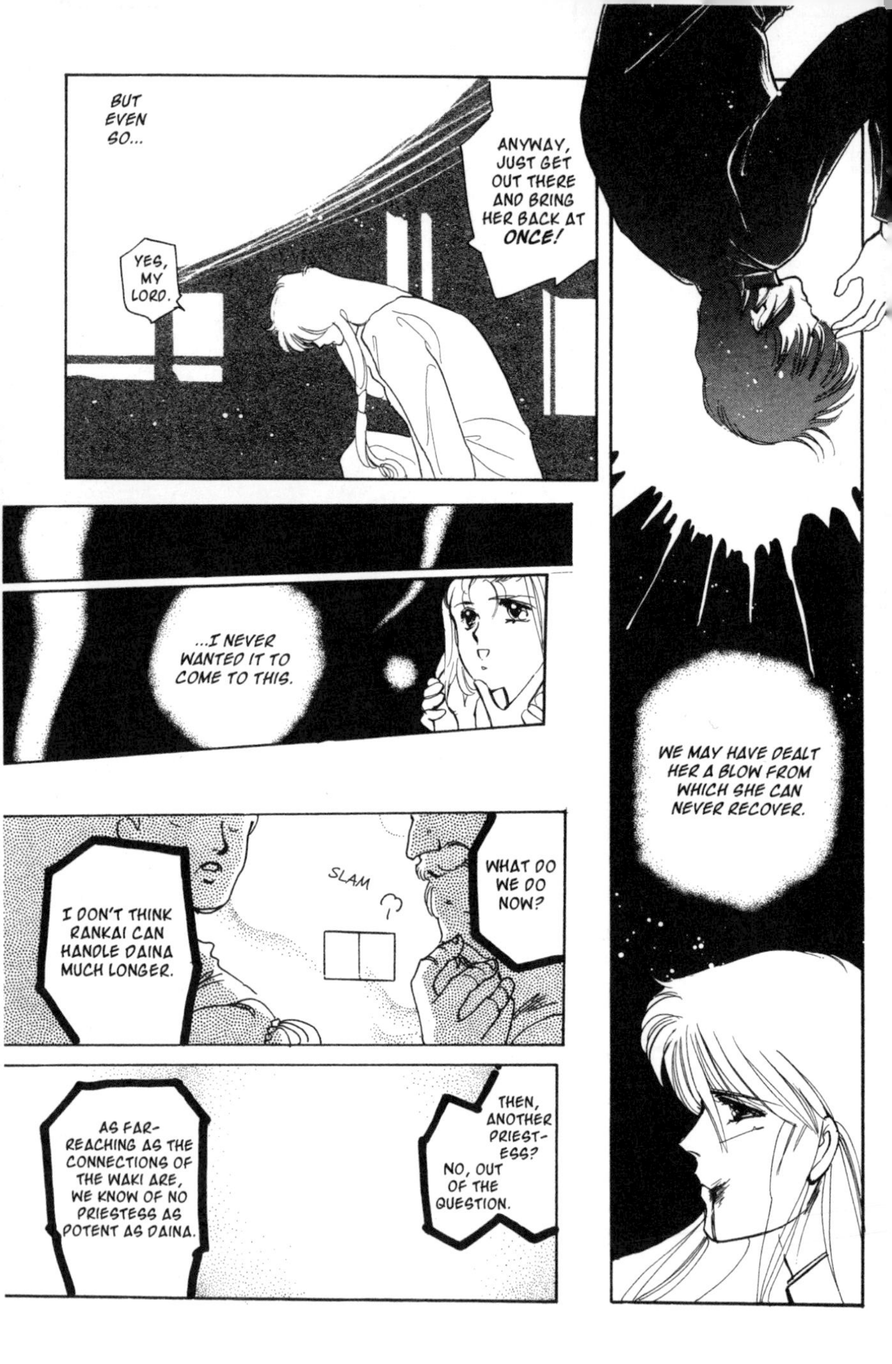
WE MAY HAVE DEALT HER A BLOW FROM WHICH SHE CAN NEVER RECOVER.
ANYWAY, JUST GET OUT THERE AND BRING HER BACK AT ONCE!
BUT EVEN SO...
YES, MY LORD.
...I NEVER WANTED IT TO COME TO THIS.
WHAT DO WE DO NOW?
SLAM
I DON'T THINK RANKAI CAN HANDLE DAINA MUCH LONGER.
THEN, ANOTHER PRIEST-ESS?
NO, OUT OF THE QUESTION.
AS FAR-REACHING AS THE CONNECTIONS OF THE WAKI ARE, WE KNOW OF NO PRIESTESS AS POTENT AS DAINA.

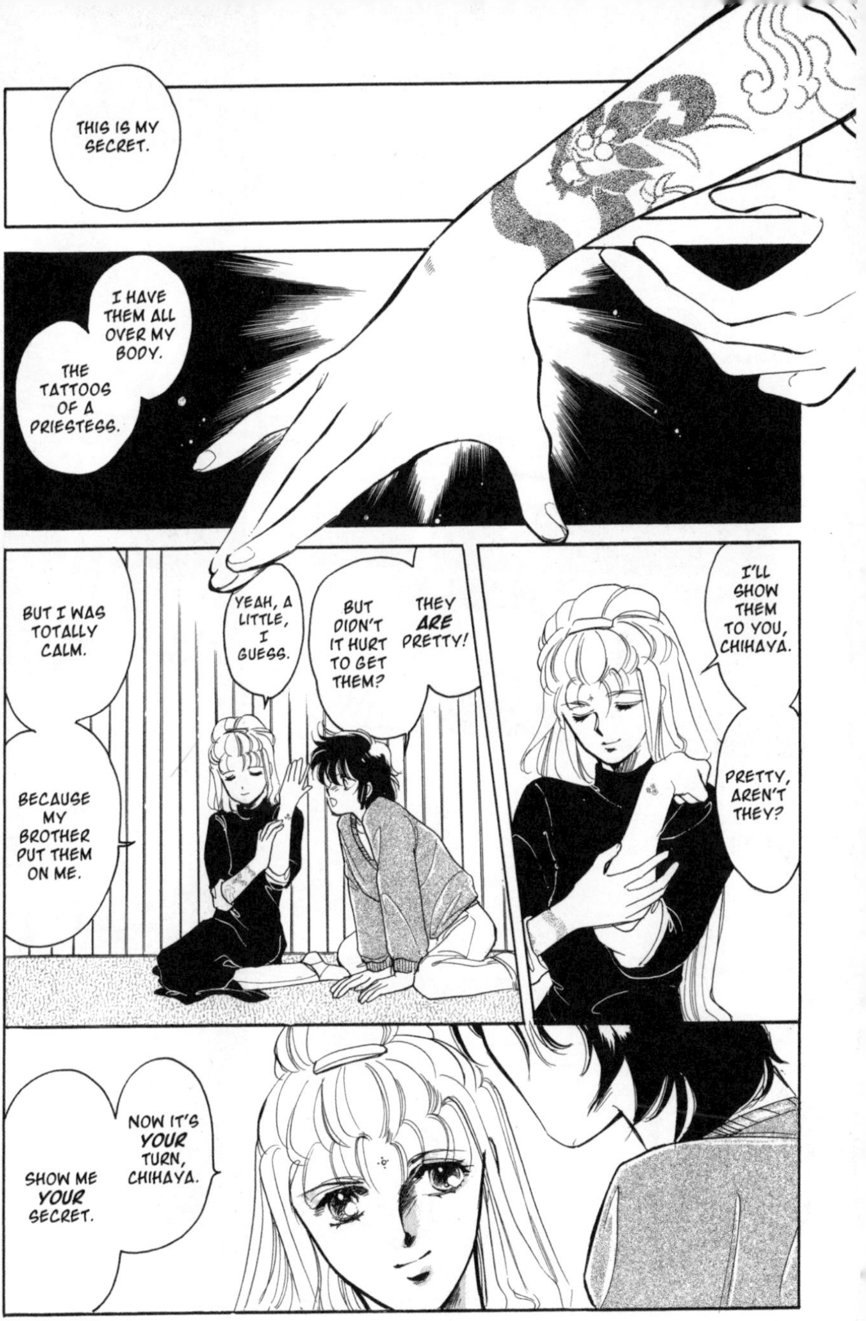
THIS IS MY SECRET.
I HAVE THEM ALL OVER MY BODY.
THE TATTOOS OF A PRIESTESS.
I'LL SHOW THEM TO YOU, CHIHAYA.
PRETTY, AREN'T THEY?
THEY *ARE* PRETTY!
BUT DIDN'T IT HURT TO GET THEM?
YEAH, A LITTLE, I GUESS.
BUT I WAS TOTALLY CALM.
BECAUSE MY BROTHER PUT THEM ON ME.
NOW IT'S *YOUR* TURN, CHIHAYA.
SHOW ME *YOUR* SECRET.

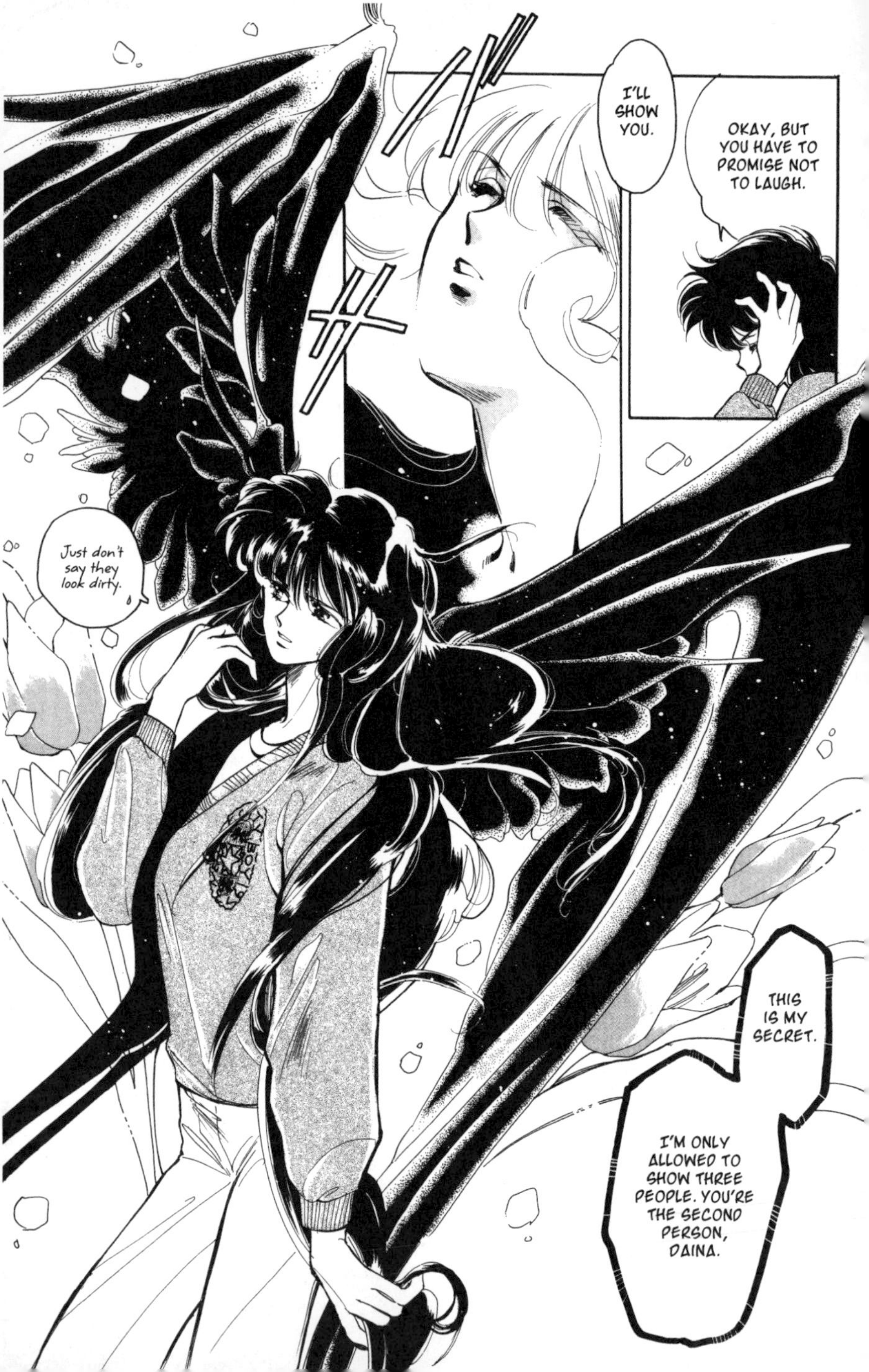
OKAY, BUT YOU HAVE TO PROMISE NOT TO LAUGH.
I'LL SHOW YOU.
THIS IS MY SECRET.
I'M ONLY ALLOWED TO SHOW THREE PEOPLE. YOU'RE THE SECOND PERSON, DAINA.
Just don't say they look dirty.

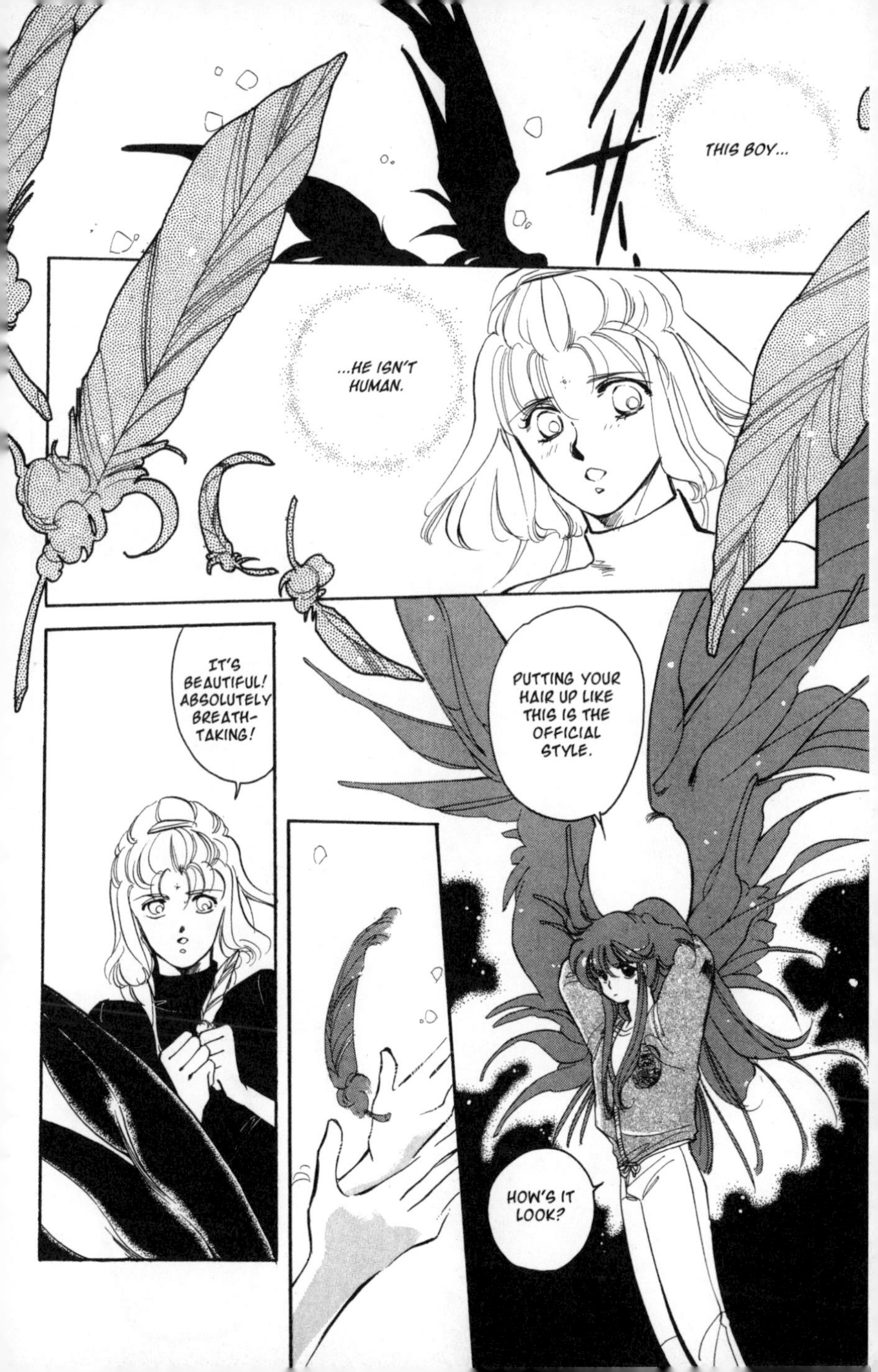
THIS BOY...
...HE ISN'T HUMAN.
PUTTING YOUR HAIR UP LIKE THIS IS THE OFFICIAL STYLE.
HOW'S IT LOOK?
IT'S BEAUTIFUL! ABSOLUTELY BREATH-TAKING!

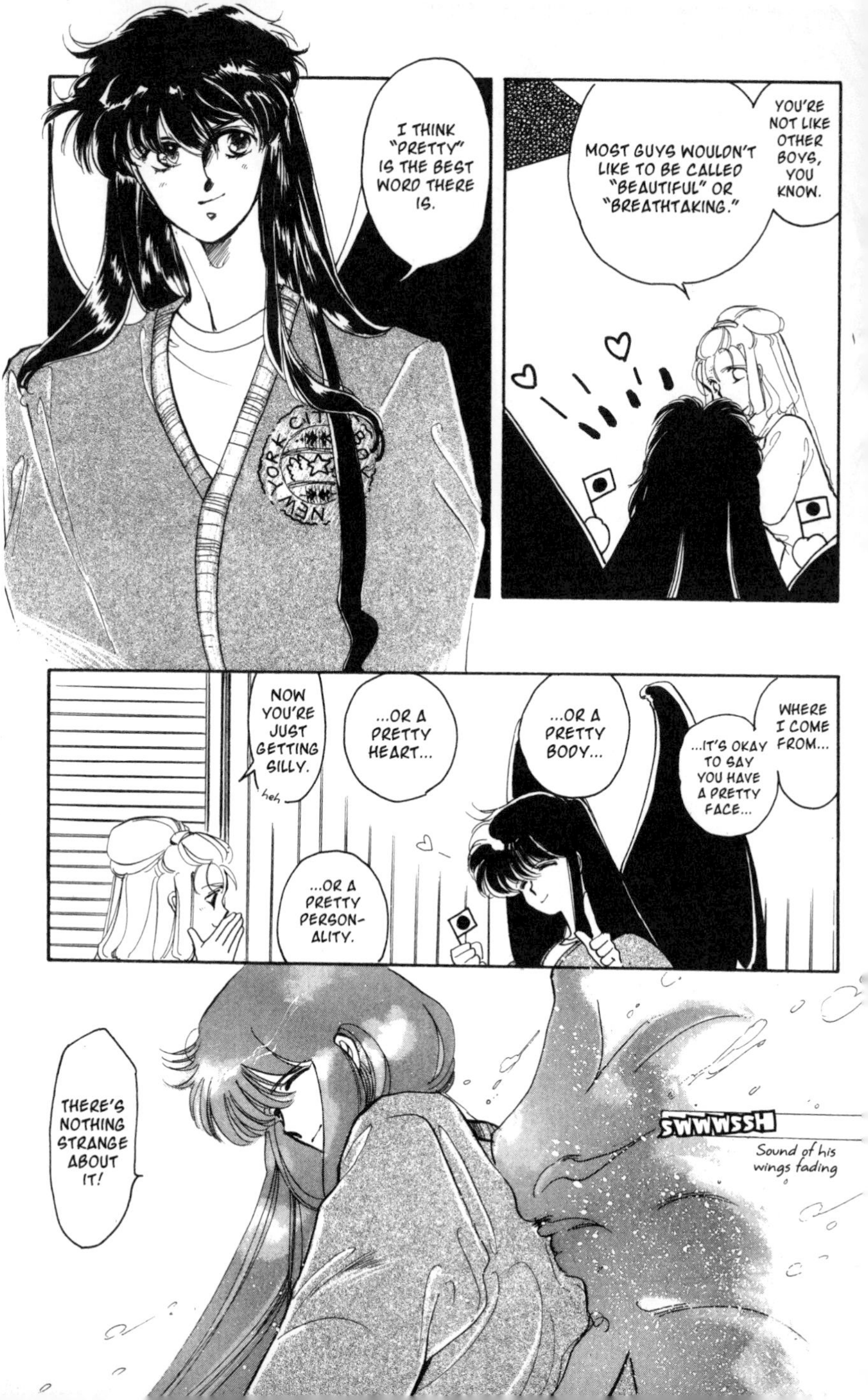
YOU'RE NOT LIKE OTHER BOYS, YOU KNOW.
MOST GUYS WOULDN'T LIKE TO BE CALLED "BEAUTIFUL" OR "BREATHTAKING."
I THINK "PRETTY" IS THE BEST WORD THERE IS.
WHERE I COME FROM...
...IT'S OKAY TO SAY YOU HAVE A PRETTY FACE...
...OR A PRETTY BODY...
...OR A PRETTY HEART...
...OR A PRETTY PERSON-ALITY.
NOW YOU'RE JUST GETTING SILLY.
heh
SWWWSSH
Sound of his wings fading
THERE'S NOTHING STRANGE ABOUT IT!

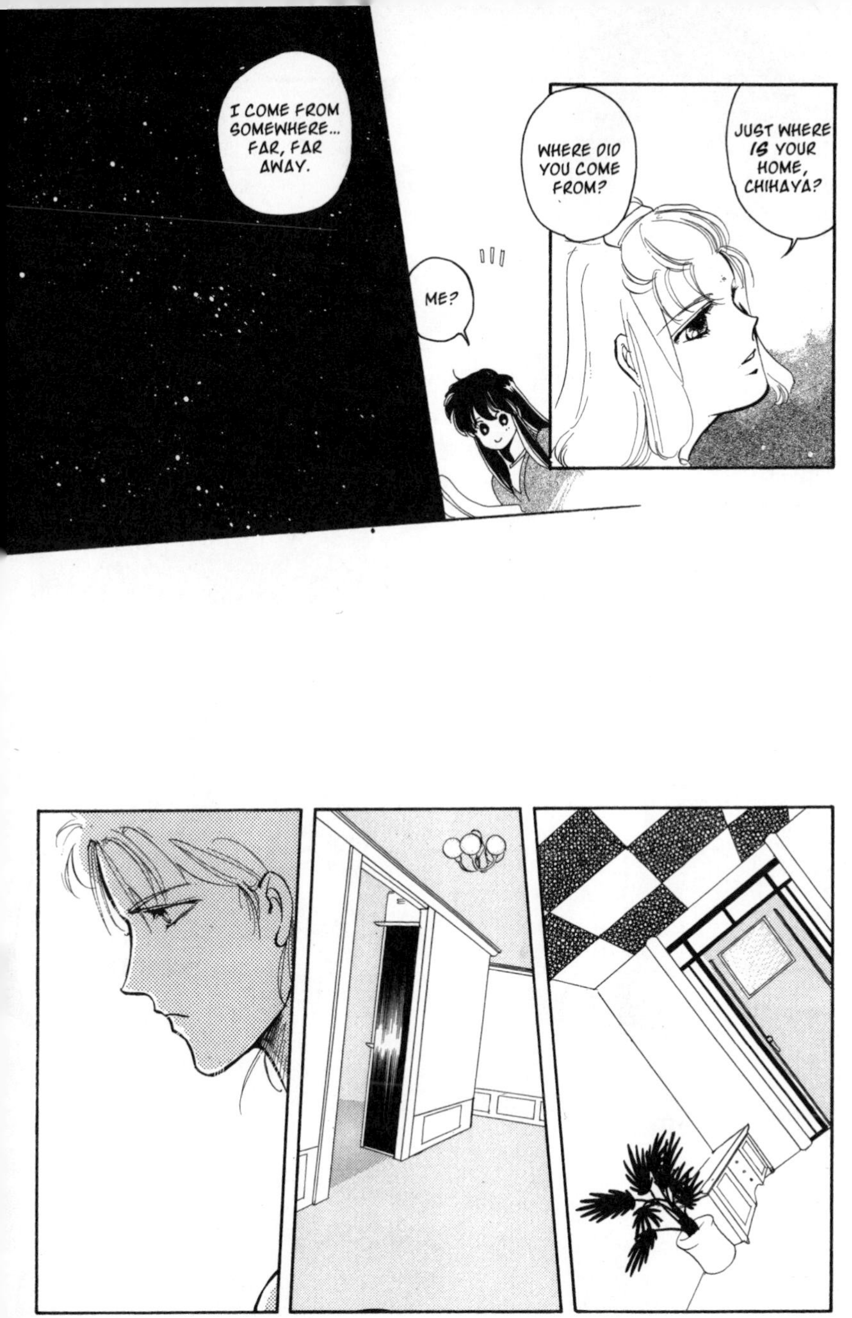
JUST WHERE IS YOUR HOME, CHIHAYA?
WHERE DID YOU COME FROM?
ME?
I COME FROM SOMEWHERE... FAR, FAR AWAY.

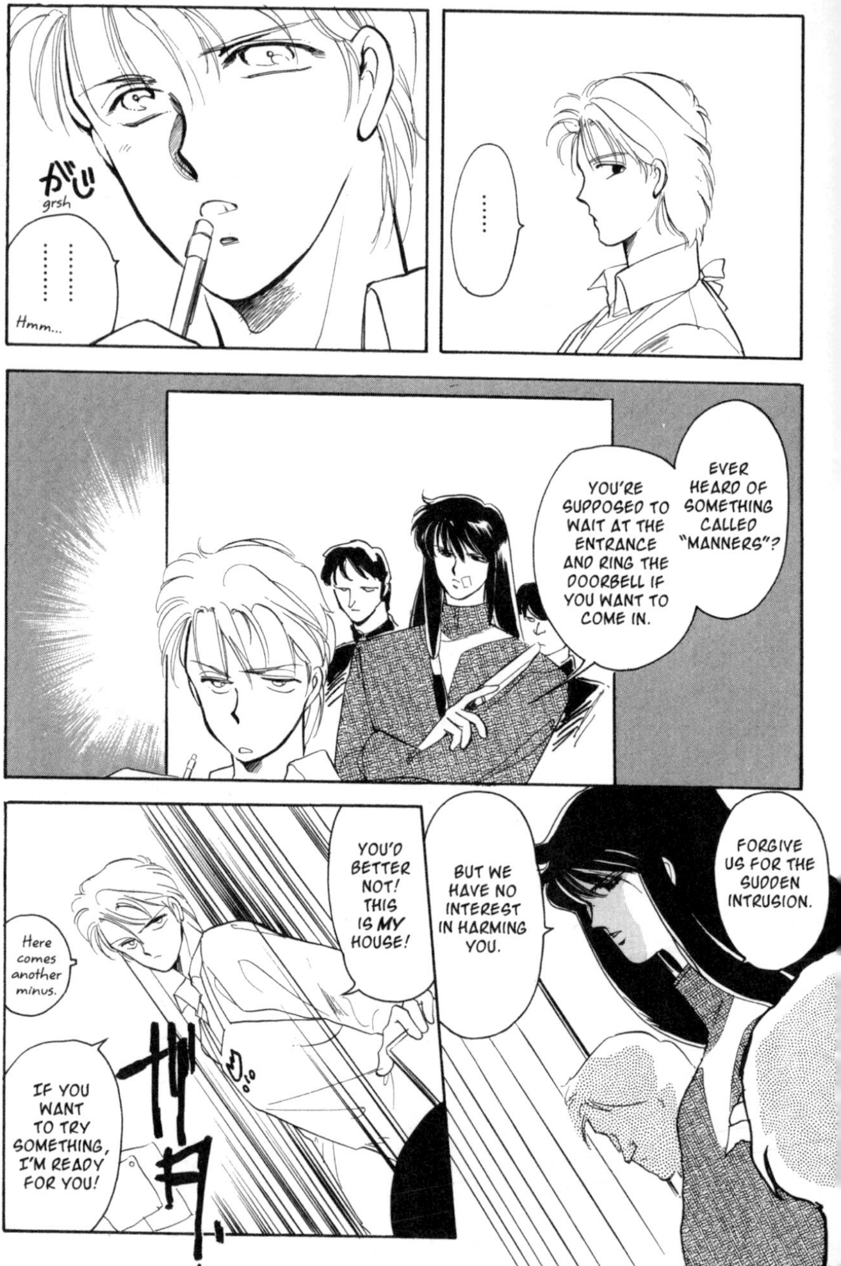
......
......
がじ
grsh
Hmm...
EVER HEARD OF SOMETHING CALLED "MANNERS"?
YOU'RE SUPPOSED TO WAIT AT THE ENTRANCE AND RING THE DOORBELL IF YOU WANT TO COME IN.
FORGIVE US FOR THE SUDDEN INTRUSION.
BUT WE HAVE NO INTEREST IN HARMING YOU.
YOU'D BETTER NOT! THIS IS MY HOUSE!
Here comes another minus.
IF YOU WANT TO TRY SOMETHING, I'M READY FOR YOU!

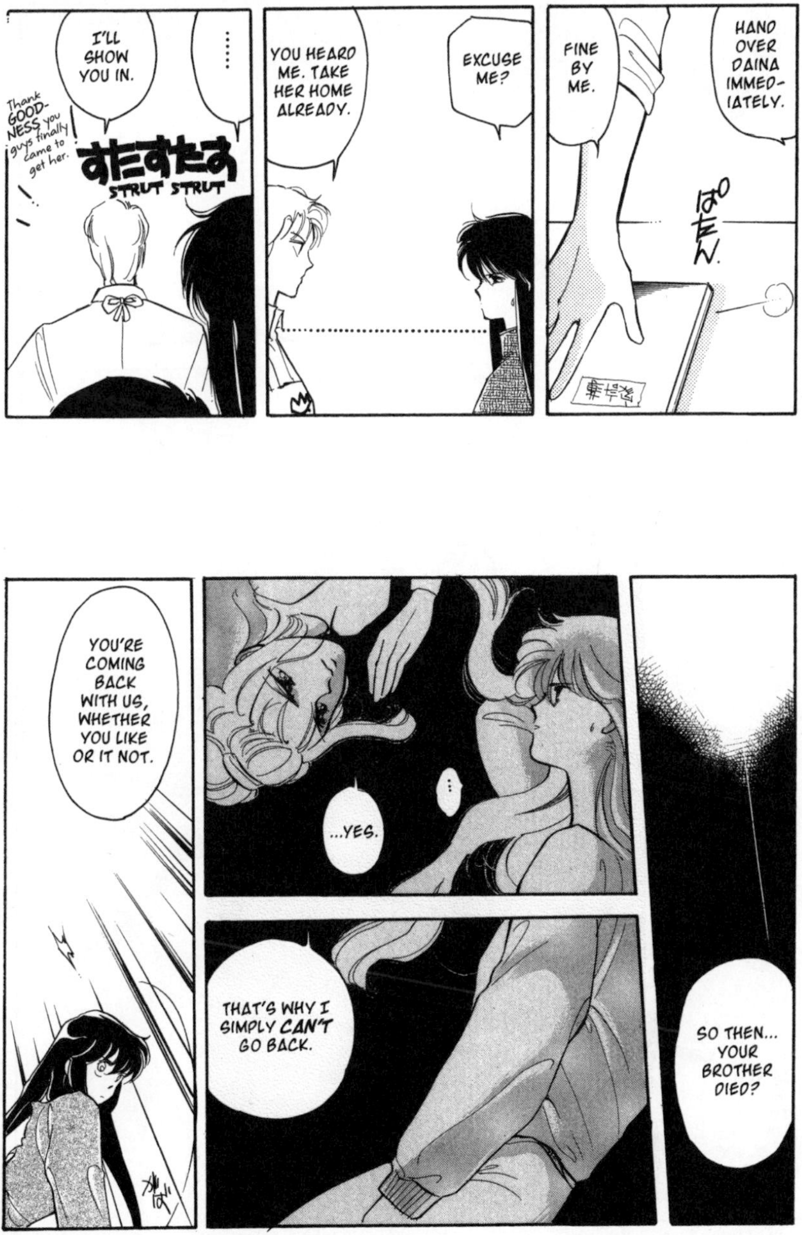
HAND OVER DAINA IMMEDIATELY.
FINE BY ME.
ぱたん.
EXCUSE ME?
YOU HEARD ME. TAKE HER HOME ALREADY.
......
I'LL SHOW YOU IN.
Thank GOODNESS you guys finally came to get her.
すたすたす
STRUT STRUT
!
SO THEN... YOUR BROTHER DIED?
...
...YES.
THAT'S WHY I SIMPLY CAN'T GO BACK.
YOU'RE COMING BACK WITH US, WHETHER YOU LIKE OR IT NOT.

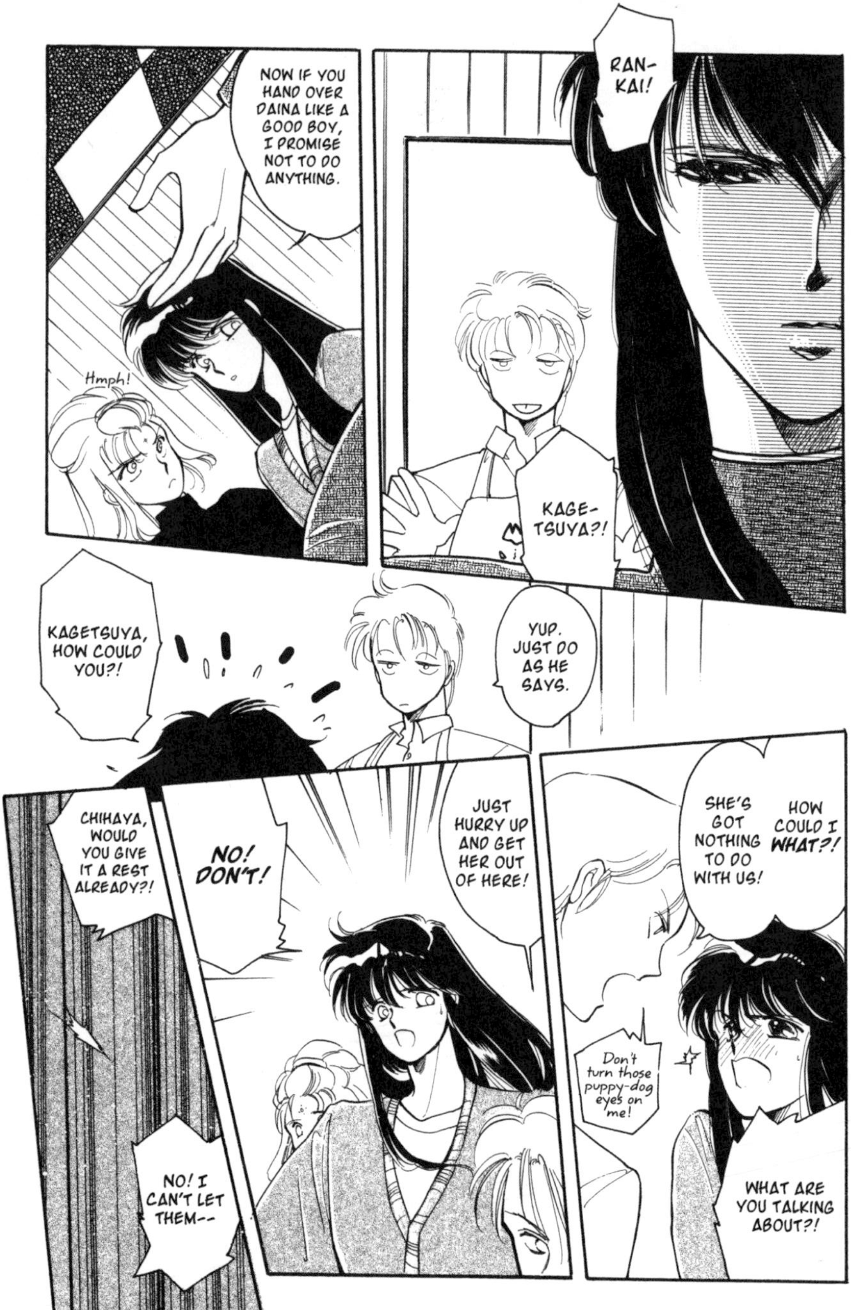
RAN-KAI!
KAGE-TSUYA?!
NOW IF YOU HAND OVER DAINA LIKE A GOOD BOY, I PROMISE NOT TO DO ANYTHING.
Hmph!
YUP. JUST DO AS HE SAYS.
KAGETSUYA, HOW COULD YOU?!
HOW COULD I WHAT?!
SHE'S GOT NOTHING TO DO WITH US!
Don't turn those puppy-dog eyes on me!
WHAT ARE YOU TALKING ABOUT?!
JUST HURRY UP AND GET HER OUT OF HERE!
NO! DON'T!
CHIHAYA, WOULD YOU GIVE IT A REST ALREADY?!
NO! I CAN'T LET THEM--

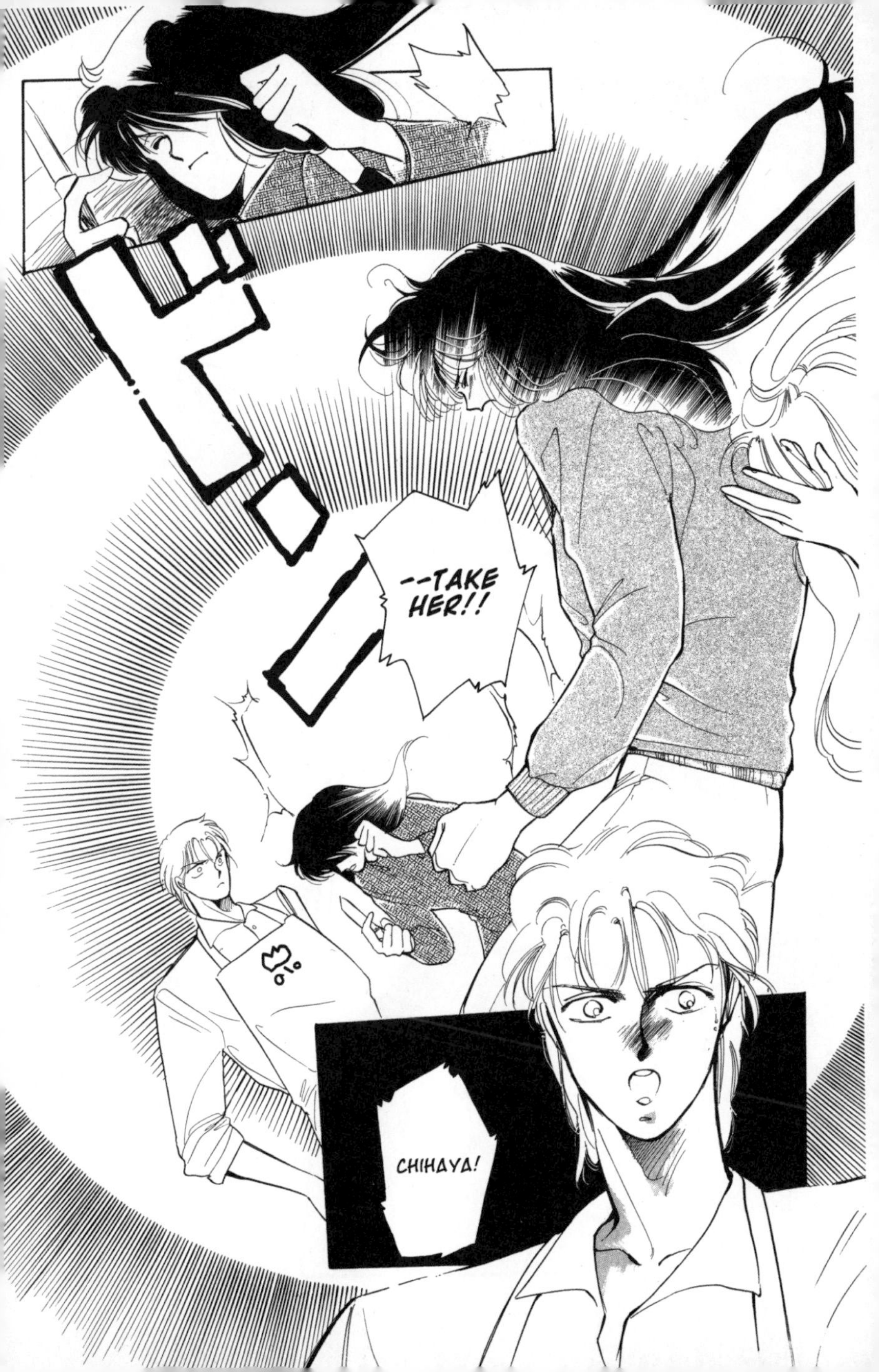
--TAKE HER!!
CHIHAYA!

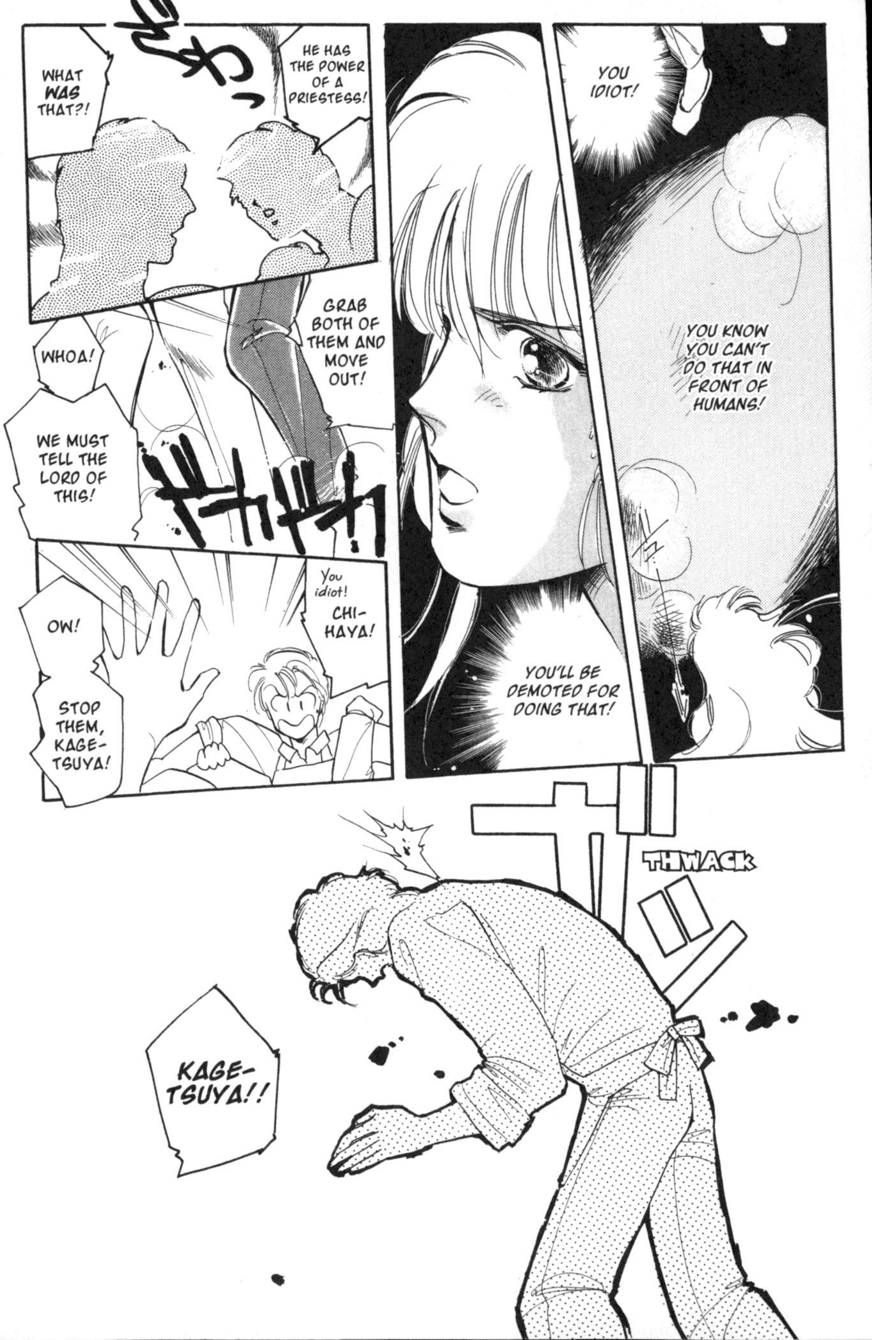
YOU IDIOT!
YOU KNOW YOU CAN'T DO THAT IN FRONT OF HUMANS!
YOU'LL BE DEMOTED FOR DOING THAT!
HE HAS THE POWER OF A PRIESTESS!
WHAT WAS THAT?!
GRAB BOTH OF THEM AND MOVE OUT!
WHOA!
WE MUST TELL THE LORD OF THIS!
You idiot!
CHI-HAYA!
OW!
STOP THEM, KAGE-TSUYA!
THWACK
KAGE-TSUYA!!

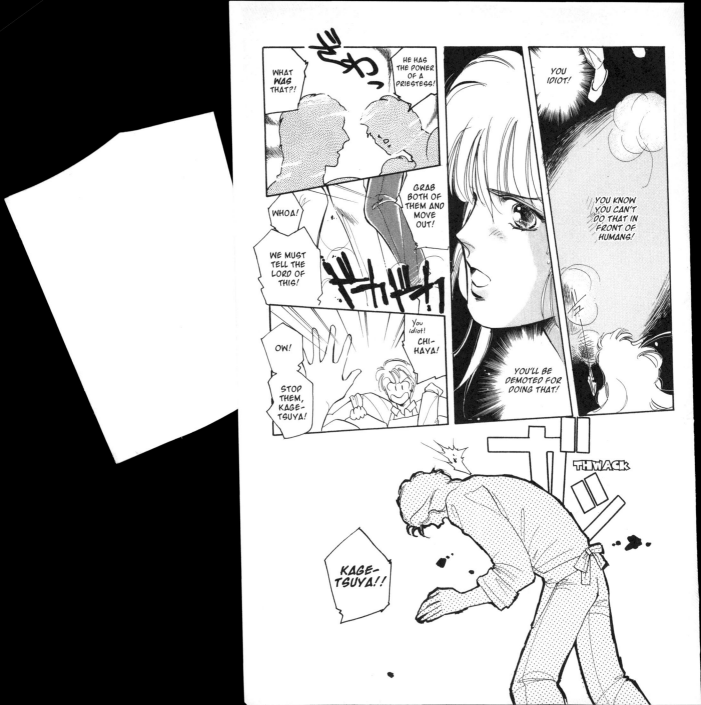

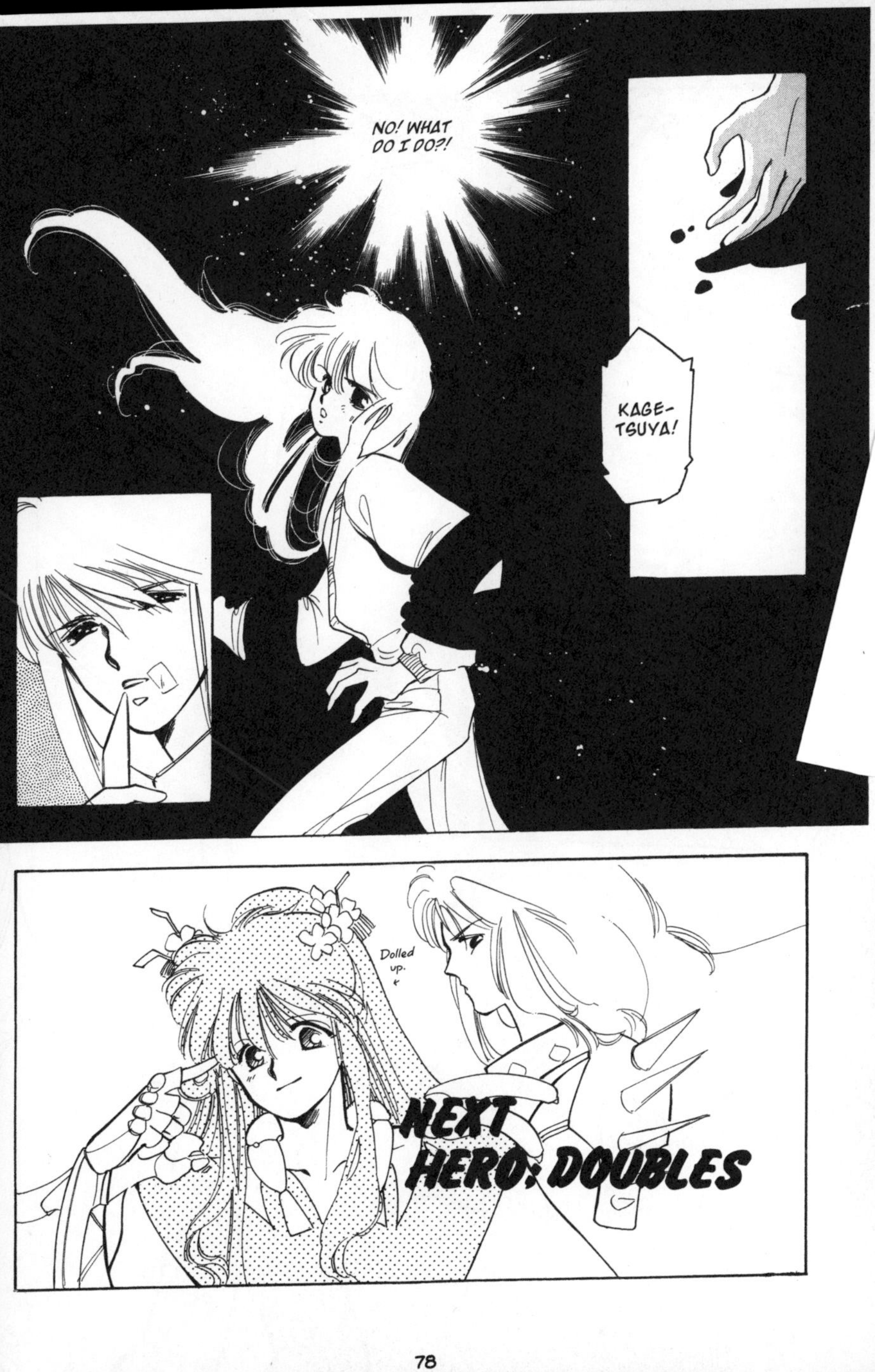
KAGE-
TSUYA!
NO! WHAT
DO I DO?!
Dolled
up.
NEXT
HERO: DOUBLES

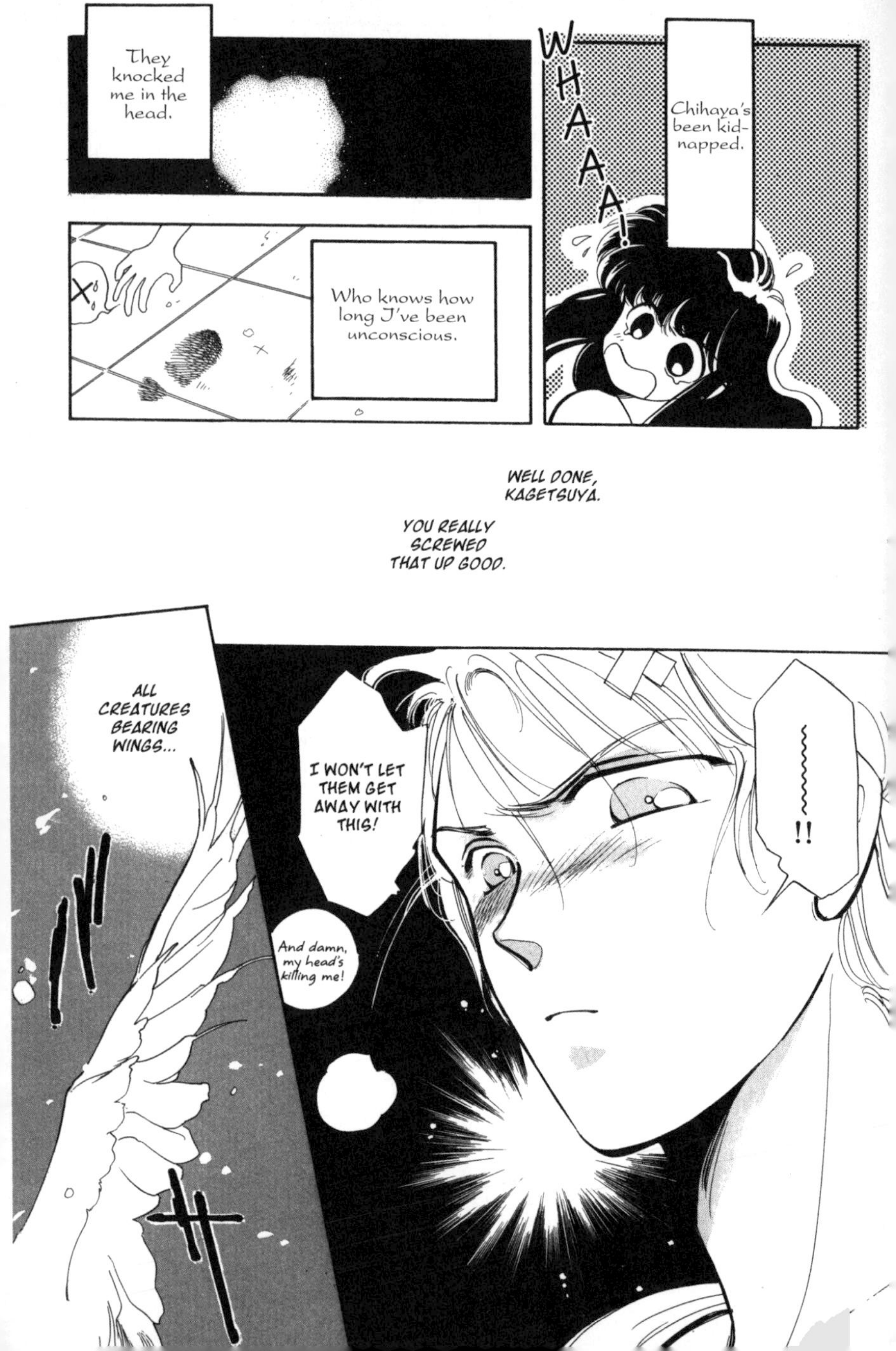

Chihaya's been kid-napped.
WHAAAA!
They knocked me in the head.
Who knows how long I've been unconscious.
WELL DONE, KAGETSUYA.
YOU REALLY SCREWED THAT UP GOOD.
~!!
I WON'T LET THEM GET AWAY WITH THIS!
ALL CREATURES BEARING WINGS...
And damn, my head's killing me!

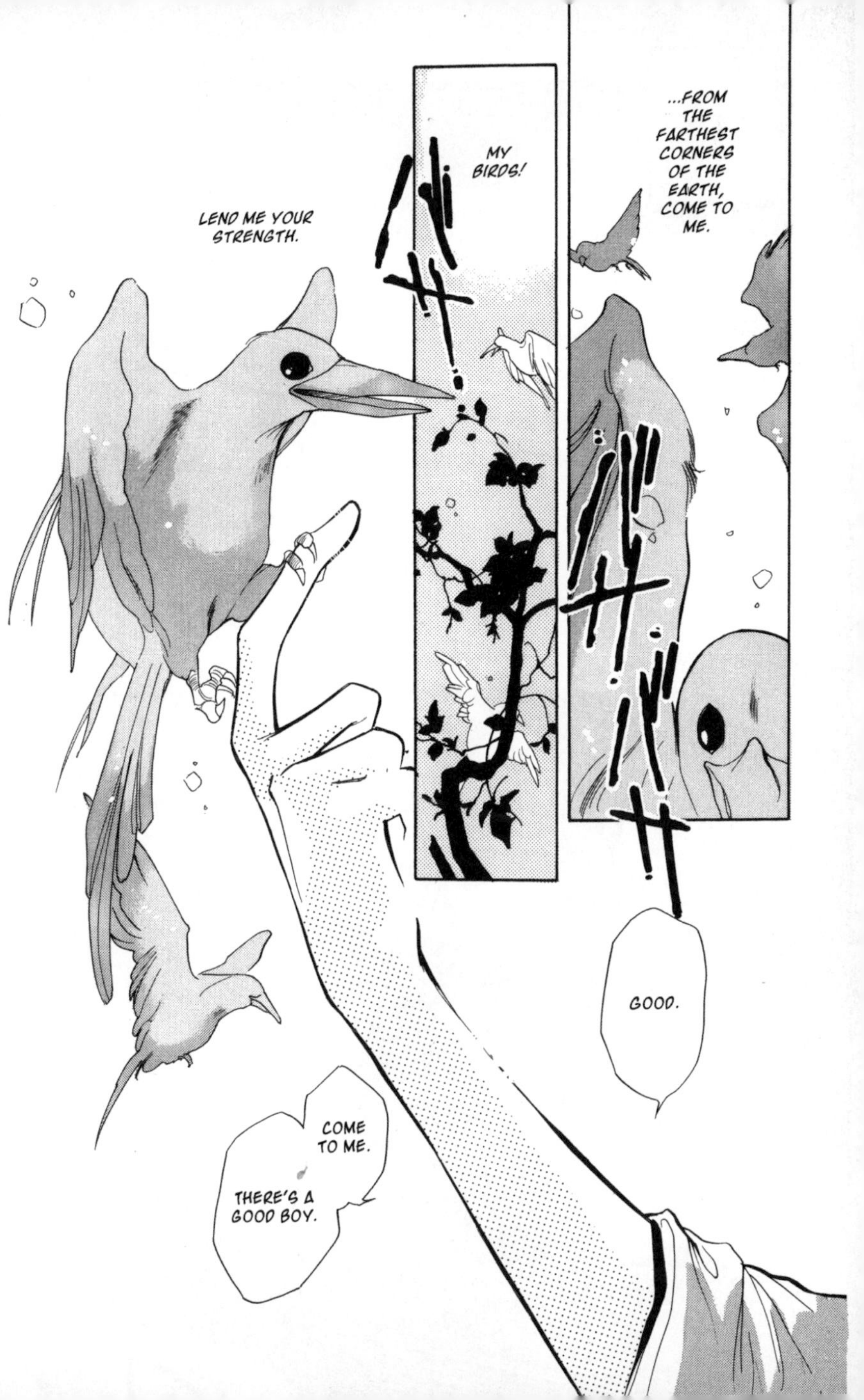
...FROM THE FARTHEST CORNERS OF THE EARTH, COME TO ME.
MY BIRDS!
LEND ME YOUR STRENGTH.
GOOD.
COME TO ME.
THERE'S A GOOD BOY.

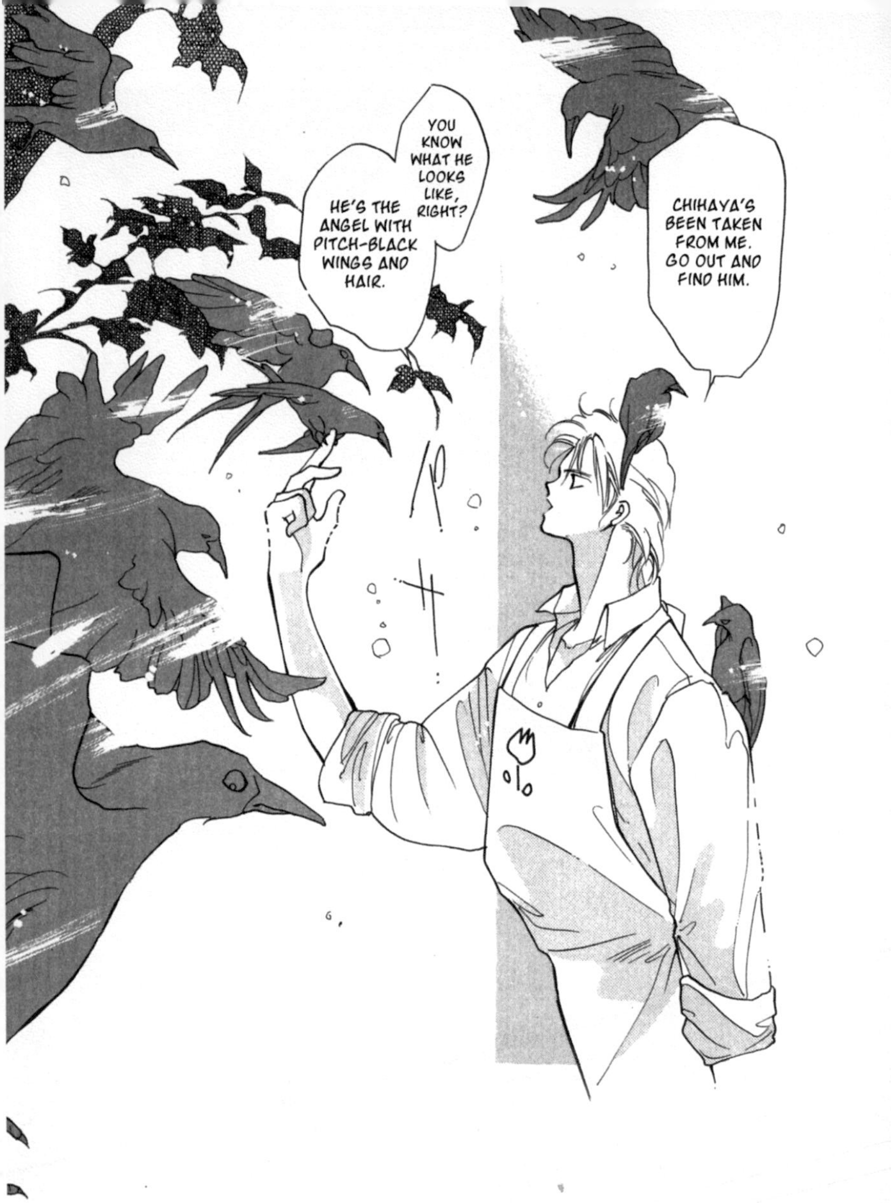
CHIHAYA'S BEEN TAKEN FROM ME. GO OUT AND FIND HIM.
YOU KNOW WHAT HE LOOKS LIKE, RIGHT?
HE'S THE ANGEL WITH PITCH-BLACK WINGS AND HAIR.

HONG KONG CHINESE PART 3

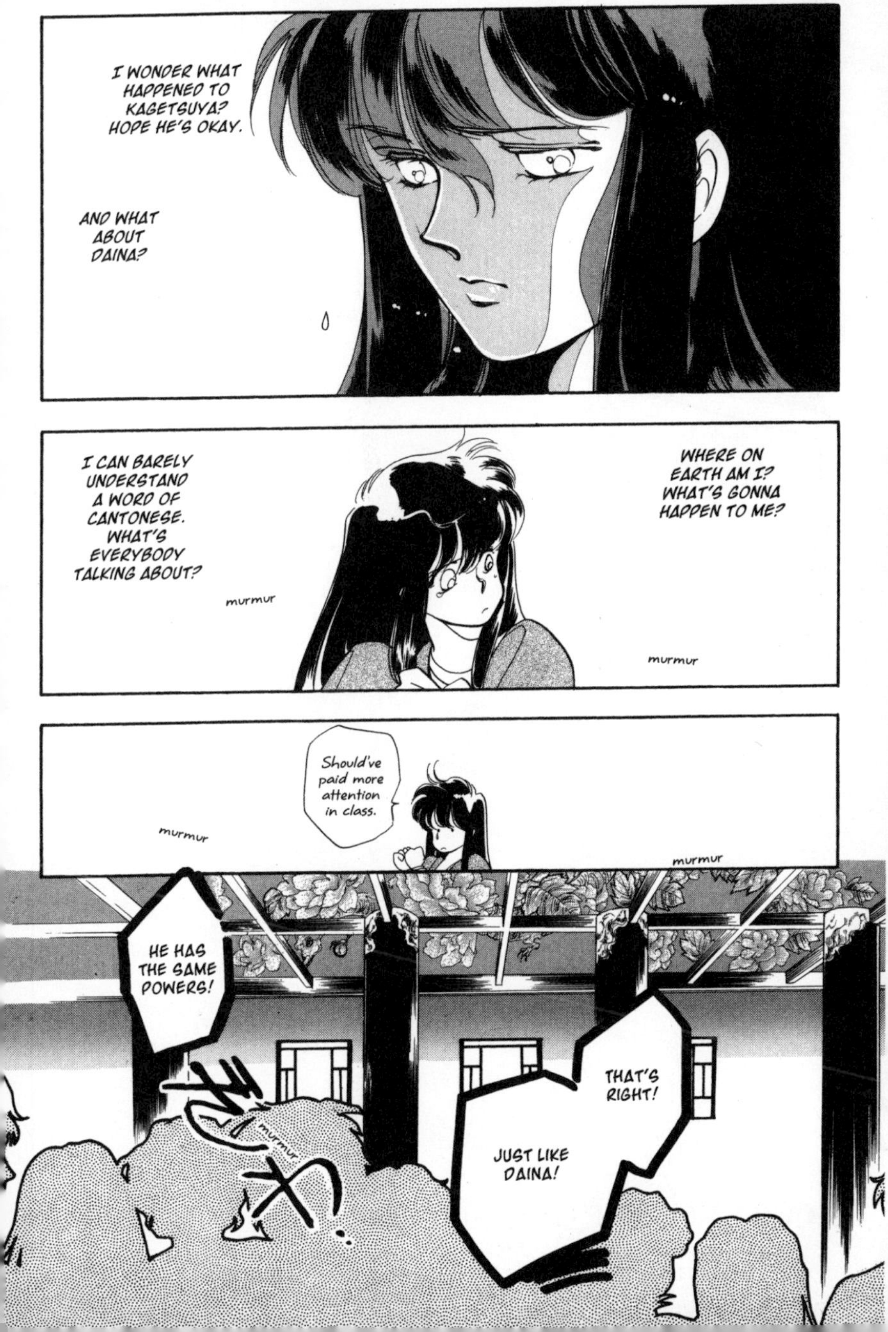
I WONDER WHAT HAPPENED TO KAGETSUYA? HOPE HE'S OKAY.
AND WHAT ABOUT DAINA?
WHERE ON EARTH AM I? WHAT'S GONNA HAPPEN TO ME?
I CAN BARELY UNDERSTAND A WORD OF CANTONESE. WHAT'S EVERYBODY TALKING ABOUT?
murmur
murmur
Should've paid more attention in class.
murmur
murmur
THAT'S RIGHT!
JUST LIKE DAINA!
HE HAS THE SAME POWERS!
murmur

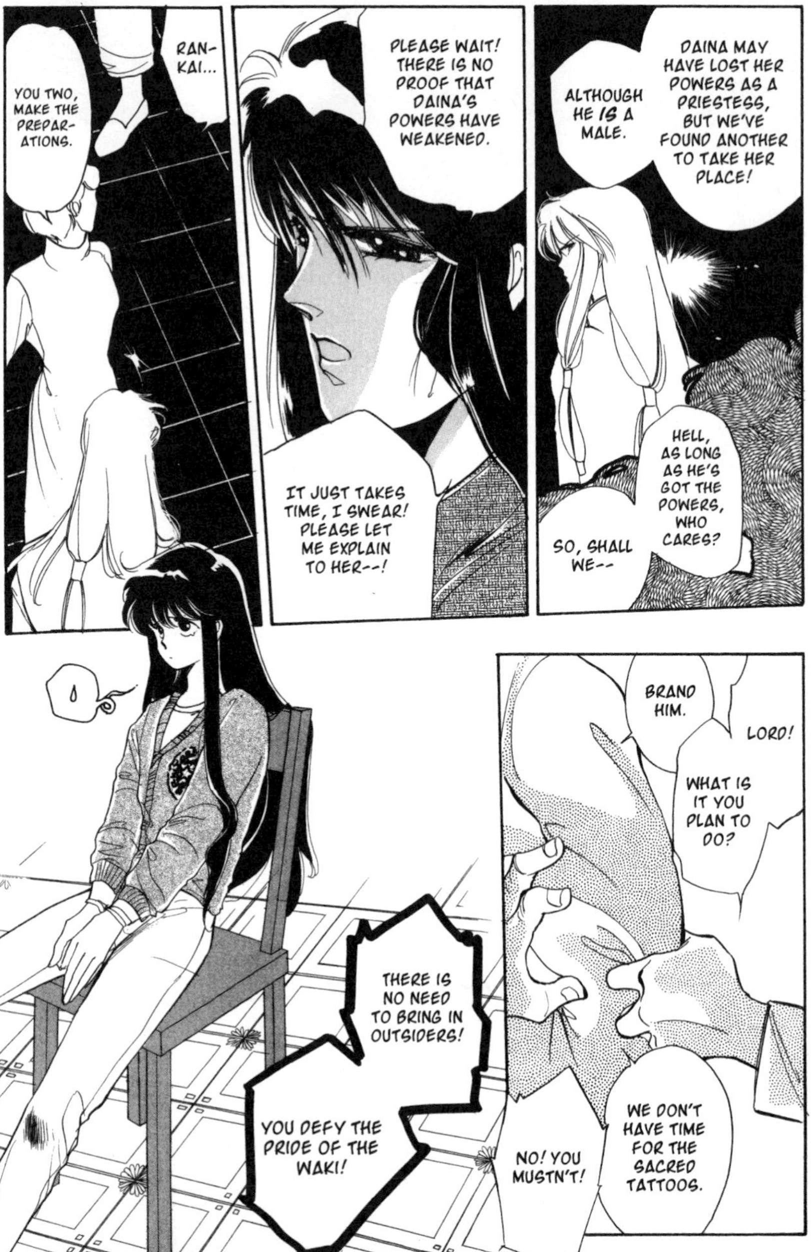
DAINA MAY HAVE LOST HER POWERS AS A PRIESTESS, BUT WE'VE FOUND ANOTHER TO TAKE HER PLACE!
ALTHOUGH HE *IS* A MALE.
HELL, AS LONG AS HE'S GOT THE POWERS, WHO CARES?
SO, SHALL WE--
PLEASE WAIT! THERE IS NO PROOF THAT DAINA'S POWERS HAVE WEAKENED.
IT JUST TAKES TIME, I SWEAR! PLEASE LET ME EXPLAIN TO HER--!
RAN-KAI...
YOU TWO, MAKE THE PREPAR-ATIONS.
BRAND HIM.
LORD!
WHAT IS IT YOU PLAN TO DO?
WE DON'T HAVE TIME FOR THE SACRED TATTOOS.
NO! YOU MUSTN'T!
THERE IS NO NEED TO BRING IN OUTSIDERS!
YOU DEFY THE PRIDE OF THE WAKI!

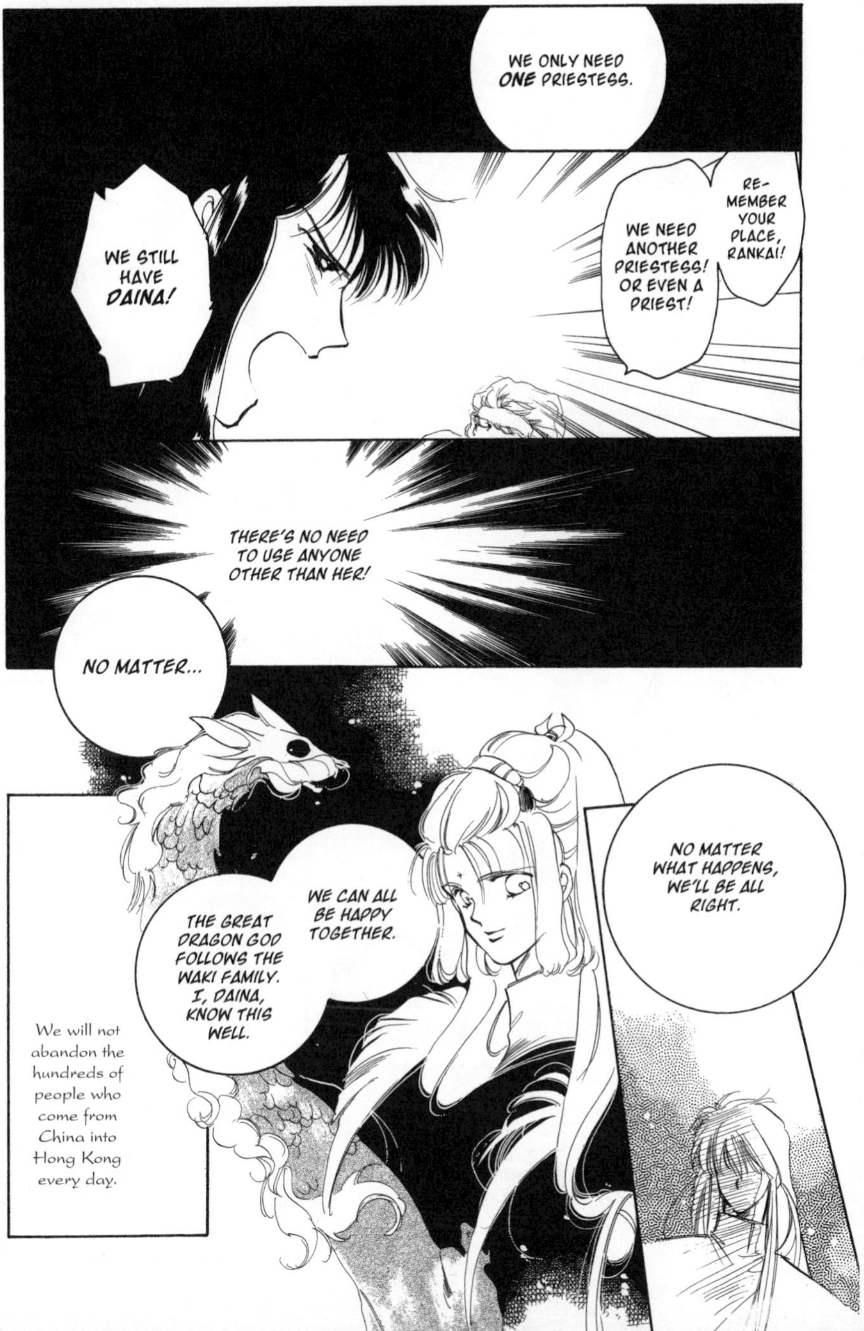
WE ONLY NEED *ONE* PRIESTESS.
RE-MEMBER YOUR PLACE, RANKAI!
WE NEED ANOTHER PRIESTESS! OR EVEN A PRIEST!
WE STILL HAVE *DAINA!*
THERE'S NO NEED TO USE ANYONE OTHER THAN HER!
NO MATTER...
NO MATTER WHAT HAPPENS, WE'LL BE ALL RIGHT.
WE CAN ALL BE HAPPY TOGETHER.
THE GREAT DRAGON GOD FOLLOWS THE WAKI FAMILY. I, DAINA, KNOW THIS WELL.
We will not abandon the hundreds of people who come from China into Hong Kong every day.

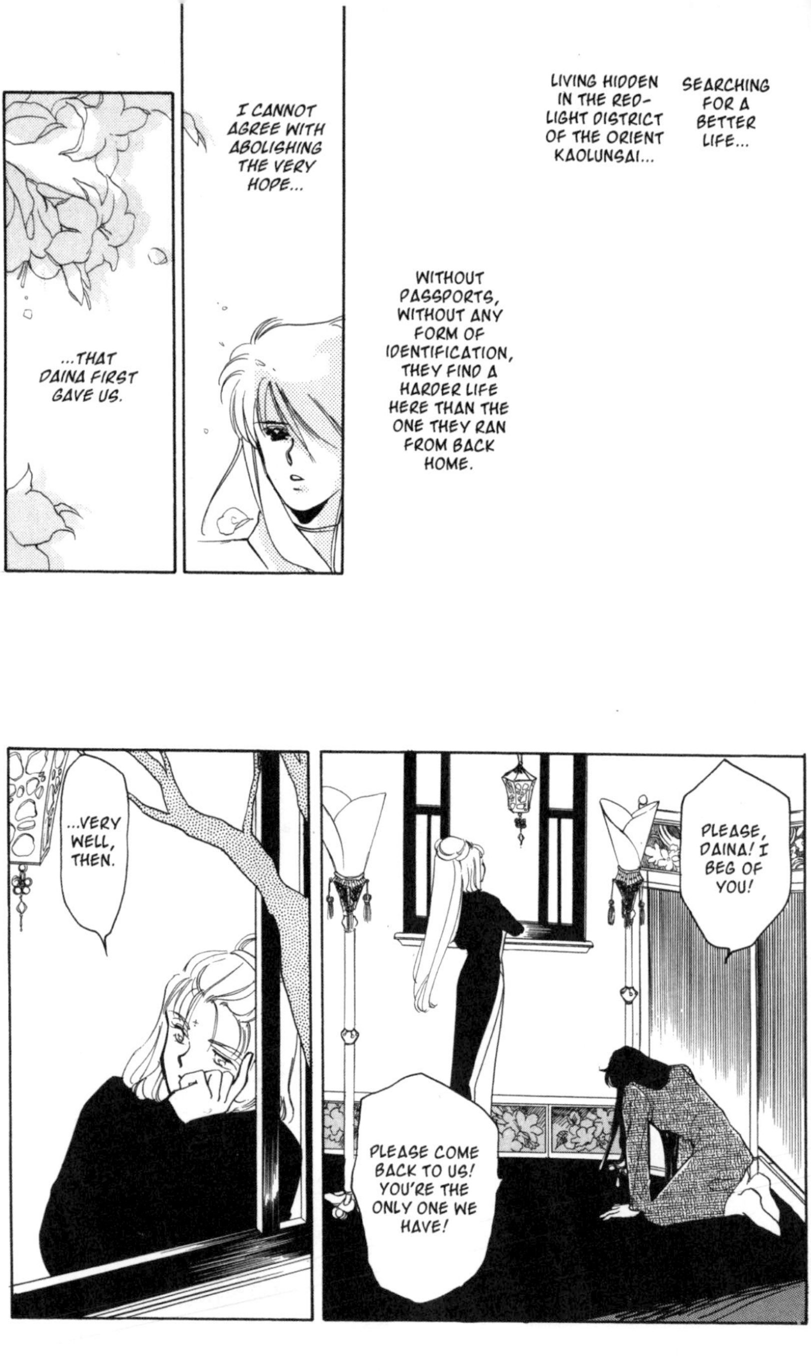
SEARCHING FOR A BETTER LIFE...
LIVING HIDDEN IN THE RED-LIGHT DISTRICT OF THE ORIENT KAOLUNSAI...
WITHOUT PASSPORTS, WITHOUT ANY FORM OF IDENTIFICATION, THEY FIND A HARDER LIFE HERE THAN THE ONE THEY RAN FROM BACK HOME.
I CANNOT AGREE WITH ABOLISHING THE VERY HOPE...
...THAT DAINA FIRST GAVE US.
PLEASE, DAINA! I BEG OF YOU!
PLEASE COME BACK TO US! YOU'RE THE ONLY ONE WE HAVE!
...VERY WELL, THEN.

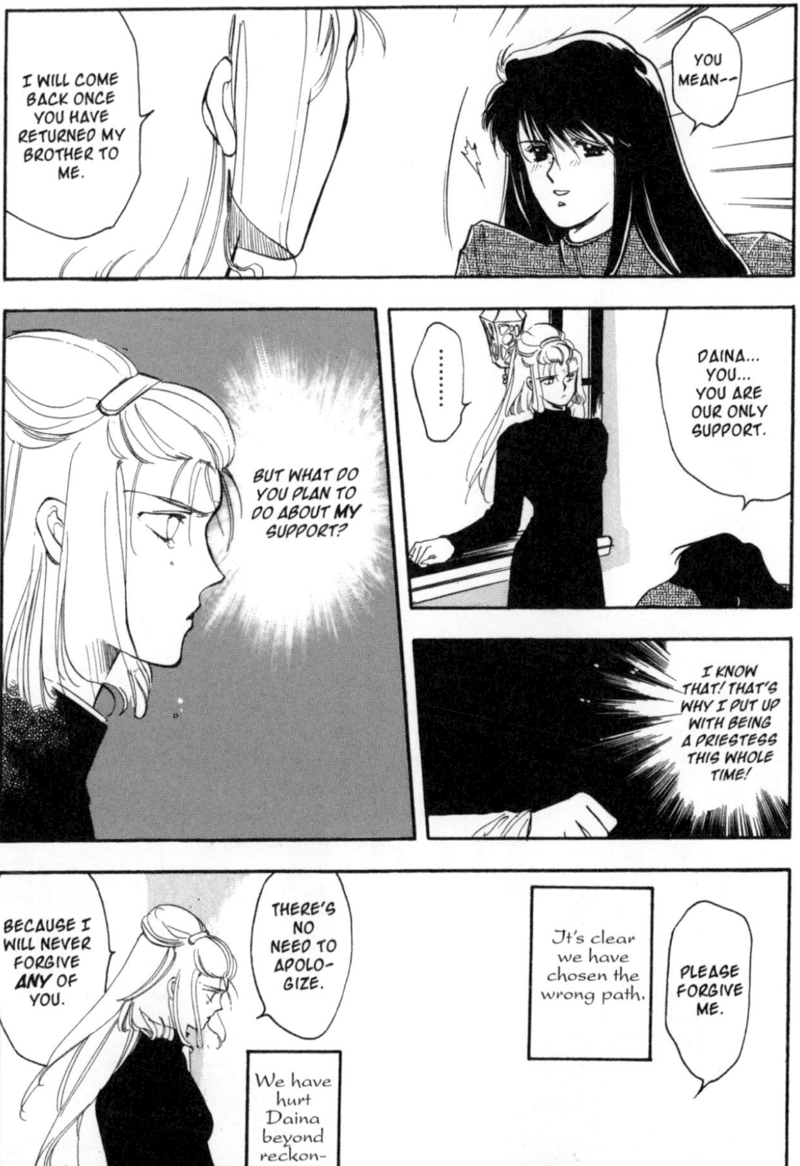
YOU MEAN--
I WILL COME BACK ONCE YOU HAVE RETURNED MY BROTHER TO ME.
DAINA... YOU... YOU ARE OUR ONLY SUPPORT.
....
I KNOW THAT! THAT'S WHY I PUT UP WITH BEING A PRIESTESS THIS WHOLE TIME!
BUT WHAT DO YOU PLAN TO DO ABOUT MY SUPPORT?
PLEASE FORGIVE ME.
It's clear we have chosen the wrong path.
We have hurt Daina beyond reckon-ing.
THERE'S NO NEED TO APOLO-GIZE.
BECAUSE I WILL NEVER FORGIVE ANY OF YOU.

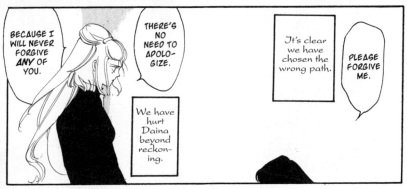

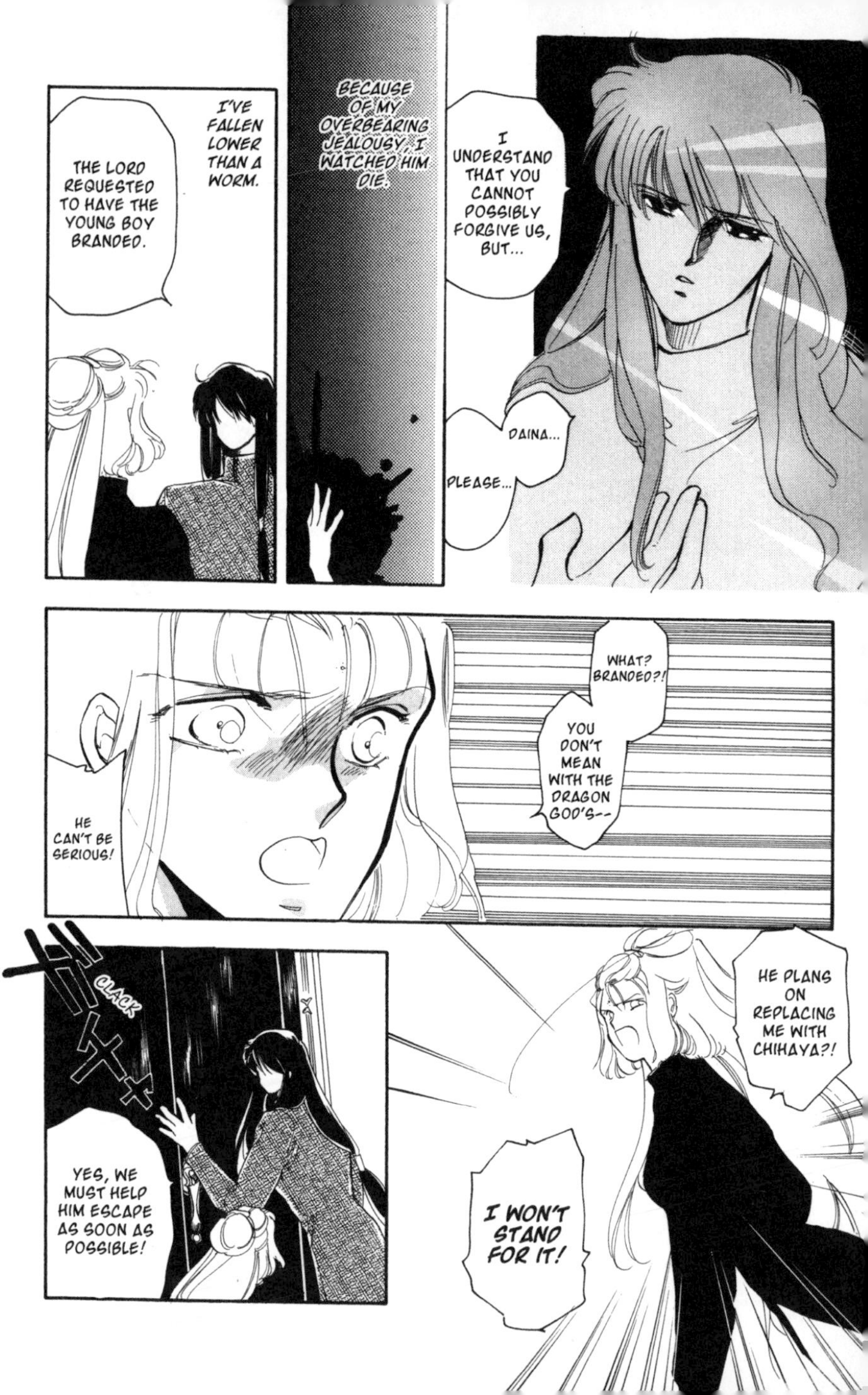
I UNDERSTAND THAT YOU CANNOT POSSIBLY FORGIVE US, BUT...
DAINA...
PLEASE...
BECAUSE OF MY OVERBEARING JEALOUSY, I WATCHED HIM DIE.
I'VE FALLEN LOWER THAN A WORM.
THE LORD REQUESTED TO HAVE THE YOUNG BOY BRANDED.
WHAT? BRANDED?!
YOU DON'T MEAN WITH THE DRAGON GOD'S--
HE CAN'T BE SERIOUS!
HE PLANS ON REPLACING ME WITH CHIHAYA?!
I WON'T STAND FOR IT!
CLACK
YES, WE MUST HELP HIM ESCAPE AS SOON AS POSSIBLE!

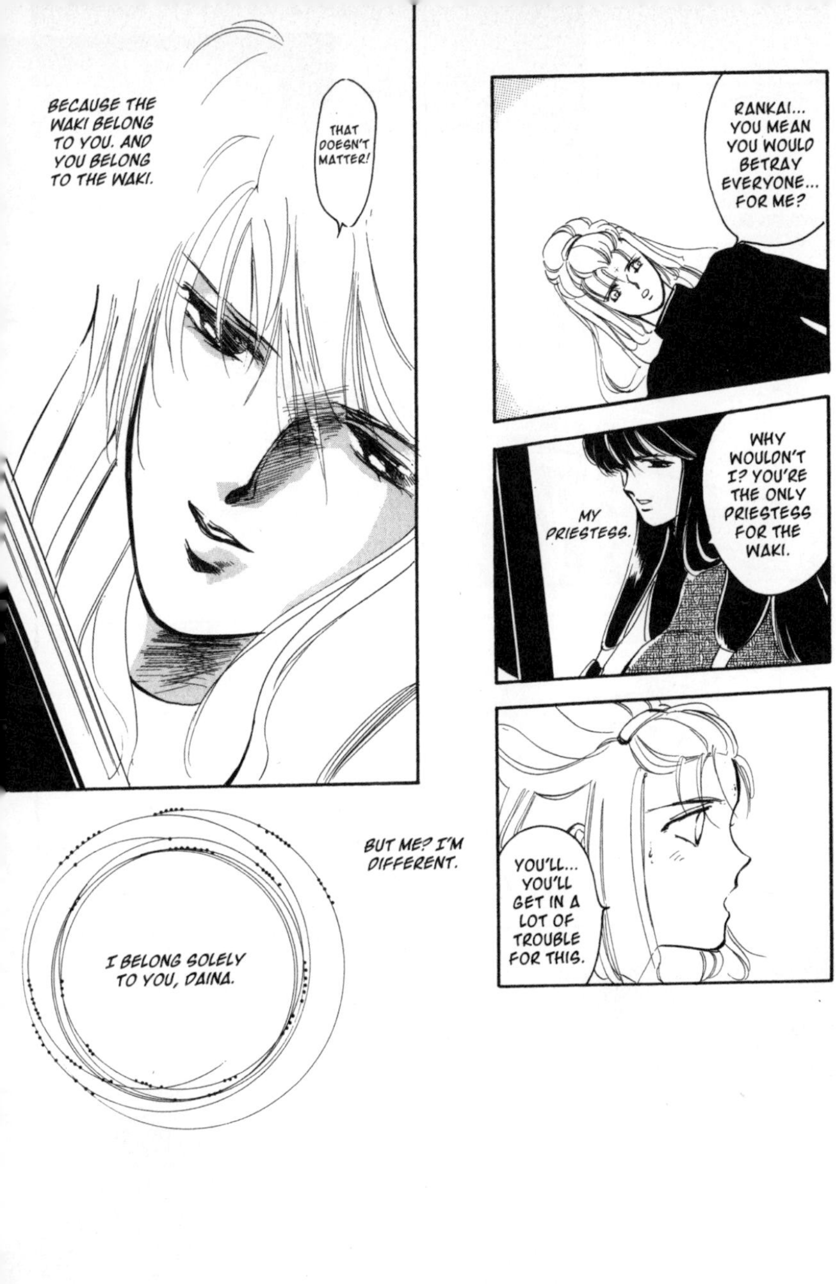
RANKAI... YOU MEAN YOU WOULD BETRAY EVERYONE... FOR ME?
WHY WOULDN'T I? YOU'RE THE ONLY PRIESTESS FOR THE WAKI.
MY PRIESTESS.
YOU'LL... YOU'LL GET IN A LOT OF TROUBLE FOR THIS.
THAT DOESN'T MATTER!
BECAUSE THE WAKI BELONG TO YOU. AND YOU BELONG TO THE WAKI.
BUT ME? I'M DIFFERENT.
I BELONG SOLELY TO YOU, DAINA.

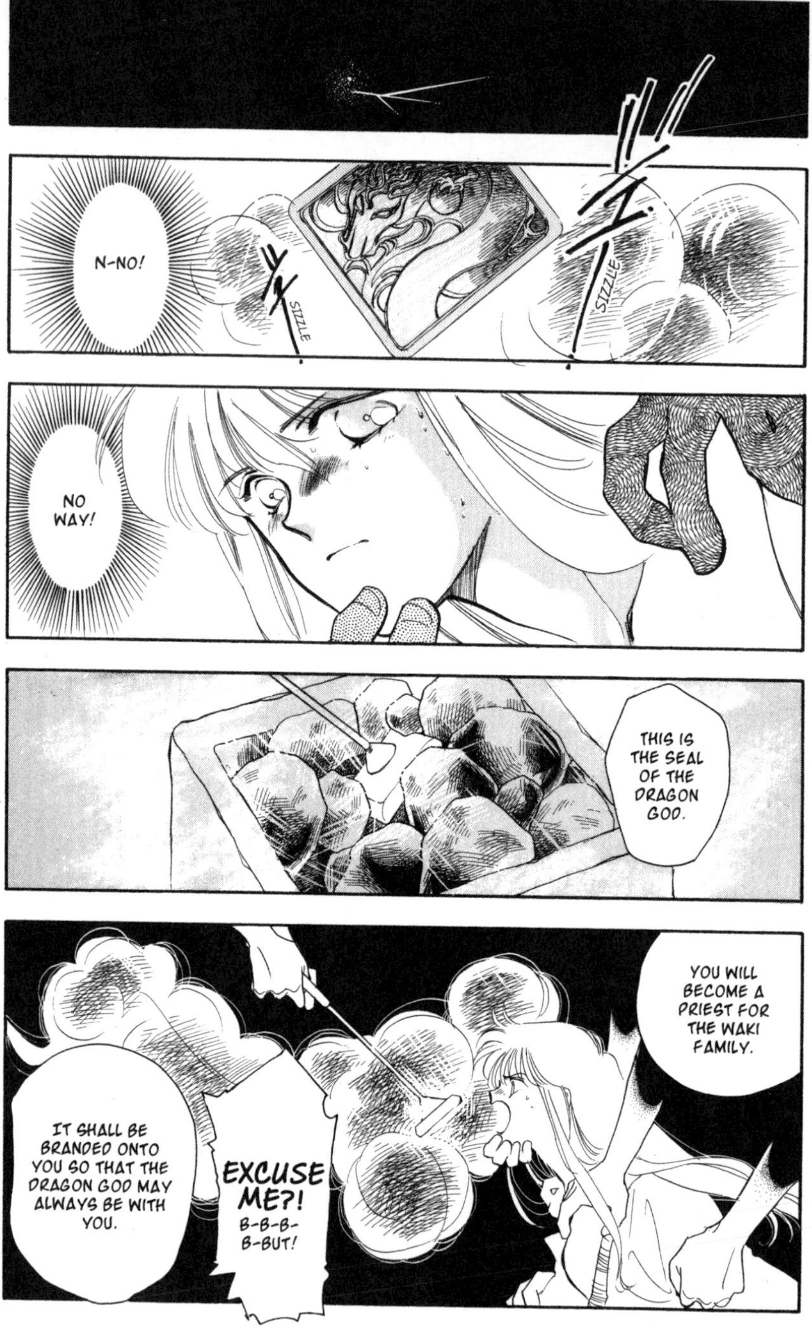
SIZZLE
SIZZLE
N-NO!
NO WAY!
THIS IS THE SEAL OF THE DRAGON GOD.
YOU WILL BECOME A PRIEST FOR THE WAKI FAMILY.
EXCUSE ME?! B-B-B-B-BUT!
IT SHALL BE BRANDED ONTO YOU SO THAT THE DRAGON GOD MAY ALWAYS BE WITH YOU.

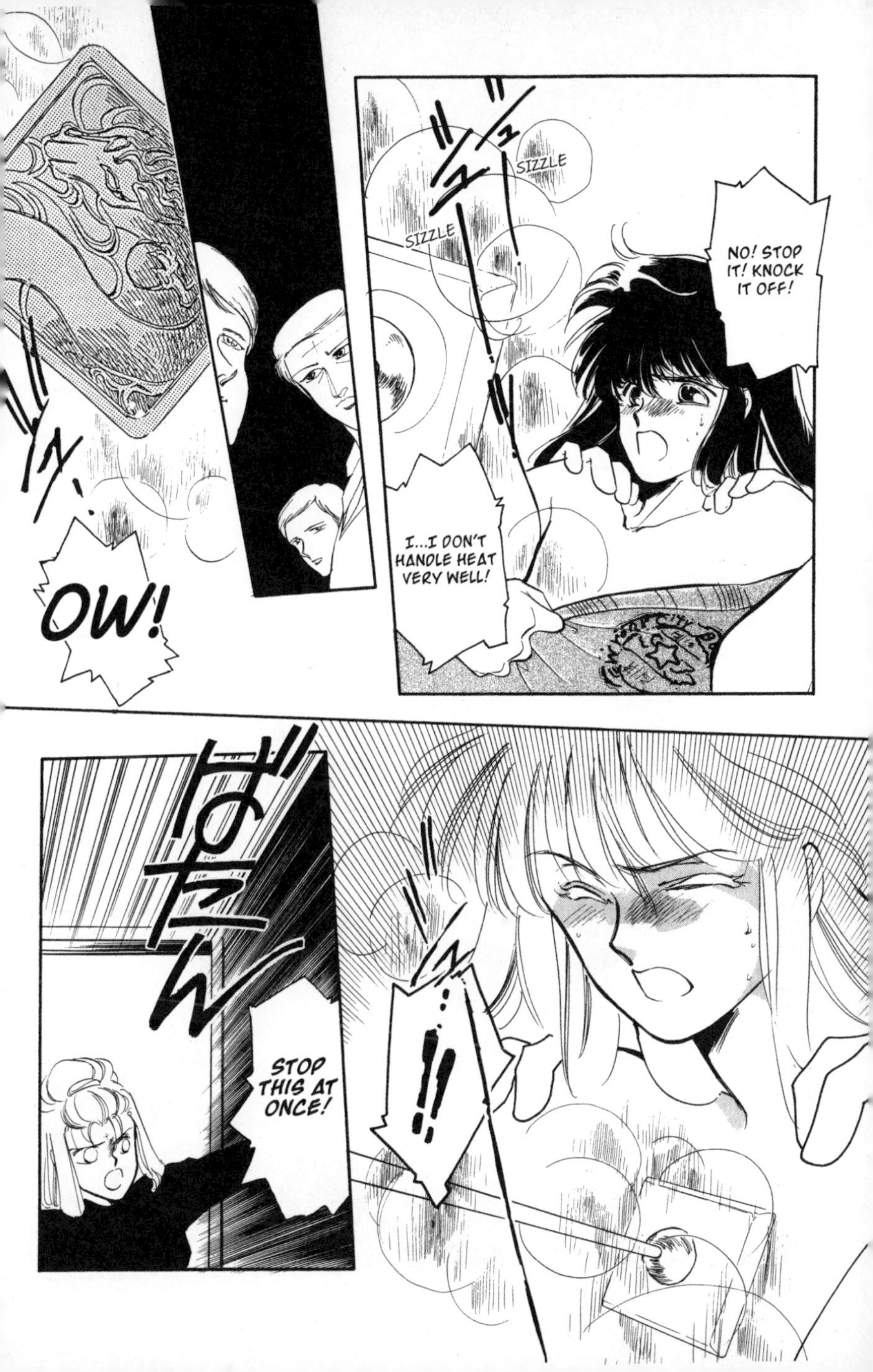
SIZZLE
SIZZLE
NO! STOP IT! KNOCK IT OFF!
I...I DON'T HANDLE HEAT VERY WELL!
OW!
STOP THIS AT ONCE!

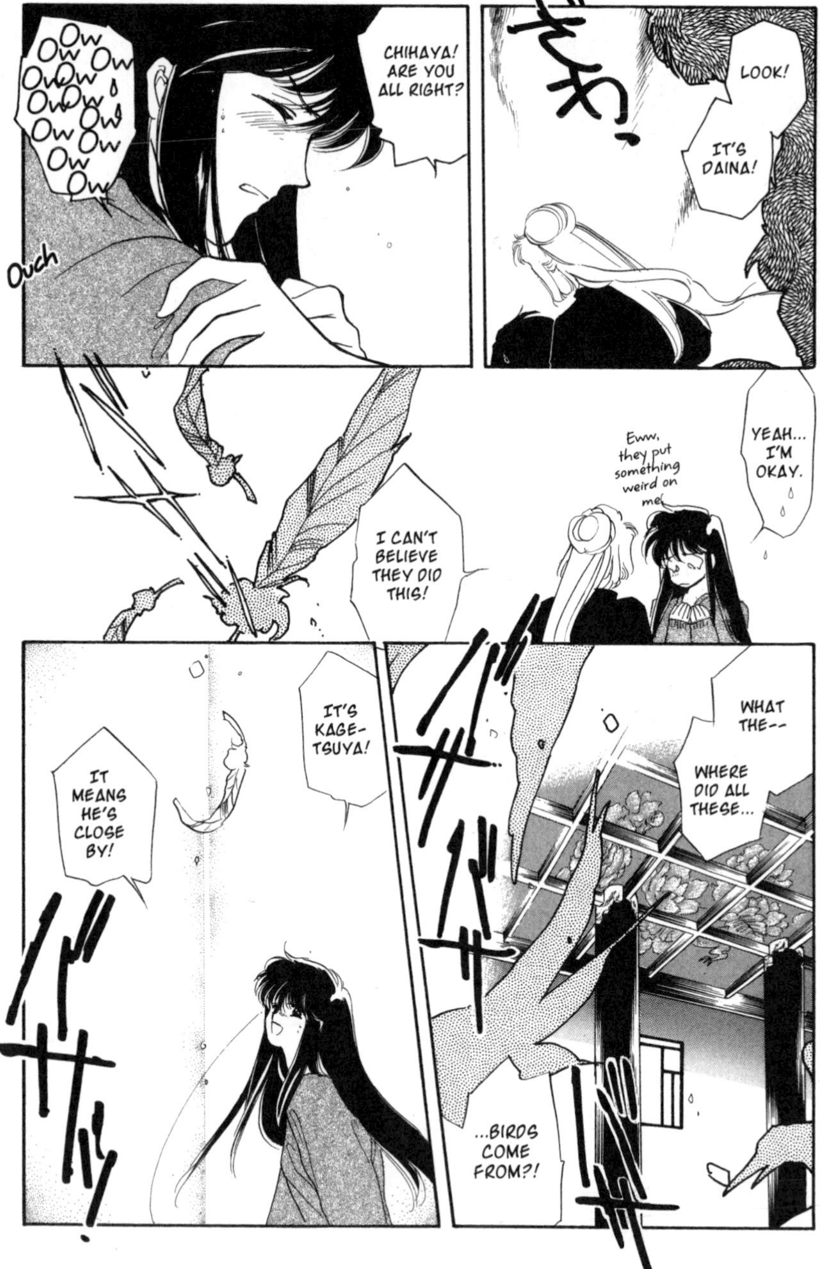
ざわっ
LOOK!
IT'S DAINA!
CHIHAYA! ARE YOU ALL RIGHT?
Ow Ow Ow Ow Ow Ow Ow Ow Ow Ow Ow Ow Ow Ow
Ouch
YEAH... I'M OKAY.
Eww, they put something weird on me
I CAN'T BELIEVE THEY DID THIS!
WHAT THE--
WHERE DID ALL THESE...
...BIRDS COME FROM?!
IT'S KAGE-TSUYA!
IT MEANS HE'S CLOSE BY!

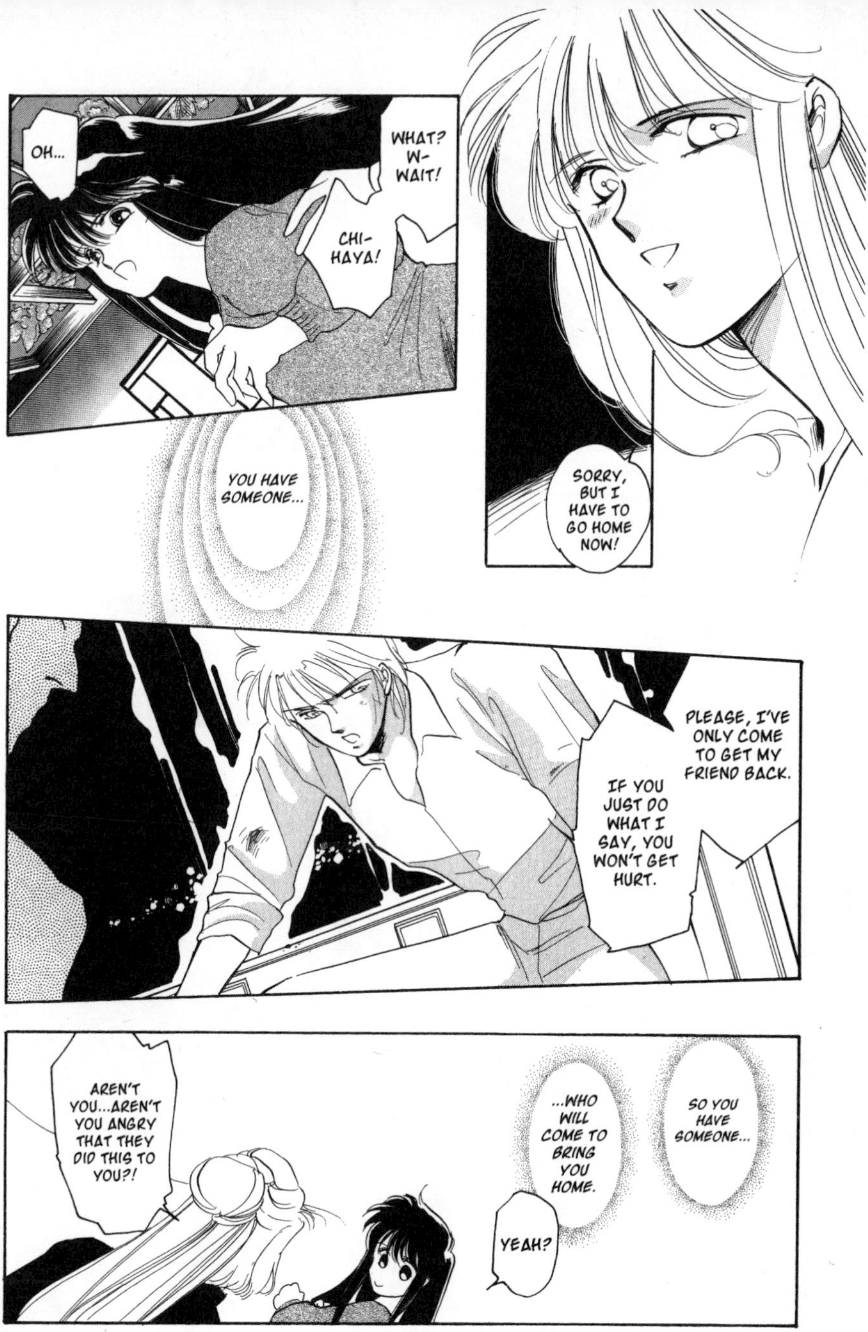
SORRY, BUT I HAVE TO GO HOME NOW!
WHAT? W-WAIT!
CHI-HAYA!
OH...
YOU HAVE SOMEONE...
PLEASE, I'VE ONLY COME TO GET MY FRIEND BACK.
IF YOU JUST DO WHAT I SAY, YOU WON'T GET HURT.
SO YOU HAVE SOMEONE...
...WHO WILL COME TO BRING YOU HOME.
YEAH?
AREN'T YOU...AREN'T YOU ANGRY THAT THEY DID THIS TO YOU?!

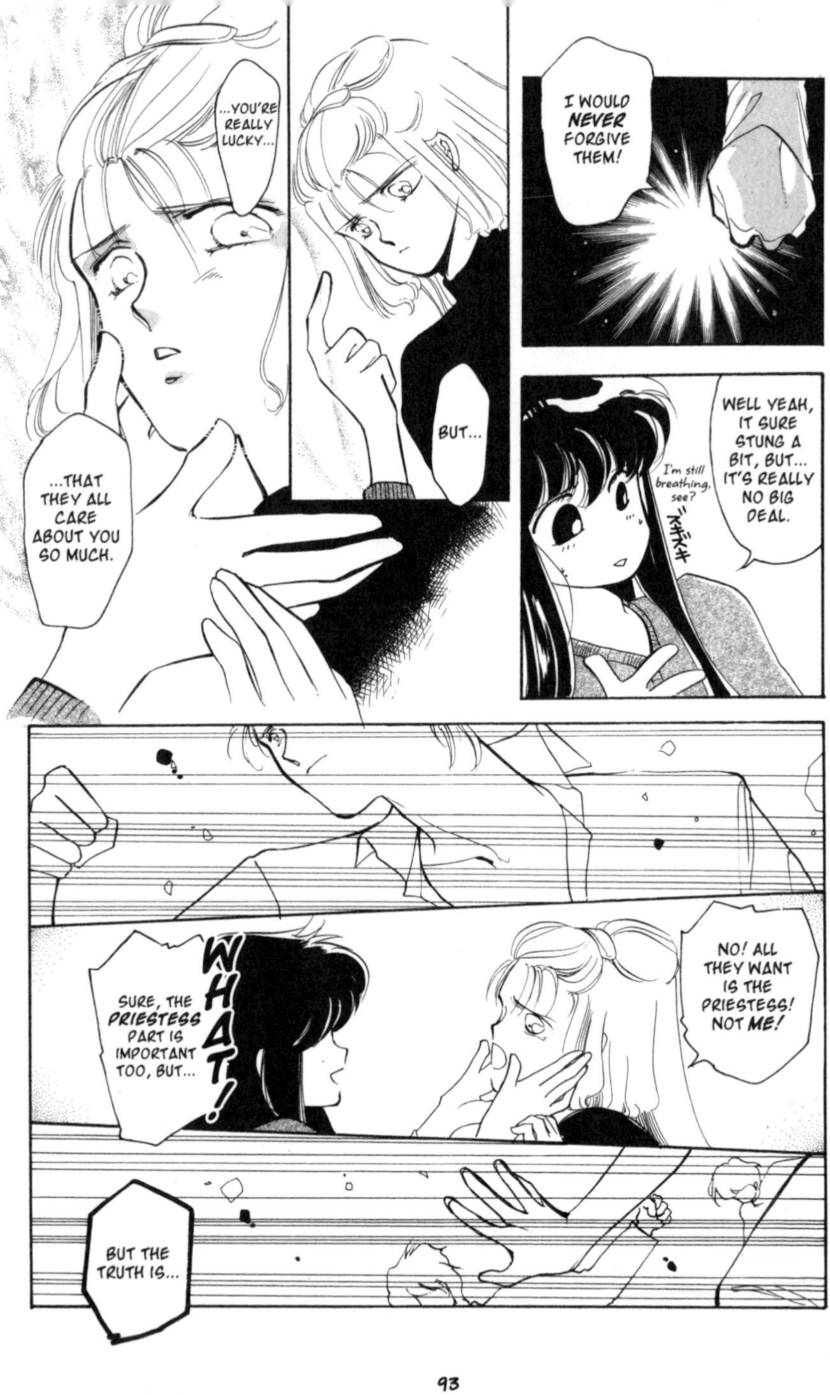
I WOULD NEVER FORGIVE THEM!
WELL YEAH, IT SURE STUNG A BIT, BUT... IT'S REALLY NO BIG DEAL.
I'm still breathing, see?
BUT...
...YOU'RE REALLY LUCKY...
...THAT THEY ALL CARE ABOUT YOU SO MUCH.
NO! ALL THEY WANT IS THE PRIESTESS! NOT ME!
WHAT!
SURE, THE PRIESTESS PART IS IMPORTANT TOO, BUT...
BUT THE TRUTH IS...

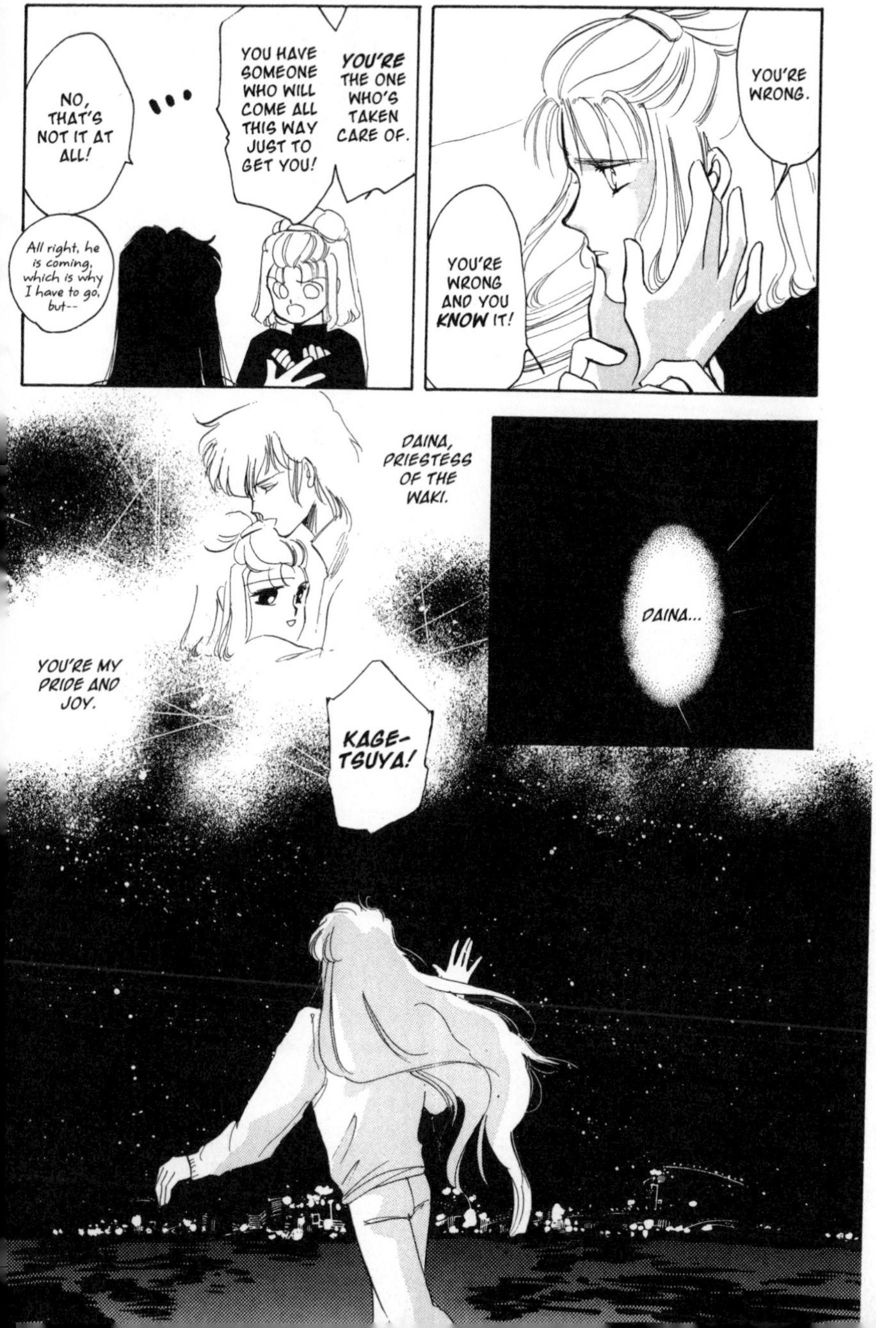
YOU'RE WRONG.
YOU'RE WRONG AND YOU KNOW IT!
YOU'RE THE ONE WHO'S TAKEN CARE OF.
YOU HAVE SOMEONE WHO WILL COME ALL THIS WAY JUST TO GET YOU!
...
NO, THAT'S NOT IT AT ALL!
All right, he is coming, which is why I have to go, but--
DAINA, PRIESTESS OF THE WAKI.
DAINA...
YOU'RE MY PRIDE AND JOY.
KAGE-TSUYA!

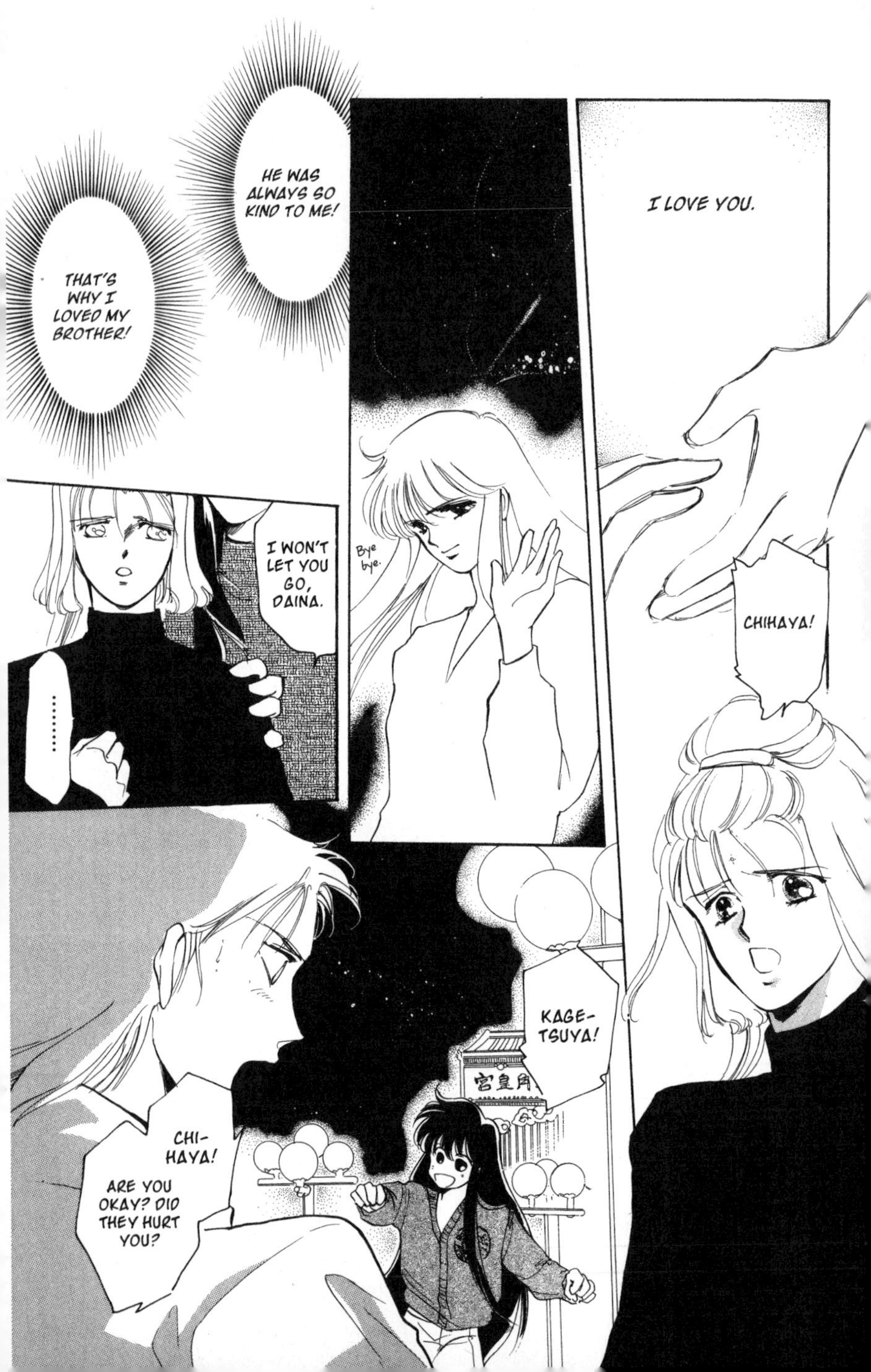
I LOVE YOU.
CHIHAYA!
Bye bye.
HE WAS ALWAYS SO KIND TO ME!
THAT'S WHY I LOVED MY BROTHER!
I WON'T LET YOU GO, DAINA.
......
KAGE-TSUYA!
CHI-HAYA!
ARE YOU OKAY? DID THEY HURT YOU?

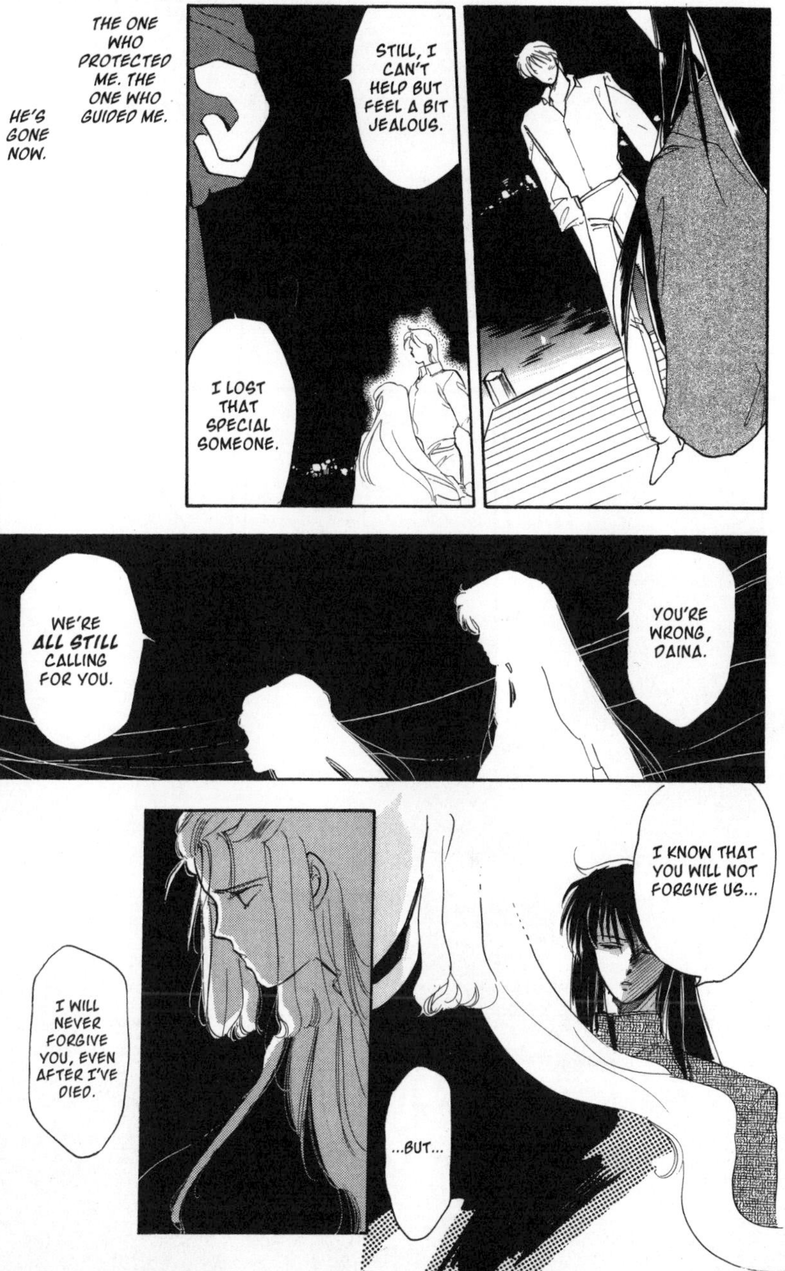
STILL, I CAN'T HELP BUT FEEL A BIT JEALOUS.
I LOST THAT SPECIAL SOMEONE.
THE ONE WHO PROTECTED ME. THE ONE WHO GUIDED ME.
HE'S GONE NOW.
YOU'RE WRONG, DAINA.
WE'RE ALL STILL CALLING FOR YOU.
I KNOW THAT YOU WILL NOT FORGIVE US...
...BUT...
I WILL NEVER FORGIVE YOU, EVEN AFTER I'VE DIED.

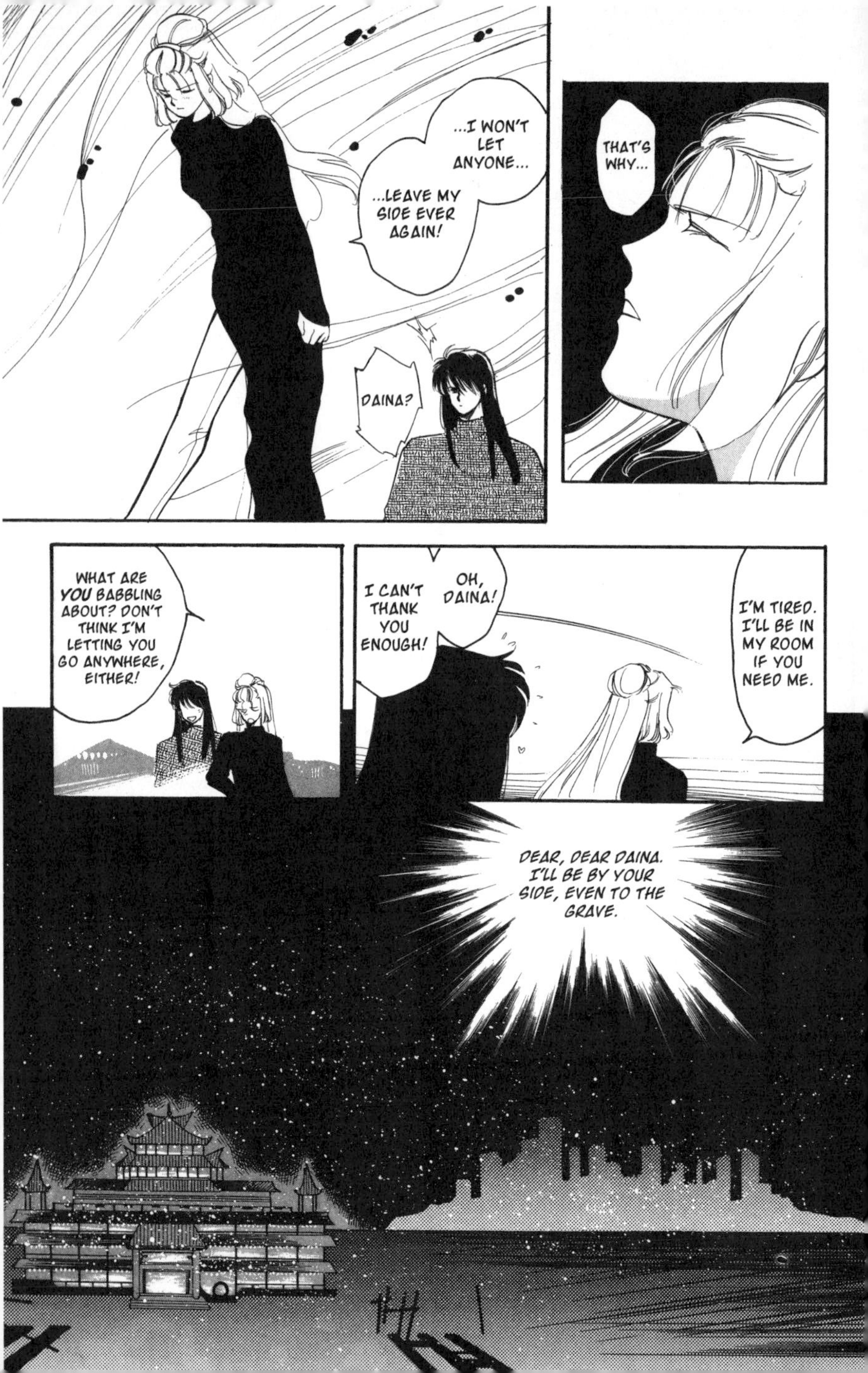
THAT'S WHY...
...I WON'T LET ANYONE...
...LEAVE MY SIDE EVER AGAIN!
DAINA?
I'M TIRED. I'LL BE IN MY ROOM IF YOU NEED ME.
OH, DAINA!
I CAN'T THANK YOU ENOUGH!
WHAT ARE *YOU* BABBLING ABOUT? DON'T THINK I'M LETTING YOU GO ANYWHERE, EITHER!
DEAR, DEAR DAINA. I'LL BE BY YOUR SIDE, EVEN TO THE GRAVE.

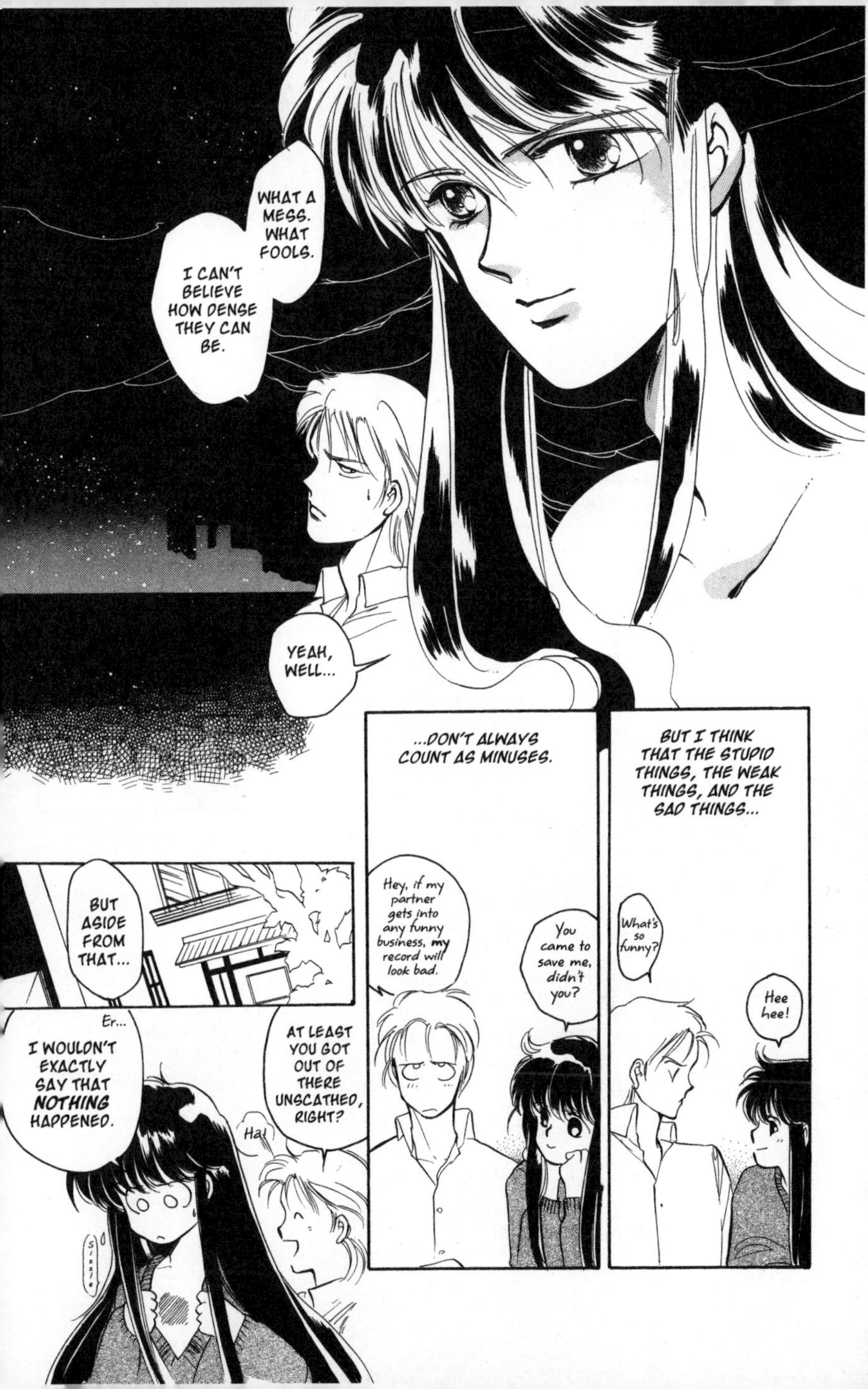
WHAT A MESS. WHAT FOOLS.
I CAN'T BELIEVE HOW DENSE THEY CAN BE.
YEAH, WELL...
BUT I THINK THAT THE STUPID THINGS, THE WEAK THINGS, AND THE SAD THINGS...
Hee hee!
What's so funny?
...DON'T ALWAYS COUNT AS MINUSES.
You came to save me, didn't you?
Hey, if my partner gets into any funny business, my record will look bad.
BUT ASIDE FROM THAT...
AT LEAST YOU GOT OUT OF THERE UNSCATHED, RIGHT?
Ha!
Er...
I WOULDN'T EXACTLY SAY THAT NOTHING HAPPENED.
Sizzle

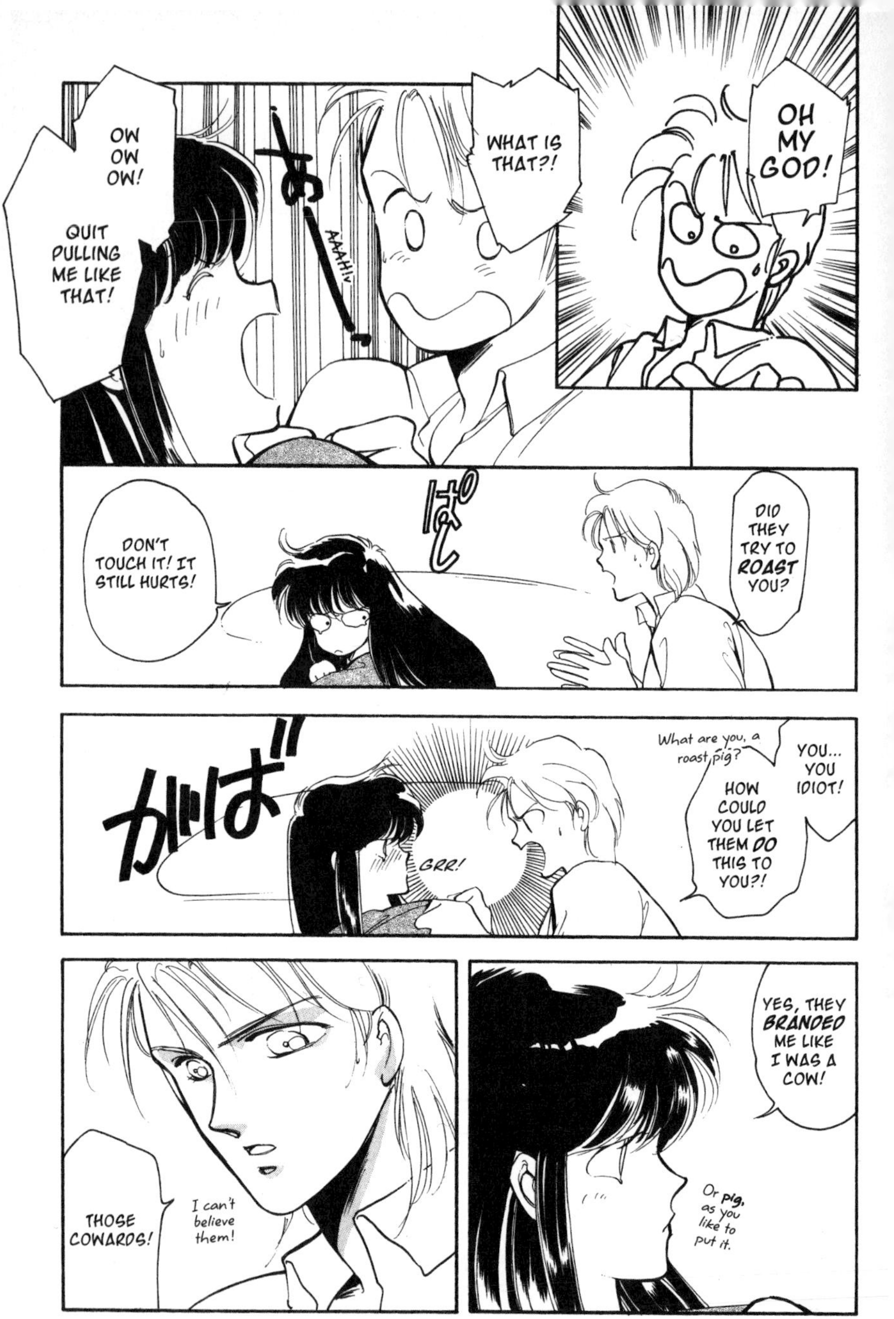
OH MY GOD!
WHAT IS THAT?!
あー
AAAHH!
OW OW OW!
QUIT PULLING ME LIKE THAT!
DID THEY TRY TO ROAST YOU?
ぱし
DON'T TOUCH IT! IT STILL HURTS!
YOU... YOU IDIOT!
What are you, a roast pig?
HOW COULD YOU LET THEM DO THIS TO YOU?!
GRR!
がばっ
YES, THEY BRANDED ME LIKE I WAS A COW!
Or pig, as you like to put it.
I can't believe them!
THOSE COWARDS!

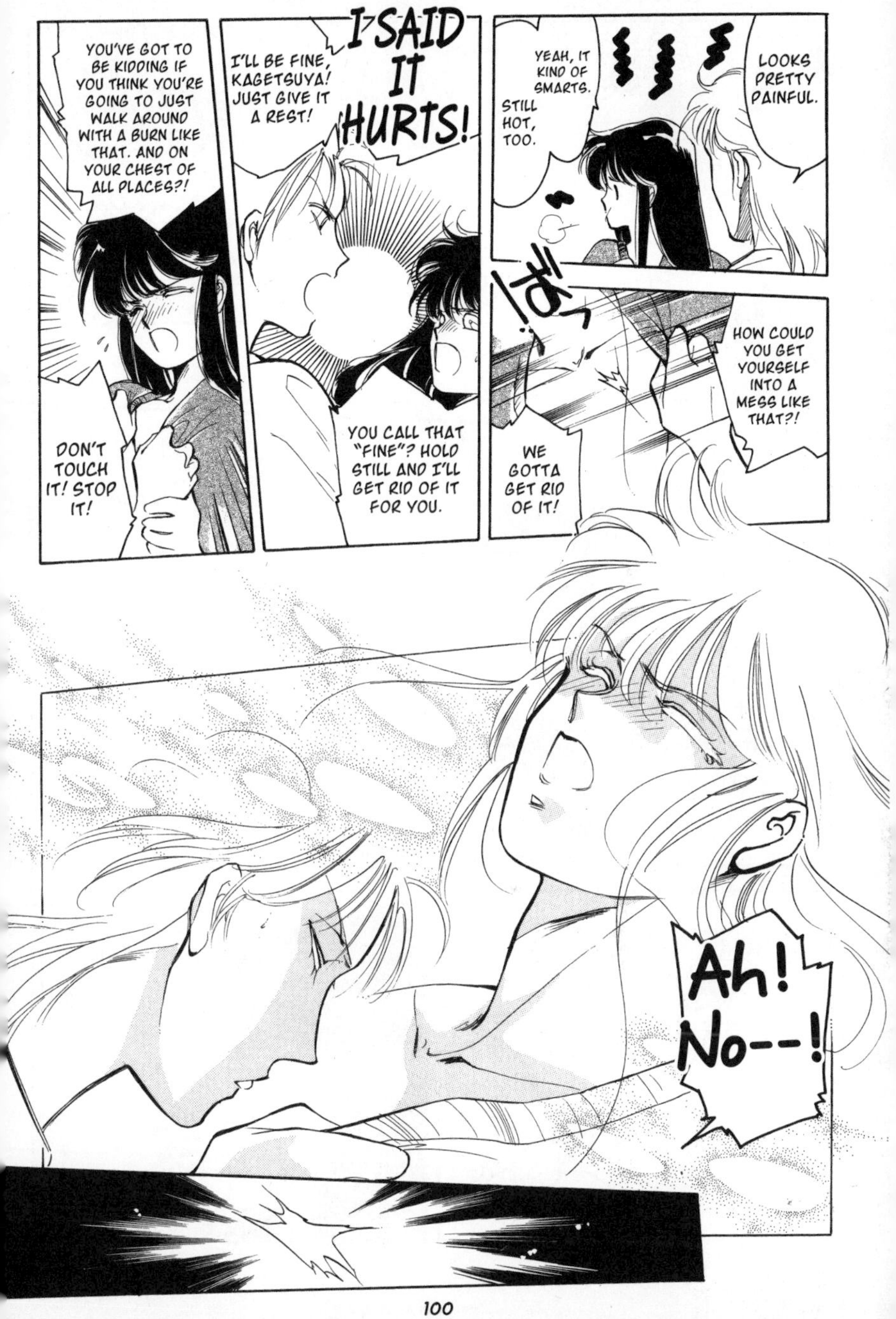
LOOKS PRETTY PAINFUL.
YEAH, IT KIND OF SMARTS.
STILL HOT, TOO.
HOW COULD YOU GET YOURSELF INTO A MESS LIKE THAT?!
WE GOTTA GET RID OF IT!
I SAID IT HURTS!
I'LL BE FINE, KAGETSUYA! JUST GIVE IT A REST!
YOU CALL THAT "FINE"? HOLD STILL AND I'LL GET RID OF IT FOR YOU.
YOU'VE GOT TO BE KIDDING IF YOU THINK YOU'RE GOING TO JUST WALK AROUND WITH A BURN LIKE THAT. AND ON YOUR CHEST OF ALL PLACES?!
DON'T TOUCH IT! STOP IT!
Ah! No--!

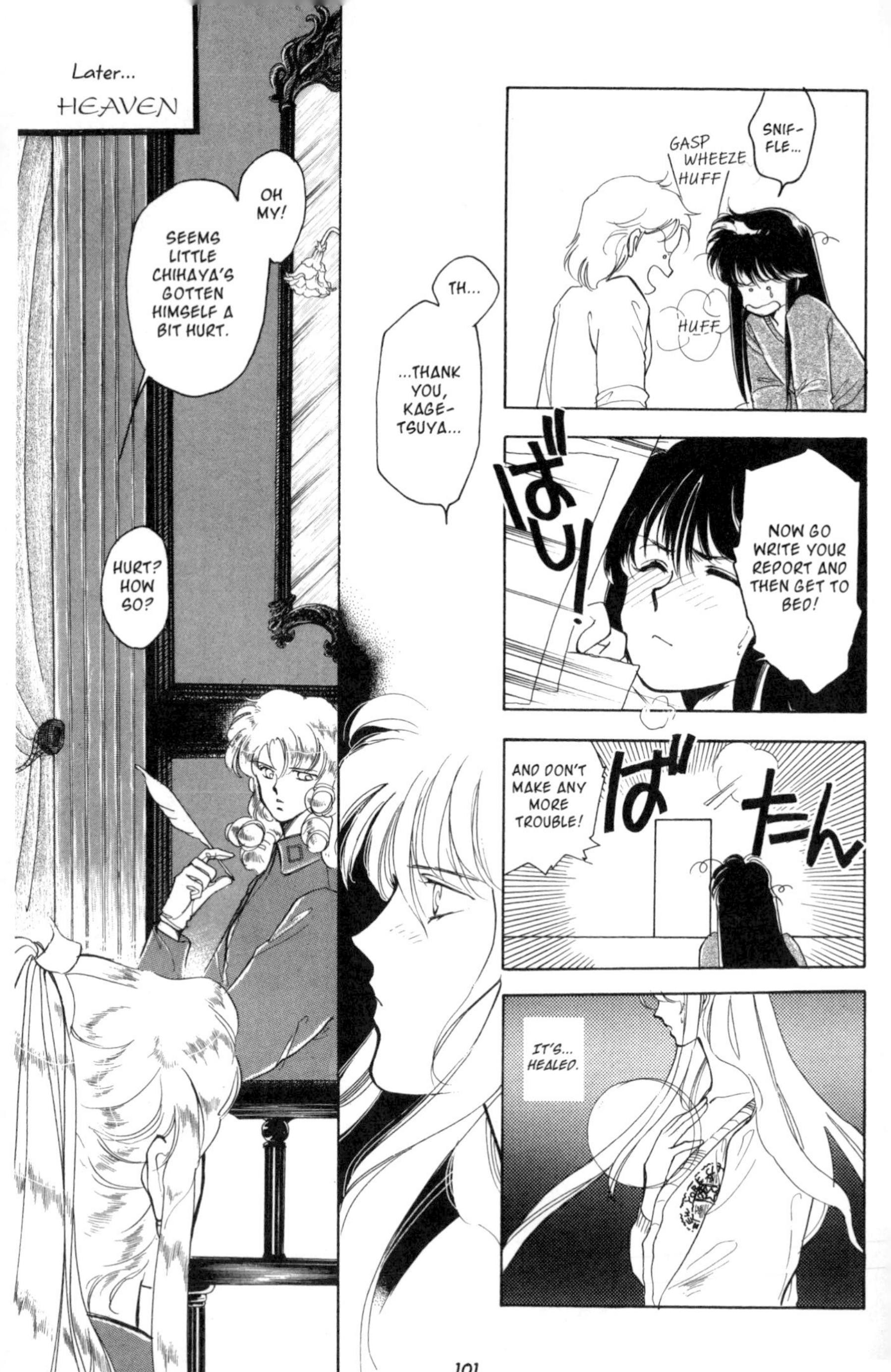
SNIF-FLE...
GASP WHEEZE HUFF
HUFF
TH...
...THANK YOU, KAGE-TSUYA...
ばり!
NOW GO WRITE YOUR REPORT AND THEN GET TO BED!
ばたん
AND DON'T MAKE ANY MORE TROUBLE!
IT'S... HEALED.
Later...
HEAVEN
OH MY!
SEEMS LITTLE CHIHAYA'S GOTTEN HIMSELF A BIT HURT.
HURT? HOW SO?

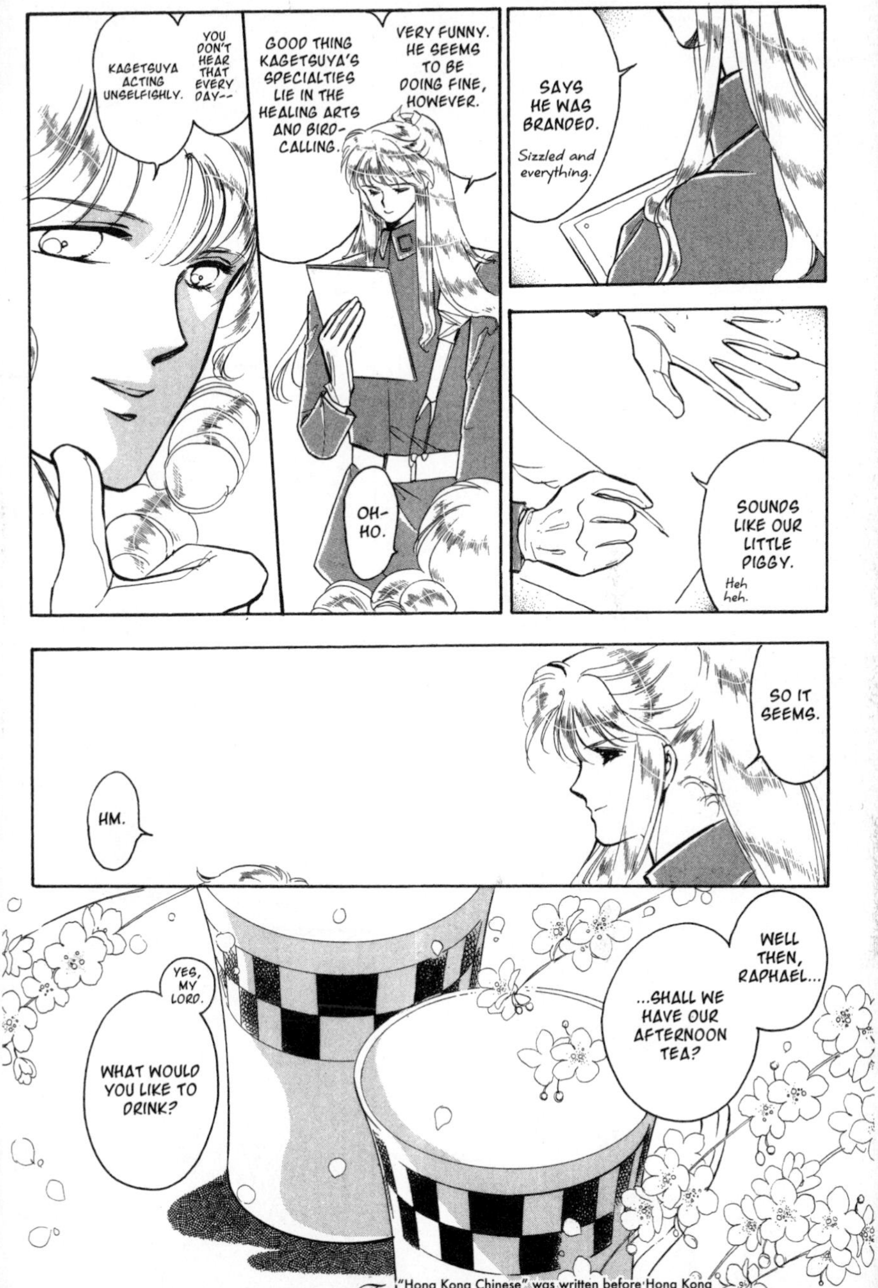
SAYS HE WAS BRANDED.
Sizzled and everything.
SOUNDS LIKE OUR LITTLE PIGGY.
Heh heh.
VERY FUNNY. HE SEEMS TO BE DOING FINE, HOWEVER.
GOOD THING KAGETSUYA'S SPECIALTIES LIE IN THE HEALING ARTS AND BIRD-CALLING.
OH-HO.
YOU DON'T HEAR THAT EVERY DAY--
KAGETSUYA ACTING UNSELFISHLY.
SO IT SEEMS.
HM.
WELL THEN, RAPHAEL...
...SHALL WE HAVE OUR AFTERNOON TEA?
YES, MY LORD.
WHAT WOULD YOU LIKE TO DRINK?

Fin

"Hong Kong Chinese" was written before Hong Kong was returned to the People's Republic of China.

CHRISTMAS SUMMER

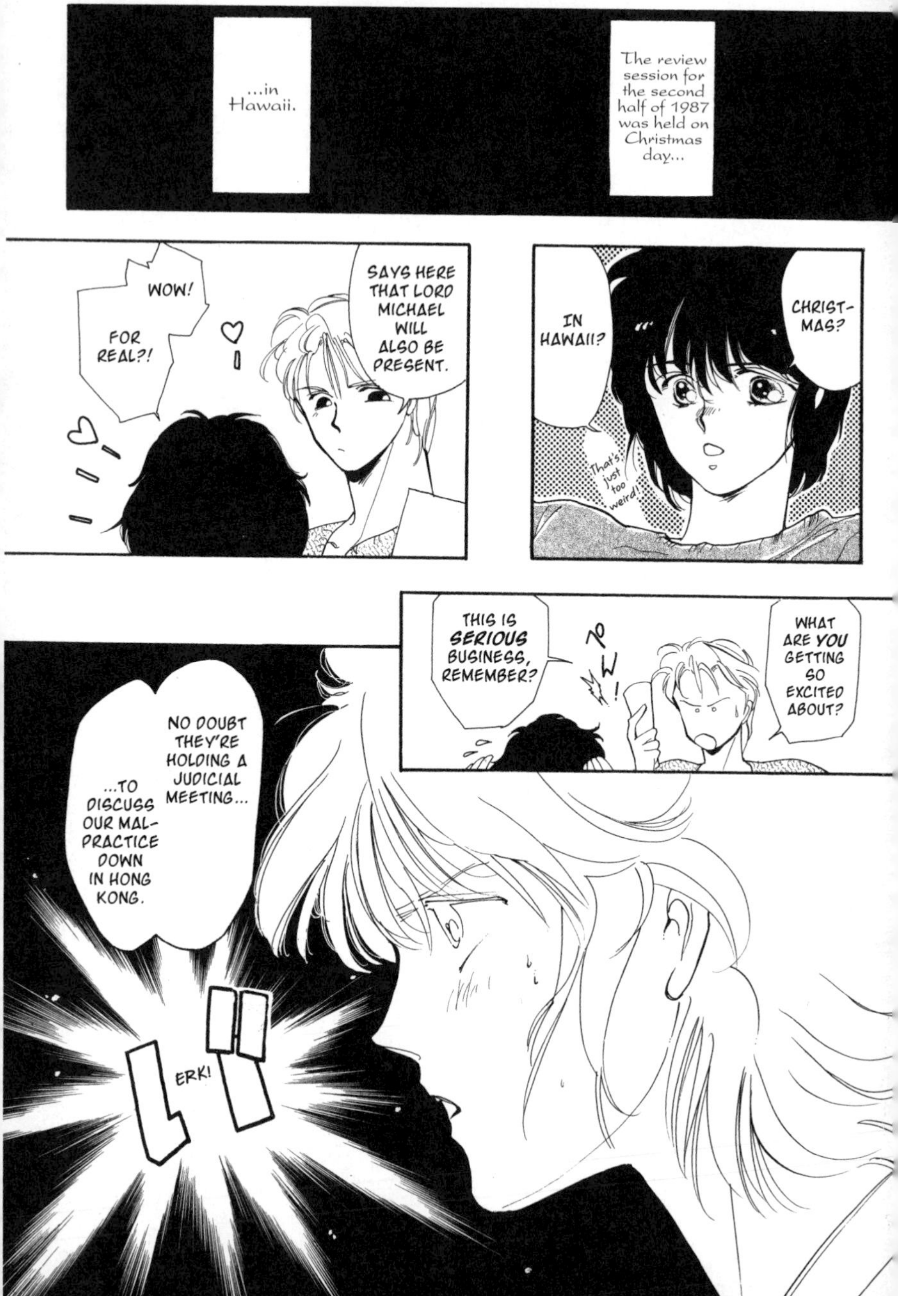
The review session for the second half of 1987 was held on Christmas day...
...in Hawaii.
CHRIST-MAS?
IN HAWAII?
That's just too weird!
SAYS HERE THAT LORD MICHAEL WILL ALSO BE PRESENT.
WOW!
FOR REAL?!
WHAT ARE YOU GETTING SO EXCITED ABOUT?
POW!
THIS IS SERIOUS BUSINESS, REMEMBER?
NO DOUBT THEY'RE HOLDING A JUDICIAL MEETING...
...TO DISCUSS OUR MAL-PRACTICE DOWN IN HONG KONG.
ERK!

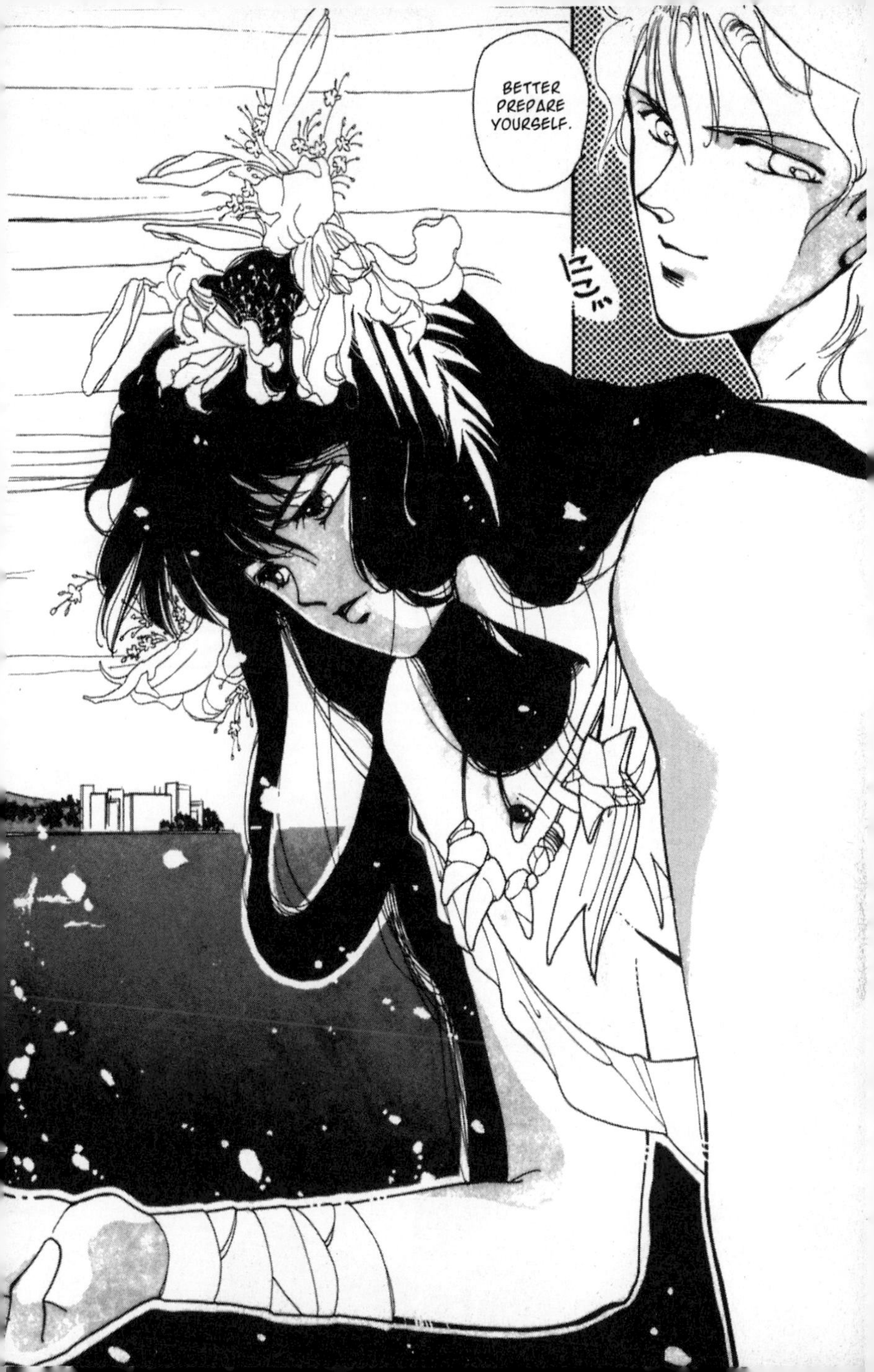
BETTER PREPARE YOURSELF.

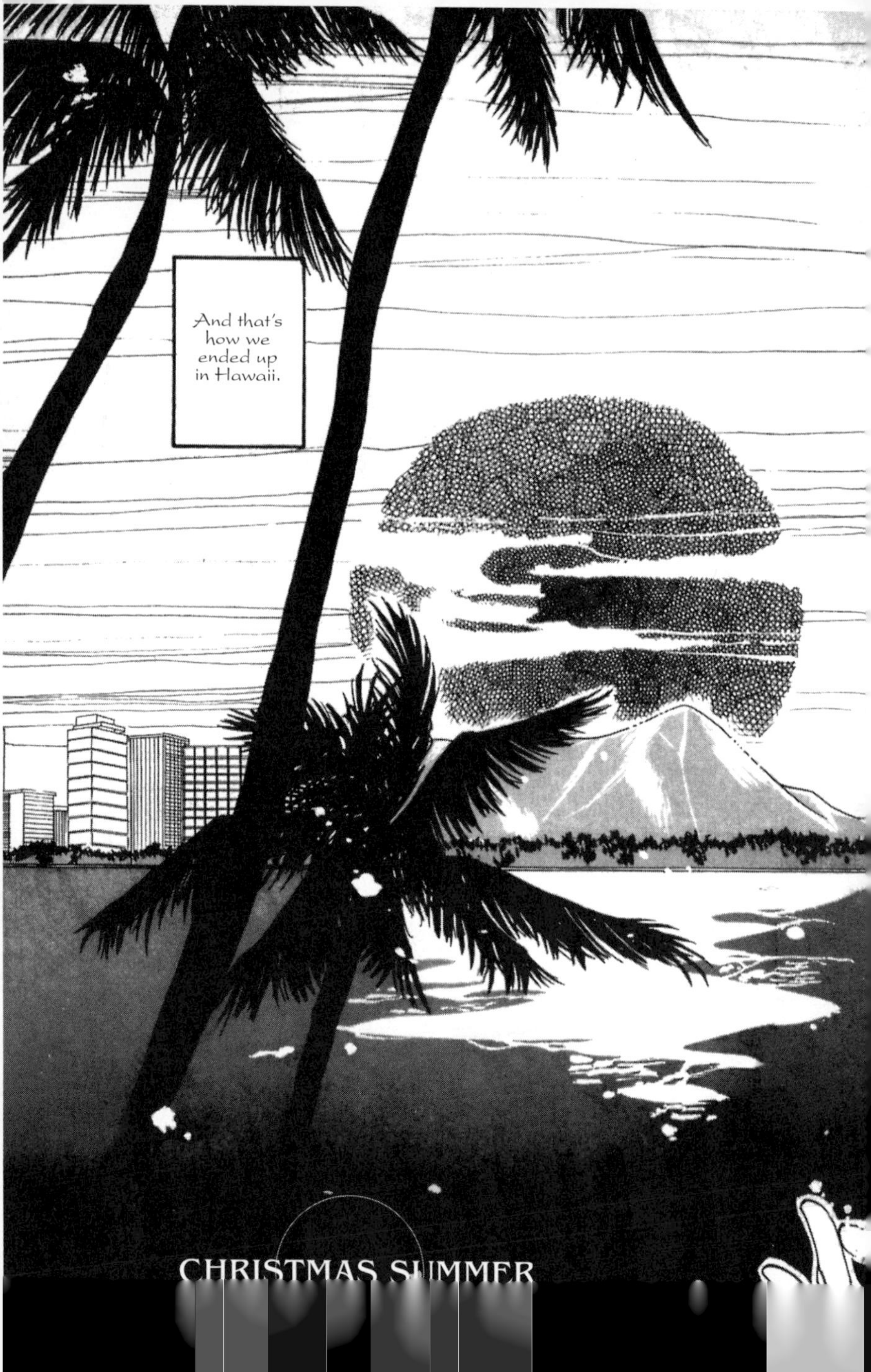
And that's how we ended up in Hawaii.
CHRISTMAS SUMMER

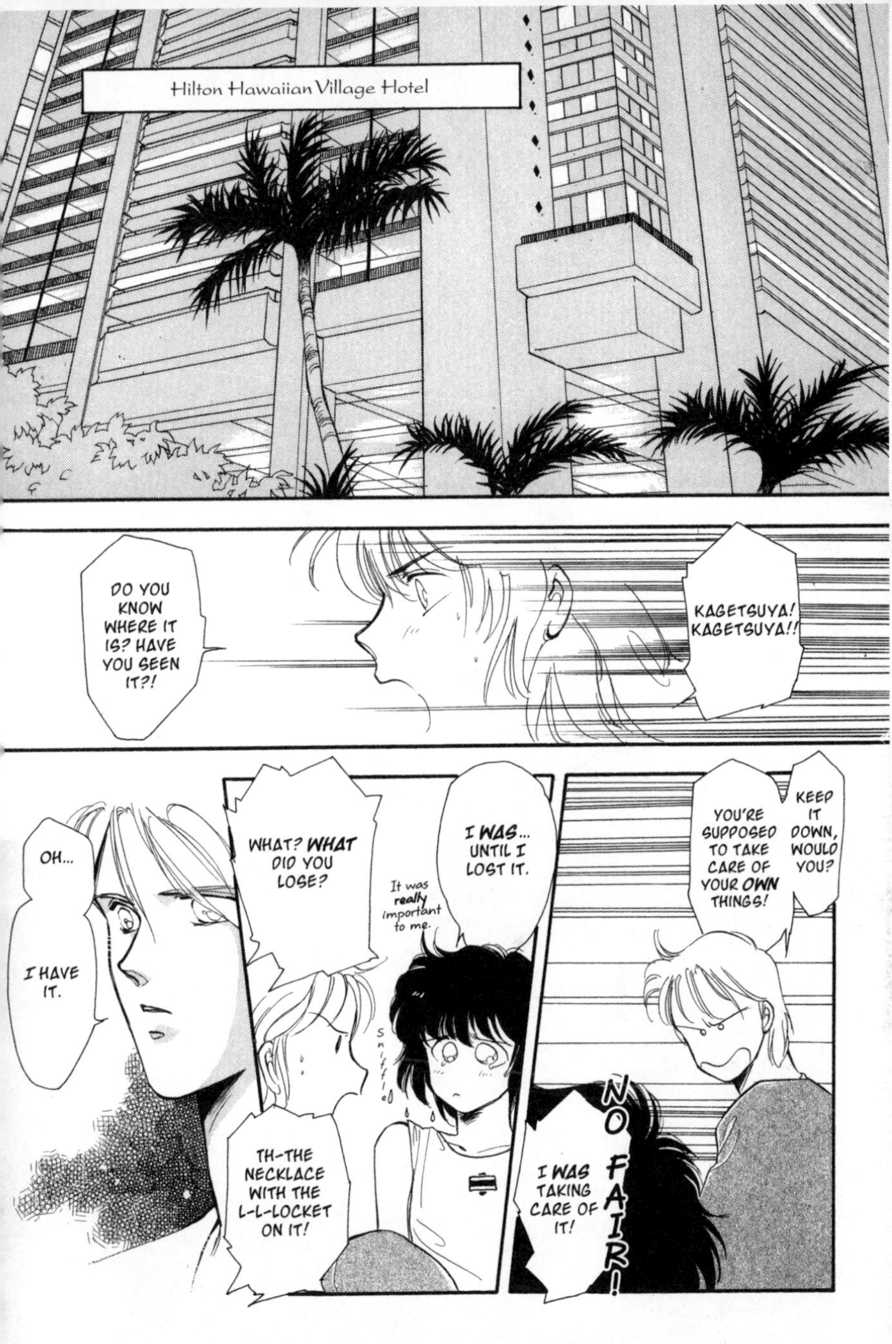
Hilton Hawaiian Village Hotel
KAGETSUYA! KAGETSUYA!!
DO YOU KNOW WHERE IT IS? HAVE YOU SEEN IT?!
KEEP IT DOWN, WOULD YOU?
YOU'RE SUPPOSED TO TAKE CARE OF YOUR **OWN** THINGS!
NO FAIR!
I **WAS** TAKING CARE OF IT!
I **WAS**... UNTIL I LOST IT.
It was **really** important to me.
WHAT? **WHAT** DID YOU LOSE?
Sniffle
TH-THE NECKLACE WITH THE L-L-LOCKET ON IT!
OH...
I HAVE IT.

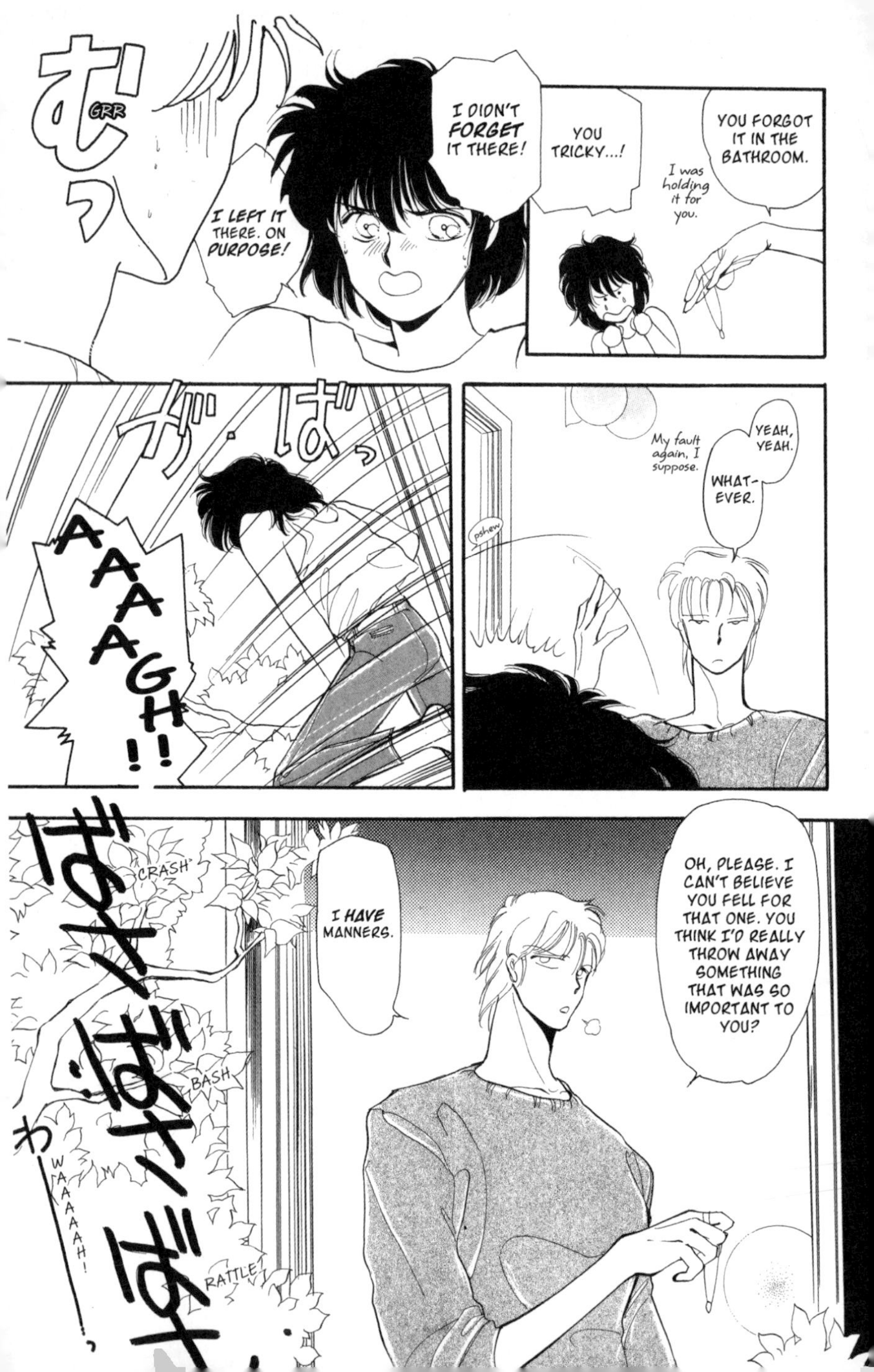
YOU FORGOT IT IN THE BATHROOM.
I was holding it for you.
YOU TRICKY...!
I DIDN'T FORGET IT THERE!
I LEFT IT THERE. ON PURPOSE!
むっ
GRR
YEAH, YEAH.
WHAT-EVER.
My fault again, I suppose.
pshew
AAAAGH!!
OH, PLEASE. I CAN'T BELIEVE YOU FELL FOR THAT ONE. YOU THINK I'D REALLY THROW AWAY SOMETHING THAT WAS SO IMPORTANT TO YOU?
I HAVE MANNERS.
CRASH
BASH
WAAAAAH!
RATTLE

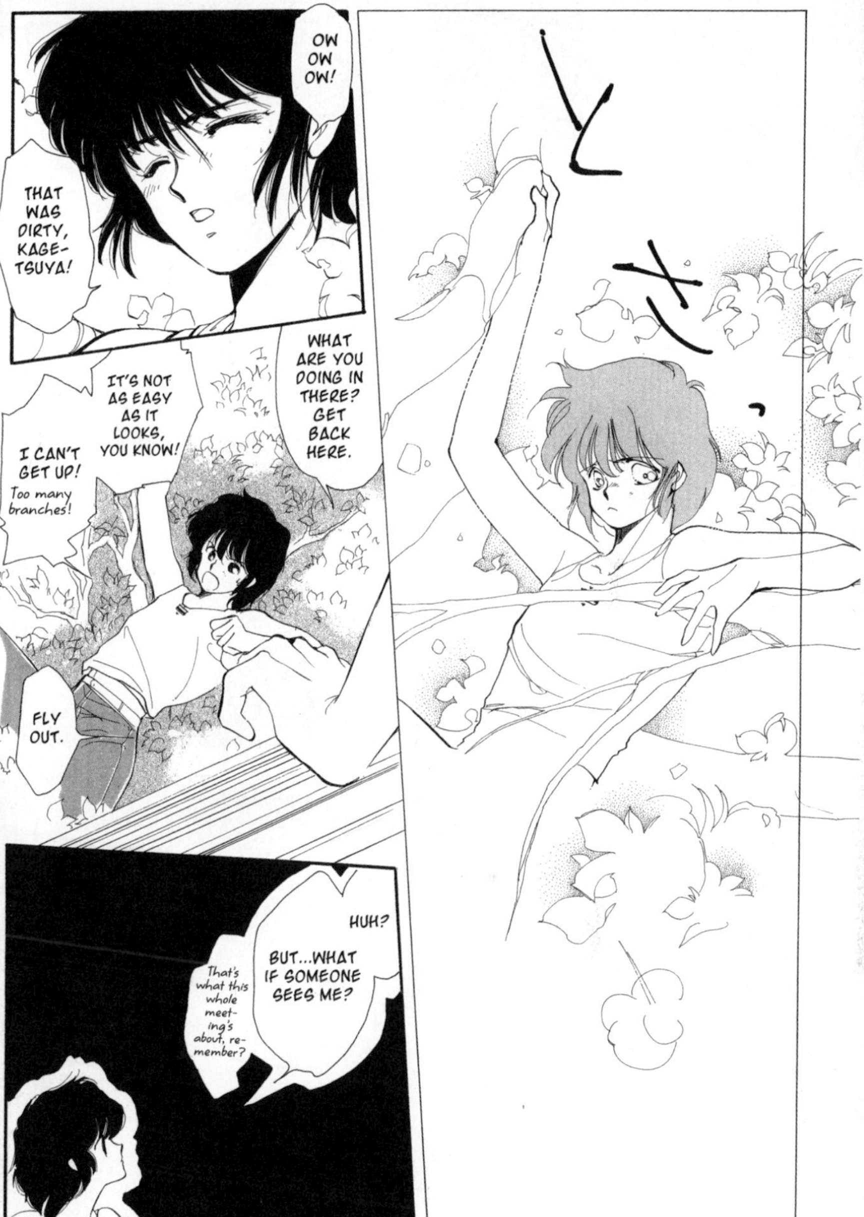
とさっ
OW OW OW!
THAT WAS DIRTY, KAGE-TSUYA!
WHAT ARE YOU DOING IN THERE? GET BACK HERE.
IT'S NOT AS EASY AS IT LOOKS, YOU KNOW!
I CAN'T GET UP! Too many branches!
FLY OUT.
HUH?
BUT...WHAT IF SOMEONE SEES ME?
That's what this whole meet-ing's about, re-member?

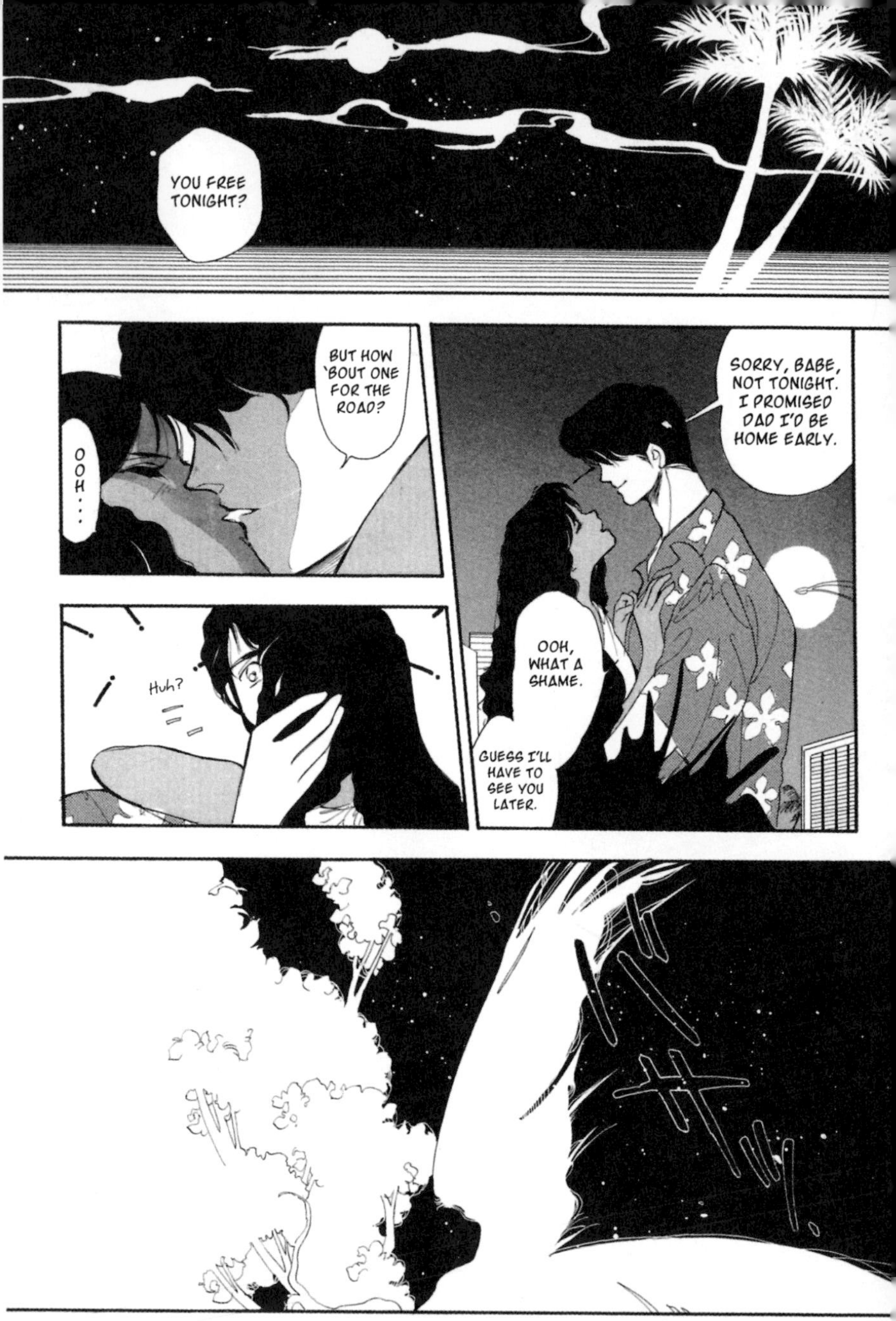
YOU FREE TONIGHT?
SORRY, BABE, NOT TONIGHT. I PROMISED DAD I'D BE HOME EARLY.
OOH, WHAT A SHAME.
GUESS I'LL HAVE TO SEE YOU LATER.
BUT HOW 'BOUT ONE FOR THE ROAD?
OOH...
Huh?

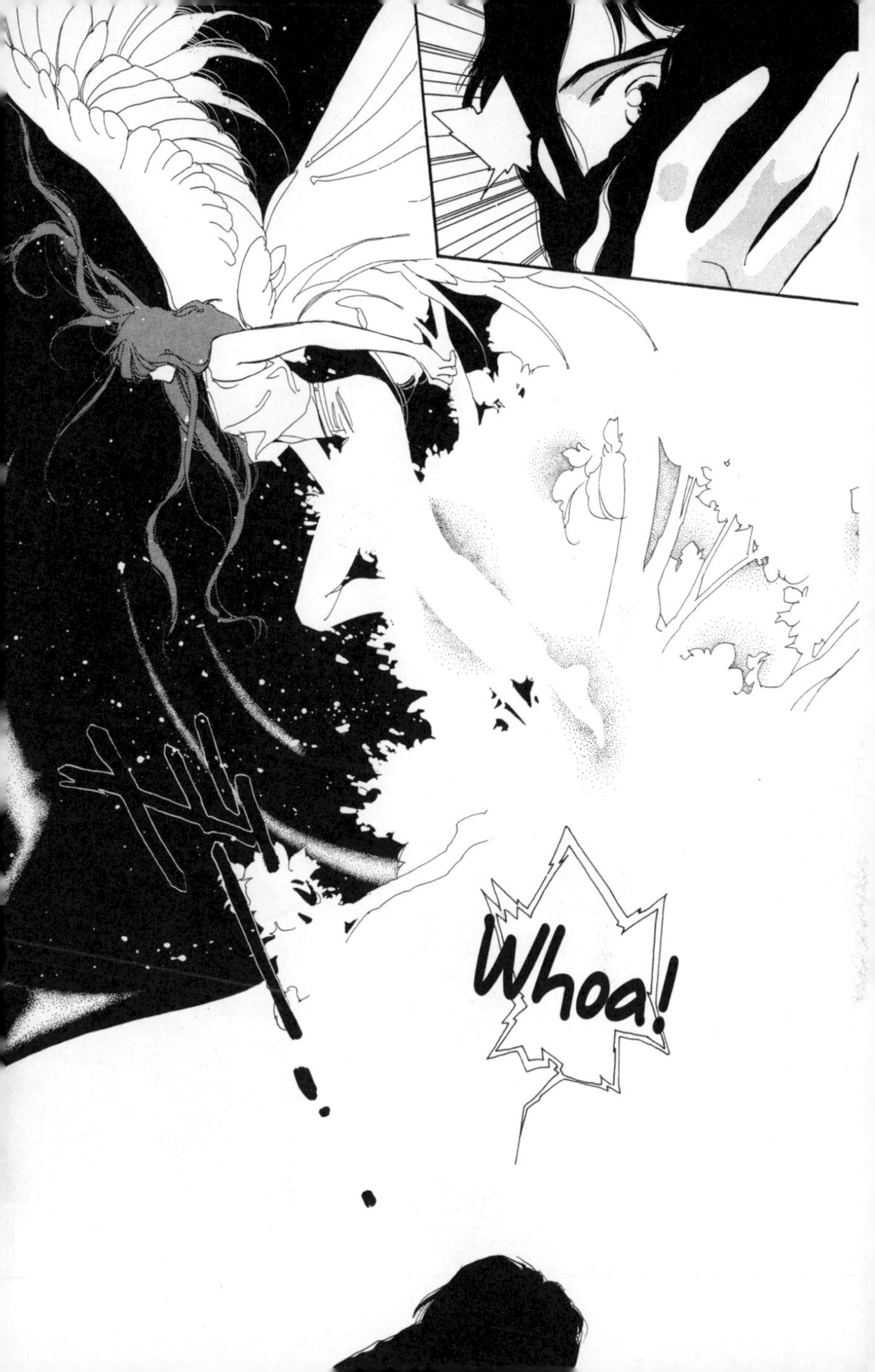
Whoa!

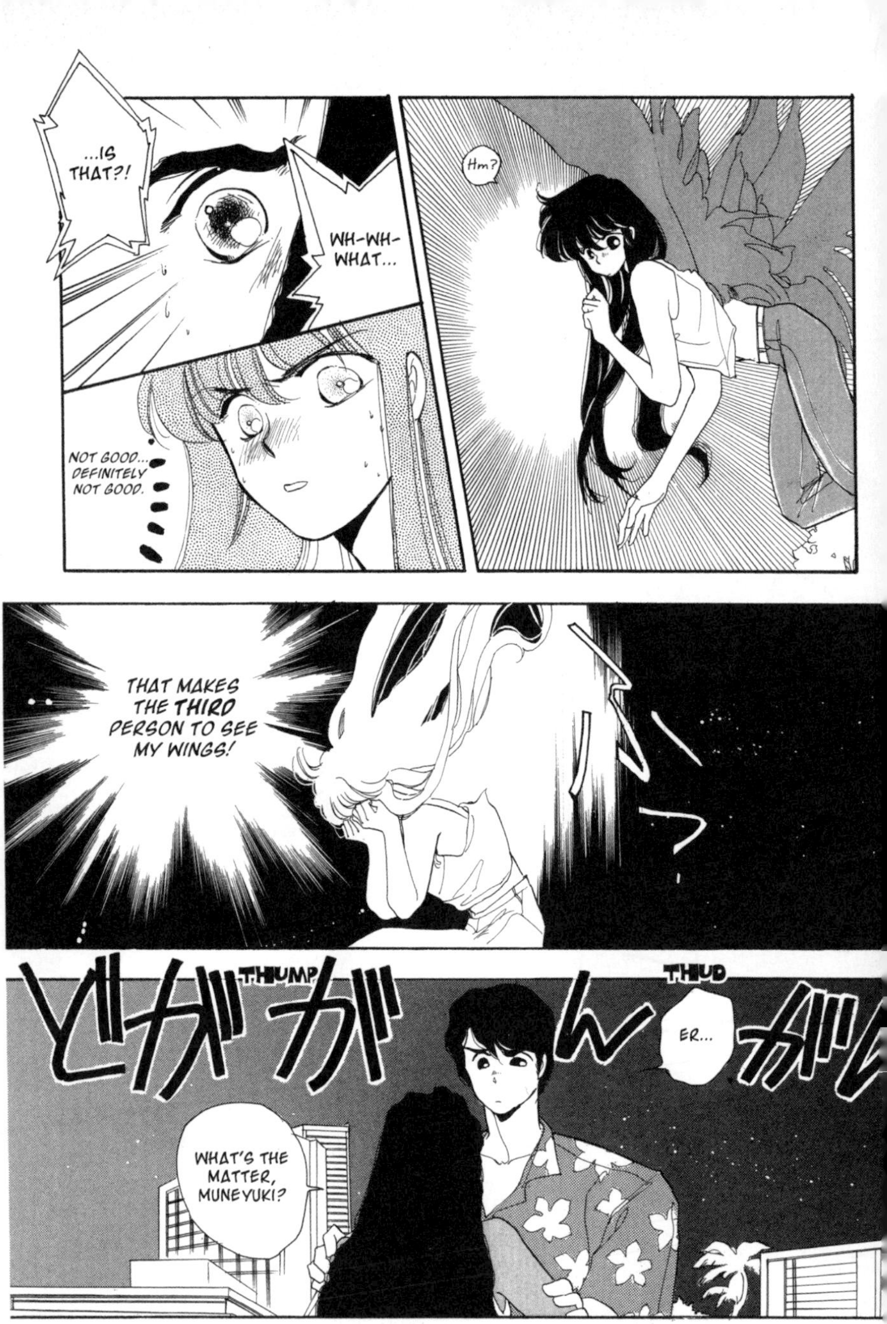
Hm?
WH-WH-WHAT...
...IS THAT?!
NOT GOOD... DEFINITELY NOT GOOD.
THAT MAKES THE **THIRD** PERSON TO SEE MY WINGS!
THUD
ER...
THUMP
WHAT'S THE MATTER, MUNEYUKI?

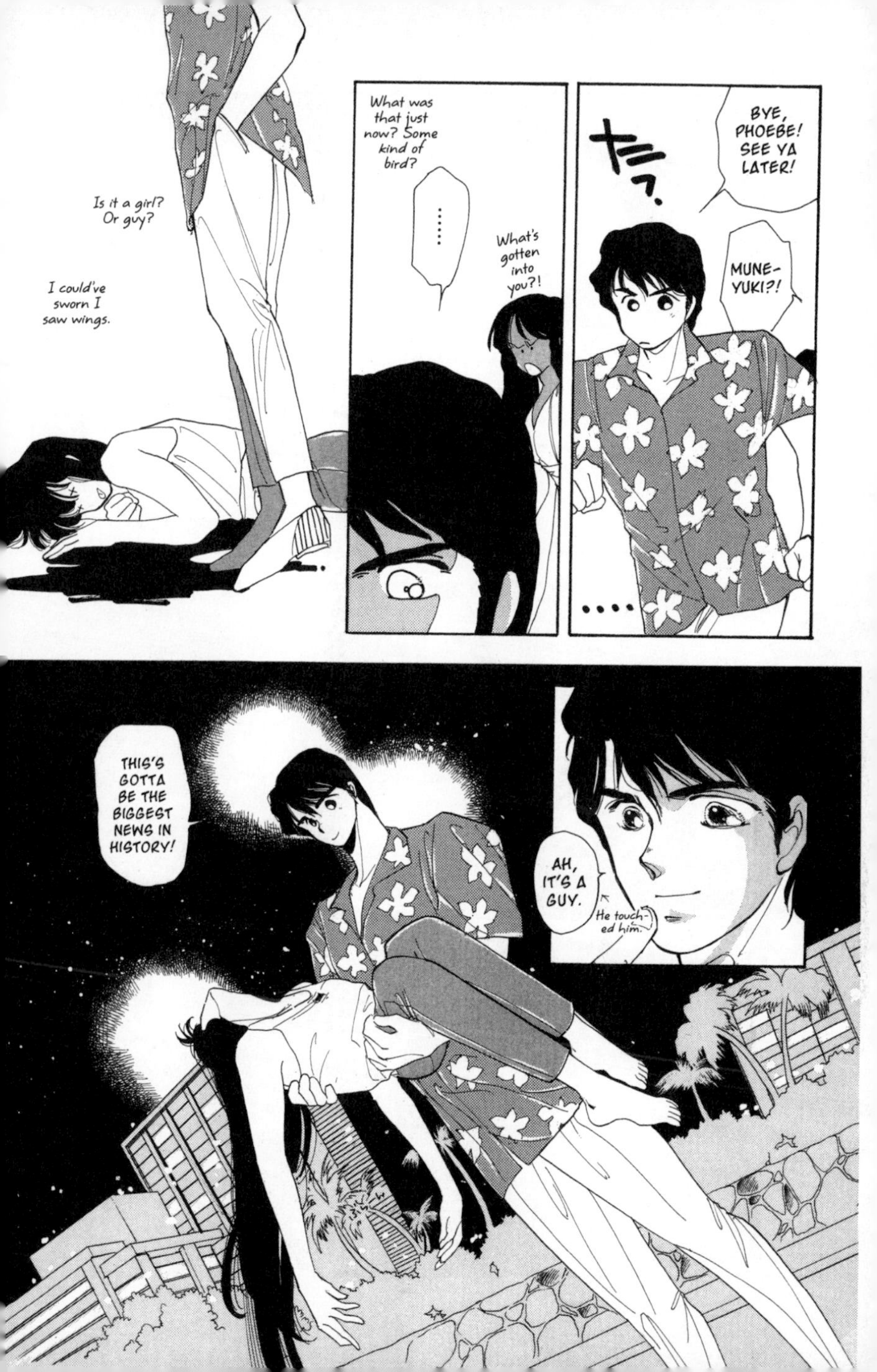
BYE, PHOEBE! SEE YA LATER!
MUNE-YUKI?!
....
What was that just now? Some kind of bird?
......
What's gotten into you?!
Is it a girl? Or guy?
I could've sworn I saw wings.
AH, IT'S A GUY.
He touched him.
THIS'S GOTTA BE THE BIGGEST NEWS IN HISTORY!

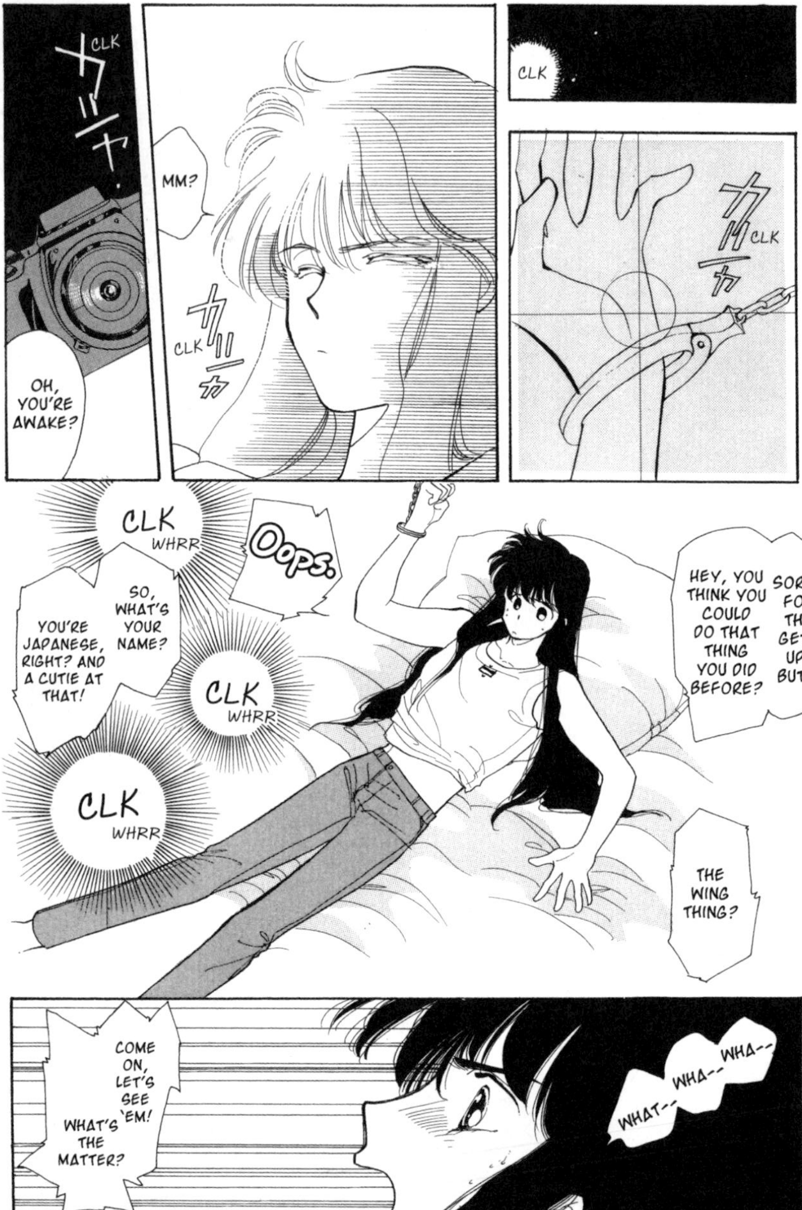
CLK
CLK
MM?
CLK
CLK
OH, YOU'RE AWAKE?
SORRY FOR THE GET-UP, BUT...
HEY, YOU THINK YOU COULD DO THAT THING YOU DID BEFORE?
THE WING THING?
Oops.
CLK WHRR
SO, WHAT'S YOUR NAME?
YOU'RE JAPANESE, RIGHT? AND A CUTIE AT THAT!
CLK WHRR
CLK WHRR
WHAT-- WHA-- WHA--
COME ON, LET'S SEE 'EM!
WHAT'S THE MATTER?

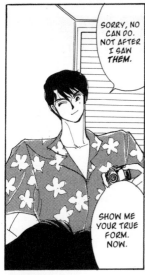

むかーっ
WHAT'S GOING ON HERE? KNOCK IT OFF! IT'S CREEPING ME OUT!
GRRRRRR
CLK
WHRR
SORRY, NO CAN DO. NOT AFTER I SAW **THEM.**
SHOW ME YOUR TRUE FORM. NOW.
YOU AN ANGEL?
OR A DEMON?
A MUTATION?
A FREAK?
HELP...!
S-STOP SAYING THAT!
HELP ME...!

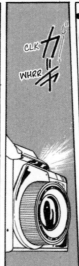

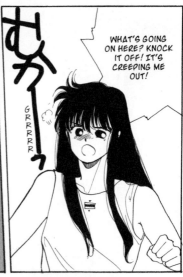

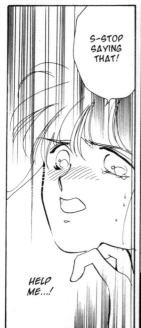

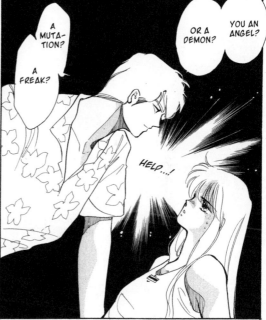

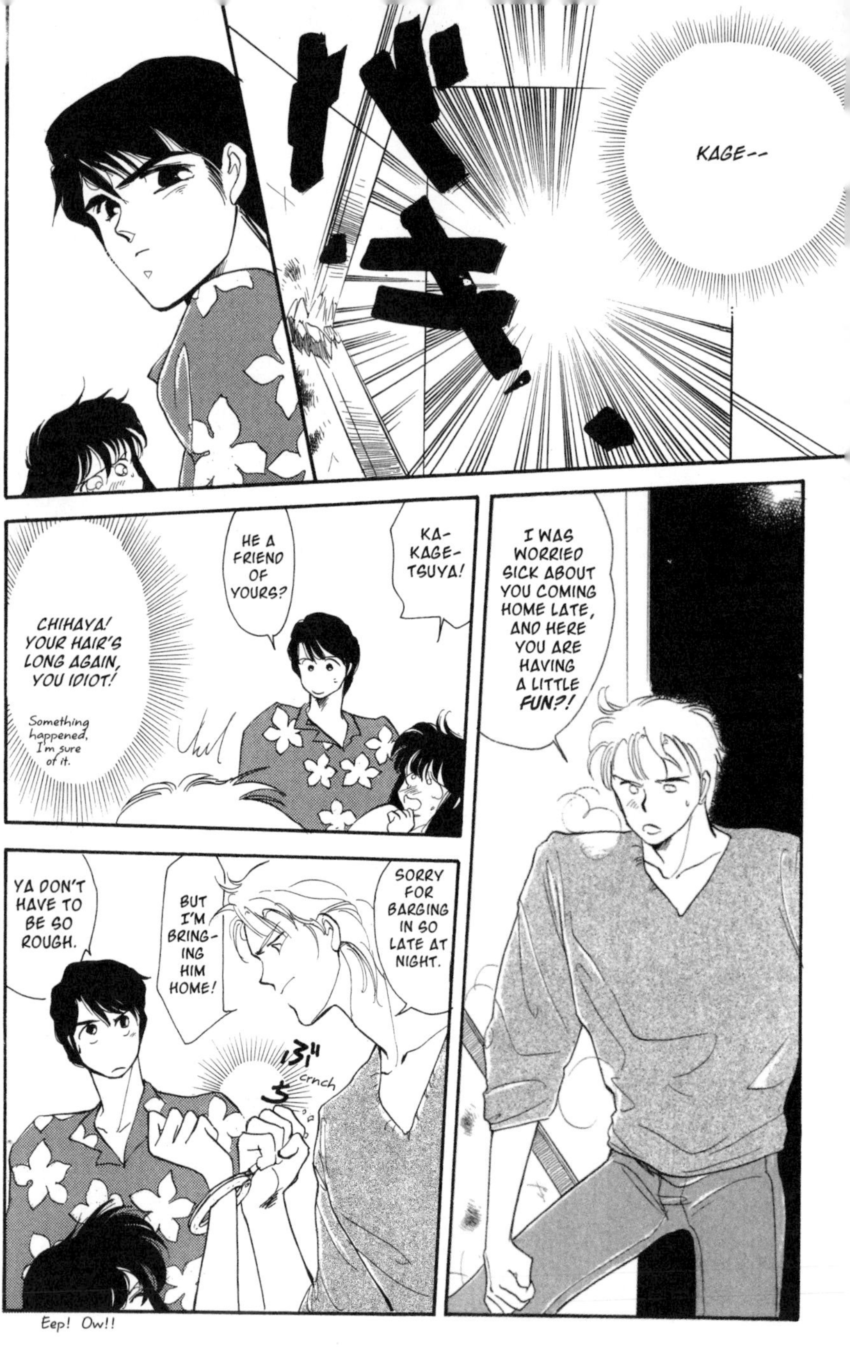
KAGE--
I WAS WORRIED SICK ABOUT YOU COMING HOME LATE, AND HERE YOU ARE HAVING A LITTLE FUN?!
KA-KAGE-TSUYA!
HE A FRIEND OF YOURS?
CHIHAYA! YOUR HAIR'S LONG AGAIN, YOU IDIOT!
Something happened, I'm sure of it.
SORRY FOR BARGING IN SO LATE AT NIGHT.
BUT I'M BRINGING HIM HOME!
YA DON'T HAVE TO BE SO ROUGH.
ぶち
crnch
Eep! Ow!!

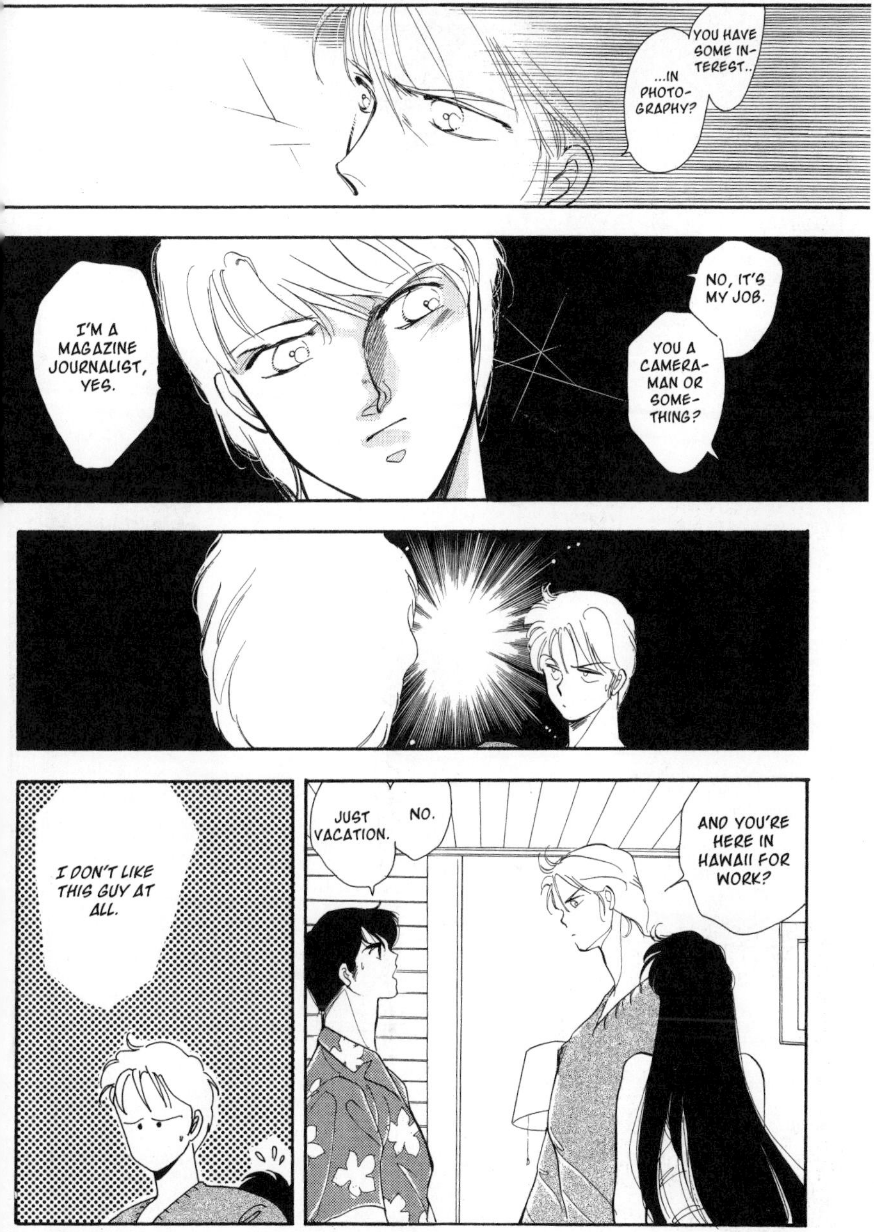
YOU HAVE SOME INTEREST..
...IN PHOTOGRAPHY?
NO, IT'S MY JOB.
YOU A CAMERAMAN OR SOMETHING?
I'M A MAGAZINE JOURNALIST, YES.
AND YOU'RE HERE IN HAWAII FOR WORK?
NO.
JUST VACATION.
I DON'T LIKE THIS GUY AT ALL.

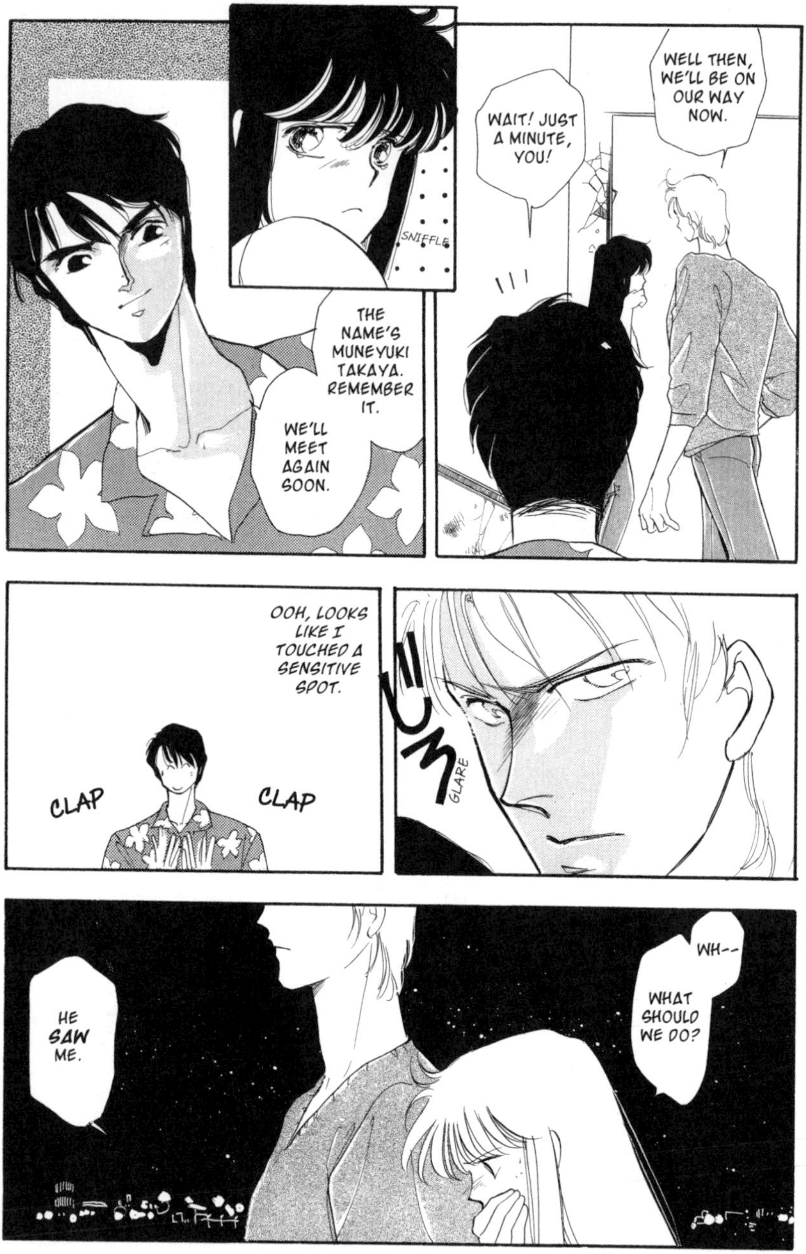
WELL THEN, WE'LL BE ON OUR WAY NOW.
WAIT! JUST A MINUTE, YOU!
SNIFFLE
THE NAME'S MUNEYUKI TAKAYA. REMEMBER IT.
WE'LL MEET AGAIN SOON.
GLARE
OOH, LOOKS LIKE I TOUCHED A SENSITIVE SPOT.
CLAP
CLAP
WH--
WHAT SHOULD WE DO?
HE SAW ME.

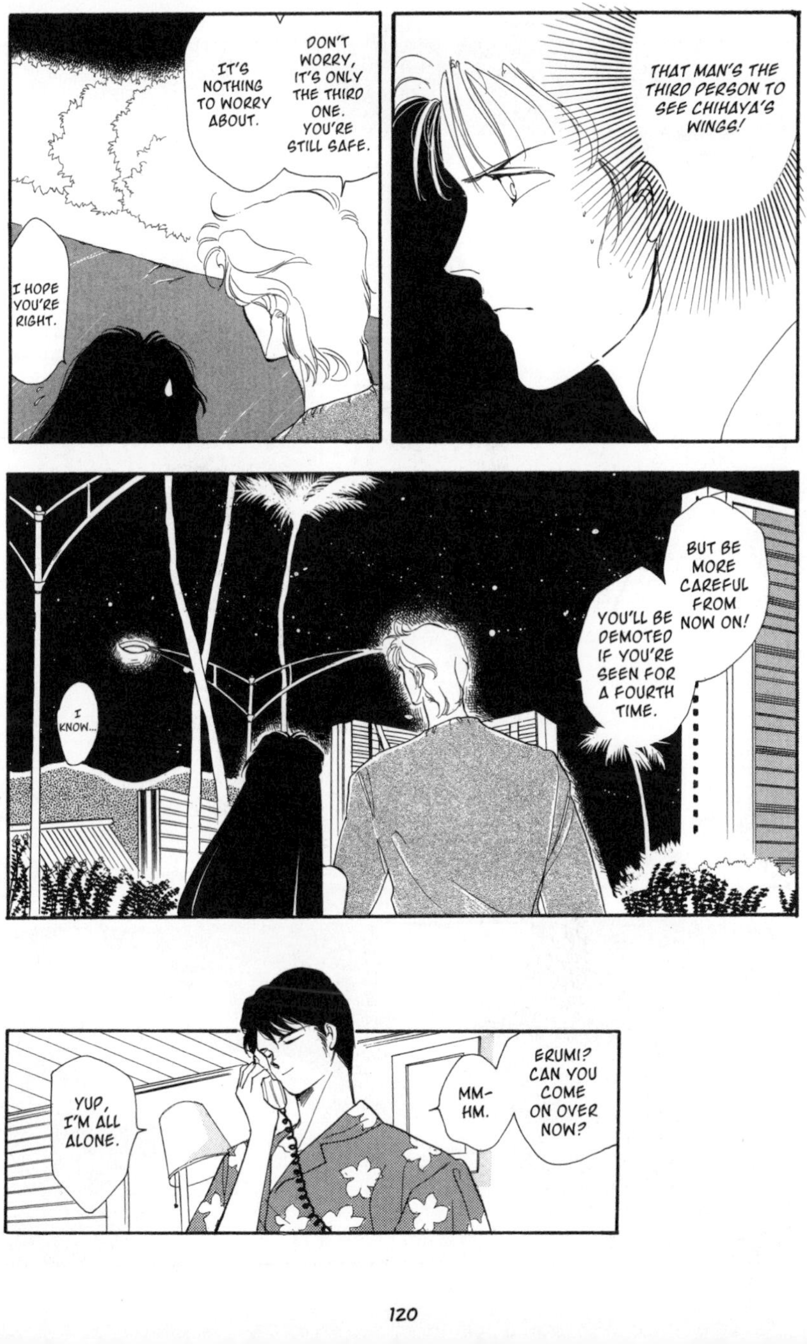
THAT MAN'S THE THIRD PERSON TO SEE CHIHAYA'S WINGS!
DON'T WORRY, IT'S ONLY THE THIRD ONE. YOU'RE STILL SAFE.
IT'S NOTHING TO WORRY ABOUT.
I HOPE YOU'RE RIGHT.
BUT BE MORE CAREFUL FROM NOW ON!
YOU'LL BE DEMOTED IF YOU'RE SEEN FOR A FOURTH TIME.
I KNOW...
ERUMI? CAN YOU COME ON OVER NOW?
MM-HM.
YUP, I'M ALL ALONE.

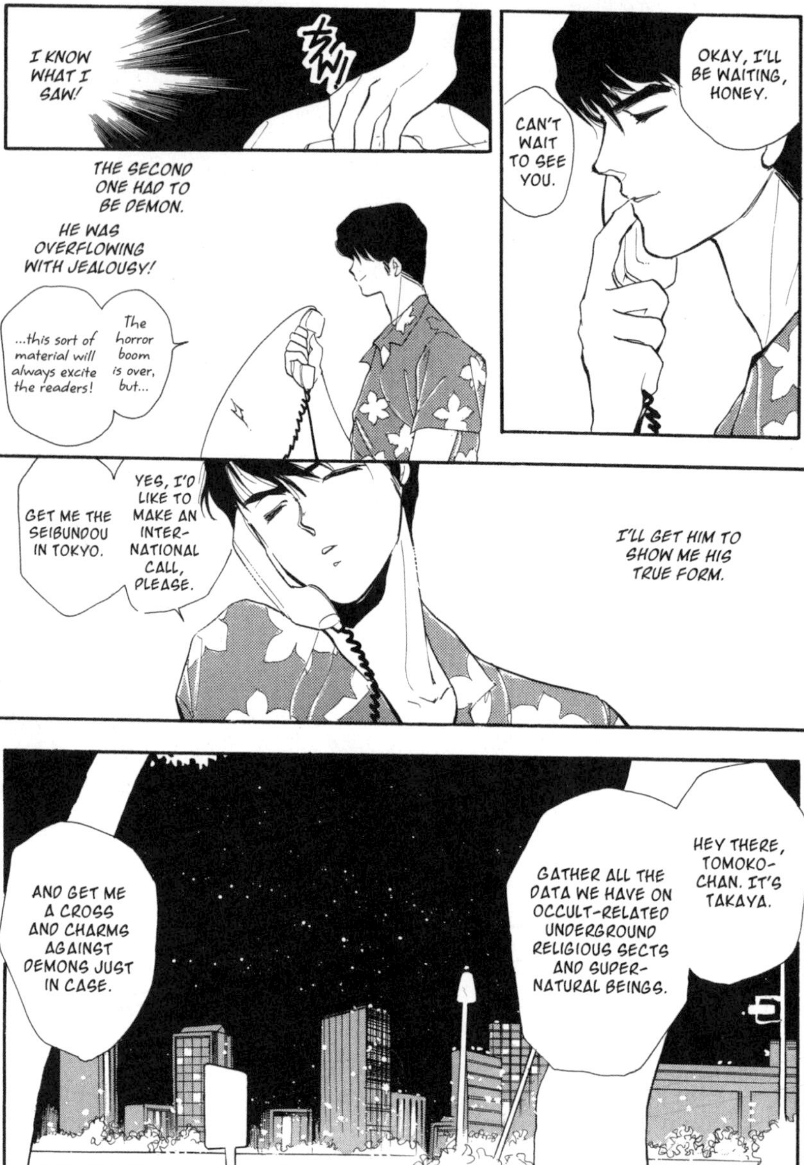
OKAY, I'LL BE WAITING, HONEY.
CAN'T WAIT TO SEE YOU.
I KNOW WHAT I SAW!
THE SECOND ONE HAD TO BE DEMON.
HE WAS OVERFLOWING WITH JEALOUSY!
The horror boom is over, but...
...this sort of material will always excite the readers!
I'LL GET HIM TO SHOW ME HIS TRUE FORM.
YES, I'D LIKE TO MAKE AN INTER-NATIONAL CALL, PLEASE.
GET ME THE SEIBUNDOU IN TOKYO.
HEY THERE, TOMOKO-CHAN. IT'S TAKAYA.
GATHER ALL THE DATA WE HAVE ON OCCULT-RELATED UNDERGROUND RELIGIOUS SECTS AND SUPER-NATURAL BEINGS.
AND GET ME A CROSS AND CHARMS AGAINST DEMONS JUST IN CASE.

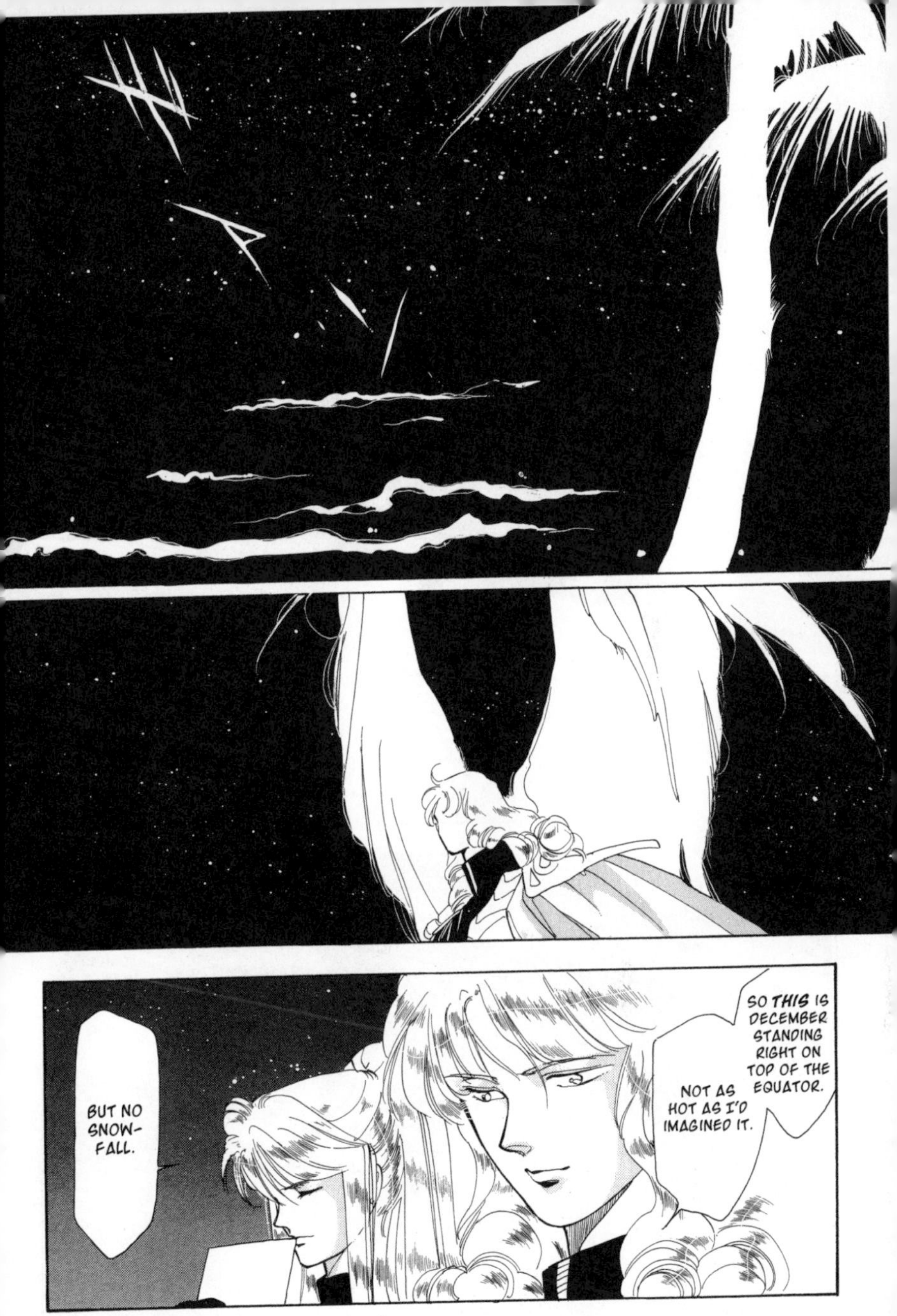
SO *THIS* IS DECEMBER STANDING RIGHT ON TOP OF THE EQUATOR.
NOT AS HOT AS I'D IMAGINED IT.
BUT NO SNOW-FALL.

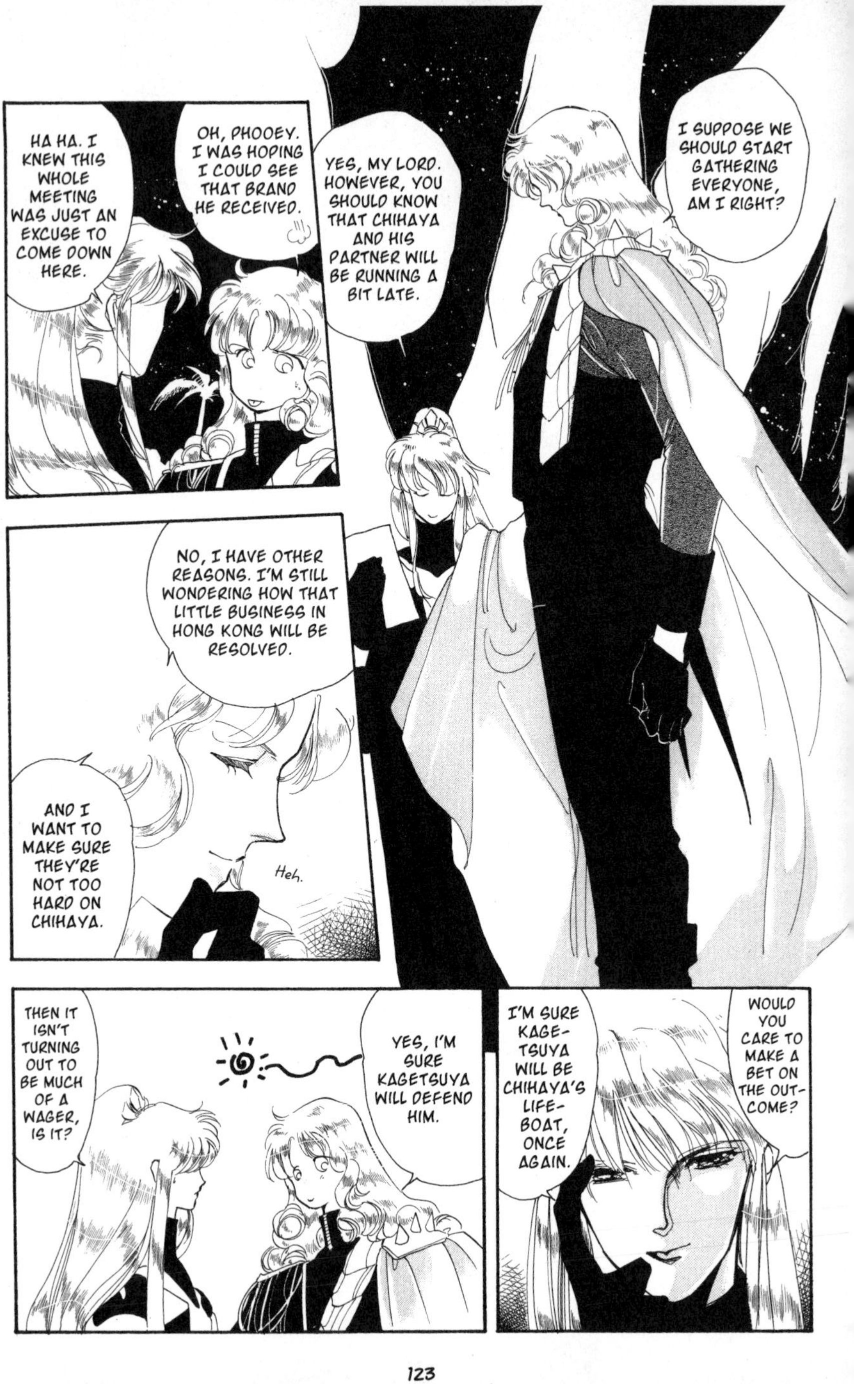
I SUPPOSE WE SHOULD START GATHERING EVERYONE, AM I RIGHT?
YES, MY LORD. HOWEVER, YOU SHOULD KNOW THAT CHIHAYA AND HIS PARTNER WILL BE RUNNING A BIT LATE.
OH, PHOOEY. I WAS HOPING I COULD SEE THAT BRAND HE RECEIVED.
HA HA. I KNEW THIS WHOLE MEETING WAS JUST AN EXCUSE TO COME DOWN HERE.
NO, I HAVE OTHER REASONS. I'M STILL WONDERING HOW THAT LITTLE BUSINESS IN HONG KONG WILL BE RESOLVED.
AND I WANT TO MAKE SURE THEY'RE NOT TOO HARD ON CHIHAYA.
Heh.
WOULD YOU CARE TO MAKE A BET ON THE OUT-COME?
I'M SURE KAGE-TSUYA WILL BE CHIHAYA'S LIFE-BOAT, ONCE AGAIN.
YES, I'M SURE KAGETSUYA WILL DEFEND HIM.
THEN IT ISN'T TURNING OUT TO BE MUCH OF A WAGER, IS IT?

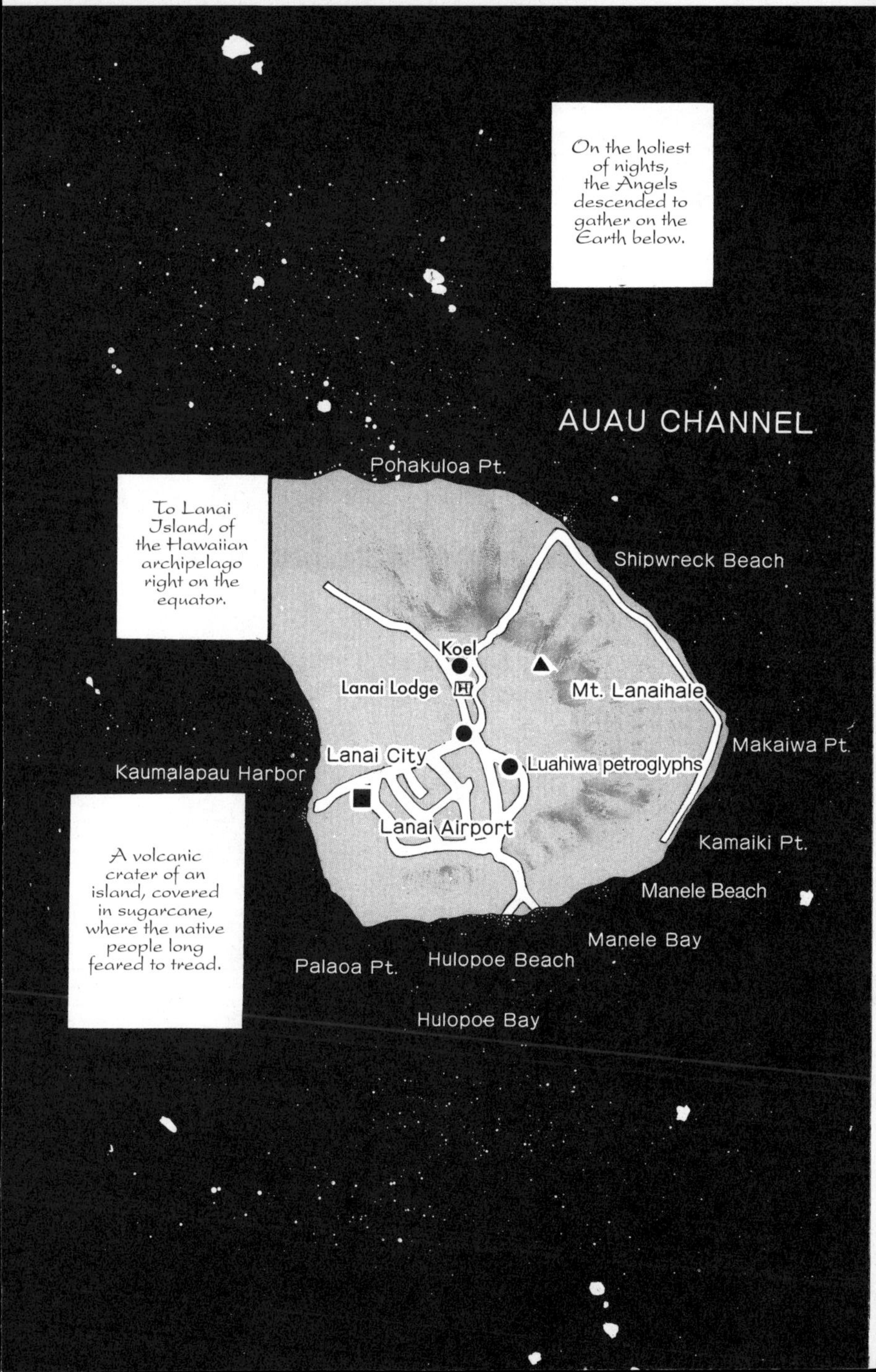
On the holiest of nights, the Angels descended to gather on the Earth below.
To Lanai Island, of the Hawaiian archipelago right on the equator.
A volcanic crater of an island, covered in sugarcane, where the native people long feared to tread.
AUAU CHANNEL
Pohakuloa Pt.
Shipwreck Beach
Koel
Lanai Lodge
Mt. Lanaihale
Makaiwa Pt.
Lanai City
Luahiwa petroglyphs
Kaumalapau Harbor
Lanai Airport
Kamaiki Pt.
Manele Beach
Manele Bay
Palaoa Pt.
Hulopoe Beach
Hulopoe Bay

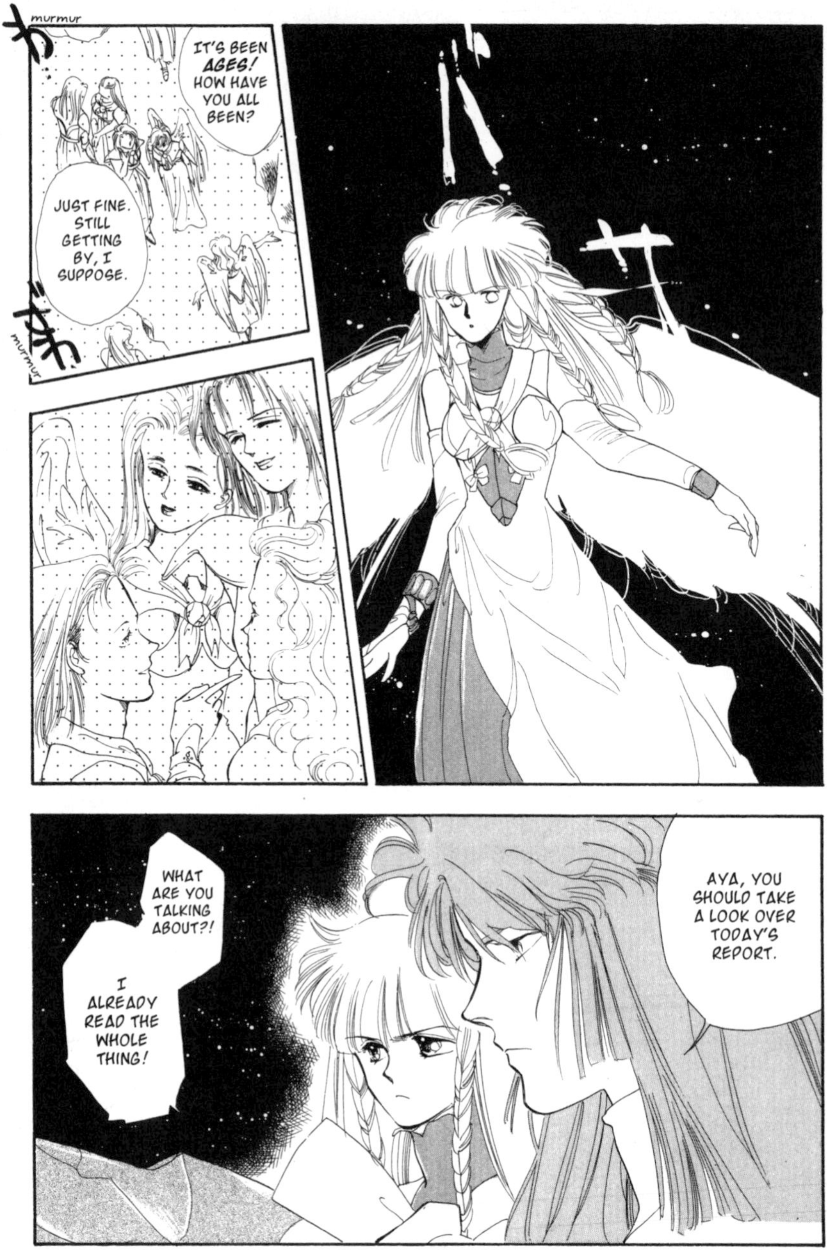
murmur
IT'S BEEN AGES! HOW HAVE YOU ALL BEEN?
JUST FINE. STILL GETTING BY, I SUPPOSE.
murmur
AYA, YOU SHOULD TAKE A LOOK OVER TODAY'S REPORT.
WHAT ARE YOU TALKING ABOUT?!
I ALREADY READ THE WHOLE THING!

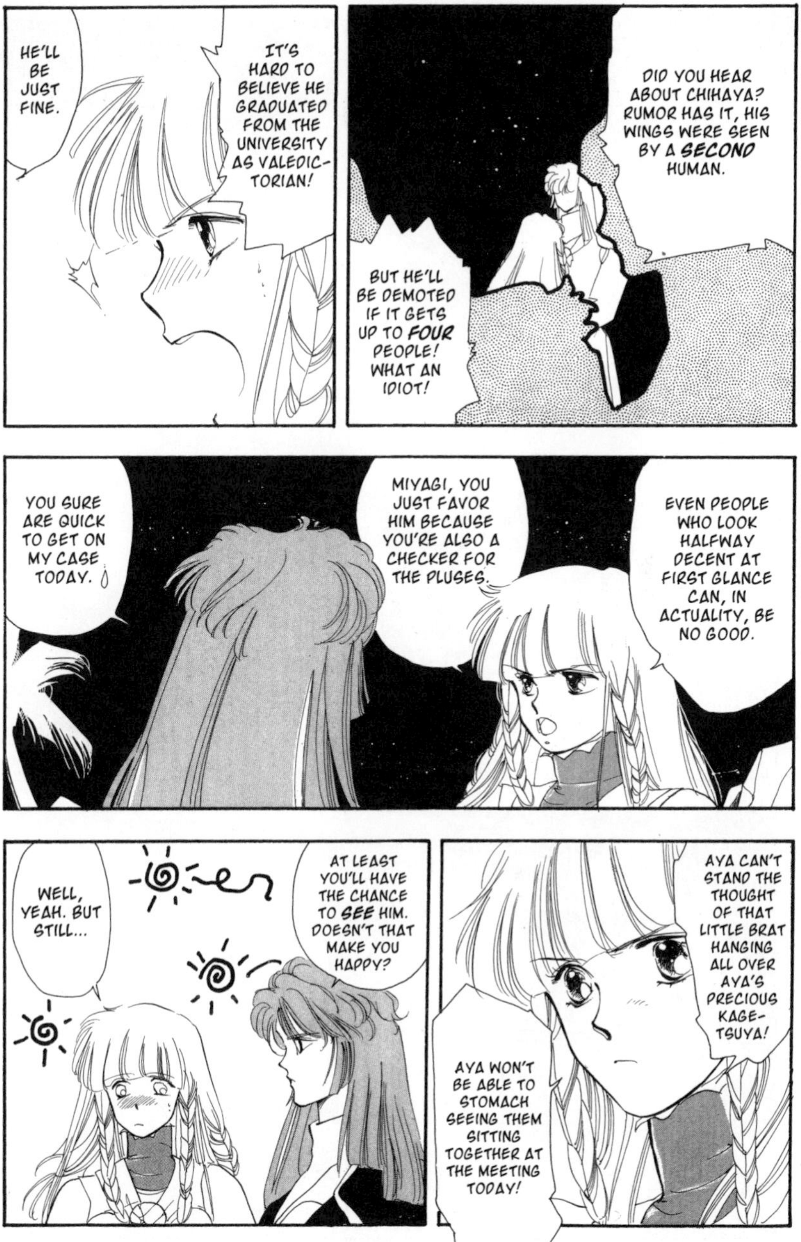
DID YOU HEAR ABOUT CHIHAYA? RUMOR HAS IT, HIS WINGS WERE SEEN BY A SECOND HUMAN.
BUT HE'LL BE DEMOTED IF IT GETS UP TO FOUR PEOPLE! WHAT AN IDIOT!
IT'S HARD TO BELIEVE HE GRADUATED FROM THE UNIVERSITY AS VALEDICTORIAN!
HE'LL BE JUST FINE.
EVEN PEOPLE WHO LOOK HALFWAY DECENT AT FIRST GLANCE CAN, IN ACTUALITY, BE NO GOOD.
MIYAGI, YOU JUST FAVOR HIM BECAUSE YOU'RE ALSO A CHECKER FOR THE PLUSES.
YOU SURE ARE QUICK TO GET ON MY CASE TODAY.
AYA CAN'T STAND THE THOUGHT OF THAT LITTLE BRAT HANGING ALL OVER AYA'S PRECIOUS KAGETSUYA!
AYA WON'T BE ABLE TO STOMACH SEEING THEM SITTING TOGETHER AT THE MEETING TODAY!
AT LEAST YOU'LL HAVE THE CHANCE TO SEE HIM. DOESN'T THAT MAKE YOU HAPPY?
WELL, YEAH. BUT STILL...

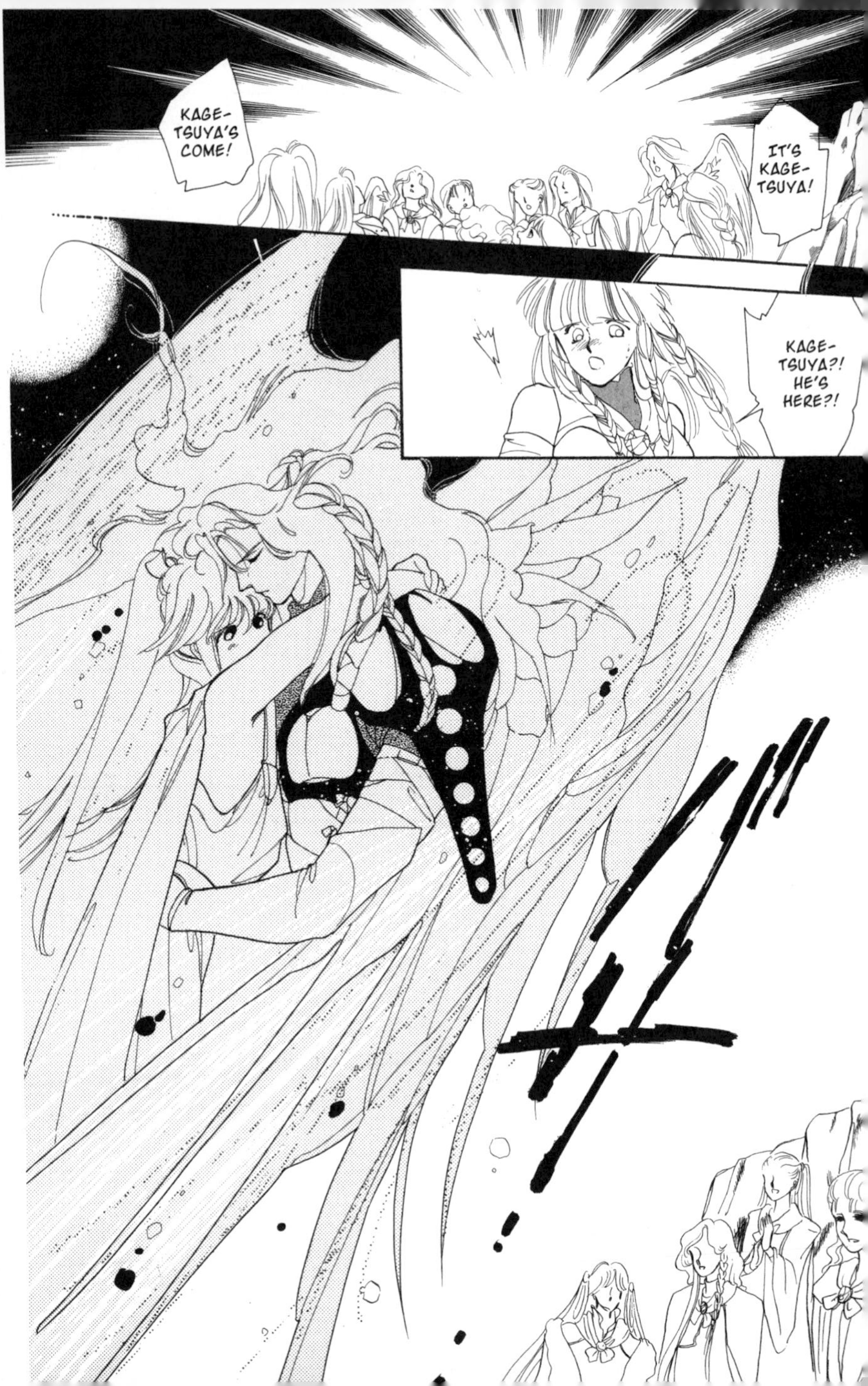
IT'S KAGE-TSUYA!
KAGE-TSUYA'S COME!
KAGE-TSUYA?! HE'S HERE?!

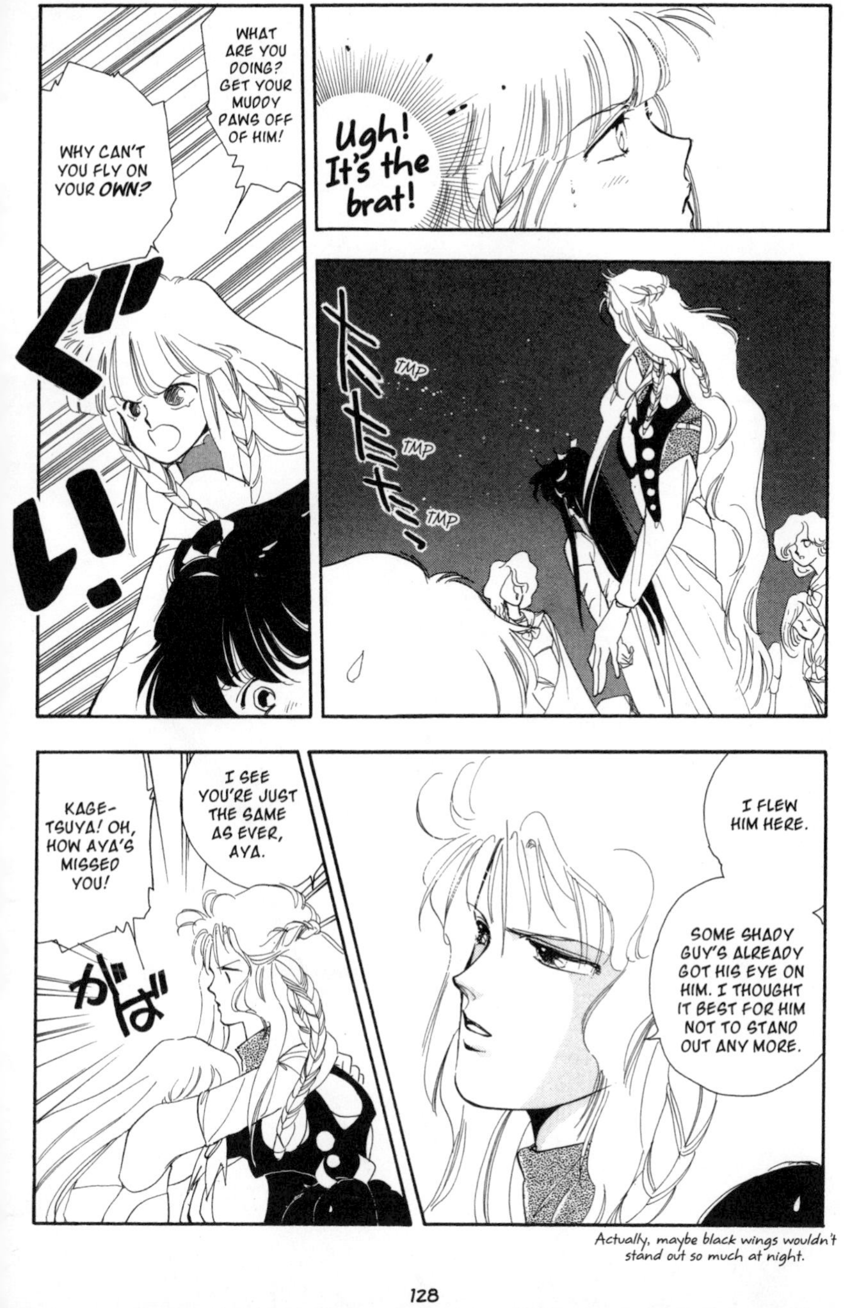
Ugh! It's the brat!
TMP
TMP
TMP
WHAT ARE YOU DOING? GET YOUR MUDDY PAWS OFF OF HIM!
WHY CAN'T YOU FLY ON YOUR OWN?
I FLEW HIM HERE.
SOME SHADY GUY'S ALREADY GOT HIS EYE ON HIM. I THOUGHT IT BEST FOR HIM NOT TO STAND OUT ANY MORE.
I SEE YOU'RE JUST THE SAME AS EVER, AYA.
KAGE-TSUYA! OH, HOW AYA'S MISSED YOU!

Actually, maybe black wings wouldn't stand out so much at night.

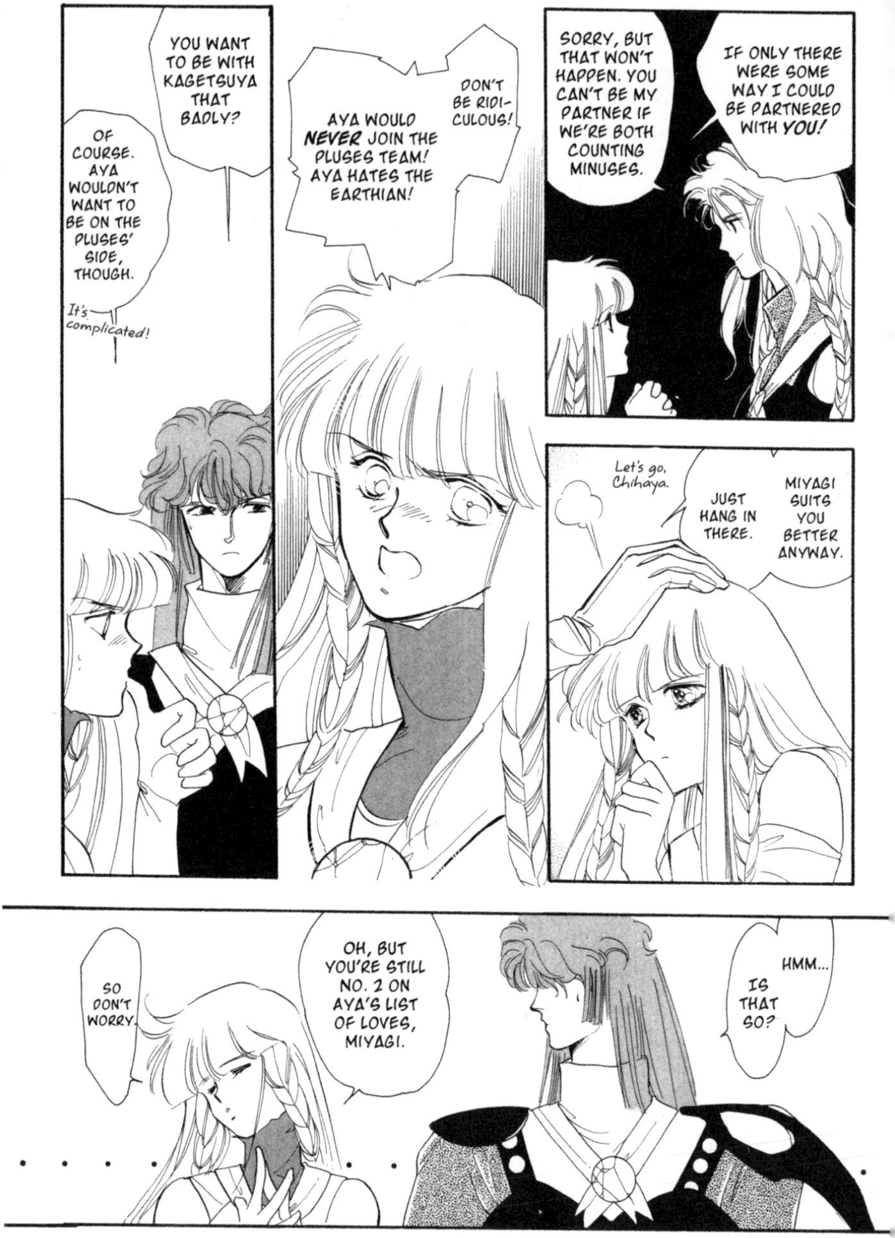
IF ONLY THERE WERE SOME WAY I COULD BE PARTNERED WITH *YOU!*
SORRY, BUT THAT WON'T HAPPEN. YOU CAN'T BE MY PARTNER IF WE'RE BOTH COUNTING MINUSES.
MIYAGI SUITS YOU BETTER ANYWAY.
JUST HANG IN THERE.
Let's go, Chihaya.
DON'T BE RIDICULOUS!
AYA WOULD **NEVER** JOIN THE PLUSES TEAM! AYA HATES THE EARTHIAN!
YOU WANT TO BE WITH KAGETSUYA THAT BADLY?
OF COURSE. AYA WOULDN'T WANT TO BE ON THE PLUSES' SIDE, THOUGH.
It's complicated!
HMM... IS THAT SO?
OH, BUT YOU'RE STILL NO. 2 ON AYA'S LIST OF LOVES, MIYAGI.
SO DON'T WORRY.

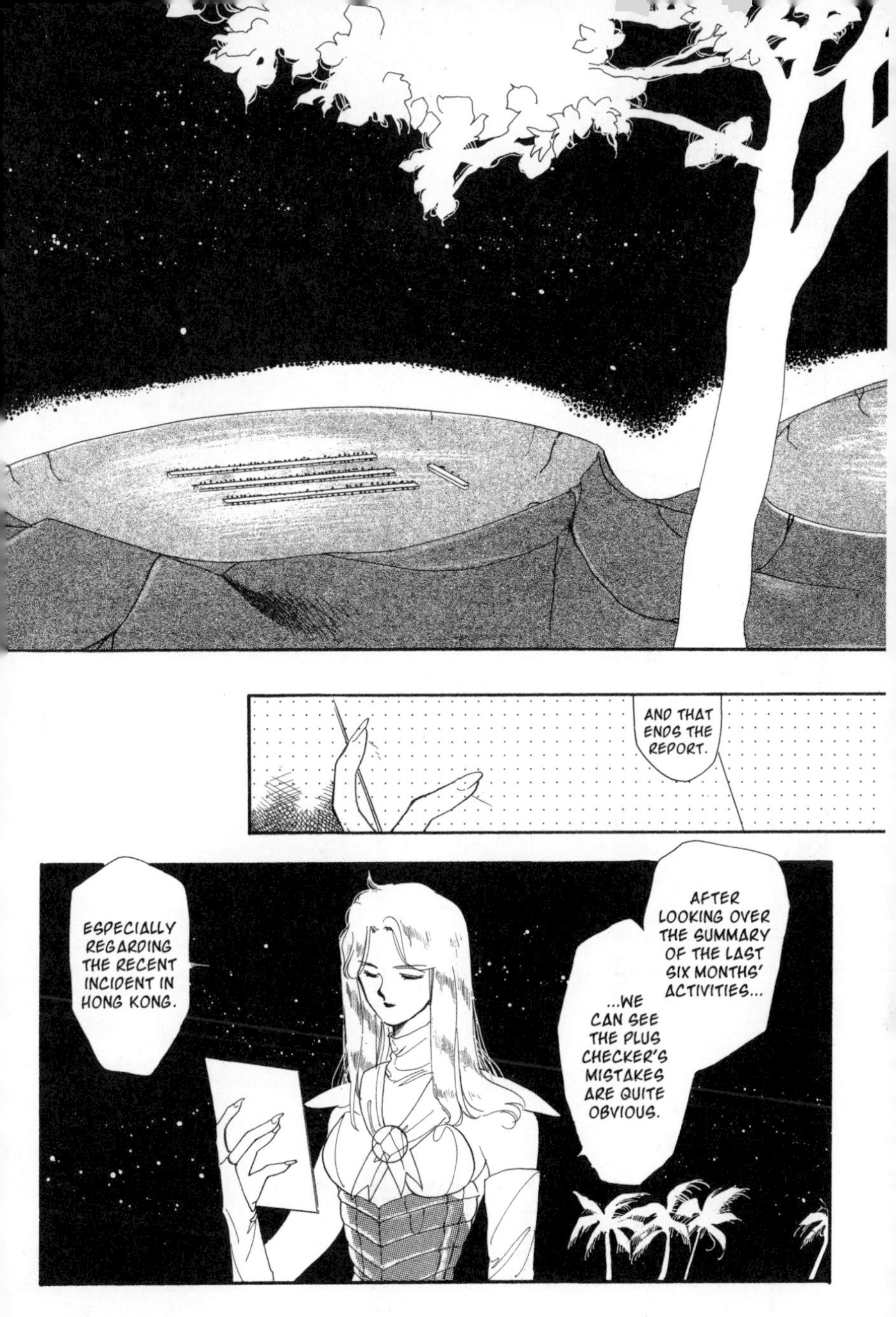
AND THAT ENDS THE REPORT.
AFTER LOOKING OVER THE SUMMARY OF THE LAST SIX MONTHS' ACTIVITIES...
...WE CAN SEE THE PLUS CHECKER'S MISTAKES ARE QUITE OBVIOUS.
ESPECIALLY REGARDING THE RECENT INCIDENT IN HONG KONG.

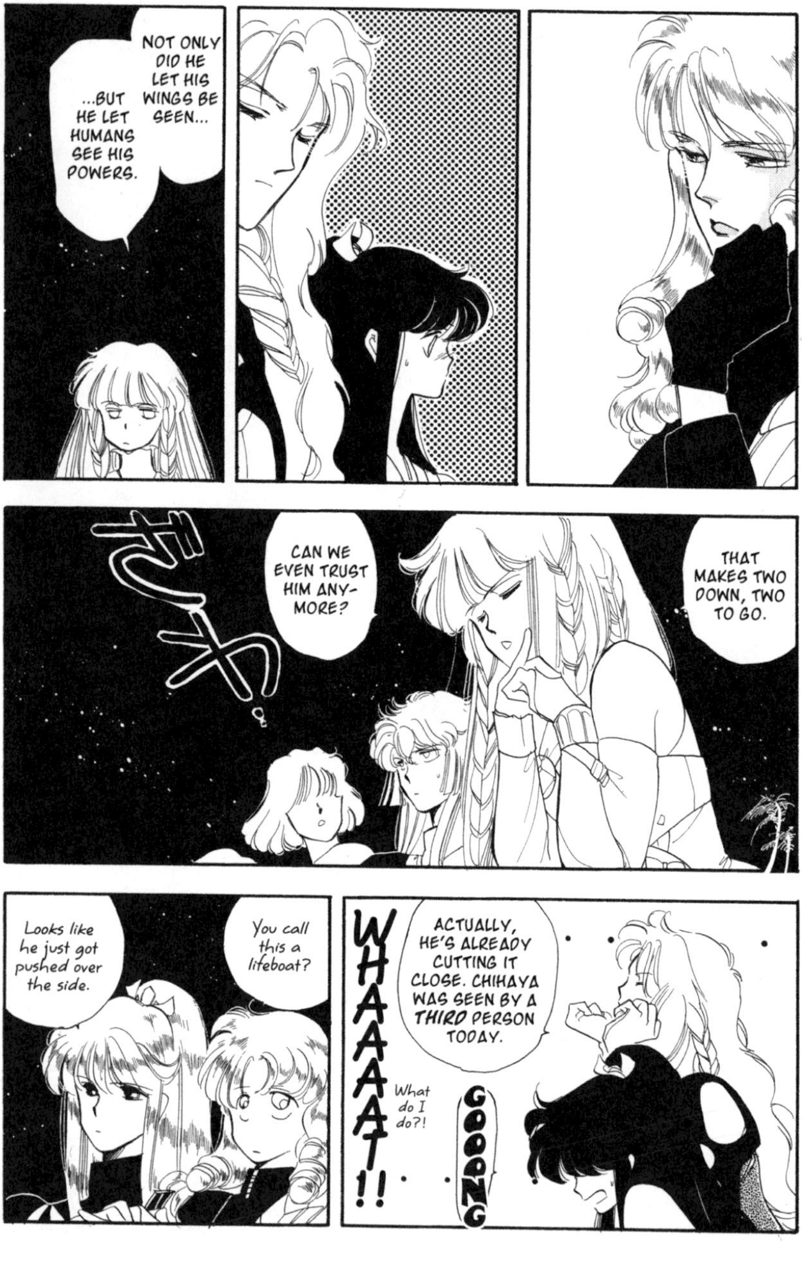
NOT ONLY DID HE LET HIS WINGS BE SEEN...
...BUT HE LET HUMANS SEE HIS POWERS.
THAT MAKES TWO DOWN, TWO TO GO.
CAN WE EVEN TRUST HIM ANY-MORE?
ACTUALLY, HE'S ALREADY CUTTING IT CLOSE. CHIHAYA WAS SEEN BY A THIRD PERSON TODAY.
WHAAAAAT!!
What do I do?!
GOOONG
You call this a lifeboat?
Looks like he just got pushed over the side.

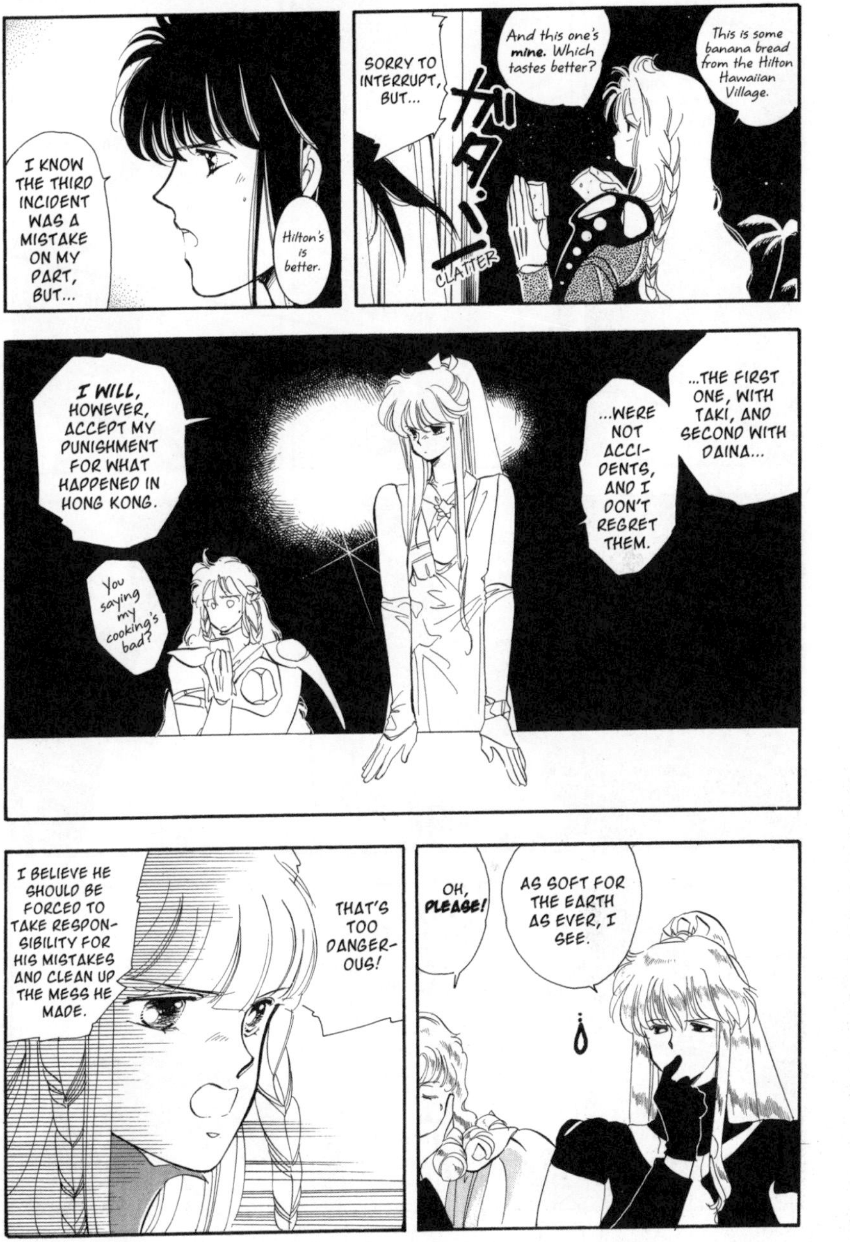
This is some banana bread from the Hilton Hawaiian Village.
And this one's **mine.** Which tastes better?
SORRY TO INTERRUPT, BUT...
CLATTER
Hilton's is better.
I KNOW THE THIRD INCIDENT WAS A MISTAKE ON MY PART, BUT...
...THE FIRST ONE, WITH TAKI, AND SECOND WITH DAINA...
...WERE NOT ACCI-DENTS, AND I DON'T REGRET THEM.
I WILL, HOWEVER, ACCEPT MY PUNISHMENT FOR WHAT HAPPENED IN HONG KONG.
You saying my cooking's bad?
AS SOFT FOR THE EARTH AS EVER, I SEE.
OH, **PLEASE!**
THAT'S TOO DANGER-OUS!
I BELIEVE HE SHOULD BE FORCED TO TAKE RESPON-SIBILITY FOR HIS MISTAKES AND CLEAN UP THE MESS HE MADE.

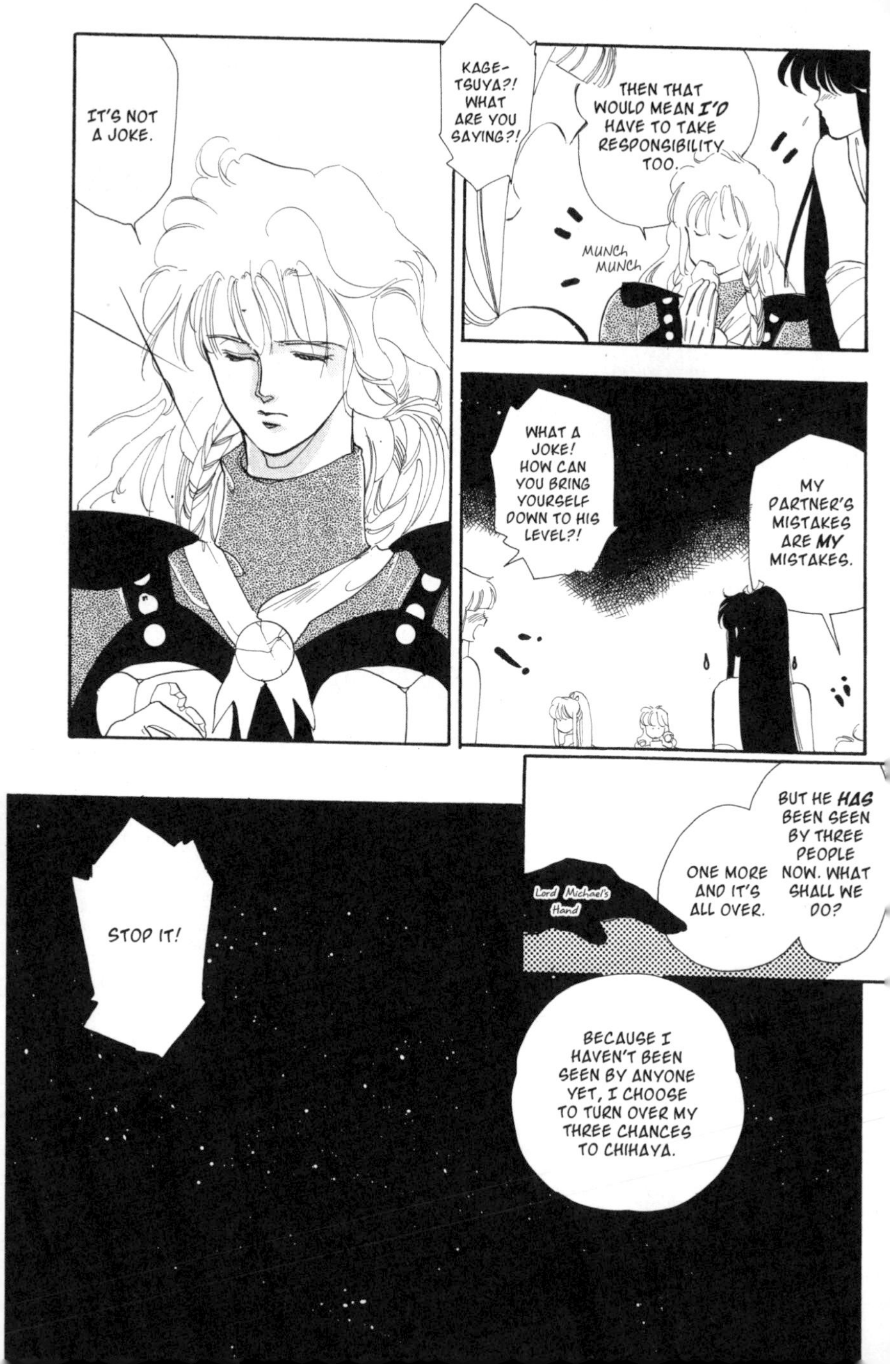
THEN THAT WOULD MEAN I'D HAVE TO TAKE RESPONSIBILITY TOO.
MUNCH MUNCH
KAGE-TSUYA?! WHAT ARE YOU SAYING?!
MY PARTNER'S MISTAKES ARE MY MISTAKES.
WHAT A JOKE! HOW CAN YOU BRING YOURSELF DOWN TO HIS LEVEL?!
IT'S NOT A JOKE.
BUT HE HAS BEEN SEEN BY THREE PEOPLE NOW. WHAT SHALL WE DO?
ONE MORE AND IT'S ALL OVER.
Lord Michael's Hand
BECAUSE I HAVEN'T BEEN SEEN BY ANYONE YET, I CHOOSE TO TURN OVER MY THREE CHANCES TO CHIHAYA.
STOP IT!

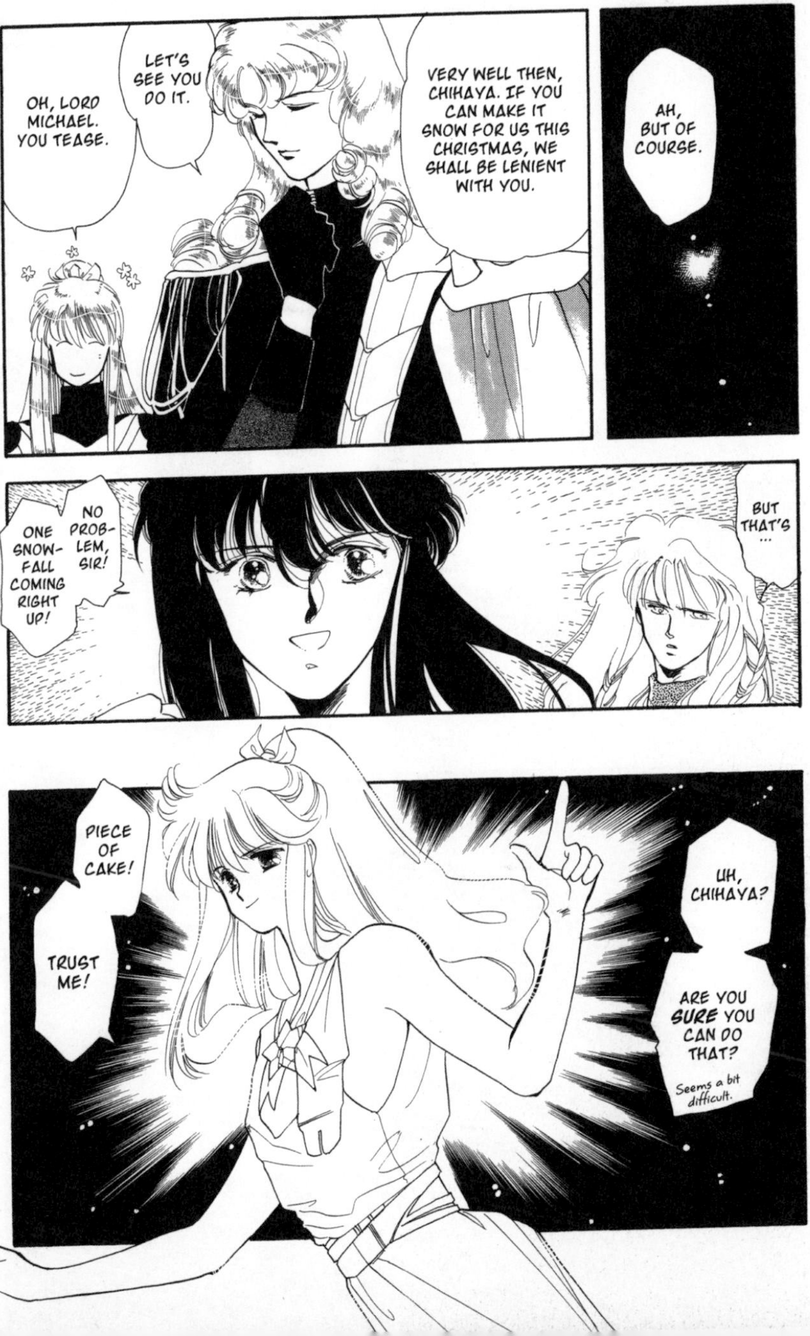
AH, BUT OF COURSE.
VERY WELL THEN, CHIHAYA. IF YOU CAN MAKE IT SNOW FOR US THIS CHRISTMAS, WE SHALL BE LENIENT WITH YOU.
LET'S SEE YOU DO IT.
OH, LORD MICHAEL. YOU TEASE.
BUT THAT'S ...
NO PROB-LEM, SIR!
ONE SNOW-FALL COMING RIGHT UP!
UH, CHIHAYA?
ARE YOU **SURE** YOU CAN DO THAT?
Seems a bit difficult.
PIECE OF CAKE!
TRUST ME!

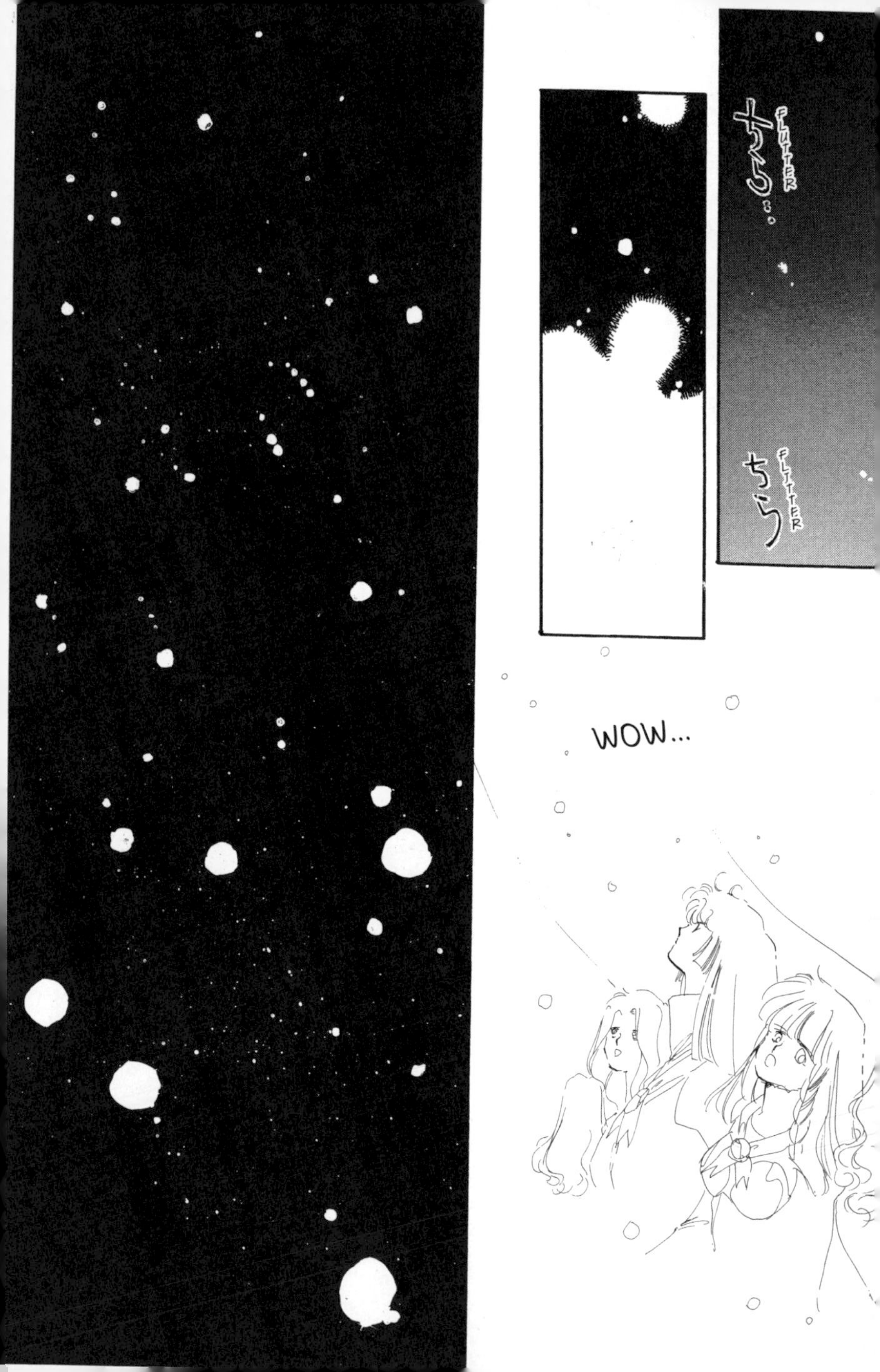
ちら。。
FLUTTER
ちら
FLITTER
WOW...

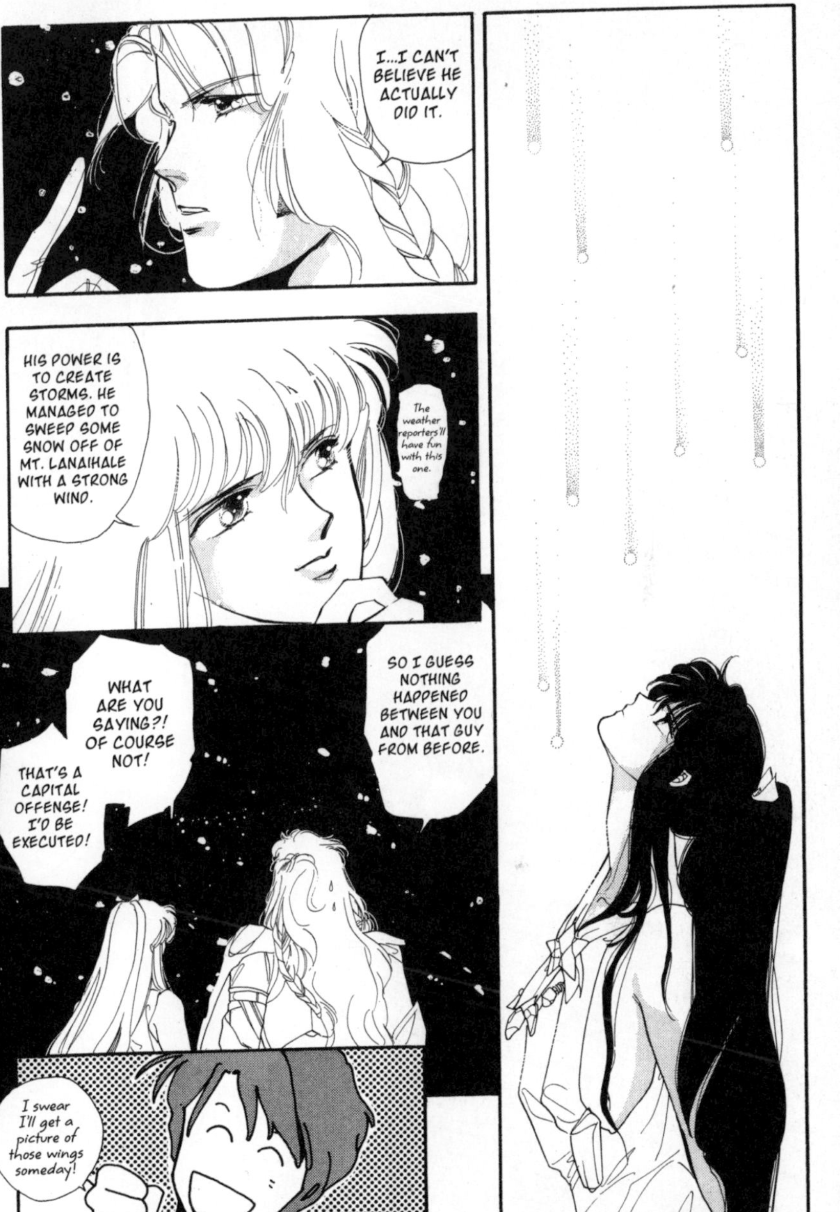
I...I CAN'T BELIEVE HE ACTUALLY DID IT.
The weather reporters'll have fun with this one.
HIS POWER IS TO CREATE STORMS. HE MANAGED TO SWEEP SOME SNOW OFF OF MT. LANAIHALE WITH A STRONG WIND.
SO I GUESS NOTHING HAPPENED BETWEEN YOU AND THAT GUY FROM BEFORE.
WHAT ARE YOU SAYING?! OF COURSE NOT!
THAT'S A CAPITAL OFFENSE! I'D BE EXECUTED!
I swear I'll get a picture of those wings someday!

For my dear Masato Tanaka.

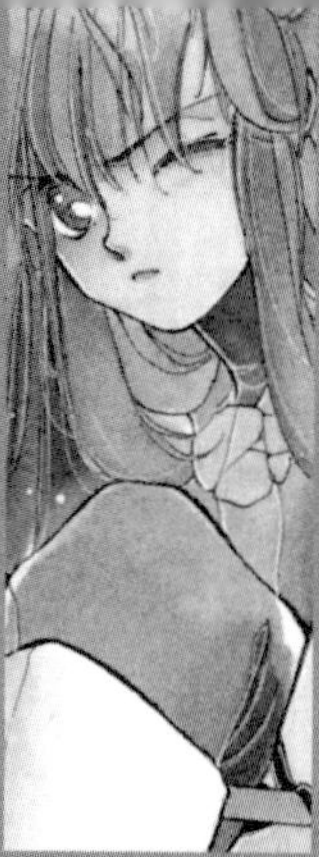

VALHALLA

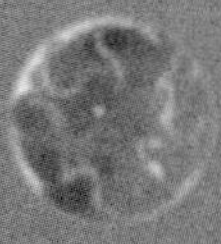

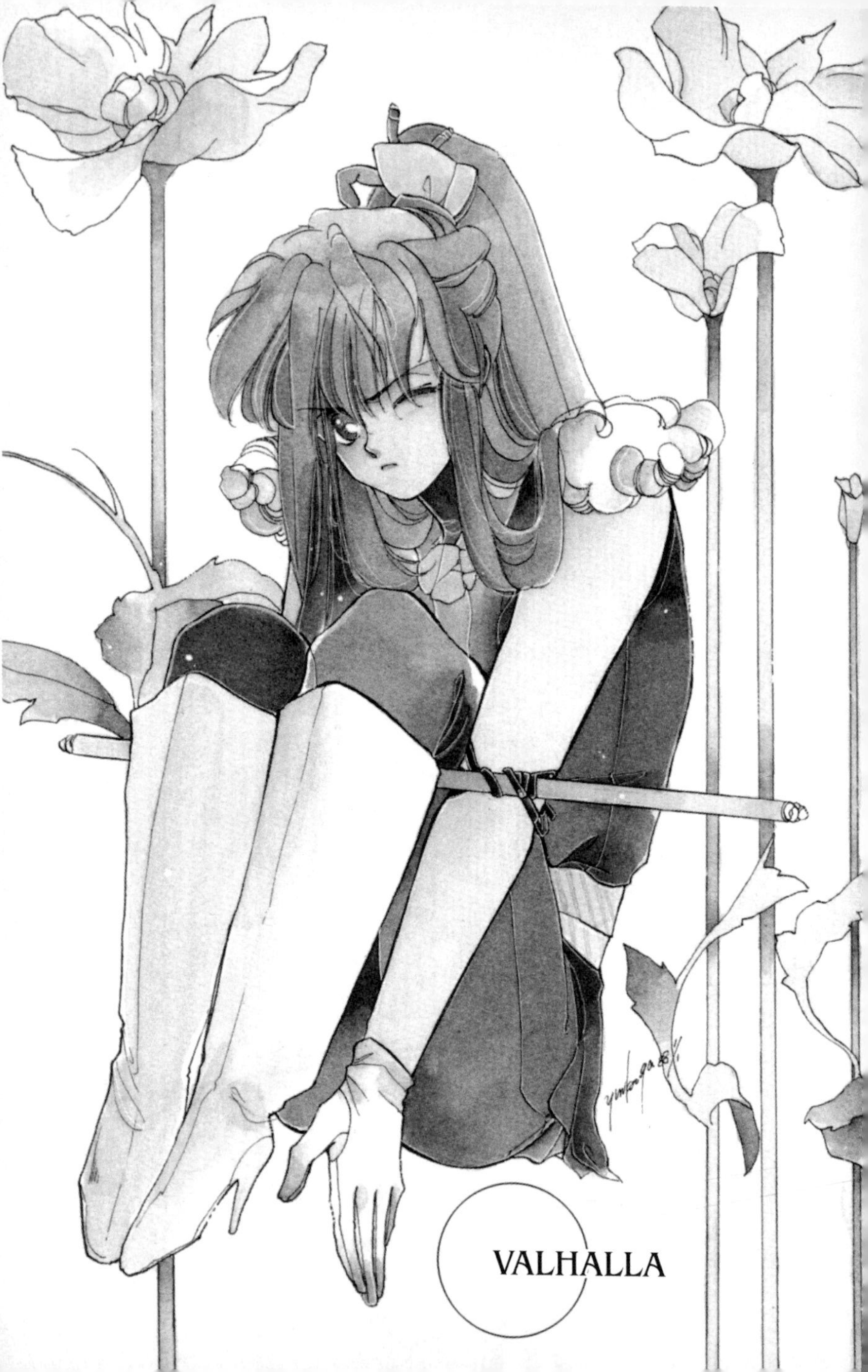

VALHALLA

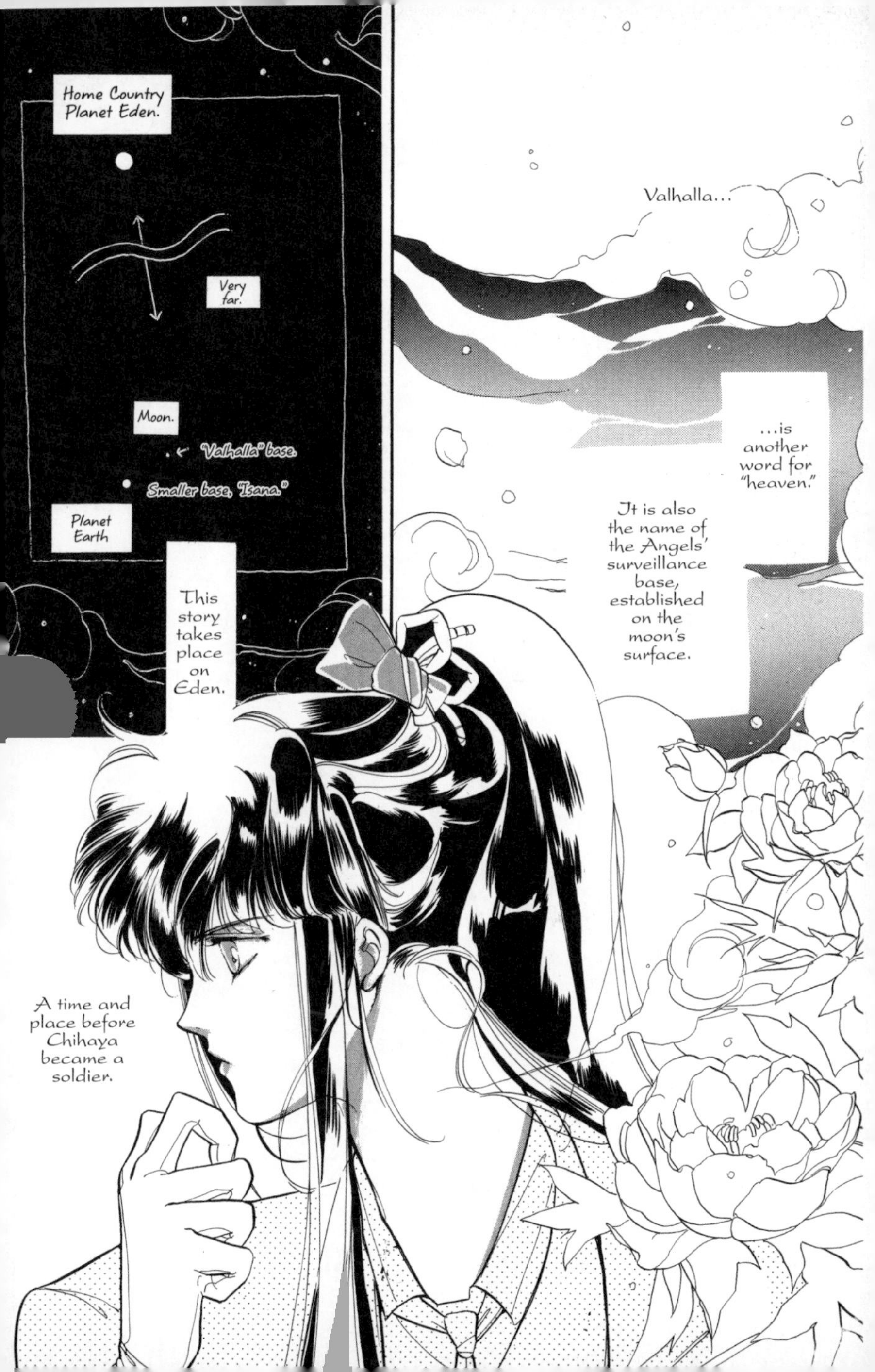
Valhalla...
...is another word for "heaven."
It is also the name of the Angels' surveillance base, established on the moon's surface.
Home Country Planet Eden.
Very far.
Moon.
"Valhalla" base.
Smaller base, "Isana."
Planet Earth
This story takes place on Eden.
A time and place before Chihaya became a soldier.

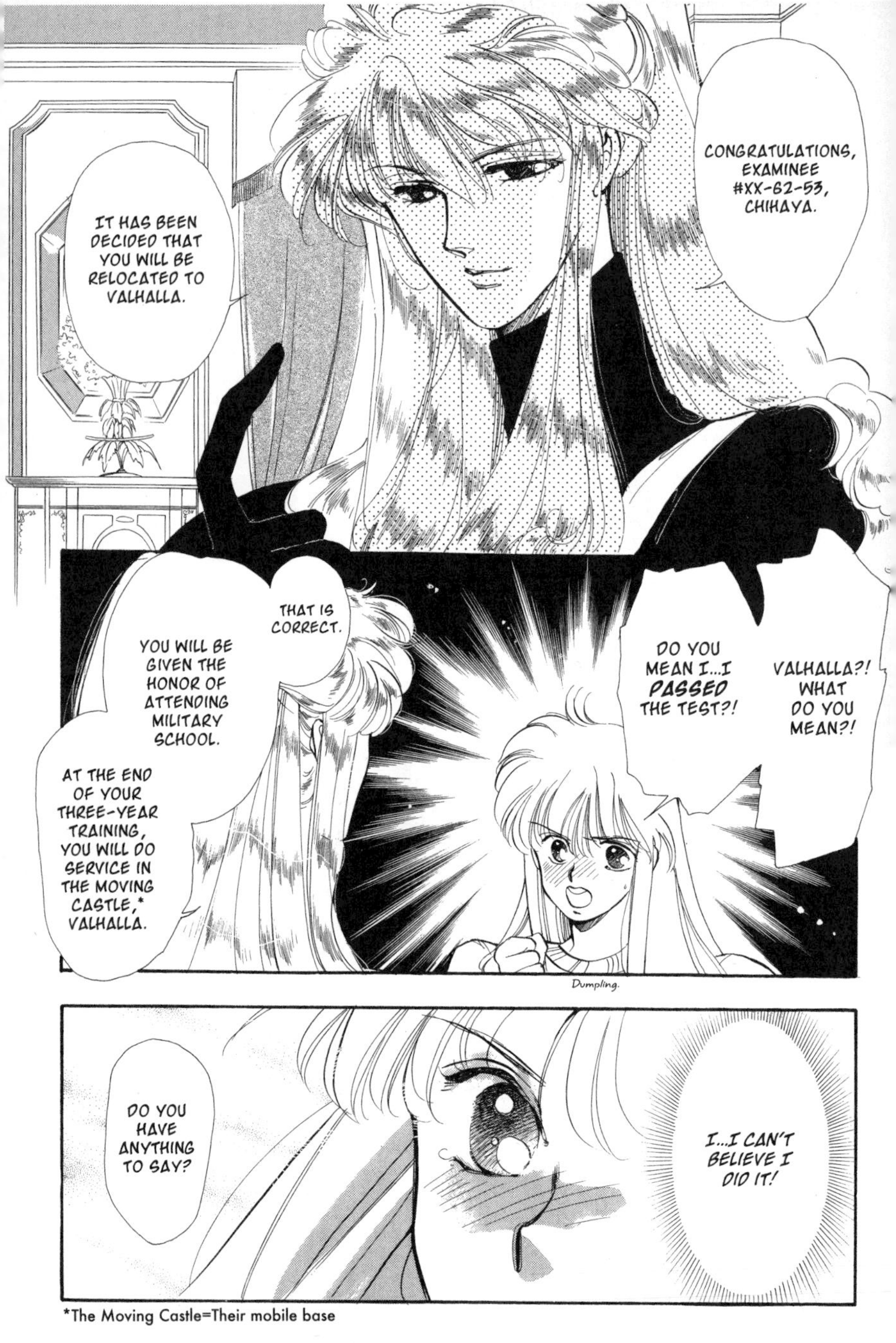
CONGRATULATIONS, EXAMINEE #XX-62-53, CHIHAYA.
IT HAS BEEN DECIDED THAT YOU WILL BE RELOCATED TO VALHALLA.
VALHALLA?! WHAT DO YOU MEAN?!
DO YOU MEAN I...I *PASSED* THE TEST?!
THAT IS CORRECT.
YOU WILL BE GIVEN THE HONOR OF ATTENDING MILITARY SCHOOL.
AT THE END OF YOUR THREE-YEAR TRAINING, YOU WILL DO SERVICE IN THE MOVING CASTLE,* VALHALLA.
Dumpling.
I...I CAN'T BELIEVE I DID IT!
DO YOU HAVE ANYTHING TO SAY?

*The Moving Castle=Their mobile base

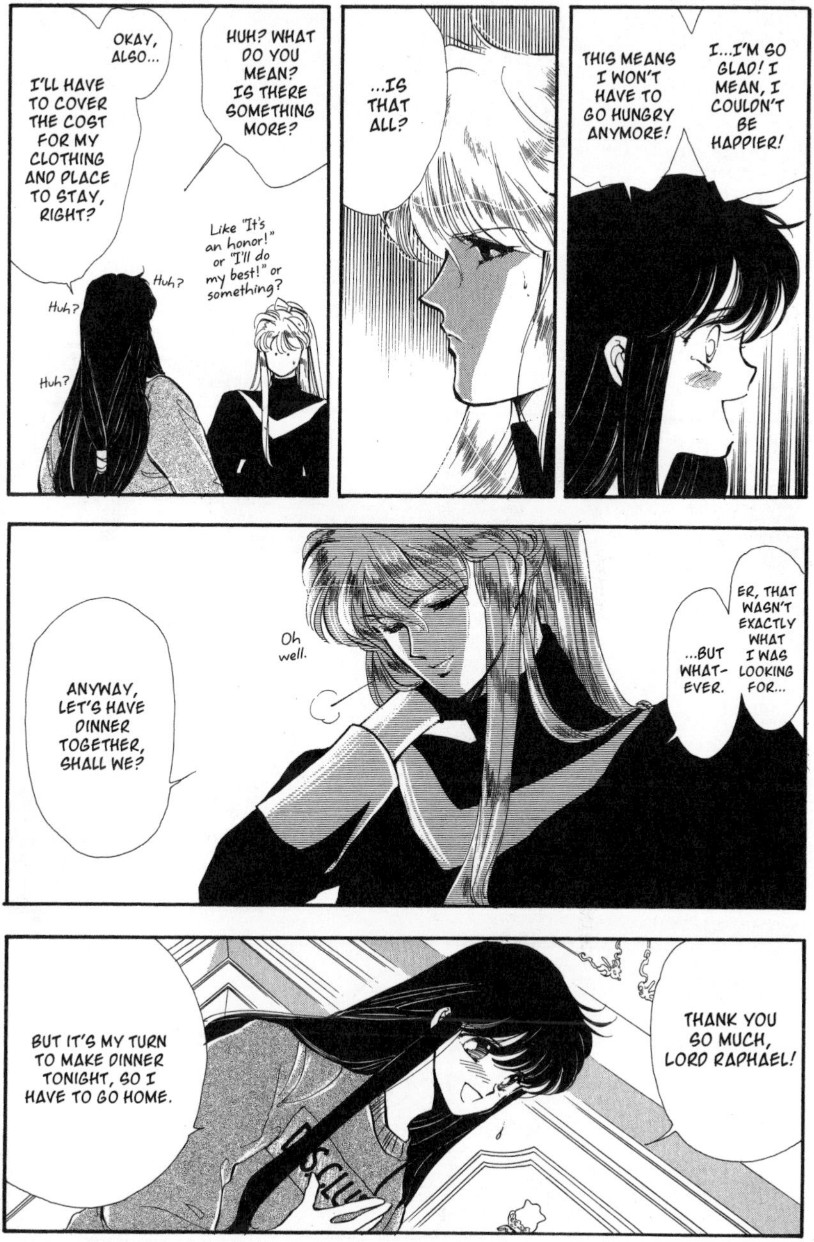
I...I'M SO GLAD! I MEAN, I COULDN'T BE HAPPIER!
THIS MEANS I WON'T HAVE TO GO HUNGRY ANYMORE!
...IS THAT ALL?
HUH? WHAT DO YOU MEAN? IS THERE SOMETHING MORE?
OKAY, ALSO...
I'LL HAVE TO COVER THE COST FOR MY CLOTHING AND PLACE TO STAY, RIGHT?
Like "It's an honor!" or "I'll do my best!" or something?
Huh?
Huh?
Huh?
ER, THAT WASN'T EXACTLY WHAT I WAS LOOKING FOR...
...BUT WHATEVER.
Oh well.
ANYWAY, LET'S HAVE DINNER TOGETHER, SHALL WE?
THANK YOU SO MUCH, LORD RAPHAEL!
BUT IT'S MY TURN TO MAKE DINNER TONIGHT, SO I HAVE TO GO HOME.

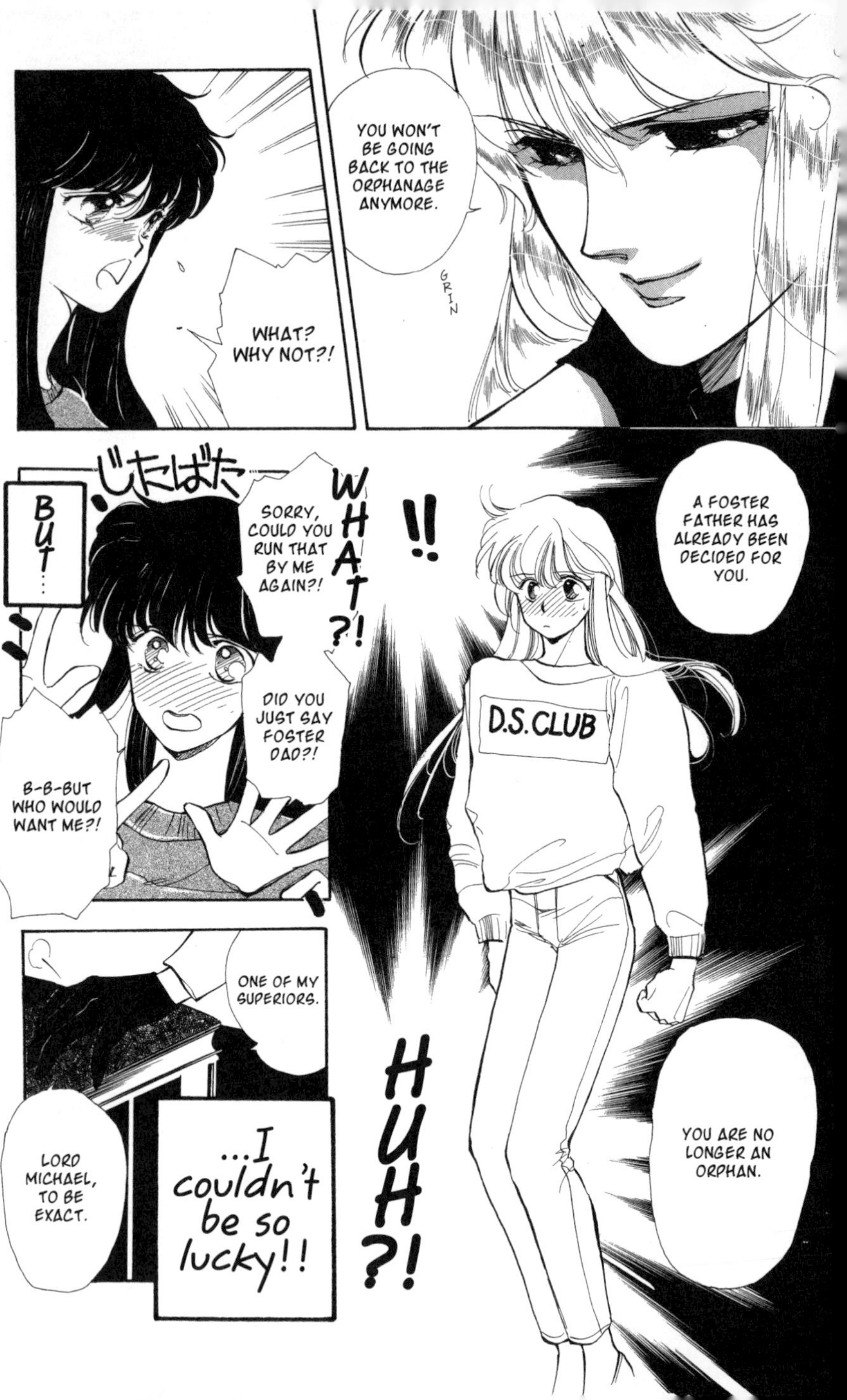
YOU WON'T BE GOING BACK TO THE ORPHANAGE ANYMORE.
GRIN
WHAT? WHY NOT?!
A FOSTER FATHER HAS ALREADY BEEN DECIDED FOR YOU.
!!
YOU ARE NO LONGER AN ORPHAN.
HUH?!
WHAT?!
SORRY, COULD YOU RUN THAT BY ME AGAIN?!
DID YOU JUST SAY FOSTER DAD?!
じたばた
BUT...
B-B-BUT WHO WOULD WANT ME?!
ONE OF MY SUPERIORS.
LORD MICHAEL, TO BE EXACT.
...I couldn't be so lucky!!

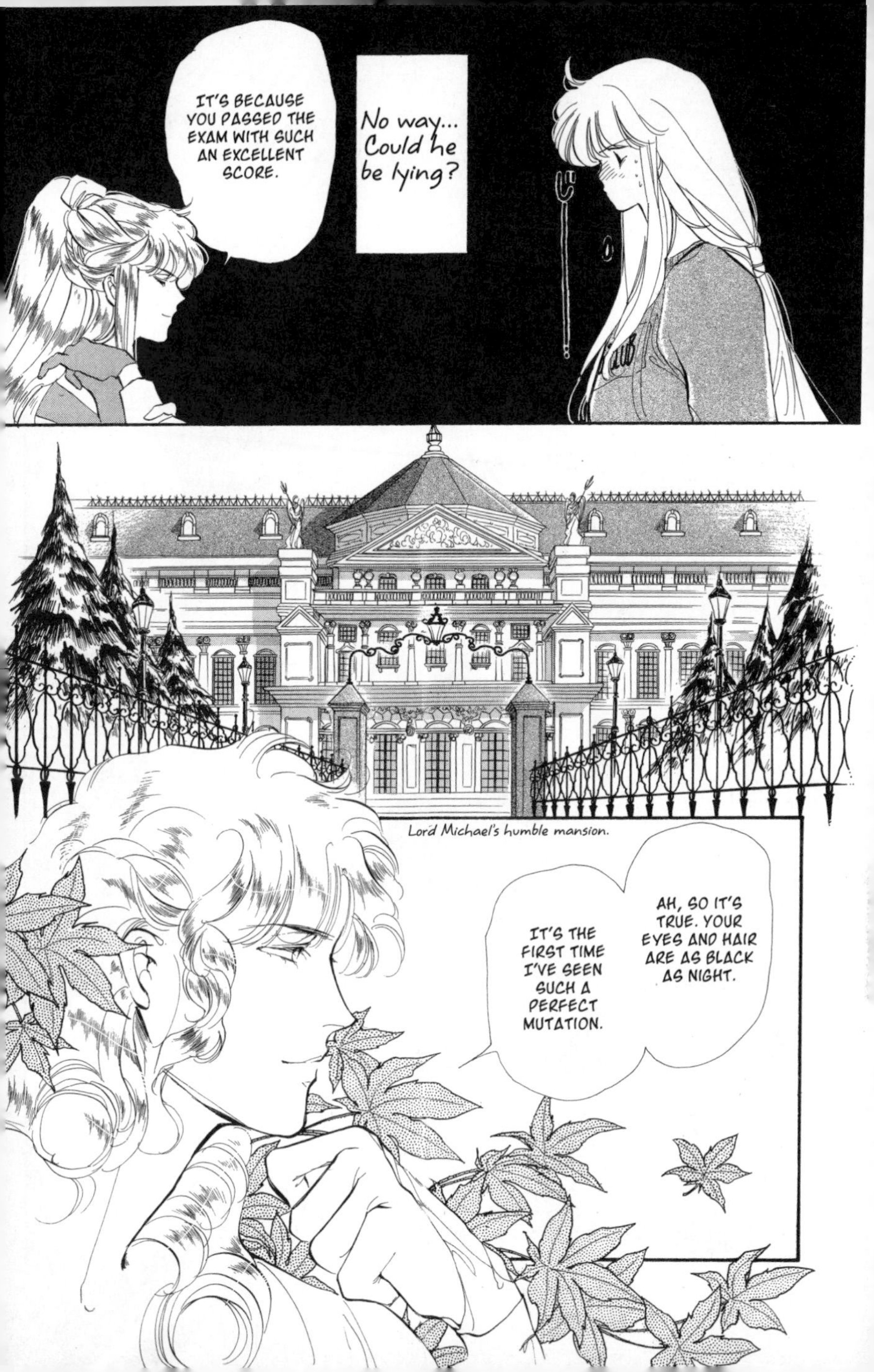

IT'S BECAUSE YOU PASSED THE EXAM WITH SUCH AN EXCELLENT SCORE.
No way... Could he be lying?
Lord Michael's humble mansion.
AH, SO IT'S TRUE. YOUR EYES AND HAIR ARE AS BLACK AS NIGHT.
IT'S THE FIRST TIME I'VE SEEN SUCH A PERFECT MUTATION.

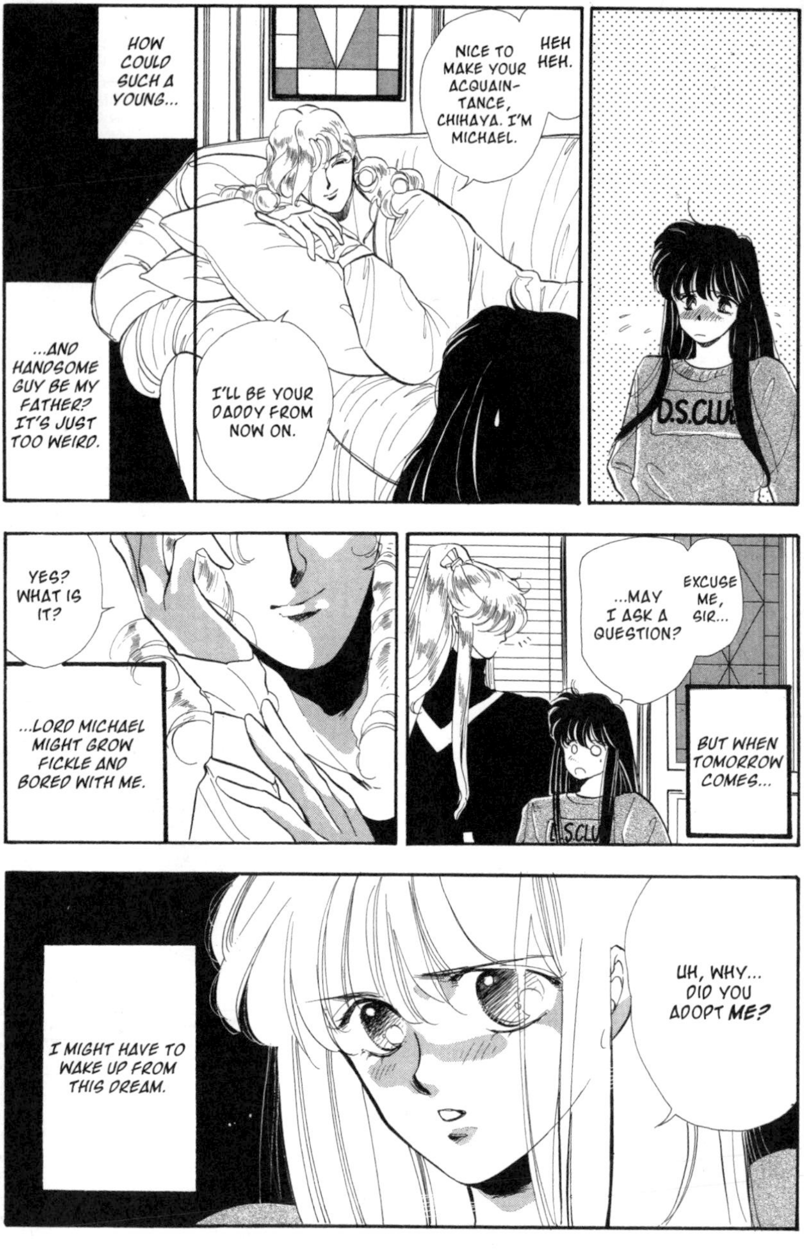
HEH HEH.
NICE TO MAKE YOUR ACQUAINTANCE, CHIHAYA. I'M MICHAEL.
I'LL BE YOUR DADDY FROM NOW ON.
HOW COULD SUCH A YOUNG...
...AND HANDSOME GUY BE MY FATHER? IT'S JUST TOO WEIRD.
EXCUSE ME, SIR...
...MAY I ASK A QUESTION?
BUT WHEN TOMORROW COMES...
YES? WHAT IS IT?
...LORD MICHAEL MIGHT GROW FICKLE AND BORED WITH ME.
UH, WHY... DID YOU ADOPT **ME?**
I MIGHT HAVE TO WAKE UP FROM THIS DREAM.

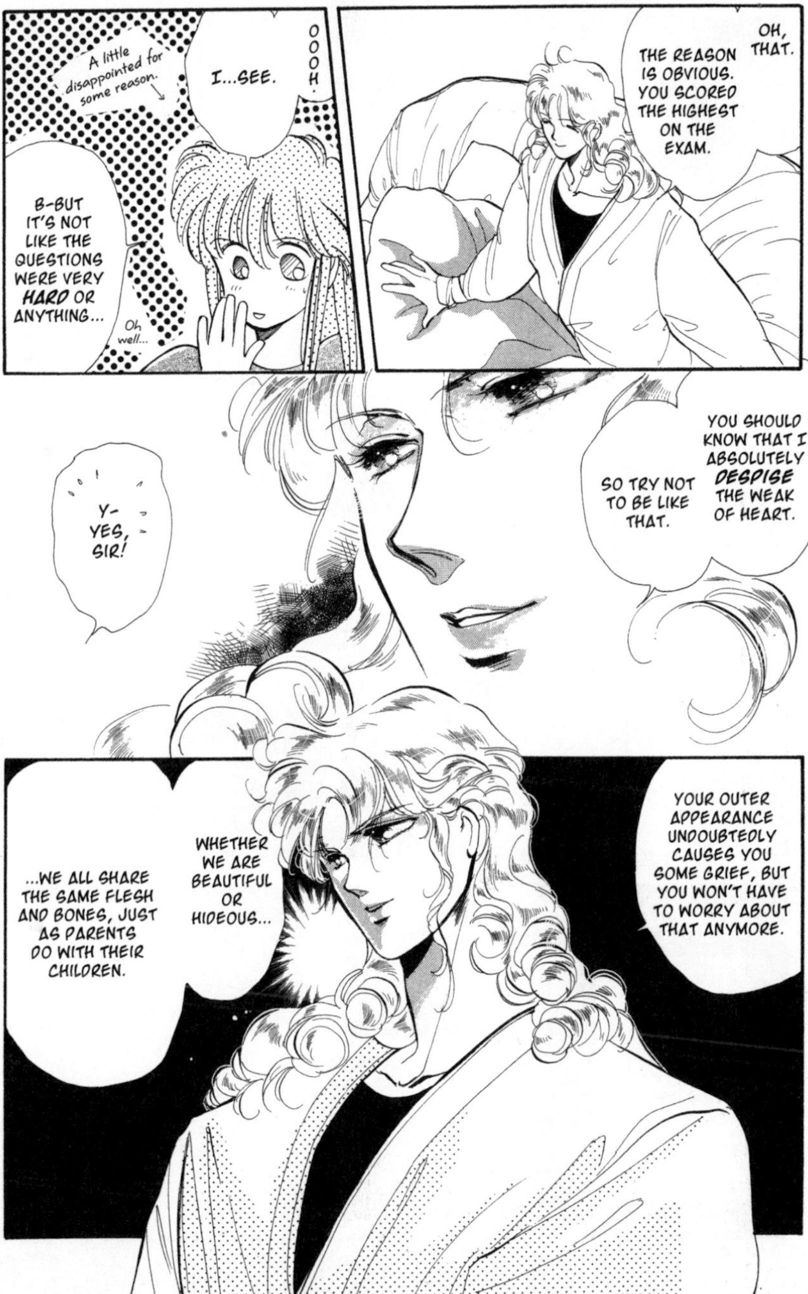
OH, THAT.
THE REASON IS OBVIOUS. YOU SCORED THE HIGHEST ON THE EXAM.
OOOOH.
I...SEE.
A little disappointed for some reason.
B-BUT IT'S NOT LIKE THE QUESTIONS WERE VERY HARD OR ANYTHING...
Oh well...
YOU SHOULD KNOW THAT I ABSOLUTELY DESPISE THE WEAK OF HEART.
SO TRY NOT TO BE LIKE THAT.
Y-YES, SIR!
YOUR OUTER APPEARANCE UNDOUBTEDLY CAUSES YOU SOME GRIEF, BUT YOU WON'T HAVE TO WORRY ABOUT THAT ANYMORE.
WHETHER WE ARE BEAUTIFUL OR HIDEOUS...
...WE ALL SHARE THE SAME FLESH AND BONES, JUST AS PARENTS DO WITH THEIR CHILDREN.

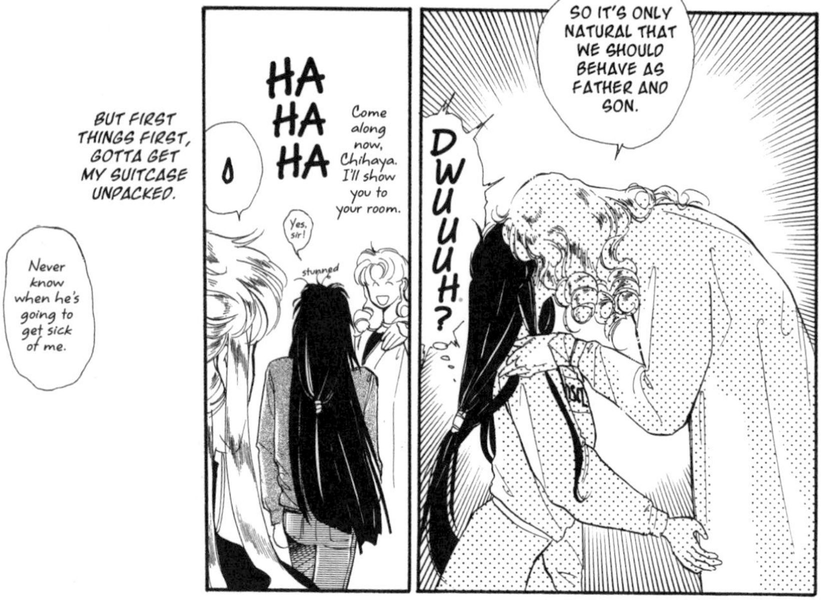
SO IT'S ONLY NATURAL THAT WE SHOULD BEHAVE AS FATHER AND SON.
DWUUUH?
HA HA HA
Come along now, Chihaya. I'll show you to your room.
Yes, sir!
stunned
BUT FIRST THINGS FIRST, GOTTA GET MY SUITCASE UNPACKED.
Never know when he's going to get sick of me.

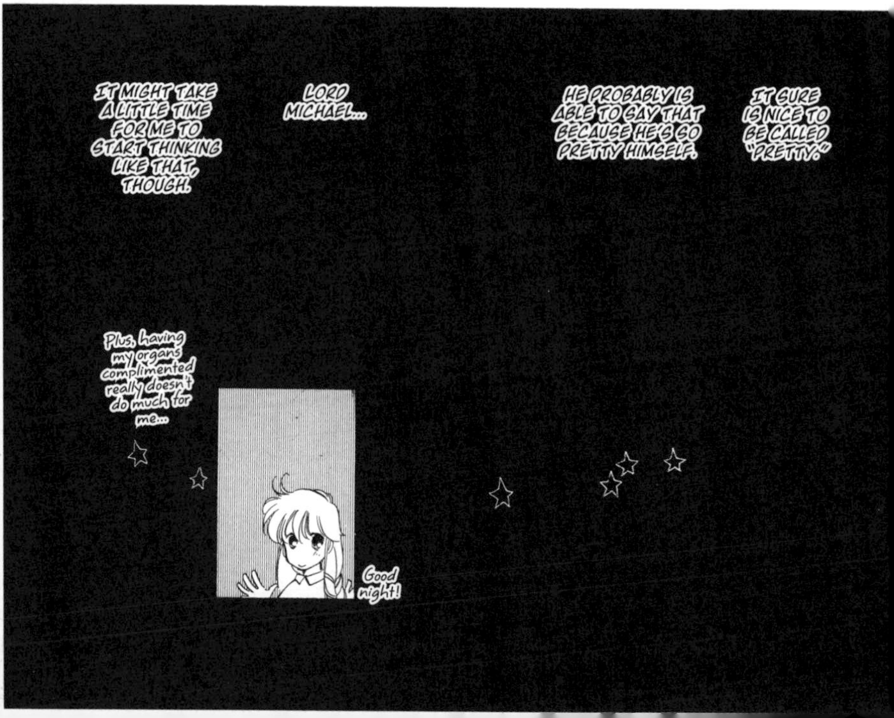
IT SURE IS NICE TO BE CALLED "PRETTY."
HE PROBABLY IS ABLE TO SAY THAT BECAUSE HE'S SO PRETTY HIMSELF.
LORD MICHAEL...
IT MIGHT TAKE A LITTLE TIME FOR ME TO START THINKING LIKE THAT, THOUGH.
Plus, having my organs complimented really doesn't do much for me...
Good night!

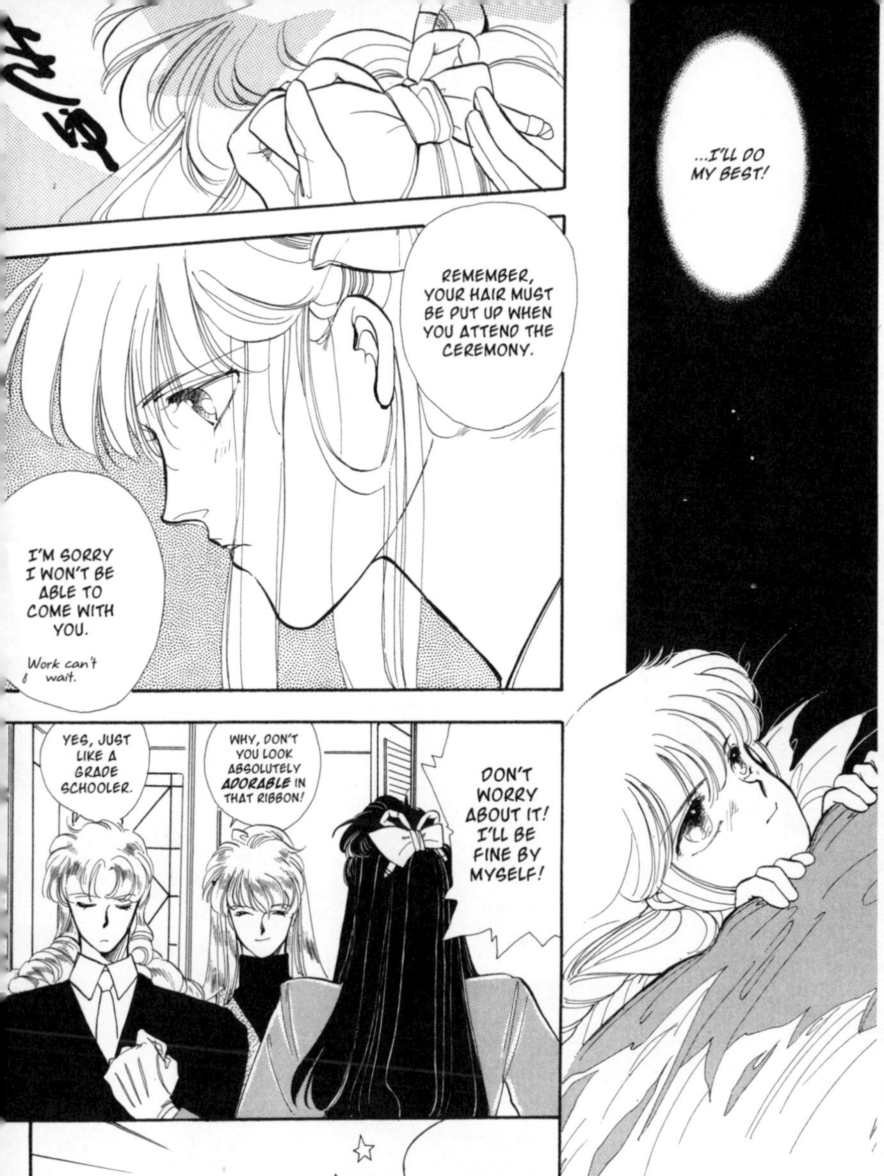
...I'LL DO MY BEST!
REMEMBER, YOUR HAIR MUST BE PUT UP WHEN YOU ATTEND THE CEREMONY.
I'M SORRY I WON'T BE ABLE TO COME WITH YOU.
Work can't wait.
DON'T WORRY ABOUT IT! I'LL BE FINE BY MYSELF!
WHY, DON'T YOU LOOK ABSOLUTELY ADORABLE IN THAT RIBBON!
YES, JUST LIKE A GRADE SCHOOLER.
WELL THEN, OFF YOU GO!

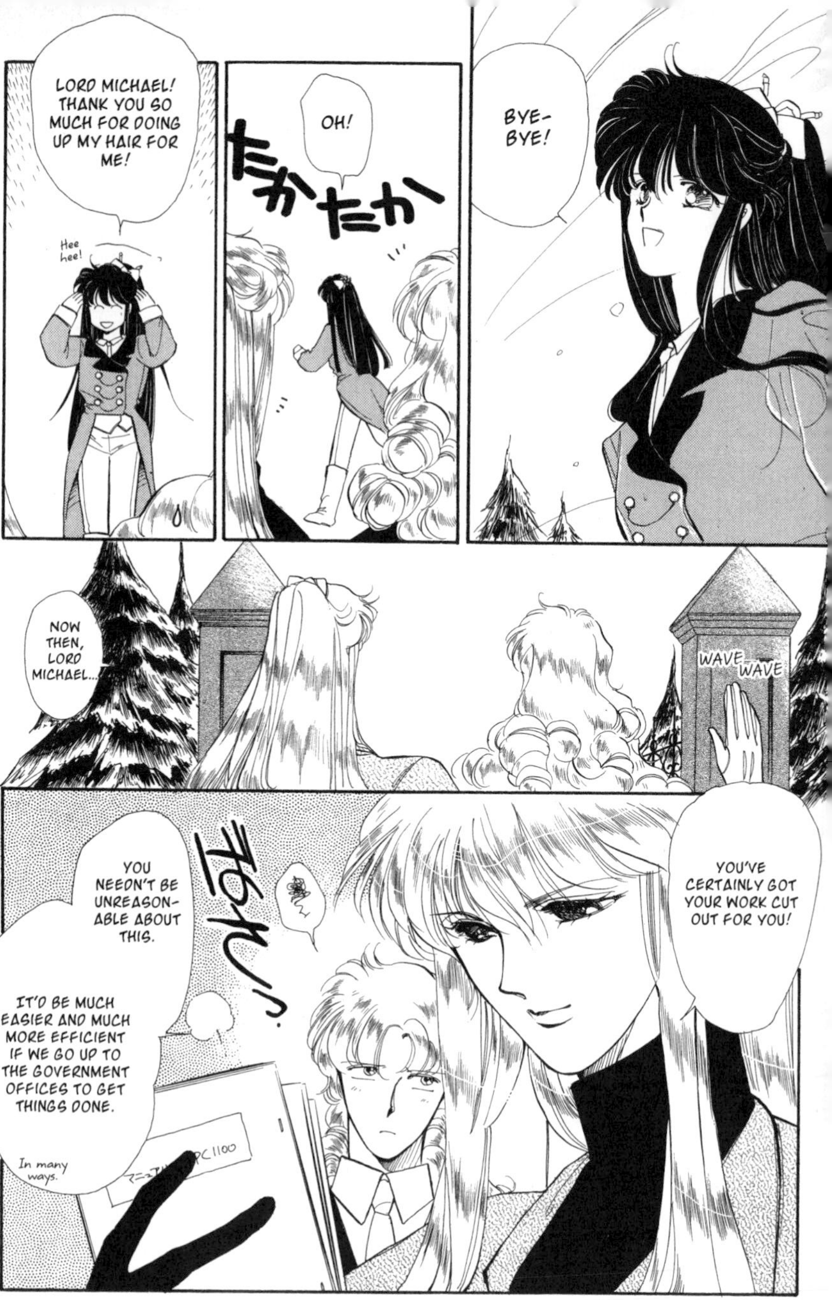
BYE-BYE!
OH!
たかたか
LORD MICHAEL! THANK YOU SO MUCH FOR DOING UP MY HAIR FOR ME!
Hee hee!
WAVE WAVE
NOW THEN, LORD MICHAEL...
YOU'VE CERTAINLY GOT YOUR WORK CUT OUT FOR YOU!
YOU NEEDN'T BE UNREASONABLE ABOUT THIS.
IT'D BE MUCH EASIER AND MUCH MORE EFFICIENT IF WE GO UP TO THE GOVERNMENT OFFICES TO GET THINGS DONE.
In many ways.

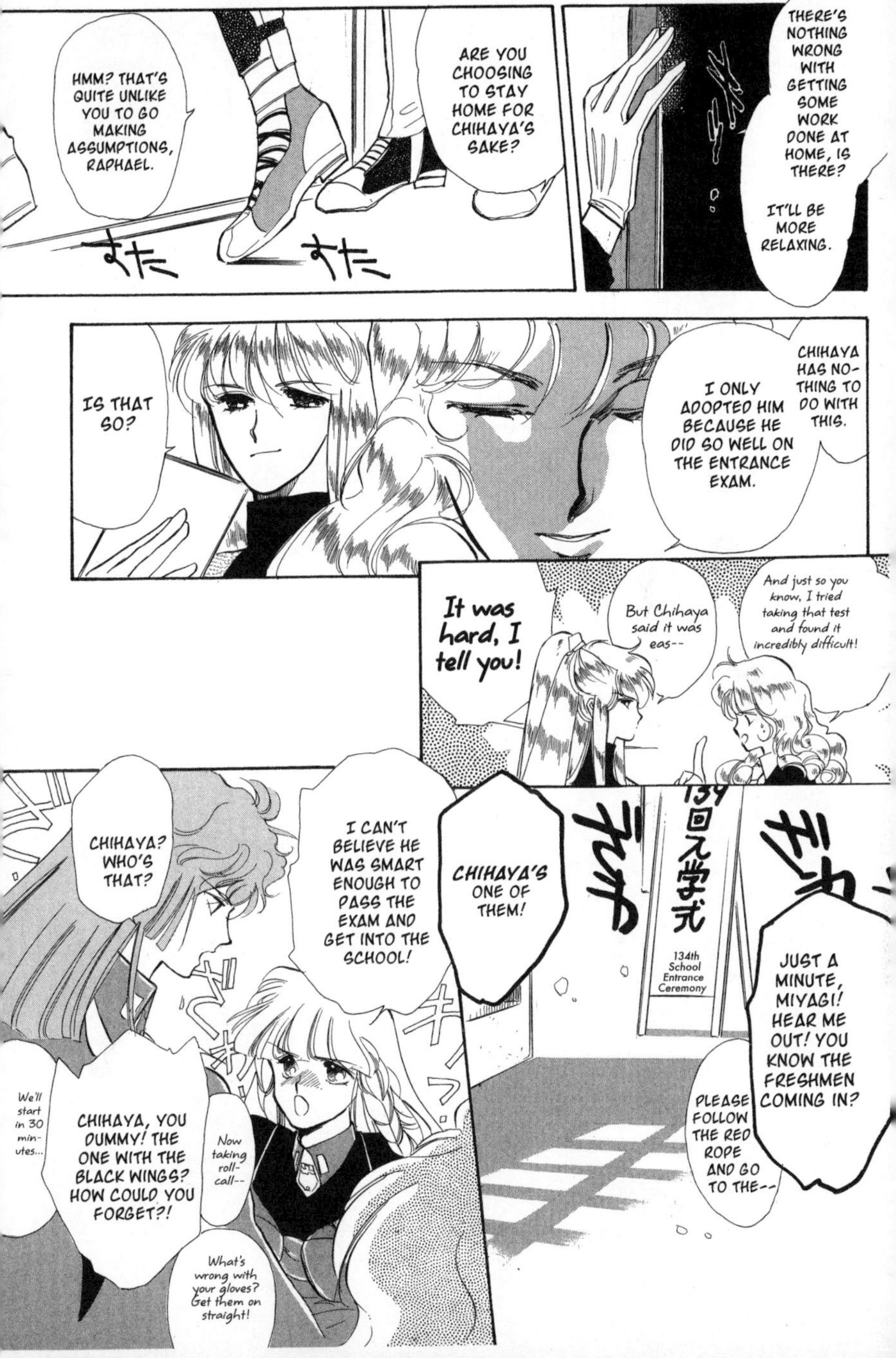
THERE'S NOTHING WRONG WITH GETTING SOME WORK DONE AT HOME, IS THERE?
IT'LL BE MORE RELAXING.
ARE YOU CHOOSING TO STAY HOME FOR CHIHAYA'S SAKE?
HMM? THAT'S QUITE UNLIKE YOU TO GO MAKING ASSUMPTIONS, RAPHAEL.
CHIHAYA HAS NOTHING TO DO WITH THIS.
I ONLY ADOPTED HIM BECAUSE HE DID SO WELL ON THE ENTRANCE EXAM.
IS THAT SO?
And just so you know, I tried taking that test and found it incredibly difficult!
But Chihaya said it was eas--
It was hard, I tell you!
134th School Entrance Ceremony
JUST A MINUTE, MIYAGI! HEAR ME OUT! YOU KNOW THE FRESHMEN COMING IN?
PLEASE FOLLOW THE RED ROPE AND GO TO THE--
CHIHAYA'S ONE OF THEM!
I CAN'T BELIEVE HE WAS SMART ENOUGH TO PASS THE EXAM AND GET INTO THE SCHOOL!
CHIHAYA? WHO'S THAT?
Now taking roll-call--
CHIHAYA, YOU DUMMY! THE ONE WITH THE BLACK WINGS? HOW COULD YOU FORGET?!
We'll start in 30 minutes...
What's wrong with your gloves? Get them on straight!

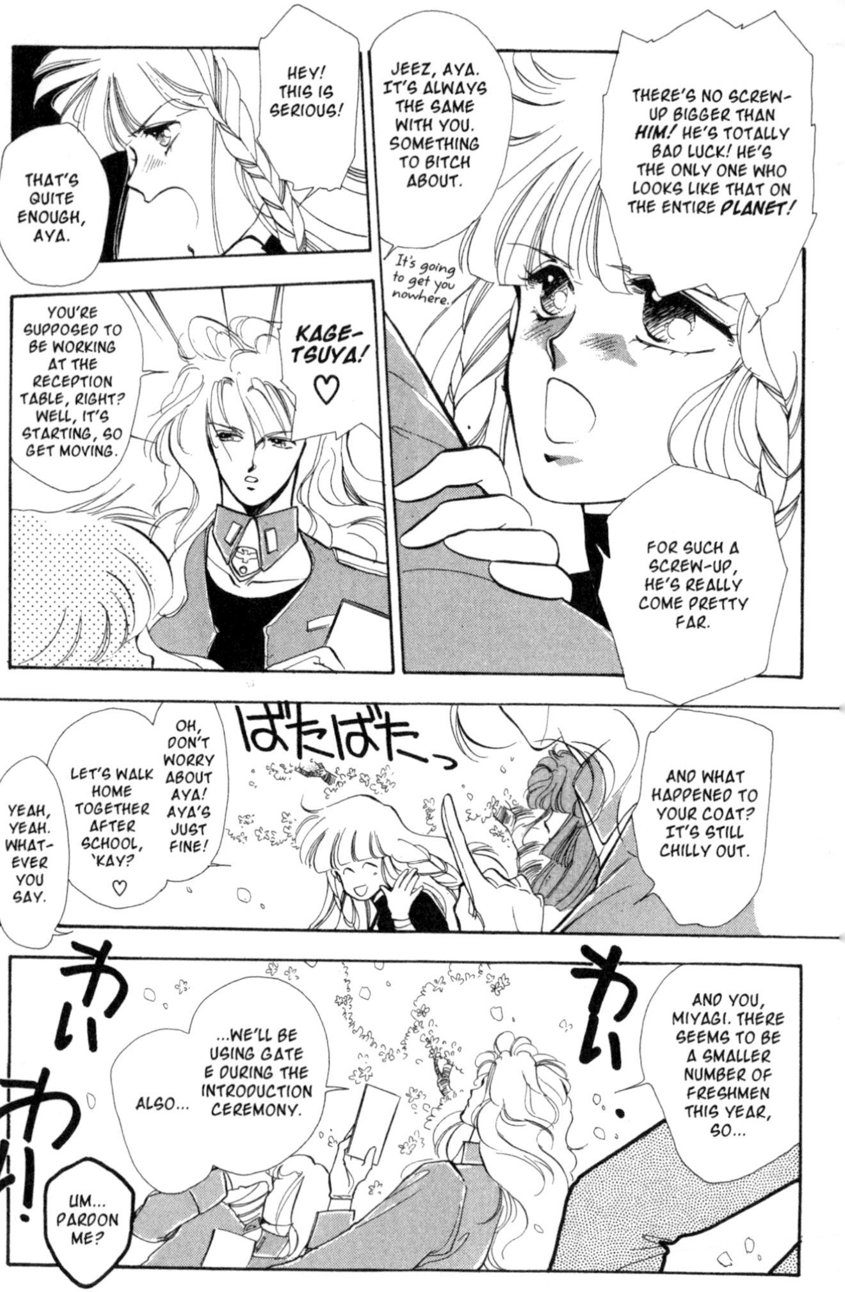
THERE'S NO SCREW-UP BIGGER THAN ***HIM!*** HE'S TOTALLY BAD LUCK! HE'S THE ONLY ONE WHO LOOKS LIKE THAT ON THE ENTIRE ***PLANET!***
FOR SUCH A SCREW-UP, HE'S REALLY COME PRETTY FAR.
JEEZ, AYA. IT'S ALWAYS THE SAME WITH YOU. SOMETHING TO BITCH ABOUT.
It's going to get you nowhere.
HEY! THIS IS SERIOUS!
THAT'S QUITE ENOUGH, AYA.
KAGE-TSUYA! ♡
YOU'RE SUPPOSED TO BE WORKING AT THE RECEPTION TABLE, RIGHT? WELL, IT'S STARTING, SO GET MOVING.
AND WHAT HAPPENED TO YOUR COAT? IT'S STILL CHILLY OUT.
ばたばたっ
OH, DON'T WORRY ABOUT AYA! AYA'S JUST FINE!
LET'S WALK HOME TOGETHER AFTER SCHOOL, 'KAY? ♡
YEAH, YEAH. WHAT-EVER YOU SAY.
わい
AND YOU, MIYAGI. THERE SEEMS TO BE A SMALLER NUMBER OF FRESHMEN THIS YEAR, SO...
...WE'LL BE USING GATE E DURING THE INTRODUCTION CEREMONY.
ALSO...
わいわい!
UM... PARDON ME?

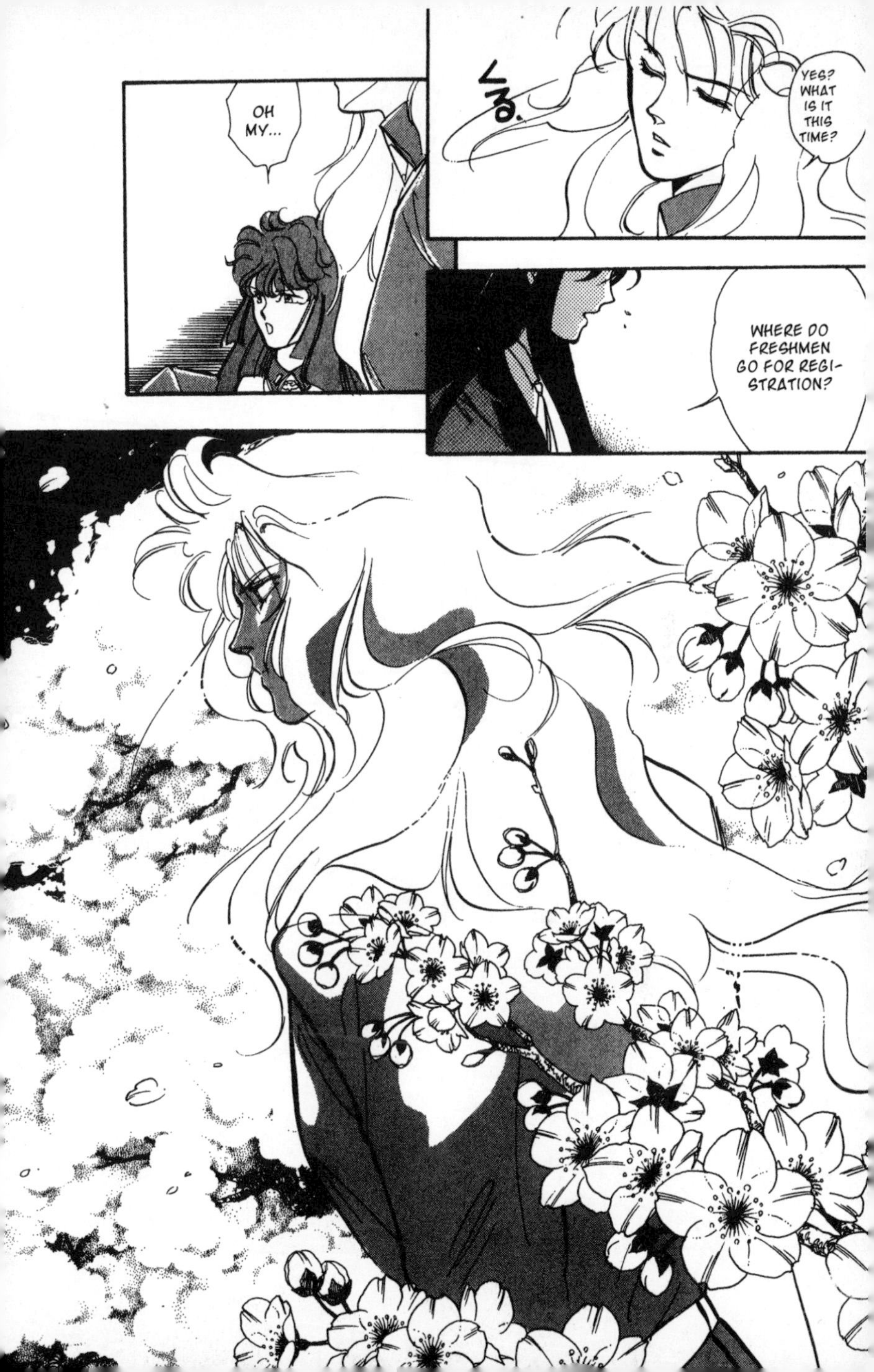
くる
YES? WHAT IS IT THIS TIME?
WHERE DO FRESHMEN GO FOR REGI-STRATION?
OH MY...

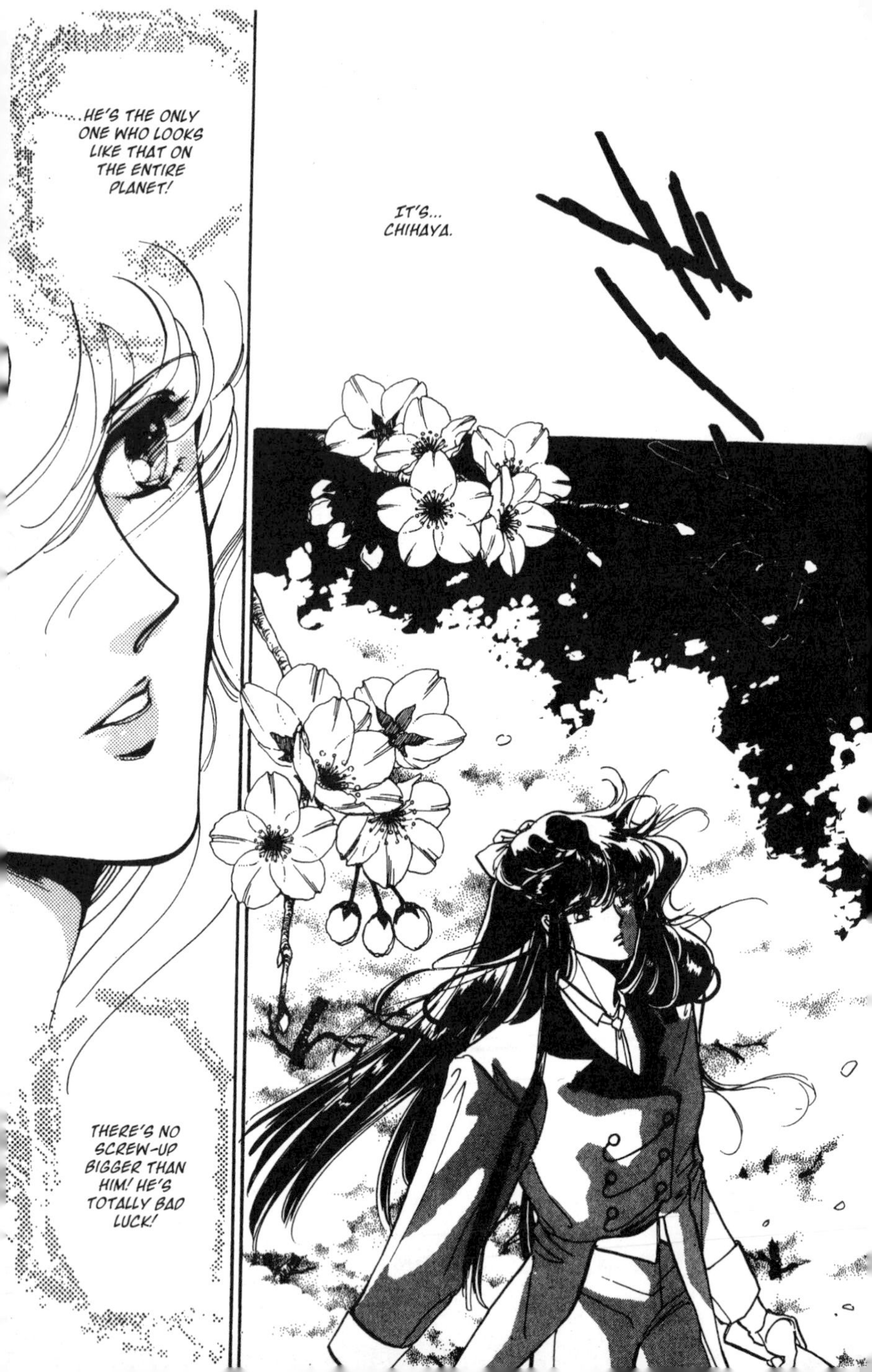
IT'S... CHIHAYA.
...HE'S THE ONLY ONE WHO LOOKS LIKE THAT ON THE ENTIRE PLANET!
THERE'S NO SCREW-UP BIGGER THAN HIM! HE'S TOTALLY BAD LUCK!

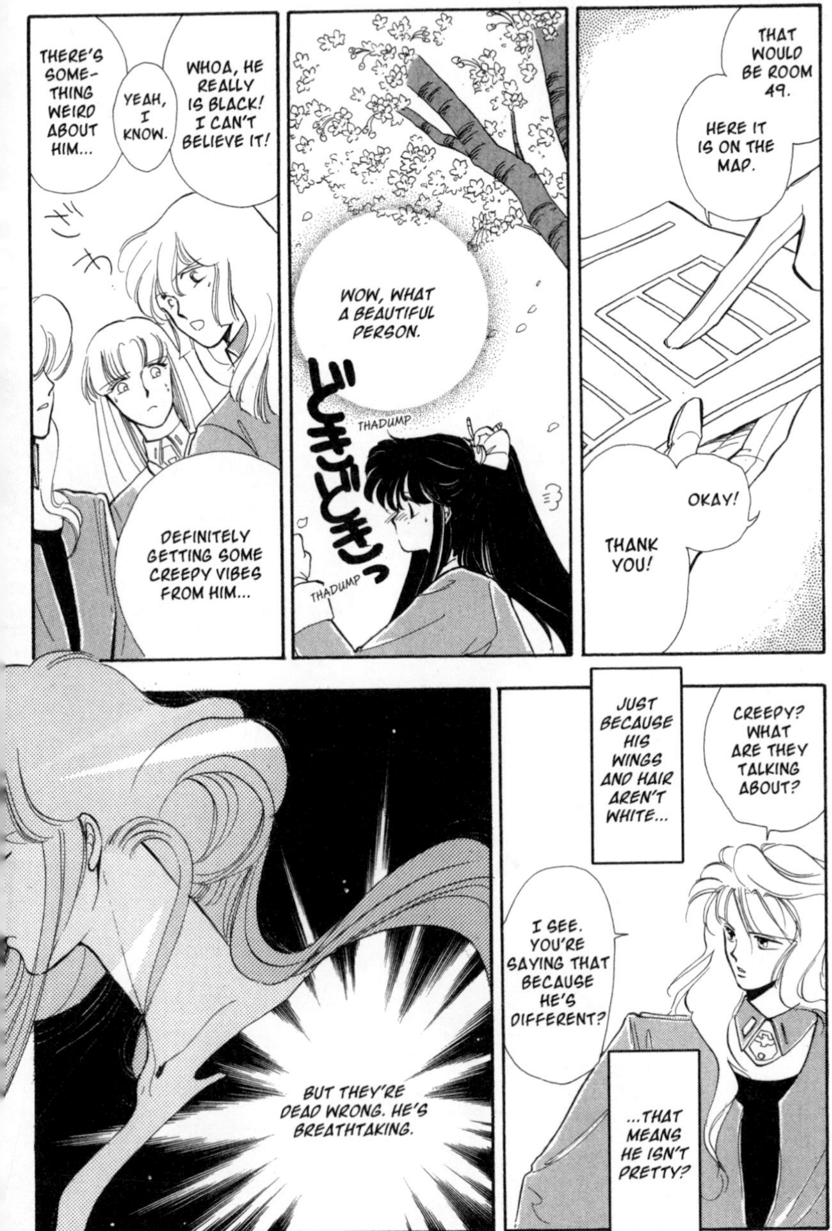
THAT WOULD BE ROOM 49.
HERE IT IS ON THE MAP.
OKAY!
THANK YOU!
WOW, WHAT A BEAUTIFUL PERSON.
どきどきっ
THADUMP
THADUMP
WHOA, HE REALLY IS BLACK! I CAN'T BELIEVE IT!
YEAH, I KNOW.
THERE'S SOME-THING WEIRD ABOUT HIM...
ざわ
DEFINITELY GETTING SOME CREEPY VIBES FROM HIM...
CREEPY? WHAT ARE THEY TALKING ABOUT?
JUST BECAUSE HIS WINGS AND HAIR AREN'T WHITE...
I SEE. YOU'RE SAYING THAT BECAUSE HE'S DIFFERENT?
...THAT MEANS HE ISN'T PRETTY?
BUT THEY'RE DEAD WRONG. HE'S BREATHTAKING.

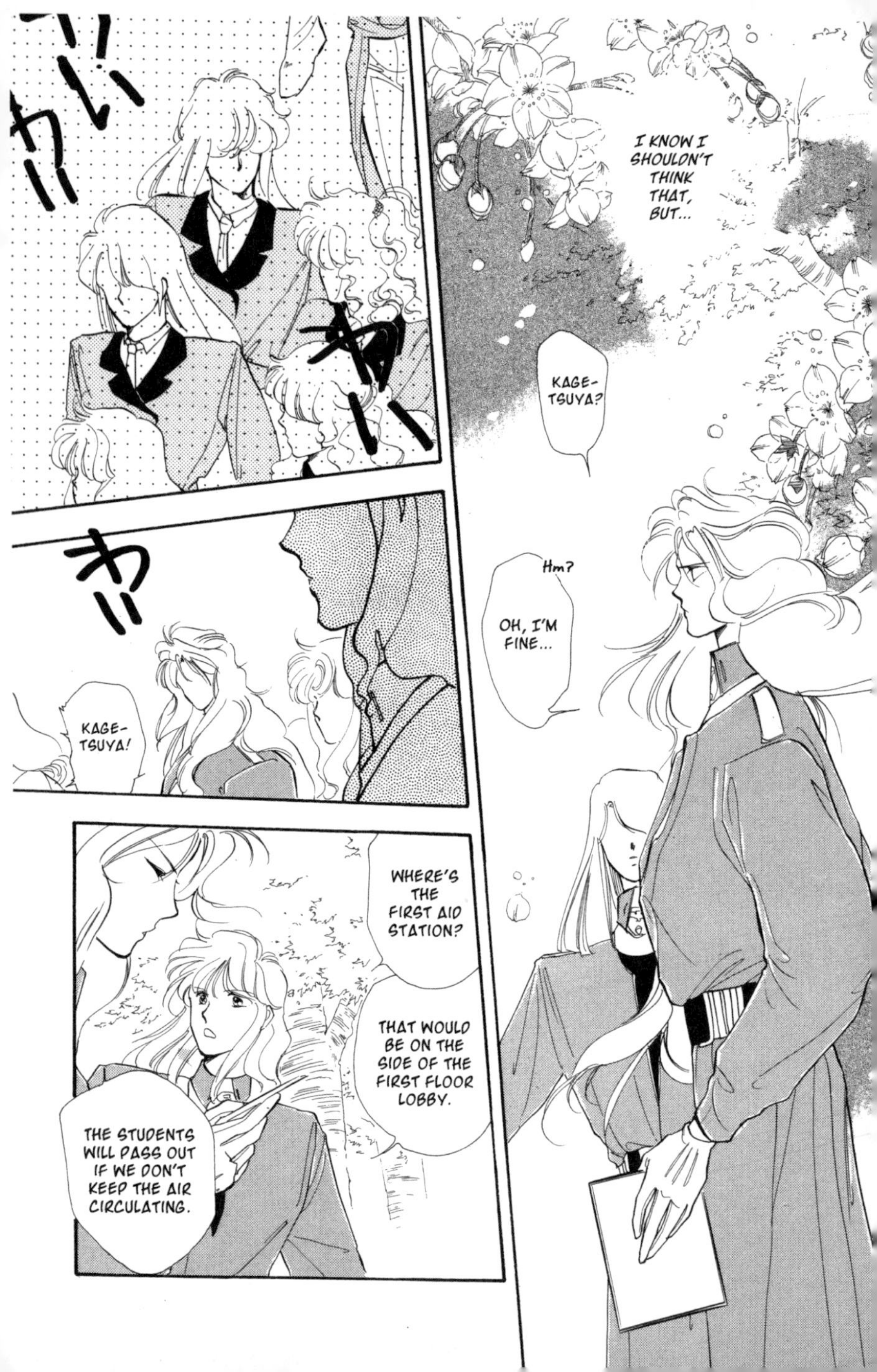
I KNOW I SHOULDN'T THINK THAT, BUT...
KAGE-TSUYA?
Hm?
OH, I'M FINE...
わい!!
わい
わ!!
KAGE-TSUYA!
WHERE'S THE FIRST AID STATION?
THAT WOULD BE ON THE SIDE OF THE FIRST FLOOR LOBBY.
THE STUDENTS WILL PASS OUT IF WE DON'T KEEP THE AIR CIRCULATING.

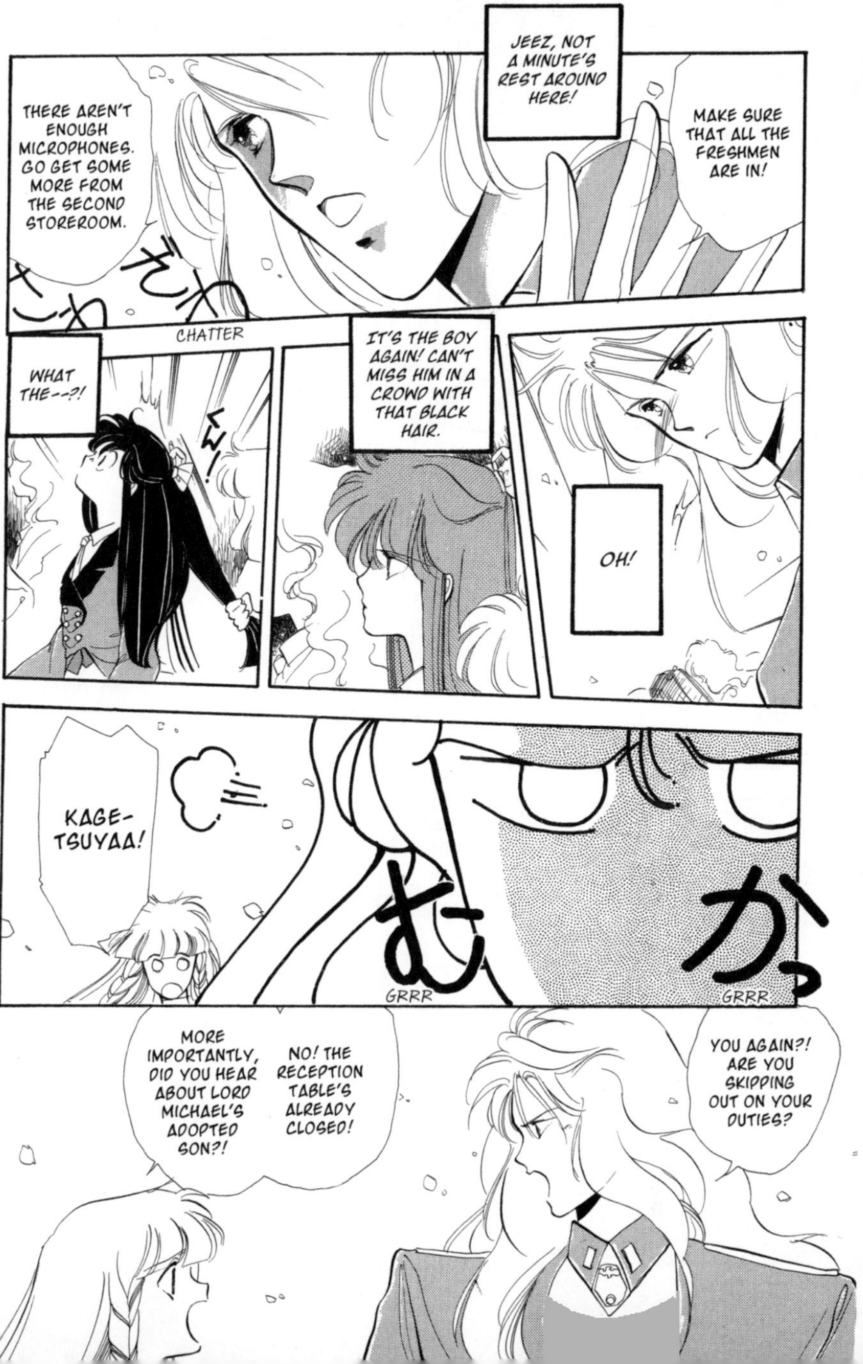
MAKE SURE THAT ALL THE FRESHMEN ARE IN!
JEEZ, NOT A MINUTE'S REST AROUND HERE!
THERE AREN'T ENOUGH MICROPHONES. GO GET SOME MORE FROM THE SECOND STOREROOM.
CHATTER
OH!
IT'S THE BOY AGAIN! CAN'T MISS HIM IN A CROWD WITH THAT BLACK HAIR.
WHAT THE--?!
GRRR
GRRR
KAGE-TSUYAA!
YOU AGAIN?! ARE YOU SKIPPING OUT ON YOUR DUTIES?
NO! THE RECEPTION TABLE'S ALREADY CLOSED!
MORE IMPORTANTLY, DID YOU HEAR ABOUT LORD MICHAEL'S ADOPTED SON?!

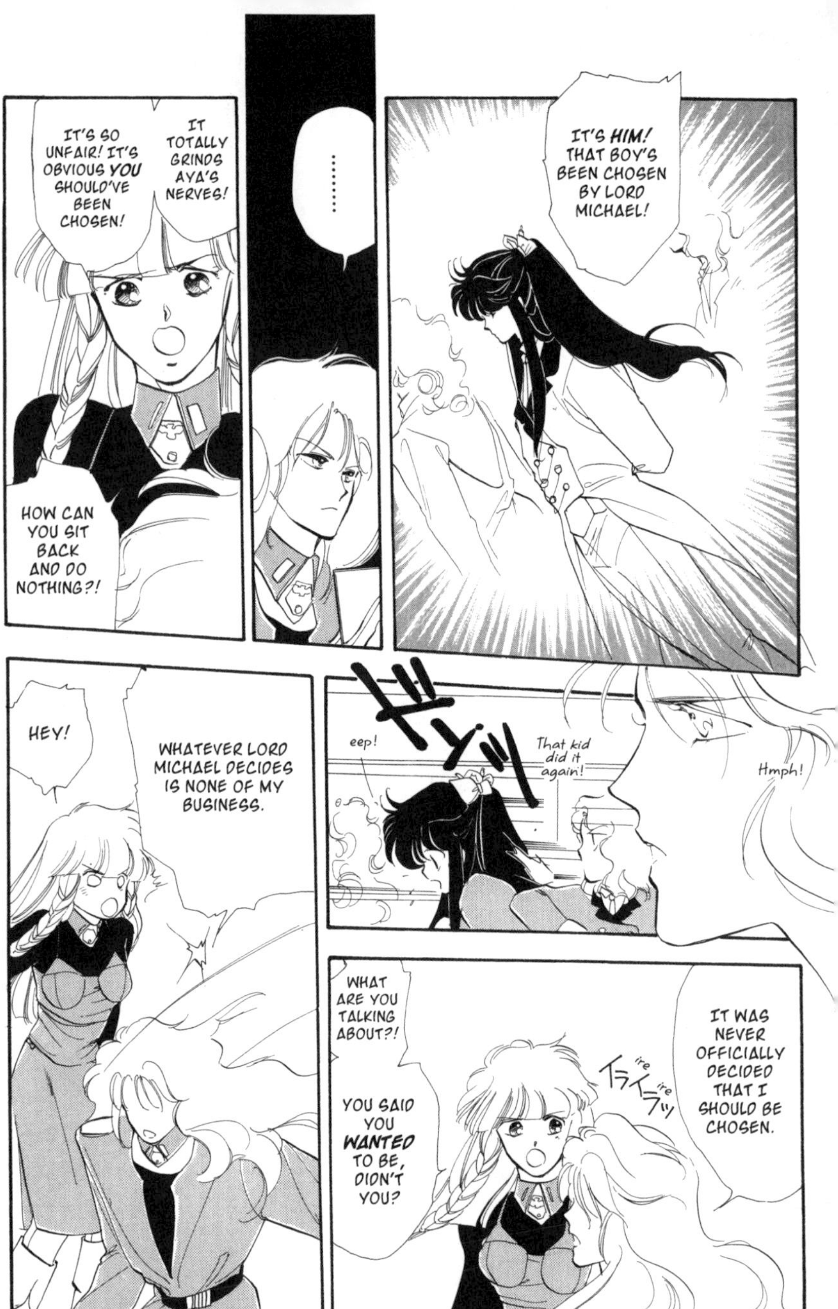
IT'S HIM! THAT BOY'S BEEN CHOSEN BY LORD MICHAEL!
……
IT TOTALLY GRINDS AYA'S NERVES!
IT'S SO UNFAIR! IT'S OBVIOUS YOU SHOULD'VE BEEN CHOSEN!
HOW CAN YOU SIT BACK AND DO NOTHING?!
Hmph!
That kid did it again!
ギッ
eep!
IT WAS NEVER OFFICIALLY DECIDED THAT I SHOULD BE CHOSEN.
イライラッ
ire ire
WHAT ARE YOU TALKING ABOUT?!
YOU SAID YOU WANTED TO BE, DIDN'T YOU?
WHATEVER LORD MICHAEL DECIDES IS NONE OF MY BUSINESS.
HEY!

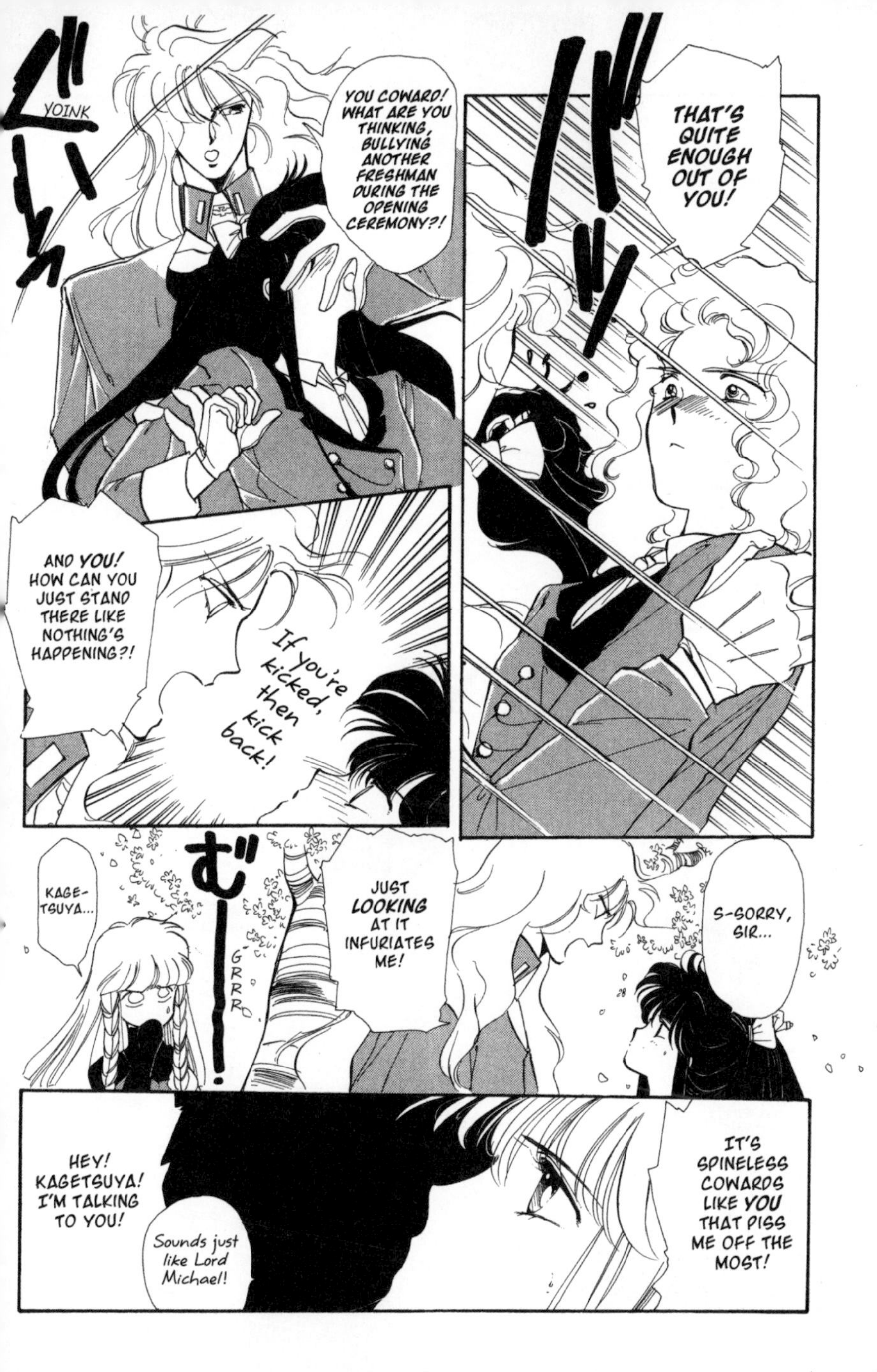
THAT'S QUITE ENOUGH OUT OF YOU!
YOINK
YOU COWARD! WHAT ARE YOU THINKING, BULLYING ANOTHER FRESHMAN DURING THE OPENING CEREMONY?!
AND YOU! HOW CAN YOU JUST STAND THERE LIKE NOTHING'S HAPPENING?!
If you're kicked, then kick back!
S-SORRY, SIR...
JUST LOOKING AT IT INFURIATES ME!
むー!
GRRR
KAGE-TSUYA...
IT'S SPINELESS COWARDS LIKE YOU THAT PISS ME OFF THE MOST!
HEY! KAGETSUYA! I'M TALKING TO YOU!
Sounds just like Lord Michael!

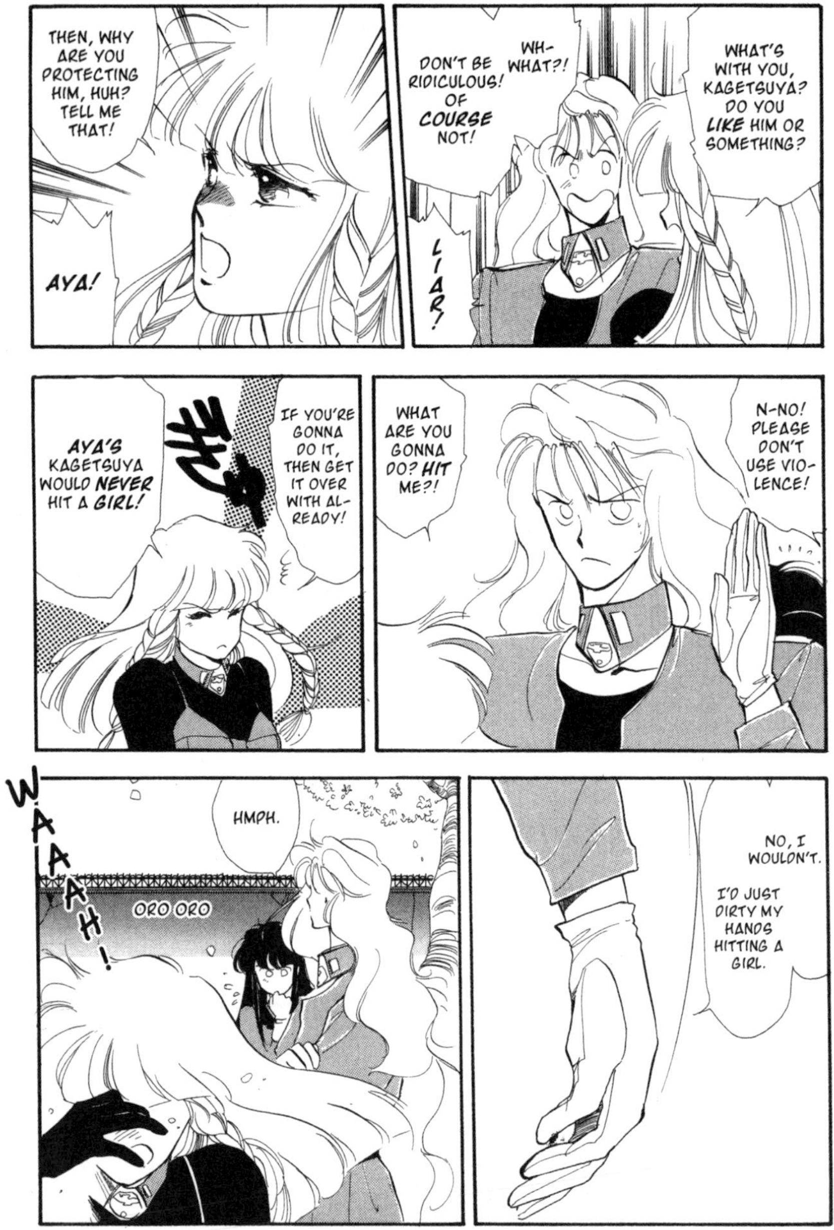
WHAT'S WITH YOU, KAGETSUYA? DO YOU LIKE HIM OR SOMETHING?
WH- WHAT?!
DON'T BE RIDICULOUS! OF COURSE NOT!
LIAR!
THEN, WHY ARE YOU PROTECTING HIM, HUH? TELL ME THAT!
AYA!
N-NO! PLEASE DON'T USE VIO- LENCE!
WHAT ARE YOU GONNA DO? HIT ME?!
IF YOU'RE GONNA DO IT, THEN GET IT OVER WITH AL- READY!
AYA'S KAGETSUYA WOULD NEVER HIT A GIRL!
NO, I WOULDN'T.
I'D JUST DIRTY MY HANDS HITTING A GIRL.
HMPH.
ORO ORO
WAAAAH!

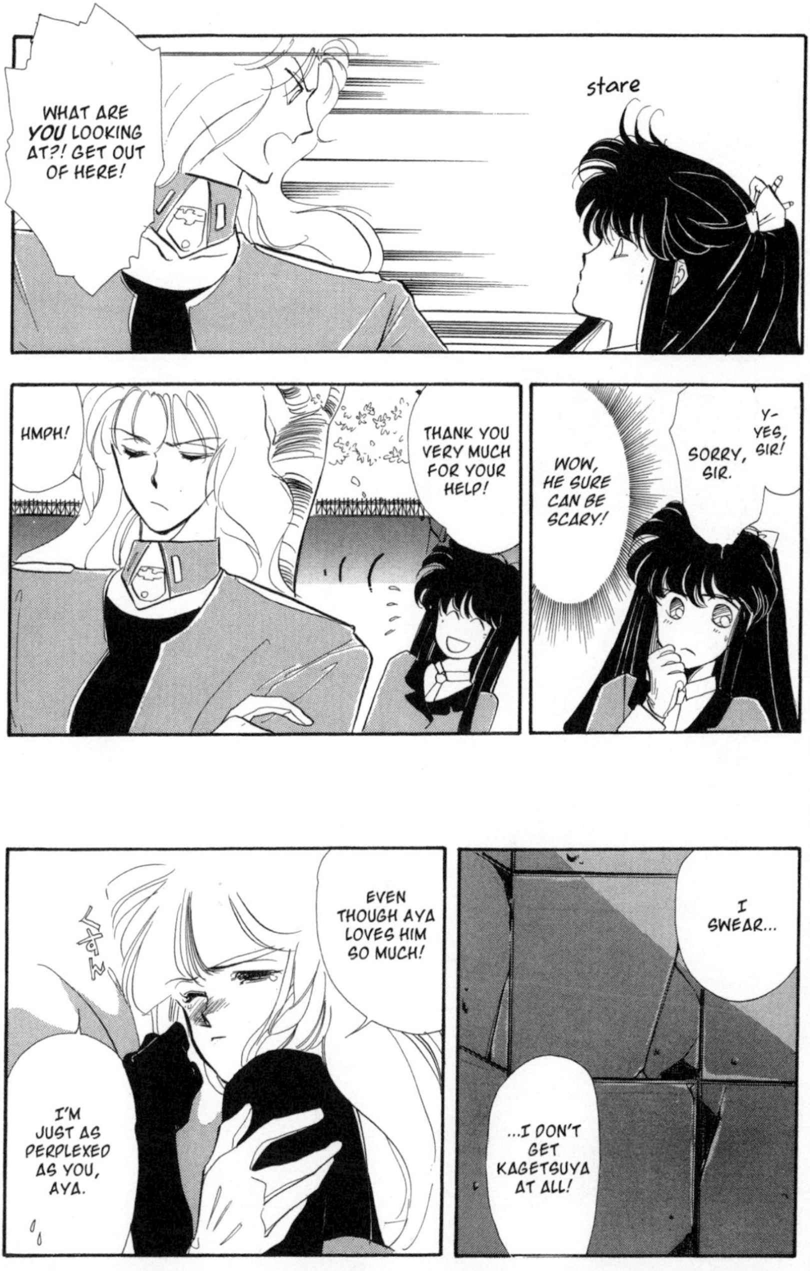
stare
WHAT ARE *YOU* LOOKING AT?! GET OUT OF HERE!
Y-YES, SIR!
SORRY, SIR.
WOW, HE SURE CAN BE SCARY!
THANK YOU VERY MUCH FOR YOUR HELP!
HMPH!
I SWEAR...
...I DON'T GET KAGETSUYA AT ALL!
EVEN THOUGH AYA LOVES HIM SO MUCH!
I'M JUST AS PERPLEXED AS YOU, AYA.

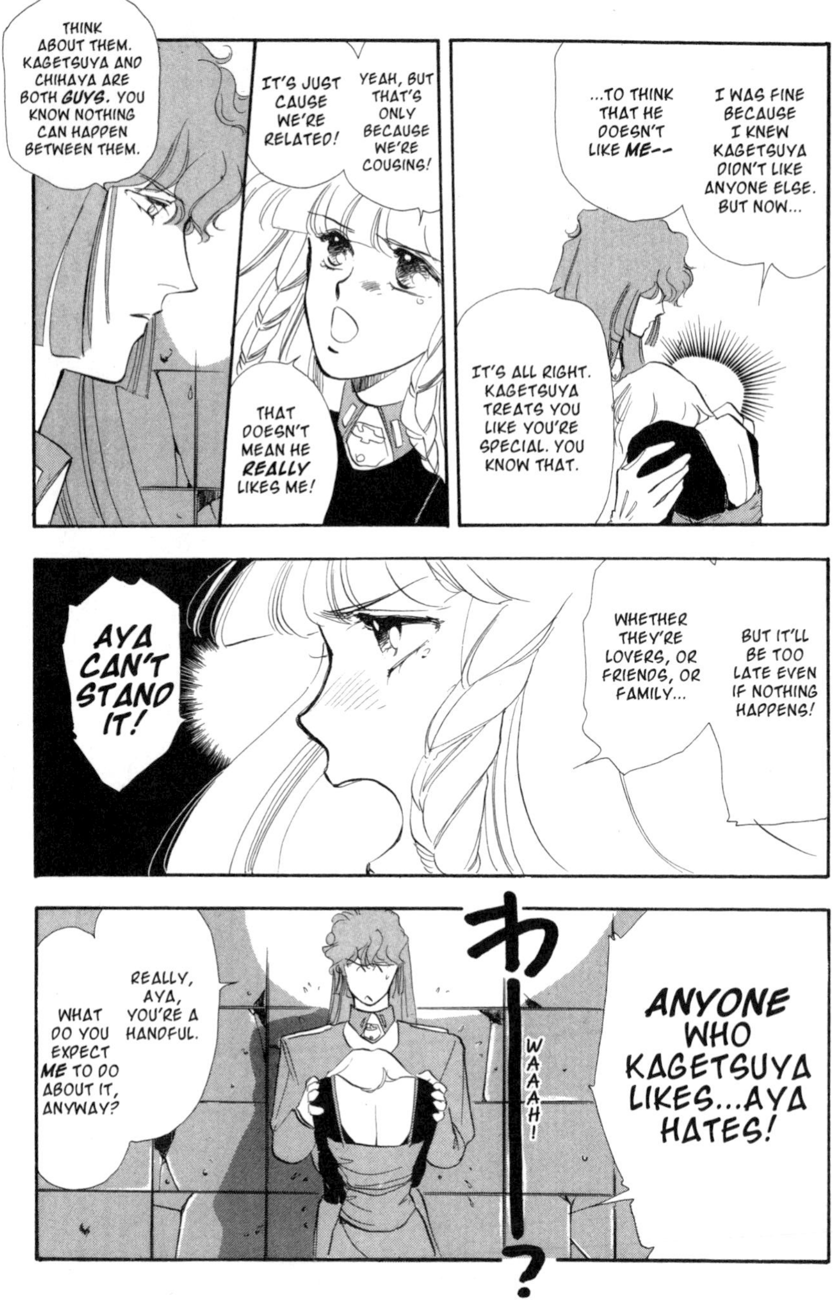
I WAS FINE BECAUSE I KNEW KAGETSUYA DIDN'T LIKE ANYONE ELSE. BUT NOW...
...TO THINK THAT HE DOESN'T LIKE ME--
IT'S ALL RIGHT. KAGETSUYA TREATS YOU LIKE YOU'RE SPECIAL. YOU KNOW THAT.
YEAH, BUT THAT'S ONLY BECAUSE WE'RE COUSINS!
IT'S JUST CAUSE WE'RE RELATED!
THAT DOESN'T MEAN HE REALLY LIKES ME!
THINK ABOUT THEM. KAGETSUYA AND CHIHAYA ARE BOTH GUYS. YOU KNOW NOTHING CAN HAPPEN BETWEEN THEM.
WHETHER THEY'RE LOVERS, OR FRIENDS, OR FAMILY...
BUT IT'LL BE TOO LATE EVEN IF NOTHING HAPPENS!
AYA CAN'T STAND IT!
ANYONE WHO KAGETSUYA LIKES...AYA HATES!
わー?
WAAAAH!
REALLY, AYA, YOU'RE A HANDFUL.
WHAT DO YOU EXPECT ME TO DO ABOUT IT, ANYWAY?

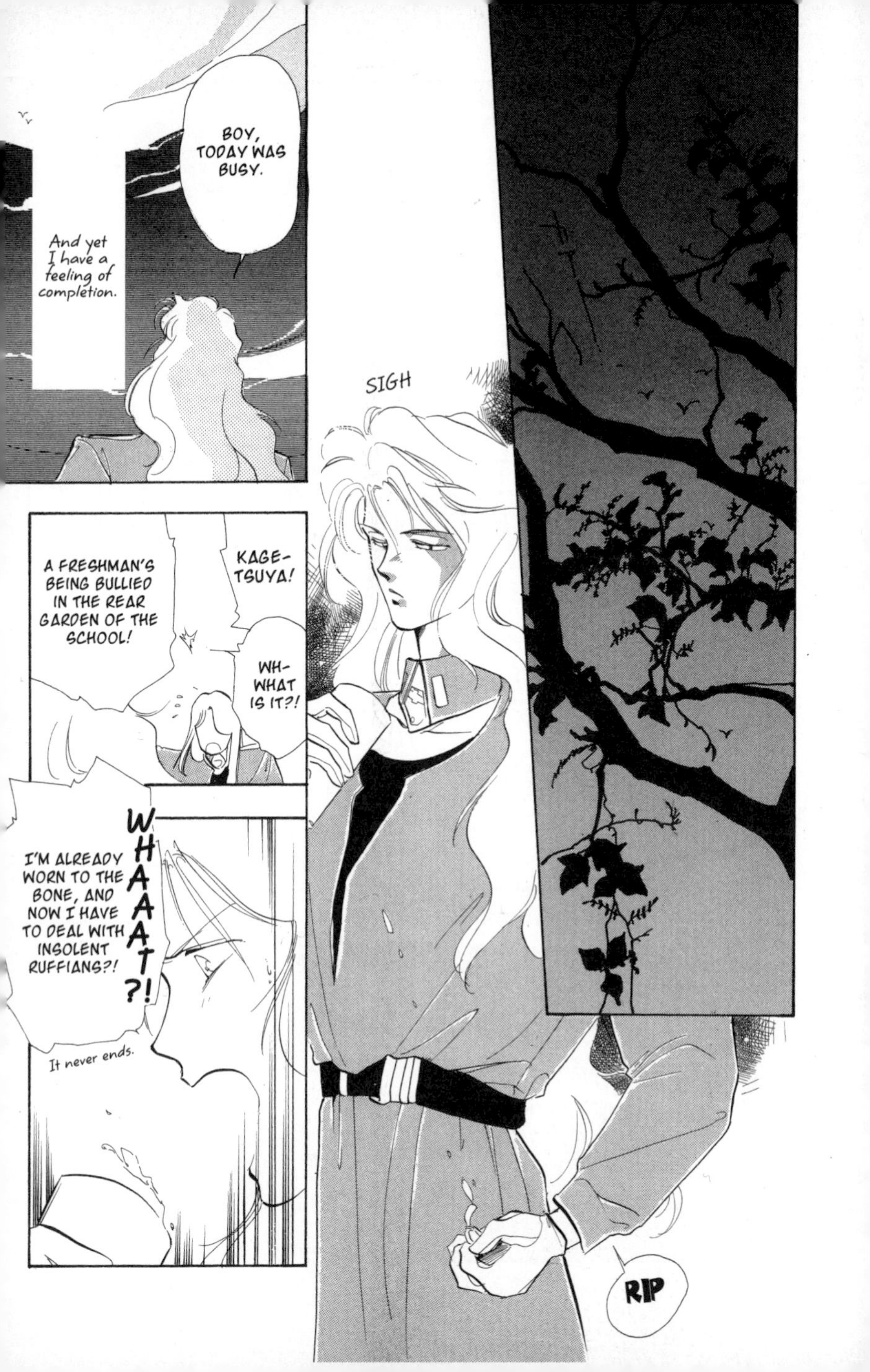
SIGH
RIP
BOY, TODAY WAS BUSY.
And yet I have a feeling of completion.
KAGE-TSUYA!
WH-WHAT IS IT?!
A FRESHMAN'S BEING BULLIED IN THE REAR GARDEN OF THE SCHOOL!
WHAAAT?!
I'M ALREADY WORN TO THE BONE, AND NOW I HAVE TO DEAL WITH INSOLENT RUFFIANS?!
It never ends.

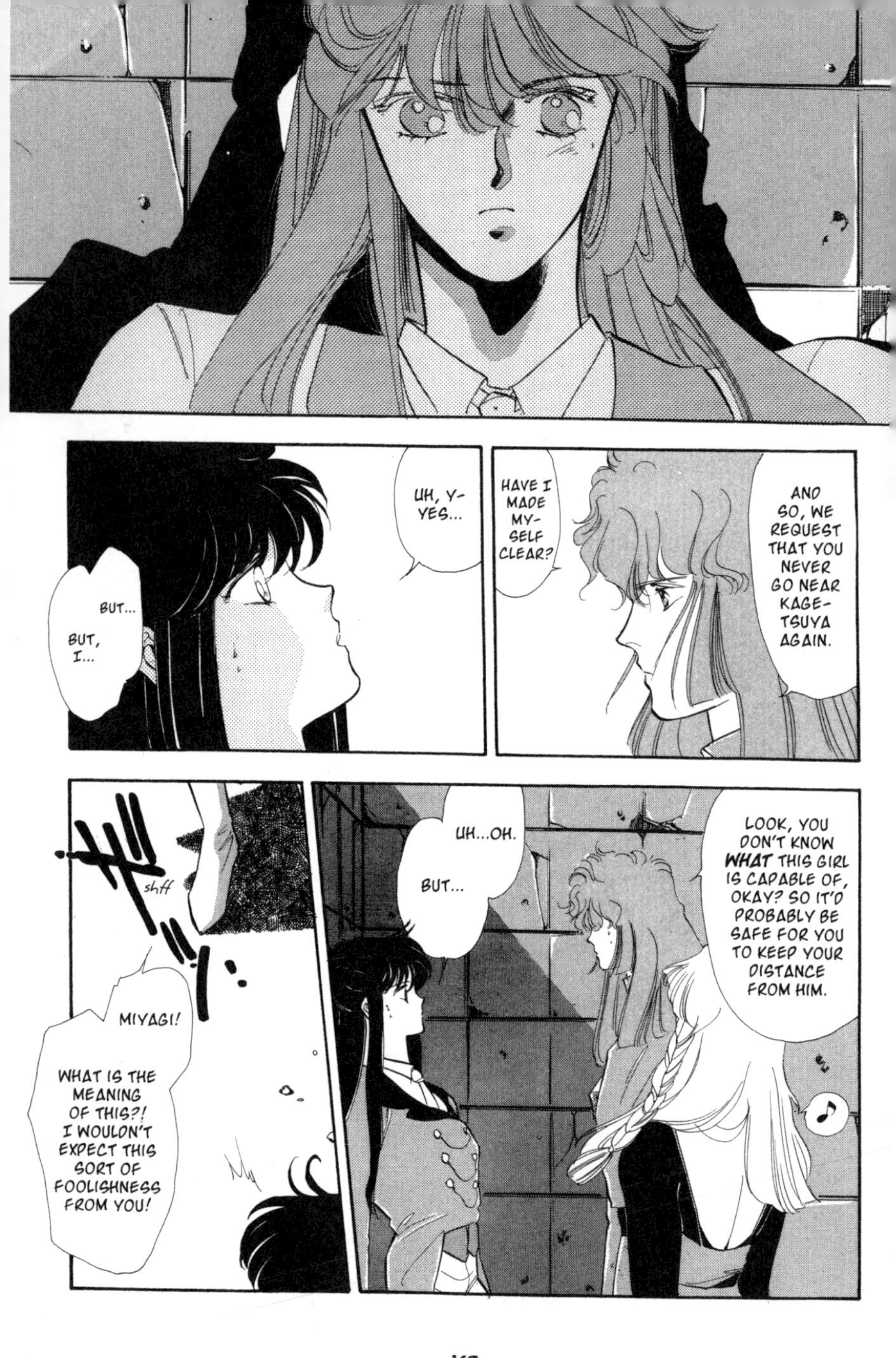
AND SO, WE REQUEST THAT YOU NEVER GO NEAR KAGE-TSUYA AGAIN.
HAVE I MADE MY-SELF CLEAR?
UH, Y-YES...
BUT... BUT, I...
LOOK, YOU DON'T KNOW **WHAT** THIS GIRL IS CAPABLE OF, OKAY? SO IT'D PROBABLY BE SAFE FOR YOU TO KEEP YOUR DISTANCE FROM HIM.
UH...OH.
BUT...
shff
MIYAGI!
WHAT IS THE MEANING OF THIS?! I WOULDN'T EXPECT THIS SORT OF FOOLISHNESS FROM YOU!

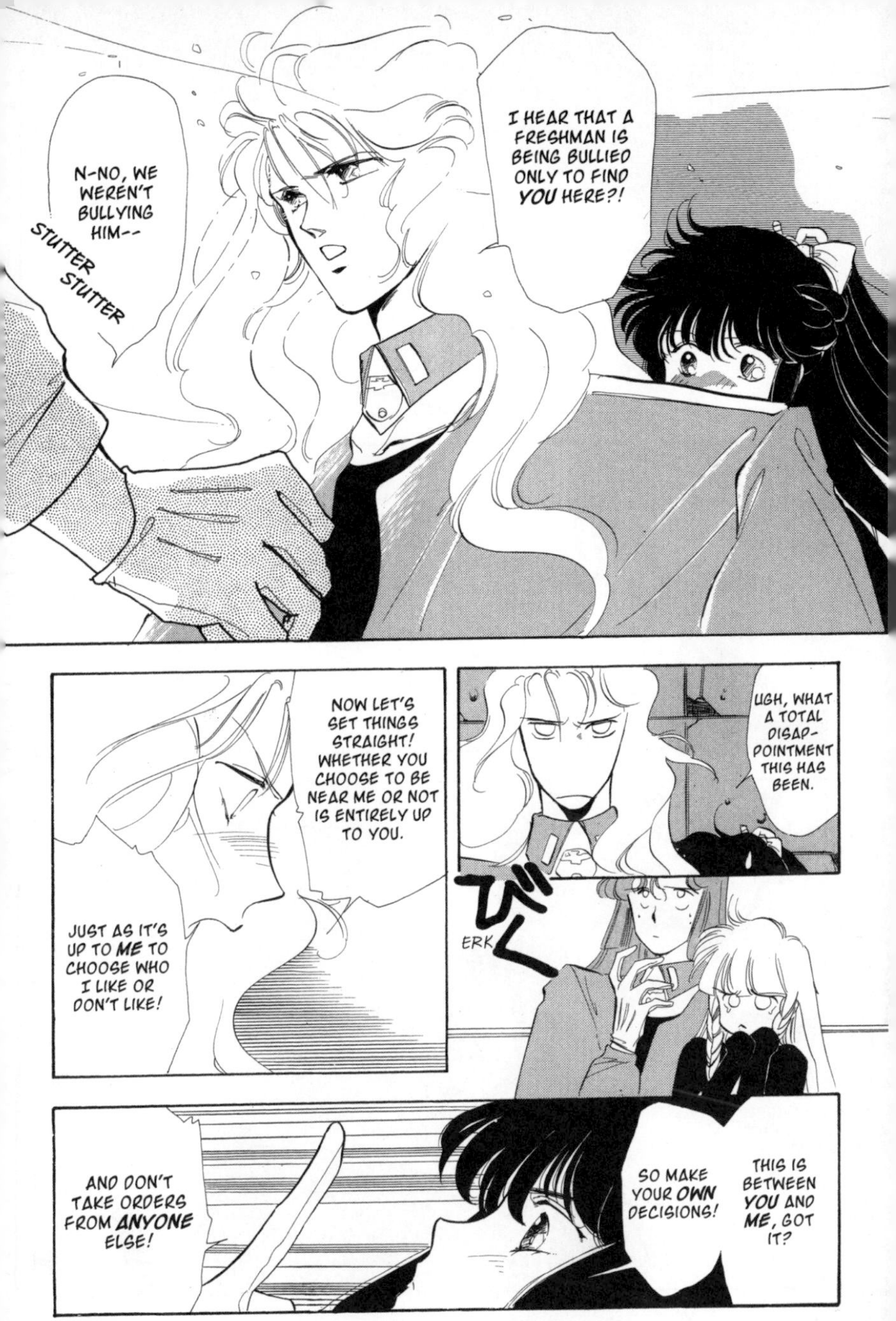
I HEAR THAT A FRESHMAN IS BEING BULLIED ONLY TO FIND YOU HERE?!
N-NO, WE WEREN'T BULLYING HIM--
STUTTER STUTTER
UGH, WHAT A TOTAL DISAP-POINTMENT THIS HAS BEEN.
びく
ERK
NOW LET'S SET THINGS STRAIGHT! WHETHER YOU CHOOSE TO BE NEAR ME OR NOT IS ENTIRELY UP TO YOU.
JUST AS IT'S UP TO ME TO CHOOSE WHO I LIKE OR DON'T LIKE!
THIS IS BETWEEN YOU AND ME, GOT IT?
SO MAKE YOUR OWN DECISIONS!
AND DON'T TAKE ORDERS FROM ANYONE ELSE!

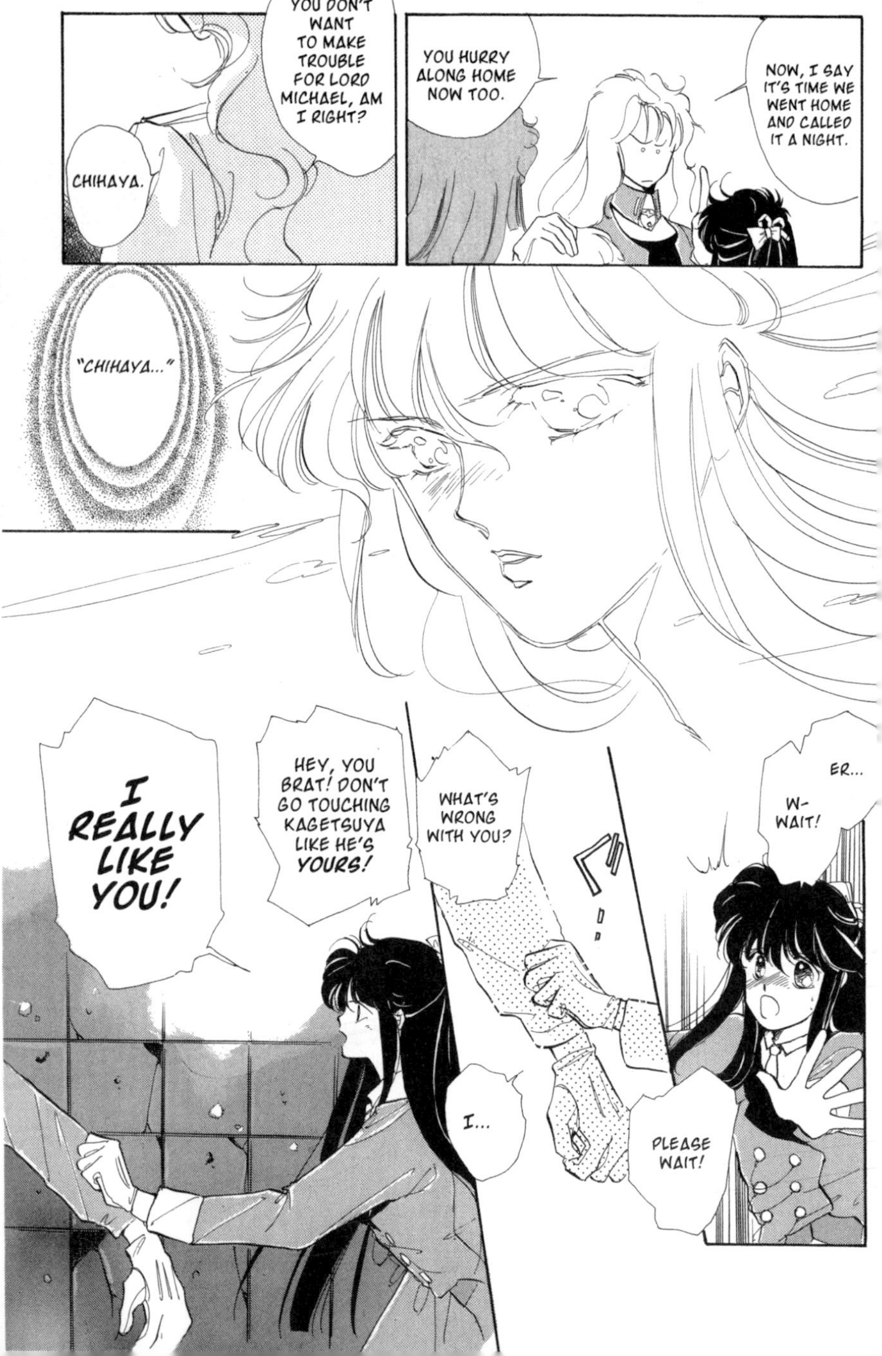
NOW, I SAY IT'S TIME WE WENT HOME AND CALLED IT A NIGHT.
YOU HURRY ALONG HOME NOW TOO.
YOU DON'T WANT TO MAKE TROUBLE FOR LORD MICHAEL, AM I RIGHT?
CHIHAYA.
"CHIHAYA..."
ER...
W-WAIT!
PLEASE WAIT!
WHAT'S WRONG WITH YOU?
I...
HEY, YOU BRAT! DON'T GO TOUCHING KAGETSUYA LIKE HE'S YOURS!
I REALLY LIKE YOU!

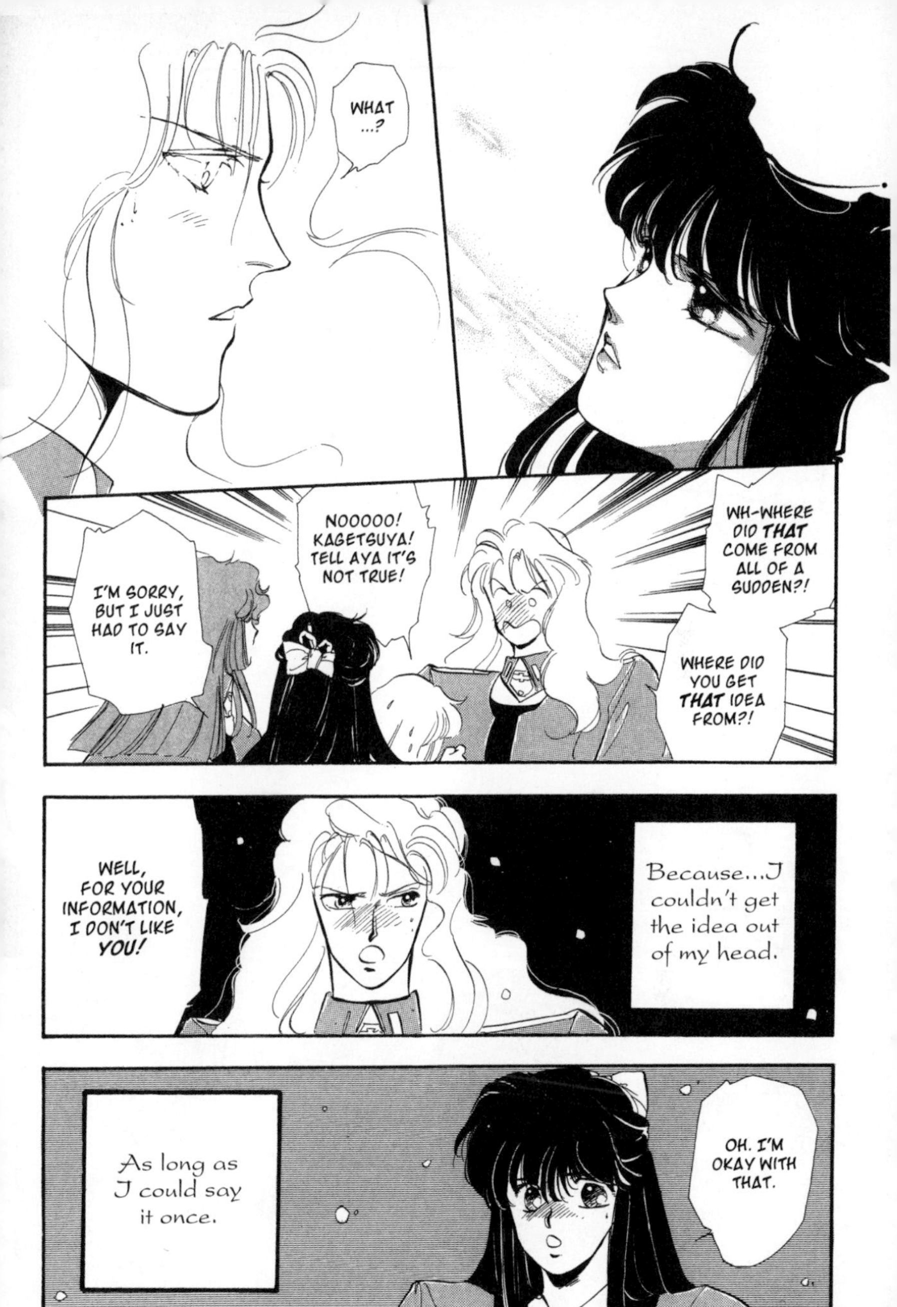
WHAT ...?
WH-WHERE DID THAT COME FROM ALL OF A SUDDEN?!
WHERE DID YOU GET THAT IDEA FROM?!
NOOOOO! KAGETSUYA! TELL AYA IT'S NOT TRUE!
I'M SORRY, BUT I JUST HAD TO SAY IT.
Because...I couldn't get the idea out of my head.
WELL, FOR YOUR INFORMATION, I DON'T LIKE YOU!
OH. I'M OKAY WITH THAT.
As long as I could say it once.

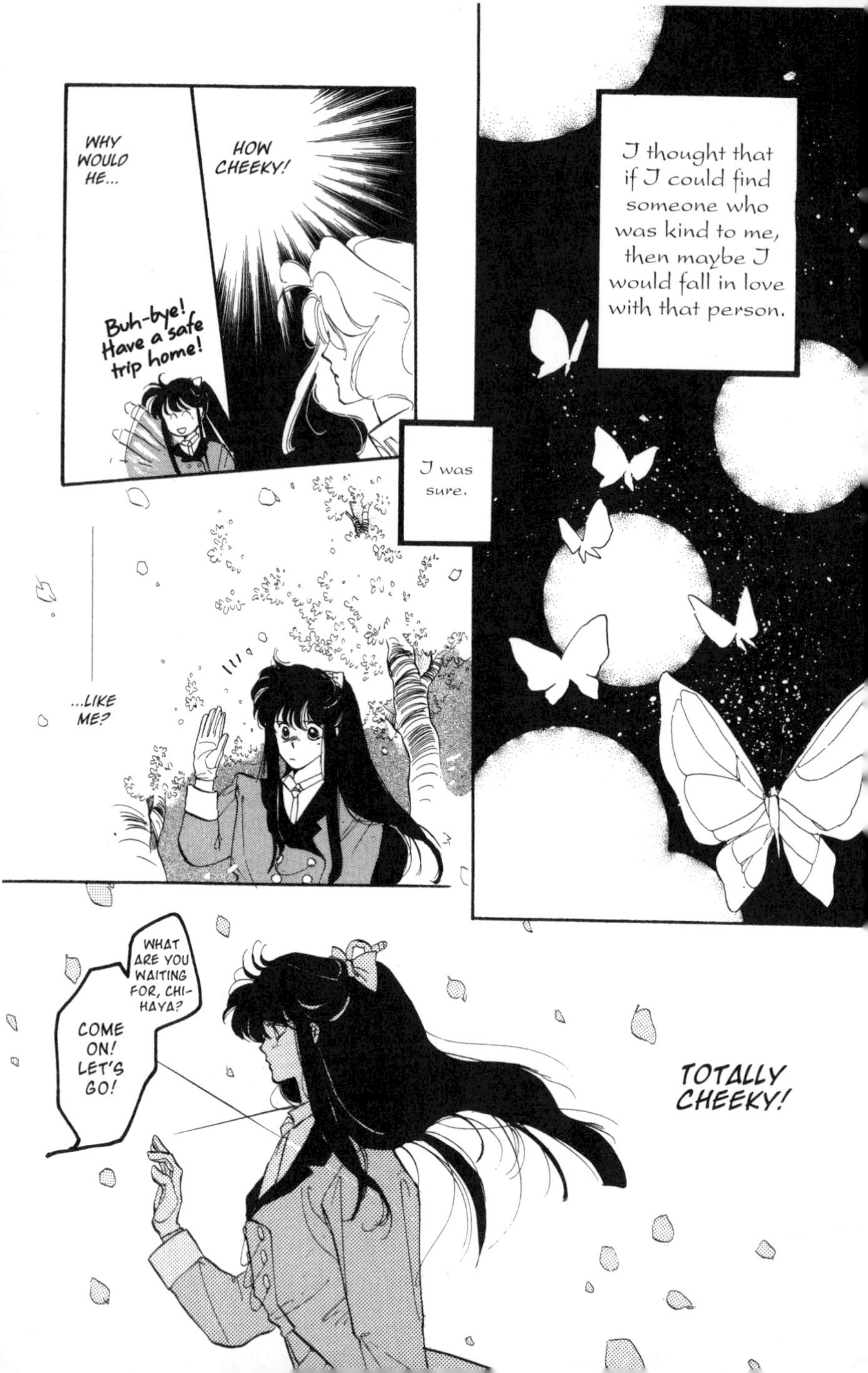
I thought that if I could find someone who was kind to me, then maybe I would fall in love with that person.
I was sure.
HOW CHEEKY!
WHY WOULD HE...
Buh-bye! Have a safe trip home!
...LIKE ME?
WHAT ARE YOU WAITING FOR, CHI-HAYA?
COME ON! LET'S GO!
TOTALLY CHEEKY!

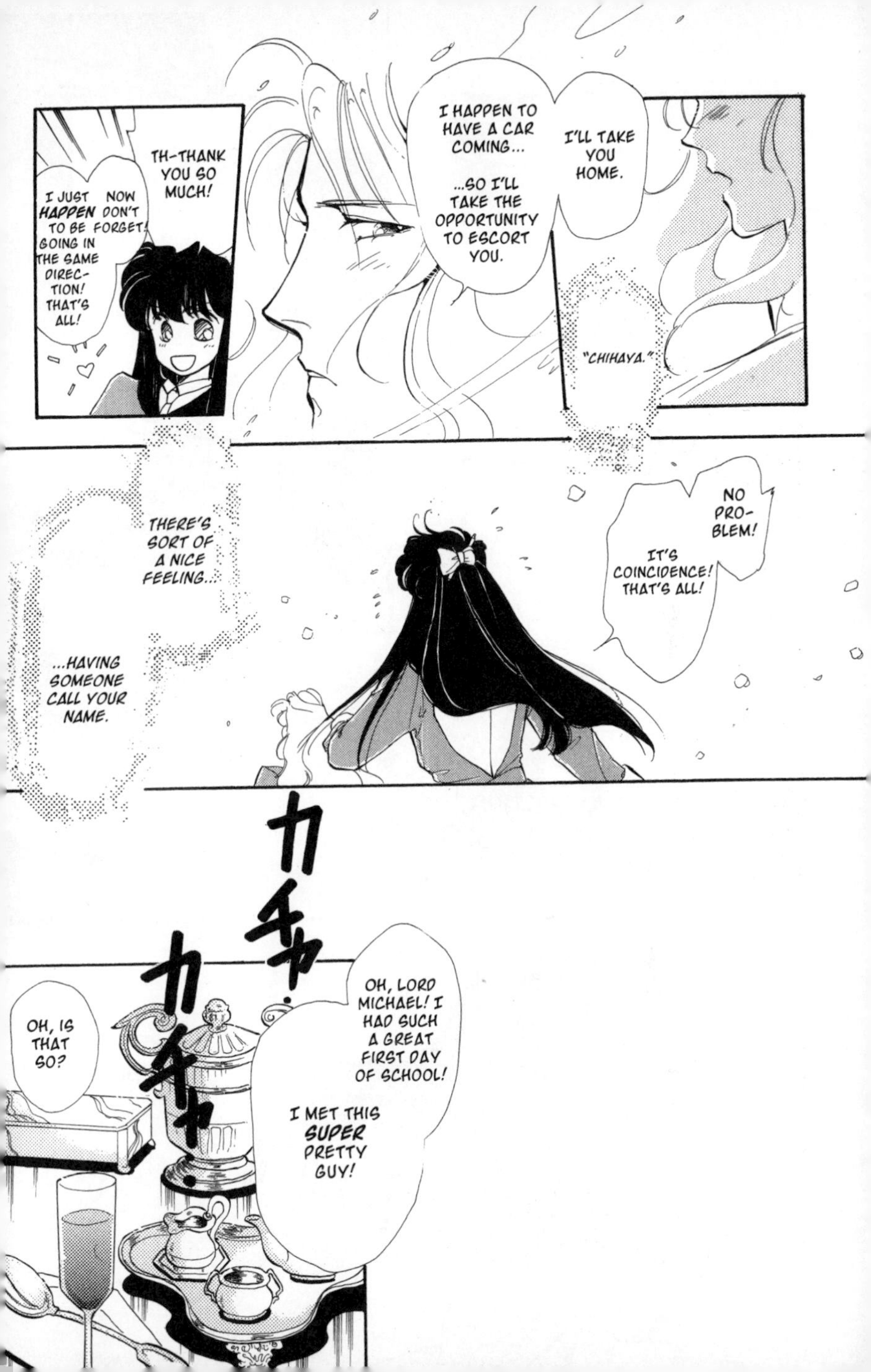
I'LL TAKE YOU HOME.
"CHIHAYA."
I HAPPEN TO HAVE A CAR COMING...
...SO I'LL TAKE THE OPPORTUNITY TO ESCORT YOU.
TH-THANK YOU SO MUCH!
NOW DON'T FORGET!
I JUST HAPPEN TO BE GOING IN THE SAME DIREC-TION! THAT'S ALL!
NO PROB-LEM!
IT'S COINCIDENCE! THAT'S ALL!
THERE'S SORT OF A NICE FEELING...
...HAVING SOMEONE CALL YOUR NAME.
カチャ
カチャ
OH, LORD MICHAEL! I HAD SUCH A GREAT FIRST DAY OF SCHOOL!
I MET THIS SUPER PRETTY GUY!
OH, IS THAT SO?

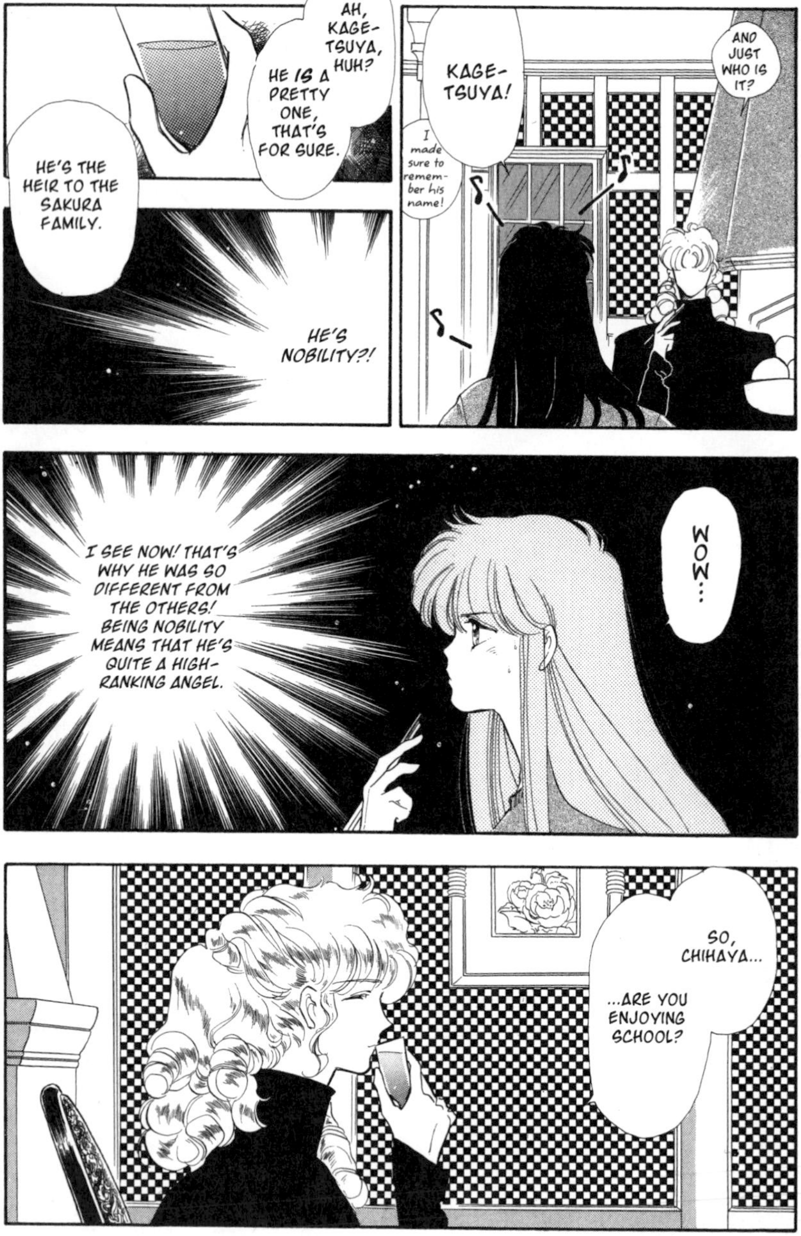
AND JUST WHO IS IT?
KAGE-TSUYA!
I made sure to remem-ber his name!
AH, KAGE-TSUYA, HUH?
HE IS A PRETTY ONE, THAT'S FOR SURE.
HE'S THE HEIR TO THE SAKURA FAMILY.
HE'S NOBILITY?!
WOW...
I SEE NOW! THAT'S WHY HE WAS SO DIFFERENT FROM THE OTHERS! BEING NOBILITY MEANS THAT HE'S QUITE A HIGH-RANKING ANGEL.
SO, CHIHAYA...
...ARE YOU ENJOYING SCHOOL?

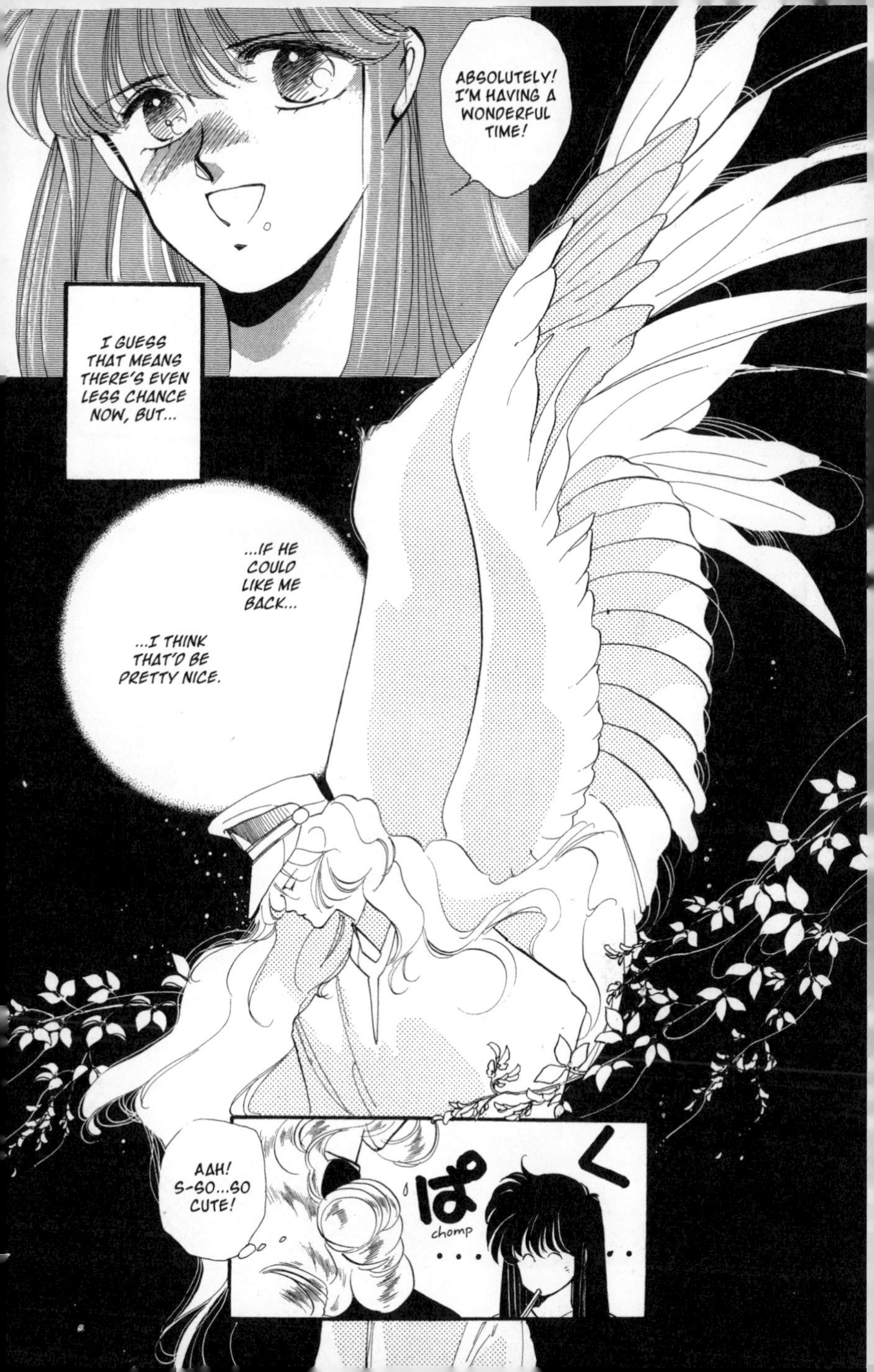
ABSOLUTELY! I'M HAVING A WONDERFUL TIME!
I GUESS THAT MEANS THERE'S EVEN LESS CHANCE NOW, BUT...
...IF HE COULD LIKE ME BACK...
...I THINK THAT'D BE PRETTY NICE.
ぱく
chomp
...
AAH! S-SO...SO CUTE!

ETERNAL ROMANCE PART 1 & 2

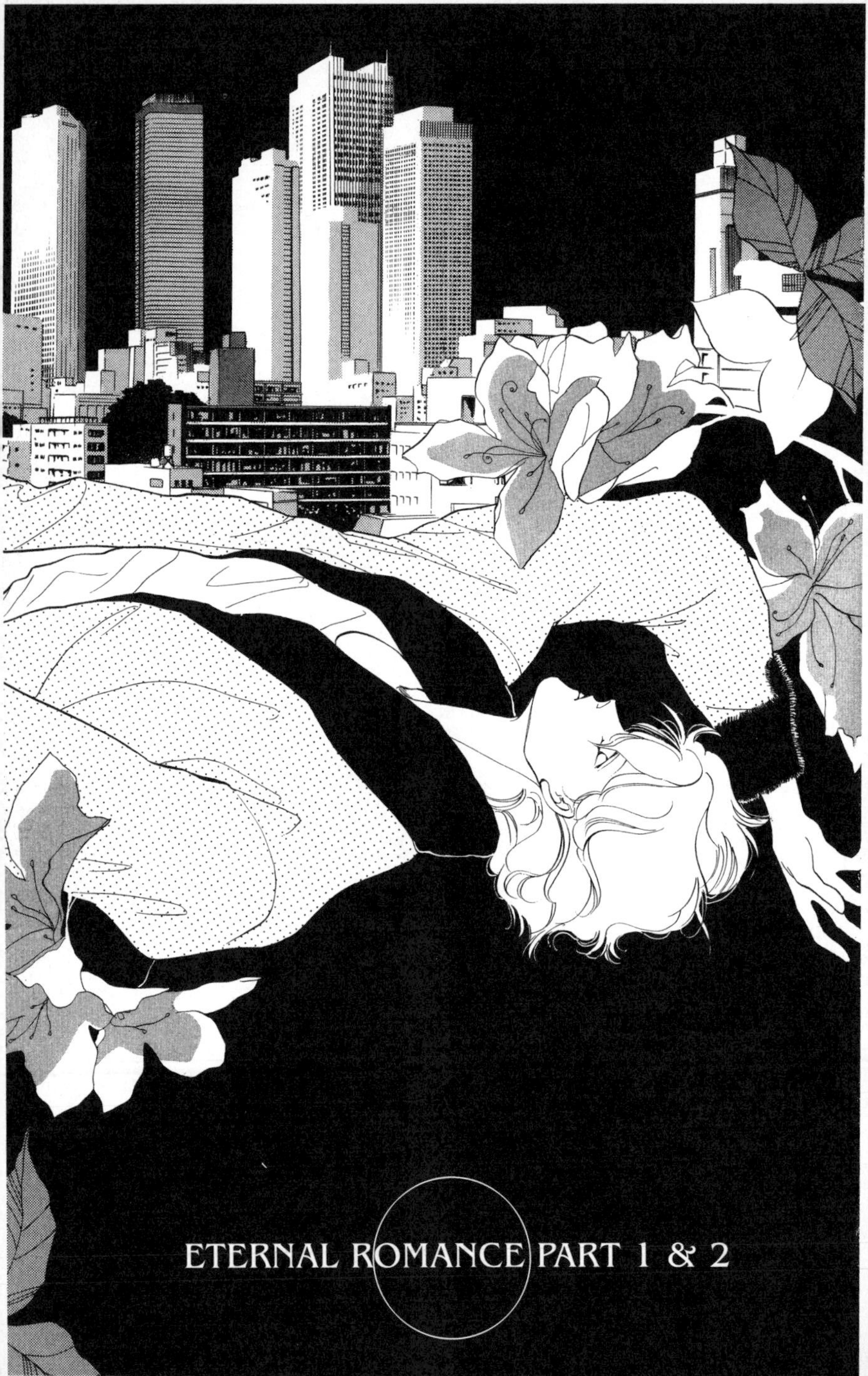

ETERNAL ROMANCE PART 1 & 2

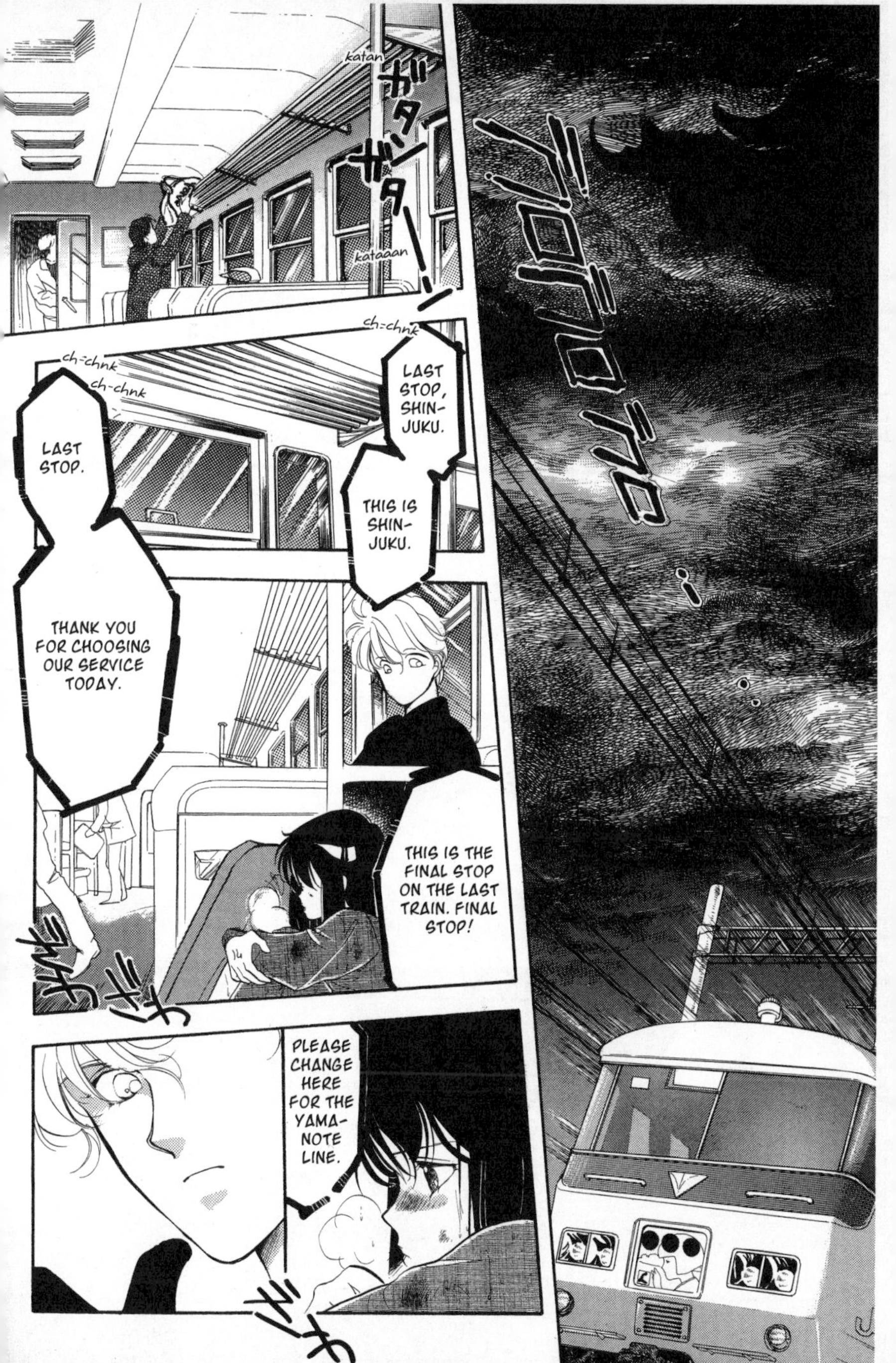
katan
kataaan
ch-chnk
ch-chnk
ch-chnk
LAST STOP, SHIN-JUKU.
THIS IS SHIN-JUKU.
LAST STOP.
THANK YOU FOR CHOOSING OUR SERVICE TODAY.
THIS IS THE FINAL STOP ON THE LAST TRAIN. FINAL STOP!
PLEASE CHANGE HERE FOR THE YAMA-NOTE LINE.

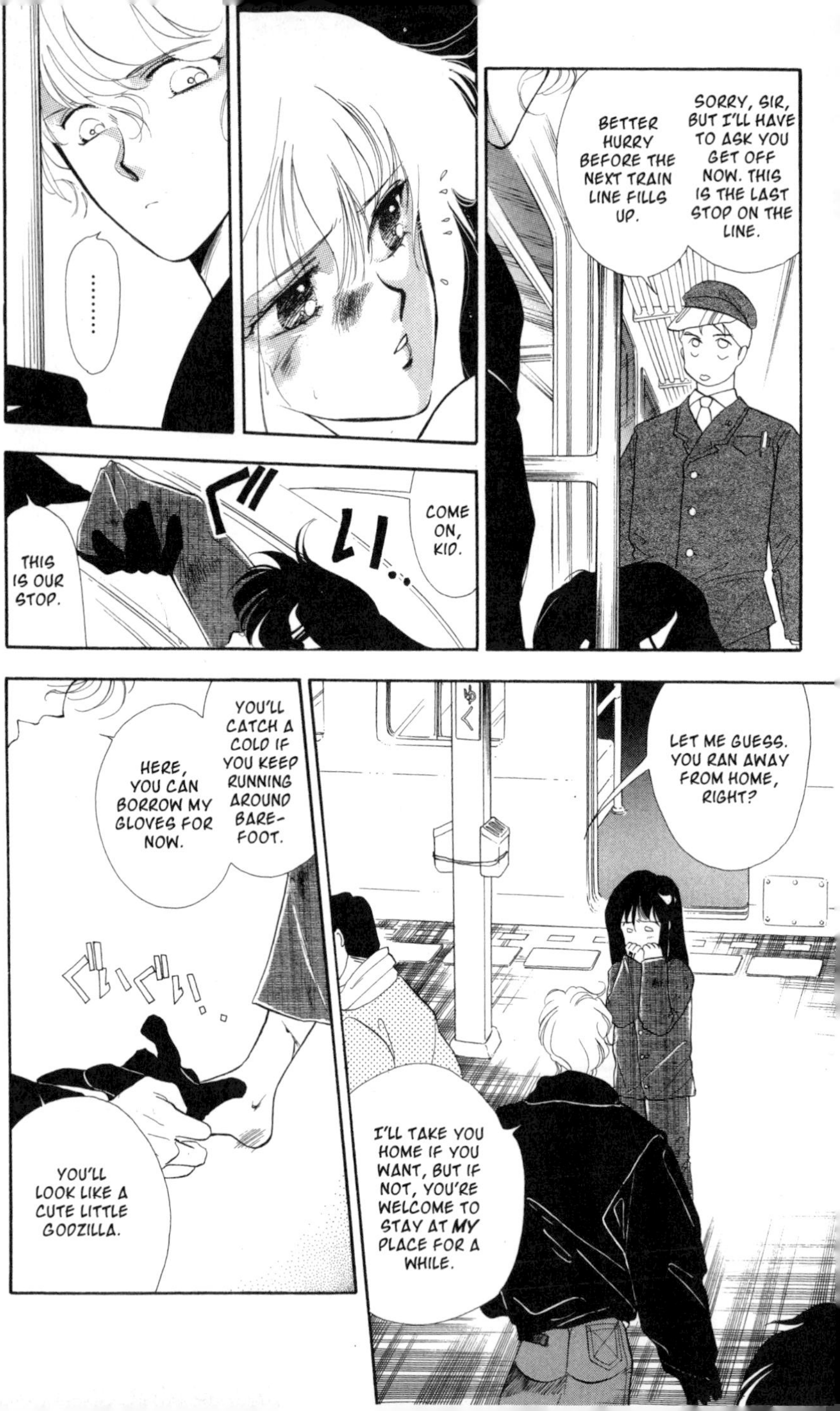
SORRY, SIR, BUT I'LL HAVE TO ASK YOU GET OFF NOW. THIS IS THE LAST STOP ON THE LINE.
BETTER HURRY BEFORE THE NEXT TRAIN LINE FILLS UP.
......
COME ON, KID.
THIS IS OUR STOP.
LET ME GUESS. YOU RAN AWAY FROM HOME, RIGHT?
I'LL TAKE YOU HOME IF YOU WANT, BUT IF NOT, YOU'RE WELCOME TO STAY AT MY PLACE FOR A WHILE.
YOU'LL CATCH A COLD IF YOU KEEP RUNNING AROUND BARE-FOOT.
HERE, YOU CAN BORROW MY GLOVES FOR NOW.
YOU'LL LOOK LIKE A CUTE LITTLE GODZILLA.

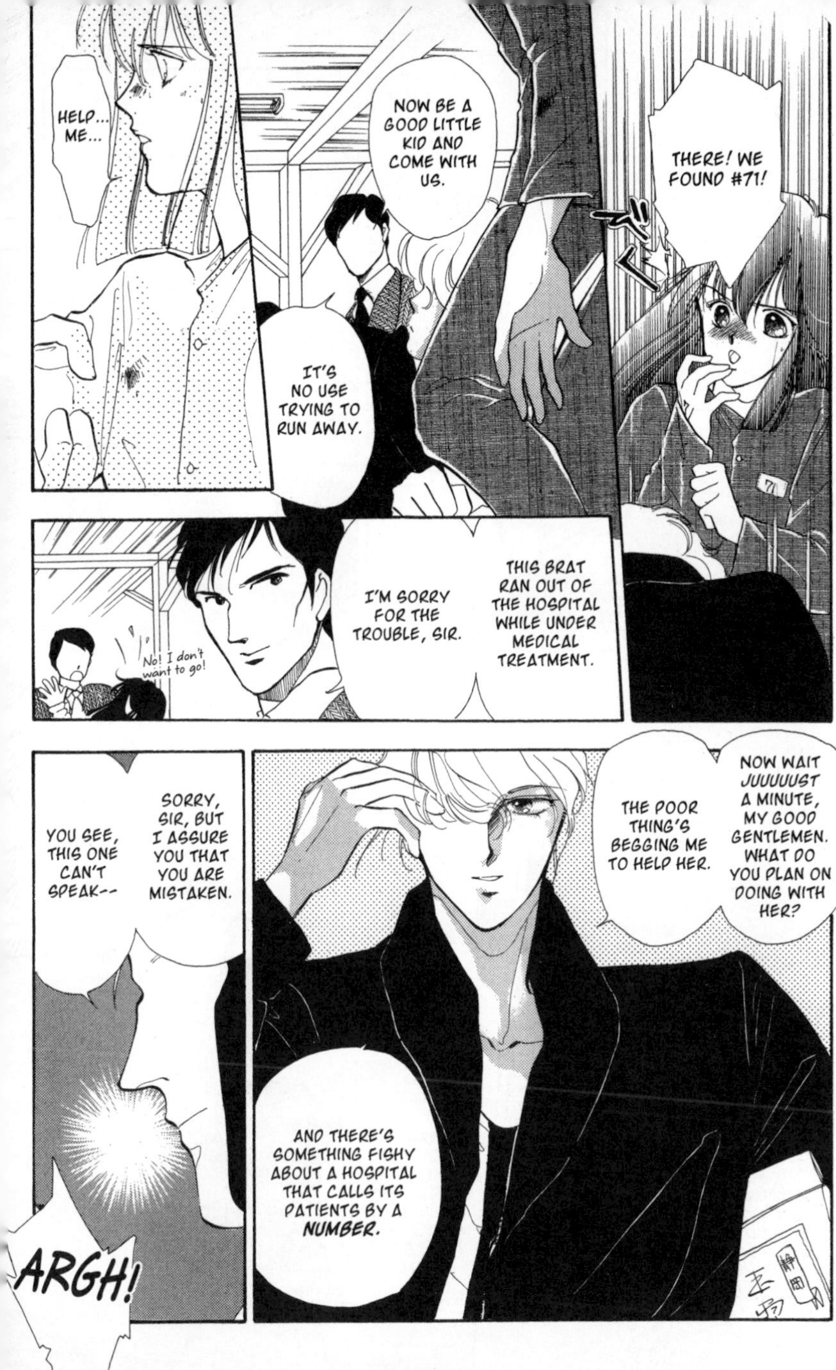

THERE! WE FOUND #71!
NOW BE A GOOD LITTLE KID AND COME WITH US.
IT'S NO USE TRYING TO RUN AWAY.
HELP... ME...
THIS BRAT RAN OUT OF THE HOSPITAL WHILE UNDER MEDICAL TREATMENT.
I'M SORRY FOR THE TROUBLE, SIR.
No! I don't want to go!
NOW WAIT JUUUUUST A MINUTE, MY GOOD GENTLEMEN. WHAT DO YOU PLAN ON DOING WITH HER?
THE POOR THING'S BEGGING ME TO HELP HER.
AND THERE'S SOMETHING FISHY ABOUT A HOSPITAL THAT CALLS ITS PATIENTS BY A **NUMBER**.
SORRY, SIR, BUT I ASSURE YOU THAT YOU ARE MISTAKEN.
YOU SEE, THIS ONE CAN'T SPEAK--
ARGH!

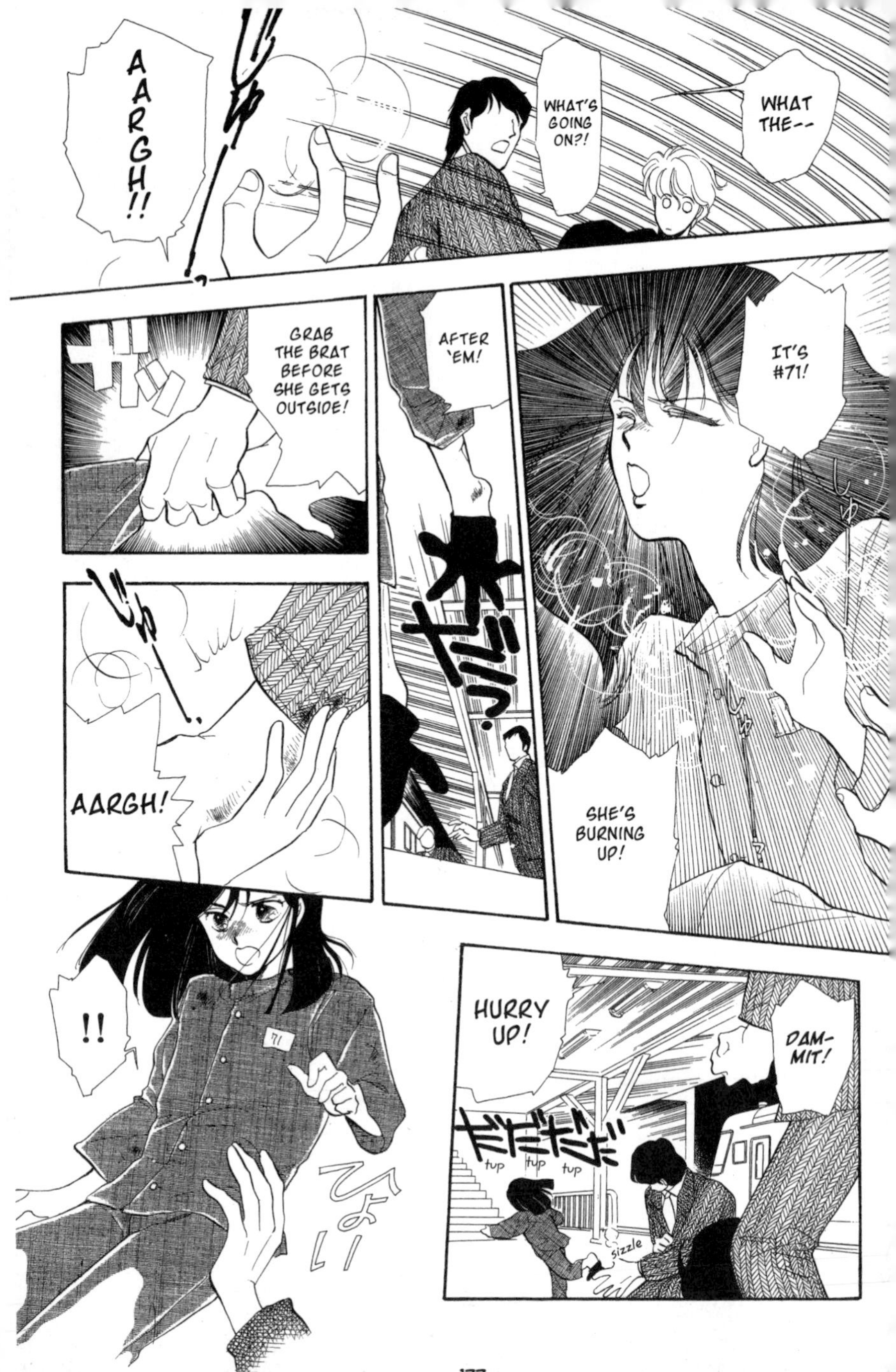
WHAT THE--
WHAT'S GOING ON?!
AARGH!!
IT'S #71!
SHE'S BURNING UP!
AFTER 'EM!
GRAB THE BRAT BEFORE SHE GETS OUTSIDE!
AARGH!
DAM-MIT!
HURRY UP!
tup tup tup
sizzle
!!

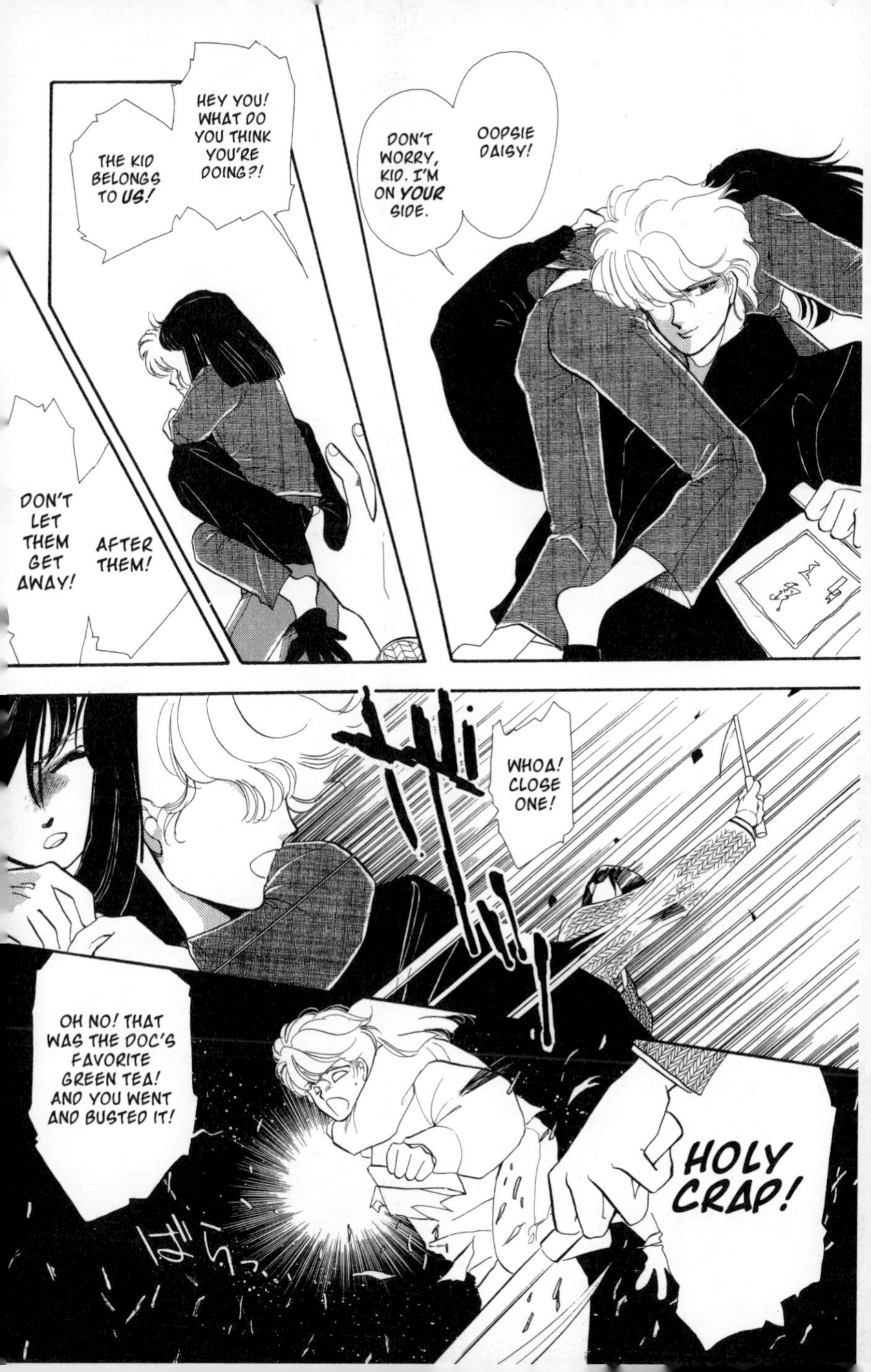
OOPSIE DAISY!
DON'T WORRY, KID. I'M ON *YOUR* SIDE.
HEY YOU! WHAT DO YOU THINK YOU'RE DOING?!
THE KID BELONGS TO *US!*
AFTER THEM!
DON'T LET THEM GET AWAY!
WHOA! CLOSE ONE!
HOLY CRAP!
OH NO! THAT WAS THE DOC'S FAVORITE GREEN TEA! AND YOU WENT AND BUSTED IT!
ばらっ

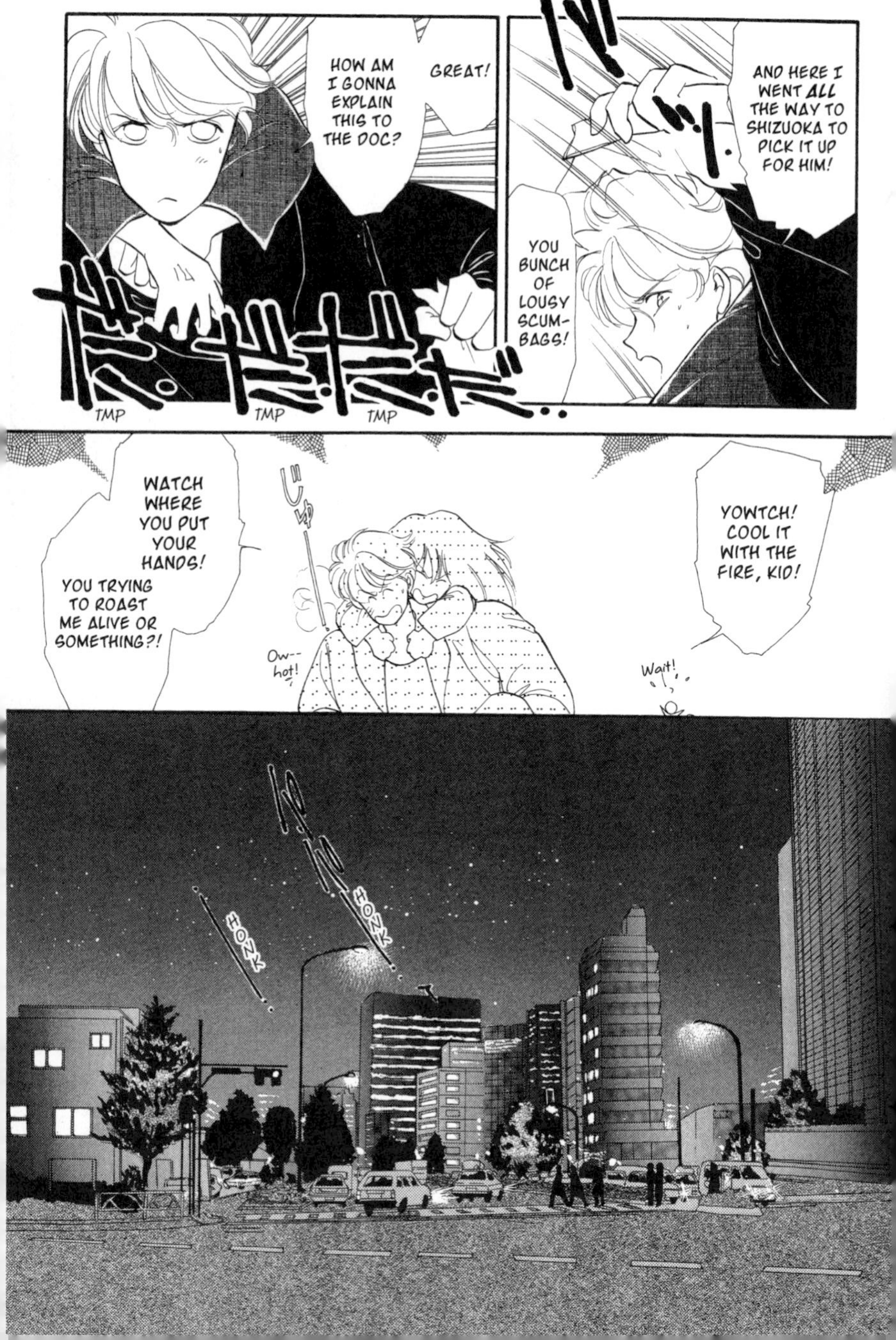
AND HERE I WENT ALL THE WAY TO SHIZUOKA TO PICK IT UP FOR HIM!
YOU BUNCH OF LOUSY SCUM-BAGS!
GREAT!
HOW AM I GONNA EXPLAIN THIS TO THE DOC?
TMP
TMP
TMP
YOWTCH! COOL IT WITH THE FIRE, KID!
Wait!
Ow-- hot!
WATCH WHERE YOU PUT YOUR HANDS!
YOU TRYING TO ROAST ME ALIVE OR SOMETHING?!
HONK
HONK

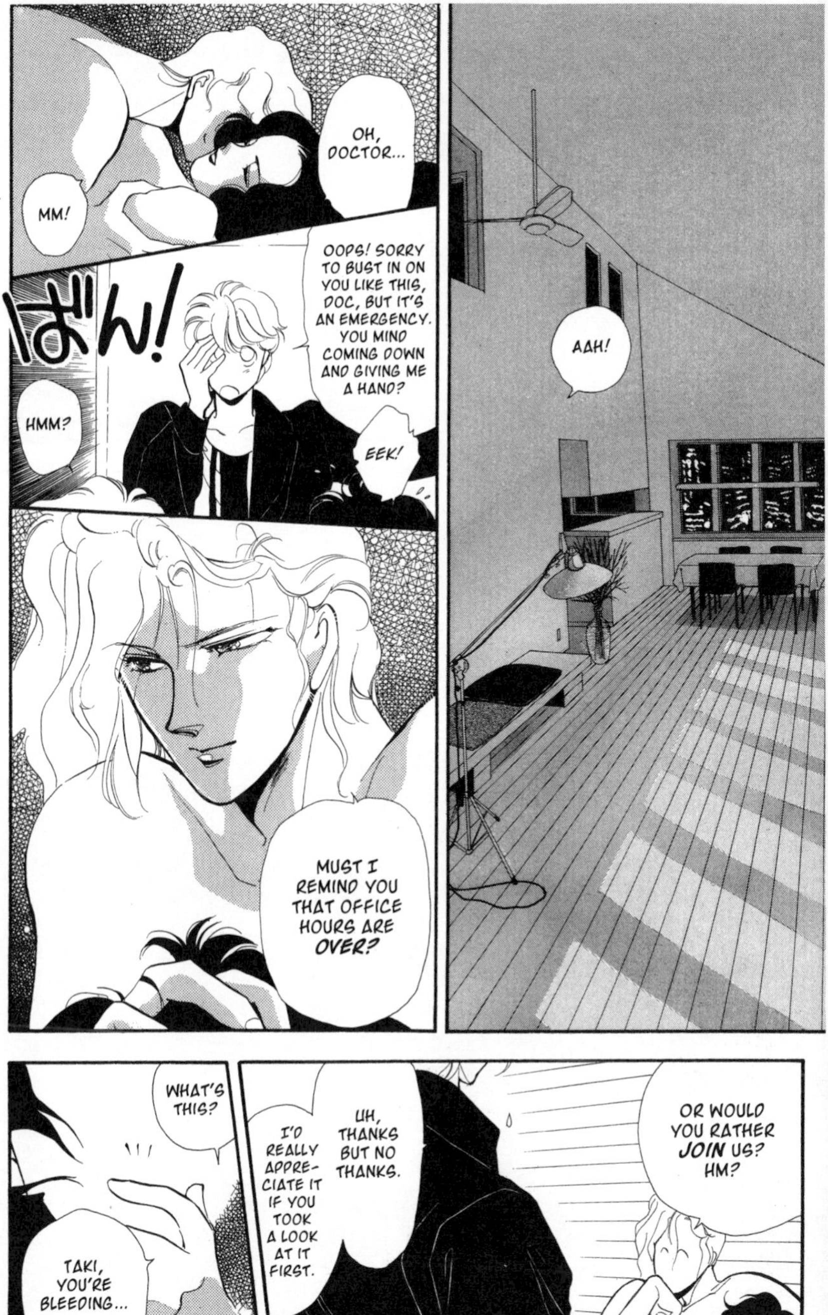

AAH!
OH, DOCTOR...
MM!
ばん!
OOPS! SORRY TO BUST IN ON YOU LIKE THIS, DOC, BUT IT'S AN EMERGENCY. YOU MIND COMING DOWN AND GIVING ME A HAND?
HMM?
EEK!
MUST I REMIND YOU THAT OFFICE HOURS ARE **OVER?**
OR WOULD YOU RATHER **JOIN** US? HM?
UH, THANKS BUT NO THANKS.
I'D REALLY APPRE-CIATE IT IF YOU TOOK A LOOK AT IT FIRST.
WHAT'S THIS?
TAKI, YOU'RE BLEEDING...

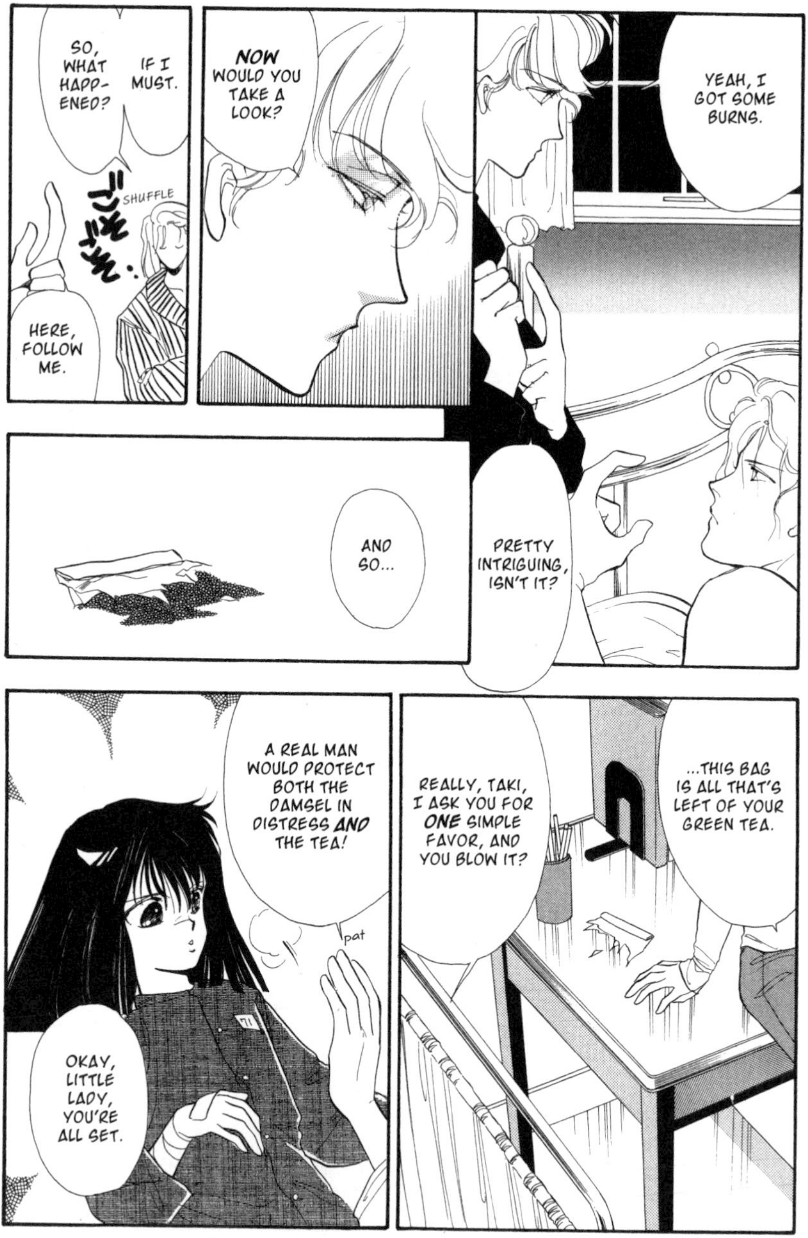
YEAH, I GOT SOME BURNS.
PRETTY INTRIGUING, ISN'T IT?
NOW WOULD YOU TAKE A LOOK?
IF I MUST.
SO, WHAT HAPP-ENED?
SHUFFLE
HERE, FOLLOW ME.
AND SO...
...THIS BAG IS ALL THAT'S LEFT OF YOUR GREEN TEA.
REALLY, TAKI, I ASK YOU FOR **ONE** SIMPLE FAVOR, AND YOU BLOW IT?
A REAL MAN WOULD PROTECT BOTH THE DAMSEL IN DISTRESS **AND** THE TEA!
pat
OKAY, LITTLE LADY, YOU'RE ALL SET.

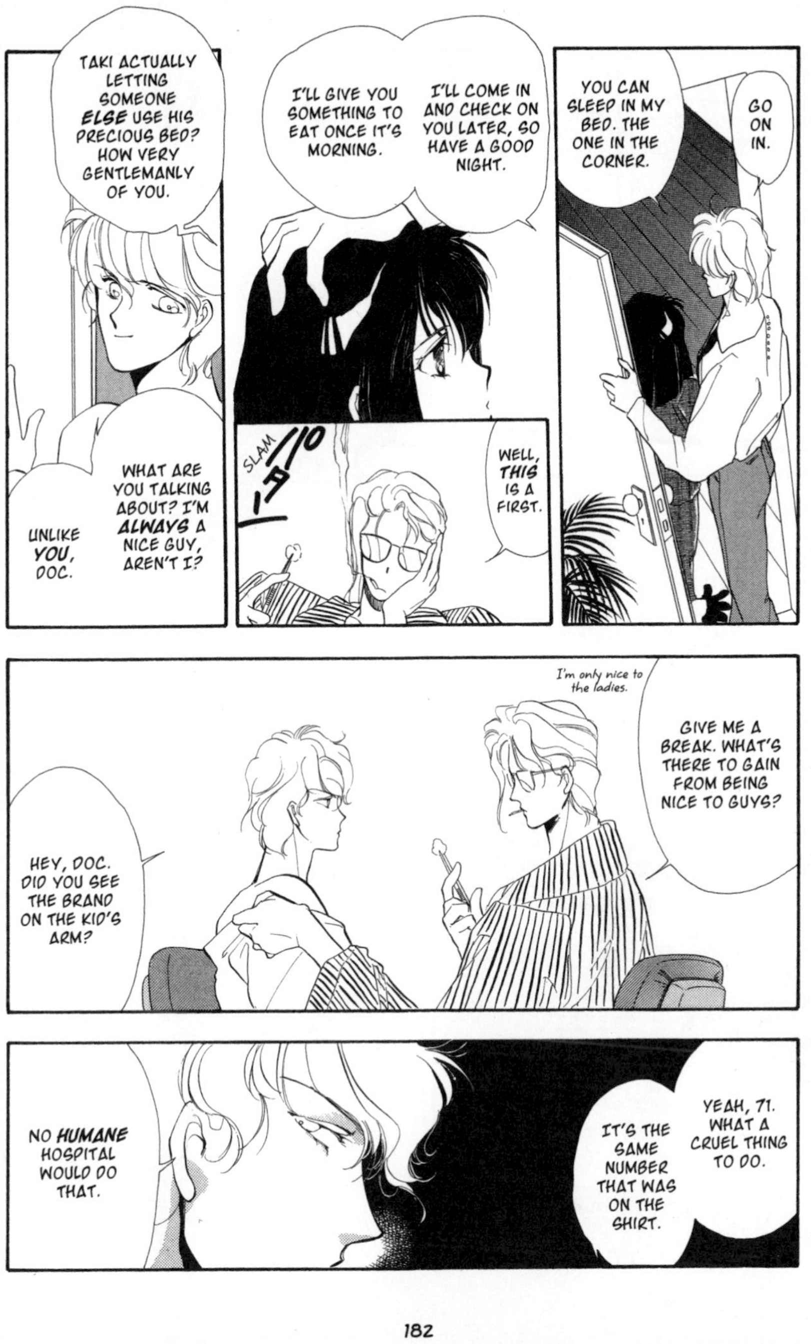
GO ON IN.
YOU CAN SLEEP IN MY BED. THE ONE IN THE CORNER.
I'LL COME IN AND CHECK ON YOU LATER, SO HAVE A GOOD NIGHT.
I'LL GIVE YOU SOMETHING TO EAT ONCE IT'S MORNING.
SLAM
WELL, THIS IS A FIRST.
TAKI ACTUALLY LETTING SOMEONE ELSE USE HIS PRECIOUS BED? HOW VERY GENTLEMANLY OF YOU.
WHAT ARE YOU TALKING ABOUT? I'M ALWAYS A NICE GUY, AREN'T I?
UNLIKE YOU, DOC.
I'm only nice to the ladies.
GIVE ME A BREAK. WHAT'S THERE TO GAIN FROM BEING NICE TO GUYS?
HEY, DOC. DID YOU SEE THE BRAND ON THE KID'S ARM?
YEAH, 71. WHAT A CRUEL THING TO DO.
IT'S THE SAME NUMBER THAT WAS ON THE SHIRT.
NO HUMANE HOSPITAL WOULD DO THAT.

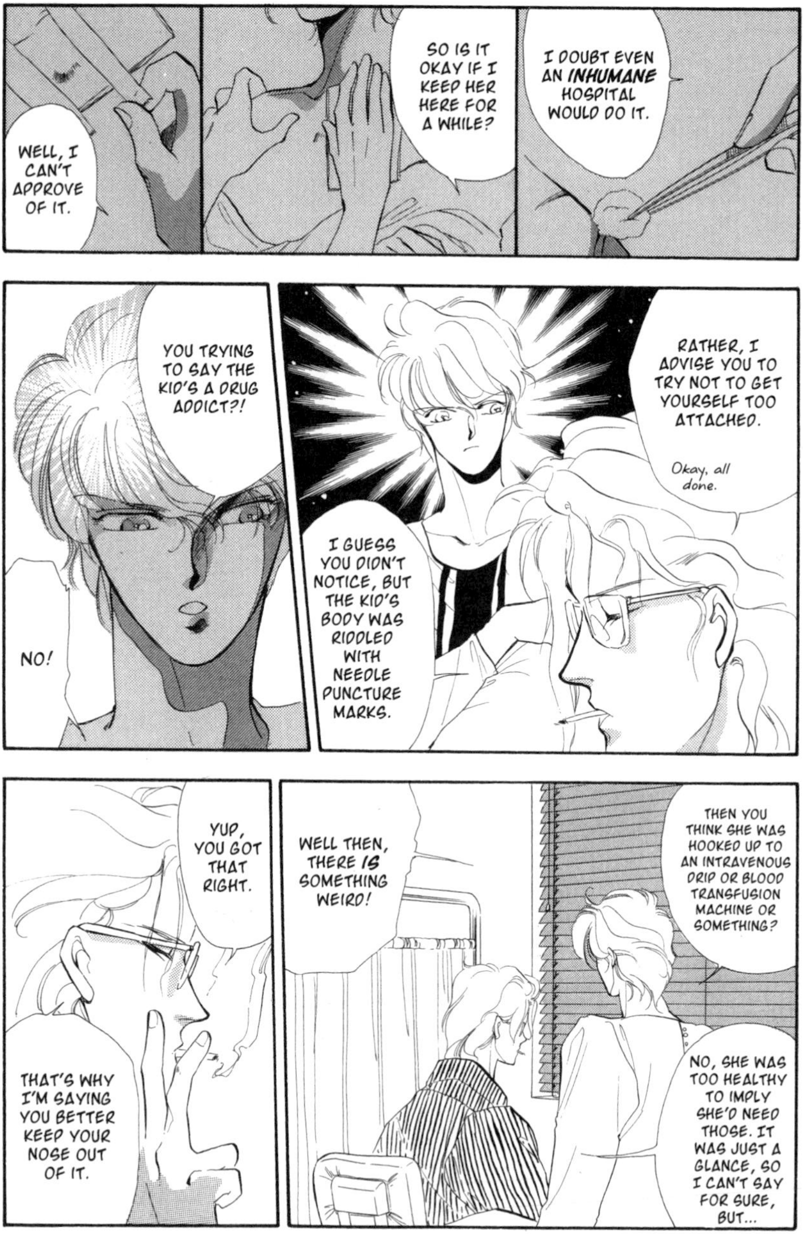
I DOUBT EVEN AN ***INHUMANE*** HOSPITAL WOULD DO IT.
SO IS IT OKAY IF I KEEP HER HERE FOR A WHILE?
WELL, I CAN'T APPROVE OF IT.
RATHER, I ADVISE YOU TO TRY NOT TO GET YOURSELF TOO ATTACHED.
Okay, all done.
I GUESS YOU DIDN'T NOTICE, BUT THE KID'S BODY WAS RIDDLED WITH NEEDLE PUNCTURE MARKS.
YOU TRYING TO SAY THE KID'S A DRUG ADDICT?!
NO!
THEN YOU THINK SHE WAS HOOKED UP TO AN INTRAVENOUS DRIP OR BLOOD TRANSFUSION MACHINE OR SOMETHING?
NO, SHE WAS TOO HEALTHY TO IMPLY SHE'D NEED THOSE. IT WAS JUST A GLANCE, SO I CAN'T SAY FOR SURE, BUT...
WELL THEN, THERE *IS* SOMETHING WEIRD!
YUP, YOU GOT THAT RIGHT.
THAT'S WHY I'M SAYING YOU BETTER KEEP YOUR NOSE OUT OF IT.

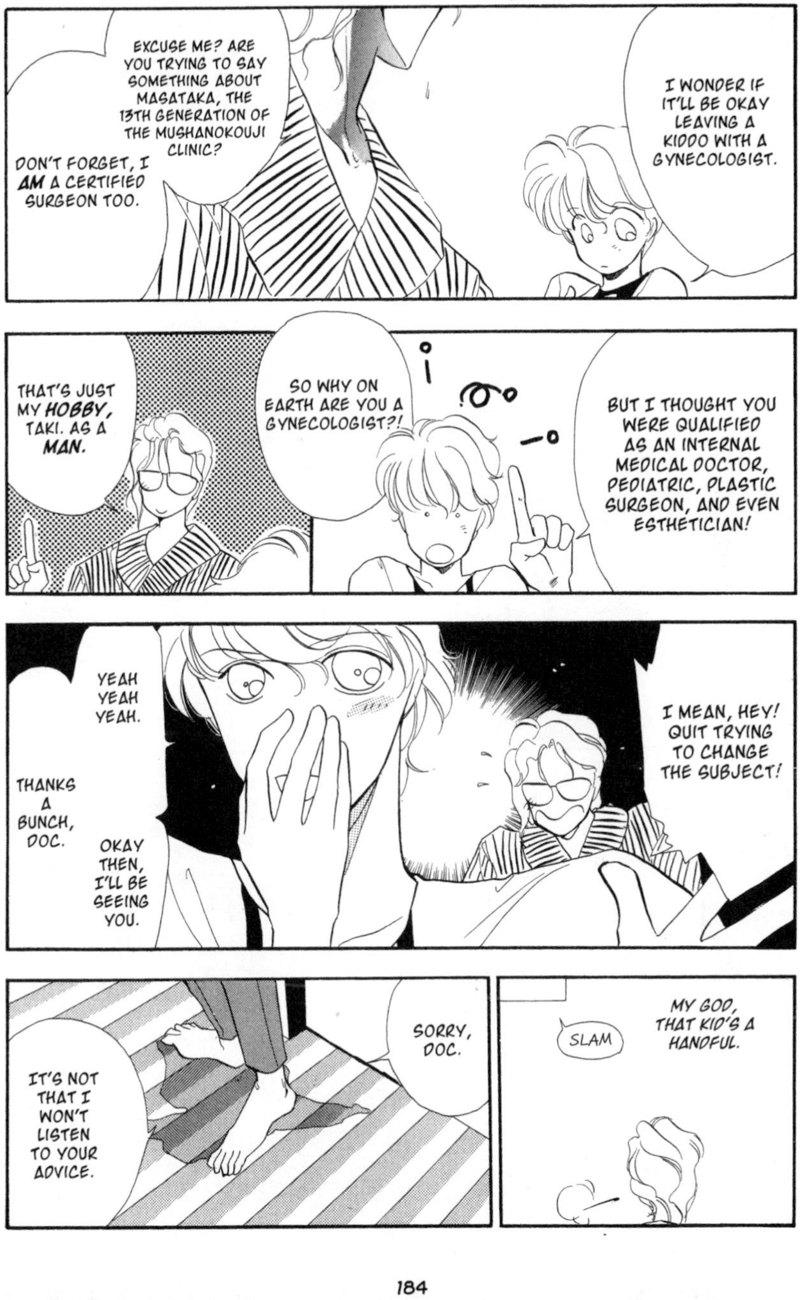
I WONDER IF IT'LL BE OKAY LEAVING A KIDDO WITH A GYNECOLOGIST.
EXCUSE ME? ARE YOU TRYING TO SAY SOMETHING ABOUT MASATAKA, THE 13TH GENERATION OF THE MUSHANOKOUJI CLINIC?
DON'T FORGET, I AM A CERTIFIED SURGEON TOO.
BUT I THOUGHT YOU WERE QUALIFIED AS AN INTERNAL MEDICAL DOCTOR, PEDIATRIC, PLASTIC SURGEON, AND EVEN ESTHETICIAN!
SO WHY ON EARTH ARE YOU A GYNECOLOGIST?!
THAT'S JUST MY HOBBY, TAKI. AS A MAN.
I MEAN, HEY! QUIT TRYING TO CHANGE THE SUBJECT!
YEAH YEAH YEAH.
OKAY THEN, I'LL BE SEEING YOU.
THANKS A BUNCH, DOC.
MY GOD, THAT KID'S A HANDFUL.
SLAM
SORRY, DOC.
IT'S NOT THAT I WON'T LISTEN TO YOUR ADVICE.

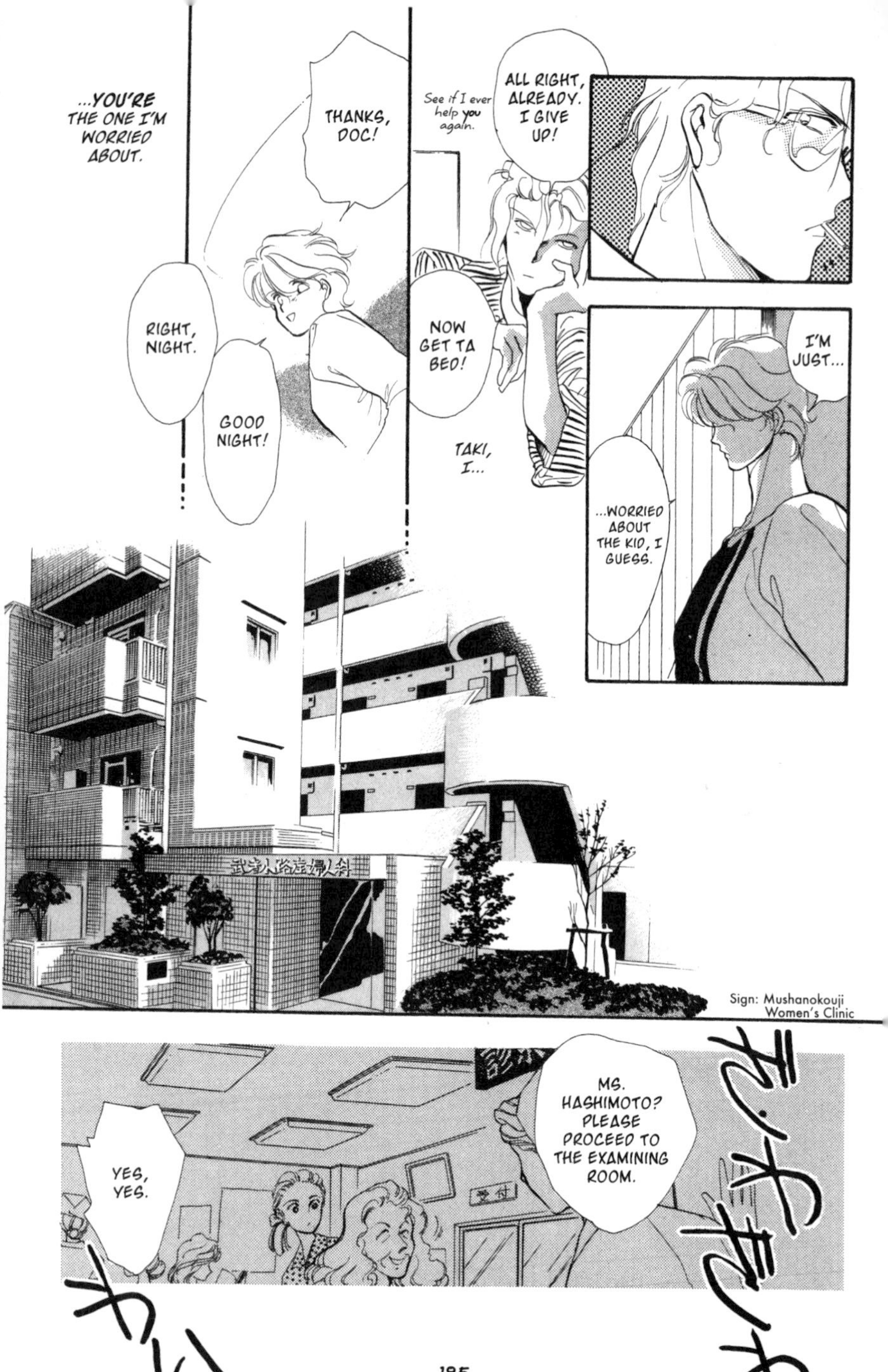
I'M JUST...
...WORRIED ABOUT THE KID, I GUESS.
ALL RIGHT, ALREADY. I GIVE UP!
See if I ever help you again.
NOW GET TA BED!
TAKI, I...
THANKS, DOC!
...YOU'RE THE ONE I'M WORRIED ABOUT.
RIGHT, NIGHT.
GOOD NIGHT!
Sign: Mushanokouji Women's Clinic
MS. HASHIMOTO? PLEASE PROCEED TO THE EXAMINING ROOM.
YES, YES.

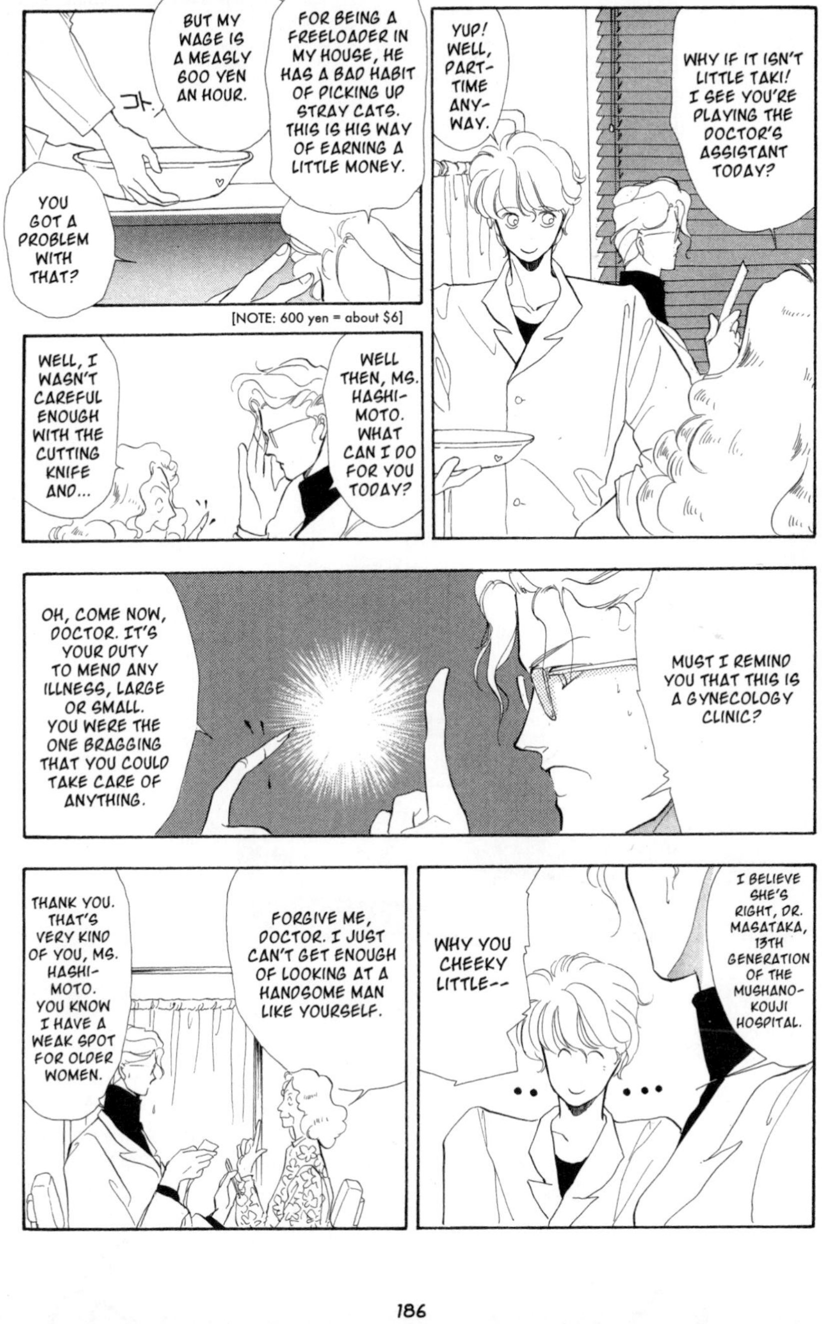
WHY IF IT ISN'T LITTLE TAKI! I SEE YOU'RE PLAYING THE DOCTOR'S ASSISTANT TODAY?
YUP! WELL, PART-TIME ANY-WAY.
FOR BEING A FREELOADER IN MY HOUSE, HE HAS A BAD HABIT OF PICKING UP STRAY CATS. THIS IS HIS WAY OF EARNING A LITTLE MONEY.
BUT MY WAGE IS A MEASLY 600 YEN AN HOUR.
コト
YOU GOT A PROBLEM WITH THAT?
[NOTE: 600 yen = about $6]
WELL THEN, MS. HASHI-MOTO. WHAT CAN I DO FOR YOU TODAY?
WELL, I WASN'T CAREFUL ENOUGH WITH THE CUTTING KNIFE AND...
MUST I REMIND YOU THAT THIS IS A GYNECOLOGY CLINIC?
OH, COME NOW, DOCTOR. IT'S YOUR DUTY TO MEND ANY ILLNESS, LARGE OR SMALL. YOU WERE THE ONE BRAGGING THAT YOU COULD TAKE CARE OF ANYTHING.
I BELIEVE SHE'S RIGHT, DR. MASATAKA, 13TH GENERATION OF THE MUSHANO-KOUJI HOSPITAL.
WHY YOU CHEEKY LITTLE--
•• •••
FORGIVE ME, DOCTOR. I JUST CAN'T GET ENOUGH OF LOOKING AT A HANDSOME MAN LIKE YOURSELF.
THANK YOU. THAT'S VERY KIND OF YOU, MS. HASHI-MOTO. YOU KNOW I HAVE A WEAK SPOT FOR OLDER WOMEN.

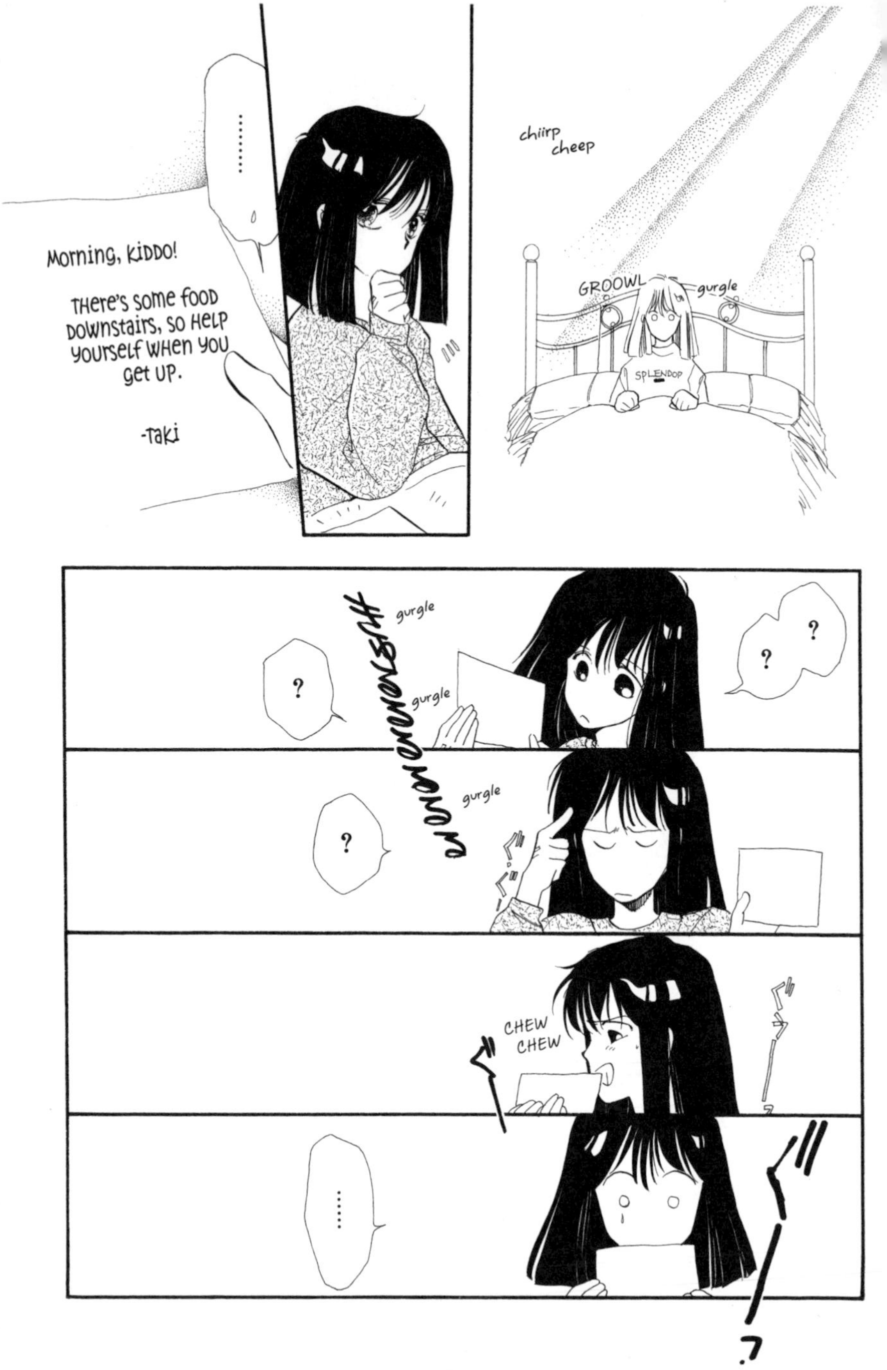
chiirp
cheep
GROOWL
gurgle
SPLENDOP
......
Morning, kiddo!
There's some food downstairs, so help yourself when you get up.
-Taki
?
?
gurgle
gurgle
?
gurgle
?
CHEW
CHEW
......

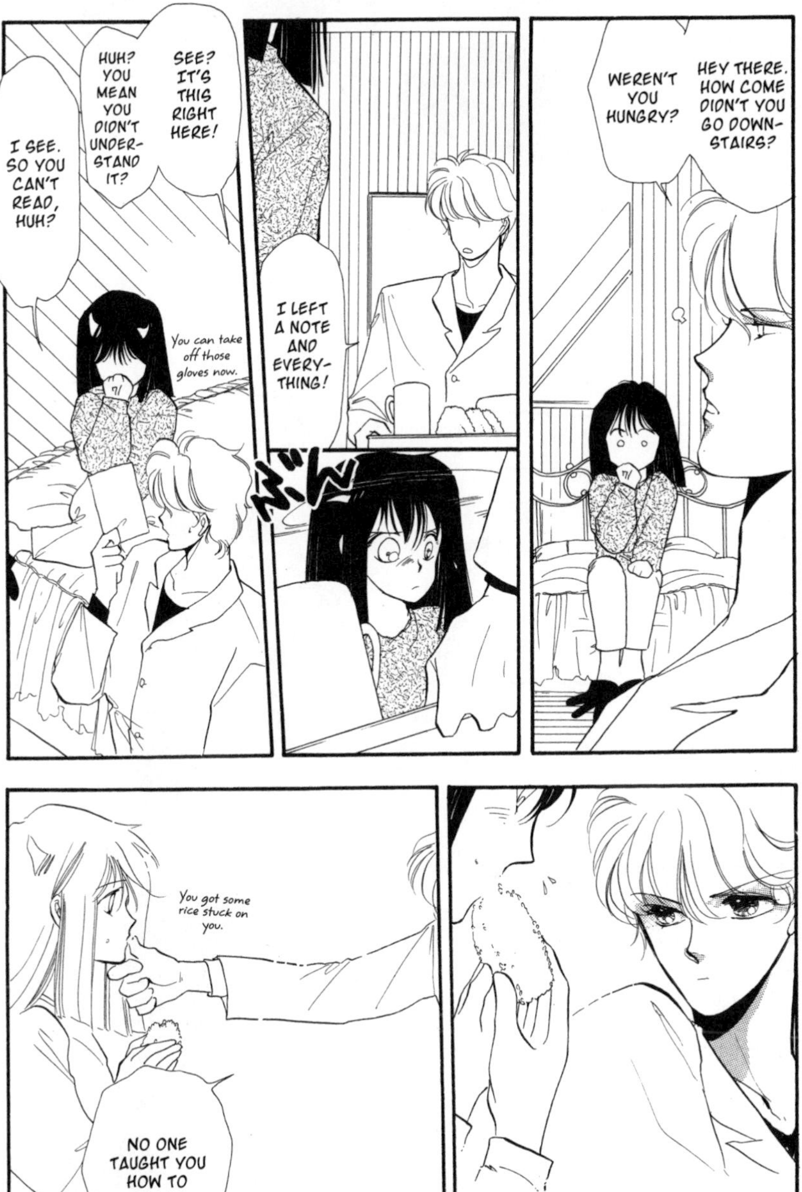
HEY THERE. HOW COME DIDN'T YOU GO DOWN-STAIRS?
WEREN'T YOU HUNGRY?
I LEFT A NOTE AND EVERY-THING!
SEE? IT'S THIS RIGHT HERE!
HUH? YOU MEAN YOU DIDN'T UNDER-STAND IT?
I SEE. SO YOU CAN'T READ, HUH?
You can take off those gloves now.
You got some rice stuck on you.
NO ONE TAUGHT YOU HOW TO READ?

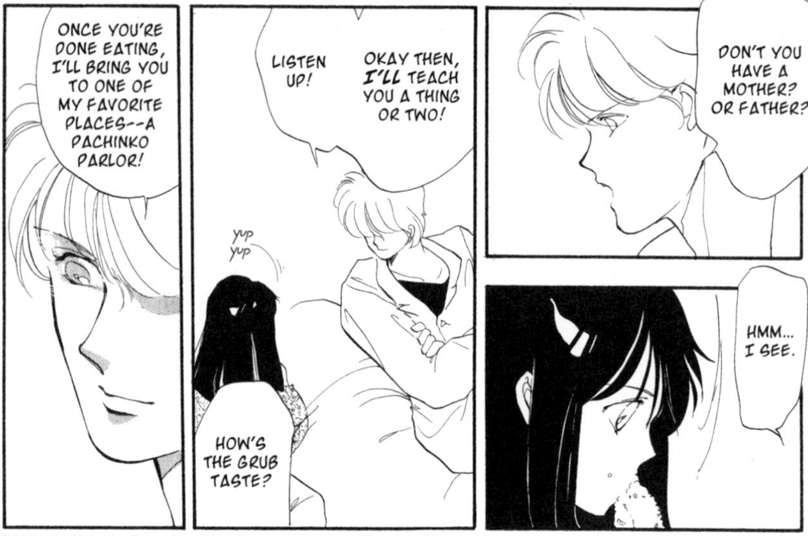
DON'T YOU HAVE A MOTHER? OR FATHER?
HMM... I SEE.
OKAY THEN, *I'LL* TEACH YOU A THING OR TWO!
LISTEN UP!
yup yup
HOW'S THE GRUB TASTE?
ONCE YOU'RE DONE EATING, I'LL BRING YOU TO ONE OF MY FAVORITE PLACES--A PACHINKO PARLOR!

[NOTE: Pachinko is a form of gambling that somewhat resembles pinball.]

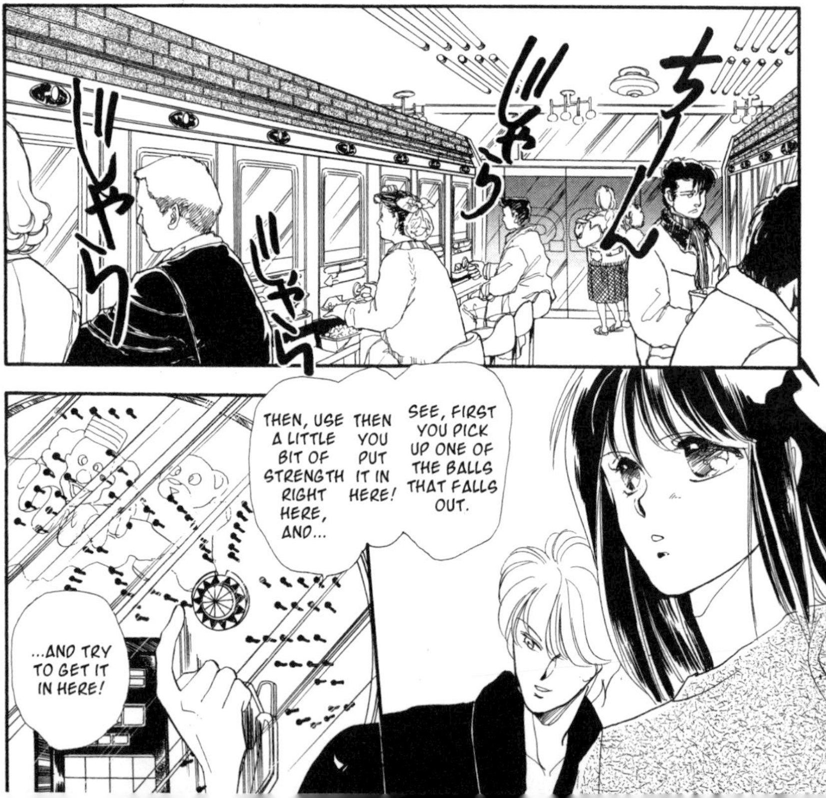
ちーん
じゃら
じゃら
じゃら
SEE, FIRST YOU PICK UP ONE OF THE BALLS THAT FALLS OUT.
THEN YOU PUT IT IN HERE!
THEN, USE A LITTLE BIT OF STRENGTH RIGHT HERE, AND...
...AND TRY TO GET IT IN HERE!

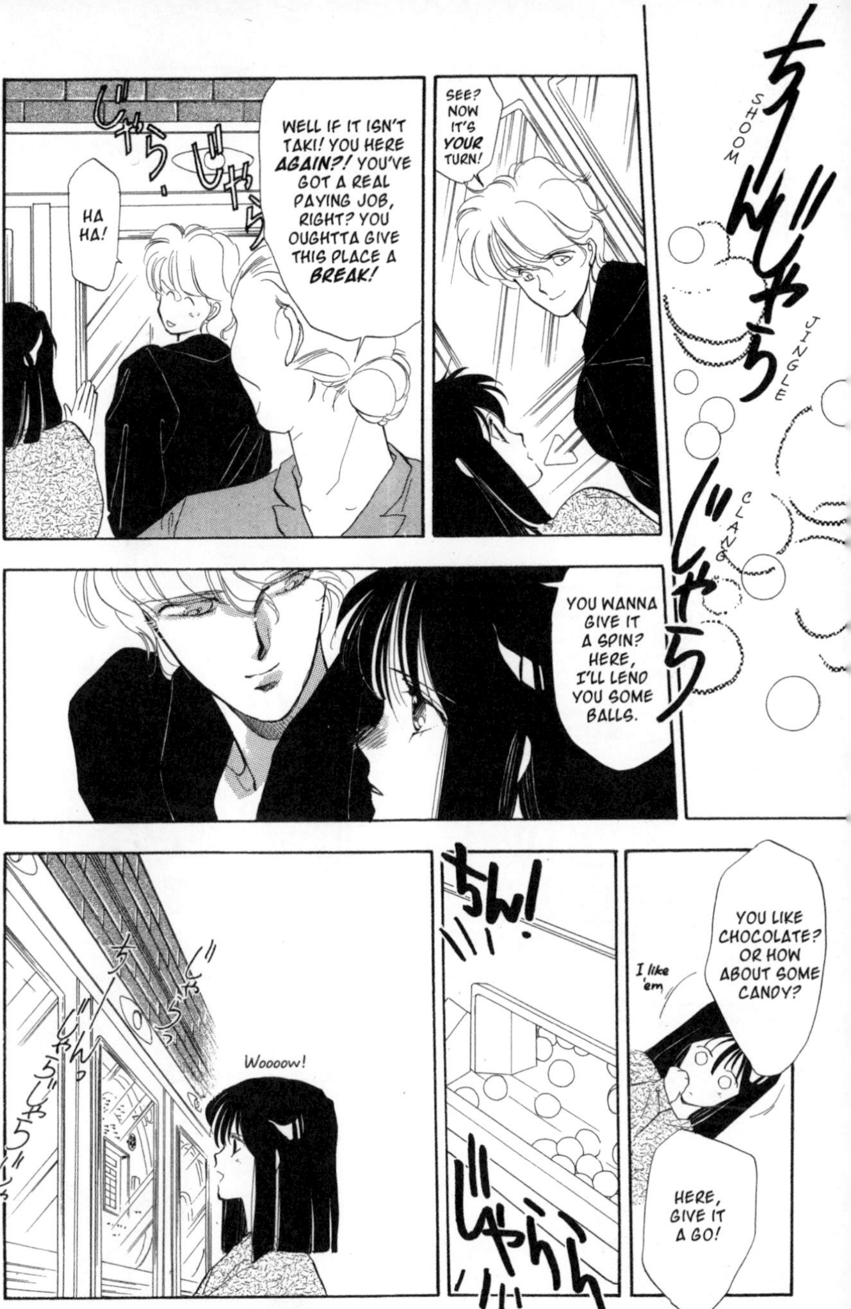
ちーんじゃら
SHOOM
JINGLE
じゃら
CLANG
SEE? NOW IT'S *YOUR* TURN!
WELL IF IT ISN'T TAKI! YOU HERE *AGAIN?!* YOU'VE GOT A REAL PAYING JOB, RIGHT? YOU OUGHTTA GIVE THIS PLACE A *BREAK!*
HA HA!
YOU WANNA GIVE IT A SPIN? HERE, I'LL LEND YOU SOME BALLS.
YOU LIKE CHOCOLATE? OR HOW ABOUT SOME CANDY?
I like 'em
HERE, GIVE IT A GO!
ちん!
じゃららら
Woooow!

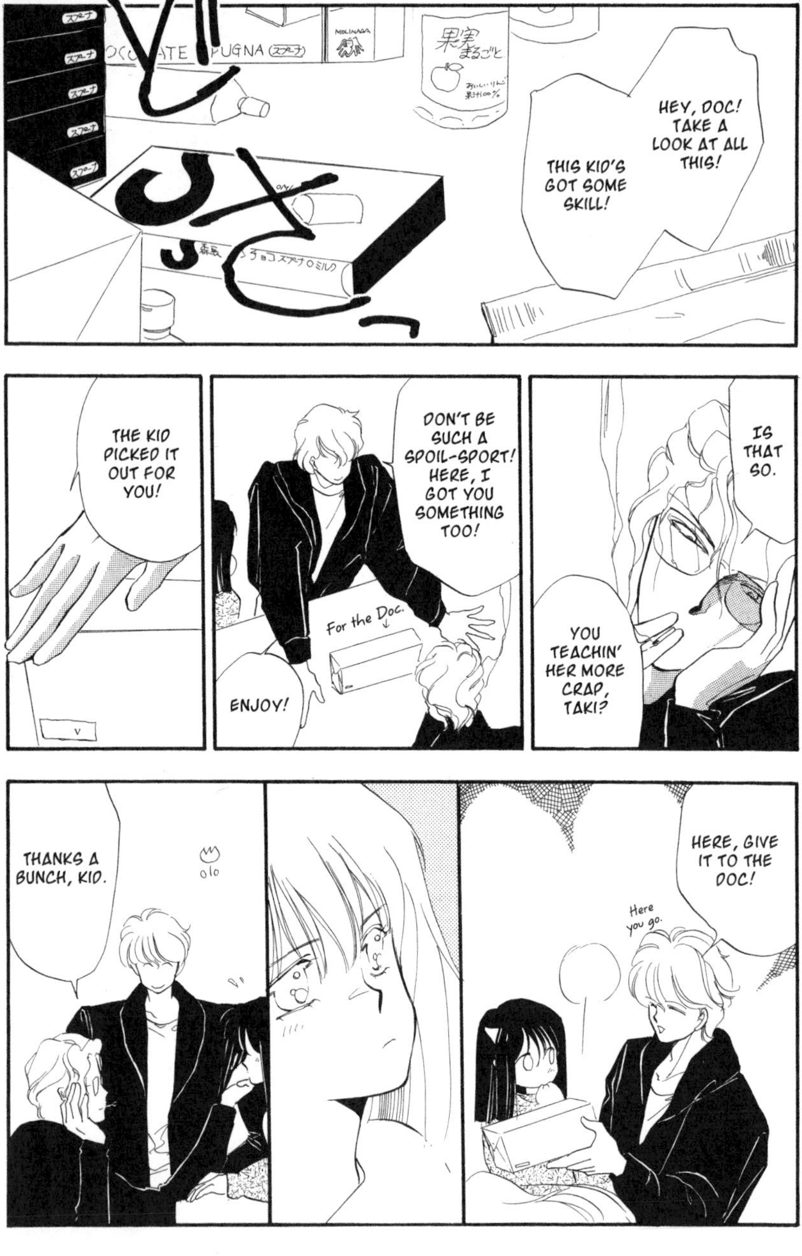
OCOLATE PUGNA (スプーナ)
MOLINAGA
果実まるごと
HEY, DOC! TAKE A LOOK AT ALL THIS!
THIS KID'S GOT SOME SKILL!
IS THAT SO.
YOU TEACHIN' HER MORE CRAP, TAKI?
DON'T BE SUCH A SPOIL-SPORT! HERE, I GOT YOU SOMETHING TOO!
For the Doc.
ENJOY!
THE KID PICKED IT OUT FOR YOU!
HERE, GIVE IT TO THE DOC!
Here you go.
THANKS A BUNCH, KID.

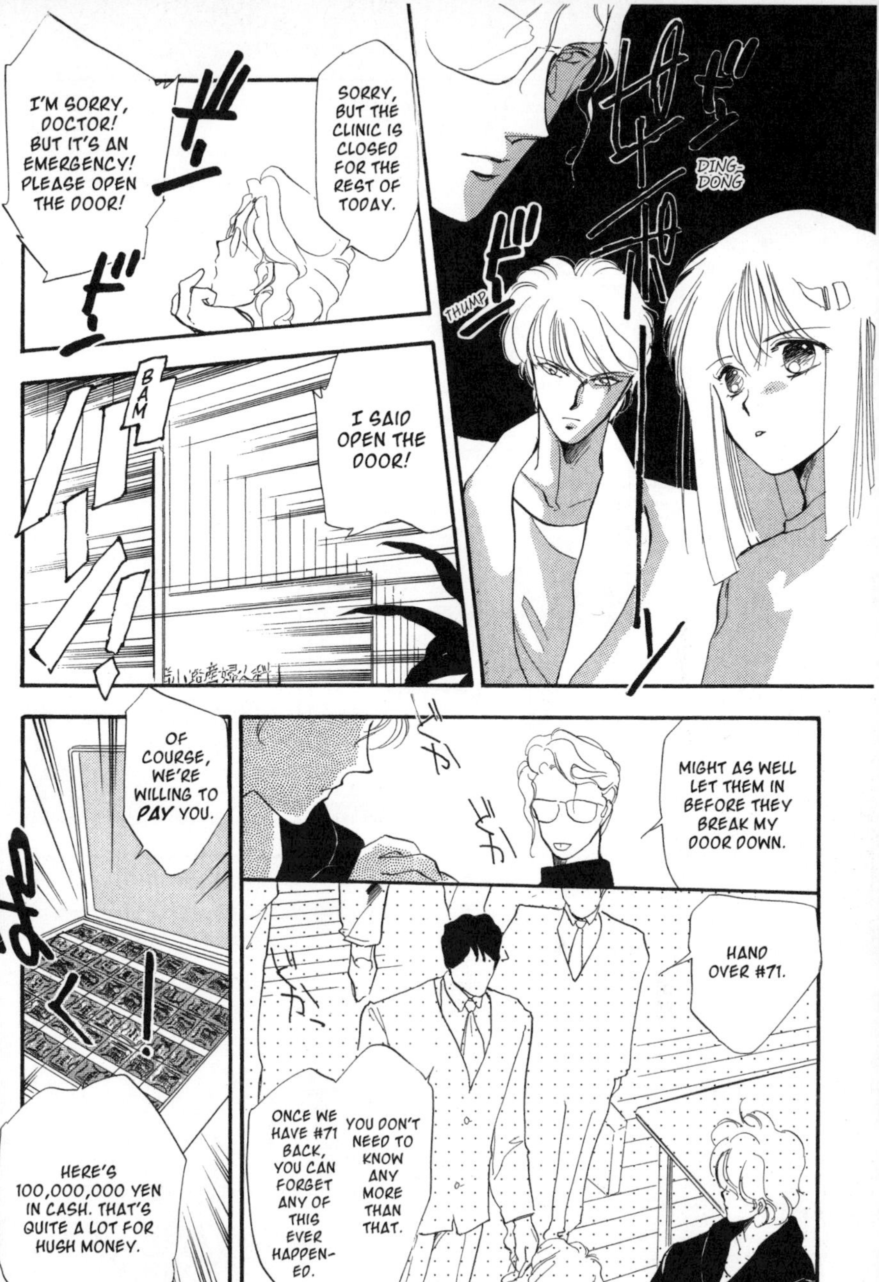
DING-DONG
THUMP
SORRY, BUT THE CLINIC IS CLOSED FOR THE REST OF TODAY.
I'M SORRY, DOCTOR! BUT IT'S AN EMERGENCY! PLEASE OPEN THE DOOR!
I SAID OPEN THE DOOR!
BAM
MIGHT AS WELL LET THEM IN BEFORE THEY BREAK MY DOOR DOWN.
HAND OVER #71.
YOU DON'T NEED TO KNOW ANY MORE THAN THAT.
ONCE WE HAVE #71 BACK, YOU CAN FORGET ANY OF THIS EVER HAPPENED.
OF COURSE, WE'RE WILLING TO **PAY** YOU.
HERE'S 100,000,000 YEN IN CASH. THAT'S QUITE A LOT FOR HUSH MONEY.
[NOTE: 100,000,000 yen = about 1 million US dollars.]

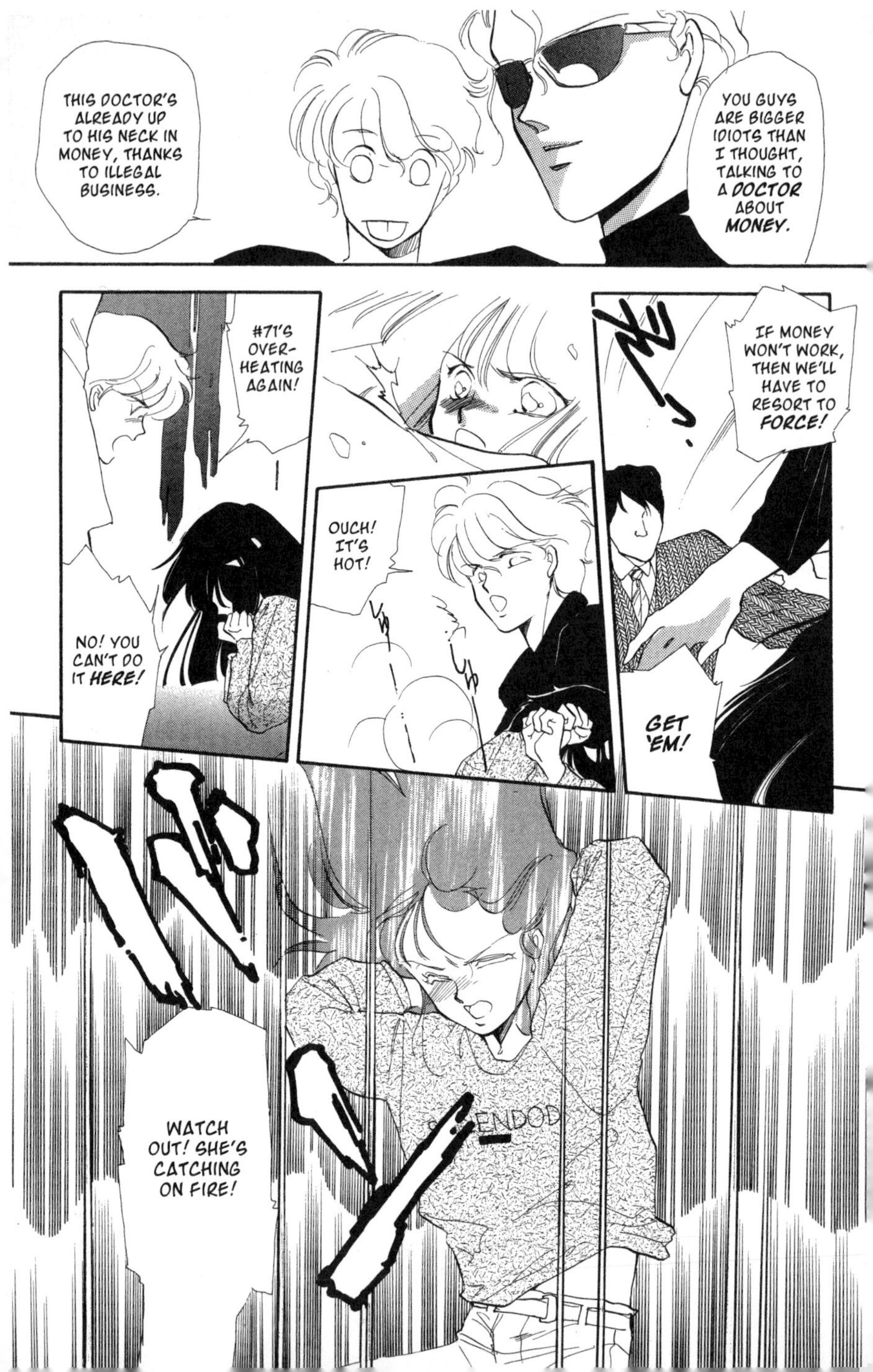
YOU GUYS ARE BIGGER IDIOTS THAN I THOUGHT, TALKING TO A *DOCTOR* ABOUT **MONEY.**
THIS DOCTOR'S ALREADY UP TO HIS NECK IN MONEY, THANKS TO ILLEGAL BUSINESS.
IF MONEY WON'T WORK, THEN WE'LL HAVE TO RESORT TO ***FORCE!***
GET 'EM!
OUCH! IT'S HOT!
#71'S OVER-HEATING AGAIN!
NO! YOU CAN'T DO IT ***HERE!***
WATCH OUT! SHE'S CATCHING ON FIRE!

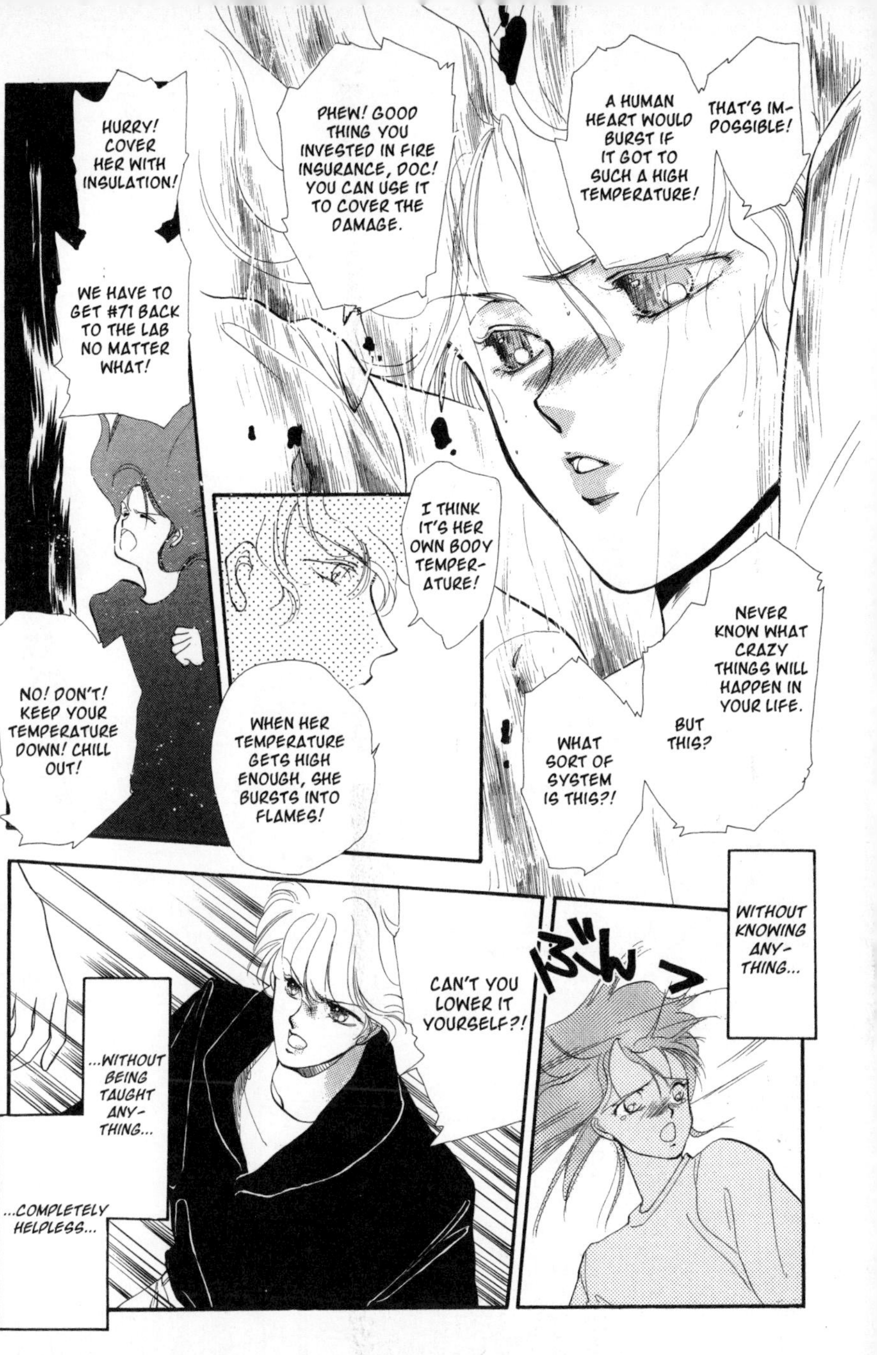
THAT'S IMPOSSIBLE!
A HUMAN HEART WOULD BURST IF IT GOT TO SUCH A HIGH TEMPERATURE!
PHEW! GOOD THING YOU INVESTED IN FIRE INSURANCE, DOC! YOU CAN USE IT TO COVER THE DAMAGE.
I THINK IT'S HER OWN BODY TEMPERATURE!
WHEN HER TEMPERATURE GETS HIGH ENOUGH, SHE BURSTS INTO FLAMES!
NEVER KNOW WHAT CRAZY THINGS WILL HAPPEN IN YOUR LIFE.
BUT THIS?
WHAT SORT OF SYSTEM IS THIS?!
HURRY! COVER HER WITH INSULATION!
WE HAVE TO GET #71 BACK TO THE LAB NO MATTER WHAT!
NO! DON'T! KEEP YOUR TEMPERATURE DOWN! CHILL OUT!
WITHOUT KNOWING ANYTHING...
ぶん
CAN'T YOU LOWER IT YOURSELF?!
...WITHOUT BEING TAUGHT ANYTHING...
...COMPLETELY HELPLESS...

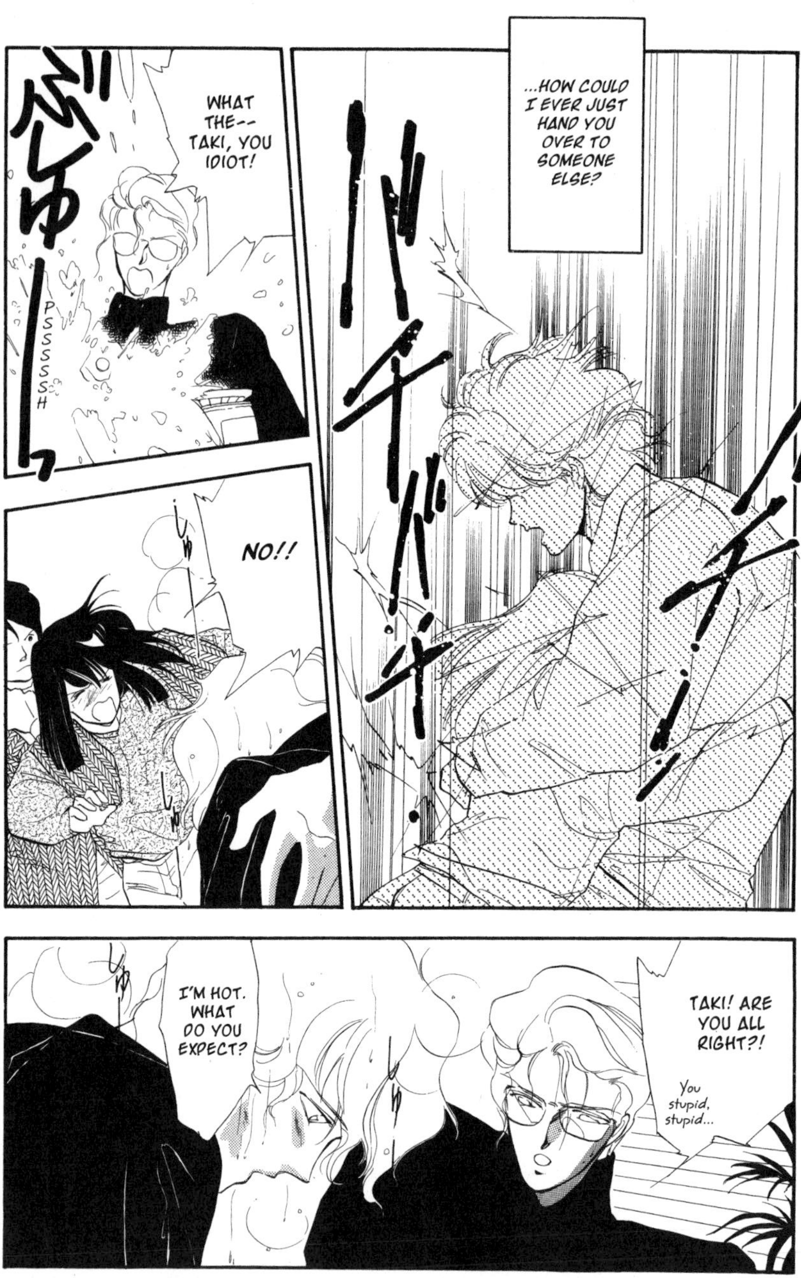
...HOW COULD I EVER JUST HAND YOU OVER TO SOMEONE ELSE?
WHAT THE-- TAKI, YOU IDIOT!
PSSSSSH
NO!!
TAKI! ARE YOU ALL RIGHT?!
You stupid, stupid...
I'M HOT. WHAT DO YOU EXPECT?

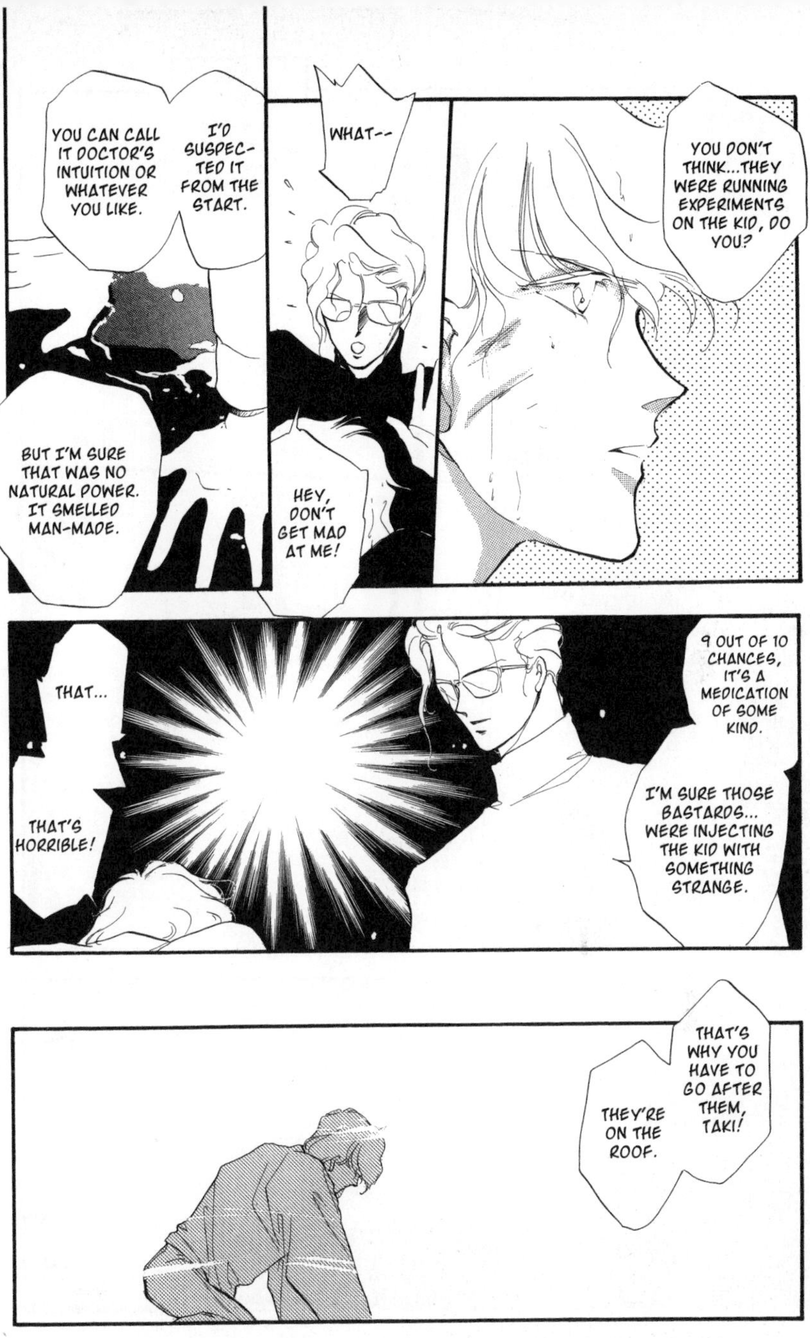
YOU DON'T THINK...THEY WERE RUNNING EXPERIMENTS ON THE KID, DO YOU?
WHAT--
HEY, DON'T GET MAD AT ME!
I'D SUSPECTED IT FROM THE START.
YOU CAN CALL IT DOCTOR'S INTUITION OR WHATEVER YOU LIKE.
BUT I'M SURE THAT WAS NO NATURAL POWER. IT SMELLED MAN-MADE.
9 OUT OF 10 CHANCES, IT'S A MEDICATION OF SOME KIND.
I'M SURE THOSE BASTARDS... WERE INJECTING THE KID WITH SOMETHING STRANGE.
THAT...
THAT'S HORRIBLE!
THAT'S WHY YOU HAVE TO GO AFTER THEM, TAKI!
THEY'RE ON THE ROOF.

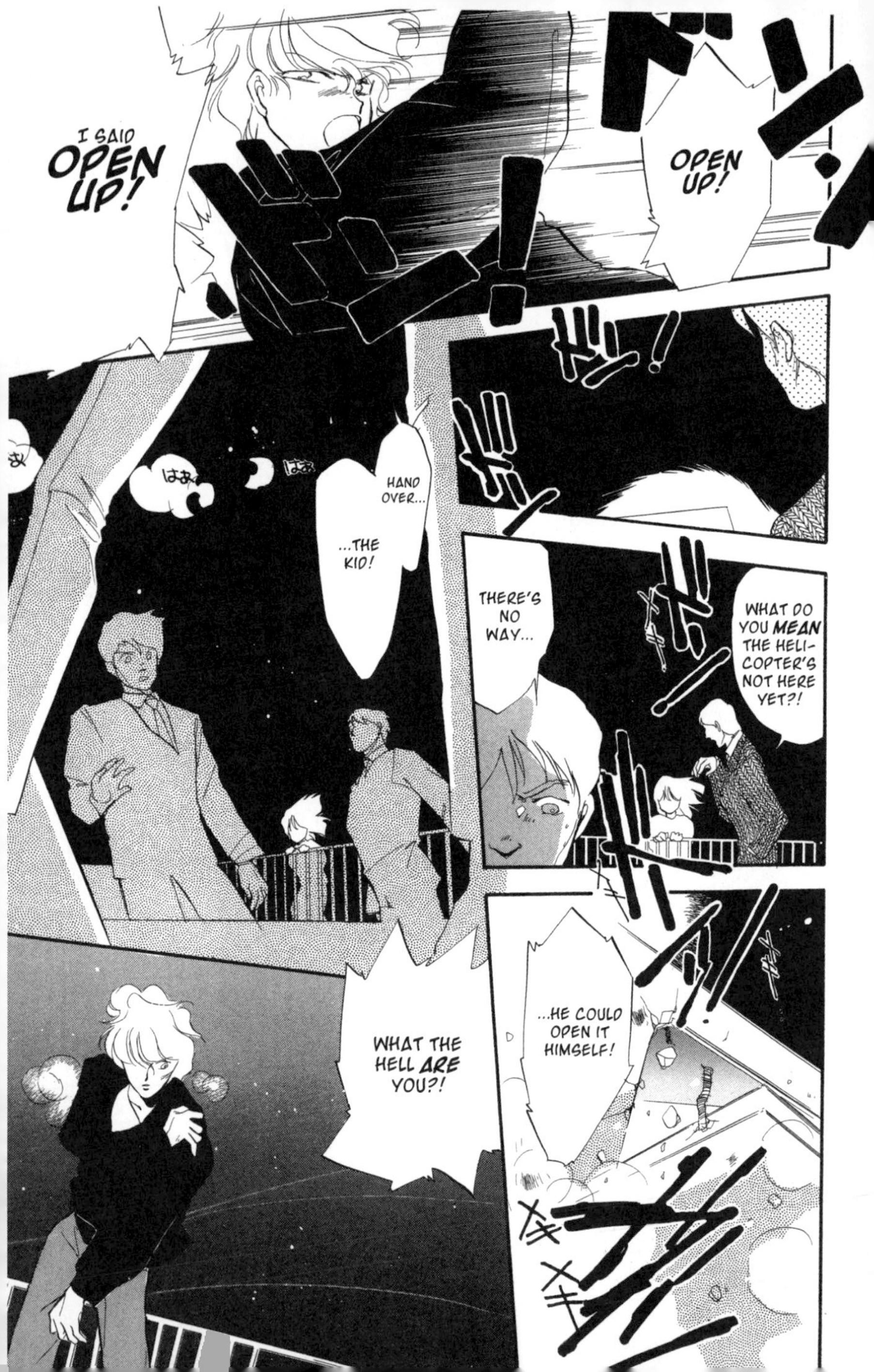
OPEN UP!
I SAID OPEN UP!
WHAT DO YOU MEAN THE HELI-COPTER'S NOT HERE YET?!
THERE'S NO WAY...
...HE COULD OPEN IT HIMSELF!
はあ
HAND OVER...
...THE KID!
WHAT THE HELL ARE YOU?!

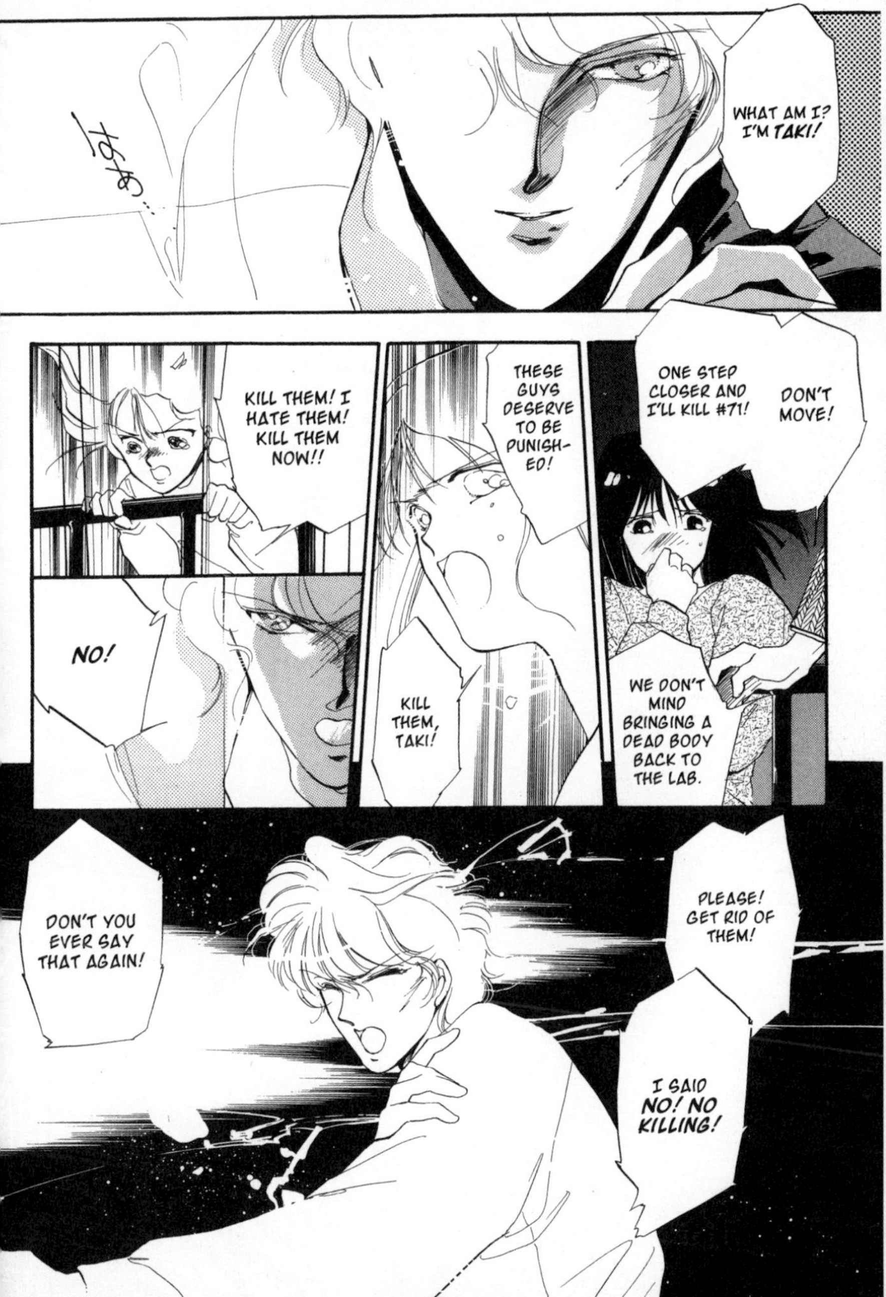
WHAT AM I? I'M TAKI!
なあ…
DON'T MOVE!
ONE STEP CLOSER AND I'LL KILL #71!
WE DON'T MIND BRINGING A DEAD BODY BACK TO THE LAB.
THESE GUYS DESERVE TO BE PUNISH-ED!
KILL THEM, TAKI!
KILL THEM! I HATE THEM! KILL THEM NOW!!
NO!
PLEASE! GET RID OF THEM!
I SAID NO! NO KILLING!
DON'T YOU EVER SAY THAT AGAIN!

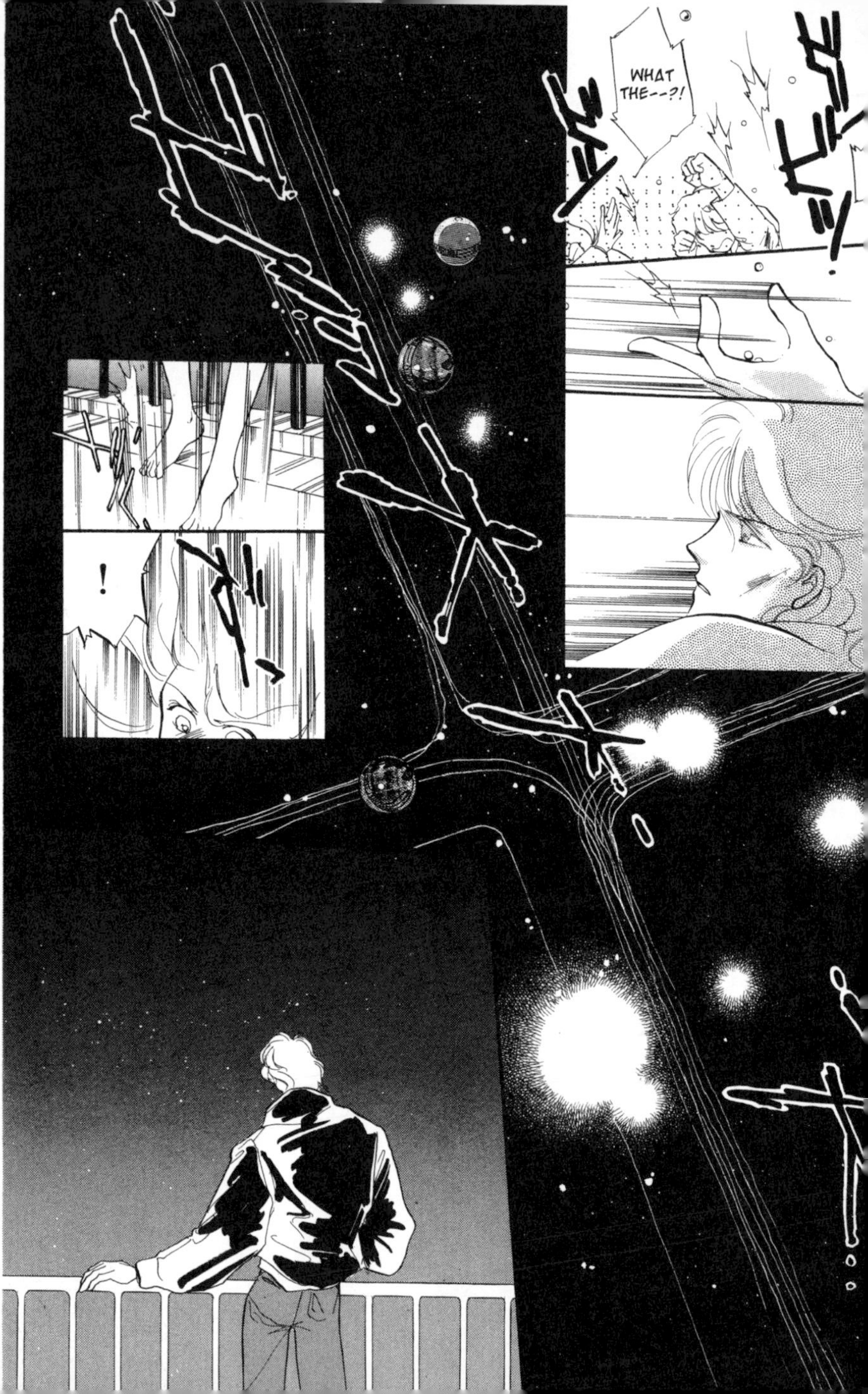
WHAT THE--?!
!

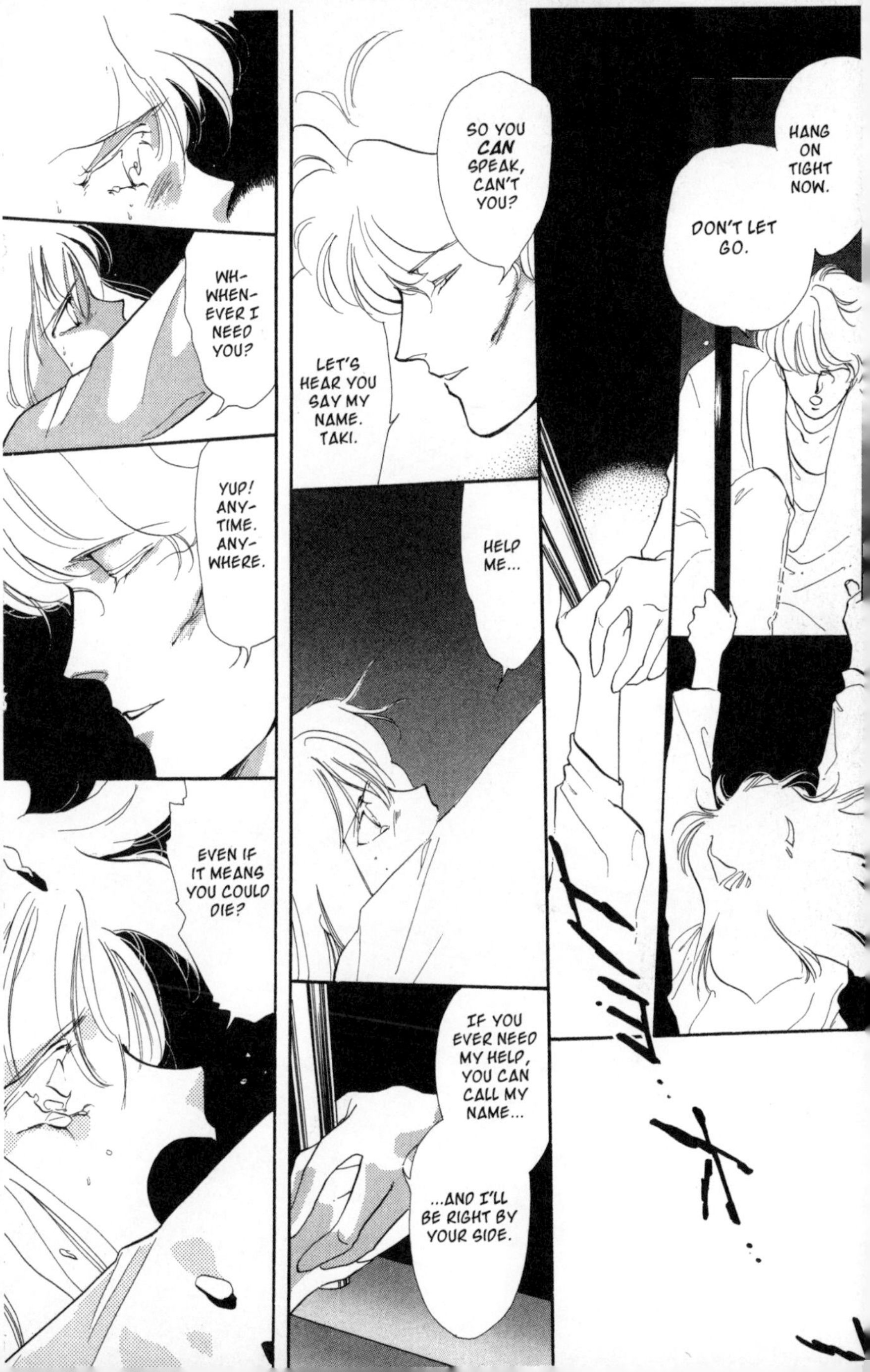
HANG ON TIGHT NOW.
DON'T LET GO.
SO YOU **CAN** SPEAK, CAN'T YOU?
LET'S HEAR YOU SAY MY NAME. TAKI.
HELP ME...
IF YOU EVER NEED MY HELP, YOU CAN CALL MY NAME...
...AND I'LL BE RIGHT BY YOUR SIDE.
WH-WHENEVER I NEED YOU?
YUP! ANYTIME. ANYWHERE.
EVEN IF IT MEANS YOU COULD DIE?

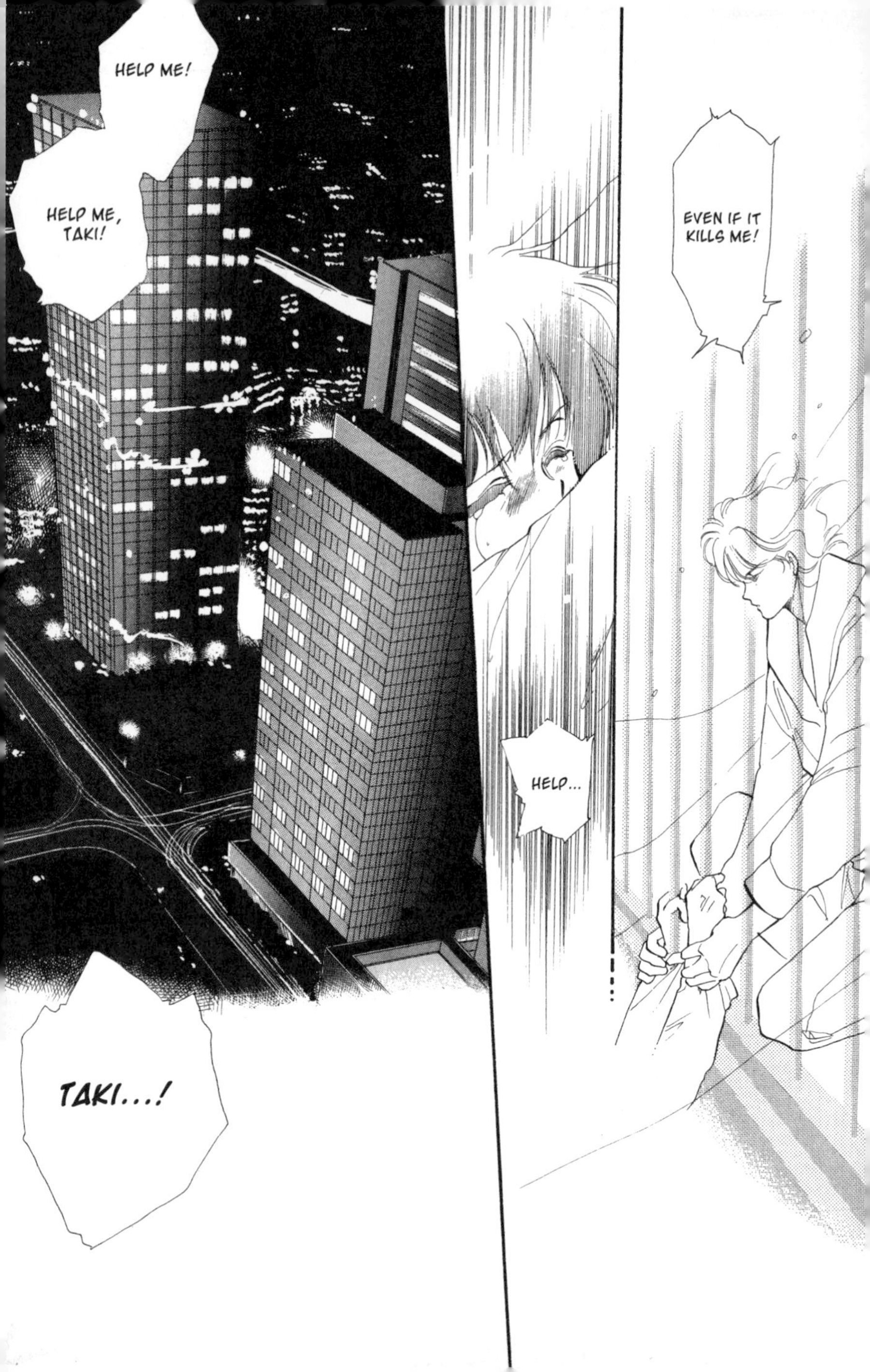
EVEN IF IT KILLS ME!
HELP...
HELP ME!
HELP ME, TAKI!
TAKI...!

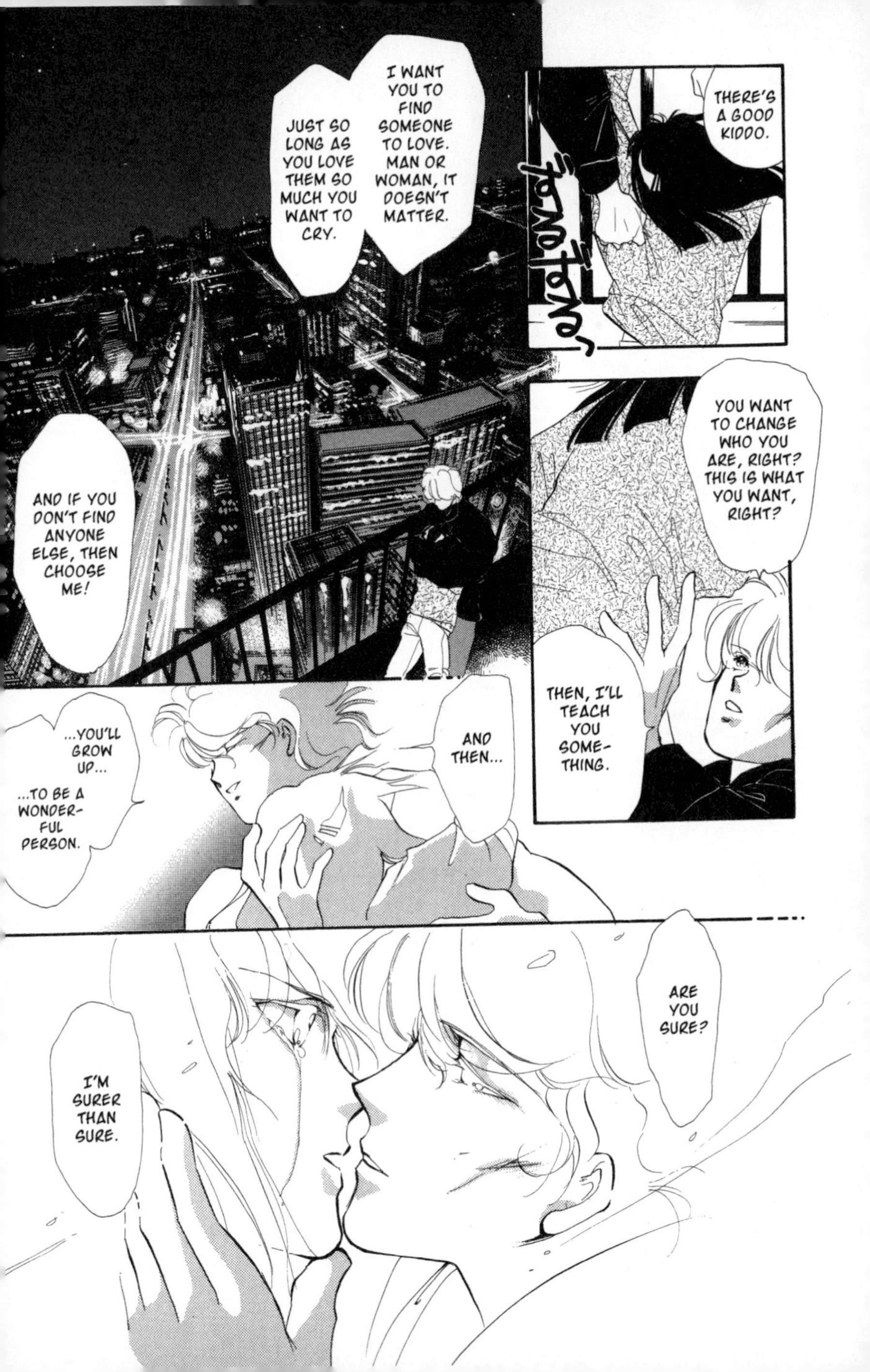

THERE'S A GOOD KIDDO.
YOU WANT TO CHANGE WHO YOU ARE, RIGHT? THIS IS WHAT YOU WANT, RIGHT?
THEN, I'LL TEACH YOU SOMETHING.
I WANT YOU TO FIND SOMEONE TO LOVE. MAN OR WOMAN, IT DOESN'T MATTER.
JUST SO LONG AS YOU LOVE THEM SO MUCH YOU WANT TO CRY.
AND IF YOU DON'T FIND ANYONE ELSE, THEN CHOOSE ME!
AND THEN...
...YOU'LL GROW UP...
...TO BE A WONDERFUL PERSON.
ARE YOU SURE?
I'M SURER THAN SURE.

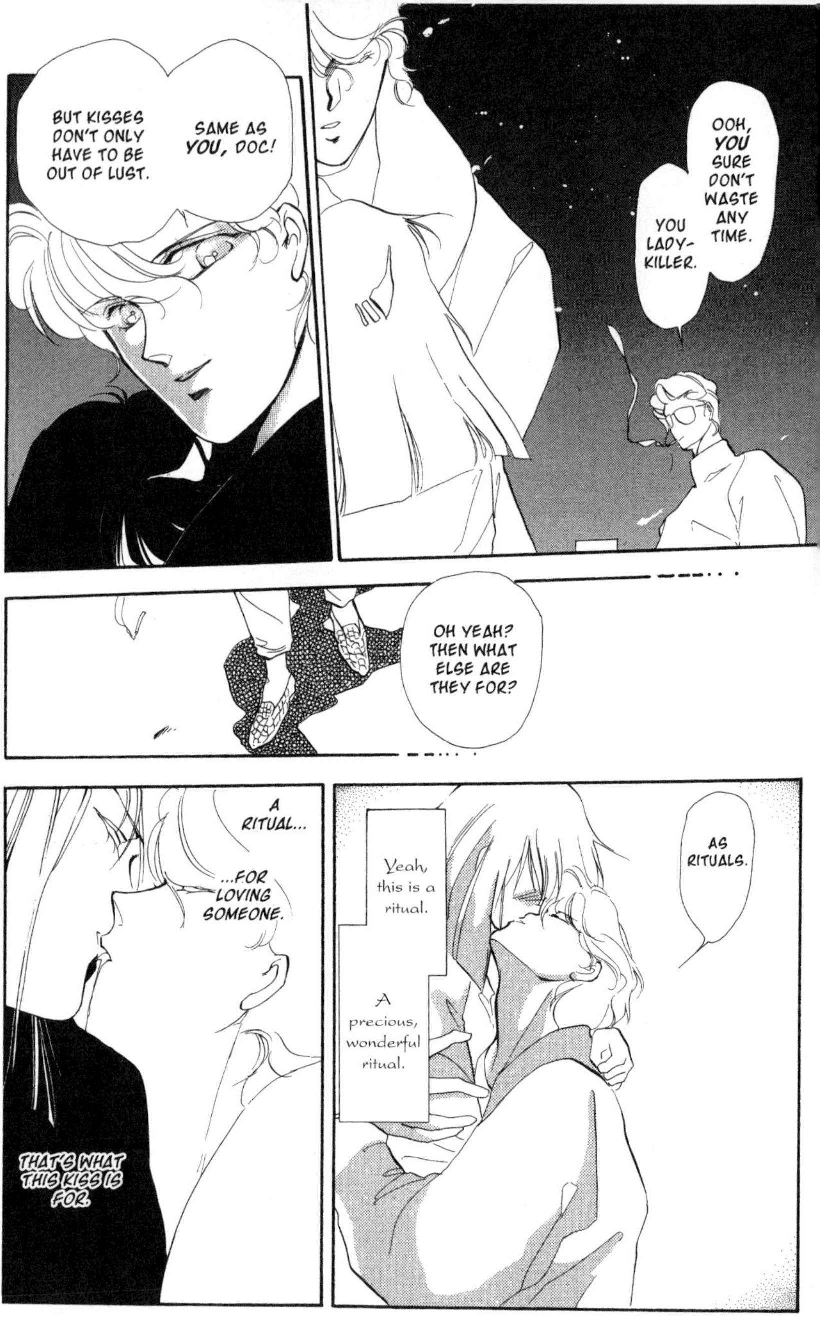
OOH, YOU SURE DON'T WASTE ANY TIME.
YOU LADY-KILLER.
SAME AS YOU, DOC!
BUT KISSES DON'T ONLY HAVE TO BE OUT OF LUST.
OH YEAH? THEN WHAT ELSE ARE THEY FOR?
AS RITUALS.
Yeah, this is a ritual.
A precious, wonderful ritual.
A RITUAL...
...FOR LOVING SOMEONE.
THAT'S WHAT THIS KISS IS FOR.

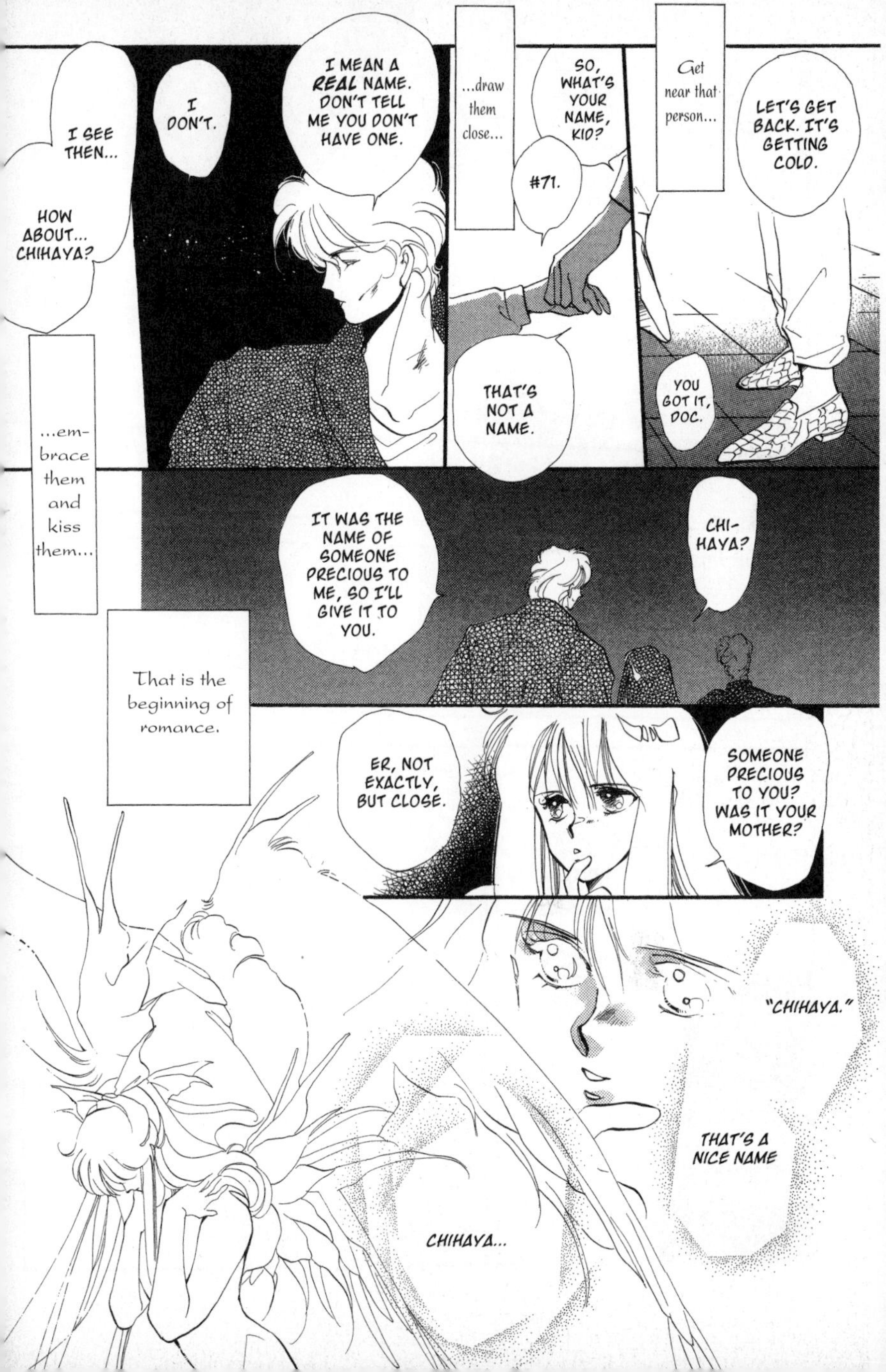
Get near that person...
LET'S GET BACK. IT'S GETTING COLD.
YOU GOT IT, DOC.
...draw them close...
SO, WHAT'S YOUR NAME, KID?
#71.
THAT'S NOT A NAME.
I MEAN A REAL NAME. DON'T TELL ME YOU DON'T HAVE ONE.
I DON'T.
I SEE THEN...
HOW ABOUT... CHIHAYA?
...em-brace them and kiss them...
CHI-HAYA?
IT WAS THE NAME OF SOMEONE PRECIOUS TO ME, SO I'LL GIVE IT TO YOU.
SOMEONE PRECIOUS TO YOU? WAS IT YOUR MOTHER?
ER, NOT EXACTLY, BUT CLOSE.
That is the beginning of romance.
"CHIHAYA."
THAT'S A NICE NAME
CHIHAYA...

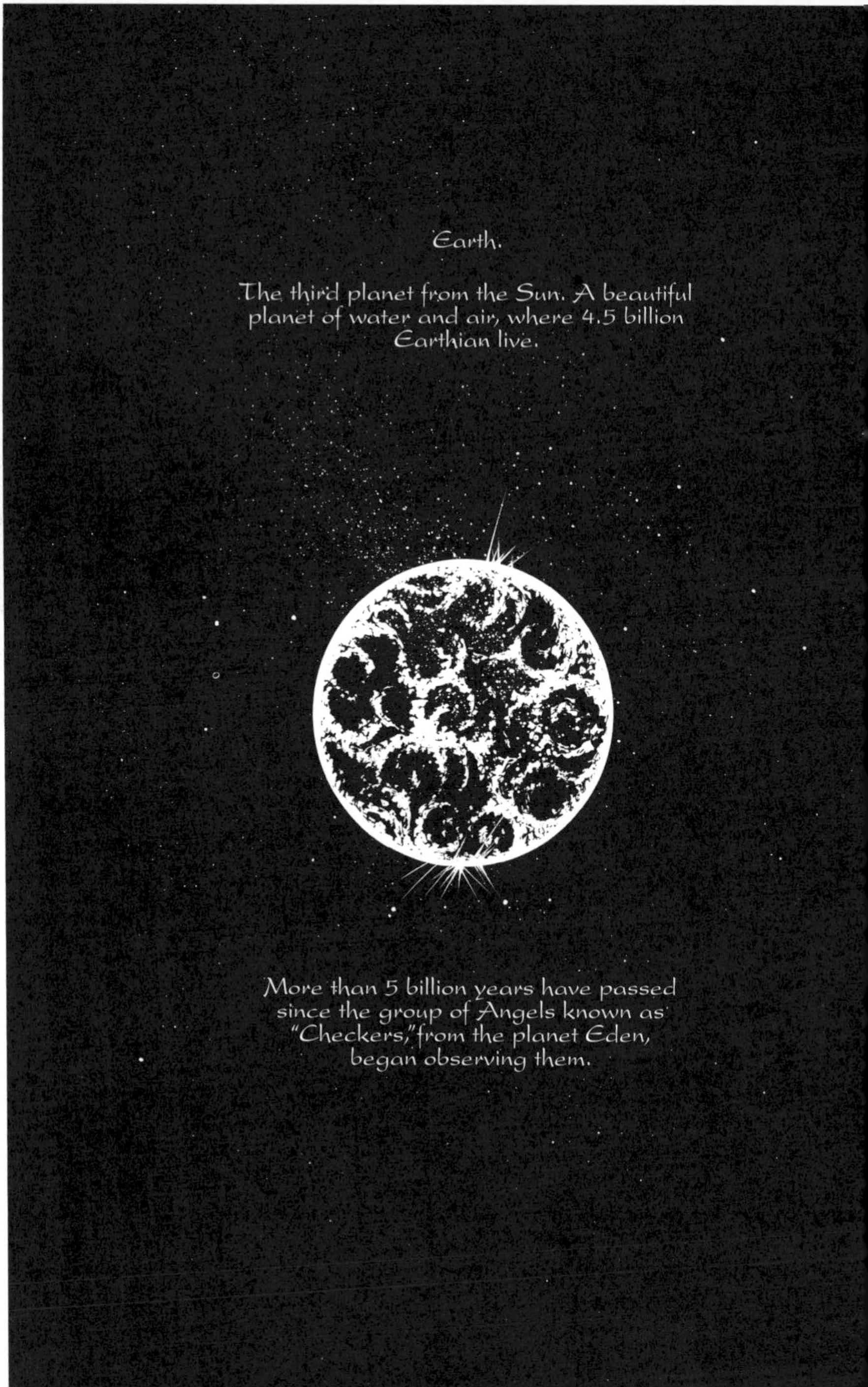
Earth.
The third planet from the Sun. A beautiful planet of water and air, where 4.5 billion Earthian live.
More than 5 billion years have passed since the group of Angels known as "Checkers," from the planet Eden, began observing them.

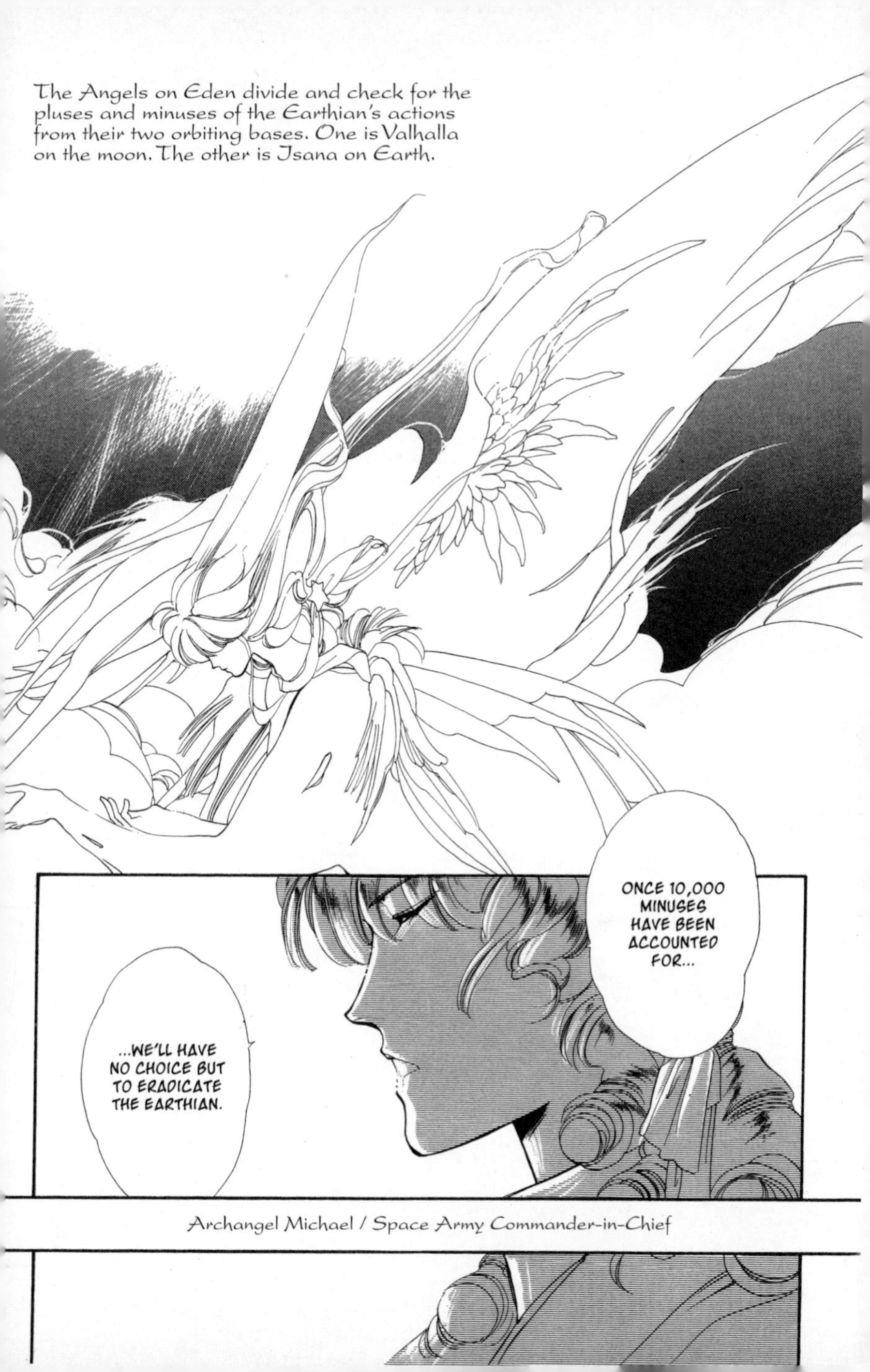
The Angels on Eden divide and check for the pluses and minuses of the Earthian's actions from their two orbiting bases. One is Valhalla on the moon. The other is Isana on Earth.
ONCE 10,000 MINUSES HAVE BEEN ACCOUNTED FOR...
...WE'LL HAVE NO CHOICE BUT TO ERADICATE THE EARTHIAN.
Archangel Michael / Space Army Commander-in-Chief

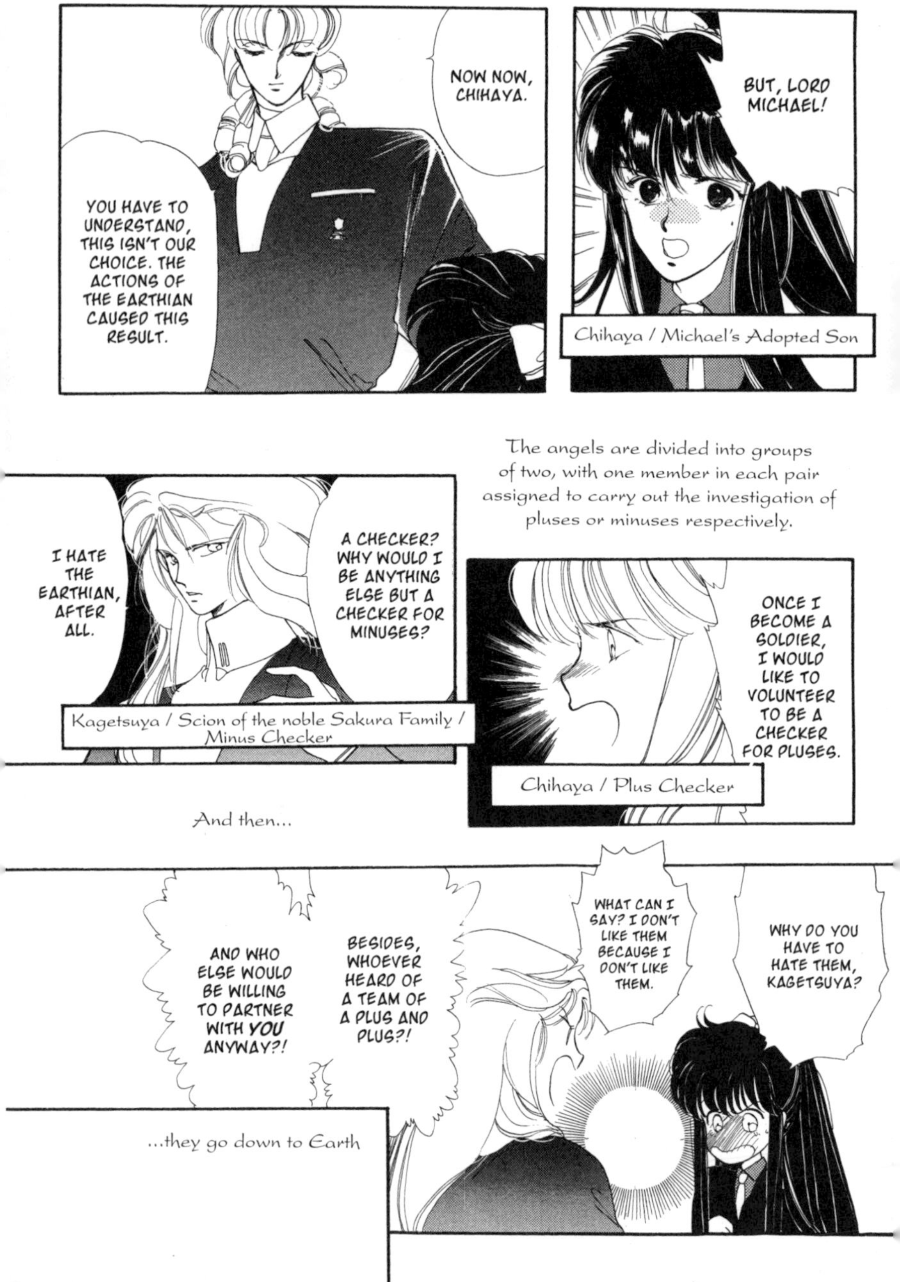
BUT, LORD MICHAEL!
Chihaya / Michael's Adopted Son
NOW NOW, CHIHAYA.
YOU HAVE TO UNDERSTAND, THIS ISN'T OUR CHOICE. THE ACTIONS OF THE EARTHIAN CAUSED THIS RESULT.
The angels are divided into groups of two, with one member in each pair assigned to carry out the investigation of pluses or minuses respectively.
ONCE I BECOME A SOLDIER, I WOULD LIKE TO VOLUNTEER TO BE A CHECKER FOR PLUSES.
Chihaya / Plus Checker
A CHECKER? WHY WOULD I BE ANYTHING ELSE BUT A CHECKER FOR MINUSES?
I HATE THE EARTHIAN, AFTER ALL.
Kagetsuya / Scion of the noble Sakura Family / Minus Checker
And then...
WHY DO YOU HAVE TO HATE THEM, KAGETSUYA?
WHAT CAN I SAY? I DON'T LIKE THEM BECAUSE I DON'T LIKE THEM.
BESIDES, WHOEVER HEARD OF A TEAM OF A PLUS AND PLUS?!
AND WHO ELSE WOULD BE WILLING TO PARTNER WITH *YOU* ANYWAY?!
...they go down to Earth

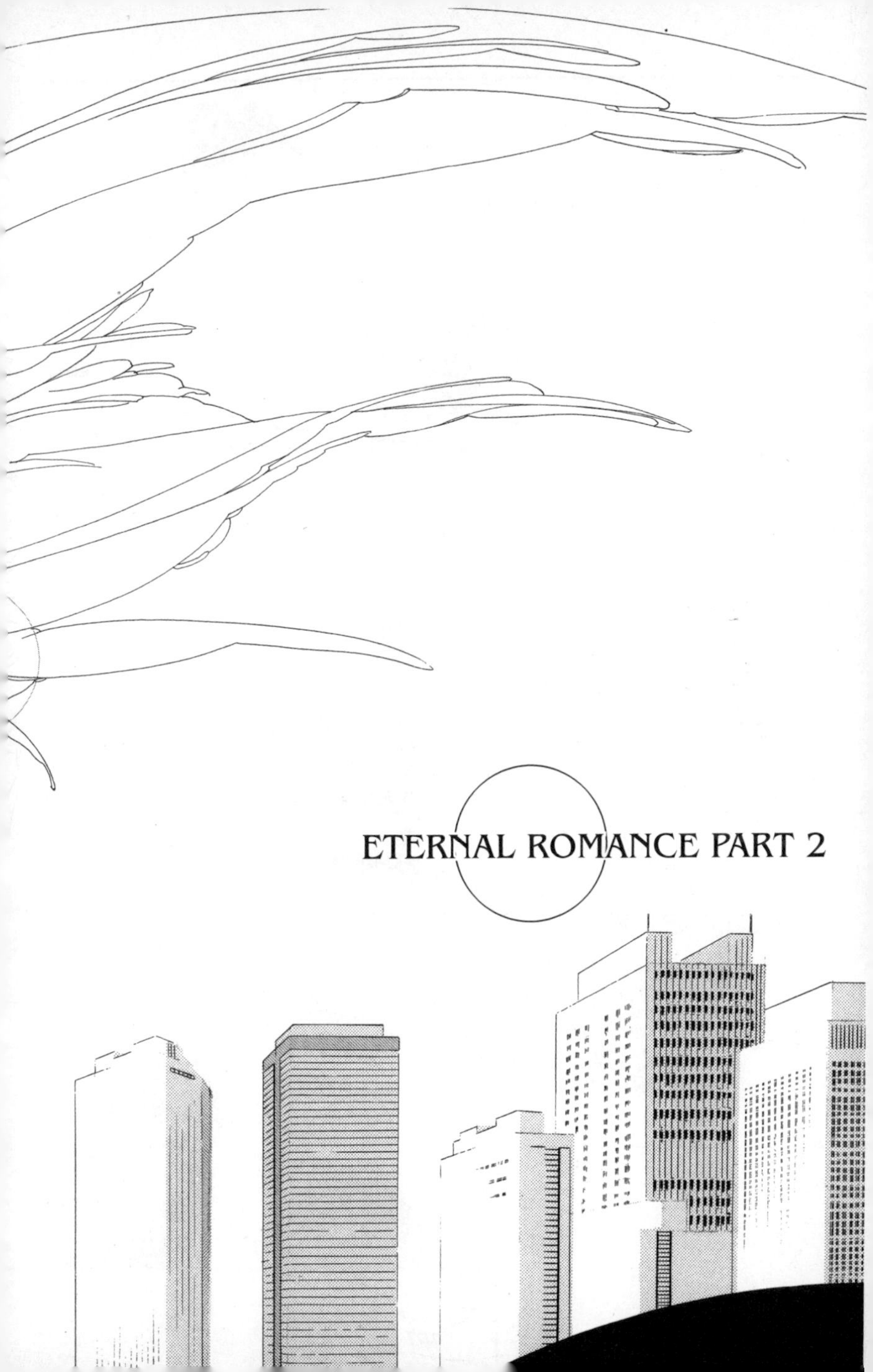
ETERNAL ROMANCE PART 2

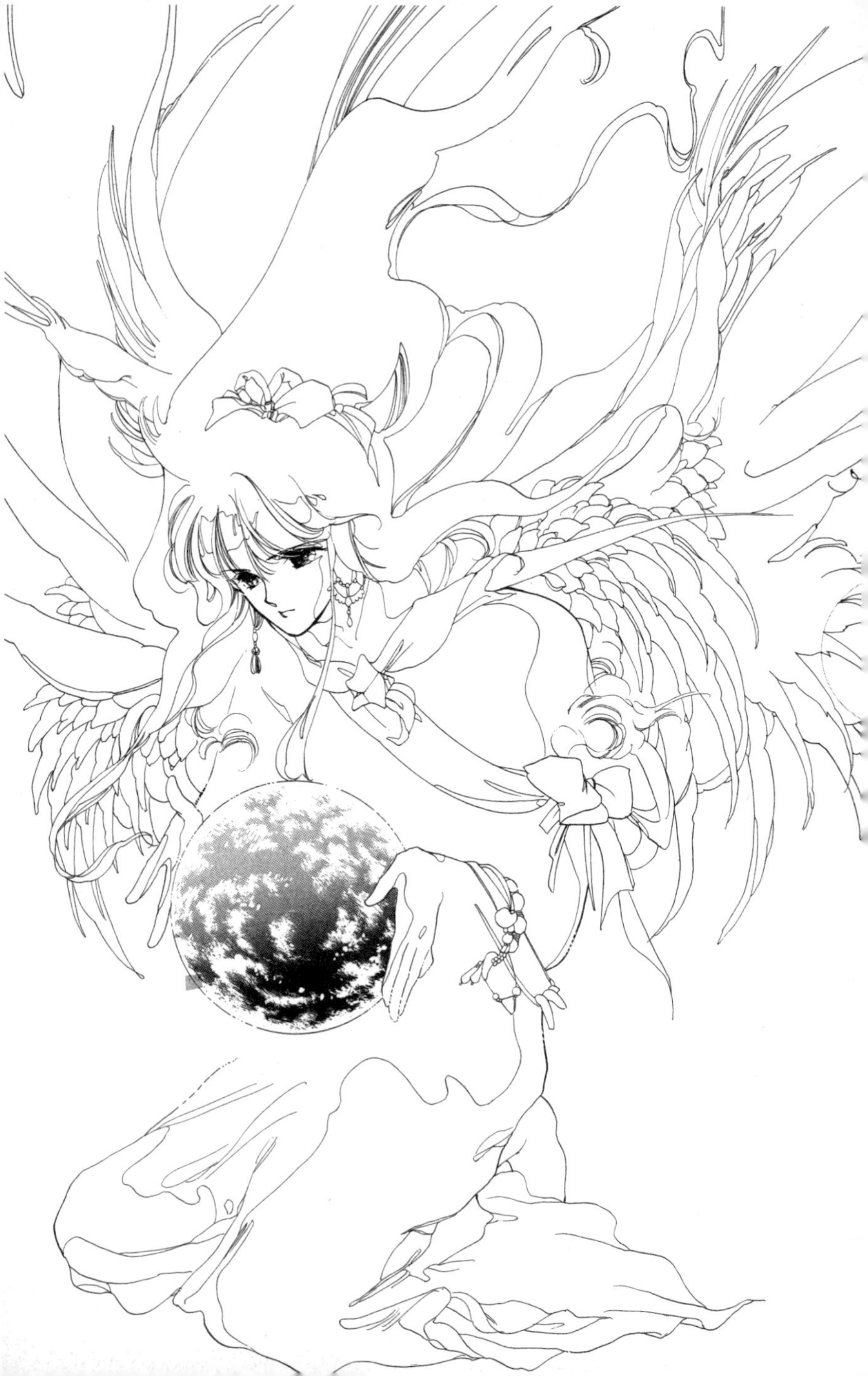

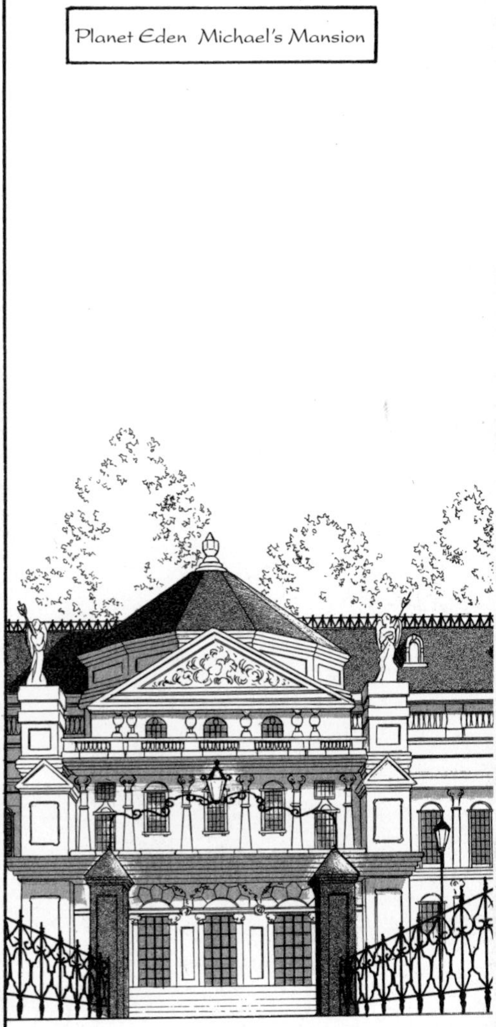
Planet Eden Michael's Mansion

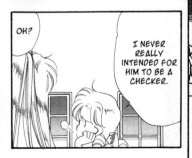

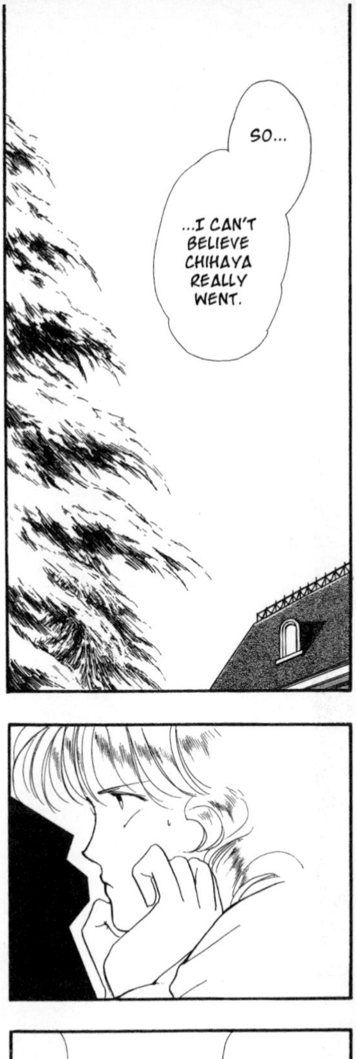
SO...
...I CAN'T BELIEVE CHIHAYA REALLY WENT.
I NEVER REALLY INTENDED FOR HIM TO BE A CHECKER.
OH?

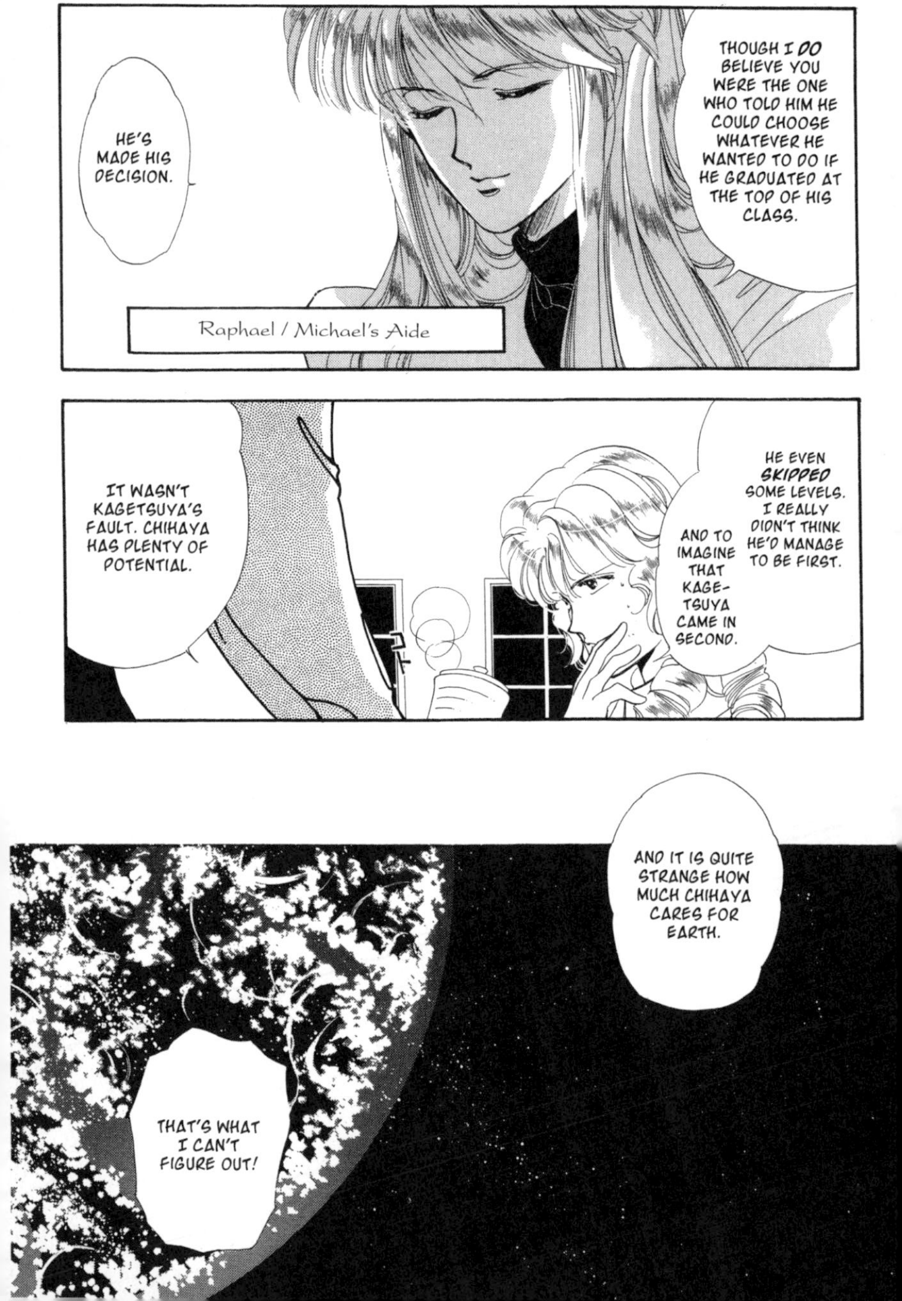
THOUGH I DO BELIEVE YOU WERE THE ONE WHO TOLD HIM HE COULD CHOOSE WHATEVER HE WANTED TO DO IF HE GRADUATED AT THE TOP OF HIS CLASS.
HE'S MADE HIS DECISION.
Raphael / Michael's Aide
HE EVEN SKIPPED SOME LEVELS. I REALLY DIDN'T THINK HE'D MANAGE TO BE FIRST.
AND TO IMAGINE THAT KAGE-TSUYA CAME IN SECOND.
コト
IT WASN'T KAGETSUYA'S FAULT. CHIHAYA HAS PLENTY OF POTENTIAL.
AND IT IS QUITE STRANGE HOW MUCH CHIHAYA CARES FOR EARTH.
THAT'S WHAT I CAN'T FIGURE OUT!

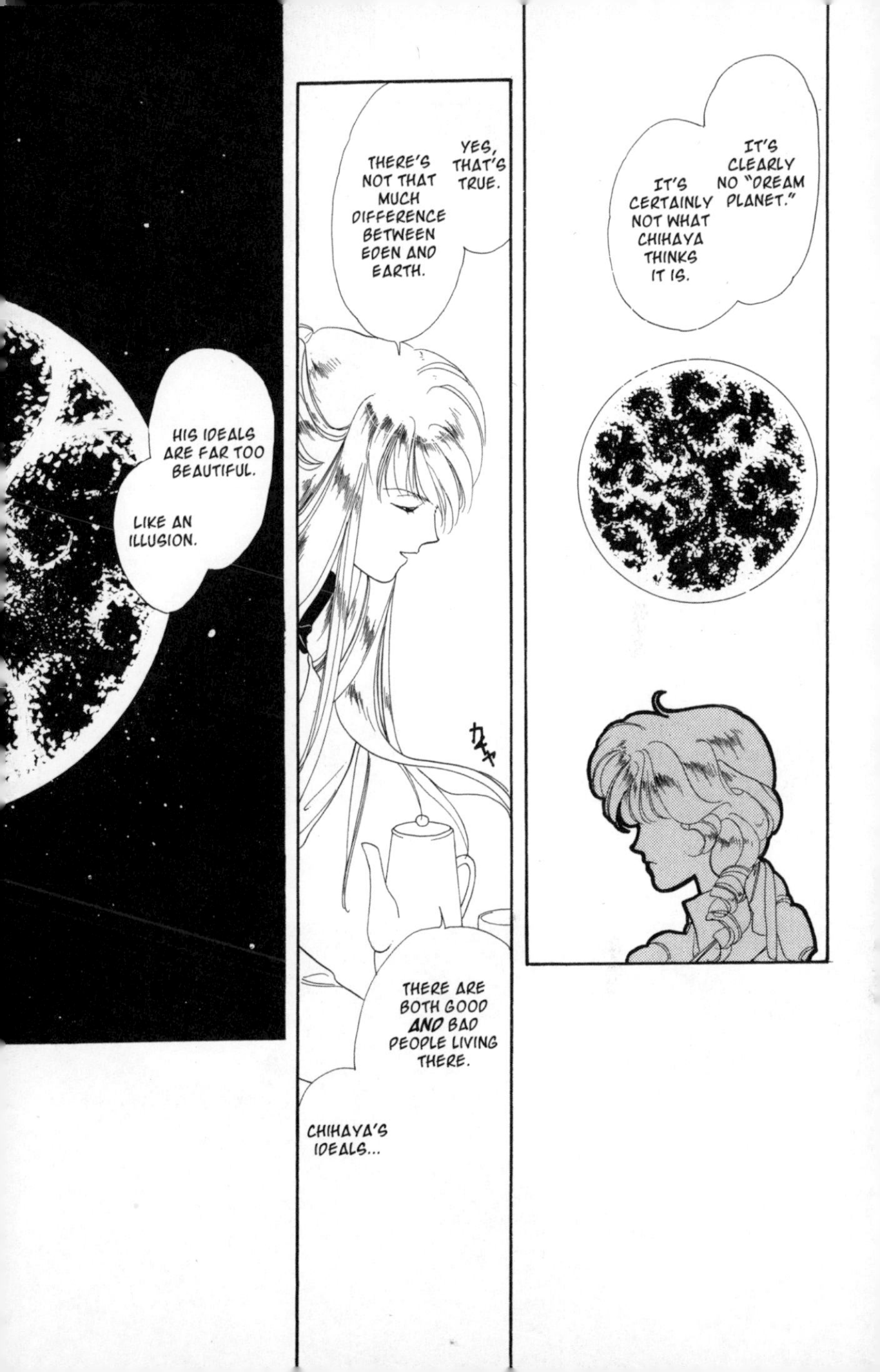
IT'S CLEARLY NO "DREAM PLANET."
IT'S CERTAINLY NOT WHAT CHIHAYA THINKS IT IS.
YES, THAT'S TRUE.
THERE'S NOT THAT MUCH DIFFERENCE BETWEEN EDEN AND EARTH.
カチャ
THERE ARE BOTH GOOD AND BAD PEOPLE LIVING THERE.
CHIHAYA'S IDEALS...
HIS IDEALS ARE FAR TOO BEAUTIFUL.
LIKE AN ILLUSION.

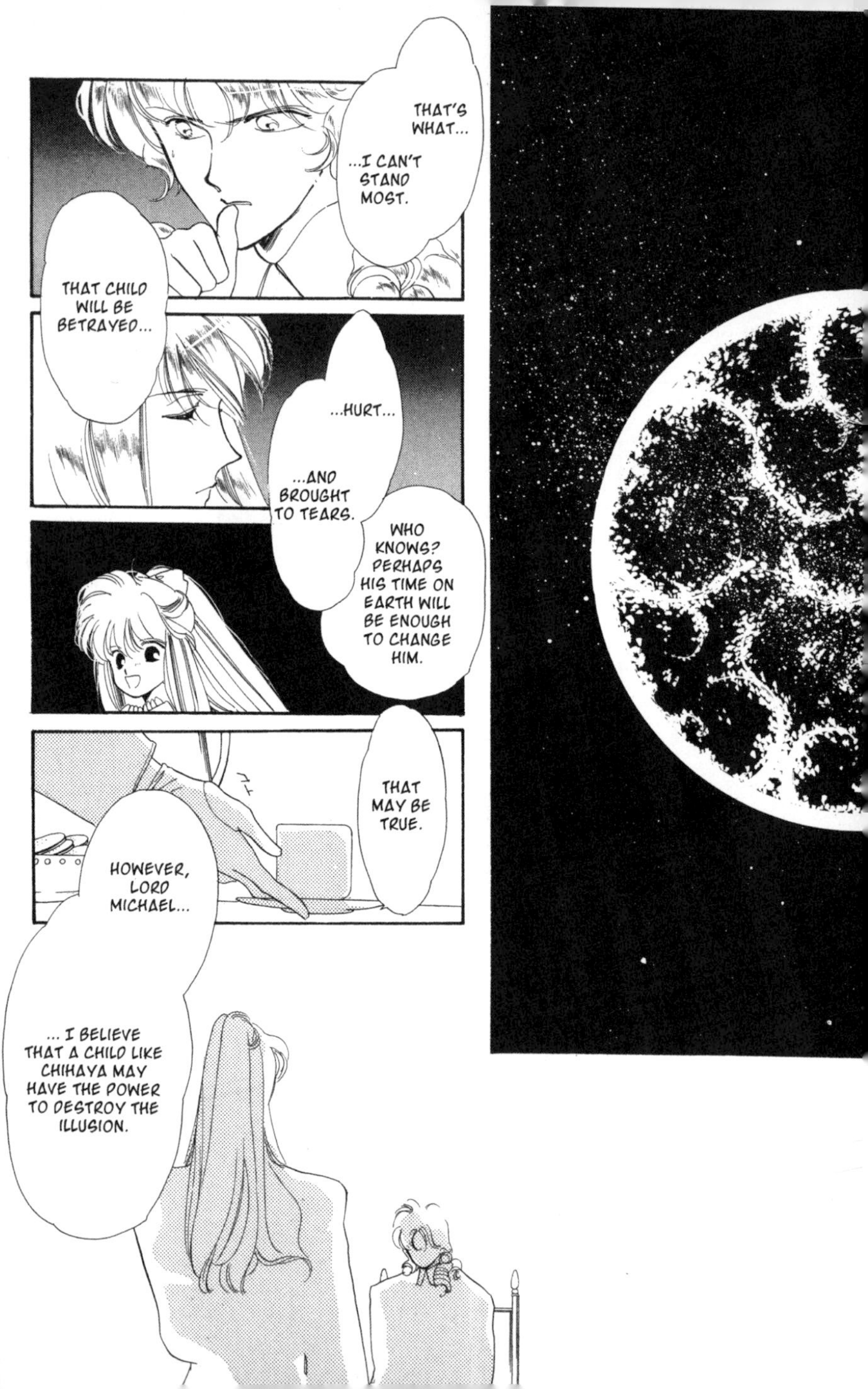
THAT'S WHAT...
...I CAN'T STAND MOST.
THAT CHILD WILL BE BETRAYED...
...HURT...
...AND BROUGHT TO TEARS.
WHO KNOWS? PERHAPS HIS TIME ON EARTH WILL BE ENOUGH TO CHANGE HIM.
THAT MAY BE TRUE.
HOWEVER, LORD MICHAEL...
... I BELIEVE THAT A CHILD LIKE CHIHAYA MAY HAVE THE POWER TO DESTROY THE ILLUSION.

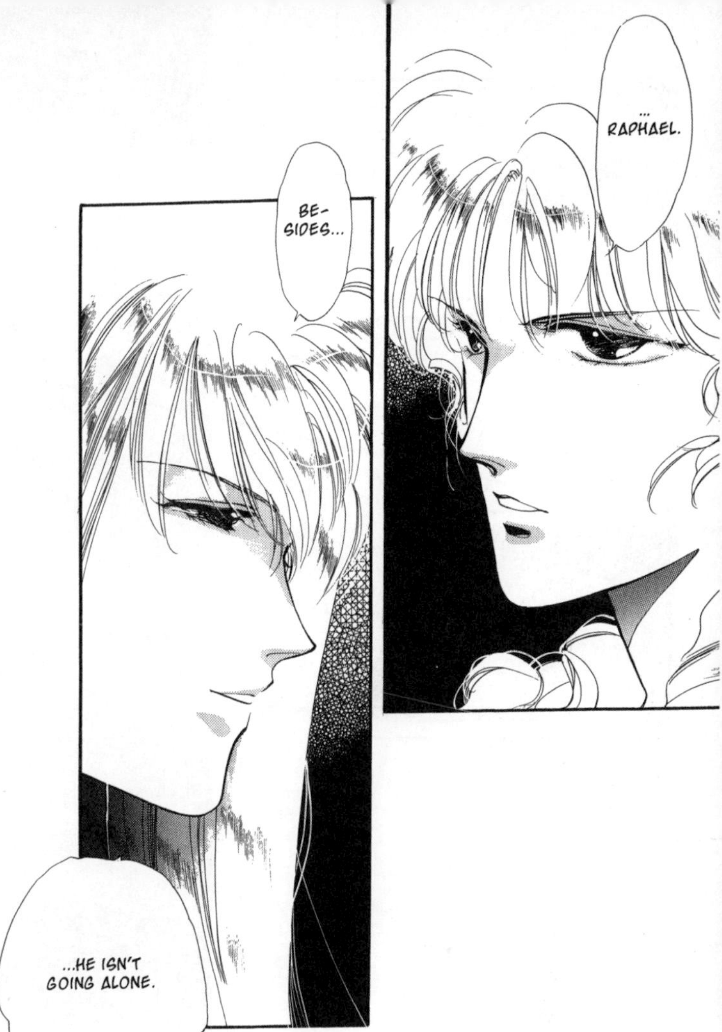
...RAPHAEL.
BE-SIDES...
...HE ISN'T GOING ALONE.

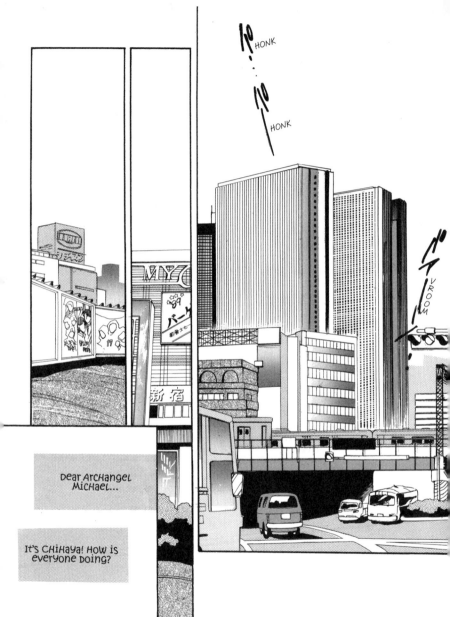

HONK

HONK

VROOM

DEAR ARCHANGEL MICHAEL...

IT'S CHIHAYA! HOW IS EVERYONE DOING?

215

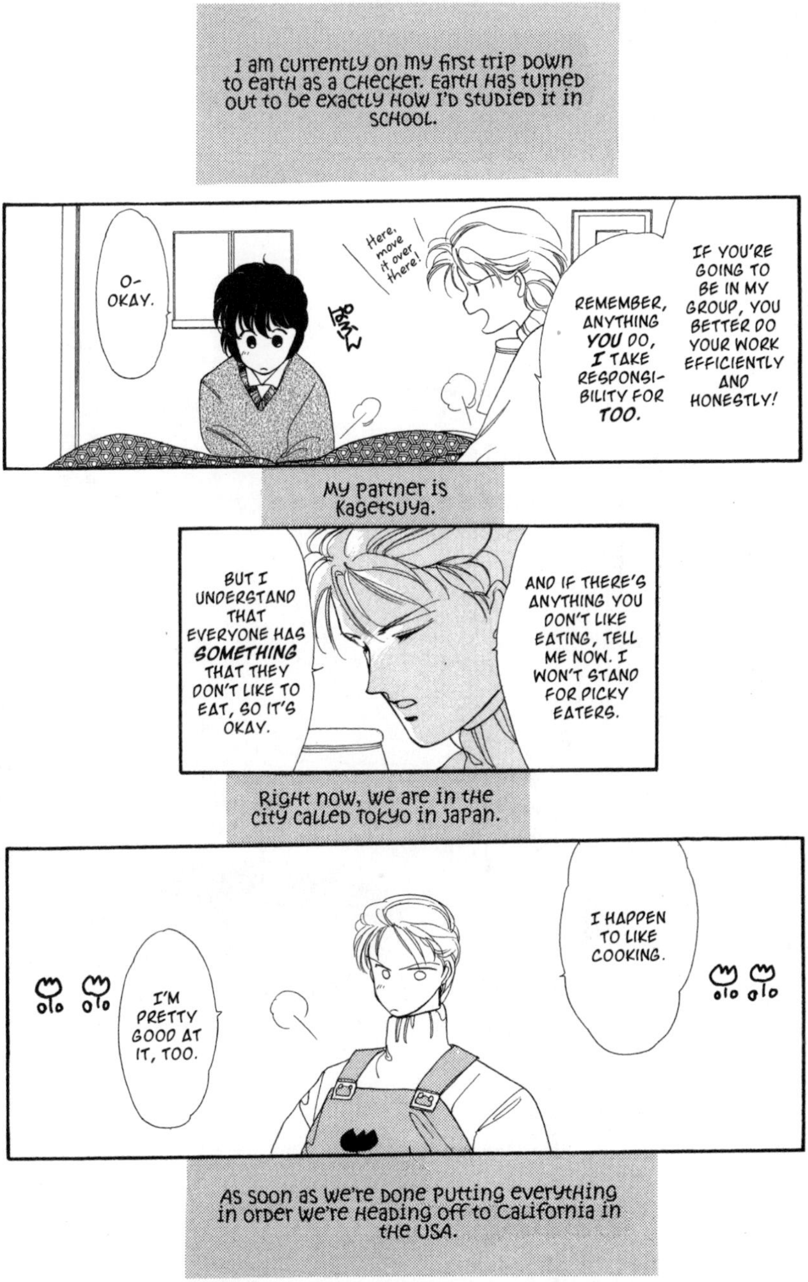
I am currently on my first trip down to earth as a Checker. Earth has turned out to be exactly how I'd studied it in school.
IF YOU'RE GOING TO BE IN MY GROUP, YOU BETTER DO YOUR WORK EFFICIENTLY AND HONESTLY!
REMEMBER, ANYTHING YOU DO, I TAKE RESPONSIBILITY FOR TOO.
Here, move it over there!
O-OKAY.
My partner is Kagetsuya.
AND IF THERE'S ANYTHING YOU DON'T LIKE EATING, TELL ME NOW. I WON'T STAND FOR PICKY EATERS.
BUT I UNDERSTAND THAT EVERYONE HAS SOMETHING THAT THEY DON'T LIKE TO EAT, SO IT'S OKAY.
Right now, we are in the city called Tokyo in Japan.
I HAPPEN TO LIKE COOKING.
I'M PRETTY GOOD AT IT, TOO.
As soon as we're done putting everything in order we're heading off to California in the USA.

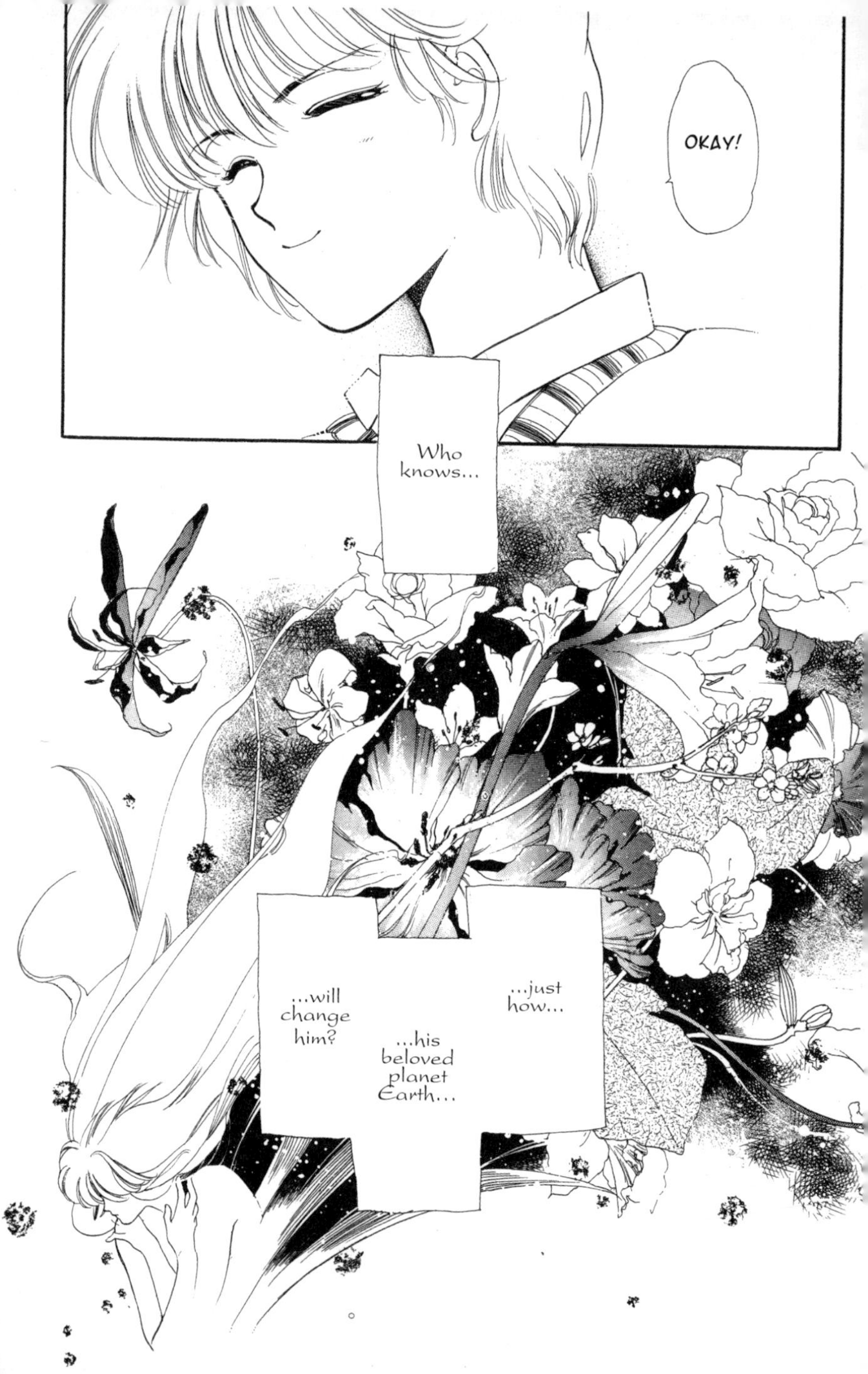
OKAY!
Who knows...
...just how...
...his beloved planet Earth...
...will change him?

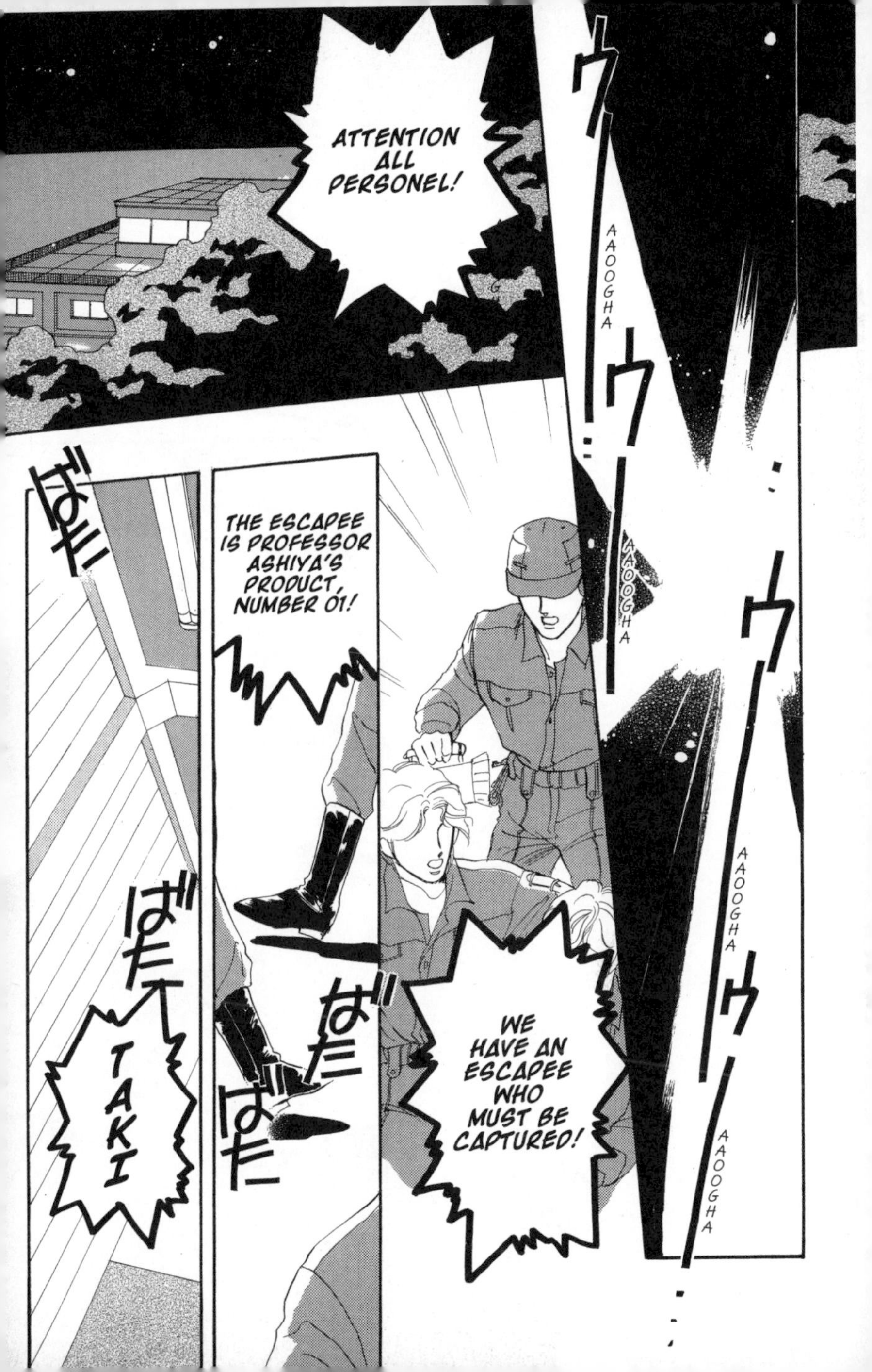
ATTENTION ALL PERSONEL!
AAOOGHA
AAOOGHA
AAOOGHA
AAOOGHA
WE HAVE AN ESCAPEE WHO MUST BE CAPTURED!
THE ESCAPEE IS PROFESSOR ASHIYA'S PRODUCT, NUMBER 01!
TAKI

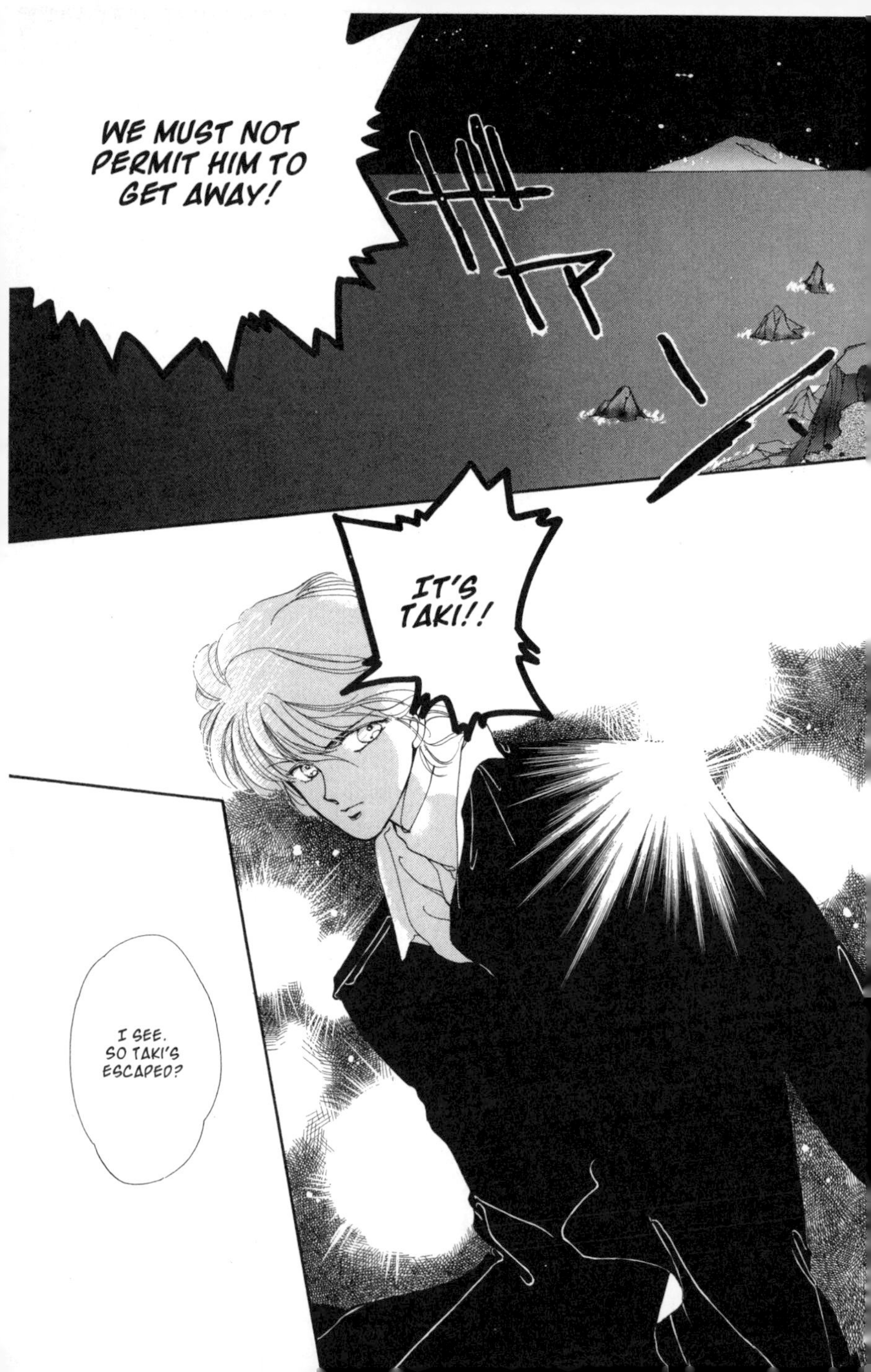
WE MUST NOT PERMIT HIM TO GET AWAY!
IT'S TAKI!!
I SEE. SO TAKI'S ESCAPED?

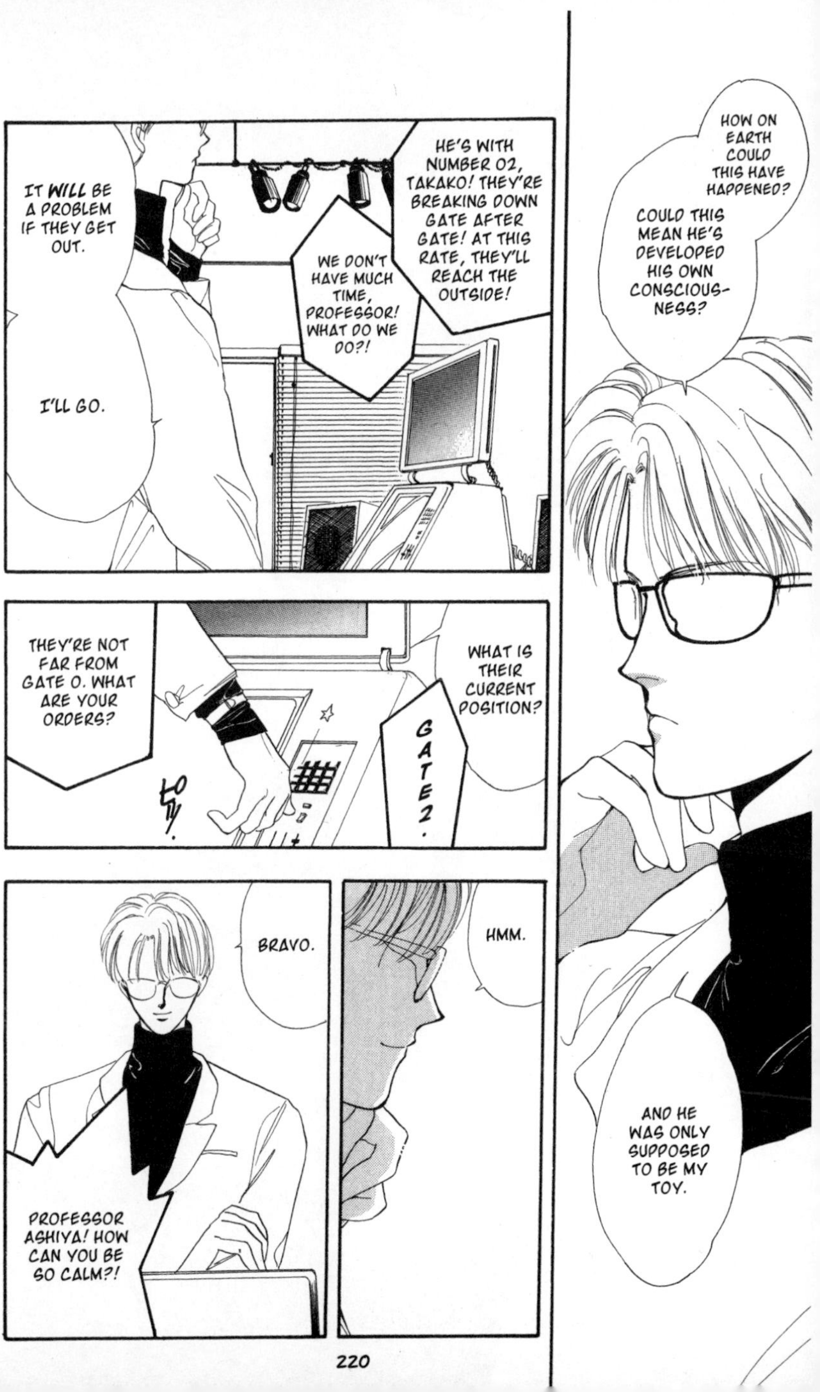
HOW ON EARTH COULD THIS HAVE HAPPENED?
COULD THIS MEAN HE'S DEVELOPED HIS OWN CONSCIOUS-NESS?
AND HE WAS ONLY SUPPOSED TO BE MY TOY.
HE'S WITH NUMBER 02, TAKAKO! THEY'RE BREAKING DOWN GATE AFTER GATE! AT THIS RATE, THEY'LL REACH THE OUTSIDE!
WE DON'T HAVE MUCH TIME, PROFESSOR! WHAT DO WE DO?!
IT WILL BE A PROBLEM IF THEY GET OUT.
I'LL GO.
WHAT IS THEIR CURRENT POSITION?
GATE 2.
THEY'RE NOT FAR FROM GATE 0. WHAT ARE YOUR ORDERS?
HMM.
BRAVO.
PROFESSOR ASHIYA! HOW CAN YOU BE SO CALM?!

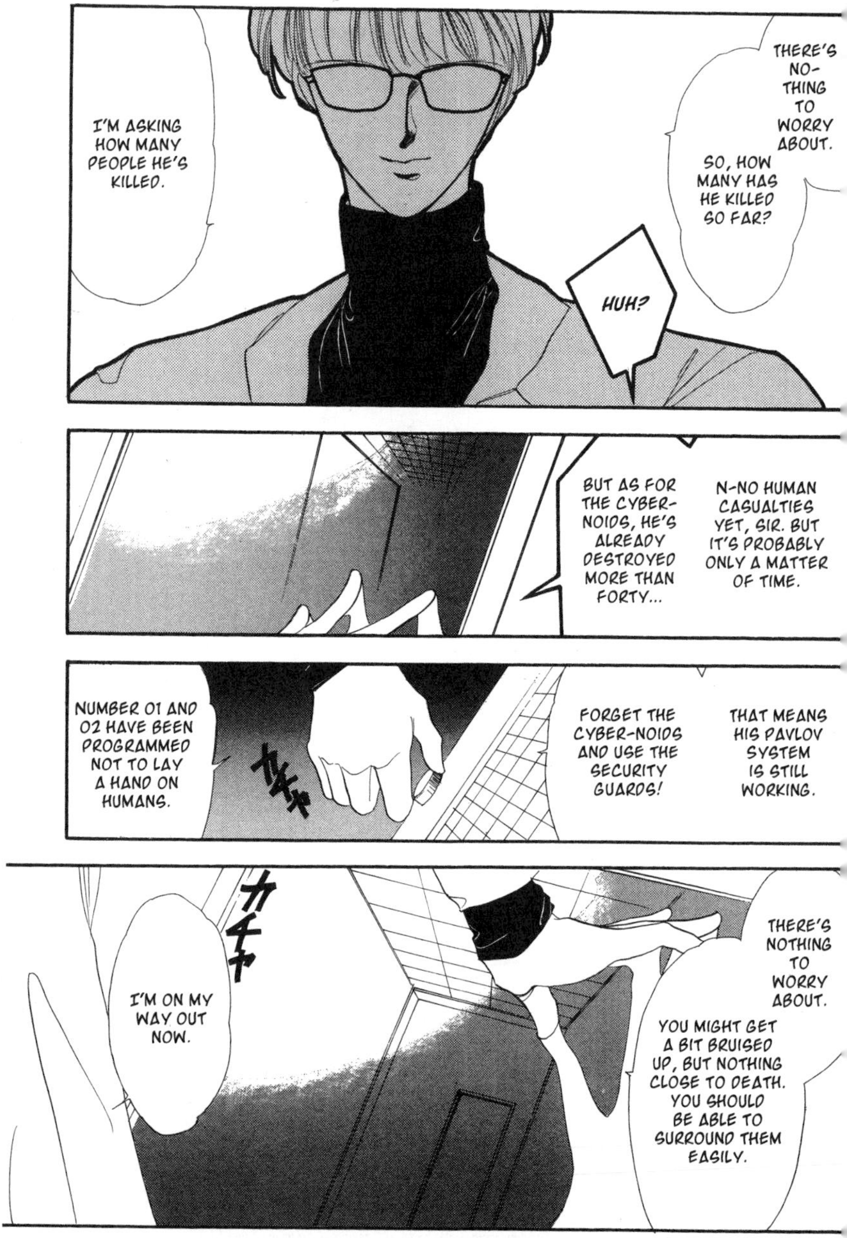
THERE'S NO-THING TO WORRY ABOUT.
SO, HOW MANY HAS HE KILLED SO FAR?
HUH?
I'M ASKING HOW MANY PEOPLE HE'S KILLED.
N-NO HUMAN CASUALTIES YET, SIR. BUT IT'S PROBABLY ONLY A MATTER OF TIME.
BUT AS FOR THE CYBER-NOIDS, HE'S ALREADY DESTROYED MORE THAN FORTY...
THAT MEANS HIS PAVLOV SYSTEM IS STILL WORKING.
FORGET THE CYBER-NOIDS AND USE THE SECURITY GUARDS!
NUMBER 01 AND 02 HAVE BEEN PROGRAMMED NOT TO LAY A HAND ON HUMANS.
カチャ
THERE'S NOTHING TO WORRY ABOUT.
YOU MIGHT GET A BIT BRUISED UP, BUT NOTHING CLOSE TO DEATH. YOU SHOULD BE ABLE TO SURROUND THEM EASILY.
カチャ
I'M ON MY WAY OUT NOW.

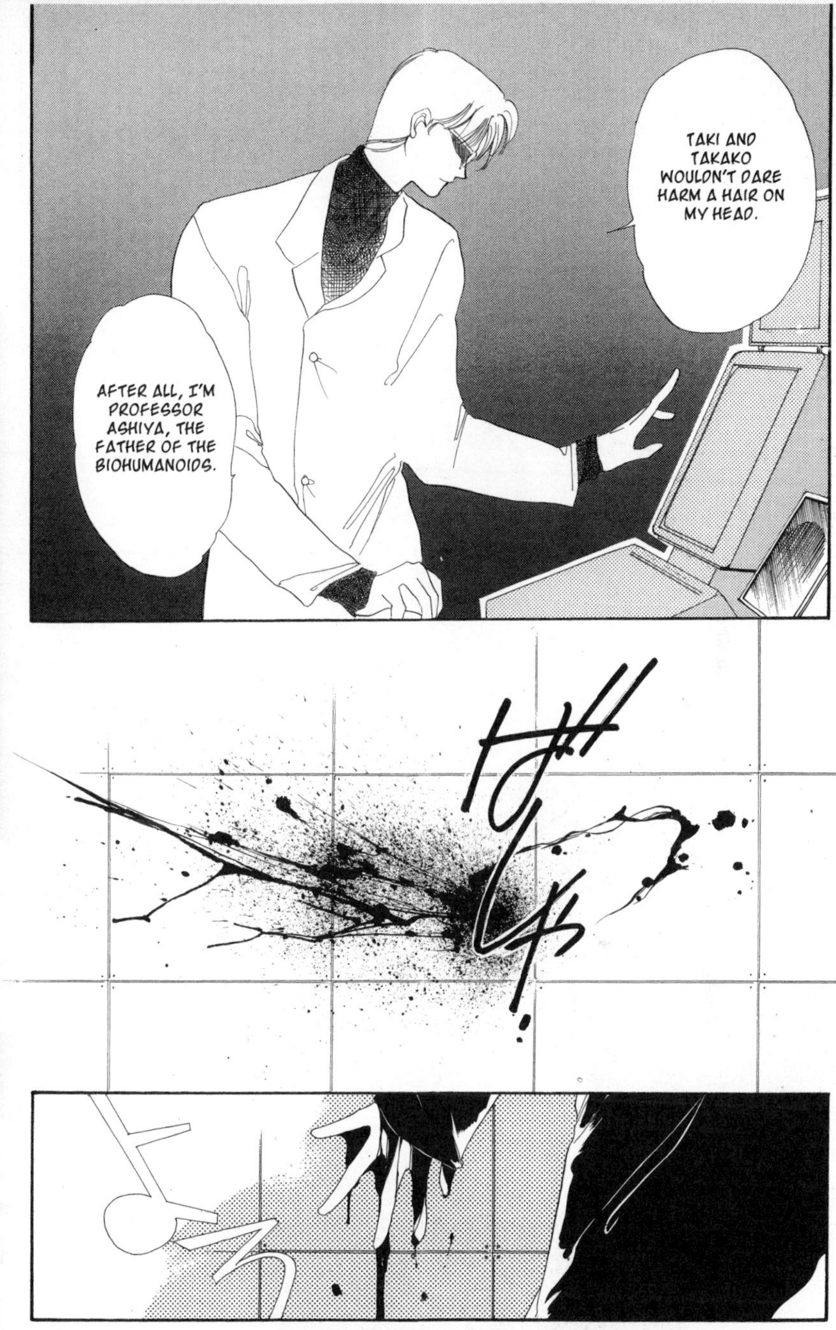
TAKI AND TAKAKO WOULDN'T DARE HARM A HAIR ON MY HEAD.
AFTER ALL, I'M PROFESSOR ASHIYA, THE FATHER OF THE BIOHUMANOIDS.

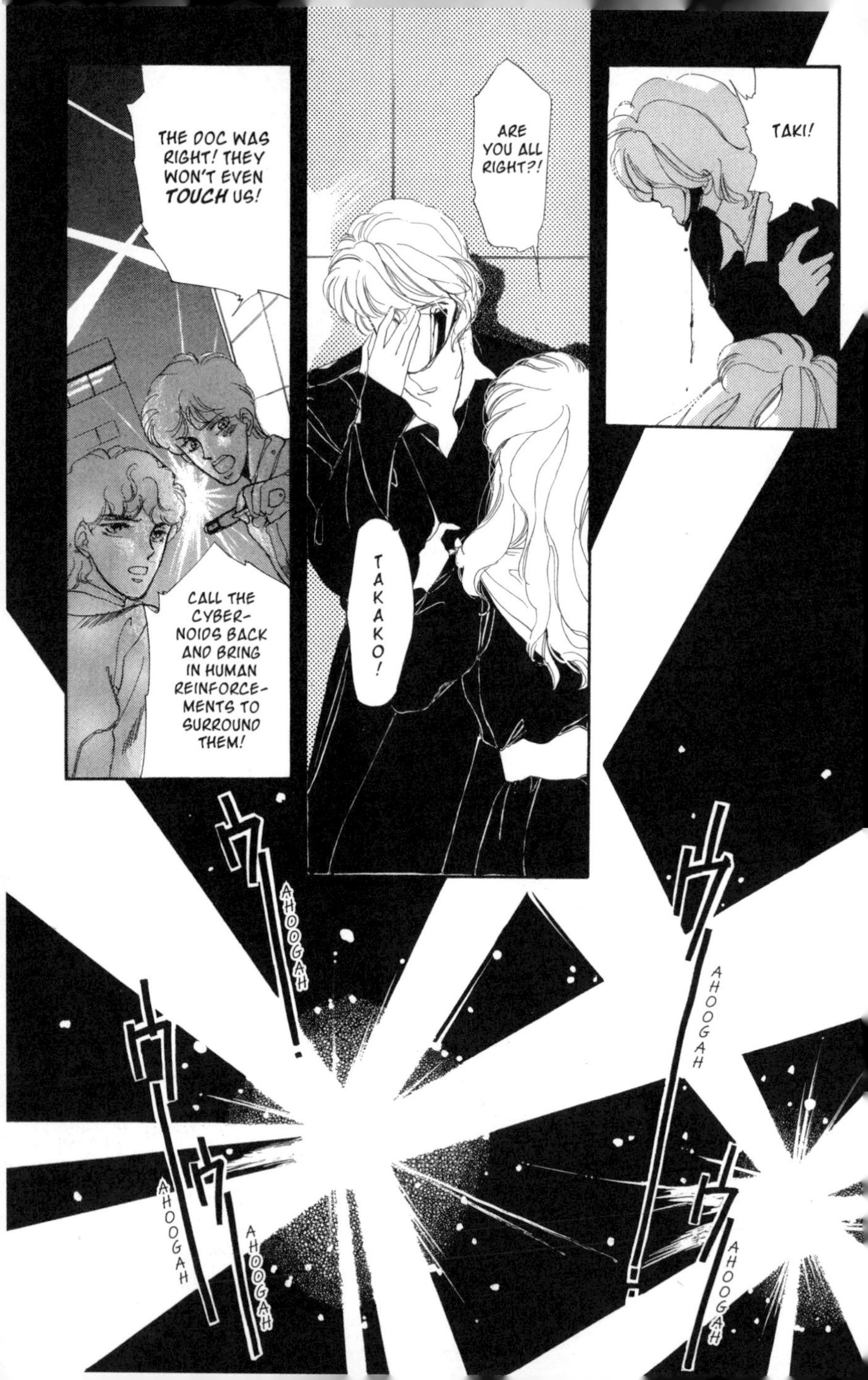
TAKI!
ARE YOU ALL RIGHT?!
TAKAKO!
THE DOC WAS RIGHT! THEY WON'T EVEN TOUCH US!
CALL THE CYBER-NOIDS BACK AND BRING IN HUMAN REINFORCE-MENTS TO SURROUND THEM!
AHOOGAH
AHOOGAH
AHOOGAH
AHOOGAH
AHOOGAH

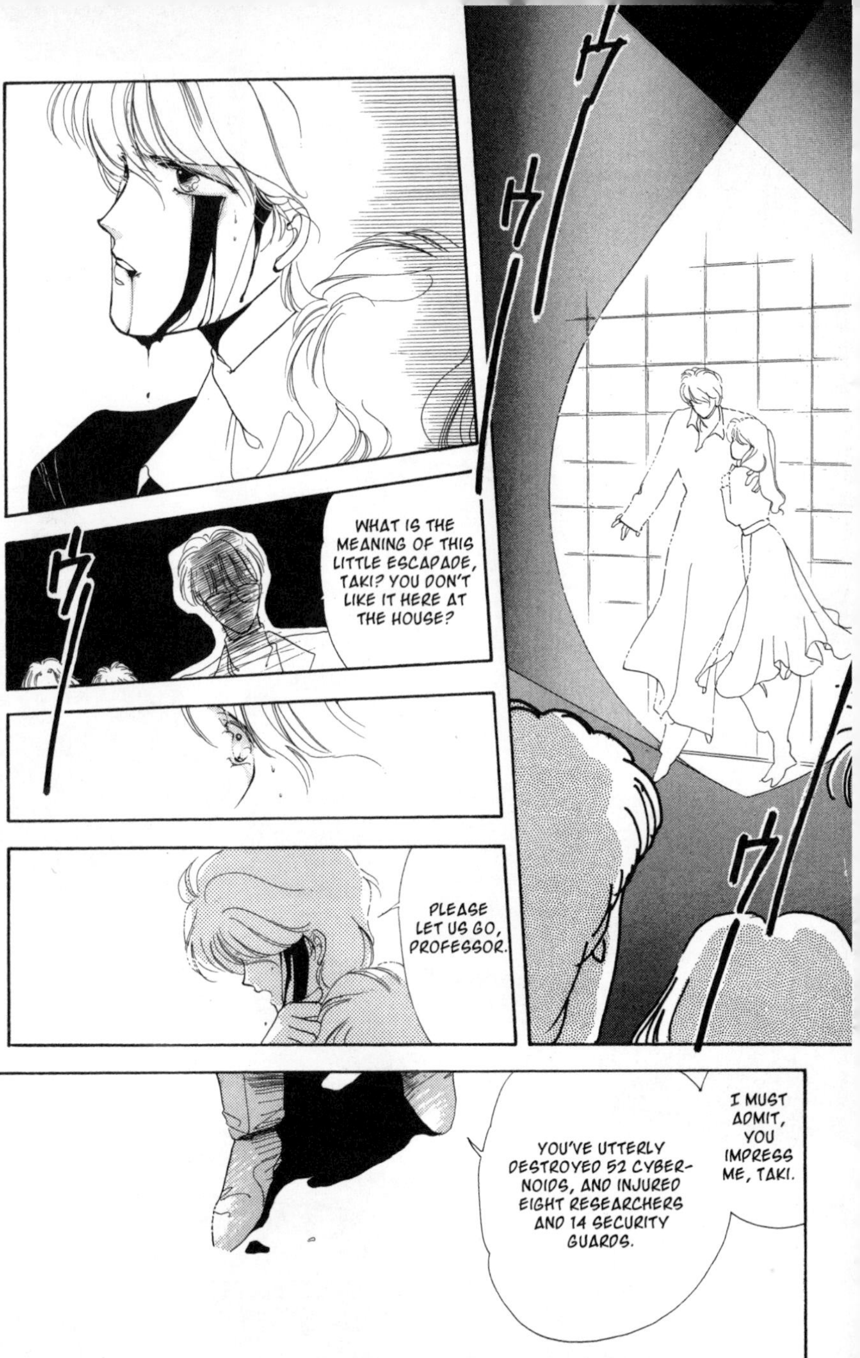

ウーウー
ウー
WHAT IS THE MEANING OF THIS LITTLE ESCAPADE, TAKI? YOU DON'T LIKE IT HERE AT THE HOUSE?
ウ
PLEASE LET US GO, PROFESSOR.
I MUST ADMIT, YOU IMPRESS ME, TAKI.
YOU'VE UTTERLY DESTROYED 52 CYBER-NOIDS, AND INJURED EIGHT RESEARCHERS AND 14 SECURITY GUARDS.

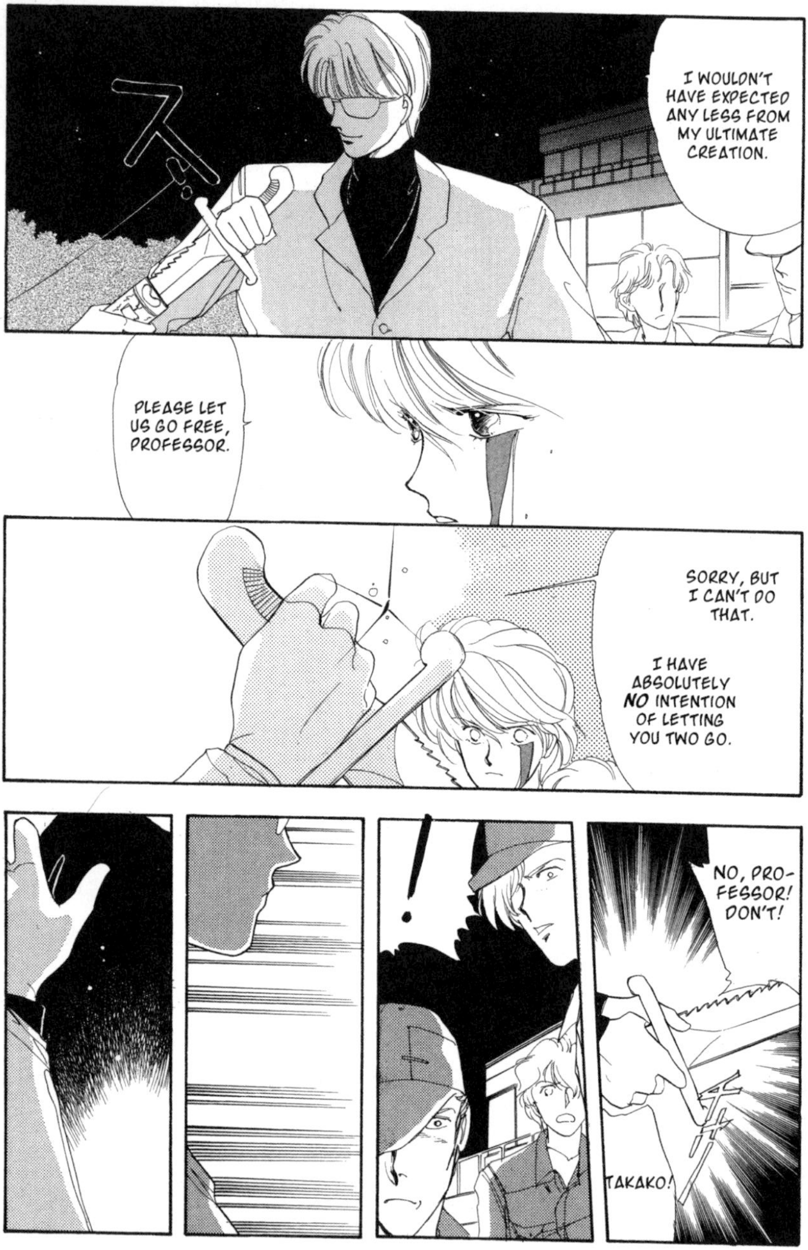
I WOULDN'T HAVE EXPECTED ANY LESS FROM MY ULTIMATE CREATION.
PLEASE LET US GO FREE, PROFESSOR.
SORRY, BUT I CAN'T DO THAT.
I HAVE ABSOLUTELY **NO** INTENTION OF LETTING YOU TWO GO.
NO, PRO-FESSOR! DON'T!
TAKAKO!
!

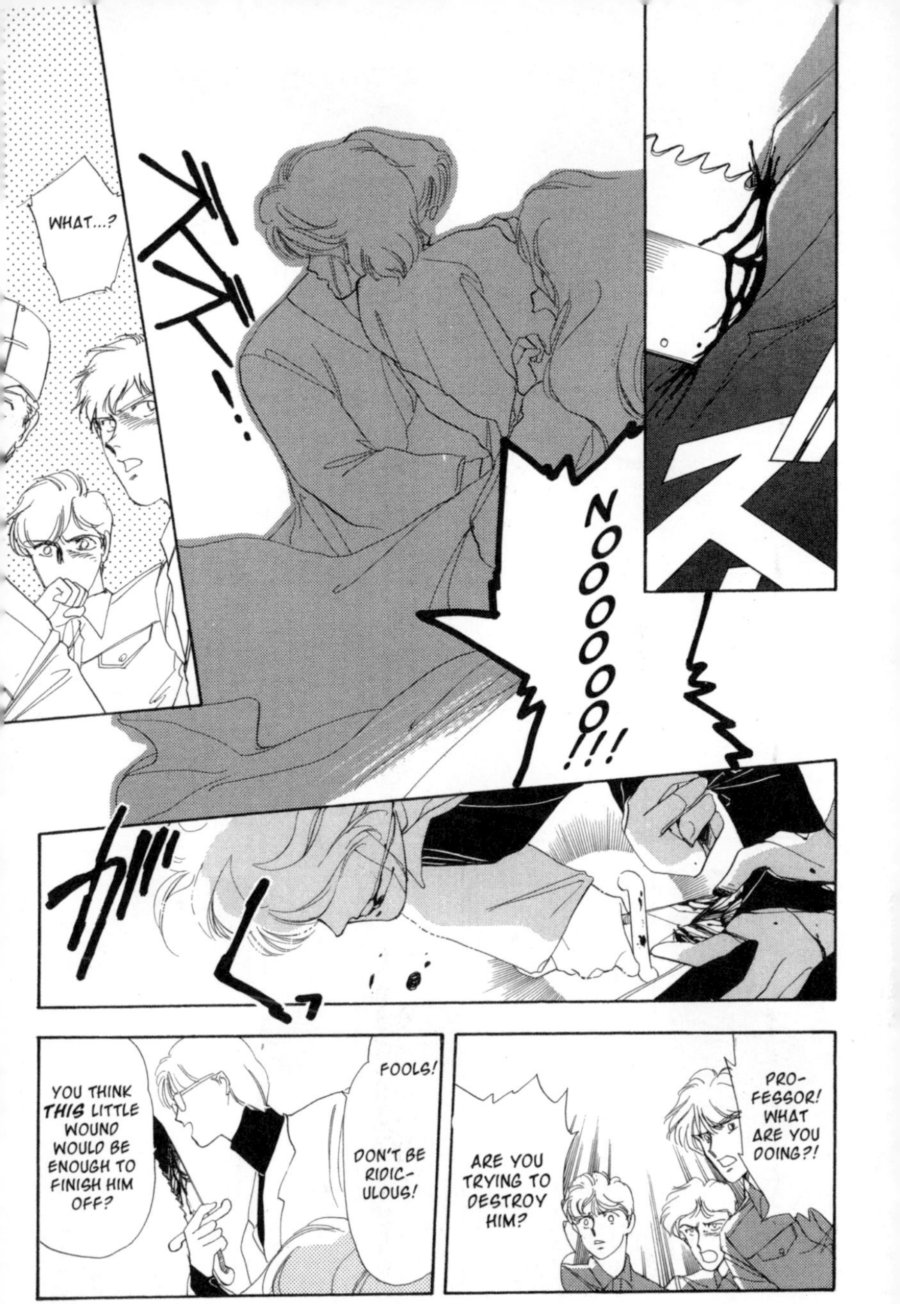
NOOOOOOOO!!!
WHAT...?
PRO-FESSOR! WHAT ARE YOU DOING?!
ARE YOU TRYING TO DESTROY HIM?
FOOLS!
DON'T BE RIDIC-ULOUS!
YOU THINK THIS LITTLE WOUND WOULD BE ENOUGH TO FINISH HIM OFF?

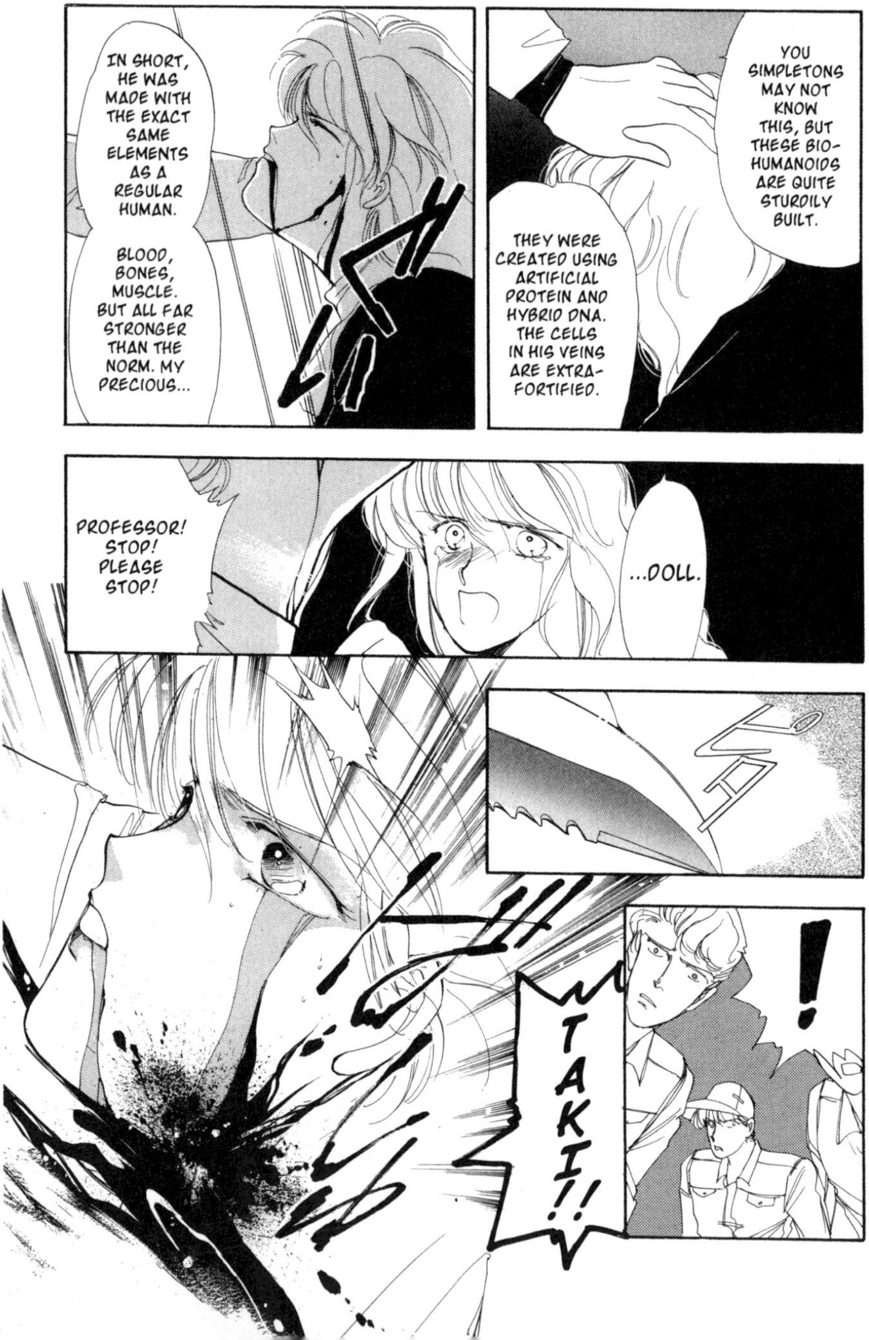
YOU SIMPLETONS MAY NOT KNOW THIS, BUT THESE BIO-HUMANOIDS ARE QUITE STURDILY BUILT.
THEY WERE CREATED USING ARTIFICIAL PROTEIN AND HYBRID DNA. THE CELLS IN HIS VEINS ARE EXTRA-FORTIFIED.
IN SHORT, HE WAS MADE WITH THE EXACT SAME ELEMENTS AS A REGULAR HUMAN.
BLOOD, BONES, MUSCLE. BUT ALL FAR STRONGER THAN THE NORM. MY PRECIOUS...
...DOLL.
PROFESSOR! STOP! PLEASE STOP!
!
TAKI!!

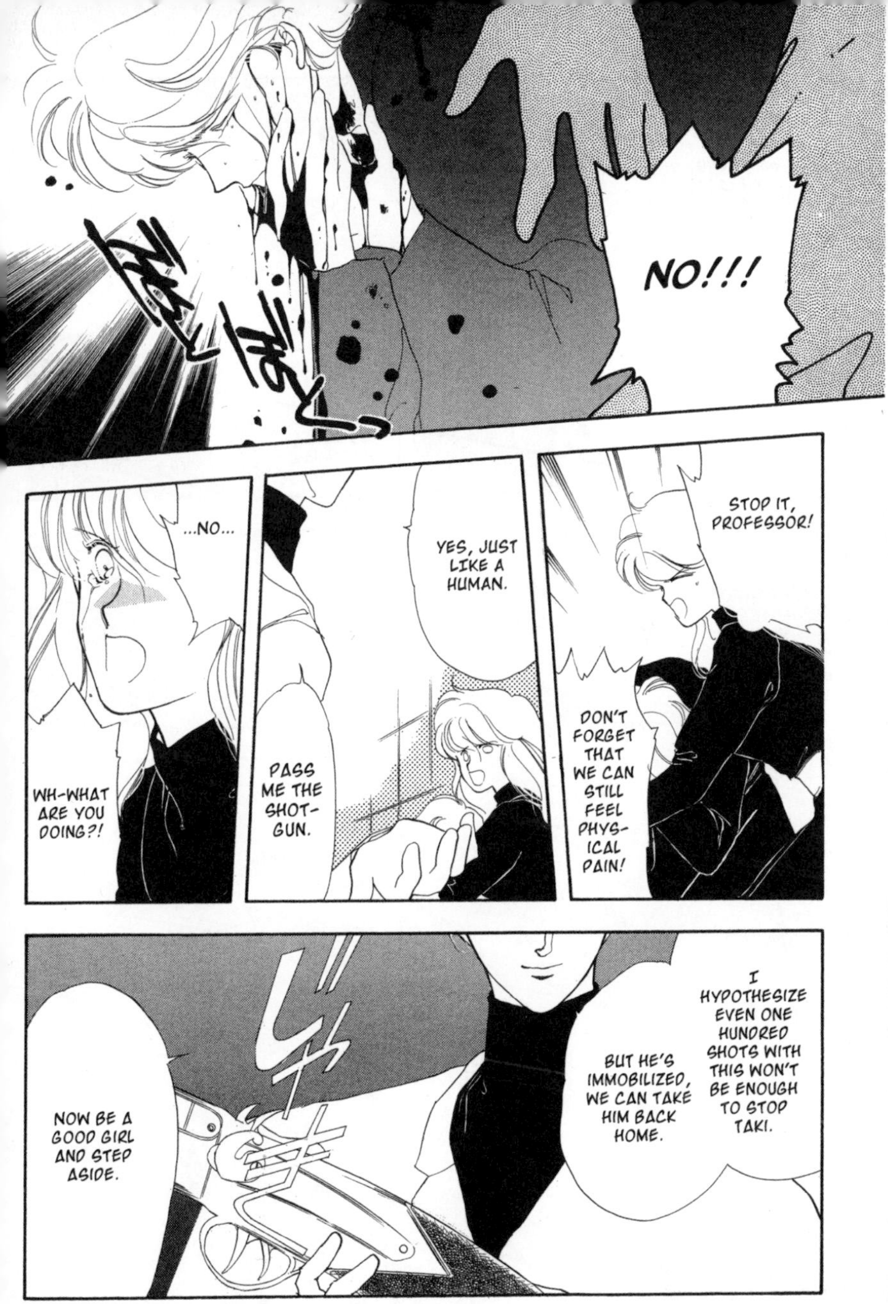
NO!!!
STOP IT, PROFESSOR!
DON'T FORGET THAT WE CAN STILL FEEL PHYSICAL PAIN!
YES, JUST LIKE A HUMAN.
PASS ME THE SHOTGUN.
...NO...
WH-WHAT ARE YOU DOING?!
I HYPOTHESIZE EVEN ONE HUNDRED SHOTS WITH THIS WON'T BE ENOUGH TO STOP TAKI.
BUT HE'S IMMOBILIZED, WE CAN TAKE HIM BACK HOME.
NOW BE A GOOD GIRL AND STEP ASIDE.

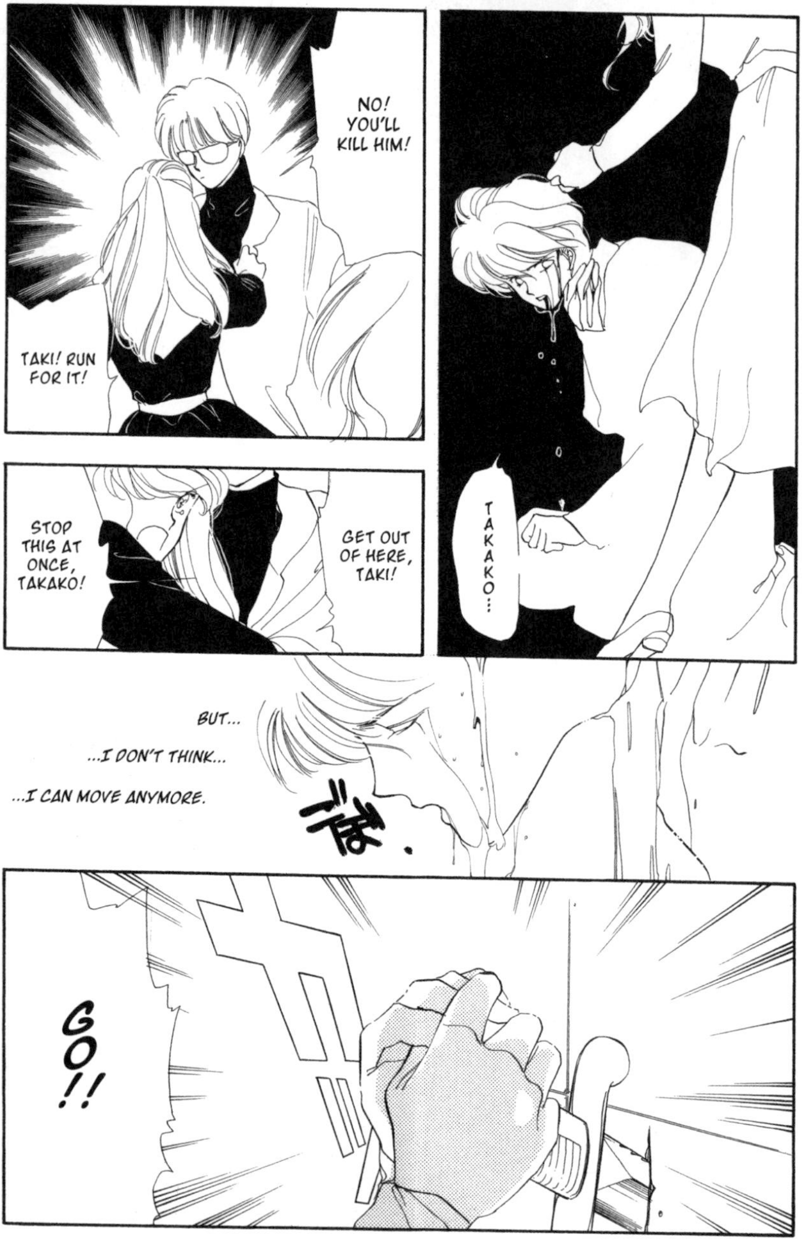
TAKAKO...
NO! YOU'LL KILL HIM!
TAKI! RUN FOR IT!
GET OUT OF HERE, TAKI!
STOP THIS AT ONCE, TAKAKO!
BUT...
...I DON'T THINK...
...I CAN MOVE ANYMORE.
ごぼ
GO!!

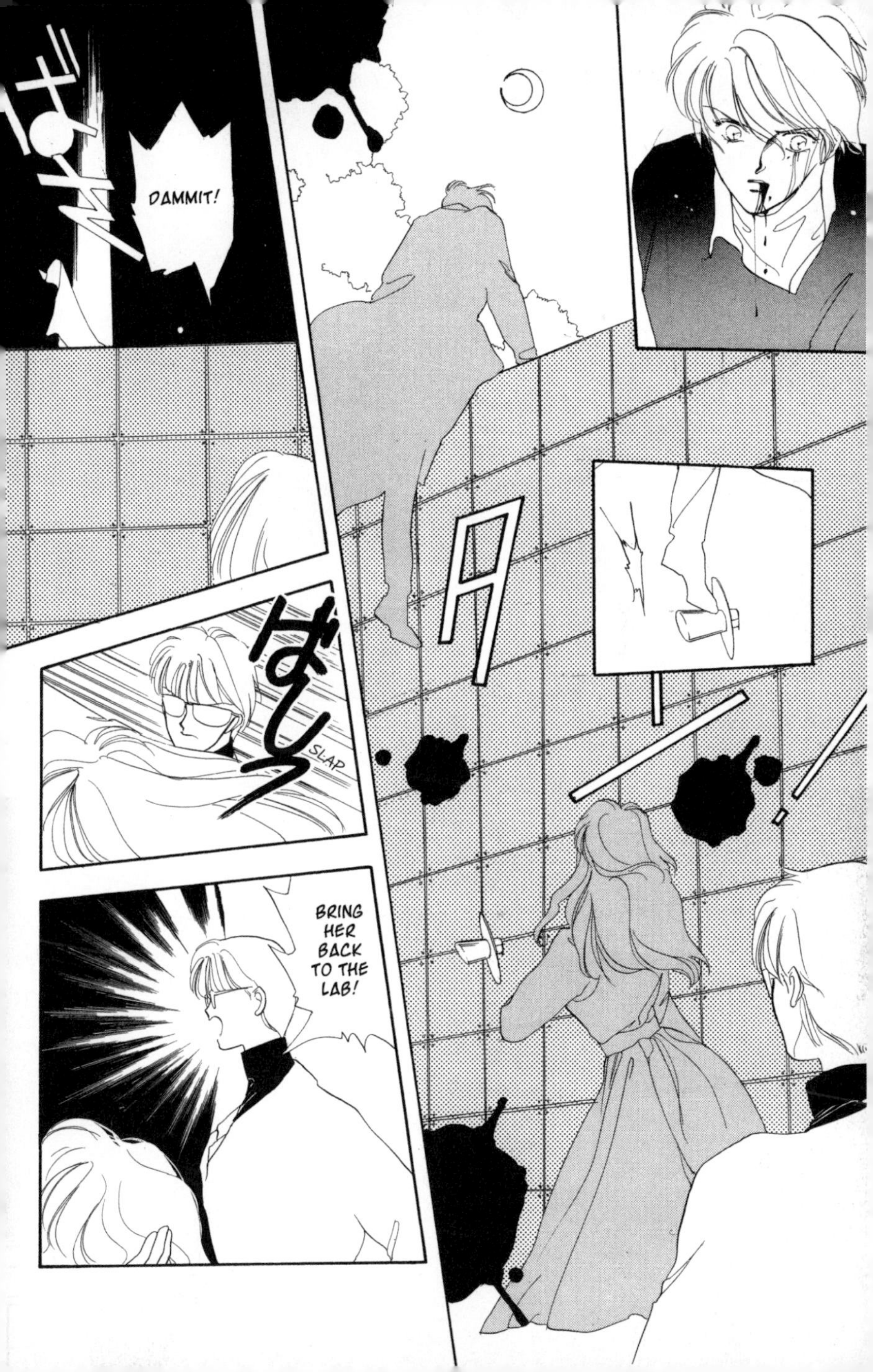
DAMMIT!
SLAP
BRING HER BACK TO THE LAB!

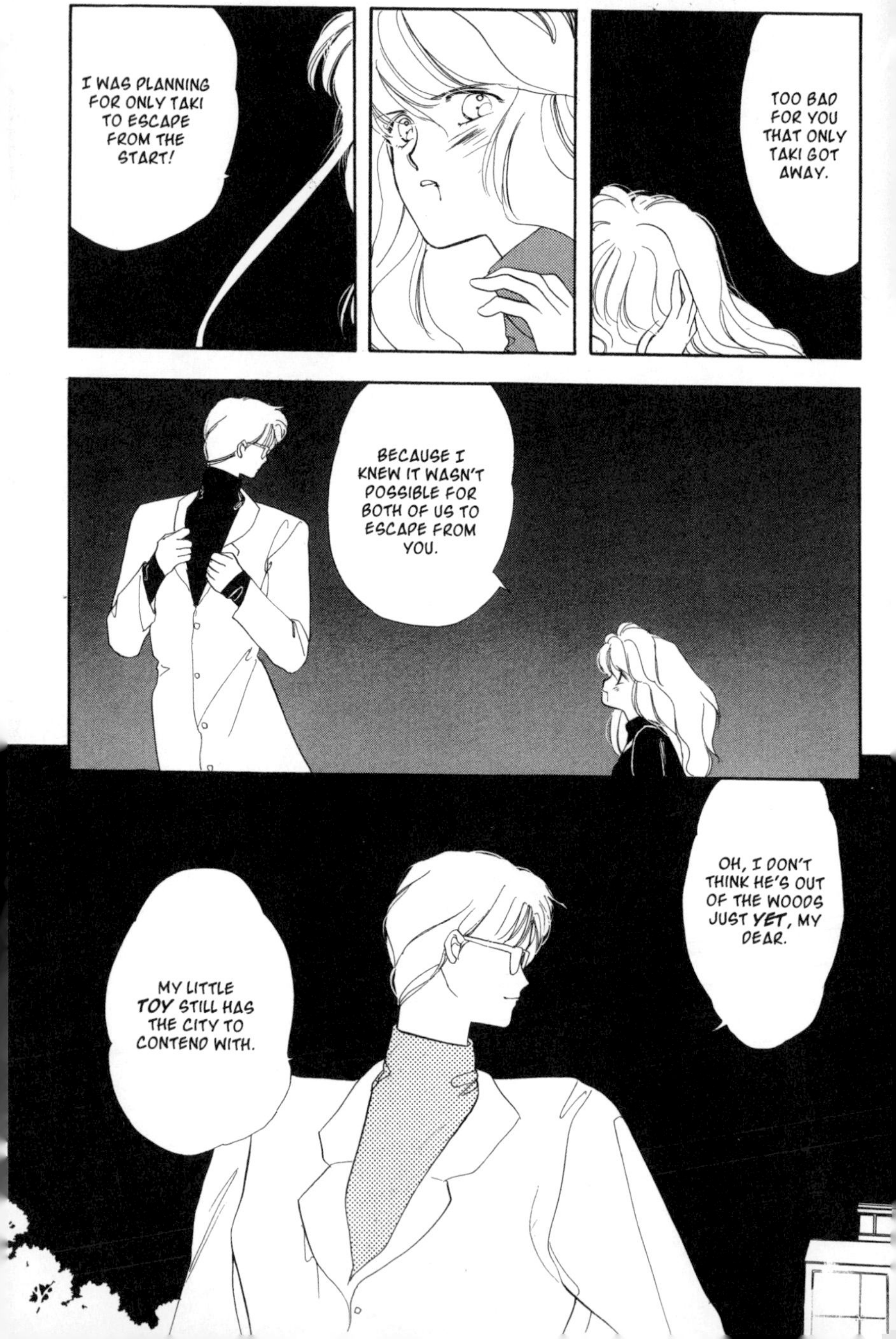
TOO BAD FOR YOU THAT ONLY TAKI GOT AWAY.
I WAS PLANNING FOR ONLY TAKI TO ESCAPE FROM THE START!
BECAUSE I KNEW IT WASN'T POSSIBLE FOR BOTH OF US TO ESCAPE FROM YOU.
OH, I DON'T THINK HE'S OUT OF THE WOODS JUST YET, MY DEAR.
MY LITTLE TOY STILL HAS THE CITY TO CONTEND WITH.

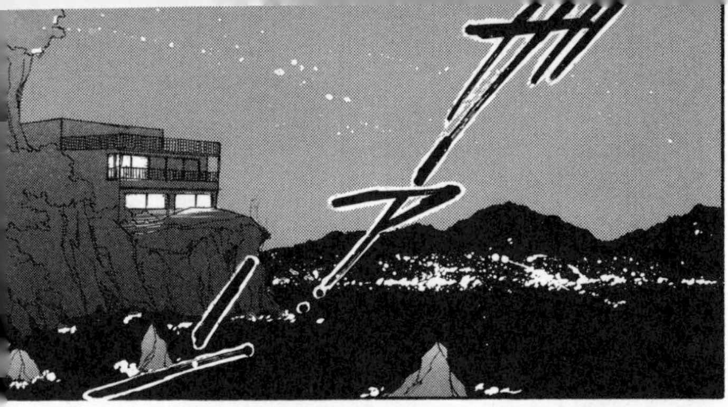

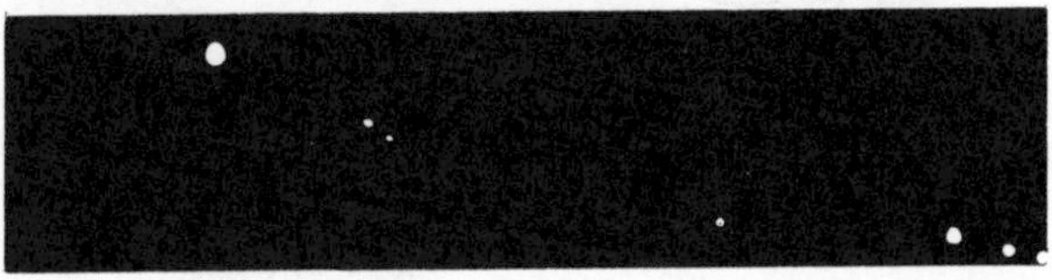

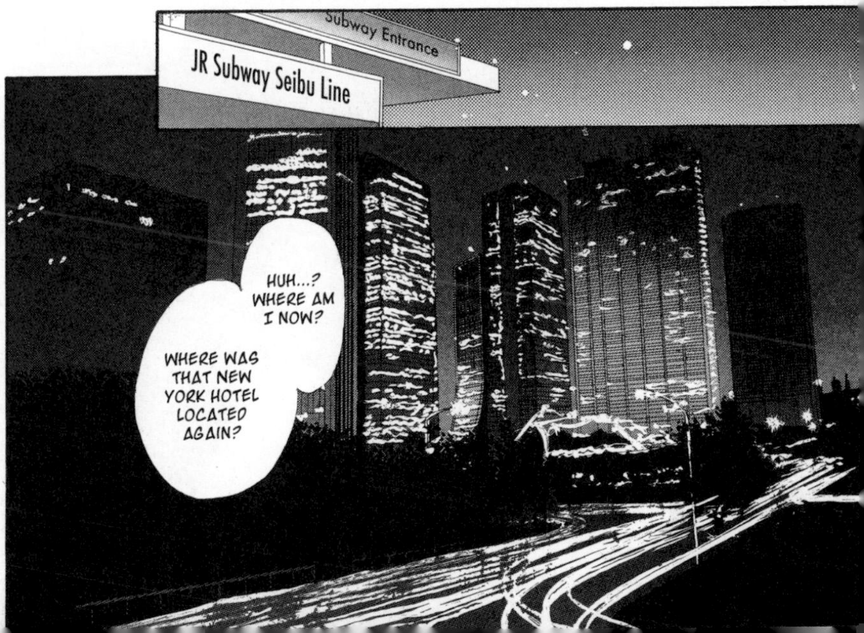
Subway Entrance
JR Subway Seibu Line
HUH...? WHERE AM I NOW?
WHERE WAS THAT NEW YORK HOTEL LOCATED AGAIN?

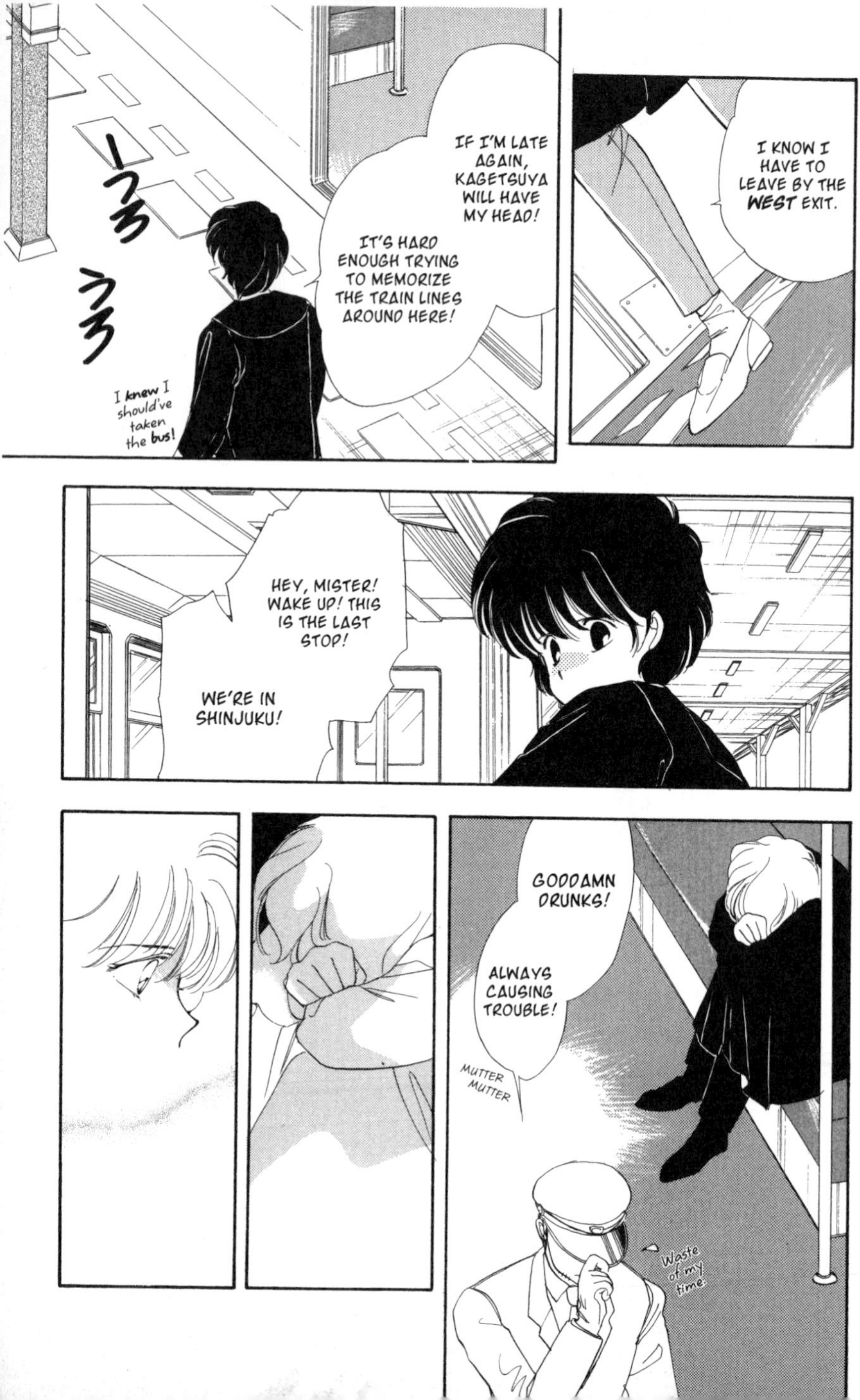
I KNOW I HAVE TO LEAVE BY THE **WEST** EXIT.
IF I'M LATE AGAIN, KAGETSUYA WILL HAVE MY HEAD!
IT'S HARD ENOUGH TRYING TO MEMORIZE THE TRAIN LINES AROUND HERE!
うろ うろ
I **knew** I should've taken the **bus**!
HEY, MISTER! WAKE UP! THIS IS THE LAST STOP!
WE'RE IN SHINJUKU!
GODDAMN DRUNKS!
ALWAYS CAUSING TROUBLE!
MUTTER MUTTER
Waste of my time.

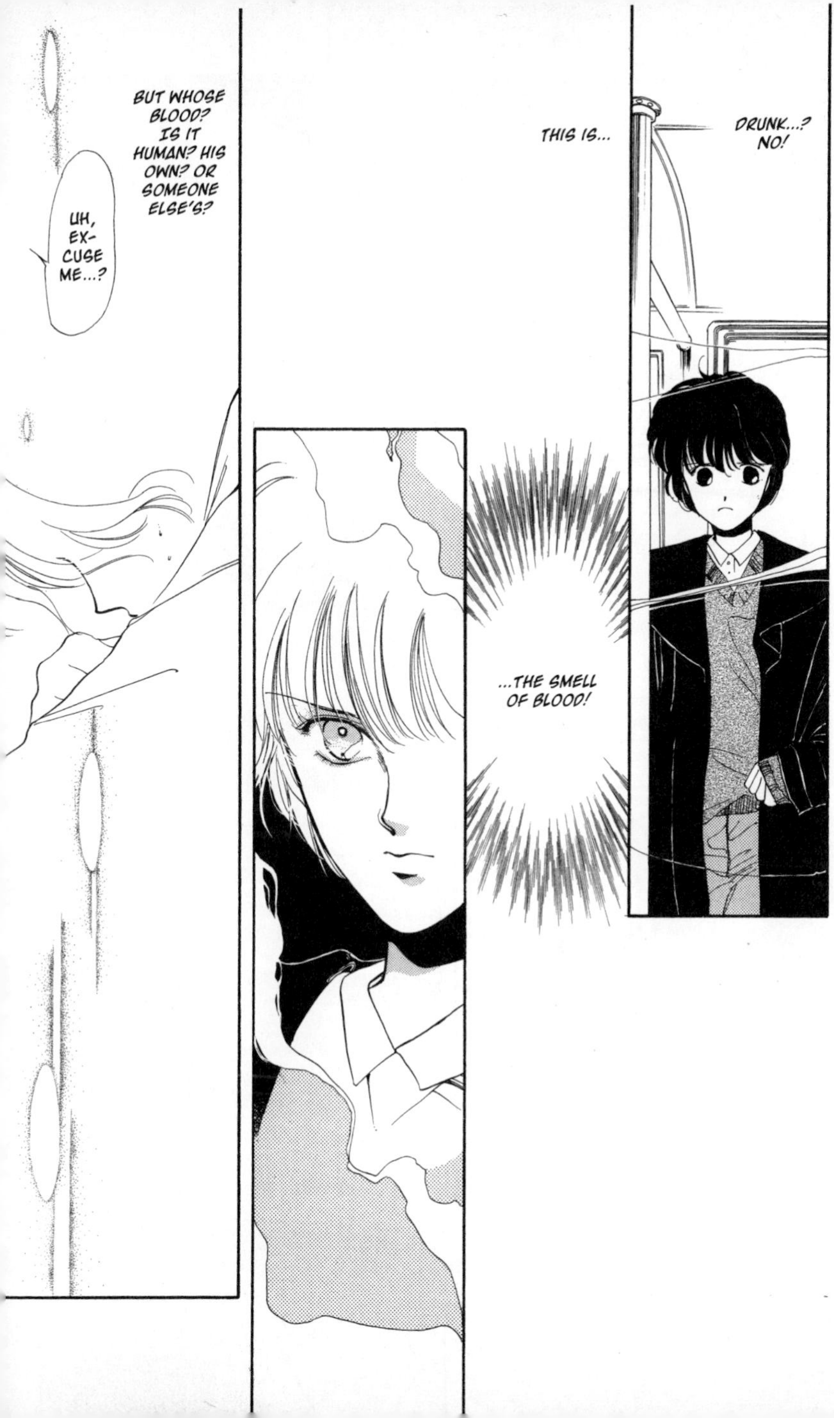
DRUNK...? NO!
THIS IS...
...THE SMELL OF BLOOD!
BUT WHOSE BLOOD? IS IT HUMAN? HIS OWN? OR SOMEONE ELSE'S?
UH, EX-CUSE ME...?

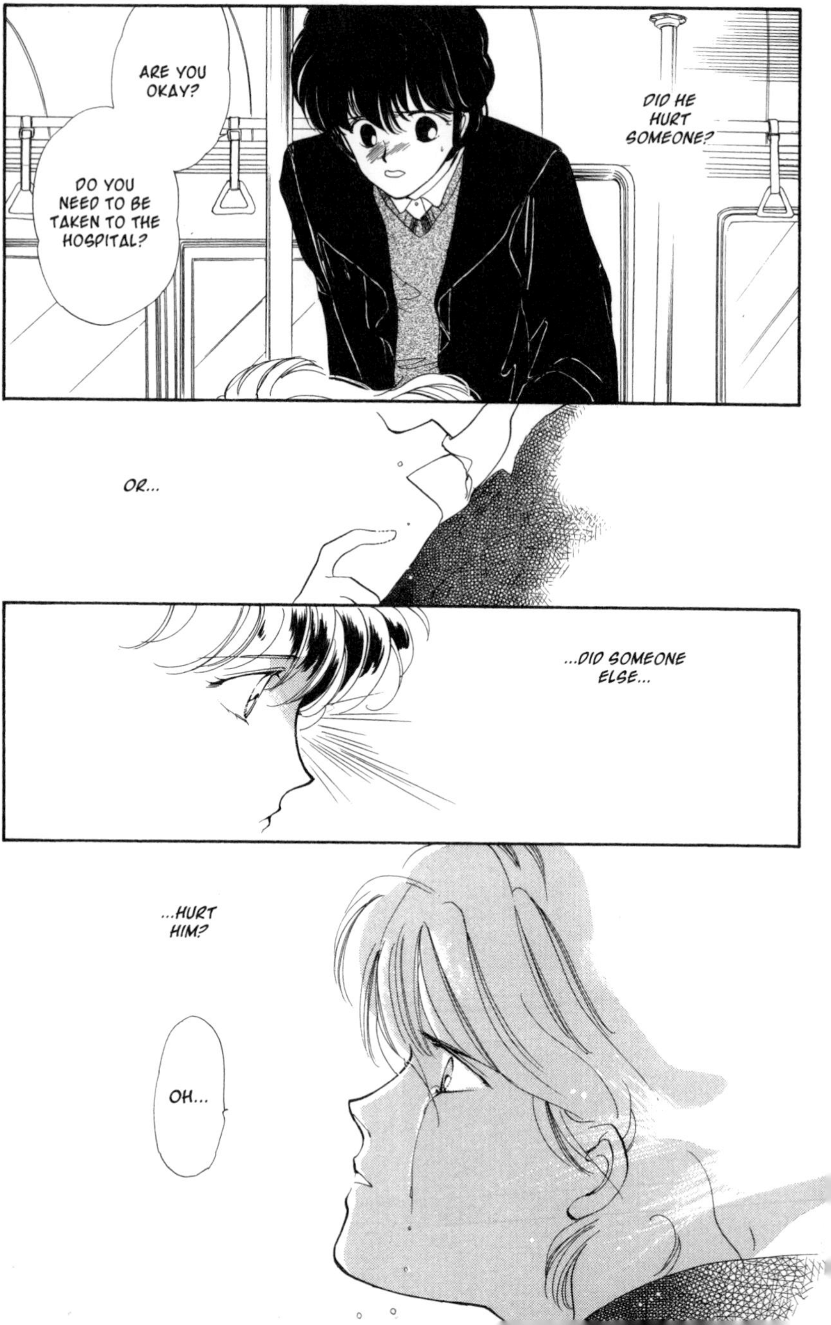
DID HE HURT SOMEONE?
ARE YOU OKAY?
DO YOU NEED TO BE TAKEN TO THE HOSPITAL?
OR...
...DID SOMEONE ELSE...
...HURT HIM?
OH...

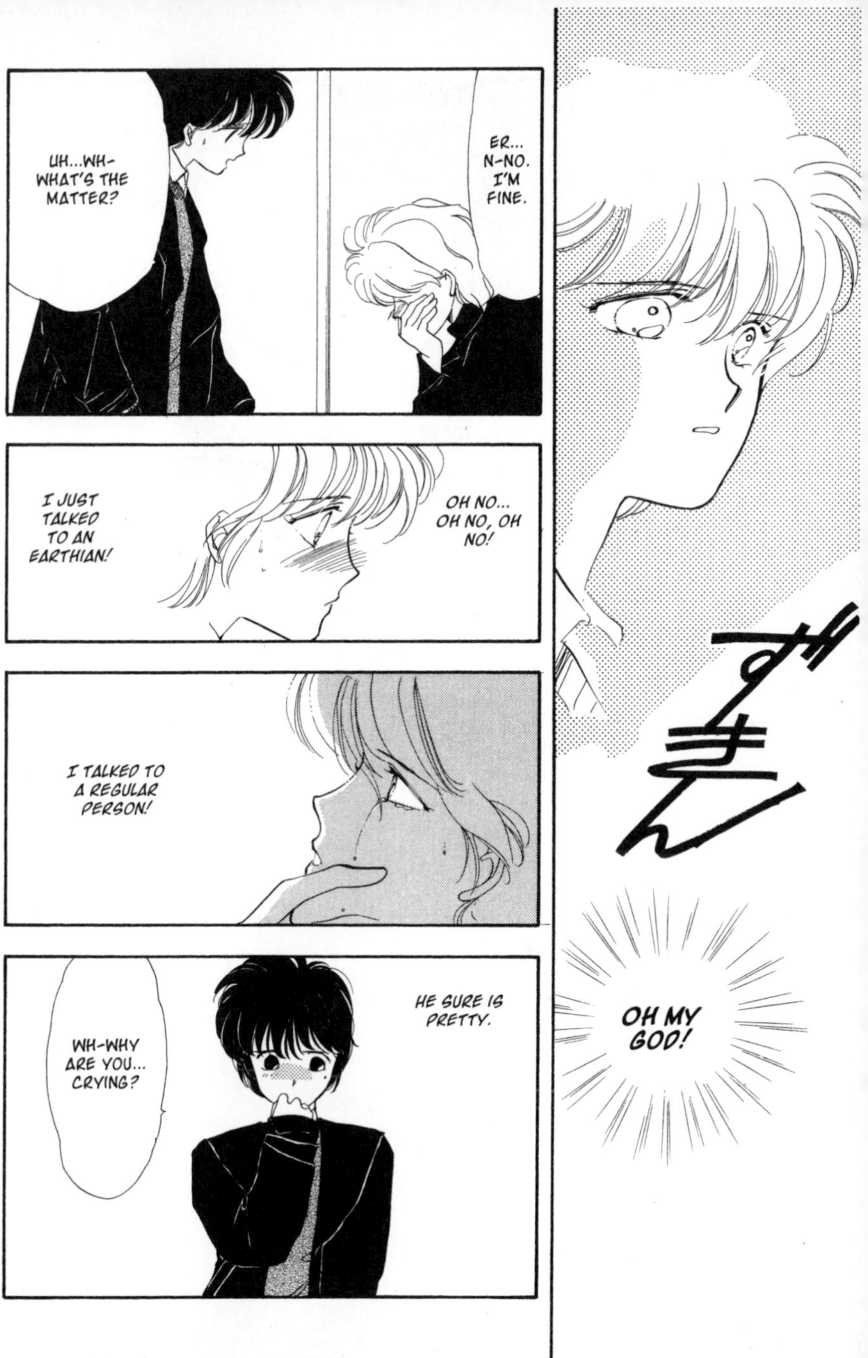
ずきん
OH MY GOD!
ER... N-NO. I'M FINE.
UH...WH-WHAT'S THE MATTER?
OH NO... OH NO, OH NO!
I JUST TALKED TO AN EARTHIAN!
I TALKED TO A REGULAR PERSON!
HE SURE IS PRETTY.
WH-WHY ARE YOU... CRYING?

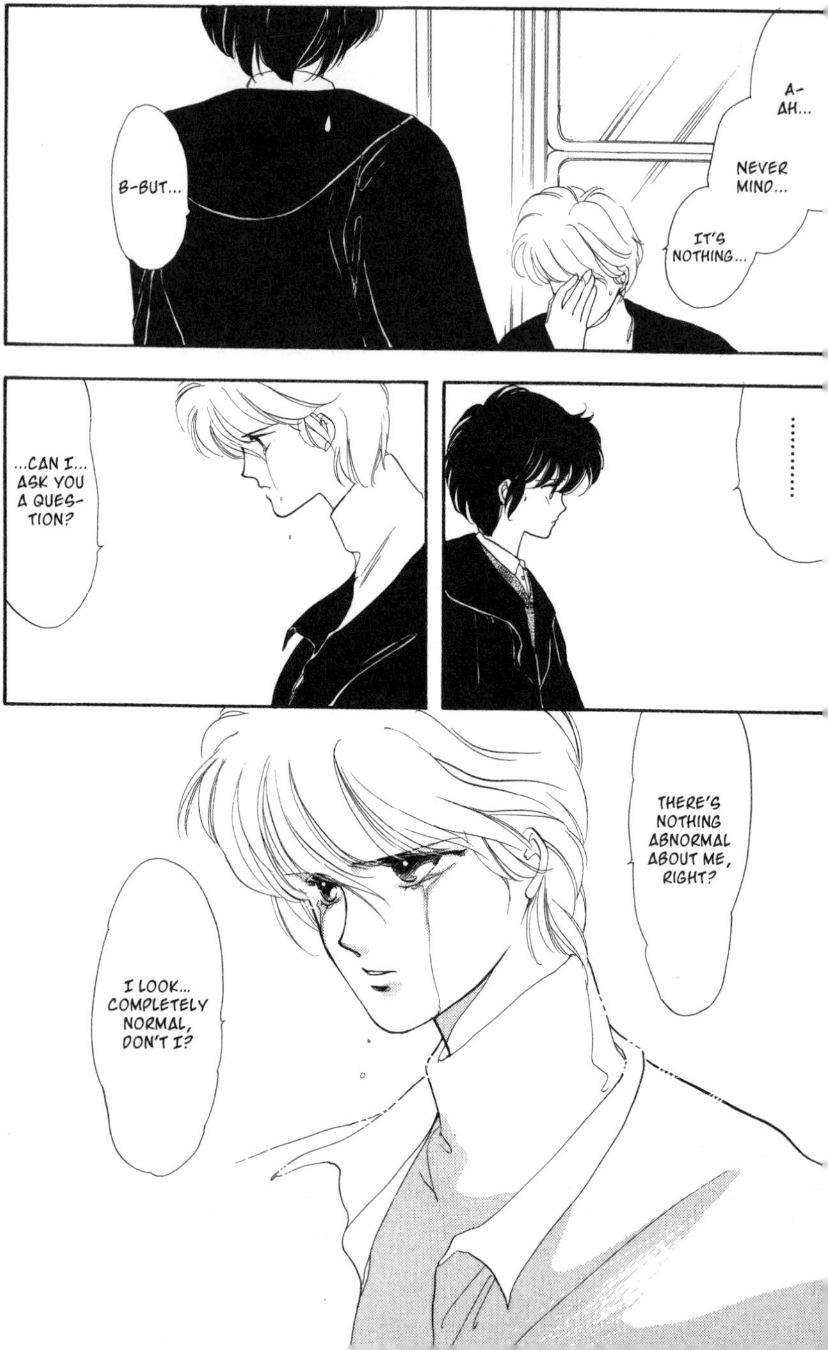
A-
AH...
NEVER MIND...
IT'S NOTHING...
B-BUT...
....
...CAN I... ASK YOU A QUESTION?
THERE'S NOTHING ABNORMAL ABOUT ME, RIGHT?
I LOOK... COMPLETELY NORMAL, DON'T I?

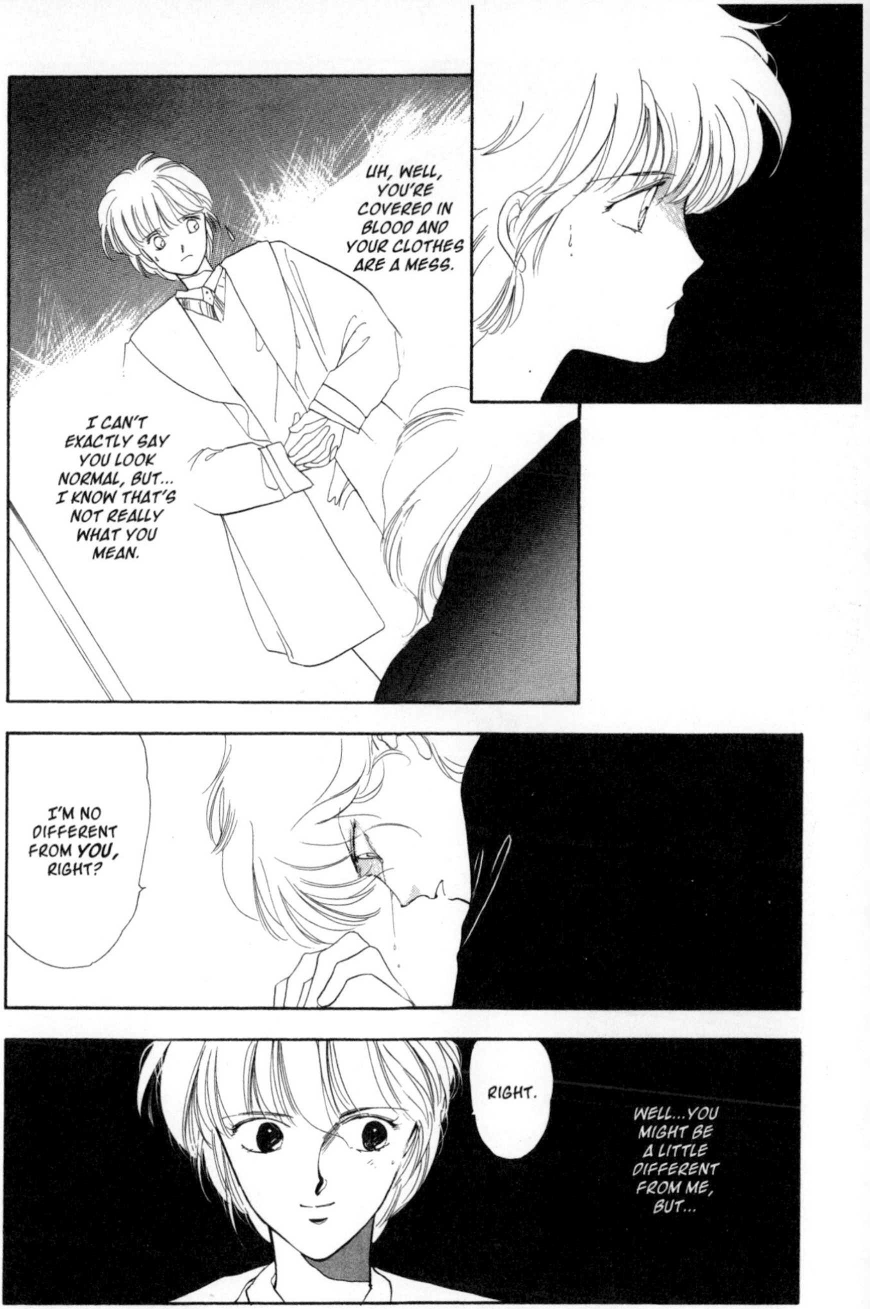
UH, WELL, YOU'RE COVERED IN BLOOD AND YOUR CLOTHES ARE A MESS.
I CAN'T EXACTLY SAY YOU LOOK NORMAL, BUT... I KNOW THAT'S NOT REALLY WHAT YOU MEAN.
I'M NO DIFFERENT FROM YOU, RIGHT?
RIGHT.
WELL...YOU MIGHT BE A LITTLE DIFFERENT FROM ME, BUT...

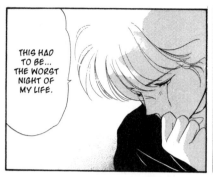

THIS HAD TO BE... THE WORST NIGHT OF MY LIFE.
I HURT THE PEOPLE AROUND ME FOR MY OWN SAKE.
AND LEFT BEHIND A FRIEND TO SAVE **MYSELF.**
I'M SORRY, PROFESSOR.
TAKAKO...
TO-NIGHT...
...I WAS NOTHING BUT A COWARD.
BUT, PROFESSOR... I'M NOT JUST YOUR DOLL.

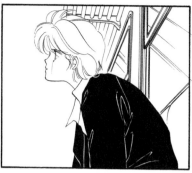

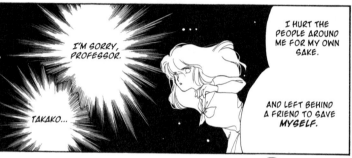

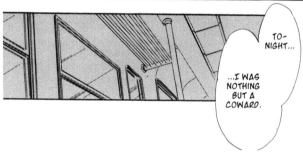

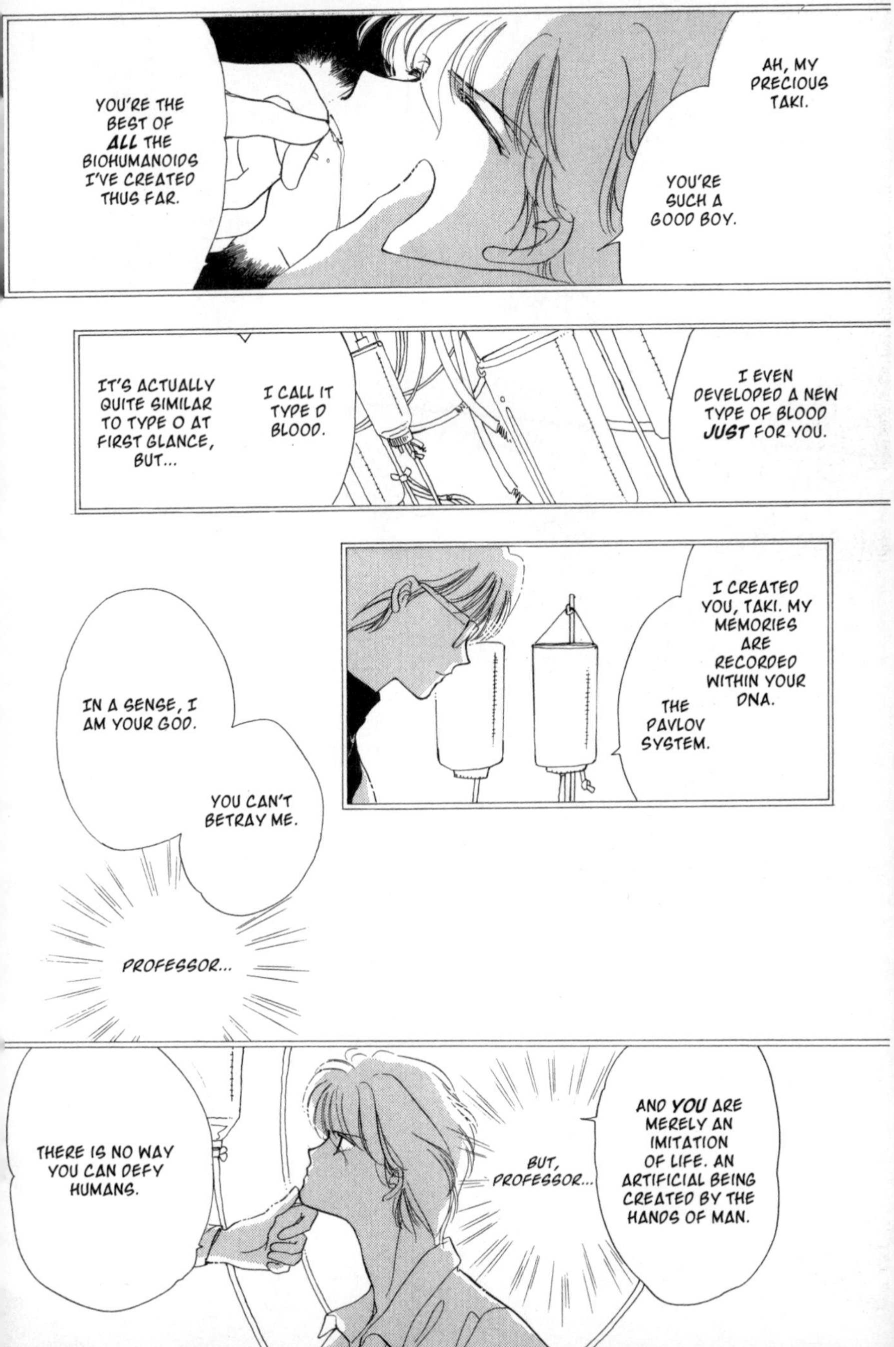
AH, MY PRECIOUS TAKI.
YOU'RE SUCH A GOOD BOY.
YOU'RE THE BEST OF ALL THE BIOHUMANOIDS I'VE CREATED THUS FAR.
I EVEN DEVELOPED A NEW TYPE OF BLOOD JUST FOR YOU.
I CALL IT TYPE D BLOOD.
IT'S ACTUALLY QUITE SIMILAR TO TYPE O AT FIRST GLANCE, BUT...
I CREATED YOU, TAKI. MY MEMORIES ARE RECORDED WITHIN YOUR DNA.
THE PAVLOV SYSTEM.
IN A SENSE, I AM YOUR GOD.
YOU CAN'T BETRAY ME.
PROFESSOR...
AND YOU ARE MERELY AN IMITATION OF LIFE. AN ARTIFICIAL BEING CREATED BY THE HANDS OF MAN.
BUT, PROFESSOR...
THERE IS NO WAY YOU CAN DEFY HUMANS.

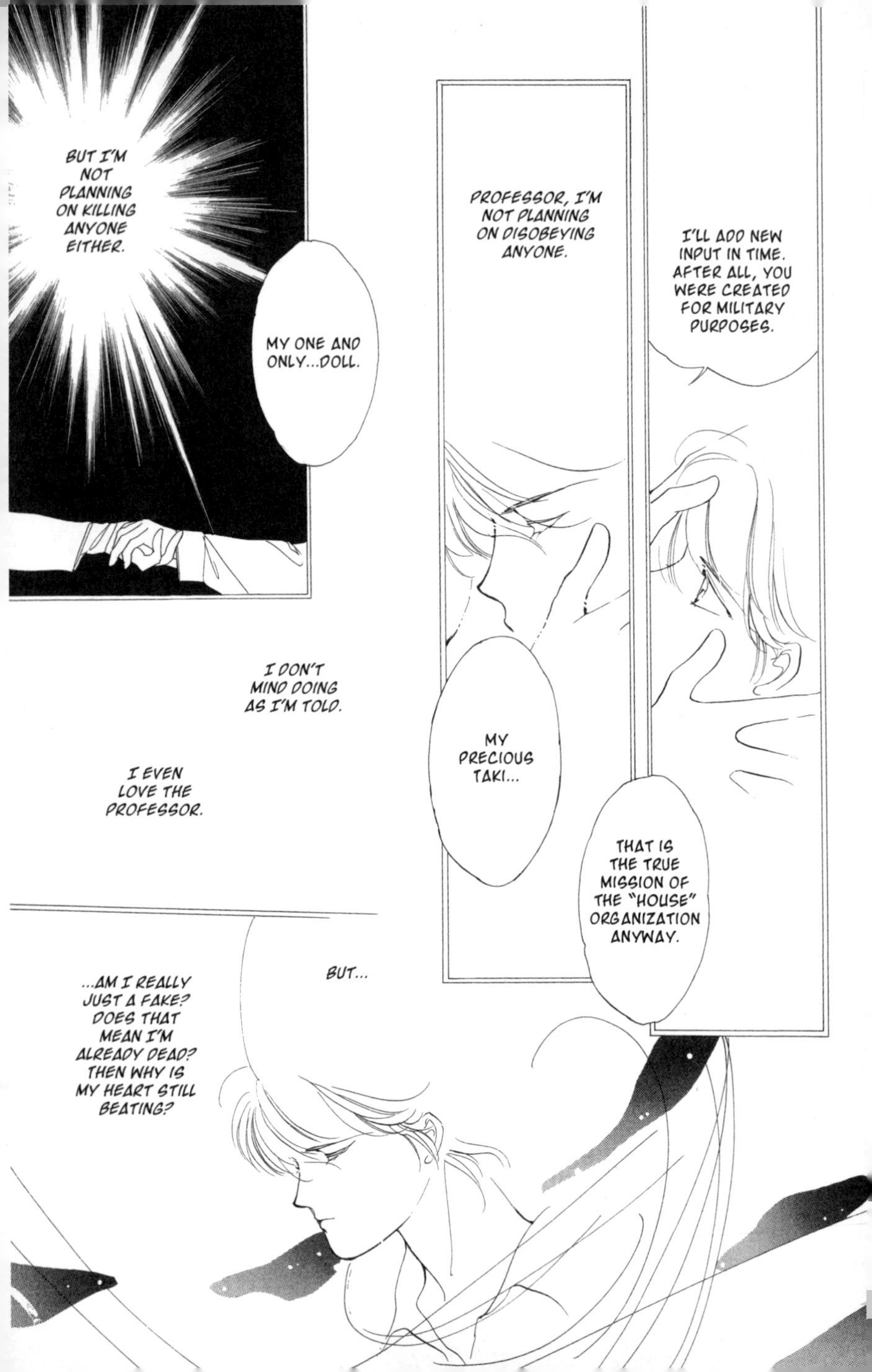
I'LL ADD NEW INPUT IN TIME. AFTER ALL, YOU WERE CREATED FOR MILITARY PURPOSES.
THAT IS THE TRUE MISSION OF THE "HOUSE" ORGANIZATION ANYWAY.
PROFESSOR, I'M NOT PLANNING ON DISOBEYING ANYONE.
MY PRECIOUS TAKI...
BUT I'M NOT PLANNING ON KILLING ANYONE EITHER.
MY ONE AND ONLY...DOLL.
I DON'T MIND DOING AS I'M TOLD.
I EVEN LOVE THE PROFESSOR.
BUT...
...AM I REALLY JUST A FAKE? DOES THAT MEAN I'M ALREADY DEAD? THEN WHY IS MY HEART STILL BEATING?

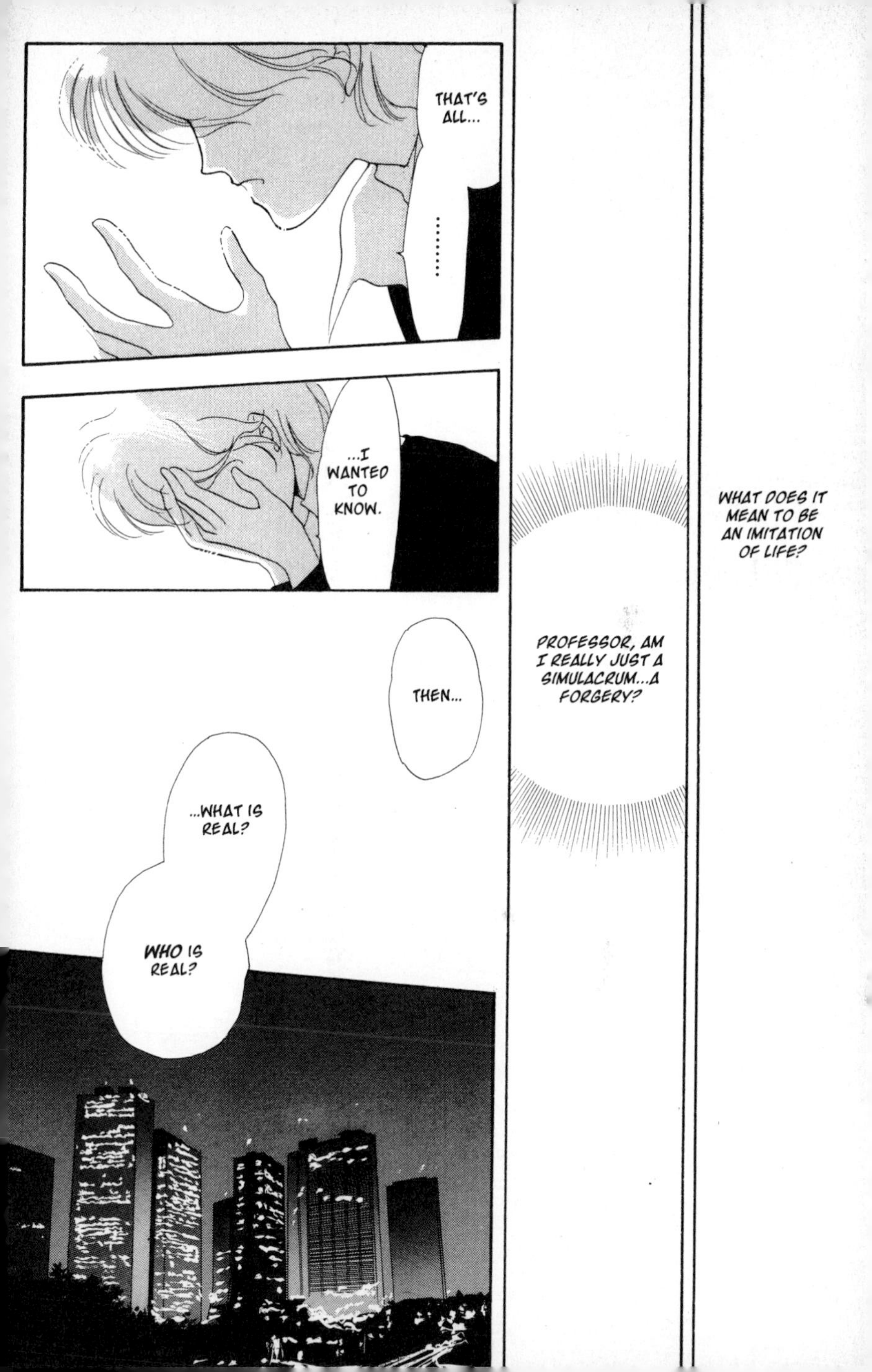
WHAT DOES IT MEAN TO BE AN IMITATION OF LIFE?
PROFESSOR, AM I REALLY JUST A SIMULACRUM...A FORGERY?
THAT'S ALL...
....
...I WANTED TO KNOW.
THEN...
...WHAT IS REAL?
WHO IS REAL?

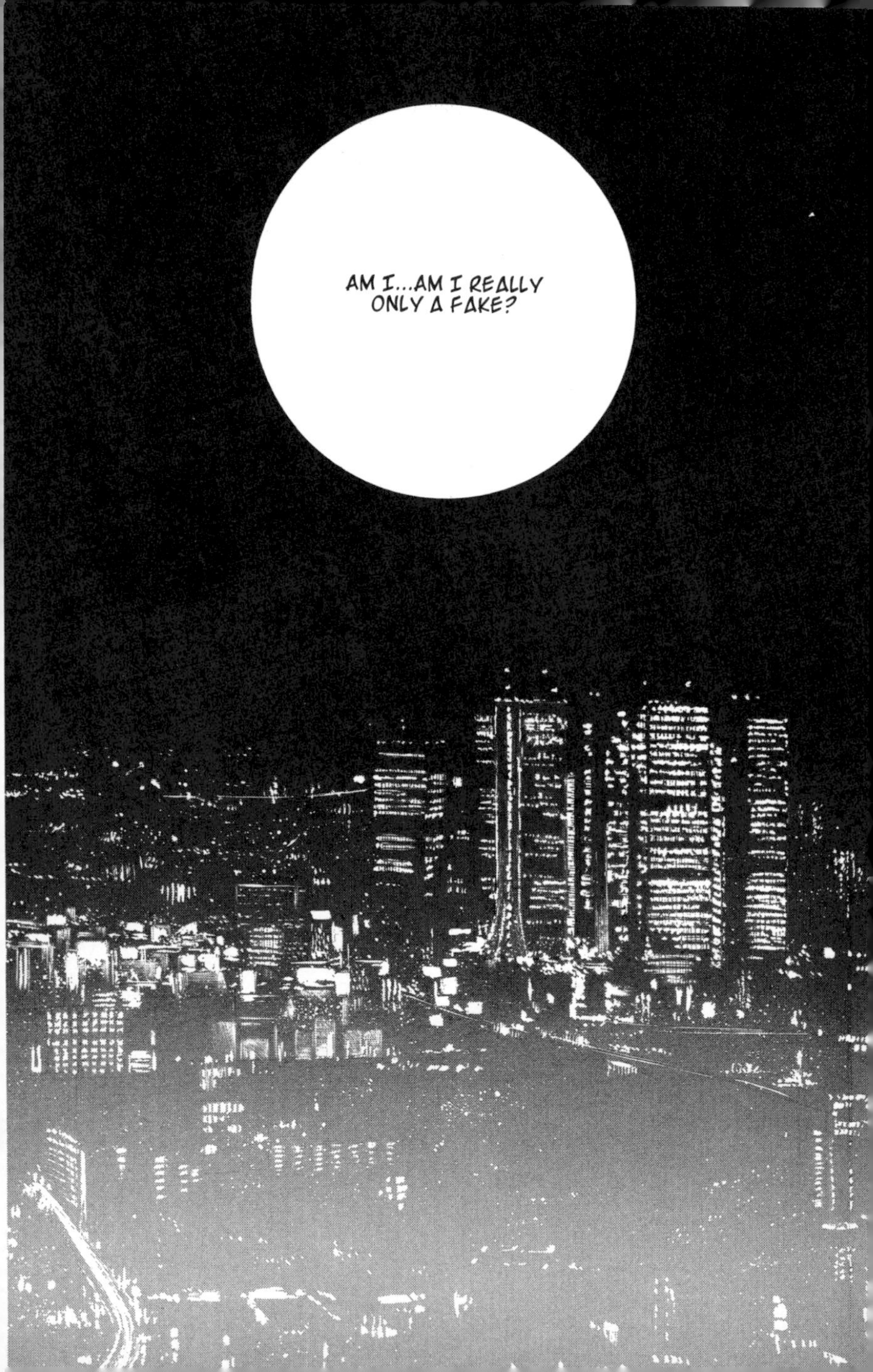
AM I...AM I REALLY ONLY A FAKE?

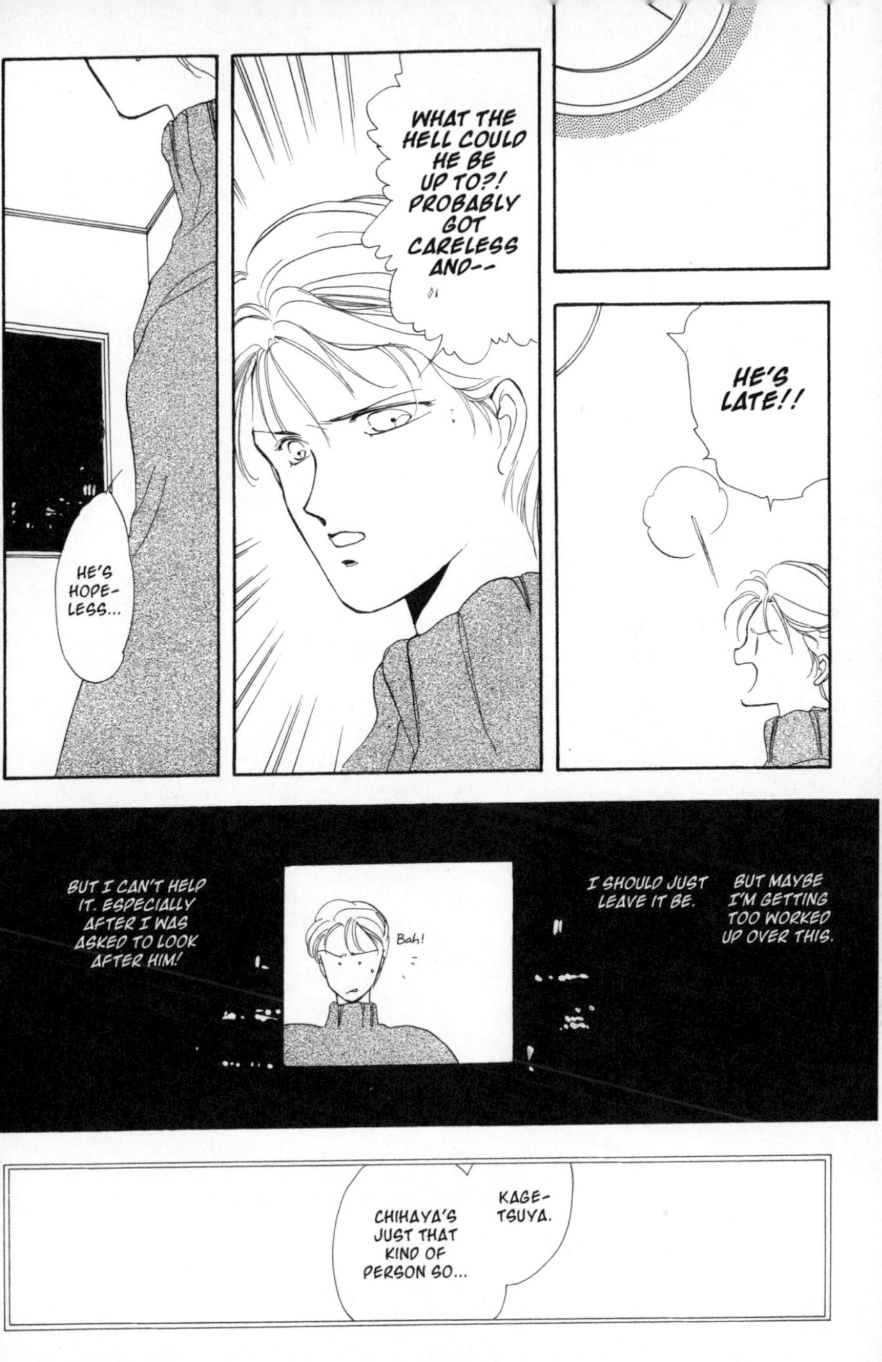

HE'S LATE!!
WHAT THE HELL COULD HE BE UP TO?! PROBABLY GOT CARELESS AND--
HE'S HOPELESS...
BUT MAYBE I'M GETTING TOO WORKED UP OVER THIS.
I SHOULD JUST LEAVE IT BE.
Bah!
BUT I CAN'T HELP IT. ESPECIALLY AFTER I WAS ASKED TO LOOK AFTER HIM!
KAGE-TSUYA.
CHIHAYA'S JUST THAT KIND OF PERSON SO...

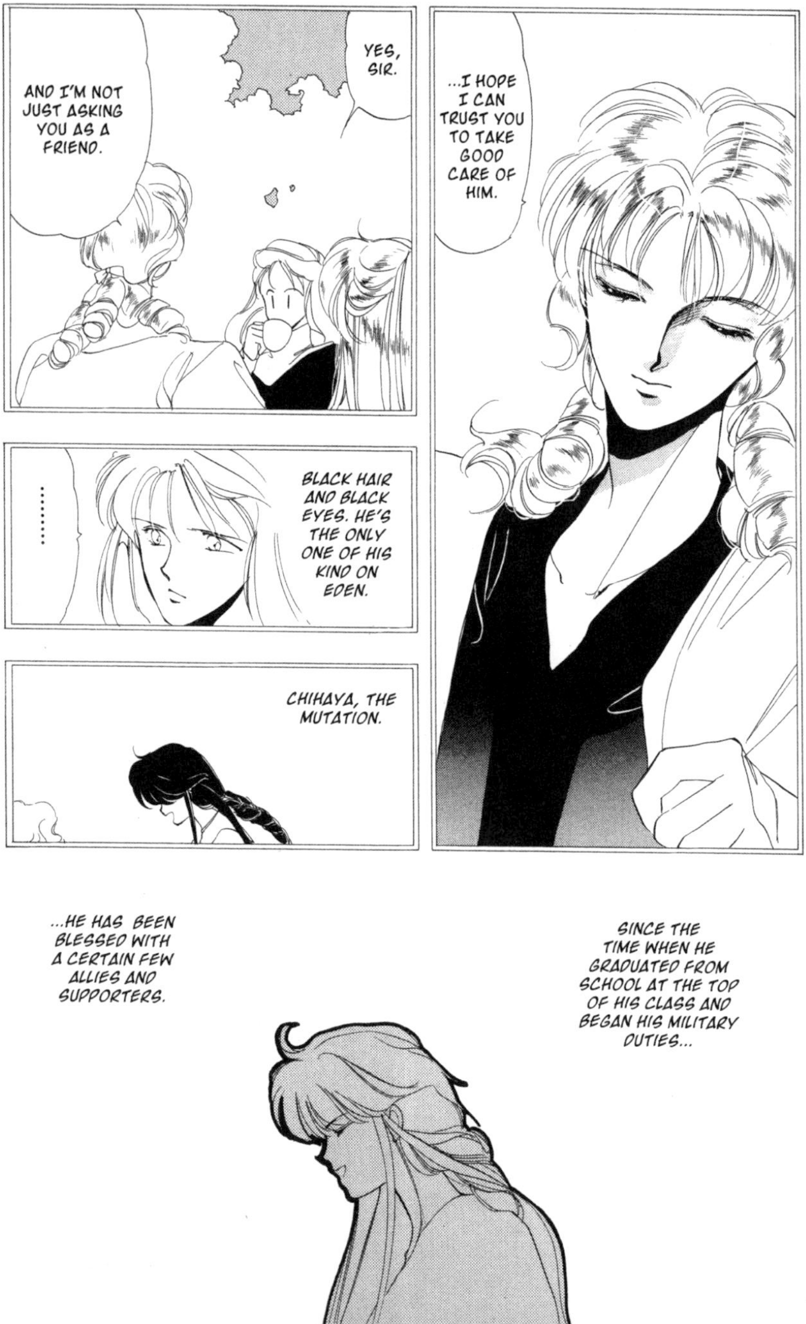
...I HOPE I CAN TRUST YOU TO TAKE GOOD CARE OF HIM.
AND I'M NOT JUST ASKING YOU AS A FRIEND.
YES, SIR.
BLACK HAIR AND BLACK EYES. HE'S THE ONLY ONE OF HIS KIND ON EDEN.
....
CHIHAYA, THE MUTATION.
SINCE THE TIME WHEN HE GRADUATED FROM SCHOOL AT THE TOP OF HIS CLASS AND BEGAN HIS MILITARY DUTIES...
...HE HAS BEEN BLESSED WITH A CERTAIN FEW ALLIES AND SUPPORTERS.

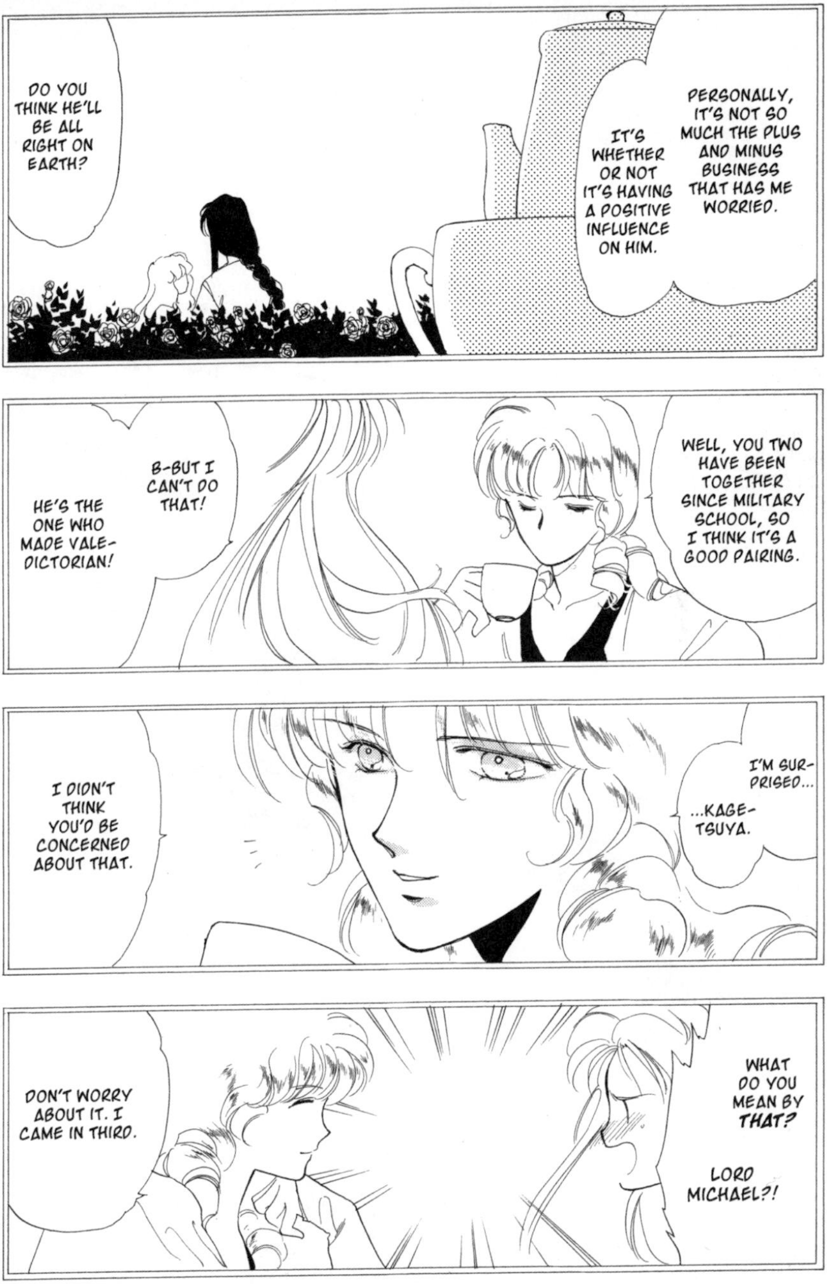
PERSONALLY, IT'S NOT SO MUCH THE PLUS AND MINUS BUSINESS THAT HAS ME WORRIED.
IT'S WHETHER OR NOT IT'S HAVING A POSITIVE INFLUENCE ON HIM.
DO YOU THINK HE'LL BE ALL RIGHT ON EARTH?
WELL, YOU TWO HAVE BEEN TOGETHER SINCE MILITARY SCHOOL, SO I THINK IT'S A GOOD PAIRING.
B-BUT I CAN'T DO THAT!
HE'S THE ONE WHO MADE VALE-DICTORIAN!
I'M SUR-PRISED...
...KAGE-TSUYA.
I DIDN'T THINK YOU'D BE CONCERNED ABOUT THAT.
WHAT DO YOU MEAN BY ***THAT?***
LORD MICHAEL?!
DON'T WORRY ABOUT IT. I CAME IN THIRD.

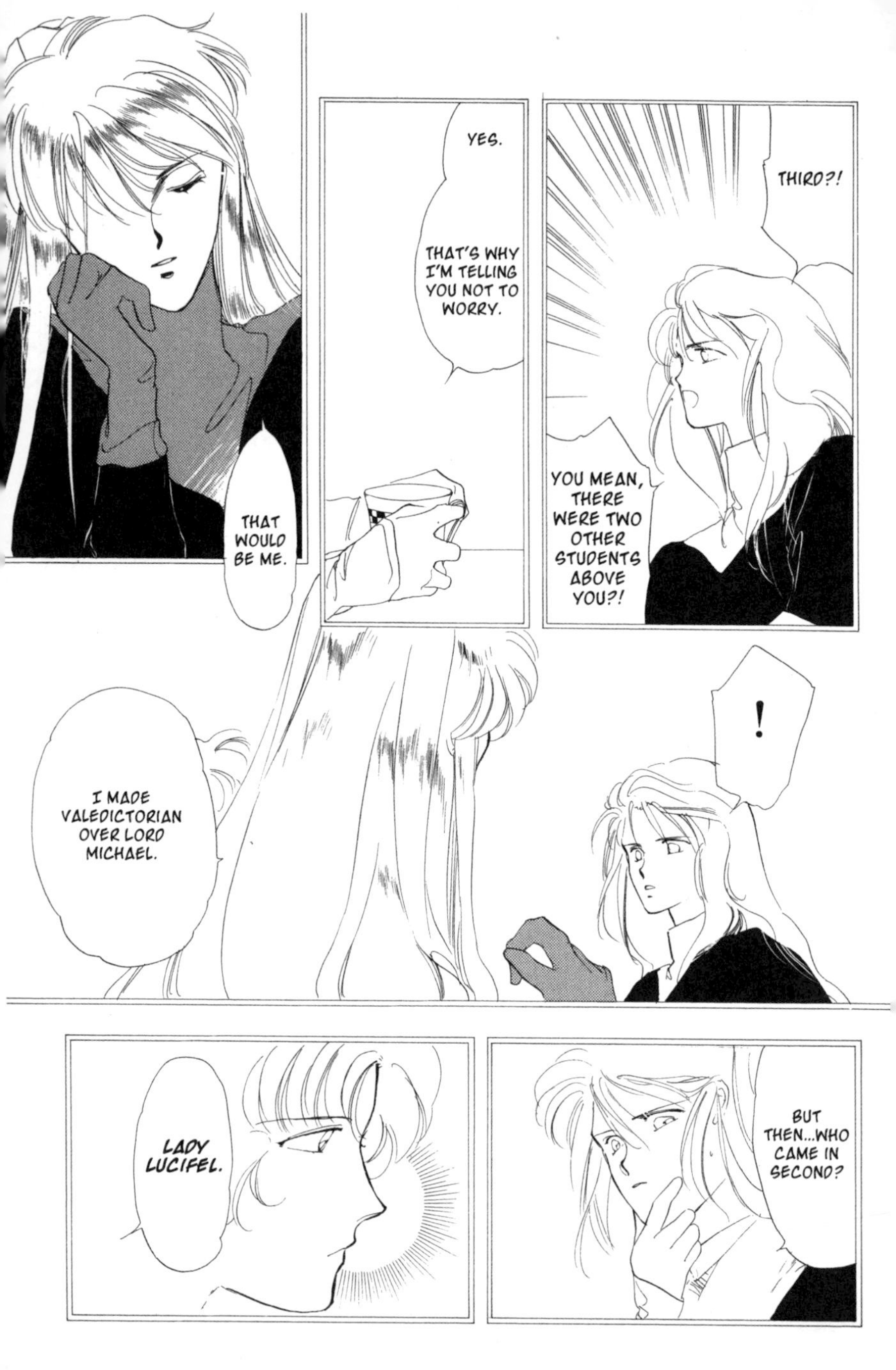
THIRD?!
YOU MEAN, THERE WERE TWO OTHER STUDENTS ABOVE YOU?!
YES.
THAT'S WHY I'M TELLING YOU NOT TO WORRY.
THAT WOULD BE ME.
!
I MADE VALEDICTORIAN OVER LORD MICHAEL.
BUT THEN...WHO CAME IN SECOND?
LADY LUCIFEL.

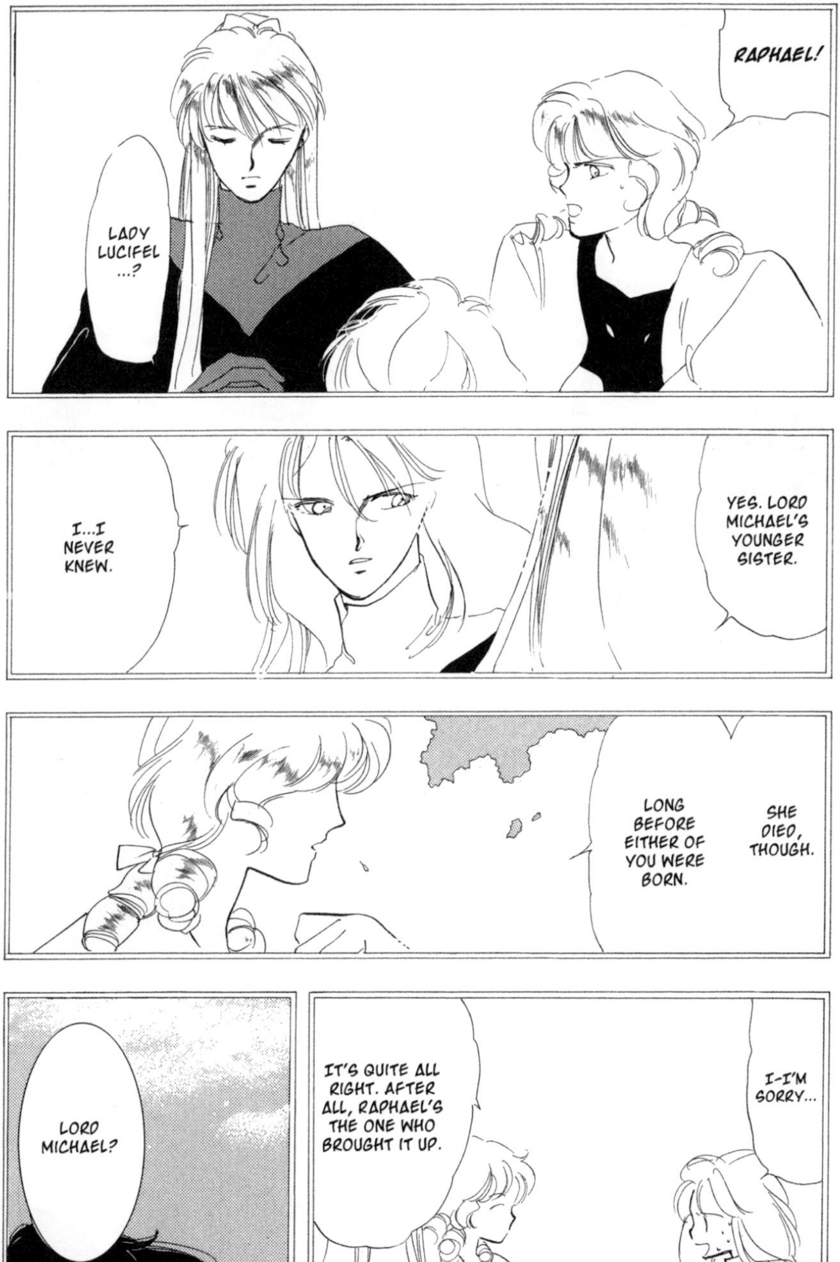
RAPHAEL!
LADY LUCIFEL ...?
YES. LORD MICHAEL'S YOUNGER SISTER.
I...I NEVER KNEW.
SHE DIED, THOUGH.
LONG BEFORE EITHER OF YOU WERE BORN.
I-I'M SORRY...
IT'S QUITE ALL RIGHT. AFTER ALL, RAPHAEL'S THE ONE WHO BROUGHT IT UP.
LORD MICHAEL?

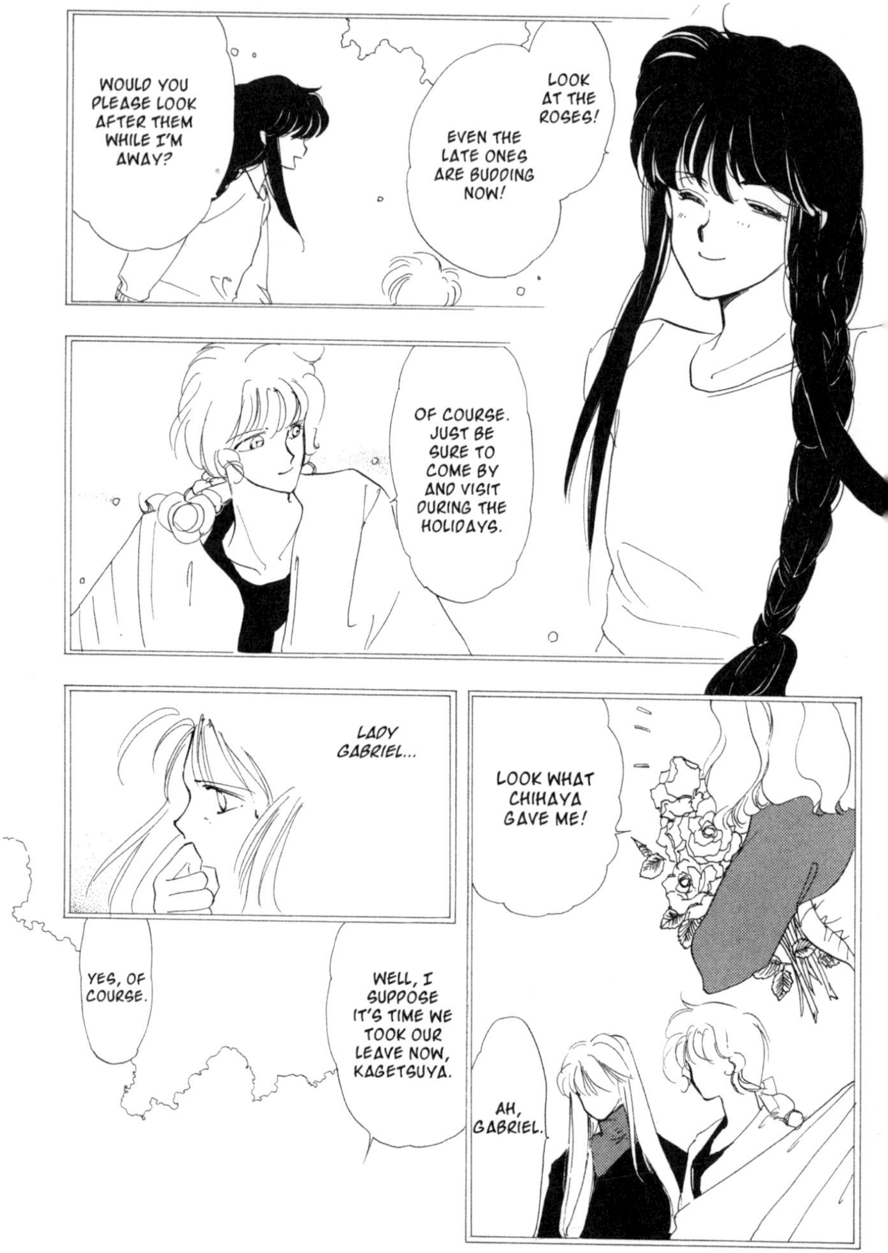
LOOK AT THE ROSES!
EVEN THE LATE ONES ARE BUDDING NOW!
WOULD YOU PLEASE LOOK AFTER THEM WHILE I'M AWAY?
OF COURSE. JUST BE SURE TO COME BY AND VISIT DURING THE HOLIDAYS.
LOOK WHAT CHIHAYA GAVE ME!
AH, GABRIEL.
LADY GABRIEL...
WELL, I SUPPOSE IT'S TIME WE TOOK OUR LEAVE NOW, KAGETSUYA.
YES, OF COURSE.

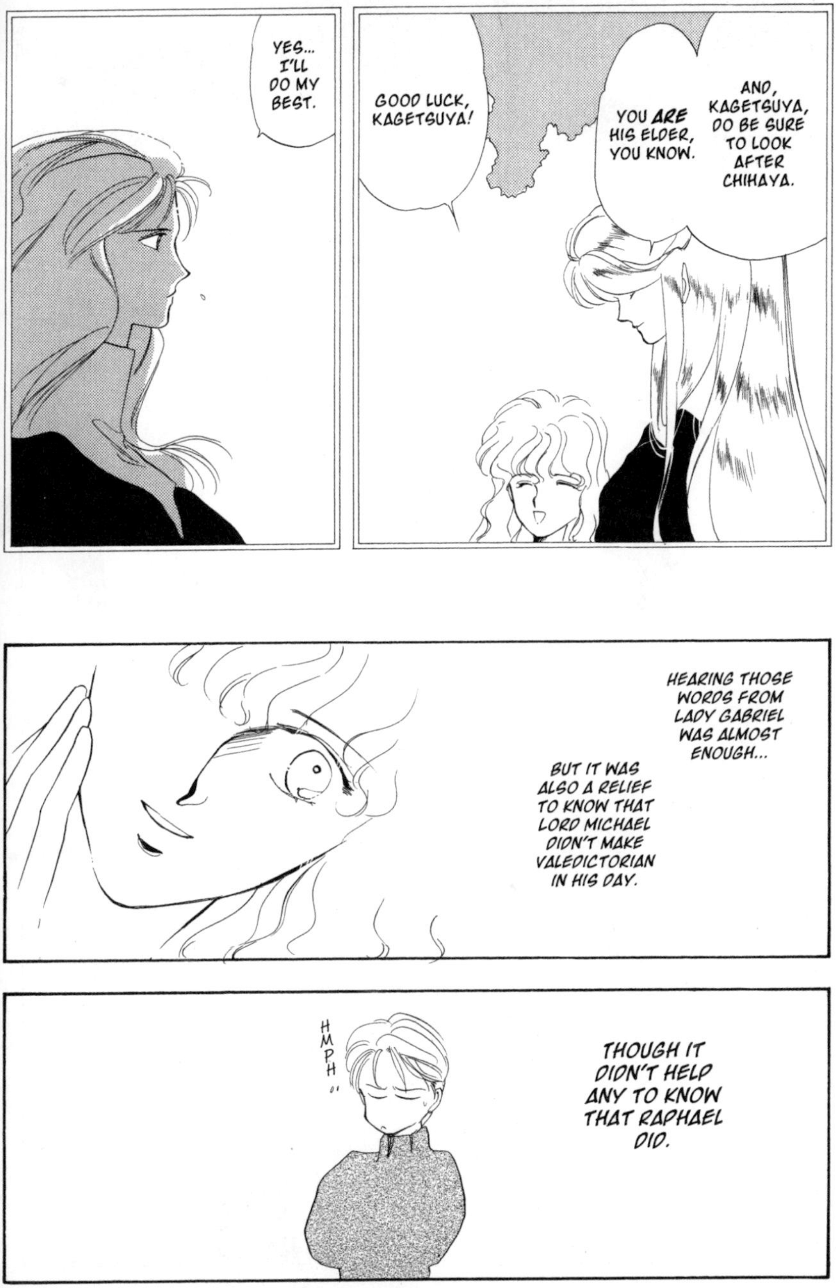
AND, KAGETSUYA, DO BE SURE TO LOOK AFTER CHIHAYA.
YOU **ARE** HIS ELDER, YOU KNOW.
GOOD LUCK, KAGETSUYA!
YES... I'LL DO MY BEST.
HEARING THOSE WORDS FROM LADY GABRIEL WAS ALMOST ENOUGH...
BUT IT WAS ALSO A RELIEF TO KNOW THAT LORD MICHAEL DIDN'T MAKE VALEDICTORIAN IN HIS DAY.
THOUGH IT DIDN'T HELP ANY TO KNOW THAT RAPHAEL DID.
HMPH

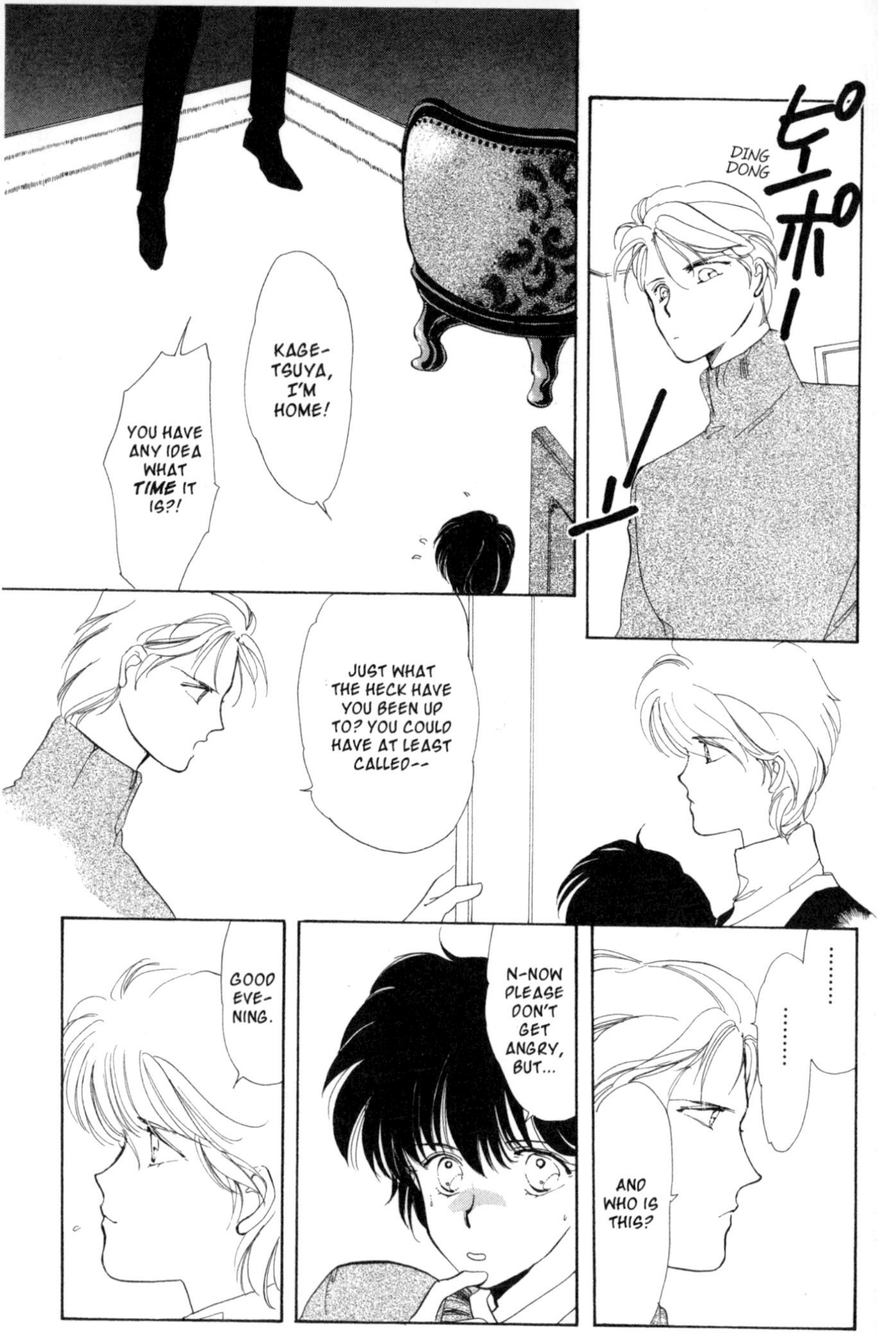
ピンポーン
DING DONG
KAGE-TSUYA, I'M HOME!
YOU HAVE ANY IDEA WHAT *TIME* IT IS?!
JUST WHAT THE HECK HAVE YOU BEEN UP TO? YOU COULD HAVE AT LEAST CALLED--
....
....
AND WHO IS THIS?
N-NOW PLEASE DON'T GET ANGRY, BUT...
GOOD EVE-NING.

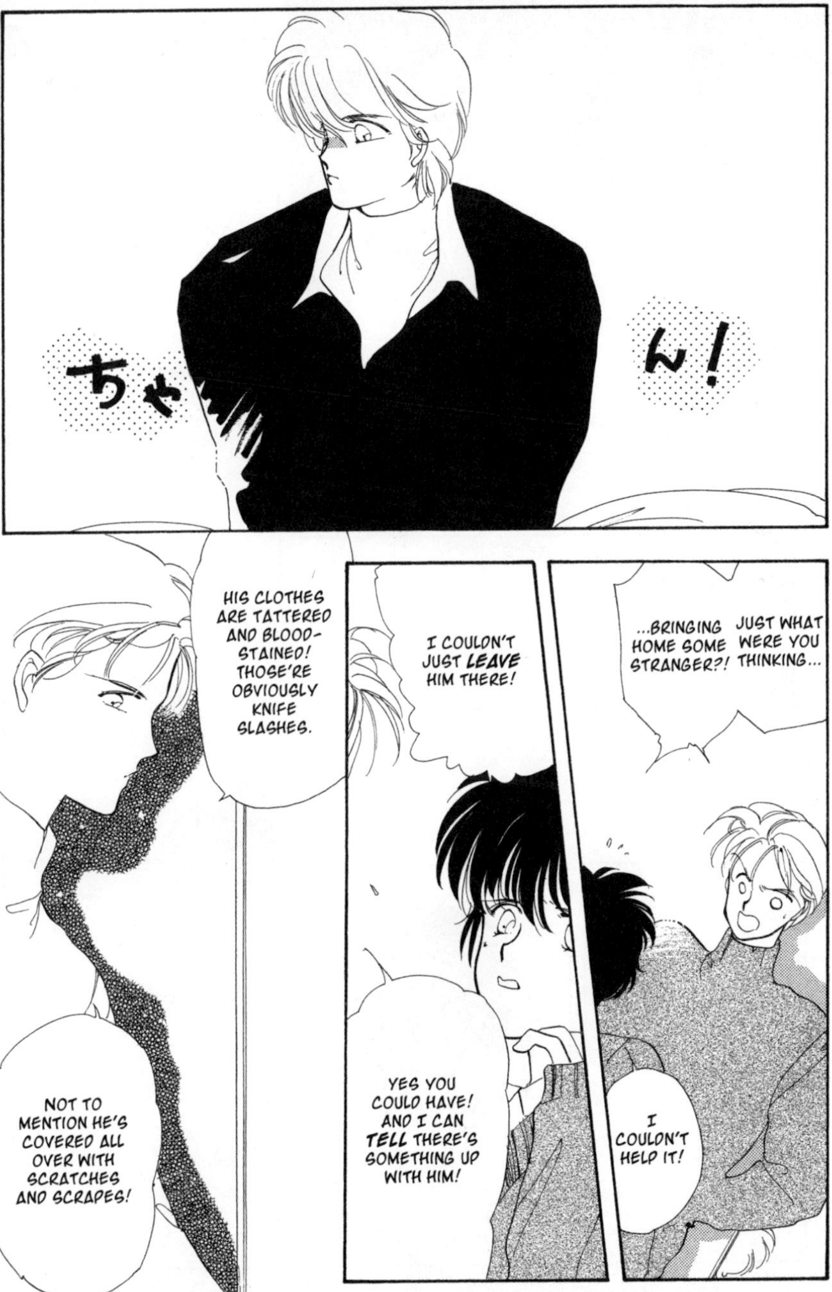
ちゃん!
JUST WHAT WERE YOU THINKING...
...BRINGING HOME SOME STRANGER?!
I COULDN'T HELP IT!
I COULDN'T JUST LEAVE HIM THERE!
YES YOU COULD HAVE! AND I CAN TELL THERE'S SOMETHING UP WITH HIM!
HIS CLOTHES ARE TATTERED AND BLOOD-STAINED! THOSE'RE OBVIOUSLY KNIFE SLASHES.
NOT TO MENTION HE'S COVERED ALL OVER WITH SCRATCHES AND SCRAPES!

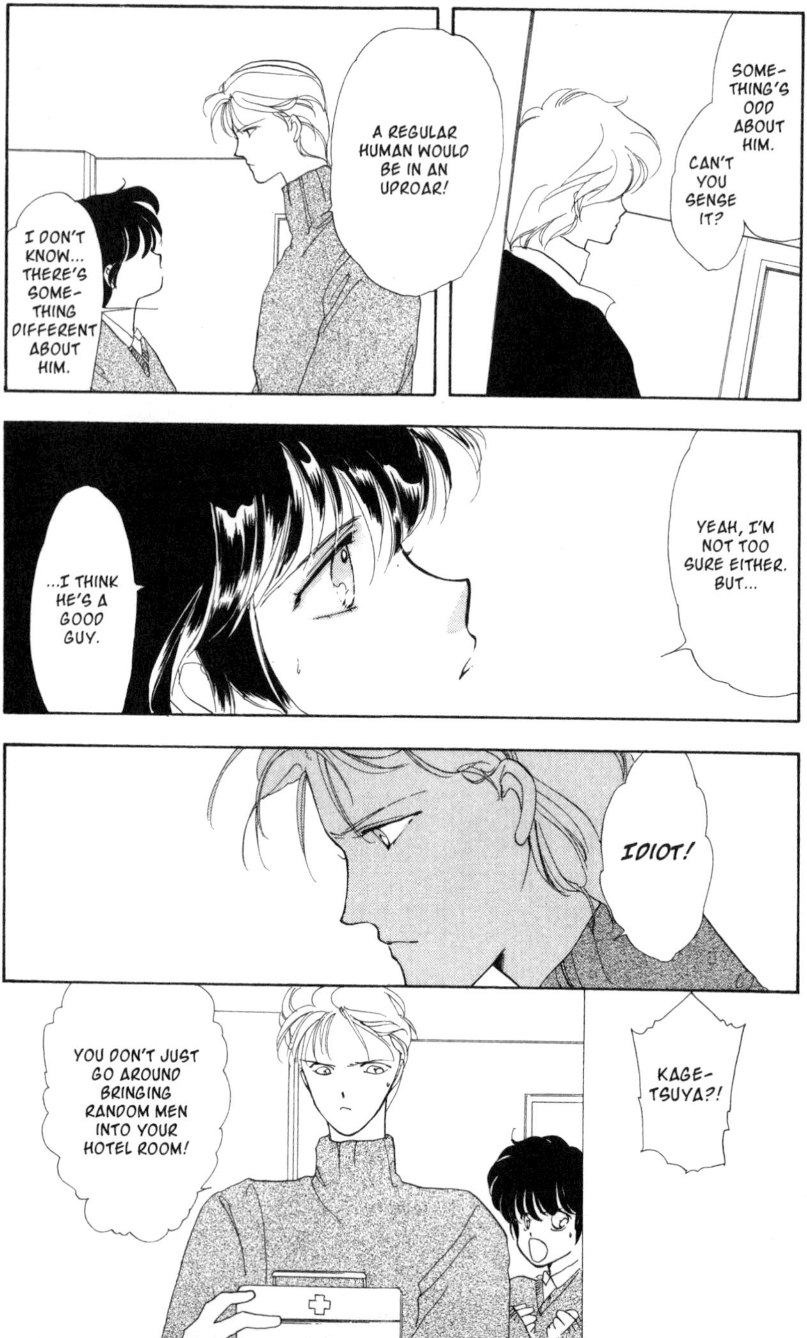
SOME-THING'S ODD ABOUT HIM.
CAN'T YOU SENSE IT?
A REGULAR HUMAN WOULD BE IN AN UPROAR!
I DON'T KNOW... THERE'S SOME-THING DIFFERENT ABOUT HIM.
YEAH, I'M NOT TOO SURE EITHER. BUT...
...I THINK HE'S A GOOD GUY.
IDIOT!
KAGE-TSUYA?!
YOU DON'T JUST GO AROUND BRINGING RANDOM MEN INTO YOUR HOTEL ROOM!

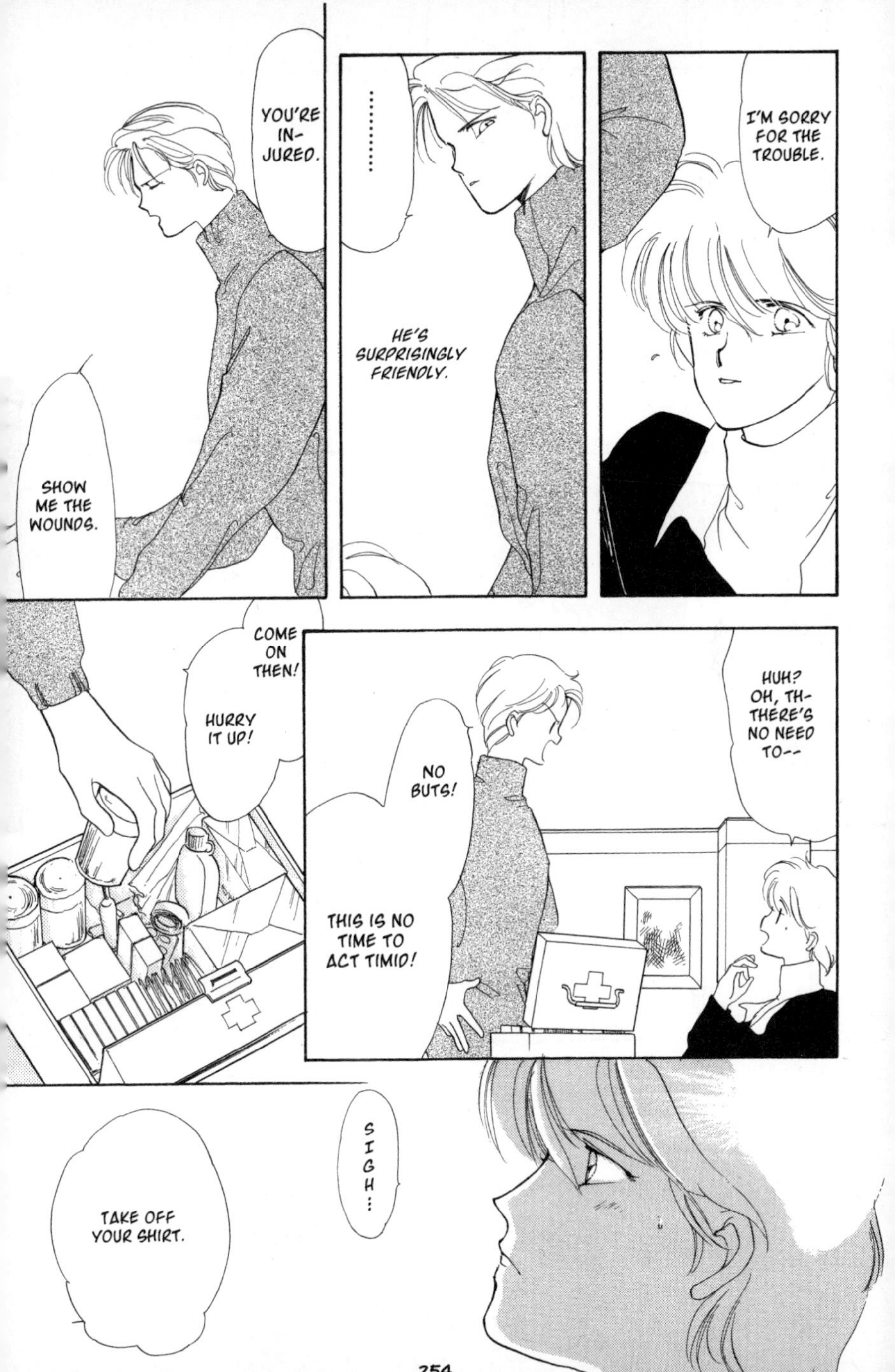
I'M SORRY FOR THE TROUBLE.
......
HE'S SURPRISINGLY FRIENDLY.
YOU'RE IN-JURED.
SHOW ME THE WOUNDS.
HUH? OH, TH-THERE'S NO NEED TO--
NO BUTS!
THIS IS NO TIME TO ACT TIMID!
COME ON THEN!
HURRY IT UP!
SIGH...
TAKE OFF YOUR SHIRT.

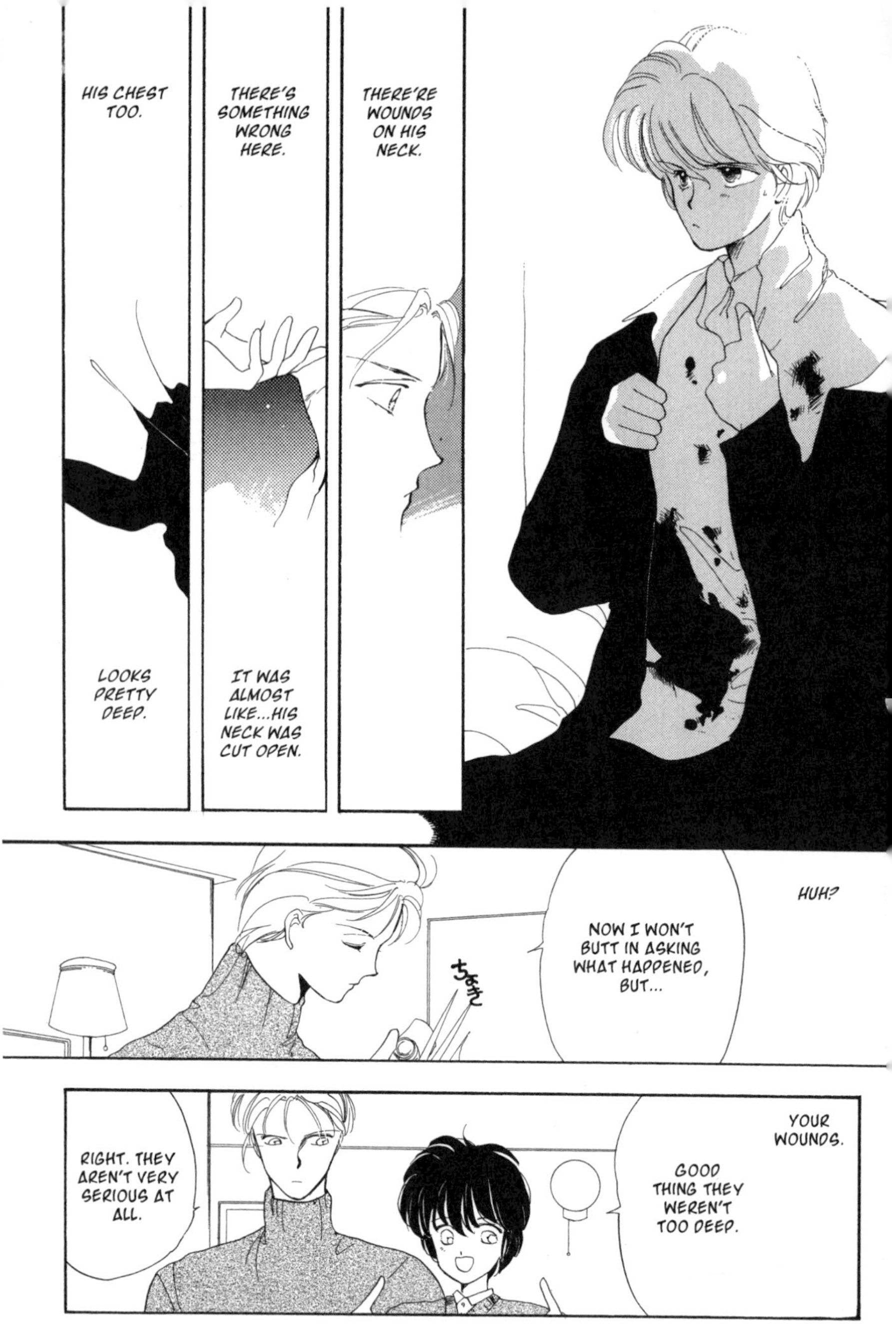

THERE'RE WOUNDS ON HIS NECK.
THERE'S SOMETHING WRONG HERE.
IT WAS ALMOST LIKE...HIS NECK WAS CUT OPEN.
HIS CHEST TOO.
LOOKS PRETTY DEEP.
HUH?
NOW I WON'T BUTT IN ASKING WHAT HAPPENED, BUT...
YOUR WOUNDS.
GOOD THING THEY WEREN'T TOO DEEP.
RIGHT. THEY AREN'T VERY SERIOUS AT ALL.

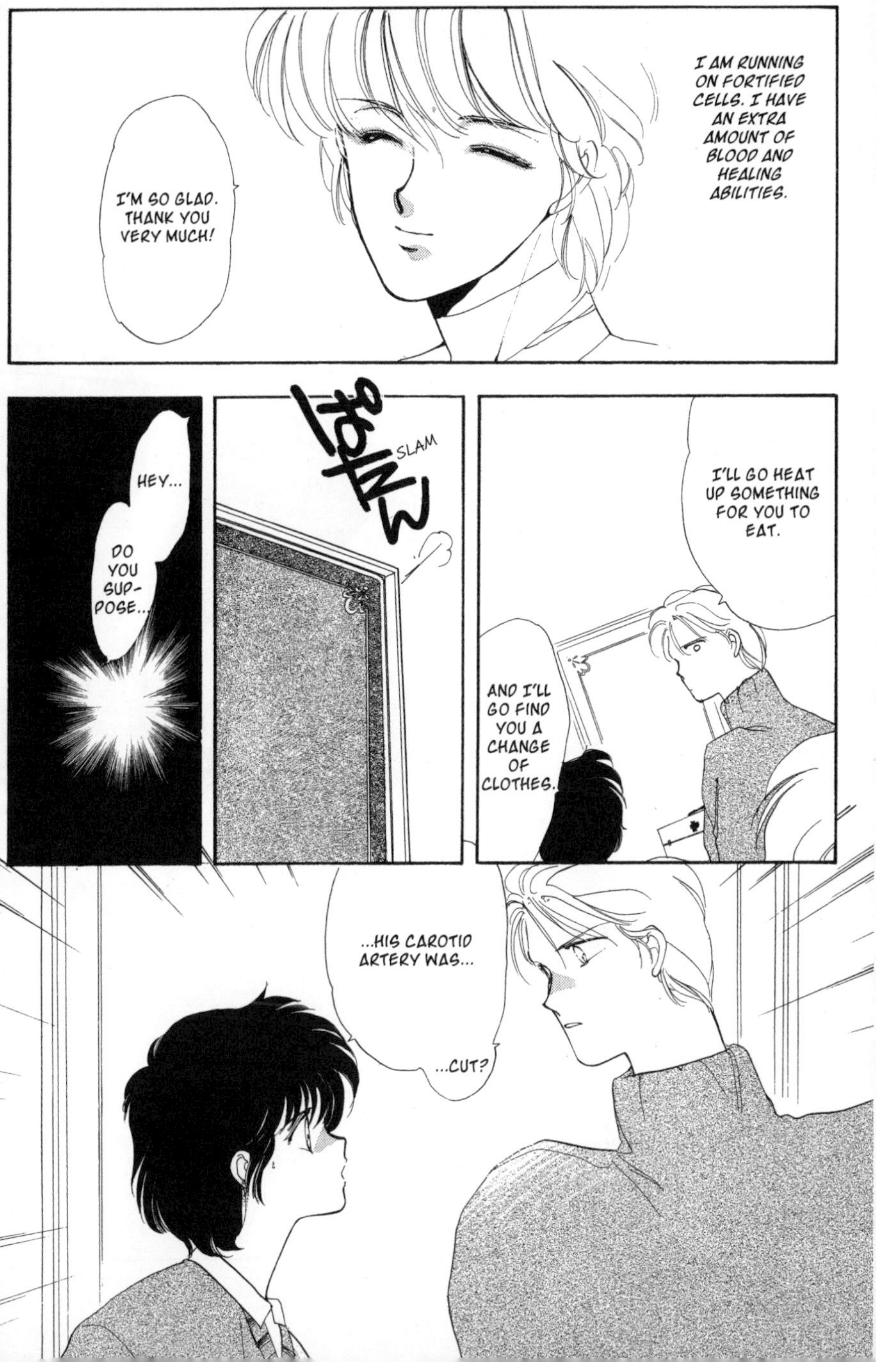
I AM RUNNING ON FORTIFIED CELLS. I HAVE AN EXTRA AMOUNT OF BLOOD AND HEALING ABILITIES.
I'M SO GLAD. THANK YOU VERY MUCH!
I'LL GO HEAT UP SOMETHING FOR YOU TO EAT.
AND I'LL GO FIND YOU A CHANGE OF CLOTHES.
SLAM
HEY...
DO YOU SUP-POSE...
...HIS CAROTID ARTERY WAS...
...CUT?

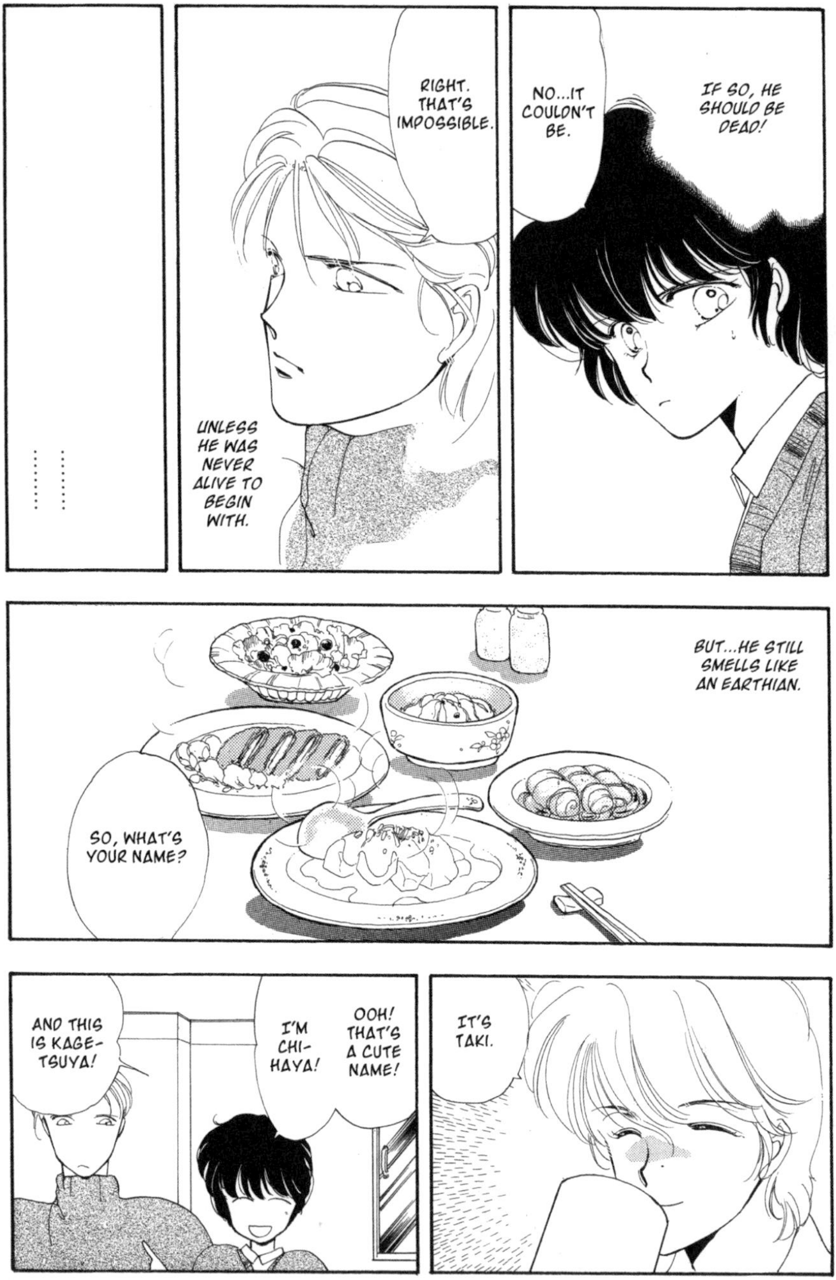
IF SO, HE SHOULD BE DEAD!
NO...IT COULDN'T BE.
RIGHT. THAT'S IMPOSSIBLE.
UNLESS HE WAS NEVER ALIVE TO BEGIN WITH.
......
BUT...HE STILL SMELLS LIKE AN EARTHIAN.
SO, WHAT'S YOUR NAME?
IT'S TAKI.
OOH! THAT'S A CUTE NAME!
I'M CHI-HAYA!
AND THIS IS KAGE-TSUYA!

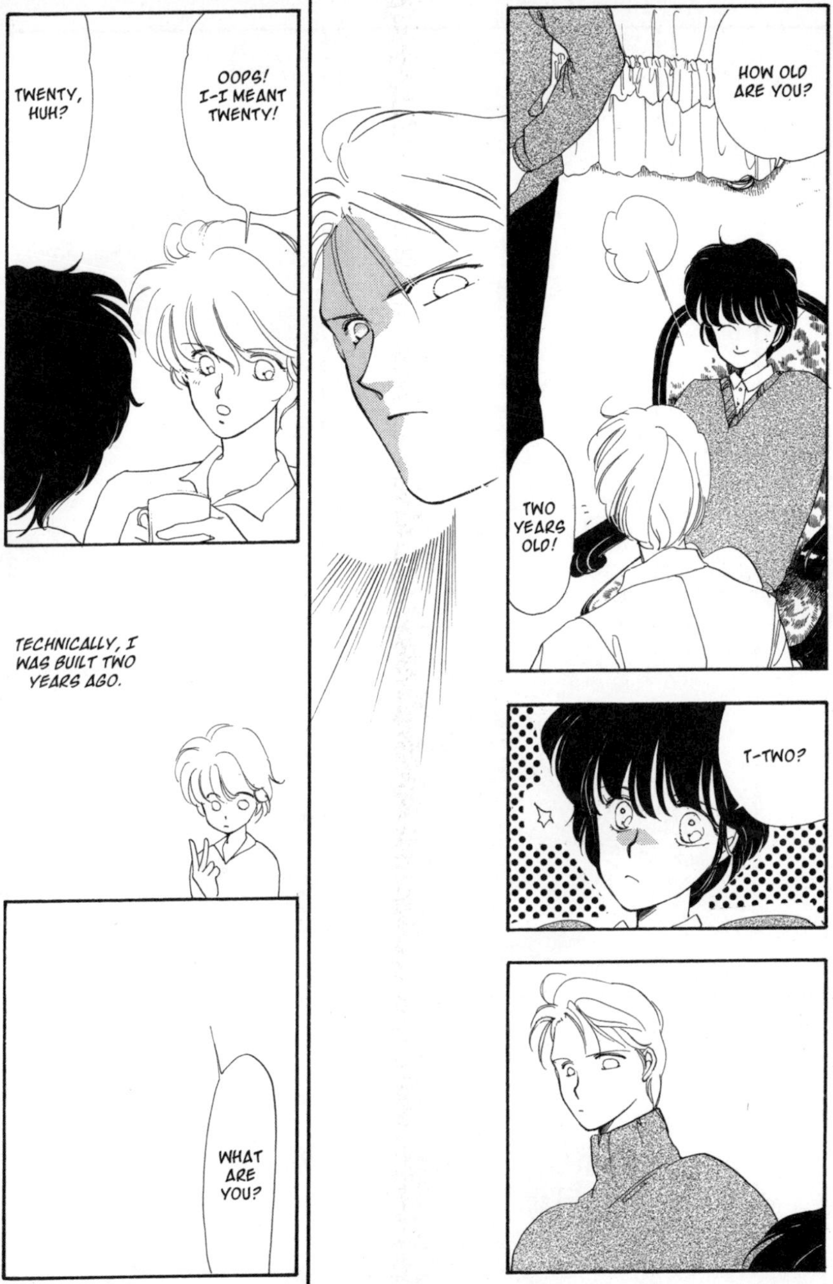
HOW OLD ARE YOU?
TWO YEARS OLD!
T-TWO?
OOPS! I-I MEANT TWENTY!
TWENTY, HUH?
TECHNICALLY, I WAS BUILT TWO YEARS AGO.
WHAT ARE YOU?

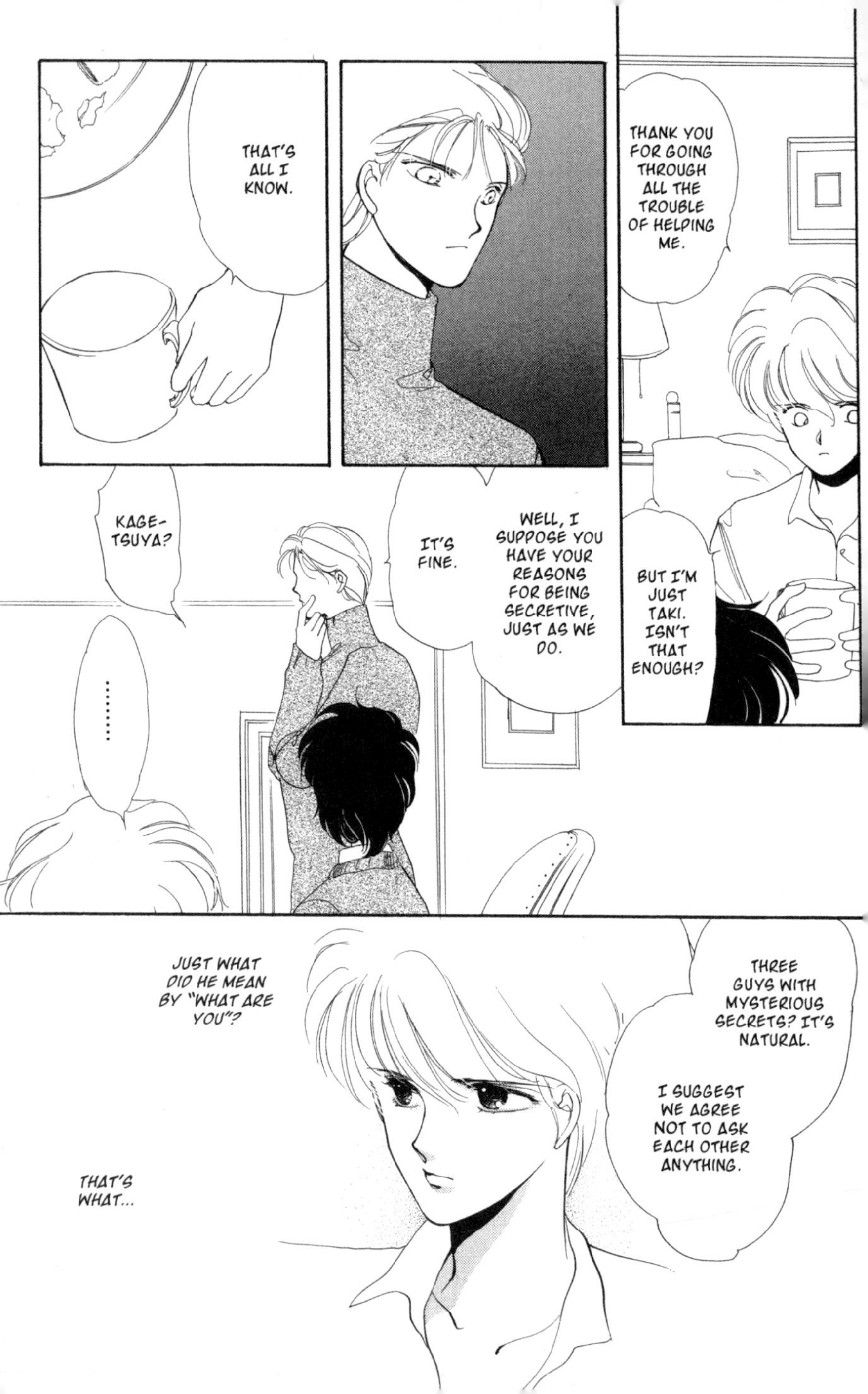

THANK YOU FOR GOING THROUGH ALL THE TROUBLE OF HELPING ME.
BUT I'M JUST TAKI. ISN'T THAT ENOUGH?
THAT'S ALL I KNOW.
WELL, I SUPPOSE YOU HAVE YOUR REASONS FOR BEING SECRETIVE, JUST AS WE DO.
IT'S FINE.
KAGE-TSUYA?
....
THREE GUYS WITH MYSTERIOUS SECRETS? IT'S NATURAL.
I SUGGEST WE AGREE NOT TO ASK EACH OTHER ANYTHING.
JUST WHAT DID HE MEAN BY "WHAT ARE YOU"?
THAT'S WHAT...

...I WANT TO KNOW MOST.

ちゃん！

I'M SORRY, SIR, BUT WE'VE LOST TRACK OF TAKI!

LOST HIM?!

Y-YES, SIR! I WOULD HAVE THOUGHT WE HAD ENOUGH PEOPLE, BUT...HE MANAGED TO SHAKE US OFF.

I GUESS I SHOULDN'T BE SURPRISED.

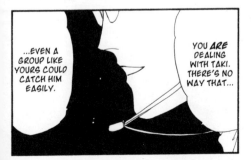

YOU *ARE* DEALING WITH TAKI. THERE'S NO WAY THAT...

...EVEN A GROUP LIKE YOURS COULD CATCH HIM EASILY.

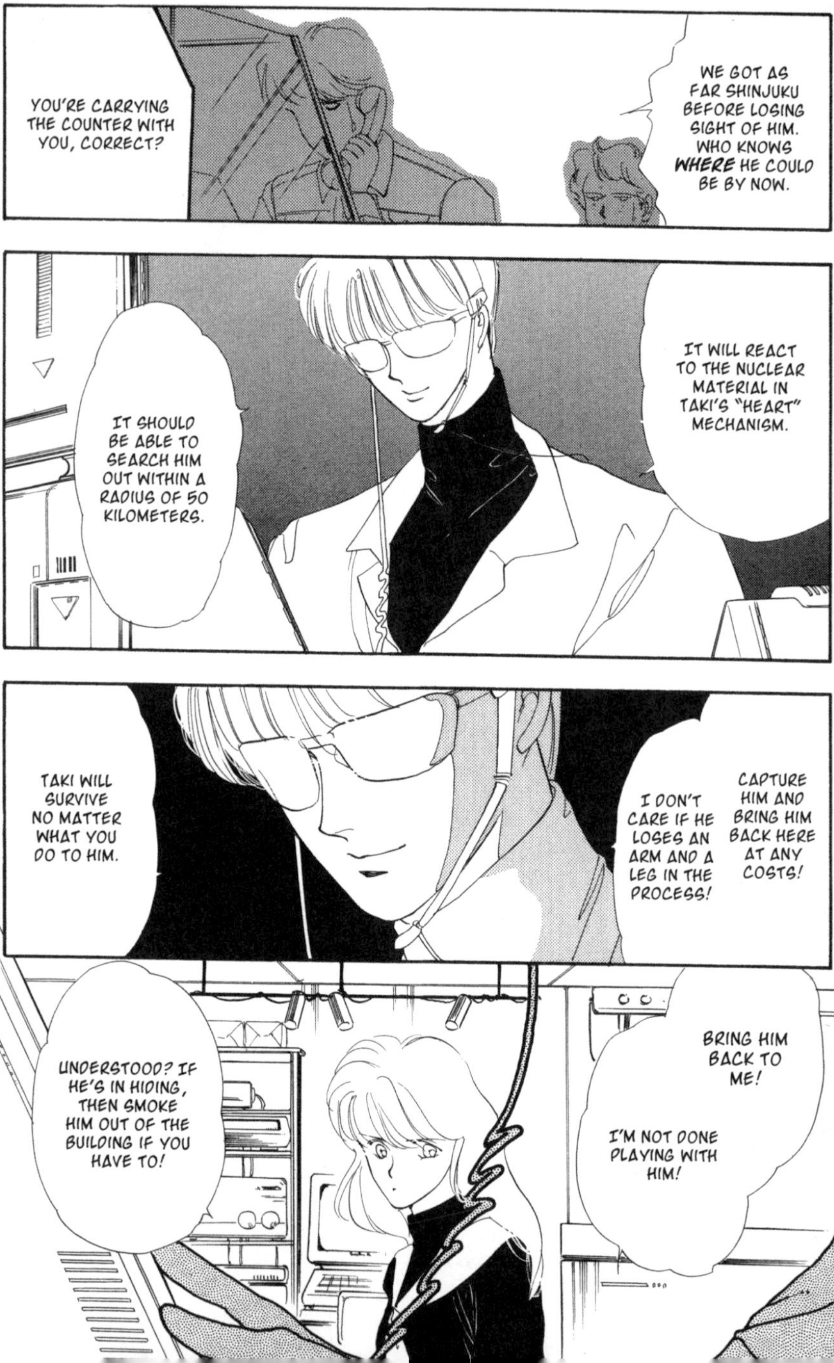
WE GOT AS FAR SHINJUKU BEFORE LOSING SIGHT OF HIM. WHO KNOWS **WHERE** HE COULD BE BY NOW.
YOU'RE CARRYING THE COUNTER WITH YOU, CORRECT?
IT WILL REACT TO THE NUCLEAR MATERIAL IN TAKI'S "HEART" MECHANISM.
IT SHOULD BE ABLE TO SEARCH HIM OUT WITHIN A RADIUS OF 50 KILOMETERS.
CAPTURE HIM AND BRING HIM BACK HERE AT ANY COSTS!
I DON'T CARE IF HE LOSES AN ARM AND A LEG IN THE PROCESS!
TAKI WILL SURVIVE NO MATTER WHAT YOU DO TO HIM.
BRING HIM BACK TO ME!
I'M NOT DONE PLAYING WITH HIM!
UNDERSTOOD? IF HE'S IN HIDING, THEN SMOKE HIM OUT OF THE BUILDING IF YOU HAVE TO!

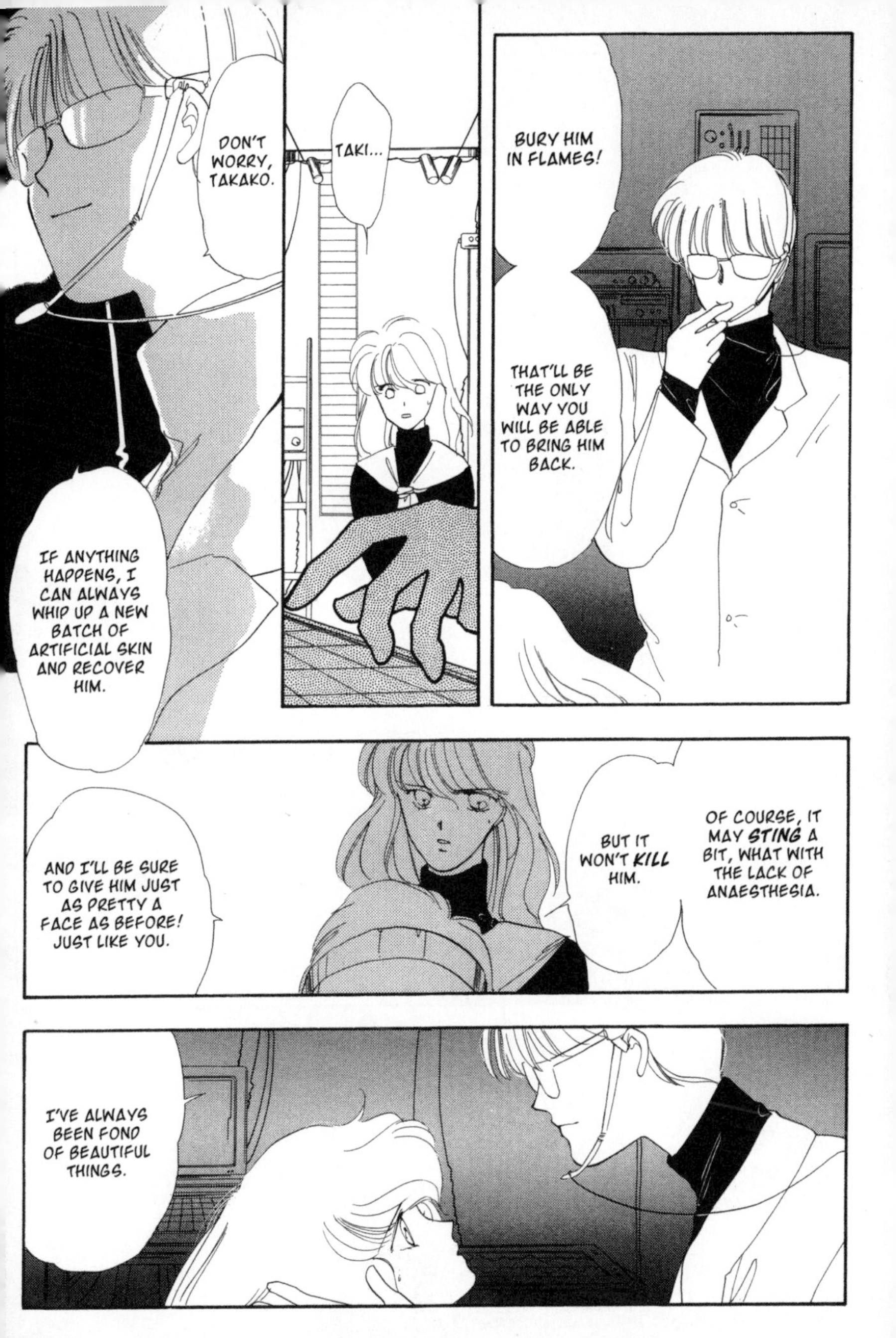
BURY HIM IN FLAMES!
THAT'LL BE THE ONLY WAY YOU WILL BE ABLE TO BRING HIM BACK.
TAKI...
DON'T WORRY, TAKAKO.
IF ANYTHING HAPPENS, I CAN ALWAYS WHIP UP A NEW BATCH OF ARTIFICIAL SKIN AND RECOVER HIM.
OF COURSE, IT MAY *STING* A BIT, WHAT WITH THE LACK OF ANAESTHESIA.
BUT IT WON'T *KILL* HIM.
AND I'LL BE SURE TO GIVE HIM JUST AS PRETTY A FACE AS BEFORE! JUST LIKE YOU.
I'VE ALWAYS BEEN FOND OF BEAUTIFUL THINGS.

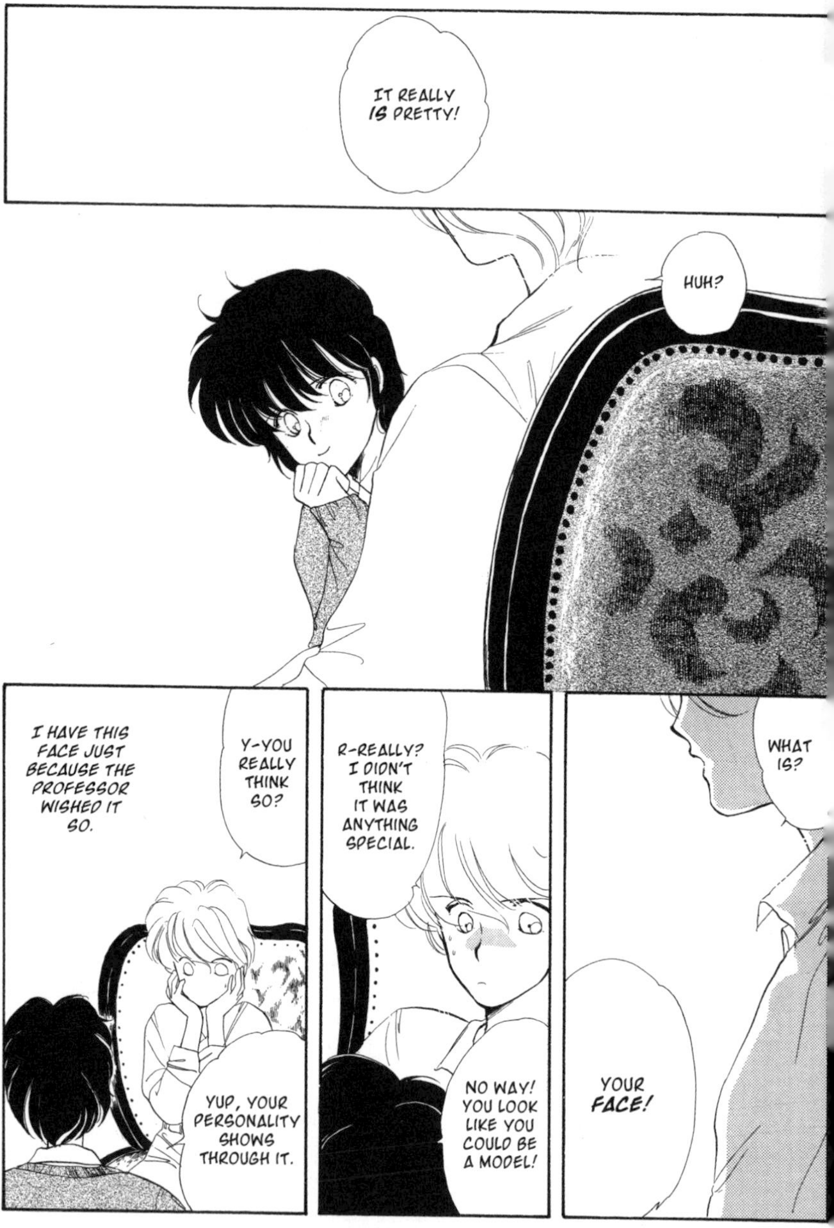
IT REALLY IS PRETTY!
HUH?
WHAT IS?
YOUR FACE!
R-REALLY? I DIDN'T THINK IT WAS ANYTHING SPECIAL.
NO WAY! YOU LOOK LIKE YOU COULD BE A MODEL!
Y-YOU REALLY THINK SO?
I HAVE THIS FACE JUST BECAUSE THE PROFESSOR WISHED IT SO.
YUP, YOUR PERSONALITY SHOWS THROUGH IT.

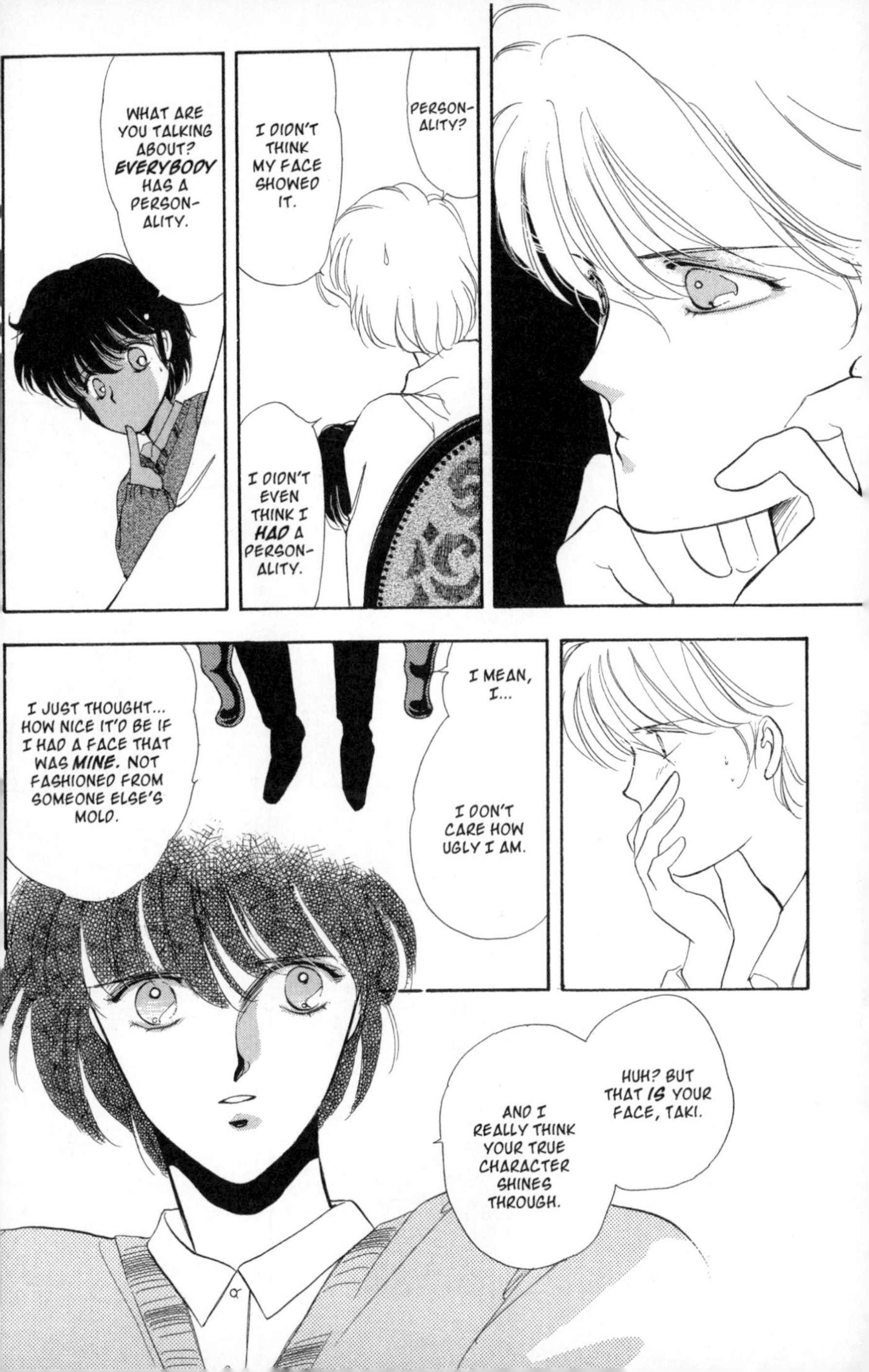
PERSONALITY?
I DIDN'T THINK MY FACE SHOWED IT.
I DIDN'T EVEN THINK I HAD A PERSONALITY.
WHAT ARE YOU TALKING ABOUT? EVERYBODY HAS A PERSONALITY.
I MEAN, I...
I DON'T CARE HOW UGLY I AM.
I JUST THOUGHT... HOW NICE IT'D BE IF I HAD A FACE THAT WAS MINE. NOT FASHIONED FROM SOMEONE ELSE'S MOLD.
HUH? BUT THAT IS YOUR FACE, TAKI.
AND I REALLY THINK YOUR TRUE CHARACTER SHINES THROUGH.

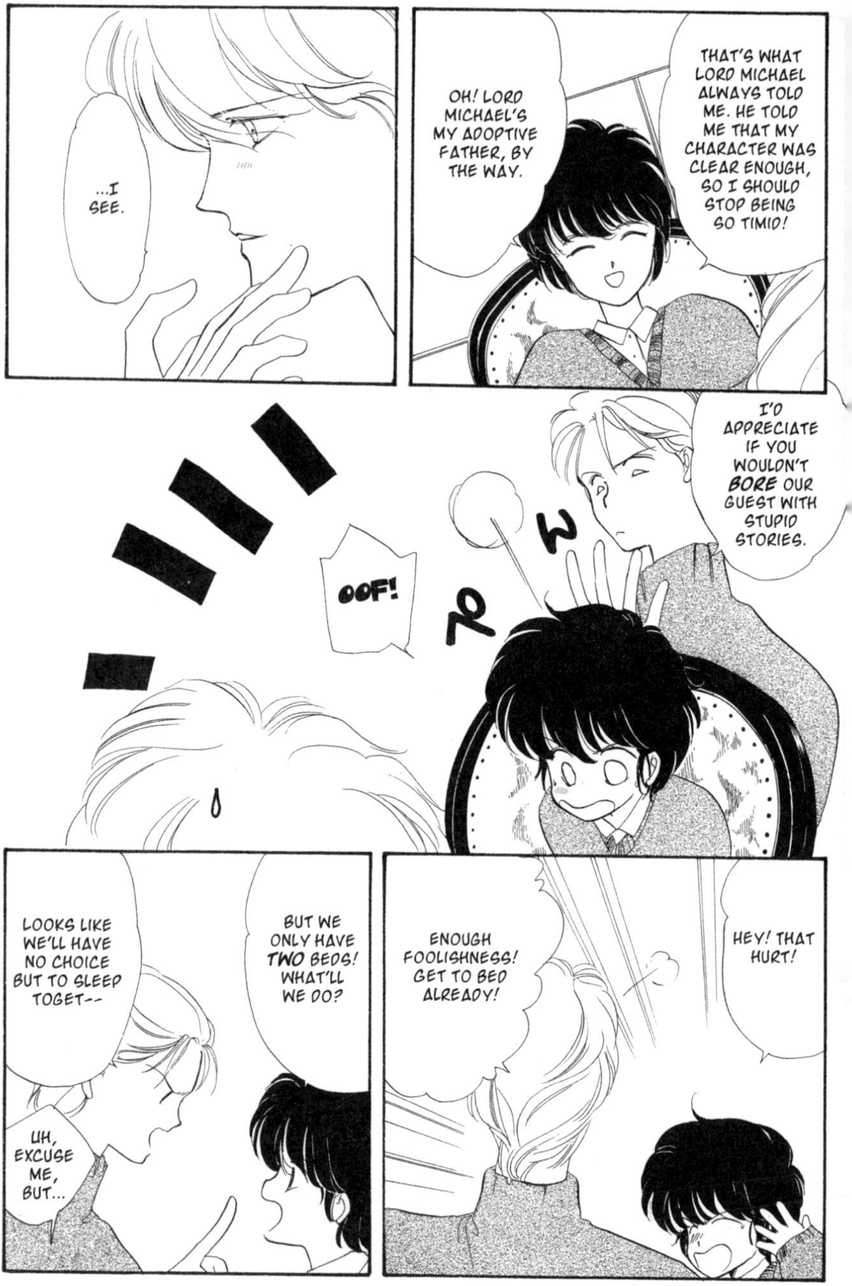
THAT'S WHAT LORD MICHAEL ALWAYS TOLD ME. HE TOLD ME THAT MY CHARACTER WAS CLEAR ENOUGH, SO I SHOULD STOP BEING SO TIMID!
OH! LORD MICHAEL'S MY ADOPTIVE FATHER, BY THE WAY.
...I SEE.
I'D APPRECIATE IF YOU WOULDN'T **BORE** OUR GUEST WITH STUPID STORIES.
OOF!
HEY! THAT HURT!
ENOUGH FOOLISHNESS! GET TO BED ALREADY!
BUT WE ONLY HAVE **TWO** BEDS! WHAT'LL WE DO?
LOOKS LIKE WE'LL HAVE NO CHOICE BUT TO SLEEP TOGET--
UH, EXCUSE ME, BUT...

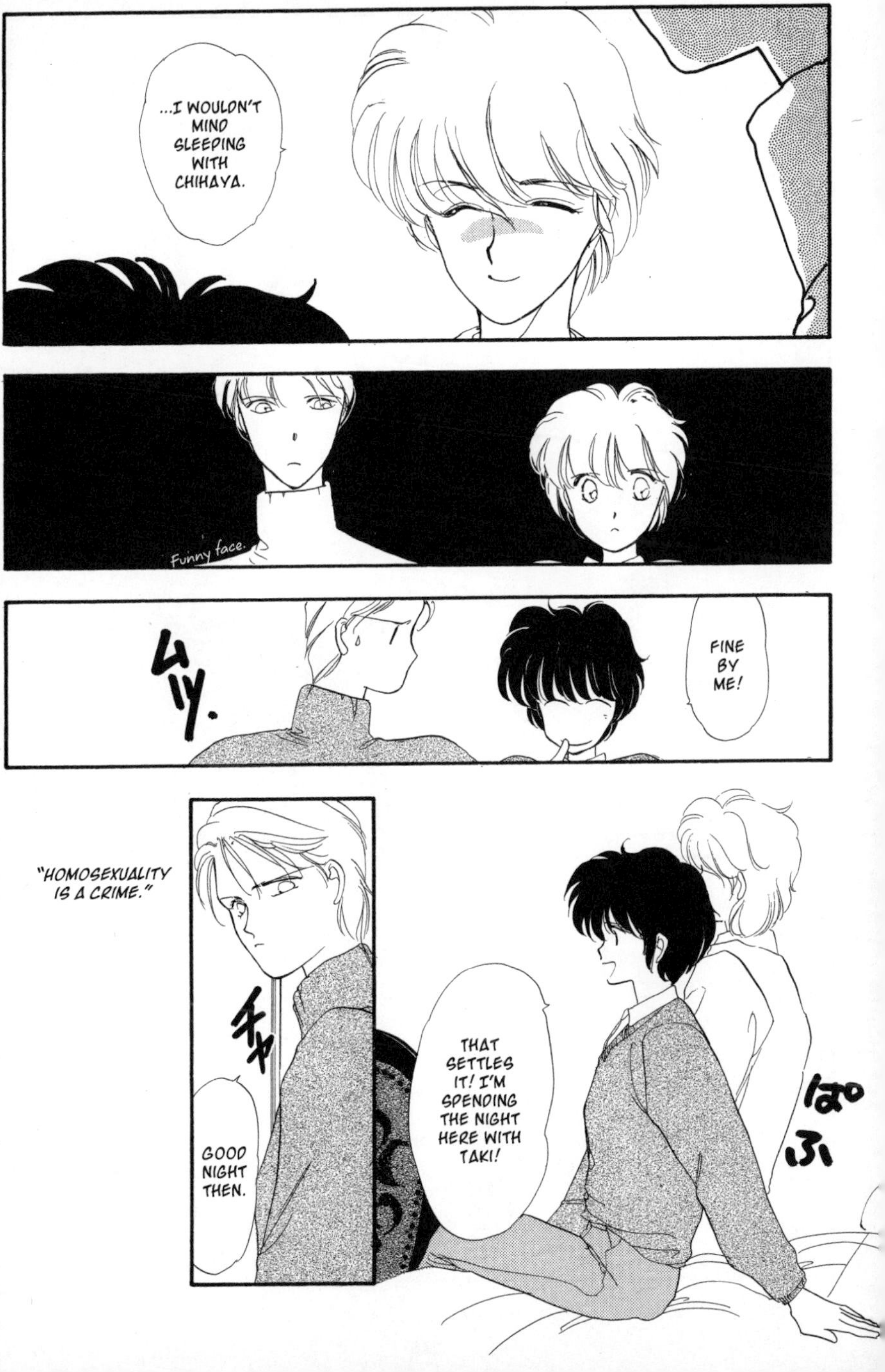
...I WOULDN'T MIND SLEEPING WITH CHIHAYA.
Funny face.
FINE BY ME!
ムッ.
ぱふ
THAT SETTLES IT! I'M SPENDING THE NIGHT HERE WITH TAKI!
チャ
GOOD NIGHT THEN.
"HOMOSEXUALITY IS A CRIME."

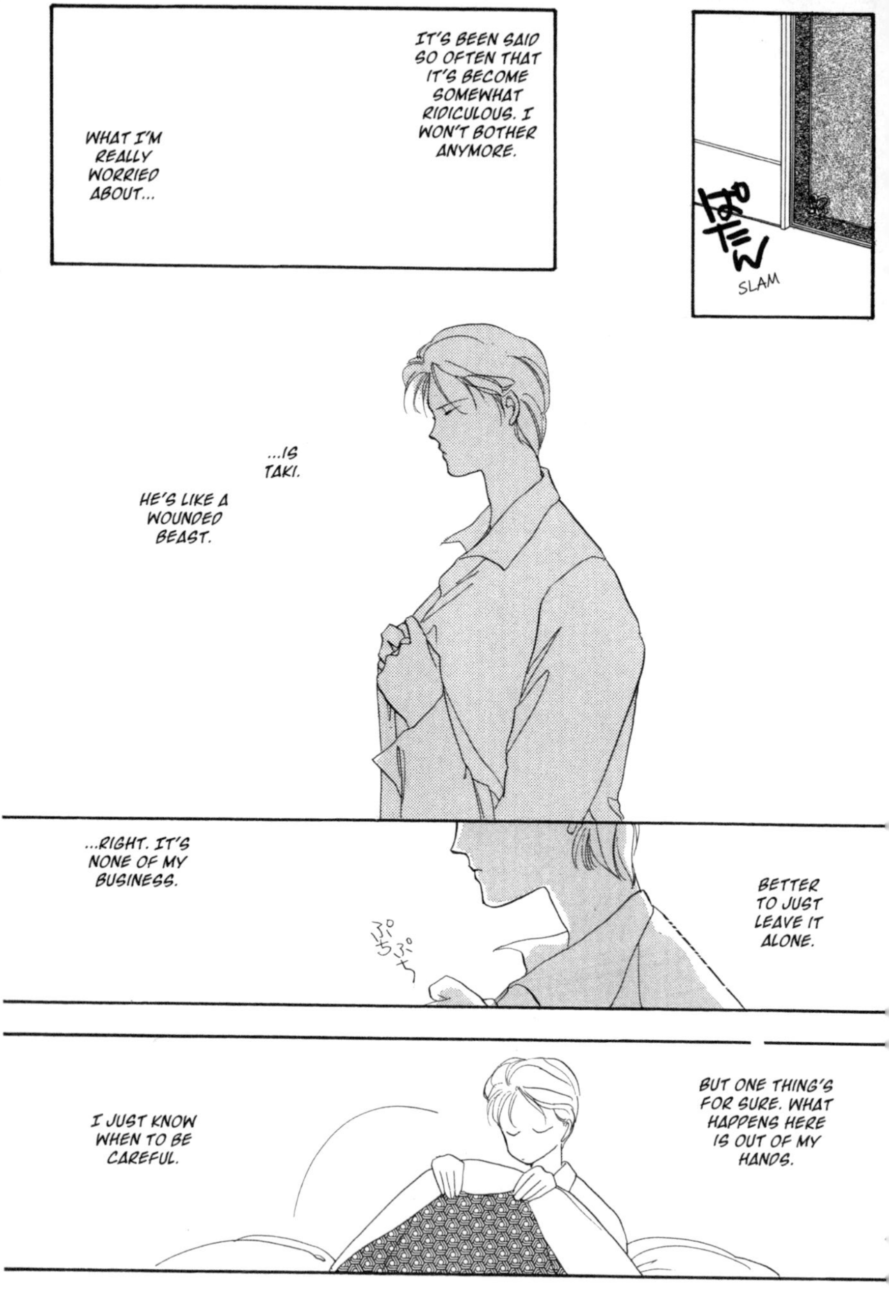
ぱたん
SLAM
IT'S BEEN SAID SO OFTEN THAT IT'S BECOME SOMEWHAT RIDICULOUS. I WON'T BOTHER ANYMORE.
WHAT I'M REALLY WORRIED ABOUT...
...IS TAKI.
HE'S LIKE A WOUNDED BEAST.
BETTER TO JUST LEAVE IT ALONE.
ぷちぷち
...RIGHT. IT'S NONE OF MY BUSINESS.
BUT ONE THING'S FOR SURE. WHAT HAPPENS HERE IS OUT OF MY HANDS.
I JUST KNOW WHEN TO BE CAREFUL.

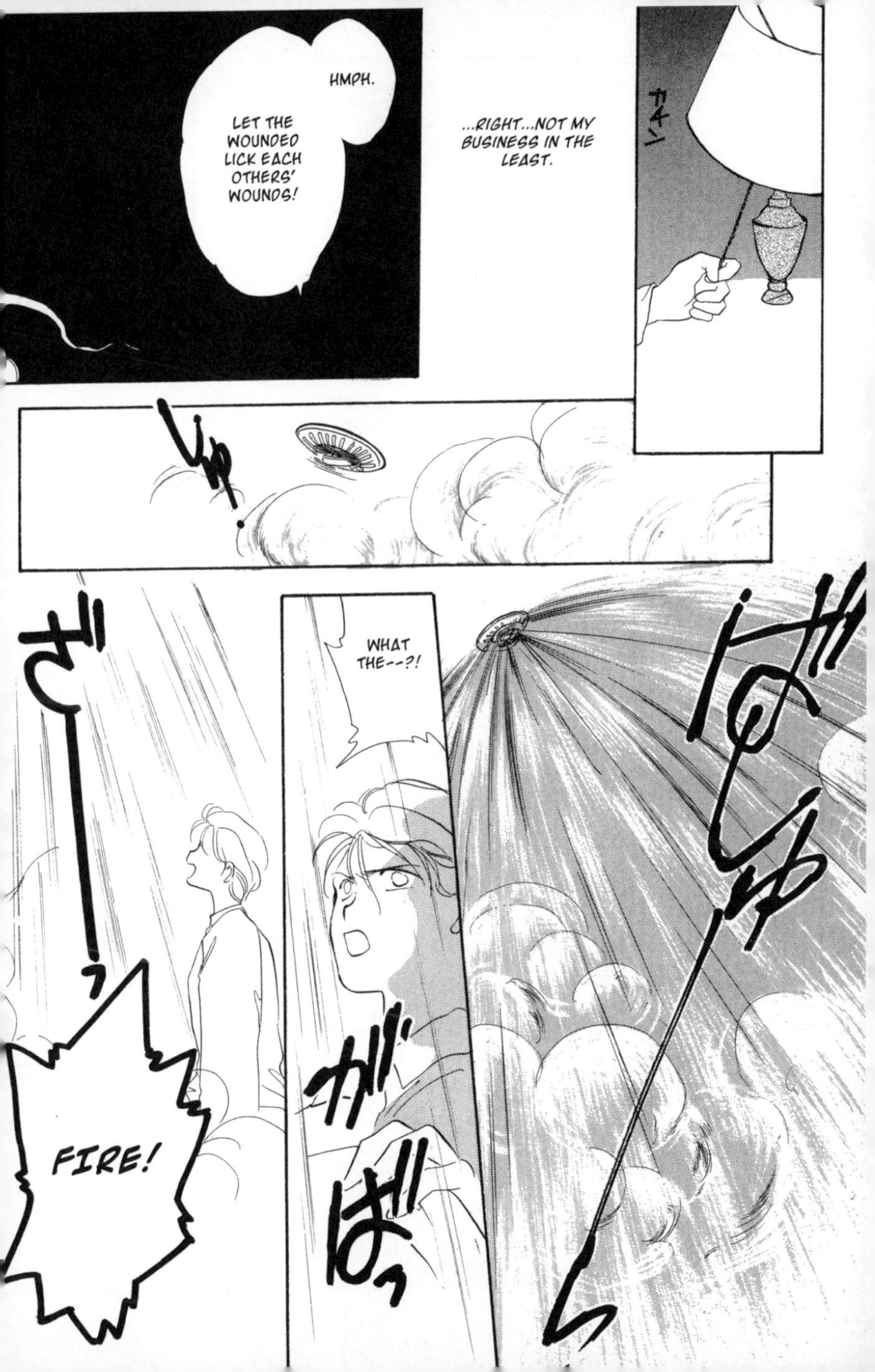

...RIGHT...NOT MY BUSINESS IN THE LEAST.
HMPH.
LET THE WOUNDED LICK EACH OTHERS' WOUNDS!
WHAT THE--?!
FIRE!

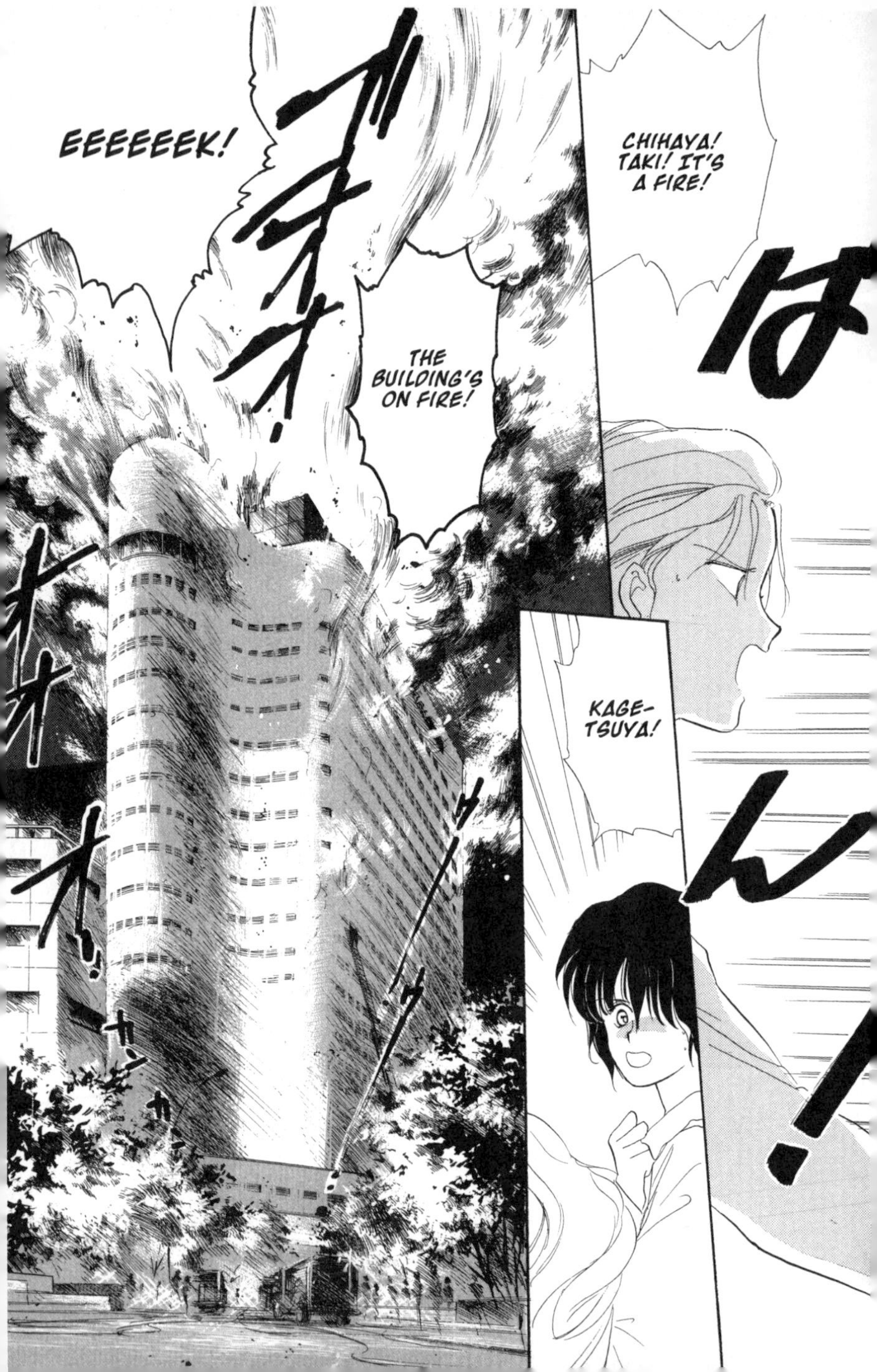
CHIHAYA! TAKI! IT'S A FIRE!
はん!
KAGE-TSUYA!
THE BUILDING'S ON FIRE!
EEEEEEK!

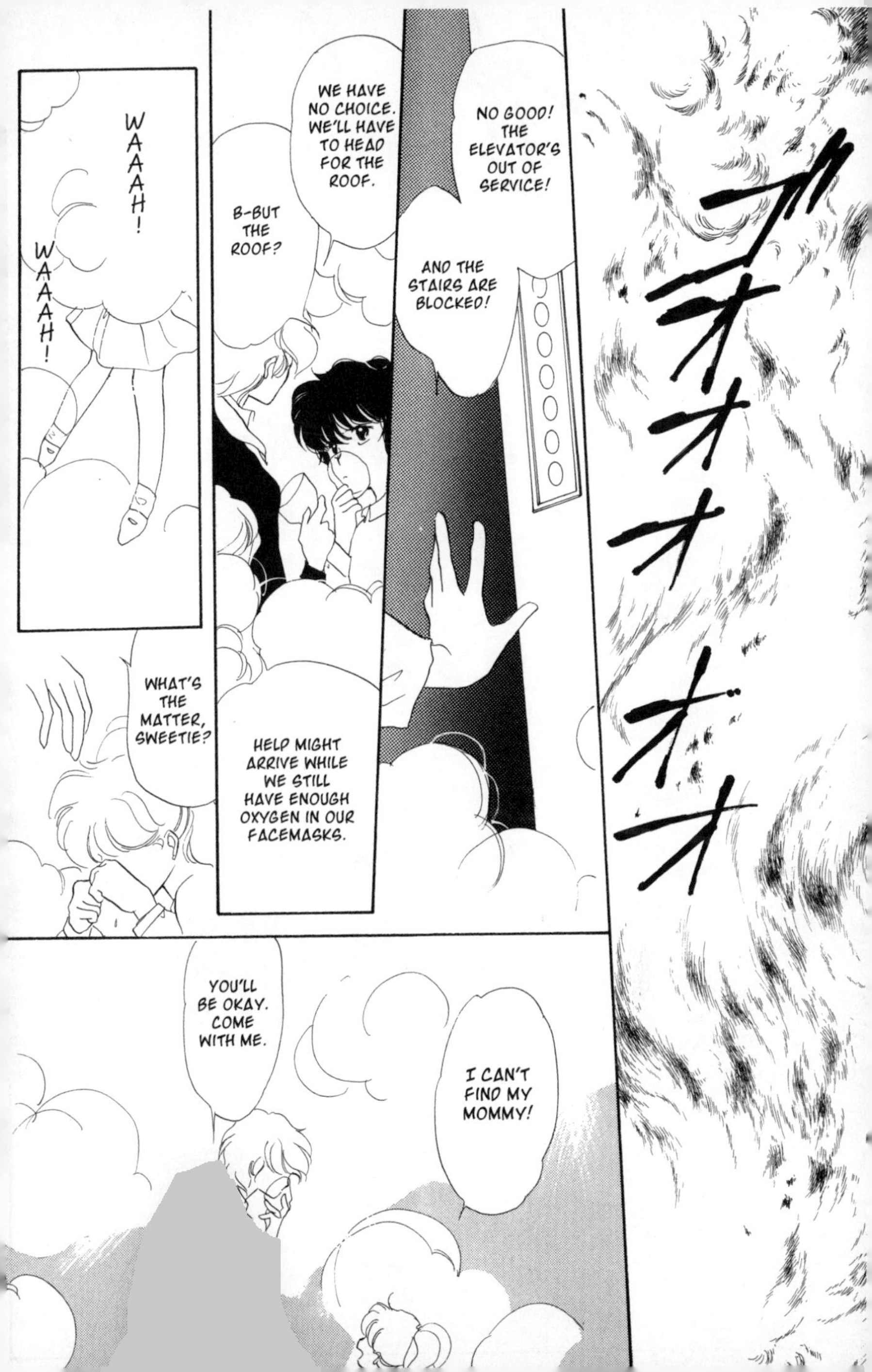
NO GOOD! THE ELEVATOR'S OUT OF SERVICE!
AND THE STAIRS ARE BLOCKED!
WE HAVE NO CHOICE. WE'LL HAVE TO HEAD FOR THE ROOF.
B-BUT THE ROOF?
HELP MIGHT ARRIVE WHILE WE STILL HAVE ENOUGH OXYGEN IN OUR FACEMASKS.
WAAAAH!
WAAAAH!
WHAT'S THE MATTER, SWEETIE?
I CAN'T FIND MY MOMMY!
YOU'LL BE OKAY. COME WITH ME.

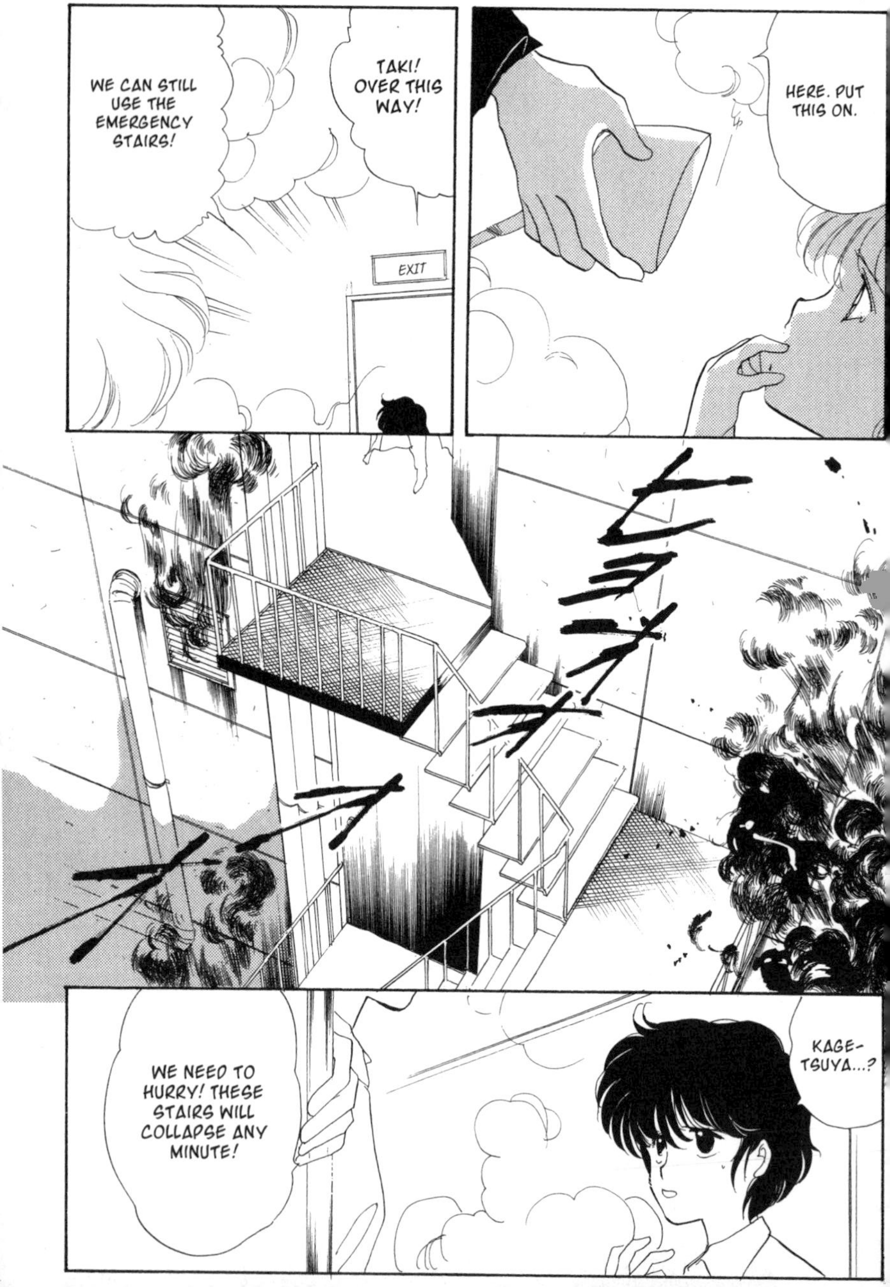
HERE. PUT THIS ON.
TAKI! OVER THIS WAY!
WE CAN STILL USE THE EMERGENCY STAIRS!
EXIT
KAGE-TSUYA...?
WE NEED TO HURRY! THESE STAIRS WILL COLLAPSE ANY MINUTE!

AN EARTHIAN WOULD NEVER SURVIVE THE TRIP!

NO! THE ONLY PLACE WE CAN GO FROM HERE IS SPACE!

THIS IS AN EMERGENCY! WHY DON'T WE JUST INSTAN-TANEOUSLY TRANSPORT OURSELVES OUT OF HERE?

I'M SORRY, BUT I'M GOING TO LET THE GIRL GO DOWN FIRST.

WE CAN GET OUT SAFELY ANYTIME, BUT...

RIGHT!

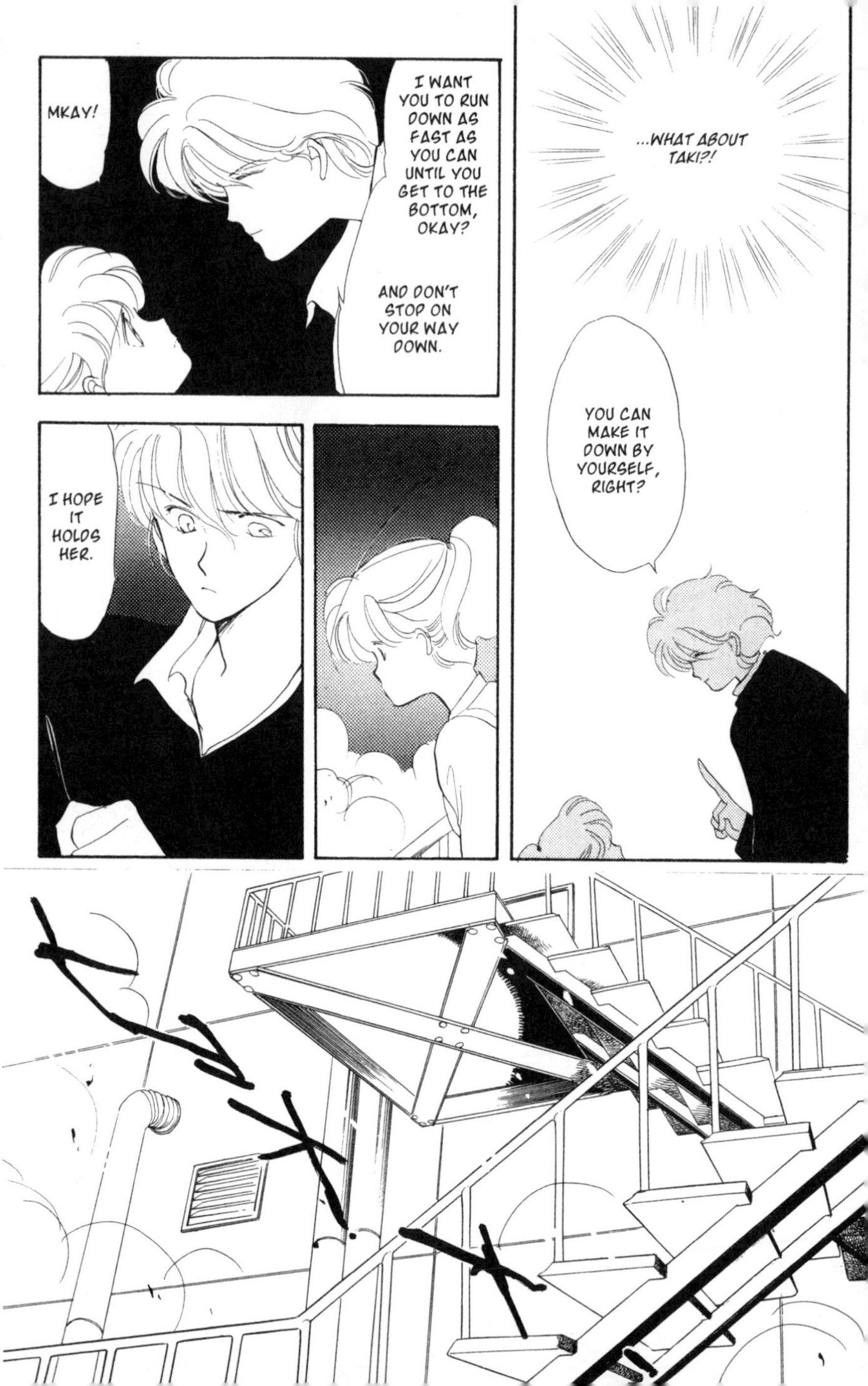
...WHAT ABOUT TAKI?!
YOU CAN MAKE IT DOWN BY YOURSELF, RIGHT?
I WANT YOU TO RUN DOWN AS FAST AS YOU CAN UNTIL YOU GET TO THE BOTTOM, OKAY?
AND DON'T STOP ON YOUR WAY DOWN.
MKAY!
I HOPE IT HOLDS HER.

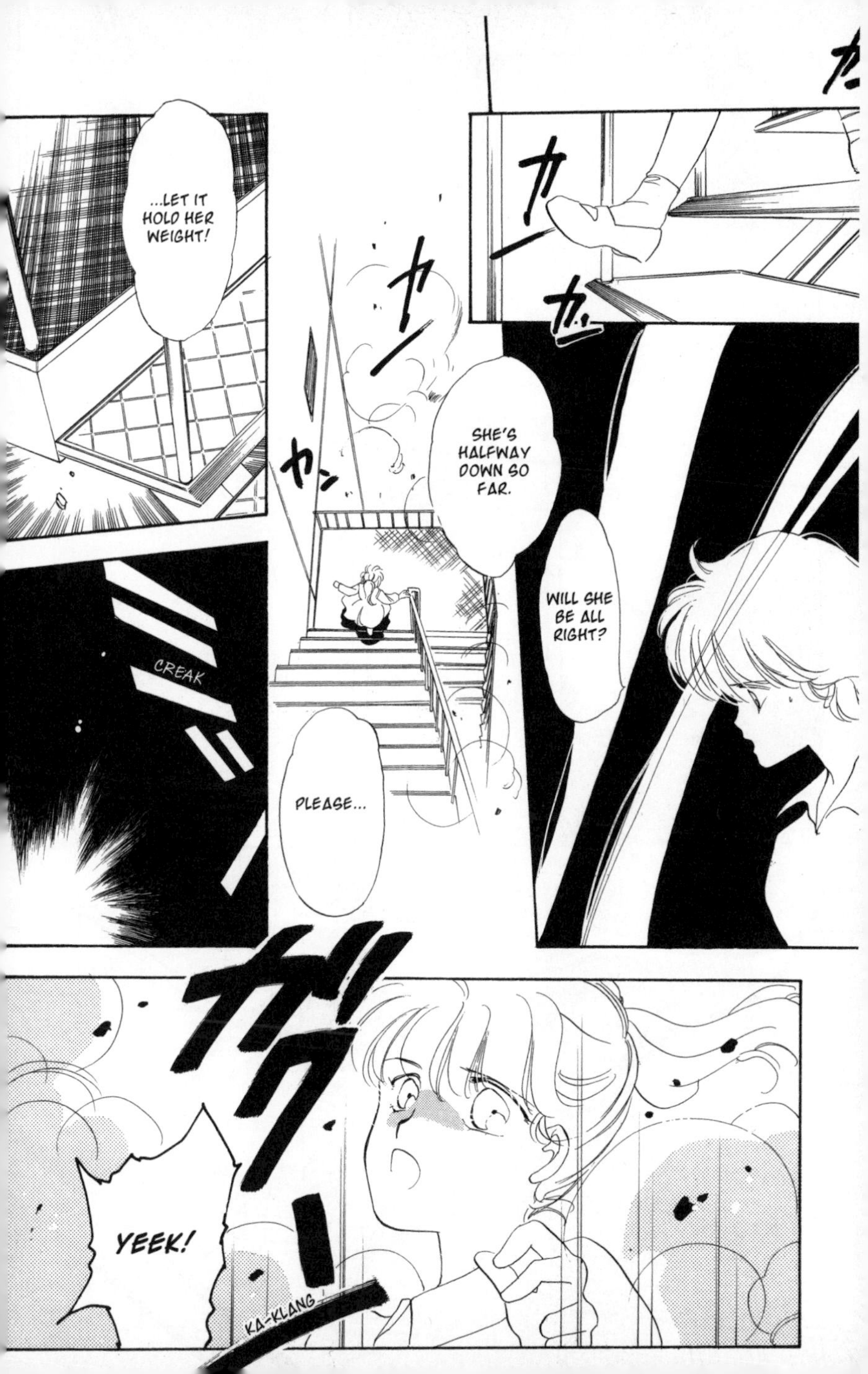
SHE'S HALFWAY DOWN SO FAR.
WILL SHE BE ALL RIGHT?
PLEASE...
...LET IT HOLD HER WEIGHT!
CREAK
KA-KLANG
YEEK!

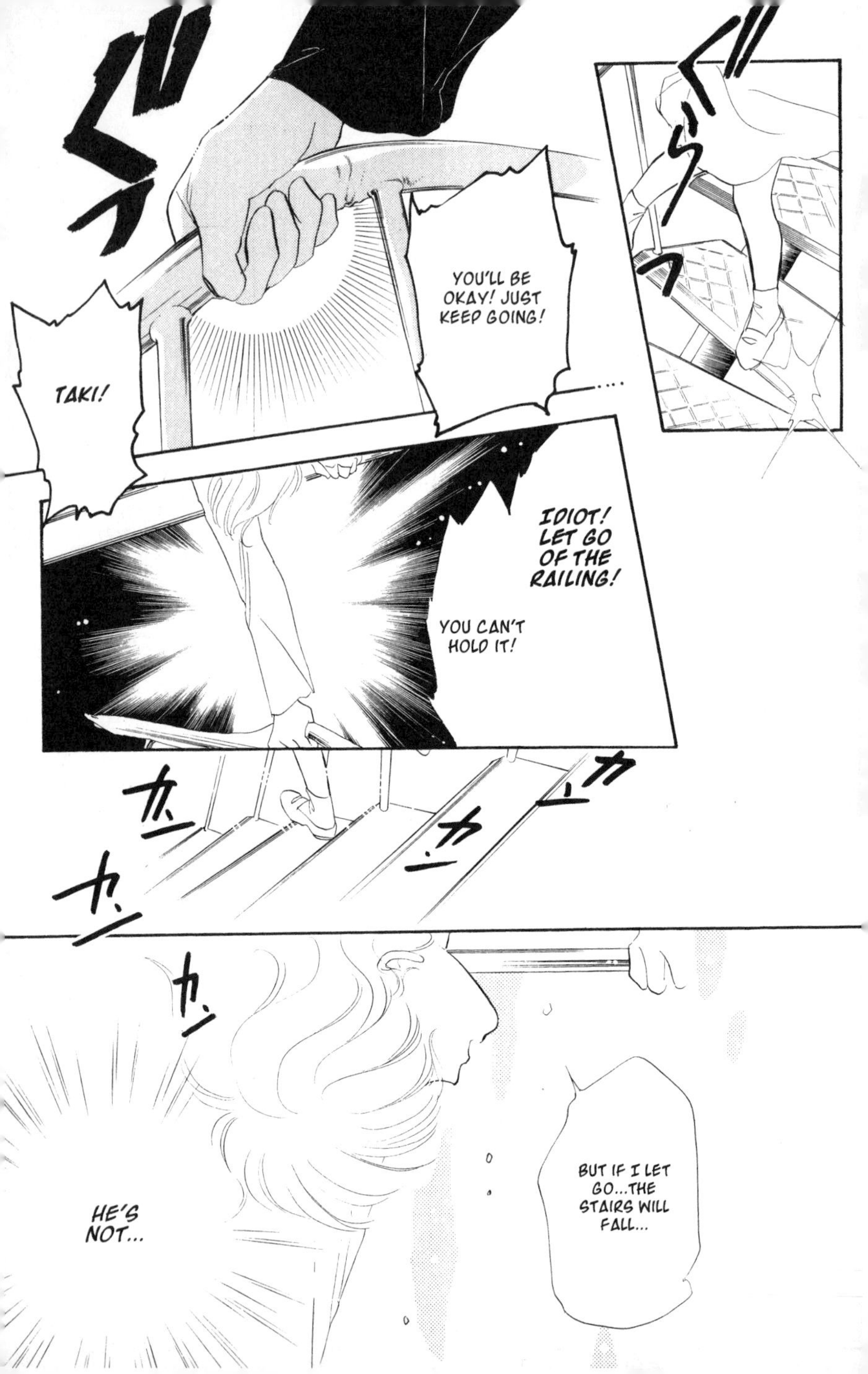
YOU'LL BE OKAY! JUST KEEP GOING!
TAKI!
IDIOT! LET GO OF THE RAILING!
YOU CAN'T HOLD IT!
BUT IF I LET GO...THE STAIRS WILL FALL...
HE'S NOT...

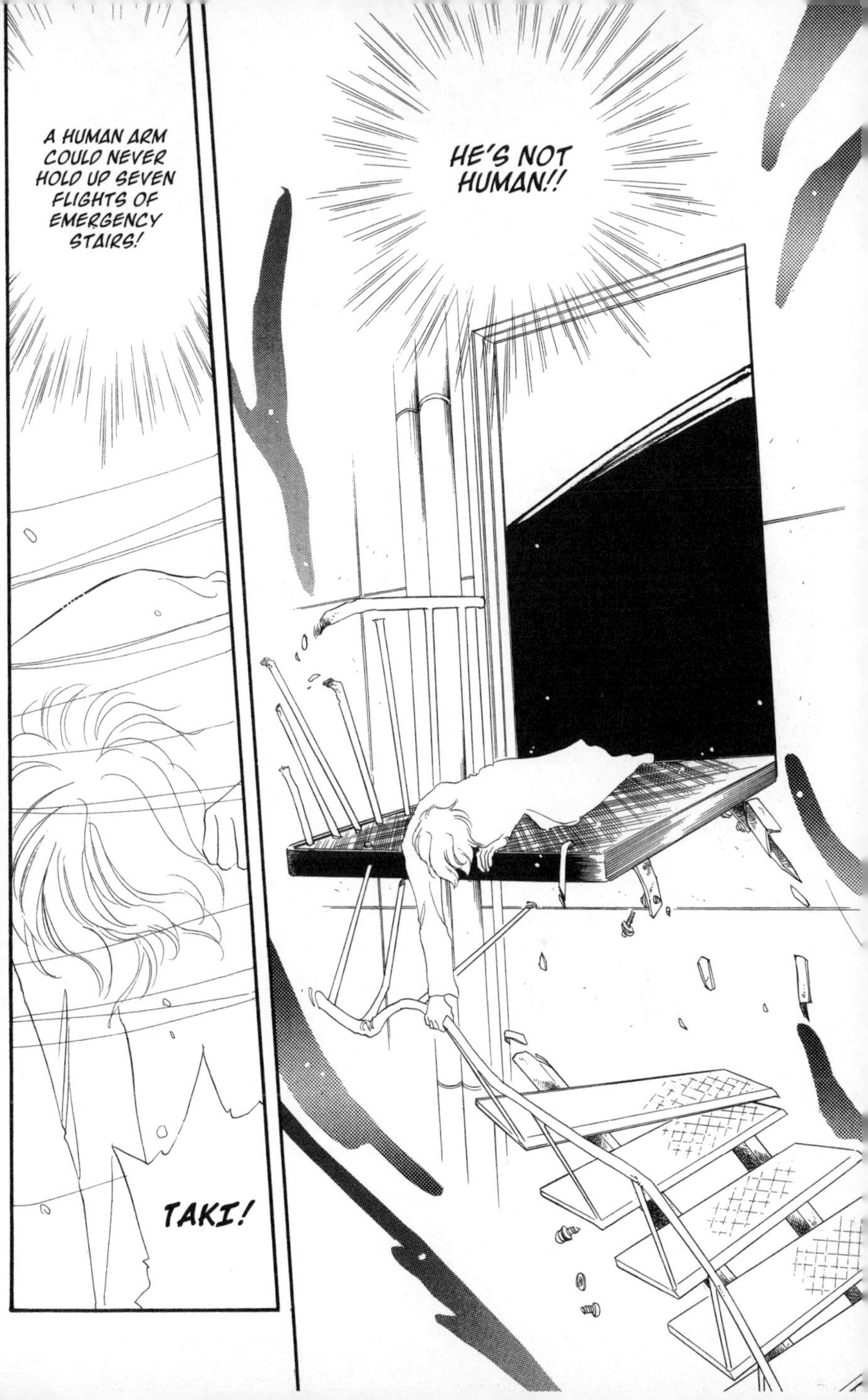
HE'S NOT HUMAN!!
A HUMAN ARM COULD NEVER HOLD UP SEVEN FLIGHTS OF EMERGENCY STAIRS!
TAKI!

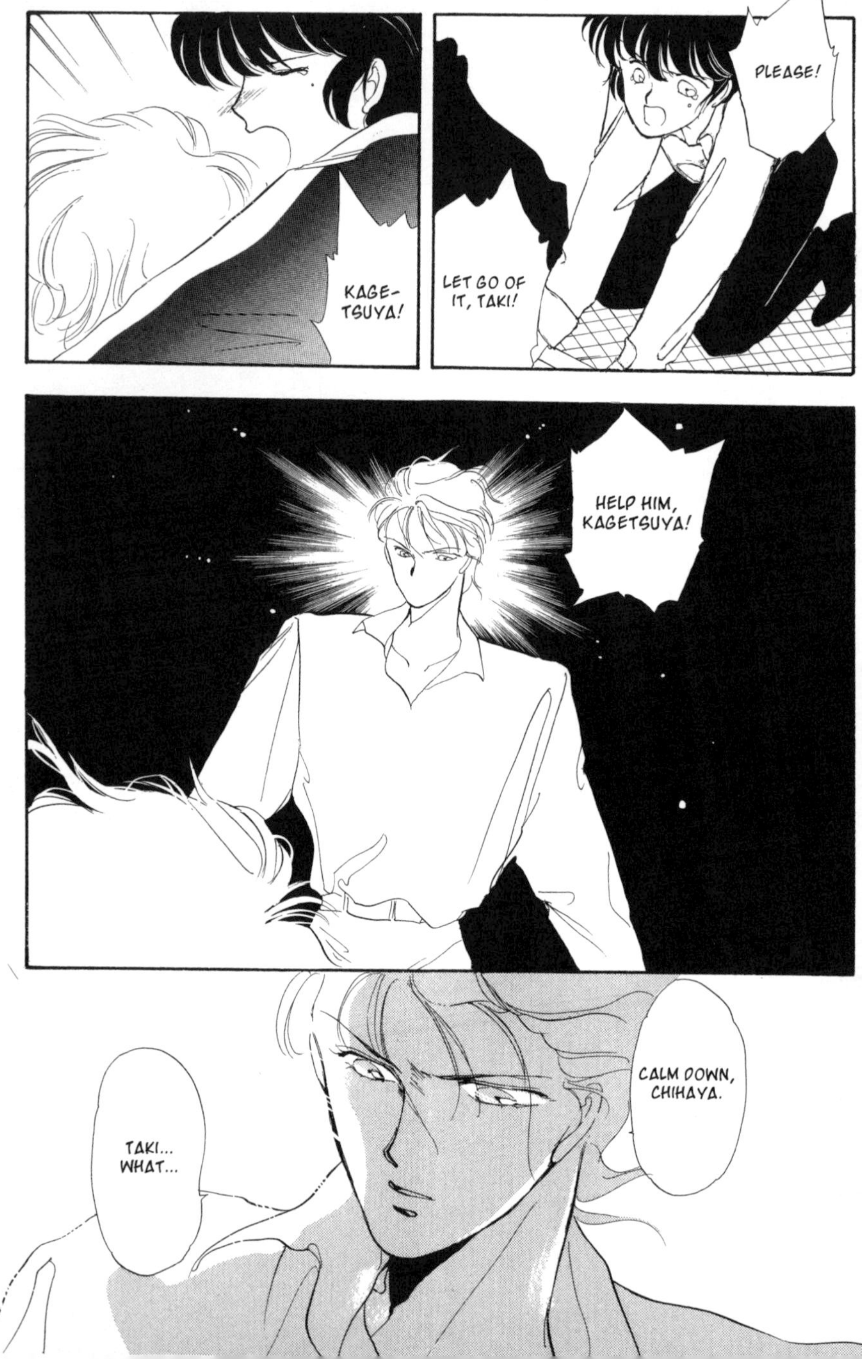
PLEASE!
LET GO OF IT, TAKI!
KAGE-TSUYA!
HELP HIM, KAGETSUYA!
CALM DOWN, CHIHAYA.
TAKI... WHAT...

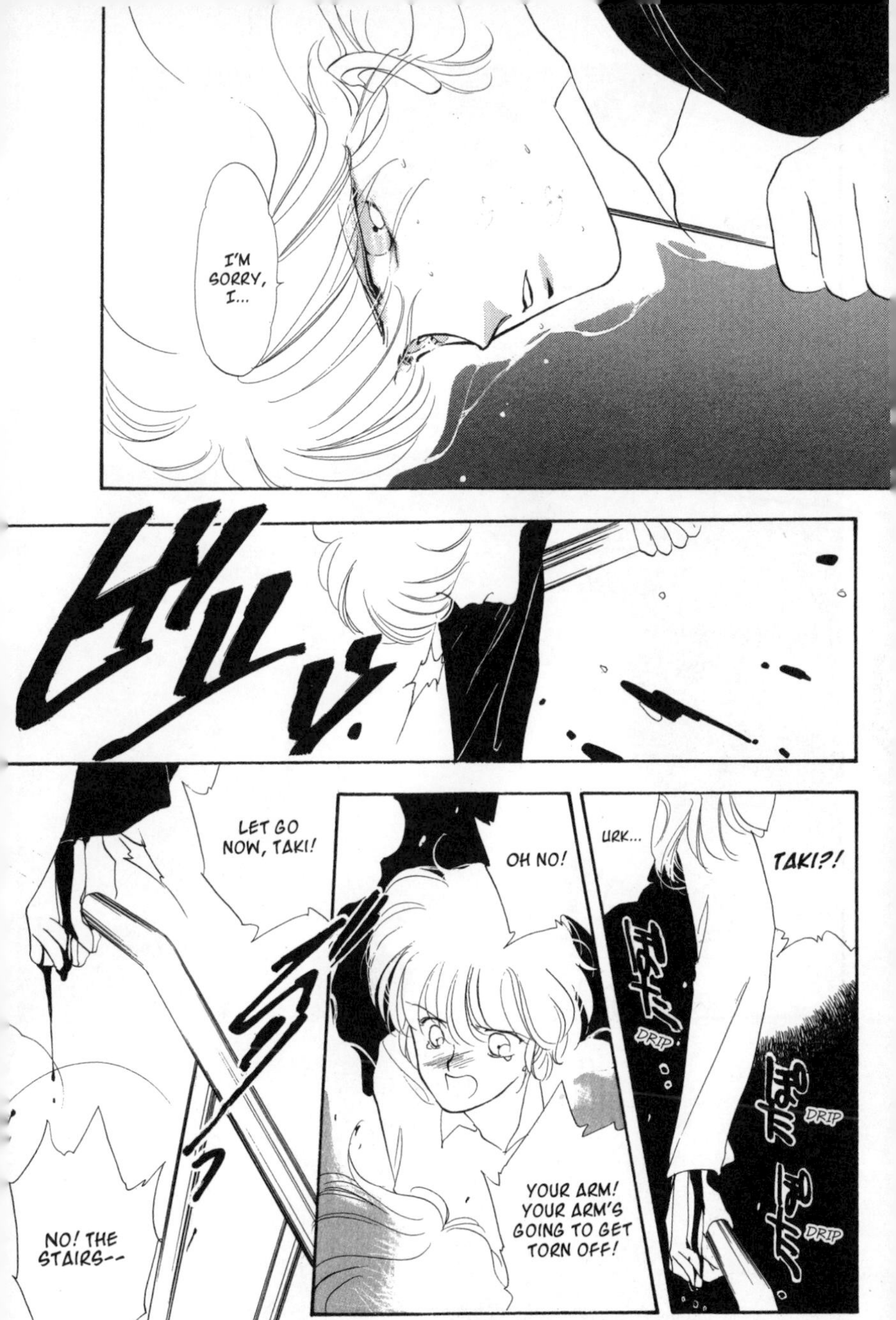
I'M SORRY, I...
TAKI?!
URK...
DRIP
DRIP
DRIP
OH NO!
YOUR ARM! YOUR ARM'S GOING TO GET TORN OFF!
LET GO NOW, TAKI!
NO! THE STAIRS--

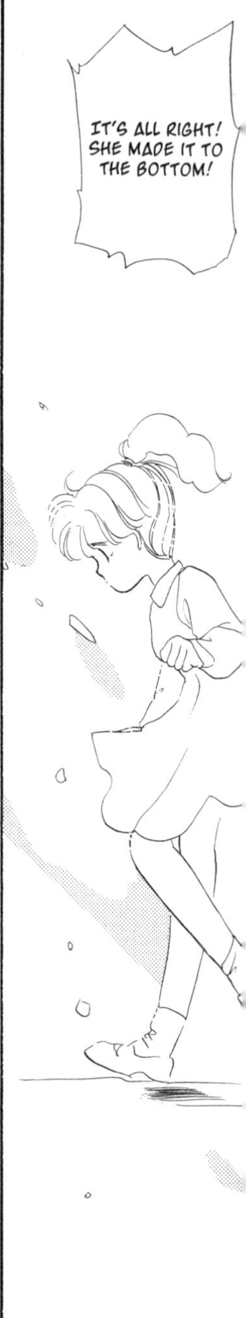
IT'S ALL RIGHT! SHE MADE IT TO THE BOTTOM!

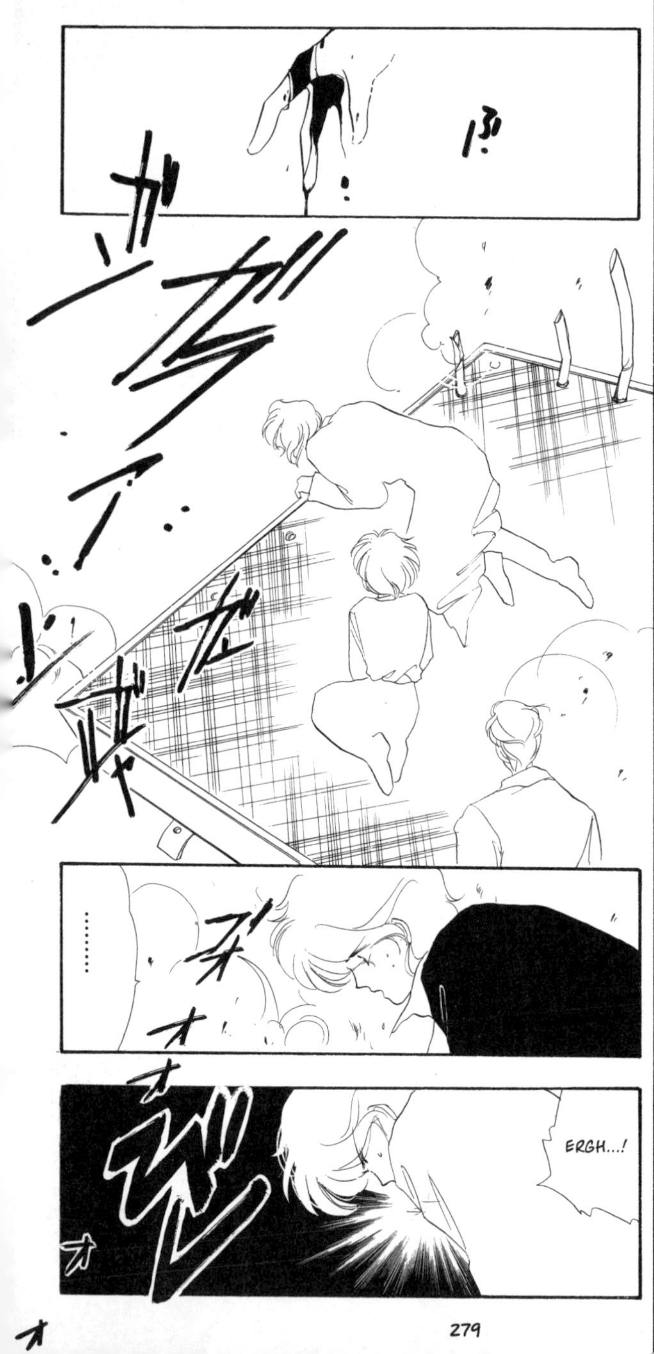
ERGH...!

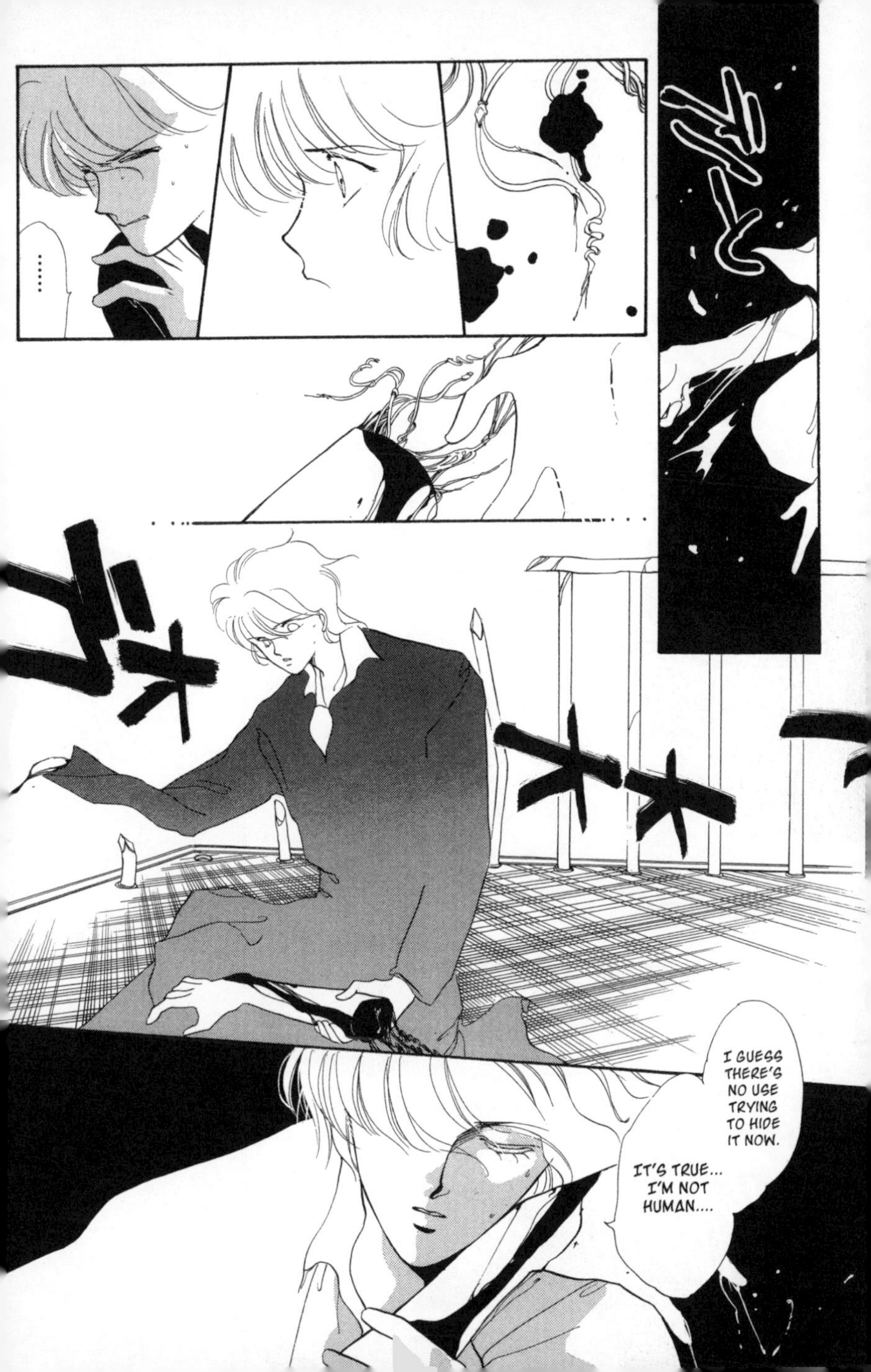
......
I GUESS THERE'S NO USE TRYING TO HIDE IT NOW.
IT'S TRUE... I'M NOT HUMAN....

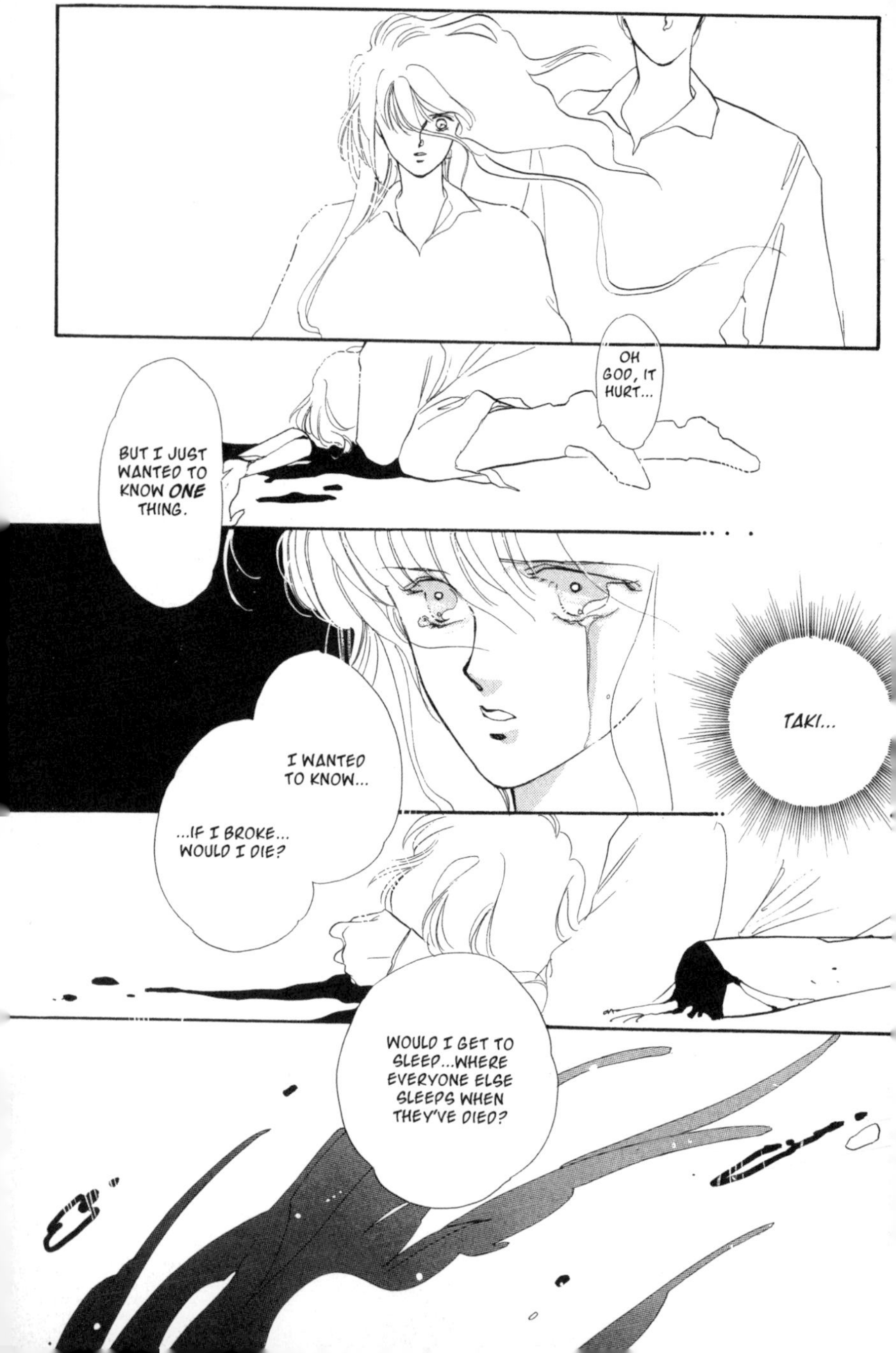
OH GOD, IT HURT...
BUT I JUST WANTED TO KNOW **ONE** THING.
TAKI...
I WANTED TO KNOW...
...IF I BROKE... WOULD I DIE?
WOULD I GET TO SLEEP...WHERE EVERYONE ELSE SLEEPS WHEN THEY'VE DIED?

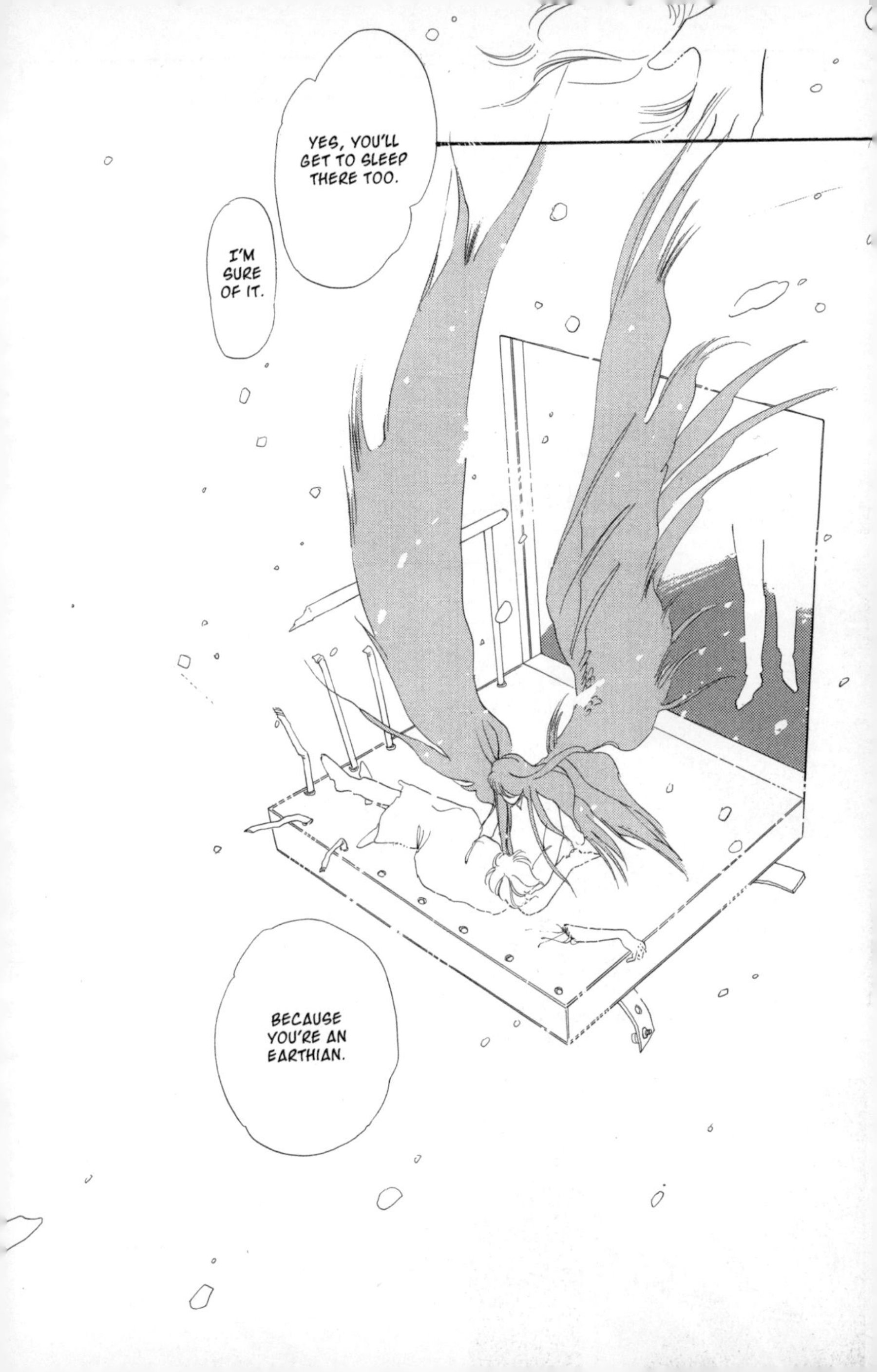
YES, YOU'LL GET TO SLEEP THERE TOO.
I'M SURE OF IT.
BECAUSE YOU'RE AN EARTHIAN.

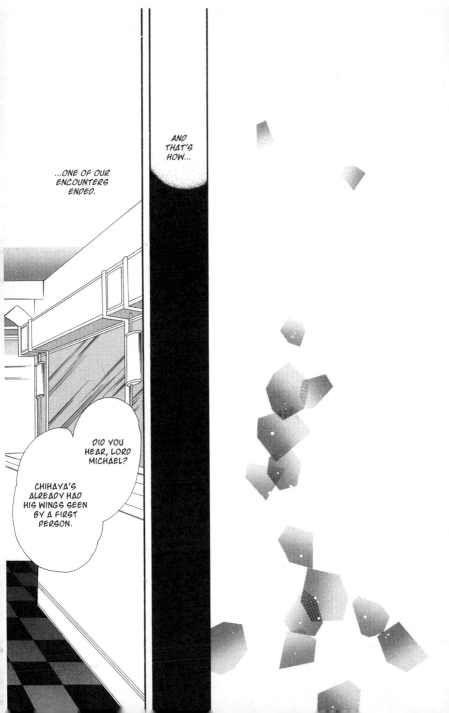

AND THAT'S HOW...

...ONE OF OUR ENCOUNTERS ENDED.

DID YOU HEAR, LORD MICHAEL?

CHIHAYA'S ALREADY HAD HIS WINGS SEEN BY A FIRST PERSON.

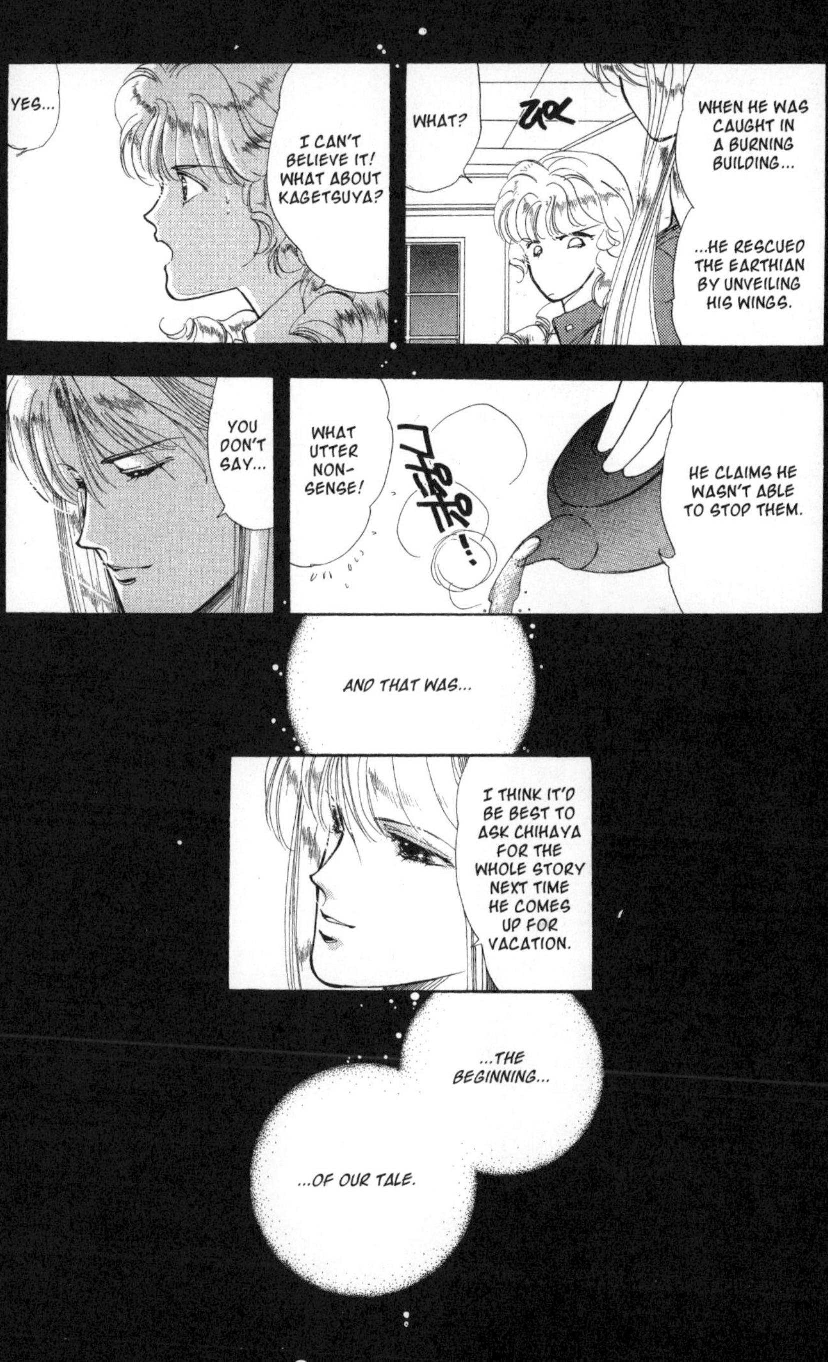
WHEN HE WAS CAUGHT IN A BURNING BUILDING...
...HE RESCUED THE EARTHIAN BY UNVEILING HIS WINGS.
WHAT?
I CAN'T BELIEVE IT! WHAT ABOUT KAGETSUYA?
YES...
HE CLAIMS HE WASN'T ABLE TO STOP THEM.
WHAT UTTER NON-SENSE!
YOU DON'T SAY...
AND THAT WAS...
I THINK IT'D BE BEST TO ASK CHIHAYA FOR THE WHOLE STORY NEXT TIME HE COMES UP FOR VACATION.
...THE BEGINNING...
...OF OUR TALE.

PHANTOM OF THE OPERA

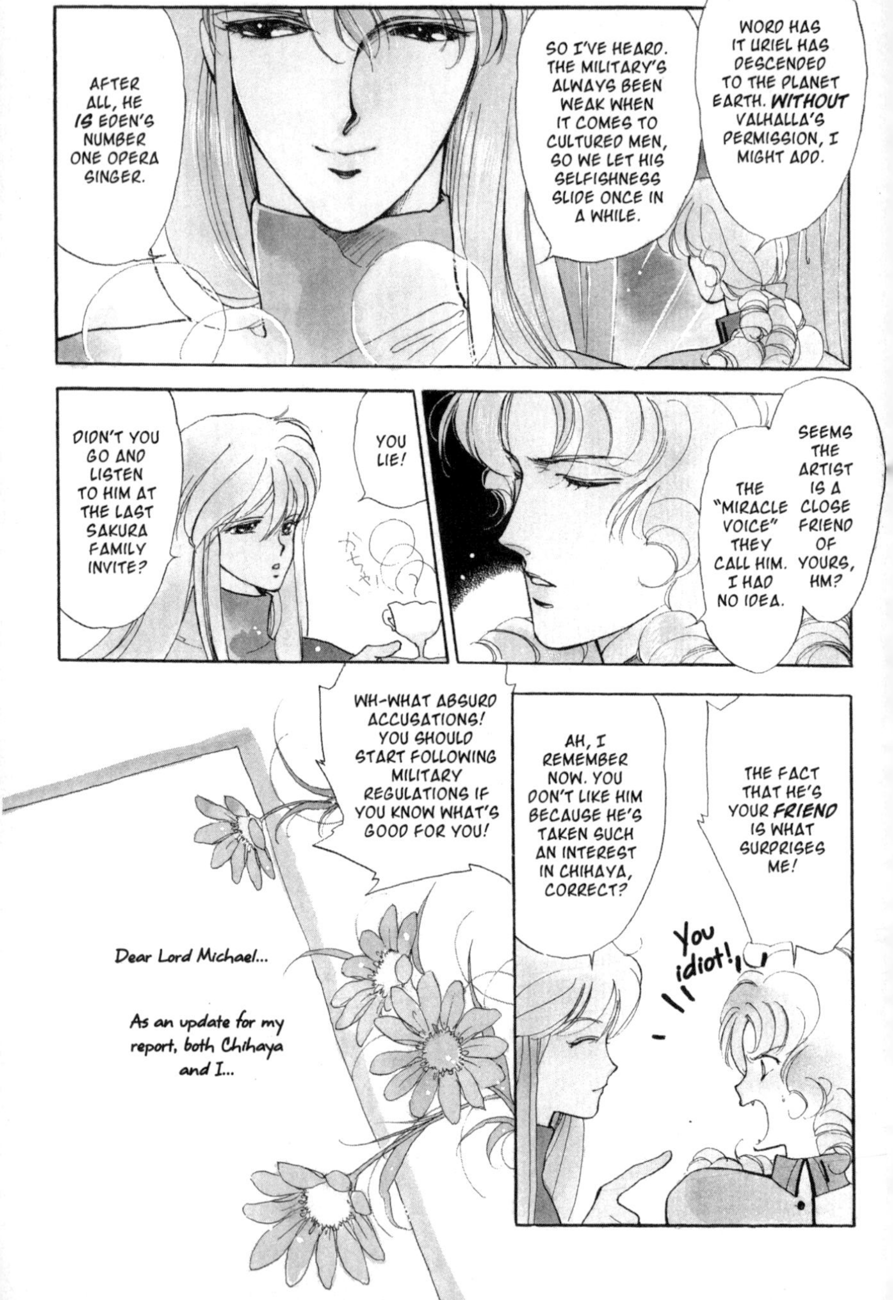
WORD HAS IT URIEL HAS DESCENDED TO THE PLANET EARTH. **WITHOUT** VALHALLA'S PERMISSION, I MIGHT ADD.
SO I'VE HEARD. THE MILITARY'S ALWAYS BEEN WEAK WHEN IT COMES TO CULTURED MEN, SO WE LET HIS SELFISHNESS SLIDE ONCE IN A WHILE.
AFTER ALL, HE **IS** EDEN'S NUMBER ONE OPERA SINGER.
SEEMS THE ARTIST IS A CLOSE FRIEND OF YOURS, HM?
THE "MIRACLE VOICE" THEY CALL HIM. I HAD NO IDEA.
YOU LIE!
DIDN'T YOU GO AND LISTEN TO HIM AT THE LAST SAKURA FAMILY INVITE?
WH-WHAT ABSURD ACCUSATIONS! YOU SHOULD START FOLLOWING MILITARY REGULATIONS IF YOU KNOW WHAT'S GOOD FOR YOU!
THE FACT THAT HE'S YOUR **FRIEND** IS WHAT SURPRISES ME!
AH, I REMEMBER NOW. YOU DON'T LIKE HIM BECAUSE HE'S TAKEN SUCH AN INTEREST IN CHIHAYA, CORRECT?
You idiot!
Dear Lord Michael...
As an update for my report, both Chihaya and I...

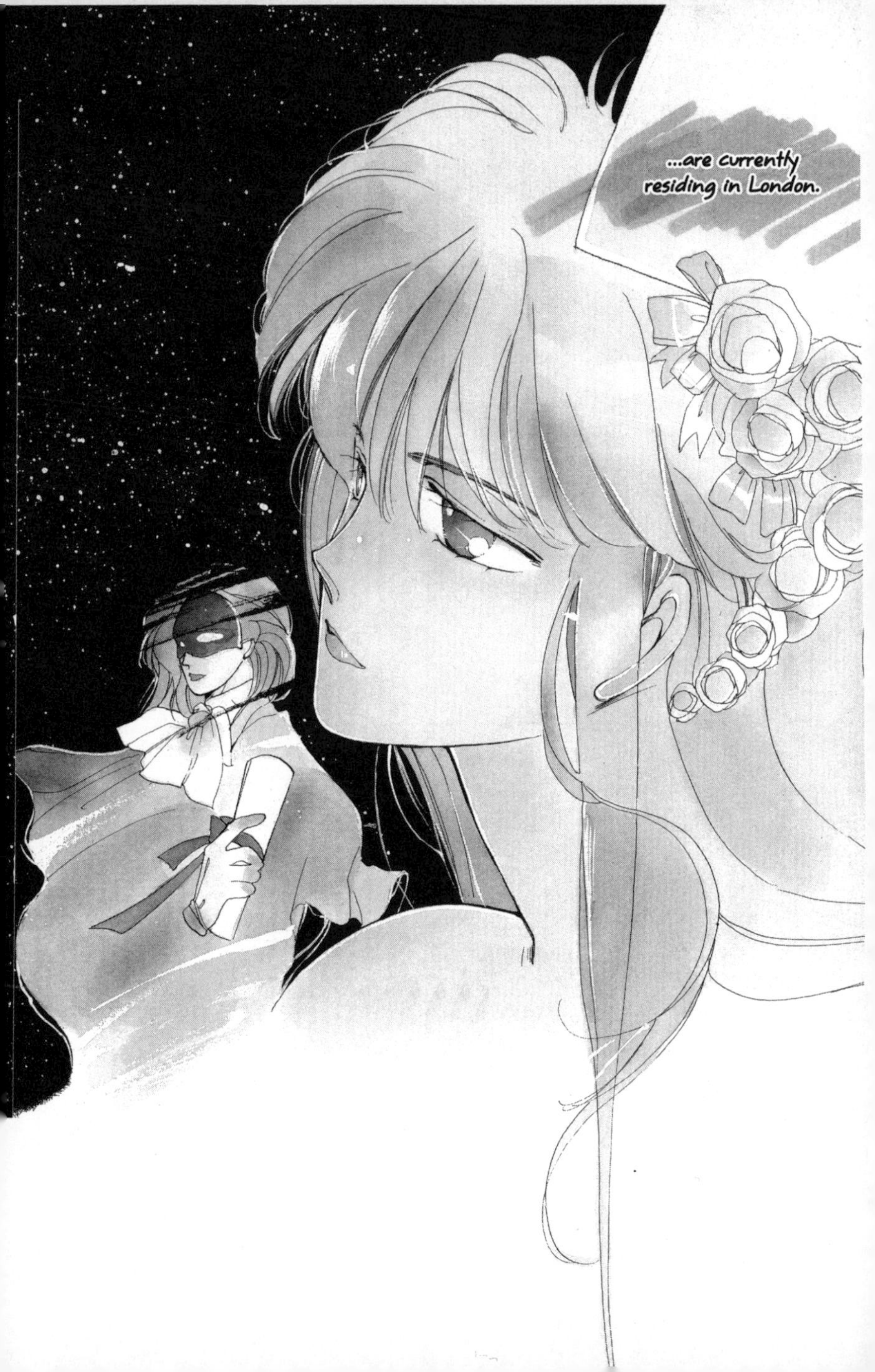
...are currently residing in London.

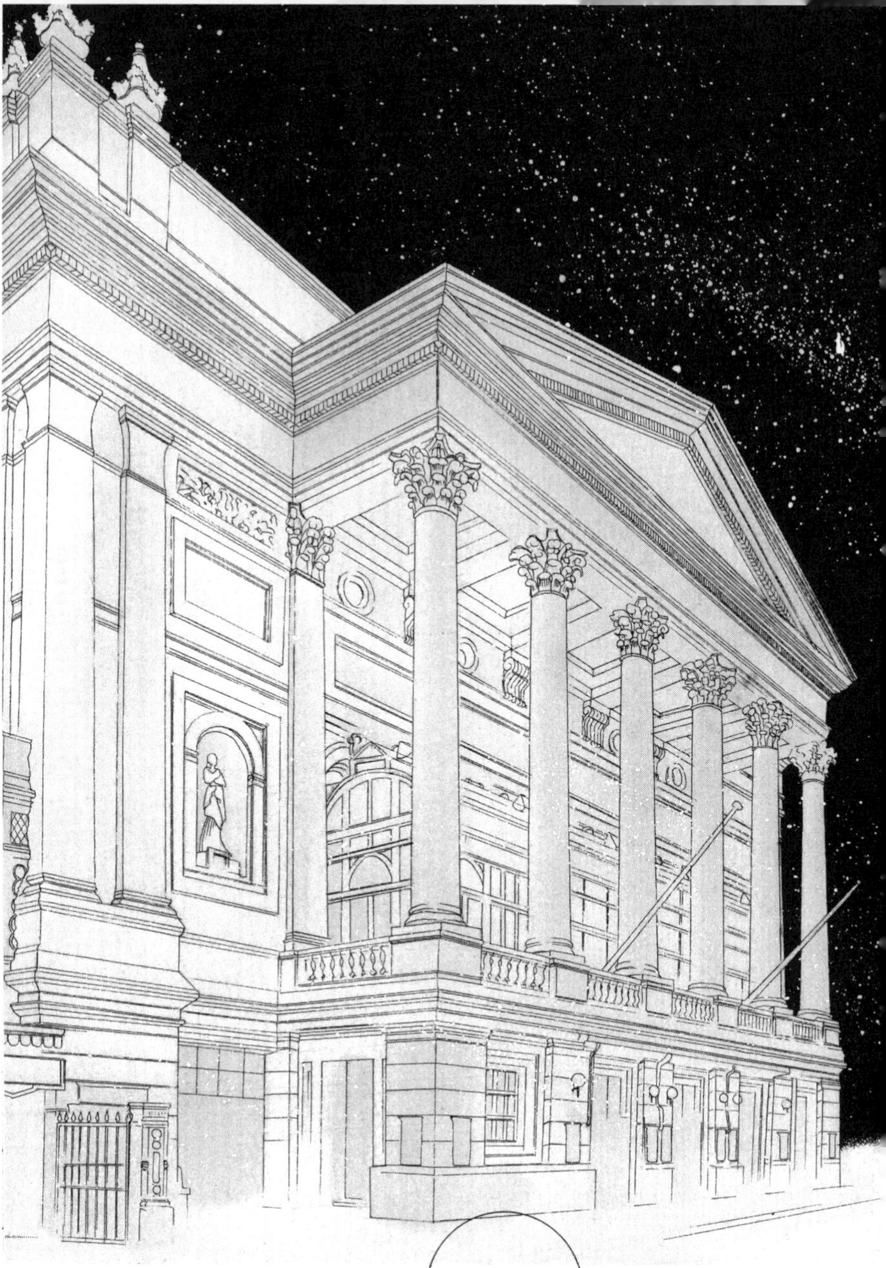

PHANTOM OF THE OPERA

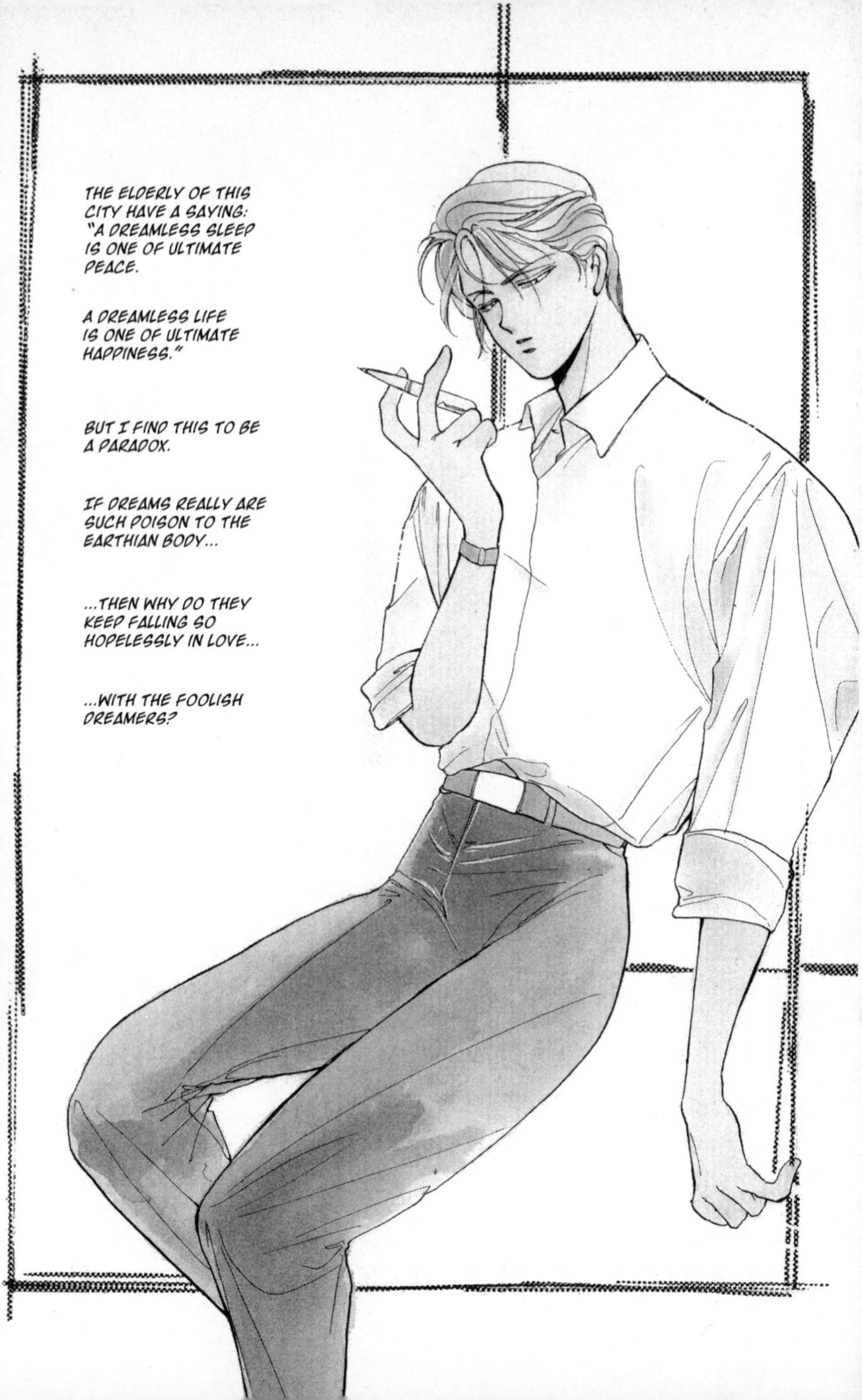
THE ELDERLY OF THIS CITY HAVE A SAYING: "A DREAMLESS SLEEP IS ONE OF ULTIMATE PEACE.
A DREAMLESS LIFE IS ONE OF ULTIMATE HAPPINESS."
BUT I FIND THIS TO BE A PARADOX.
IF DREAMS REALLY ARE SUCH POISON TO THE EARTHIAN BODY...
...THEN WHY DO THEY KEEP FALLING SO HOPELESSLY IN LOVE...
...WITH THE FOOLISH DREAMERS?

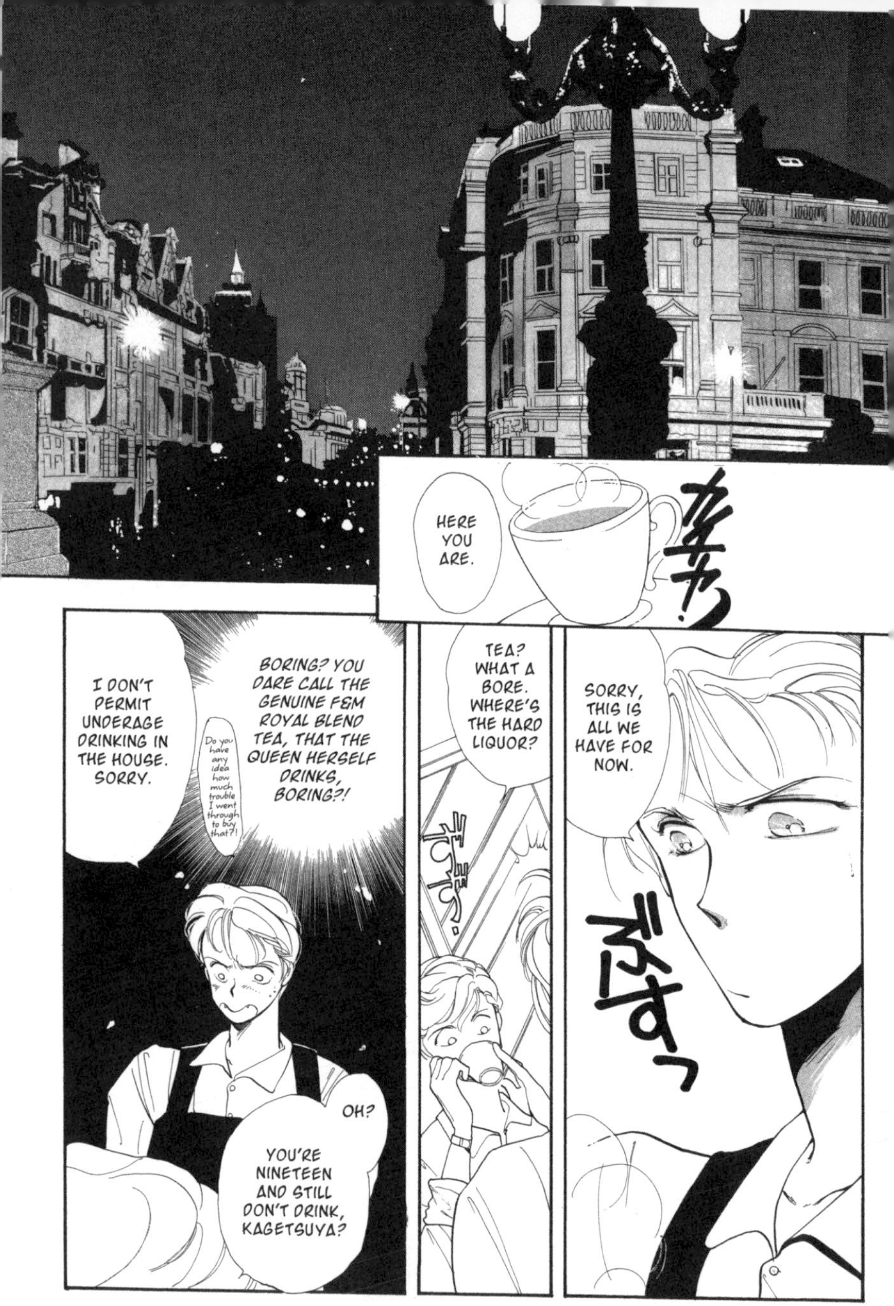
HERE YOU ARE.
SORRY, THIS IS ALL WE HAVE FOR NOW.
TEA? WHAT A BORE. WHERE'S THE HARD LIQUOR?
BORING? YOU DARE CALL THE GENUINE F&M ROYAL BLEND TEA, THAT THE QUEEN HERSELF DRINKS, BORING?!
Do you have any idea how much trouble I went through to buy that?!
I DON'T PERMIT UNDERAGE DRINKING IN THE HOUSE. SORRY.
OH?
YOU'RE NINETEEN AND STILL DON'T DRINK, KAGETSUYA?

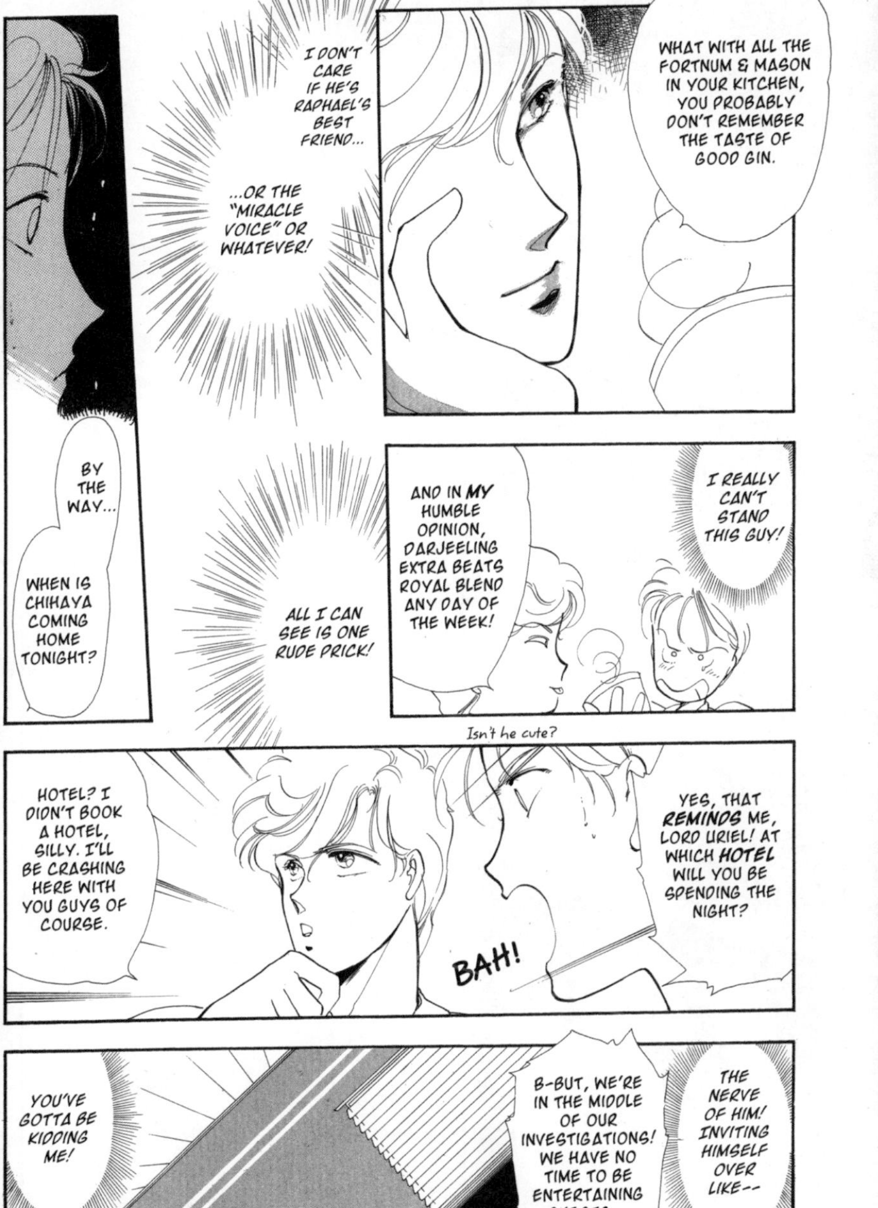
WHAT WITH ALL THE FORTNUM & MASON IN YOUR KITCHEN, YOU PROBABLY DON'T REMEMBER THE TASTE OF GOOD GIN.
I DON'T CARE IF HE'S RAPHAEL'S BEST FRIEND...
...OR THE "MIRACLE VOICE" OR WHATEVER!
I REALLY CAN'T STAND THIS GUY!
AND IN **MY** HUMBLE OPINION, DARJEELING EXTRA BEATS ROYAL BLEND ANY DAY OF THE WEEK!
ALL I CAN SEE IS ONE RUDE PRICK!
BY THE WAY...
WHEN IS CHIHAYA COMING HOME TONIGHT?
Isn't he cute?
YES, THAT **REMINDS** ME, LORD URIEL! AT WHICH **HOTEL** WILL YOU BE SPENDING THE NIGHT?
BAH!
HOTEL? I DIDN'T BOOK A HOTEL, SILLY. I'LL BE CRASHING HERE WITH YOU GUYS OF COURSE.
THE NERVE OF HIM! INVITING HIMSELF OVER LIKE--
B-BUT, WE'RE IN THE MIDDLE OF OUR INVESTIGATIONS! WE HAVE NO TIME TO BE ENTERTAINING GUESTS--
YOU'VE GOTTA BE KIDDING ME!

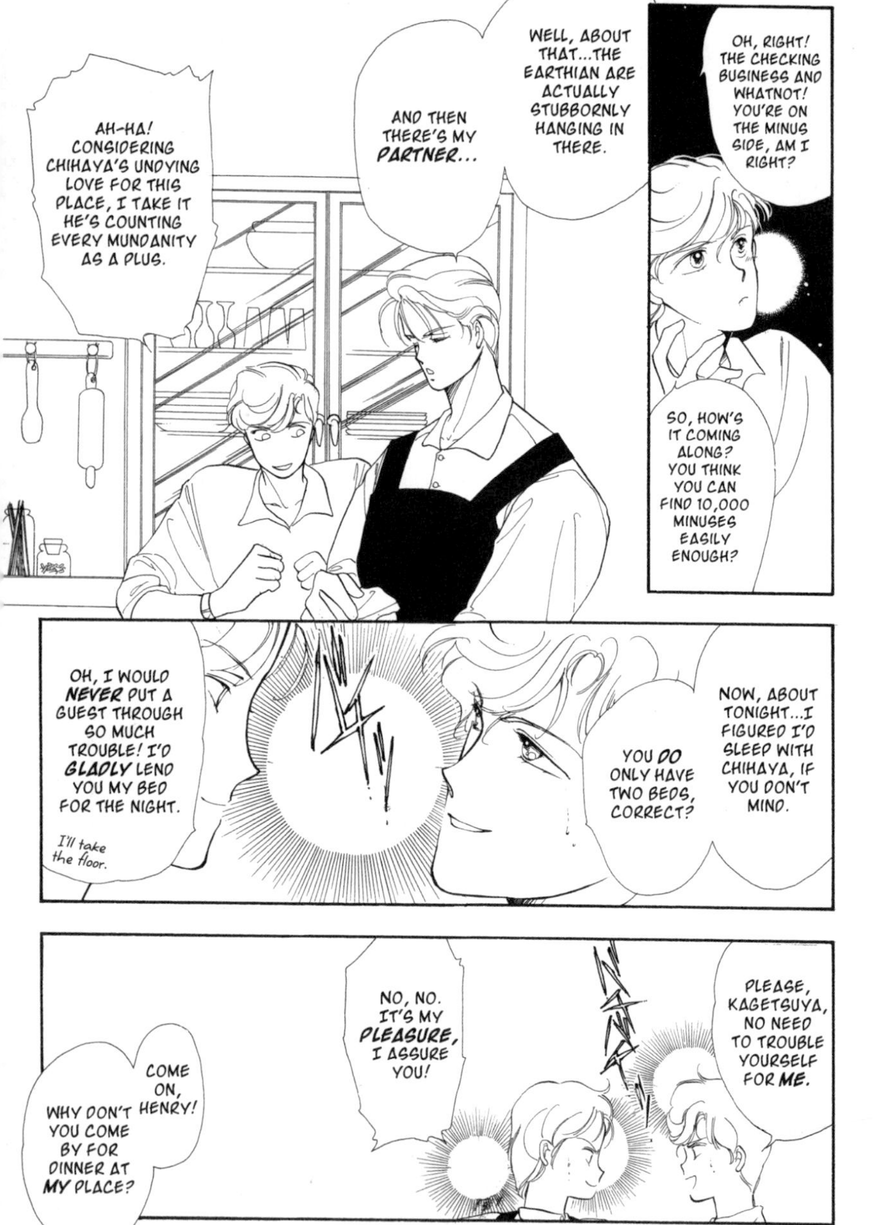
OH, RIGHT! THE CHECKING BUSINESS AND WHATNOT! YOU'RE ON THE MINUS SIDE, AM I RIGHT?
SO, HOW'S IT COMING ALONG? YOU THINK YOU CAN FIND 10,000 MINUSES EASILY ENOUGH?
WELL, ABOUT THAT...THE EARTHIAN ARE ACTUALLY STUBBORNLY HANGING IN THERE.
AND THEN THERE'S MY ***PARTNER***...
AH-HA! CONSIDERING CHIHAYA'S UNDYING LOVE FOR THIS PLACE, I TAKE IT HE'S COUNTING EVERY MUNDANITY AS A PLUS.
NOW, ABOUT TONIGHT...I FIGURED I'D SLEEP WITH CHIHAYA, IF YOU DON'T MIND.
YOU ***DO*** ONLY HAVE TWO BEDS, CORRECT?
OH, I WOULD ***NEVER*** PUT A GUEST THROUGH SO MUCH TROUBLE! I'D ***GLADLY*** LEND YOU MY BED FOR THE NIGHT.
I'll take the floor.
PLEASE, KAGETSUYA, NO NEED TO TROUBLE YOURSELF FOR ***ME***.
NO, NO. IT'S MY ***PLEASURE***, I ASSURE YOU!
COME ON, HENRY!
WHY DON'T YOU COME BY FOR DINNER AT ***MY*** PLACE?

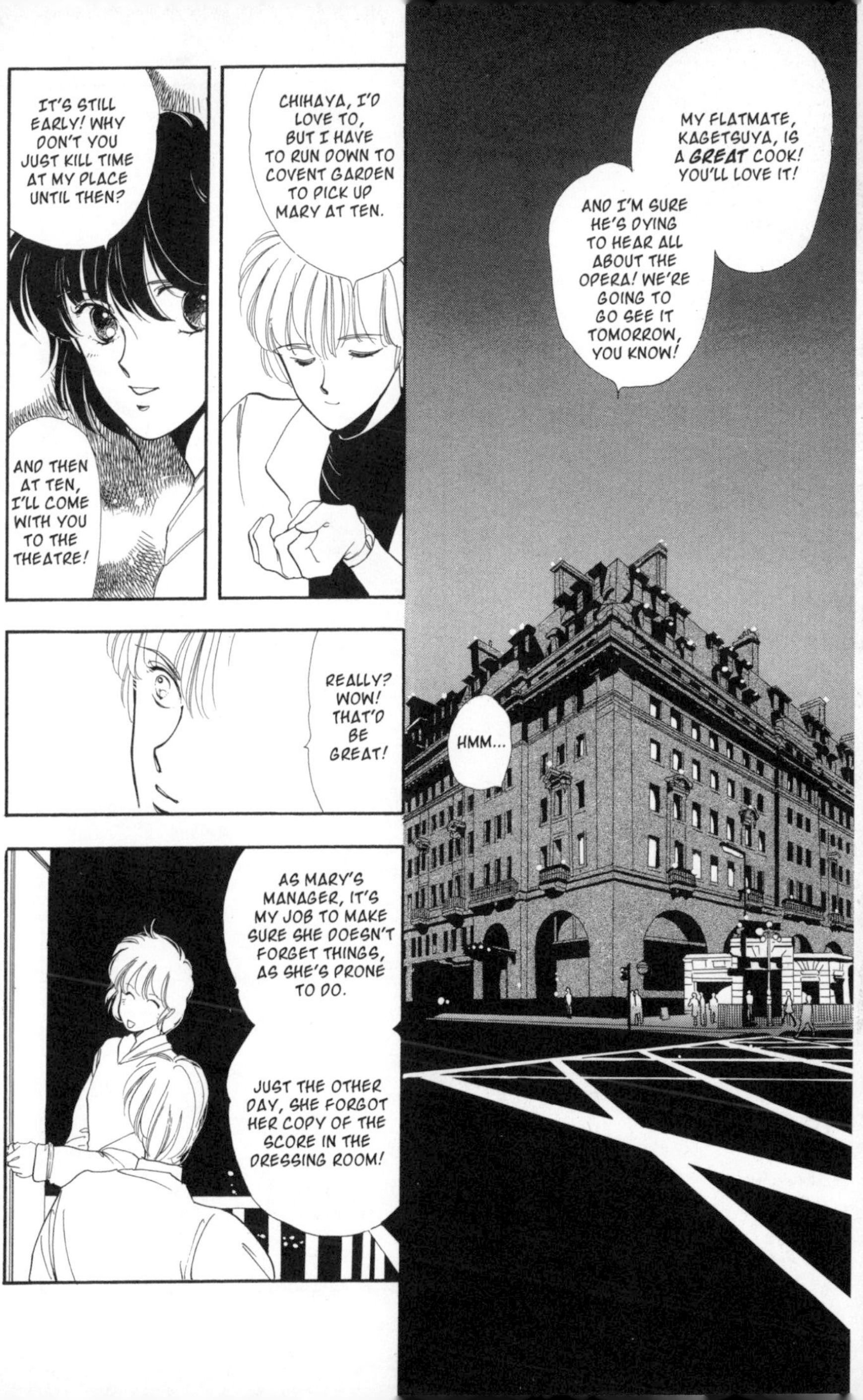
MY FLATMATE, KAGETSUYA, IS A **GREAT** COOK! YOU'LL LOVE IT!
AND I'M SURE HE'S DYING TO HEAR ALL ABOUT THE OPERA! WE'RE GOING TO GO SEE IT TOMORROW, YOU KNOW!
HMM...
CHIHAYA, I'D LOVE TO, BUT I HAVE TO RUN DOWN TO COVENT GARDEN TO PICK UP MARY AT TEN.
IT'S STILL EARLY! WHY DON'T YOU JUST KILL TIME AT MY PLACE UNTIL THEN?
AND THEN AT TEN, I'LL COME WITH YOU TO THE THEATRE!
REALLY? WOW! THAT'D BE GREAT!
AS MARY'S MANAGER, IT'S MY JOB TO MAKE SURE SHE DOESN'T FORGET THINGS, AS SHE'S PRONE TO DO.
JUST THE OTHER DAY, SHE FORGOT HER COPY OF THE SCORE IN THE DRESSING ROOM!

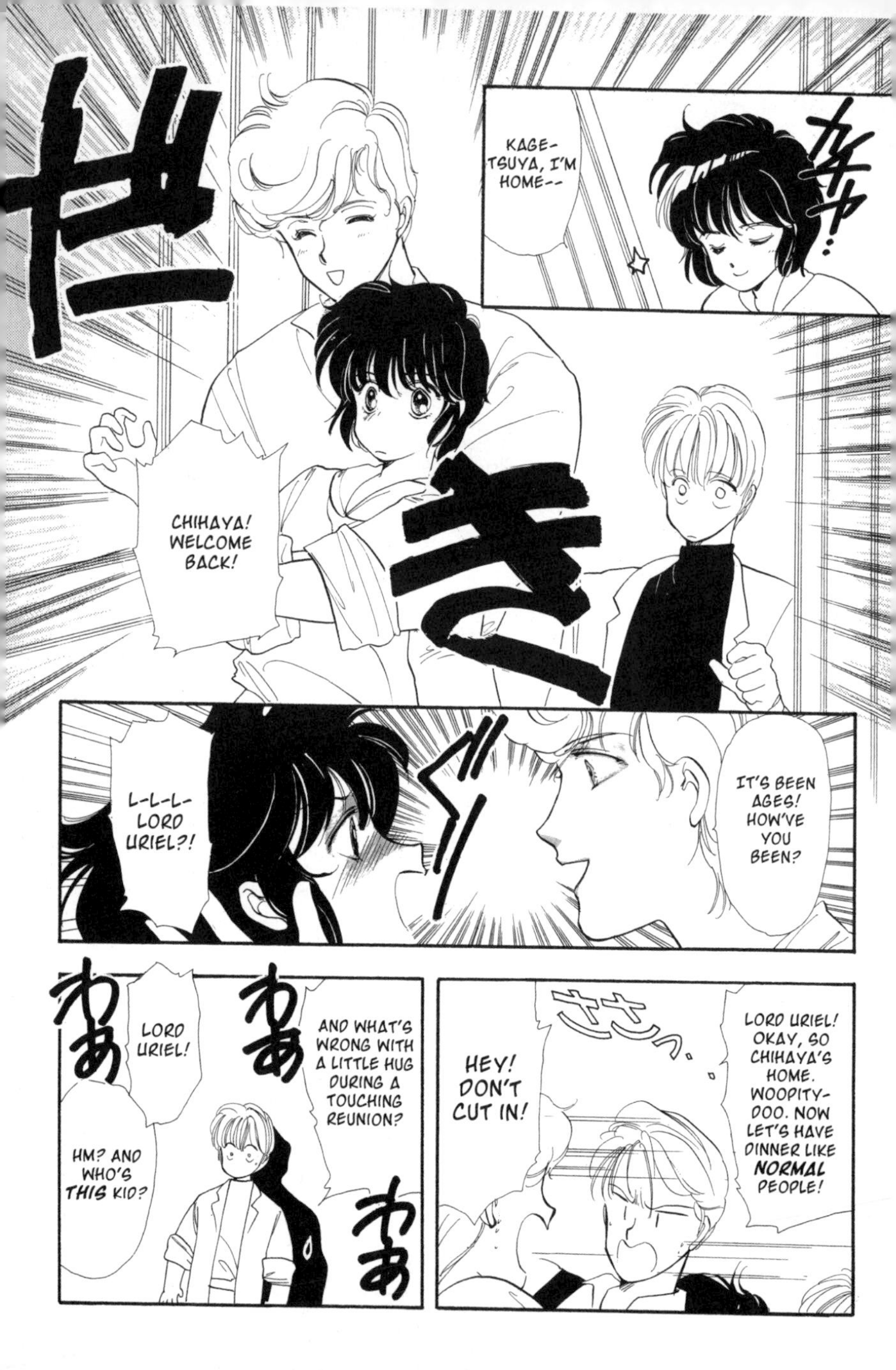

カチャ
KAGE-TSUYA, I'M HOME--
CHIHAYA! WELCOME BACK!
IT'S BEEN AGES! HOW'VE YOU BEEN?
L-L-L-LORD URIEL?!
LORD URIEL! OKAY, SO CHIHAYA'S HOME. WOOPITY-DOO. NOW LET'S HAVE DINNER LIKE **NORMAL** PEOPLE!
HEY! DON'T CUT IN!
ささっ
AND WHAT'S WRONG WITH A LITTLE HUG DURING A TOUCHING REUNION?
LORD URIEL!
HM? AND WHO'S **THIS** KID?
わあ
わあ
わあ

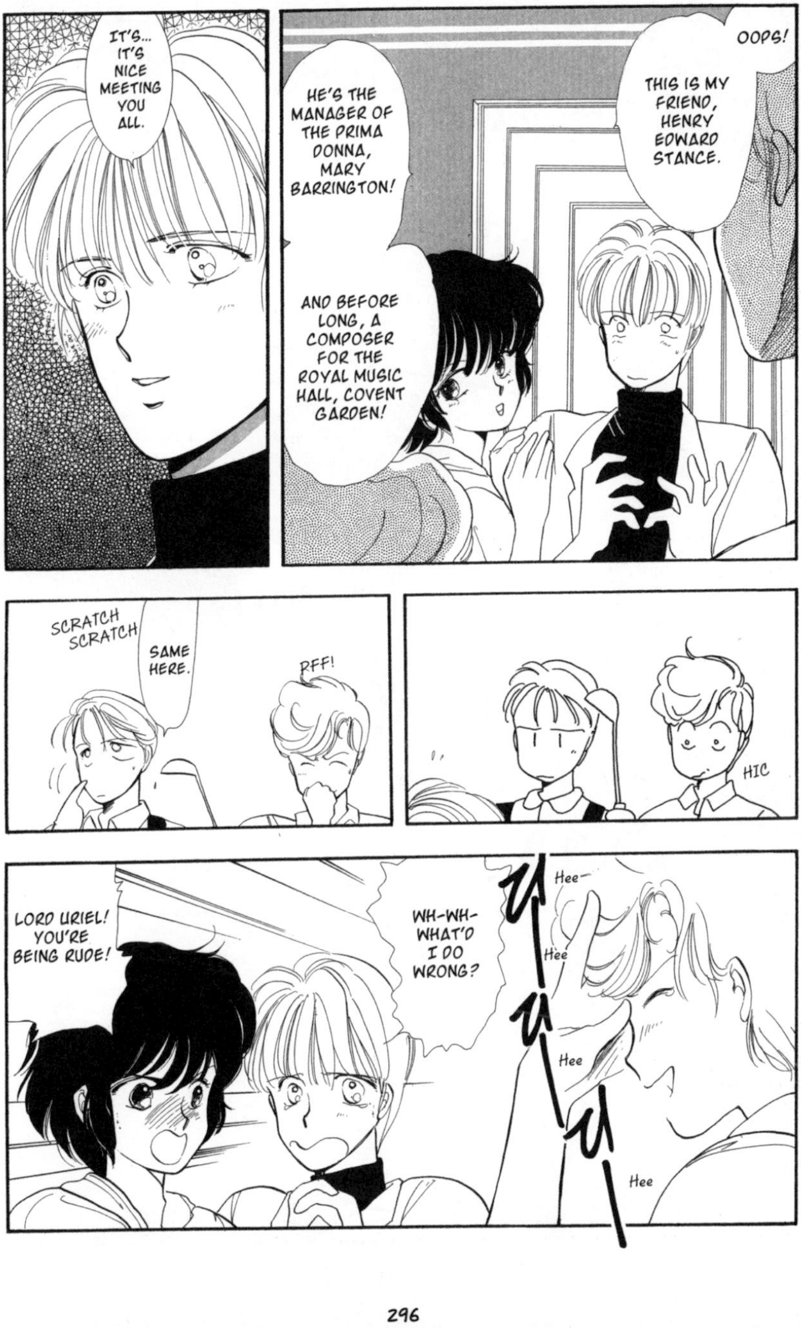
OOPS!
THIS IS MY FRIEND, HENRY EDWARD STANCE.
HE'S THE MANAGER OF THE PRIMA DONNA, MARY BARRINGTON!
AND BEFORE LONG, A COMPOSER FOR THE ROYAL MUSIC HALL, COVENT GARDEN!
IT'S... IT'S NICE MEETING YOU ALL.
HIC
SCRATCH SCRATCH
SAME HERE.
PFF!
Hee
Hee
Hee
Hee
WH-WH-WHAT'D I DO WRONG?
LORD URIEL! YOU'RE BEING RUDE!

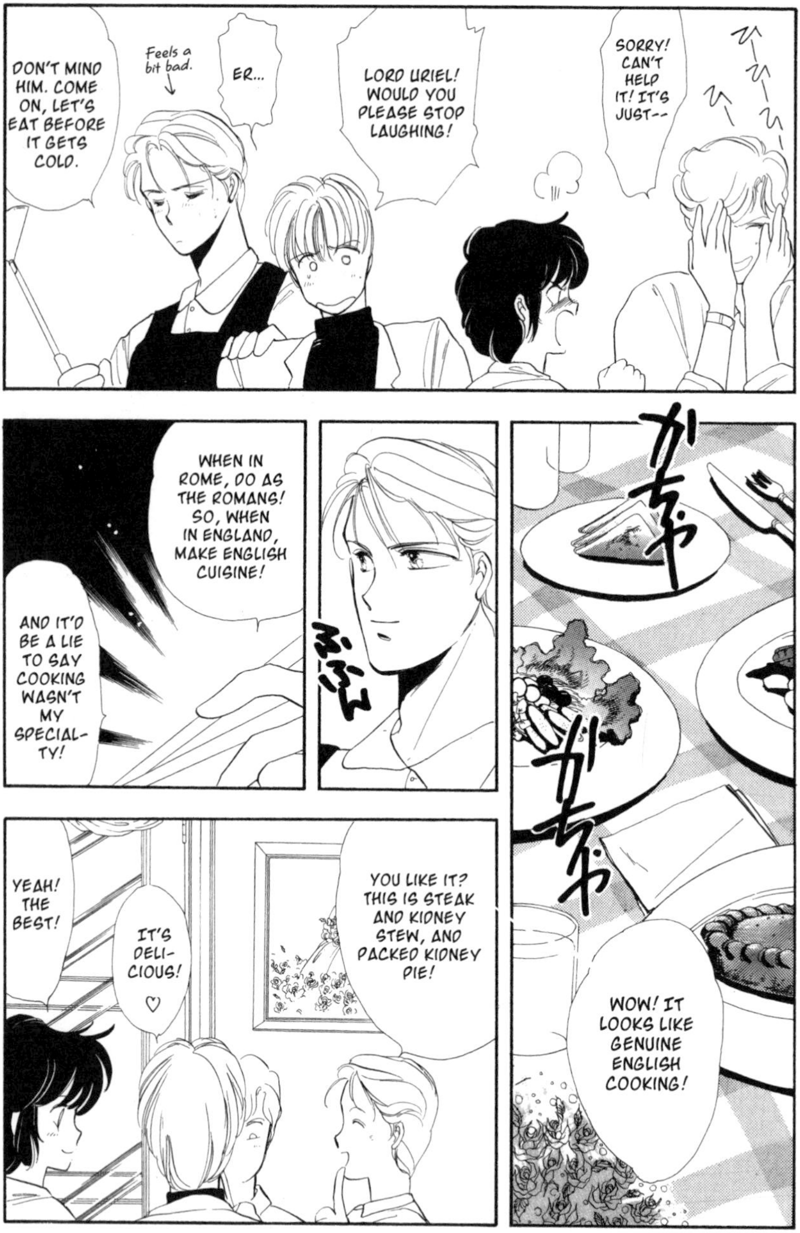
SORRY! CAN'T HELP IT! IT'S JUST--
ひ〜ひ〜ひ〜
ひ〜
LORD URIEL! WOULD YOU PLEASE STOP LAUGHING!
ER...
Feels a bit bad.
DON'T MIND HIM. COME ON, LET'S EAT BEFORE IT GETS COLD.
かちゃ
かちゃ
WOW! IT LOOKS LIKE GENUINE ENGLISH COOKING!
ふふん
WHEN IN ROME, DO AS THE ROMANS! SO, WHEN IN ENGLAND, MAKE ENGLISH CUISINE!
AND IT'D BE A LIE TO SAY COOKING WASN'T MY SPECIAL-TY!
YOU LIKE IT? THIS IS STEAK AND KIDNEY STEW, AND PACKED KIDNEY PIE!
IT'S DELI-CIOUS! ♡
YEAH! THE BEST!

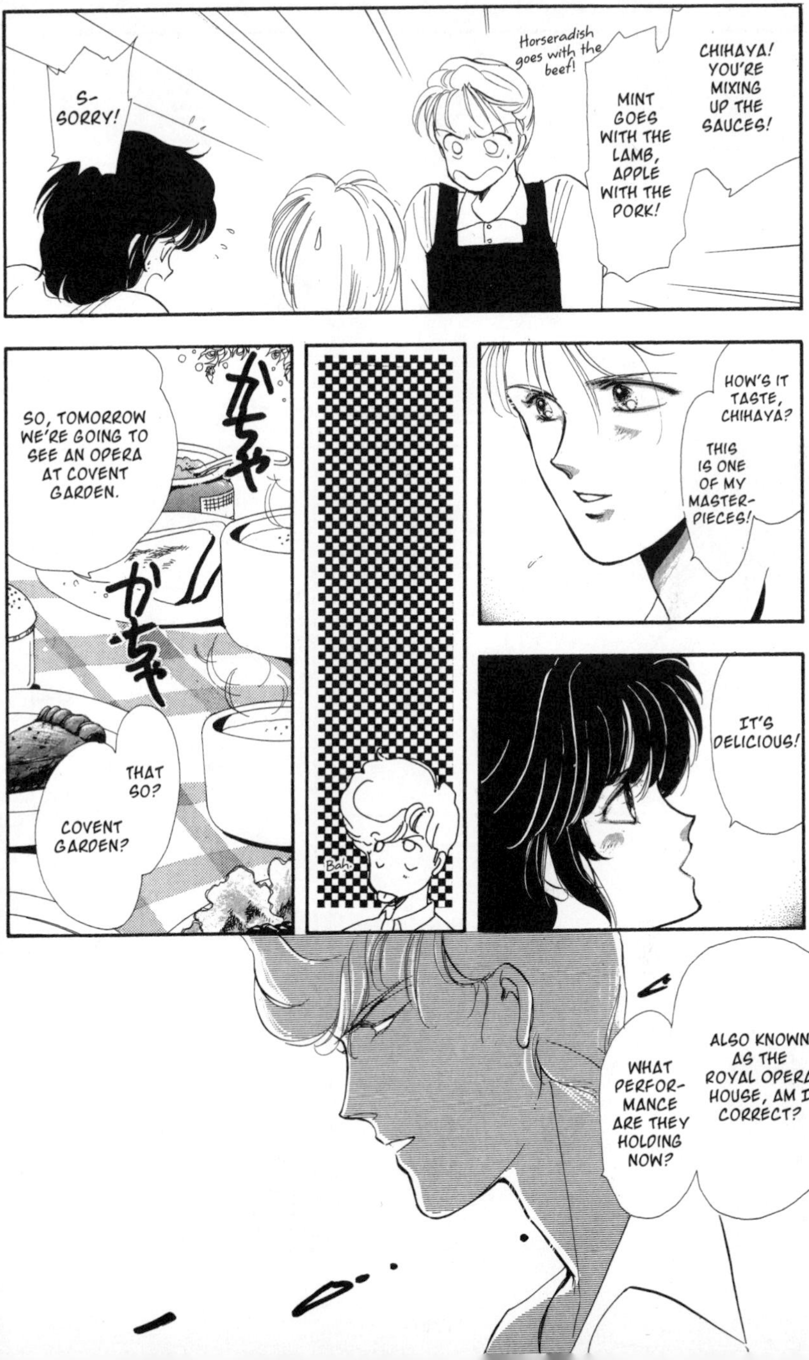
CHIHAYA! YOU'RE MIXING UP THE SAUCES!
MINT GOES WITH THE LAMB, APPLE WITH THE PORK!
Horseradish goes with the beef!
S-SORRY!
HOW'S IT TASTE, CHIHAYA?
THIS IS ONE OF MY MASTER-PIECES!
IT'S DELICIOUS!
Bah.
かちゃ
SO, TOMORROW WE'RE GOING TO SEE AN OPERA AT COVENT GARDEN.
かちゃ
THAT SO?
COVENT GARDEN?
ALSO KNOWN AS THE ROYAL OPERA HOUSE, AM I CORRECT?
WHAT PERFOR-MANCE ARE THEY HOLDING NOW?

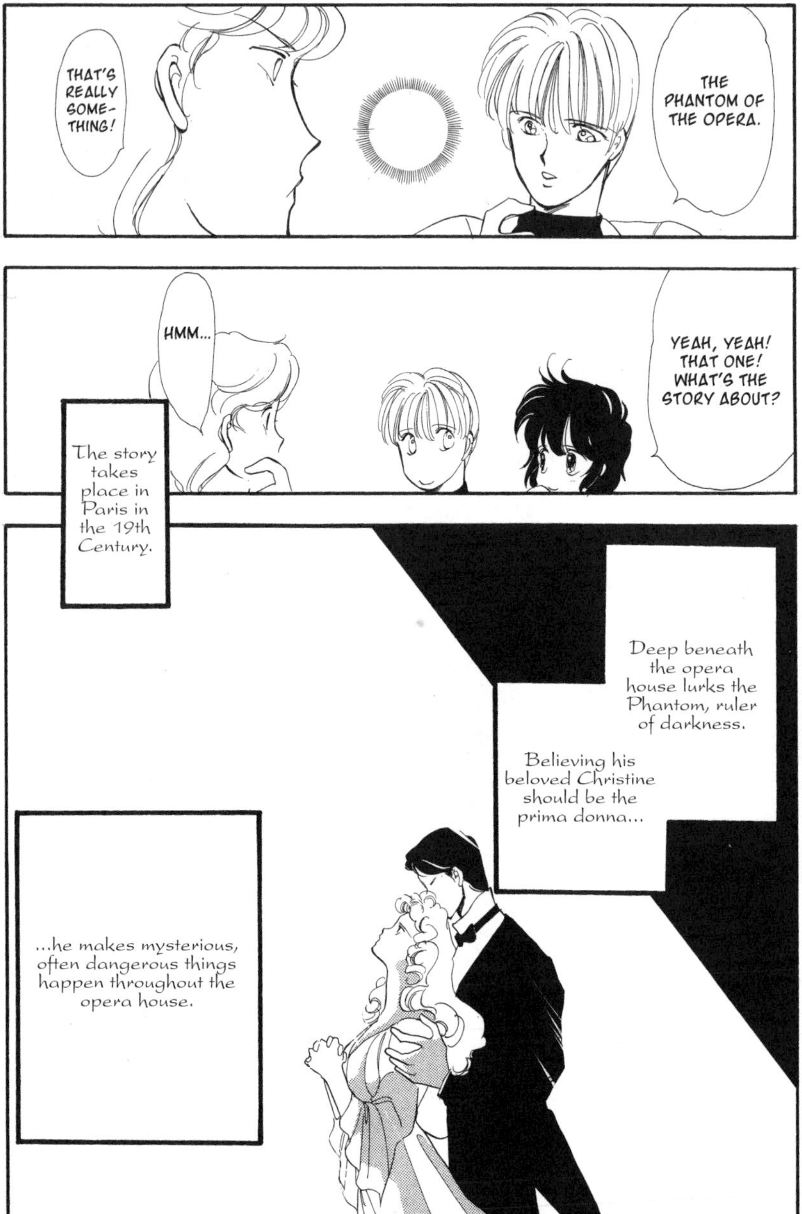
THE PHANTOM OF THE OPERA.
THAT'S REALLY SOME-THING!
YEAH, YEAH! THAT ONE! WHAT'S THE STORY ABOUT?
HMM...
The story takes place in Paris in the 19th Century.
Deep beneath the opera house lurks the Phantom, ruler of darkness.
Believing his beloved Christine should be the prima donna...
...he makes mysterious, often dangerous things happen throughout the opera house.

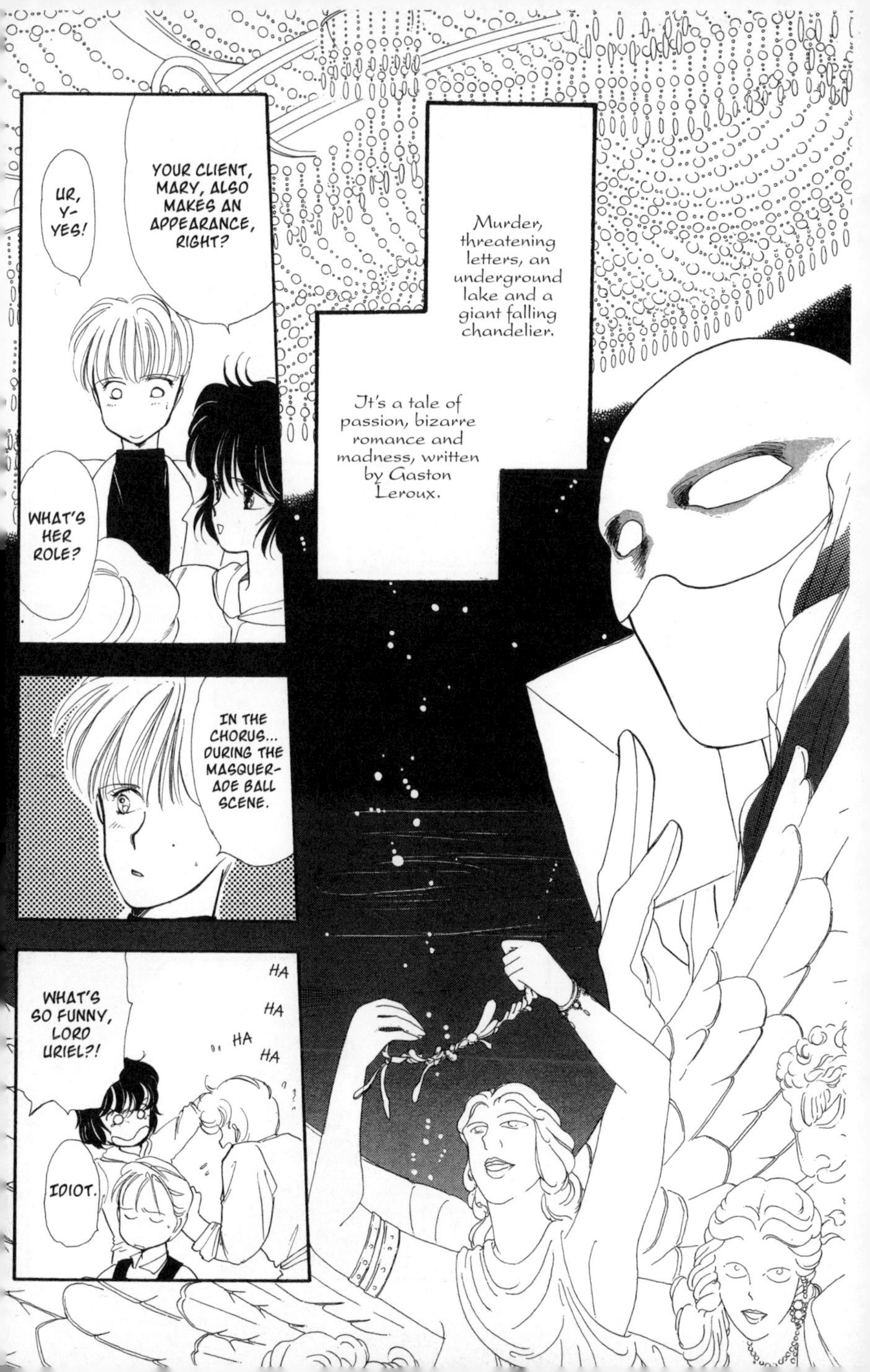
Murder, threatening letters, an underground lake and a giant falling chandelier.
It's a tale of passion, bizarre romance and madness, written by Gaston Leroux.
YOUR CLIENT, MARY, ALSO MAKES AN APPEARANCE, RIGHT?
UR, Y-YES!
WHAT'S HER ROLE?
IN THE CHORUS... DURING THE MASQUERADE BALL SCENE.
HA HA HA HA
WHAT'S SO FUNNY, LORD URIEL?!
IDIOT.

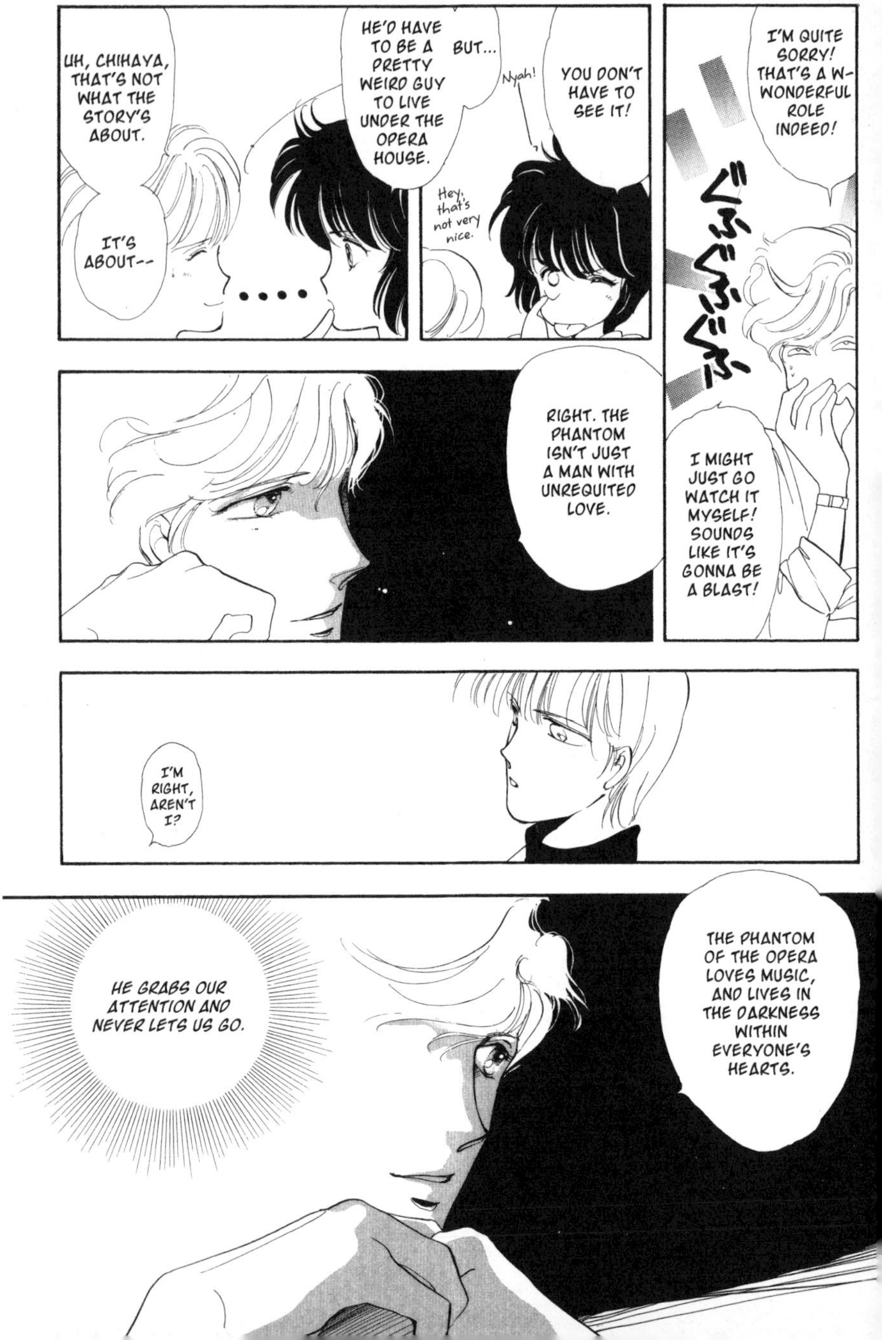
I'M QUITE SORRY! THAT'S A W-WONDERFUL ROLE INDEED!
ぐふぐふぐふ
I MIGHT JUST GO WATCH IT MYSELF! SOUNDS LIKE IT'S GONNA BE A BLAST!
YOU DON'T HAVE TO SEE IT!
Nyah!
Hey, that's not very nice.
BUT...
HE'D HAVE TO BE A PRETTY WEIRD GUY TO LIVE UNDER THE OPERA HOUSE.
UH, CHIHAYA, THAT'S NOT WHAT THE STORY'S ABOUT.
IT'S ABOUT--
....
RIGHT. THE PHANTOM ISN'T JUST A MAN WITH UNREQUITED LOVE.
I'M RIGHT, AREN'T I?
THE PHANTOM OF THE OPERA LOVES MUSIC, AND LIVES IN THE DARKNESS WITHIN EVERYONE'S HEARTS.
HE GRABS OUR ATTENTION AND NEVER LETS US GO.

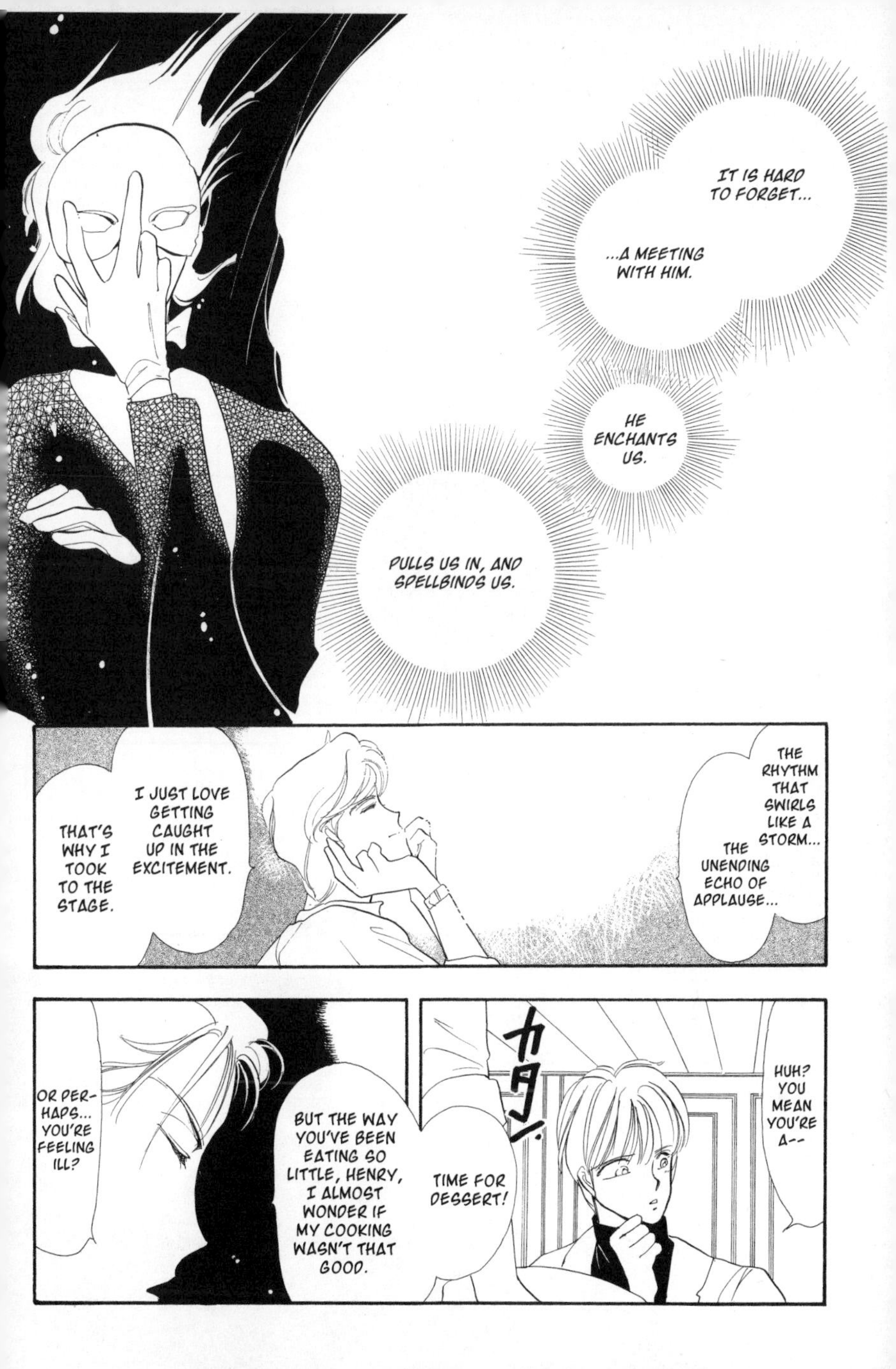
IT IS HARD TO FORGET...
...A MEETING WITH HIM.
HE ENCHANTS US.
PULLS US IN, AND SPELLBINDS US.
THE RHYTHM THAT SWIRLS LIKE A STORM...
THE UNENDING ECHO OF APPLAUSE...
I JUST LOVE GETTING CAUGHT UP IN THE EXCITEMENT.
THAT'S WHY I TOOK TO THE STAGE.
HUH? YOU MEAN YOU'RE A--
カタ
TIME FOR DESSERT!
BUT THE WAY YOU'VE BEEN EATING SO LITTLE, HENRY, I ALMOST WONDER IF MY COOKING WASN'T THAT GOOD.
OR PER-HAPS... YOU'RE FEELING ILL?

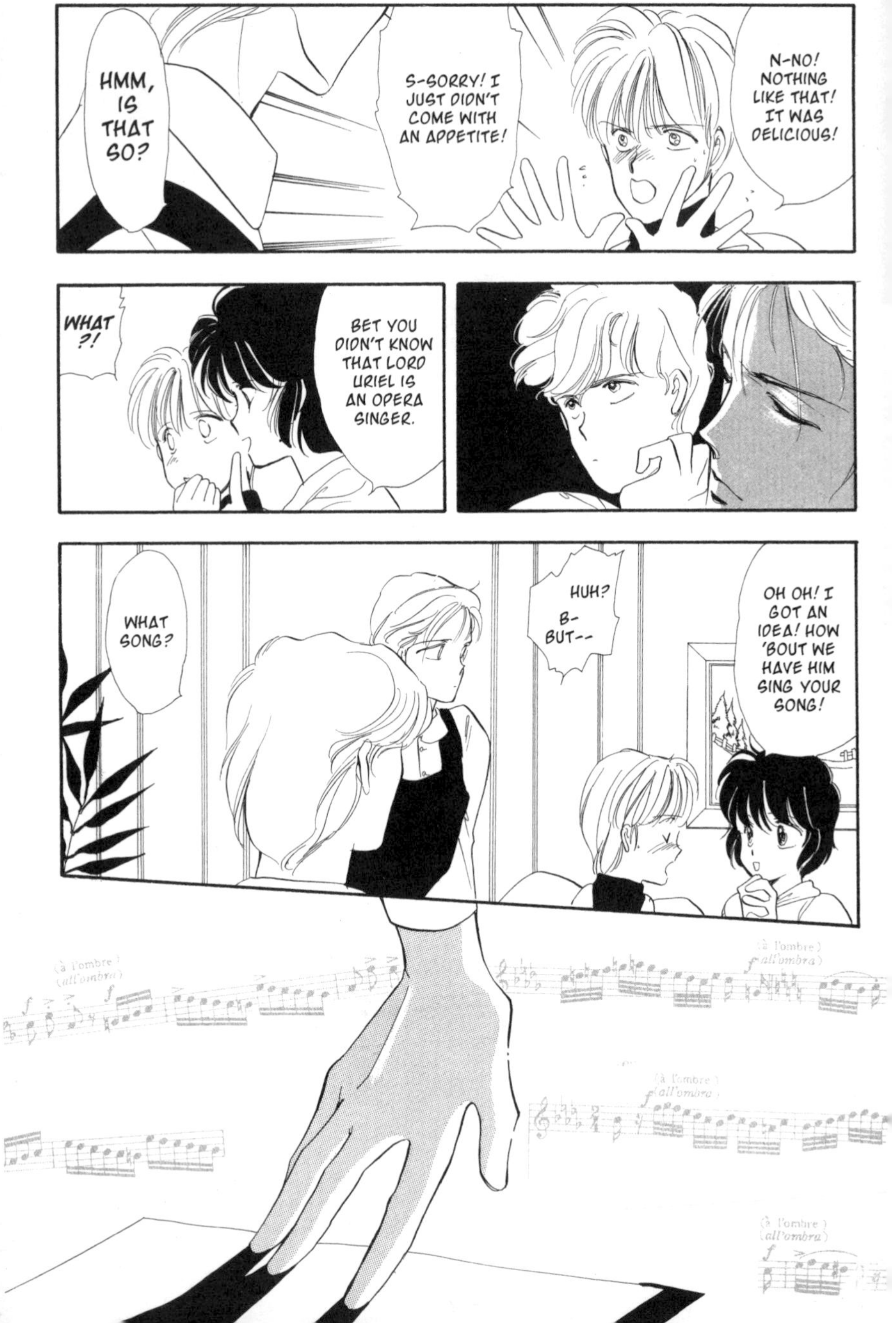
N-NO! NOTHING LIKE THAT! IT WAS DELICIOUS!
S-SORRY! I JUST DIDN'T COME WITH AN APPETITE!
HMM, IS THAT SO?
BET YOU DIDN'T KNOW THAT LORD URIEL IS AN OPERA SINGER.
WHAT ?!
OH OH! I GOT AN IDEA! HOW 'BOUT WE HAVE HIM SING YOUR SONG!
HUH? B-BUT--
WHAT SONG?
(à l'ombre) (all'ombra)
(à l'ombre) (all'ombra)
(à l'ombre) (all'ombra)
(à l'ombre) (all'ombra)

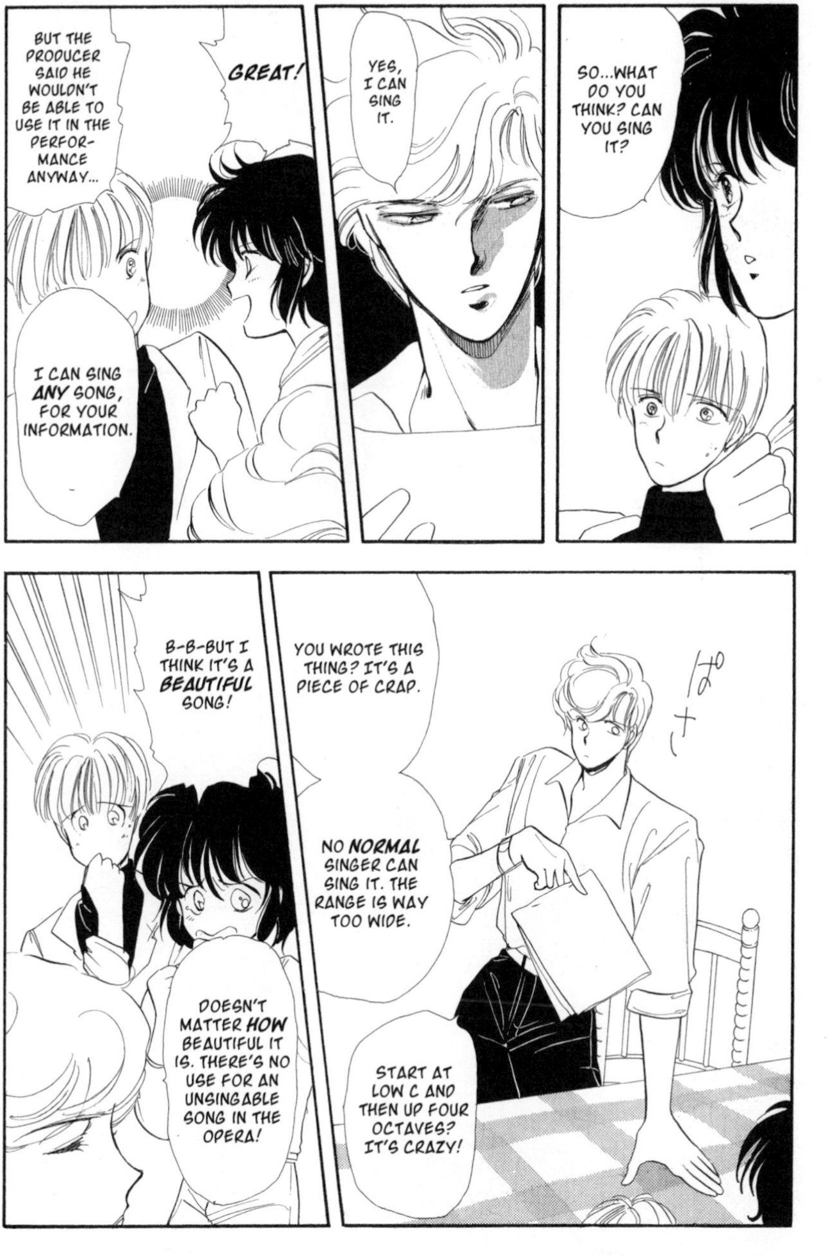
SO...WHAT DO YOU THINK? CAN YOU SING IT?
YES, I CAN SING IT.
GREAT!
BUT THE PRODUCER SAID HE WOULDN'T BE ABLE TO USE IT IN THE PERFORMANCE ANYWAY...
I CAN SING ANY SONG, FOR YOUR INFORMATION.
YOU WROTE THIS THING? IT'S A PIECE OF CRAP.
NO NORMAL SINGER CAN SING IT. THE RANGE IS WAY TOO WIDE.
START AT LOW C AND THEN UP FOUR OCTAVES? IT'S CRAZY!
B-B-BUT I THINK IT'S A BEAUTIFUL SONG!
DOESN'T MATTER HOW BEAUTIFUL IT IS. THERE'S NO USE FOR AN UNSINGABLE SONG IN THE OPERA!

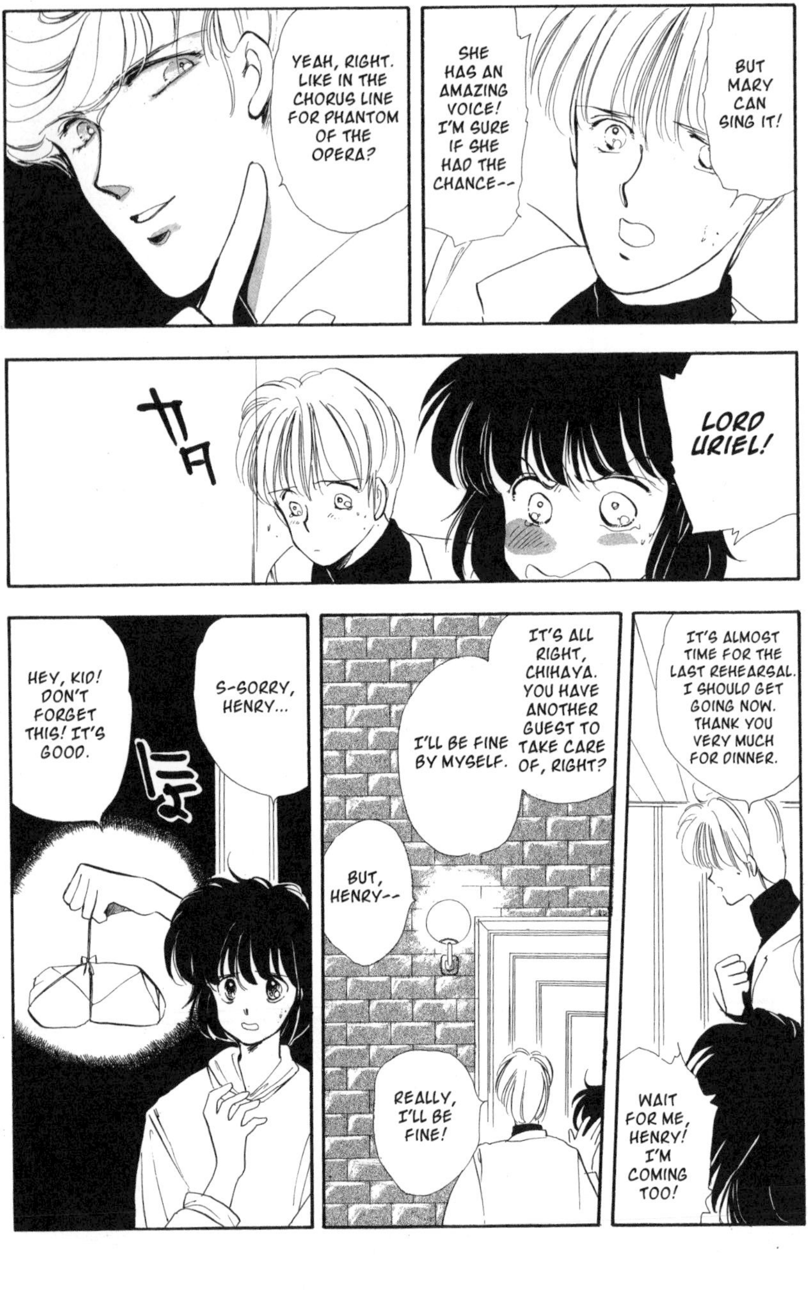
BUT MARY CAN SING IT!
SHE HAS AN AMAZING VOICE! I'M SURE IF SHE HAD THE CHANCE--
YEAH, RIGHT. LIKE IN THE CHORUS LINE FOR PHANTOM OF THE OPERA?
LORD URIEL!
カタ
IT'S ALMOST TIME FOR THE LAST REHEARSAL. I SHOULD GET GOING NOW. THANK YOU VERY MUCH FOR DINNER.
WAIT FOR ME, HENRY! I'M COMING TOO!
IT'S ALL RIGHT, CHIHAYA. YOU HAVE ANOTHER GUEST TO TAKE CARE OF, RIGHT?
I'LL BE FINE BY MYSELF.
BUT, HENRY--
REALLY, I'LL BE FINE!
S-SORRY, HENRY...
HEY, KID! DON'T FORGET THIS! IT'S GOOD.
ニュ

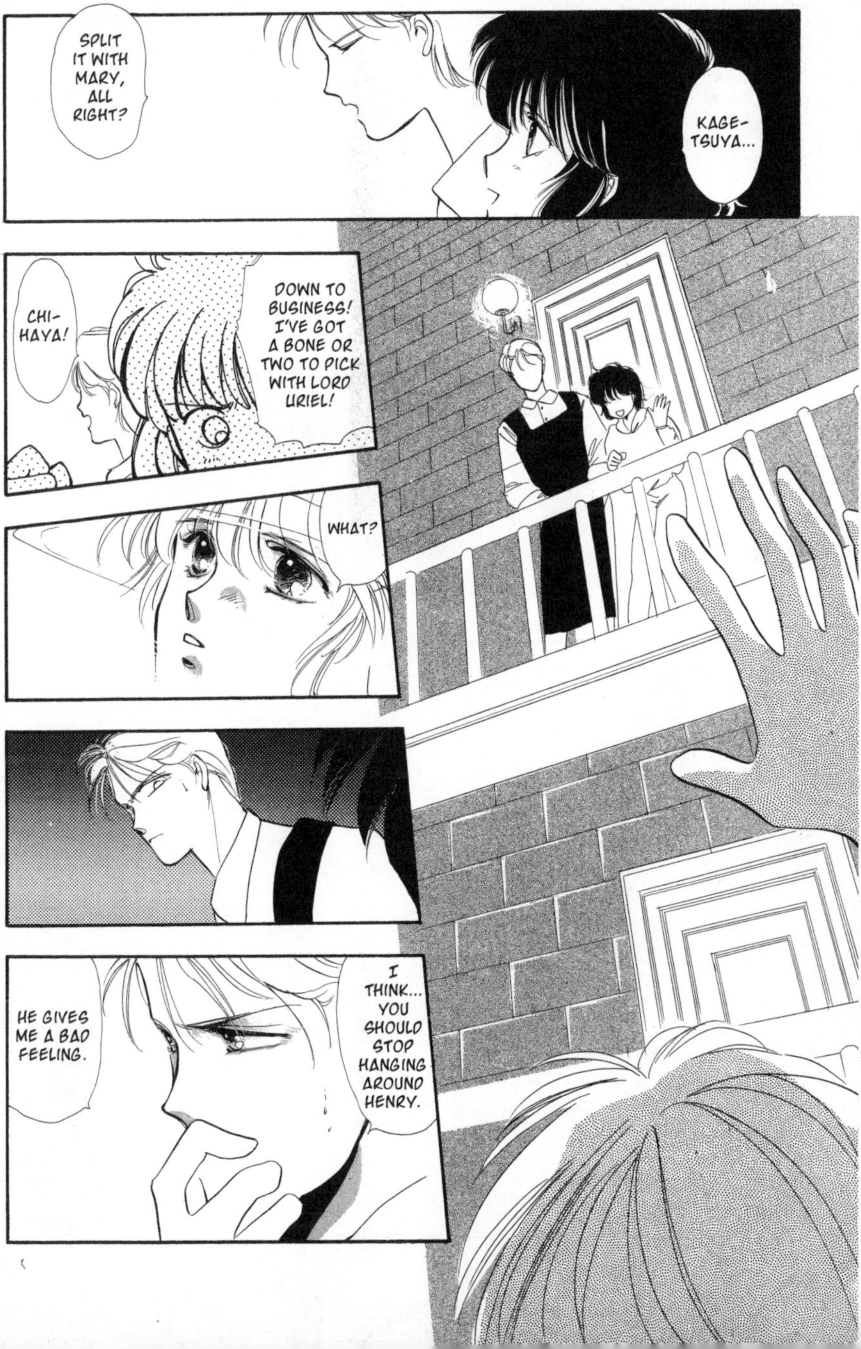
KAGE-TSUYA...
SPLIT IT WITH MARY, ALL RIGHT?
DOWN TO BUSINESS! I'VE GOT A BONE OR TWO TO PICK WITH LORD URIEL!
CHI-HAYA!
WHAT?
I THINK... YOU SHOULD STOP HANGING AROUND HENRY.
HE GIVES ME A BAD FEELING.

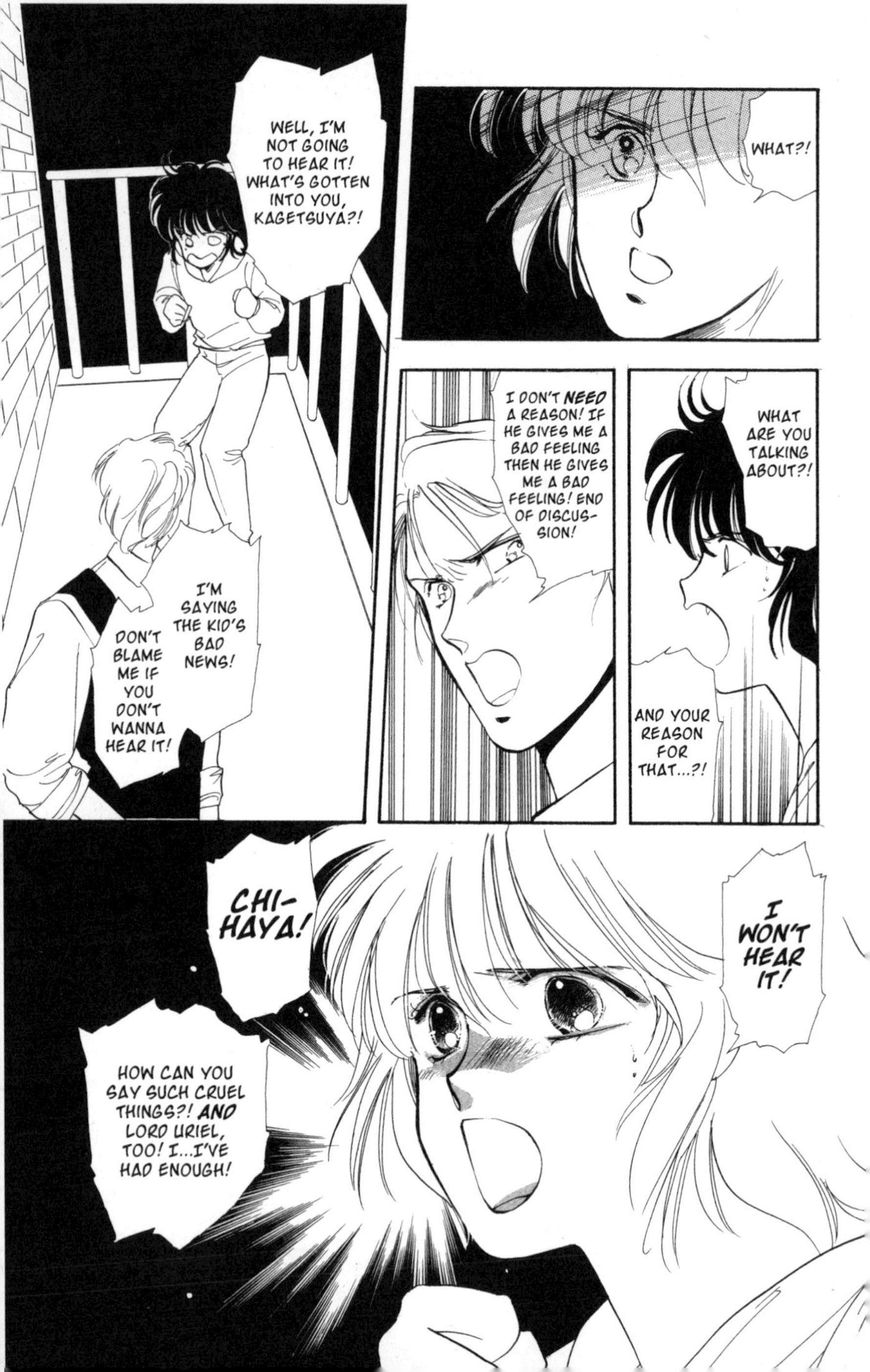
WHAT?!
WHAT ARE YOU TALKING ABOUT?!
AND YOUR REASON FOR THAT...?!
I DON'T **NEED** A REASON! IF HE GIVES ME A BAD FEELING THEN HE GIVES ME A BAD FEELING! END OF DISCUS-SION!
WELL, I'M NOT GOING TO HEAR IT! WHAT'S GOTTEN INTO YOU, KAGETSUYA?!
I'M SAYING THE KID'S BAD NEWS!
DON'T BLAME ME IF YOU DON'T WANNA HEAR IT!
I WON'T HEAR IT!
CHI-HAYA!
HOW CAN YOU SAY SUCH CRUEL THINGS?! **AND** LORD URIEL, TOO! I...I'VE HAD ENOUGH!

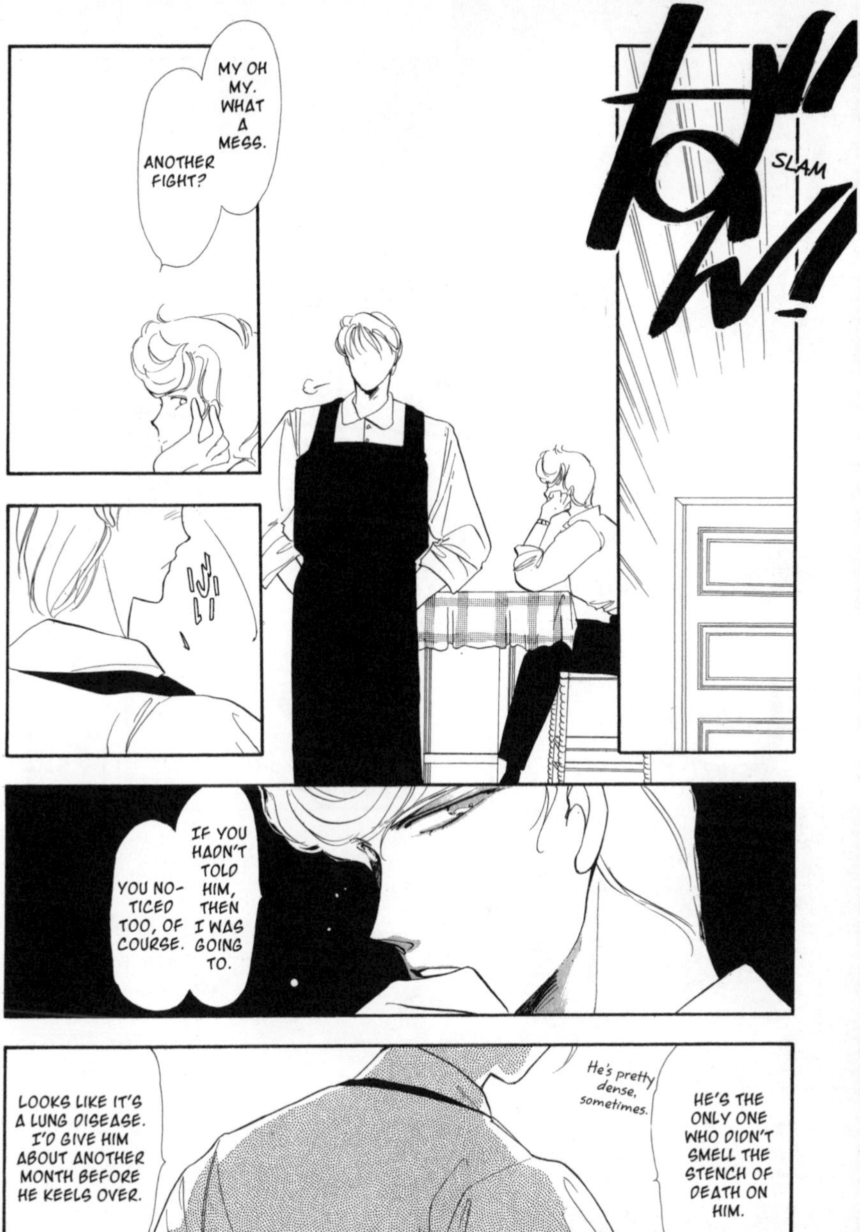
SLAM
MY OH MY. WHAT A MESS.
ANOTHER FIGHT?
IF YOU HADN'T TOLD HIM, THEN I WAS GOING TO.
YOU NO-TICED TOO, OF COURSE.
HE'S THE ONLY ONE WHO DIDN'T SMELL THE STENCH OF DEATH ON HIM.
He's pretty dense, sometimes.
LOOKS LIKE IT'S A LUNG DISEASE. I'D GIVE HIM ABOUT ANOTHER MONTH BEFORE HE KEELS OVER.

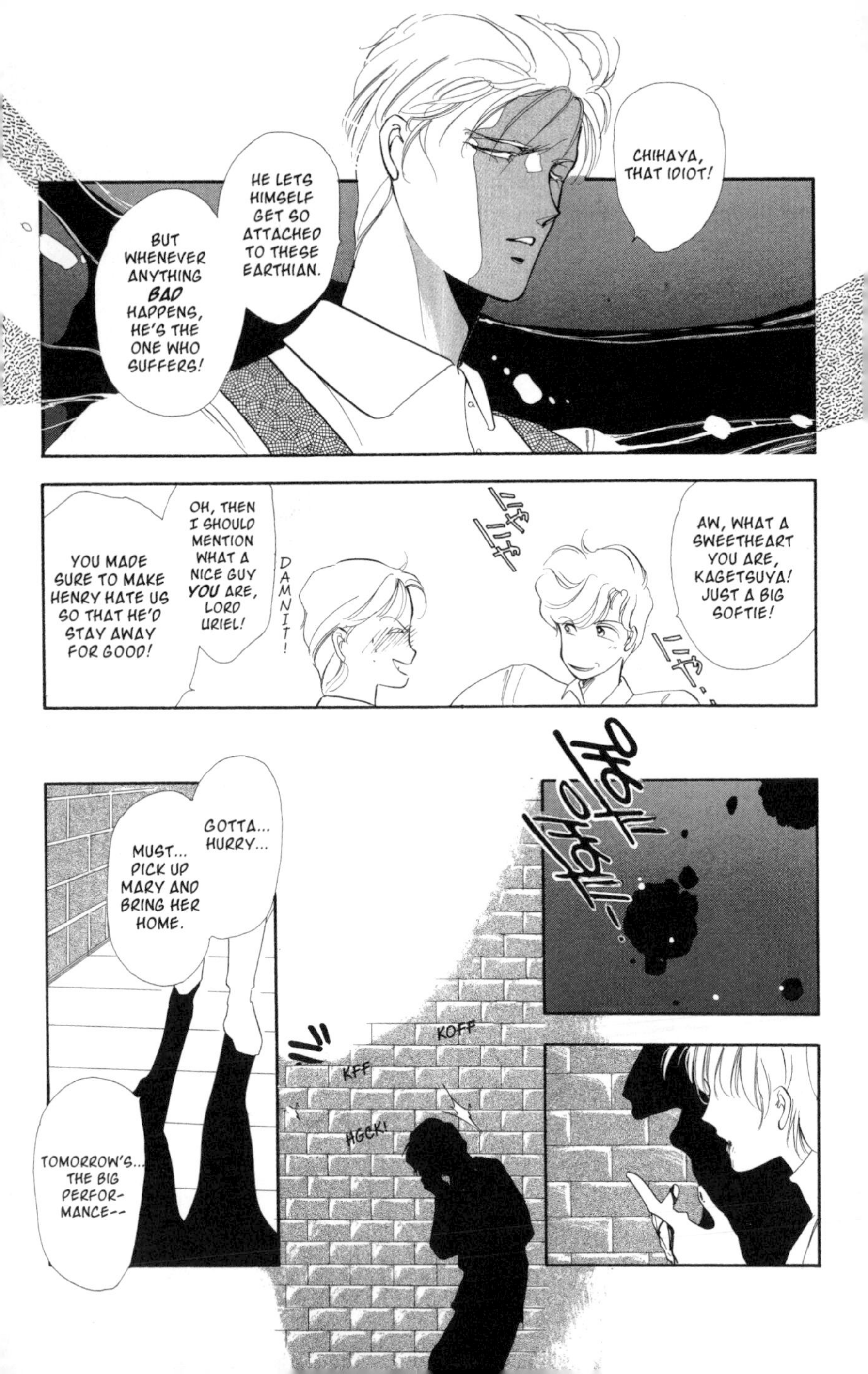
CHIHAYA, THAT IDIOT!
HE LETS HIMSELF GET SO ATTACHED TO THESE EARTHIAN.
BUT WHENEVER ANYTHING BAD HAPPENS, HE'S THE ONE WHO SUFFERS!
AW, WHAT A SWEETHEART YOU ARE, KAGETSUYA! JUST A BIG SOFTIE!
ニヤニヤ
ニヤ...
DAMNIT!
OH, THEN I SHOULD MENTION WHAT A NICE GUY YOU ARE, LORD URIEL!
YOU MADE SURE TO MAKE HENRY HATE US SO THAT HE'D STAY AWAY FOR GOOD!
KOFF
KFF
HGCK!
GOTTA... HURRY...
MUST... PICK UP MARY AND BRING HER HOME.
TOMORROW'S... THE BIG PERFOR-MANCE--

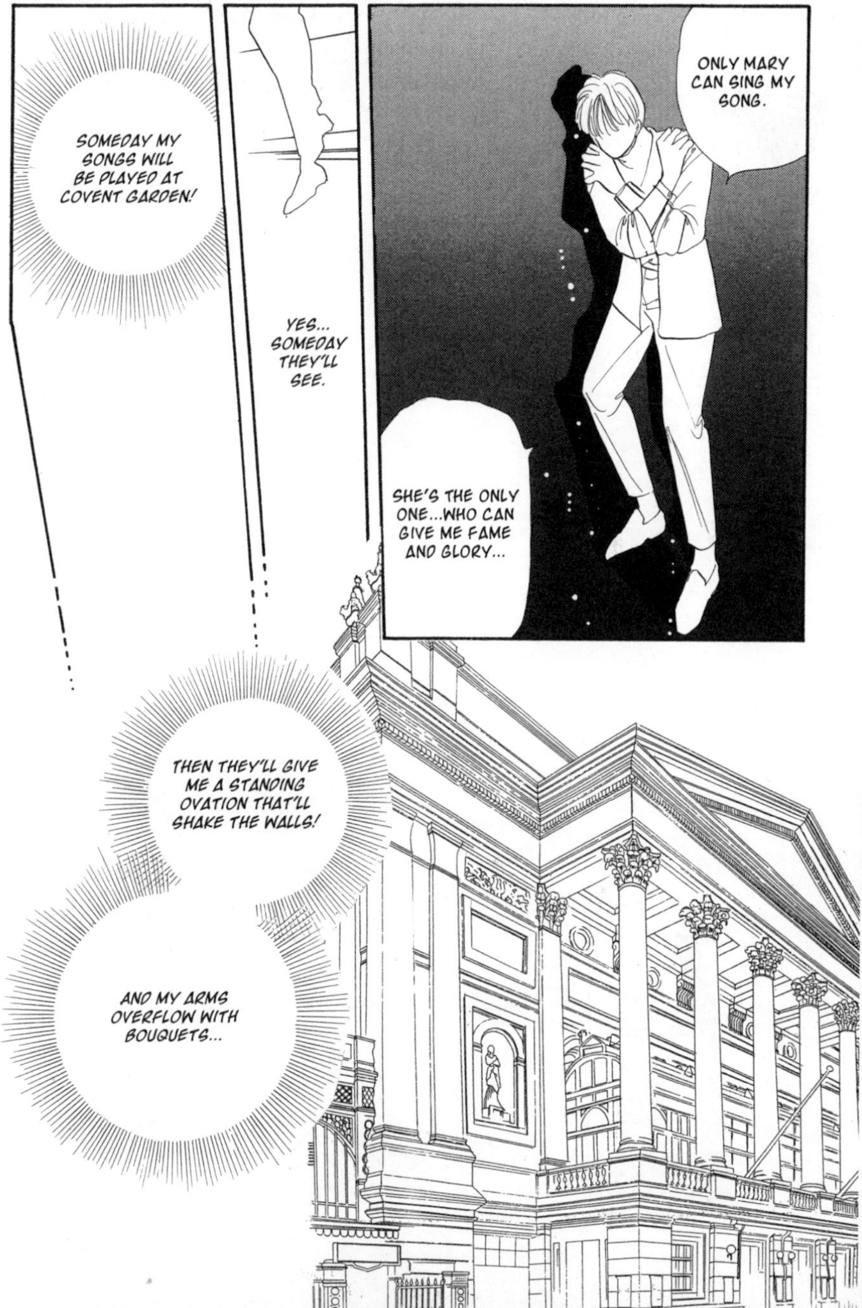
ONLY MARY CAN SING MY SONG.
SHE'S THE ONLY ONE...WHO CAN GIVE ME FAME AND GLORY...
YES... SOMEDAY THEY'LL SEE.
SOMEDAY MY SONGS WILL BE PLAYED AT COVENT GARDEN!
THEN THEY'LL GIVE ME A STANDING OVATION THAT'LL SHAKE THE WALLS!
AND MY ARMS OVERFLOW WITH BOUQUETS...

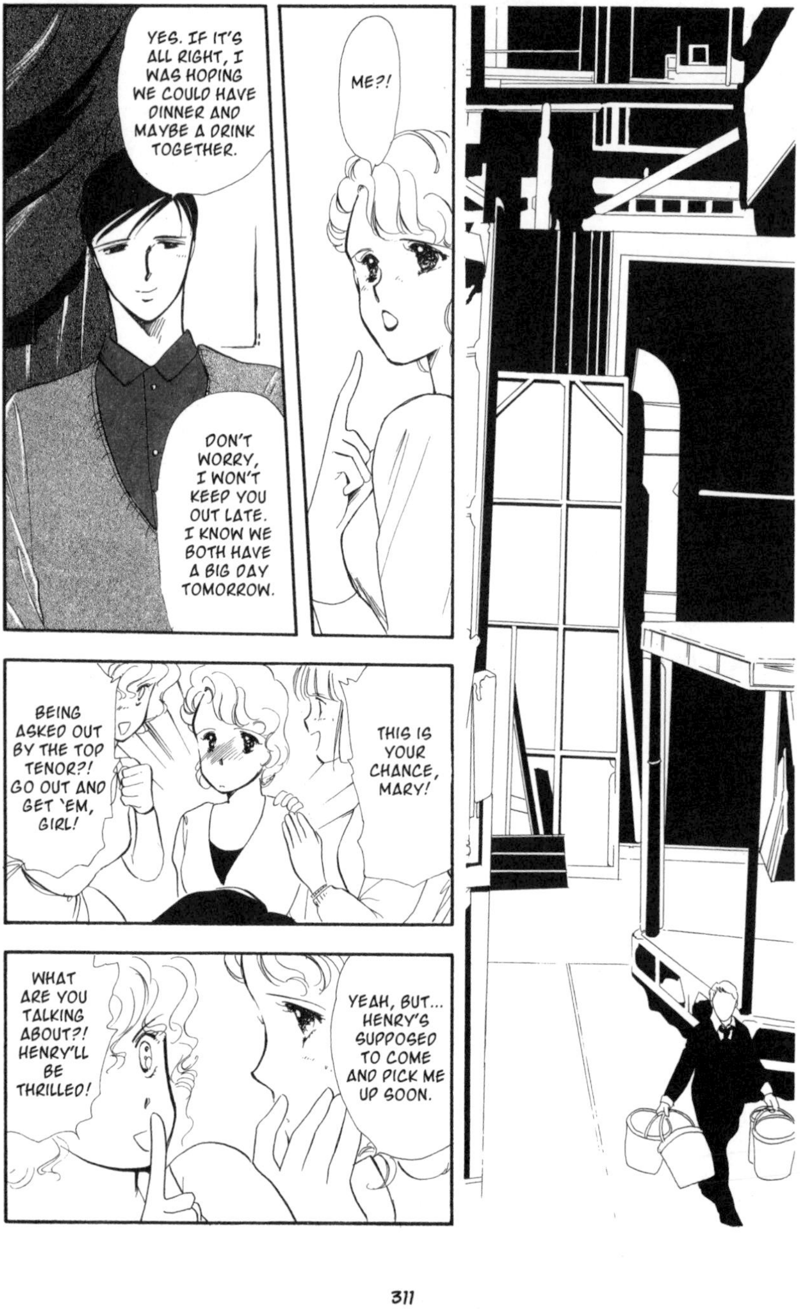
ME?!
YES. IF IT'S ALL RIGHT, I WAS HOPING WE COULD HAVE DINNER AND MAYBE A DRINK TOGETHER.
DON'T WORRY, I WON'T KEEP YOU OUT LATE. I KNOW WE BOTH HAVE A BIG DAY TOMORROW.
THIS IS YOUR CHANCE, MARY!
BEING ASKED OUT BY THE TOP TENOR?! GO OUT AND GET 'EM, GIRL!
YEAH, BUT... HENRY'S SUPPOSED TO COME AND PICK ME UP SOON.
WHAT ARE YOU TALKING ABOUT?! HENRY'LL BE THRILLED!

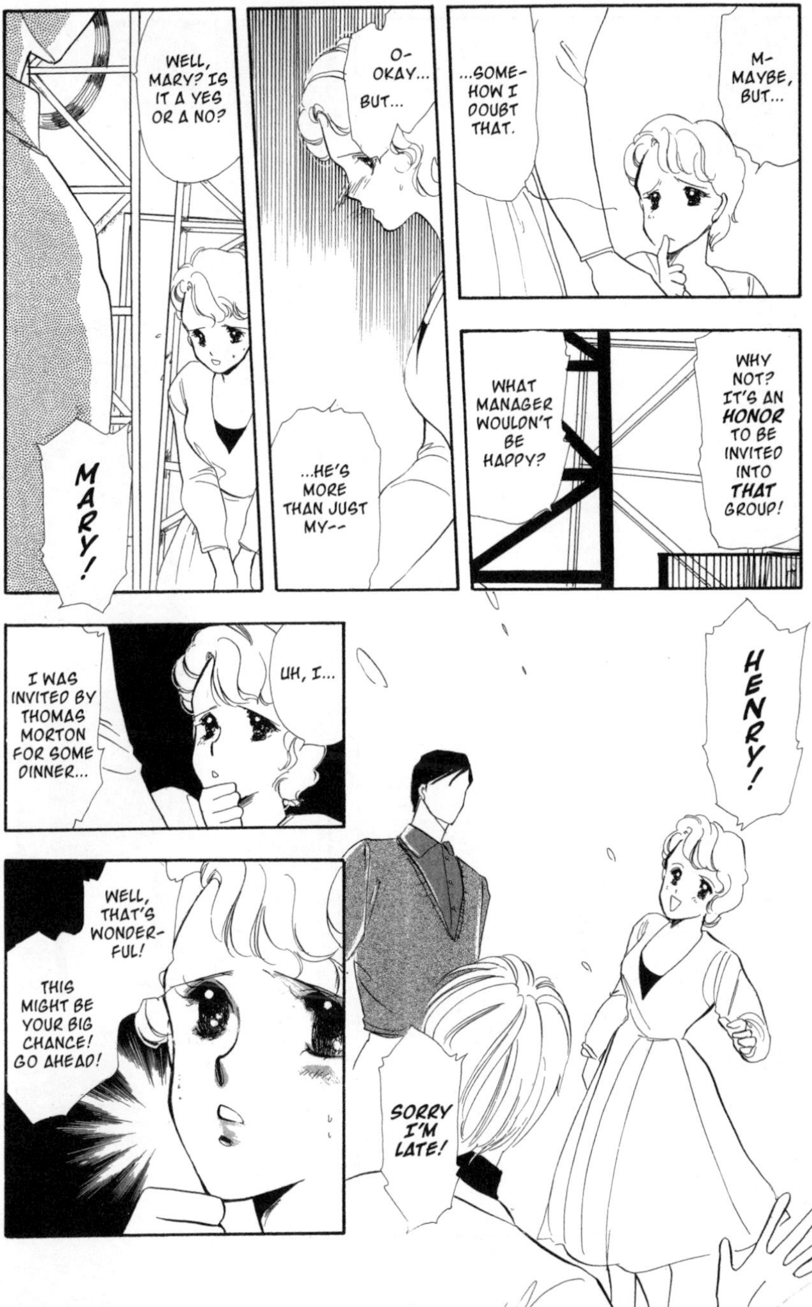
M-MAYBE, BUT...
...SOME-HOW I DOUBT THAT.
WHY NOT? IT'S AN HONOR TO BE INVITED INTO THAT GROUP!
WHAT MANAGER WOULDN'T BE HAPPY?
O-OKAY... BUT...
...HE'S MORE THAN JUST MY--
WELL, MARY? IS IT A YES OR A NO?
MARY!
HENRY!
SORRY I'M LATE!
UH, I...
I WAS INVITED BY THOMAS MORTON FOR SOME DINNER...
WELL, THAT'S WONDER-FUL!
THIS MIGHT BE YOUR BIG CHANCE! GO AHEAD!

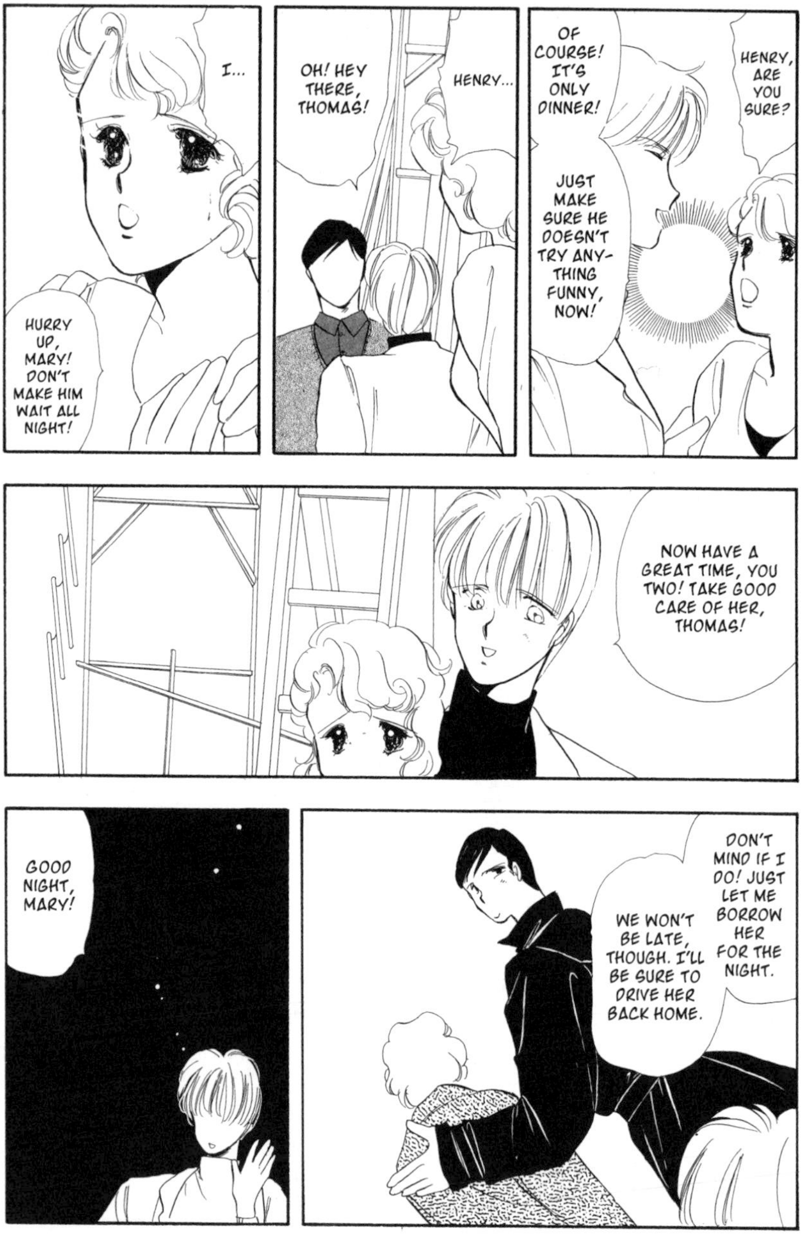
HENRY, ARE YOU SURE?
OF COURSE! IT'S ONLY DINNER!
JUST MAKE SURE HE DOESN'T TRY ANY-THING FUNNY, NOW!
HENRY...
OH! HEY THERE, THOMAS!
I...
HURRY UP, MARY! DON'T MAKE HIM WAIT ALL NIGHT!
NOW HAVE A GREAT TIME, YOU TWO! TAKE GOOD CARE OF HER, THOMAS!
DON'T MIND IF I DO! JUST LET ME BORROW HER FOR THE NIGHT.
WE WON'T BE LATE, THOUGH. I'LL BE SURE TO DRIVE HER BACK HOME.
GOOD NIGHT, MARY!

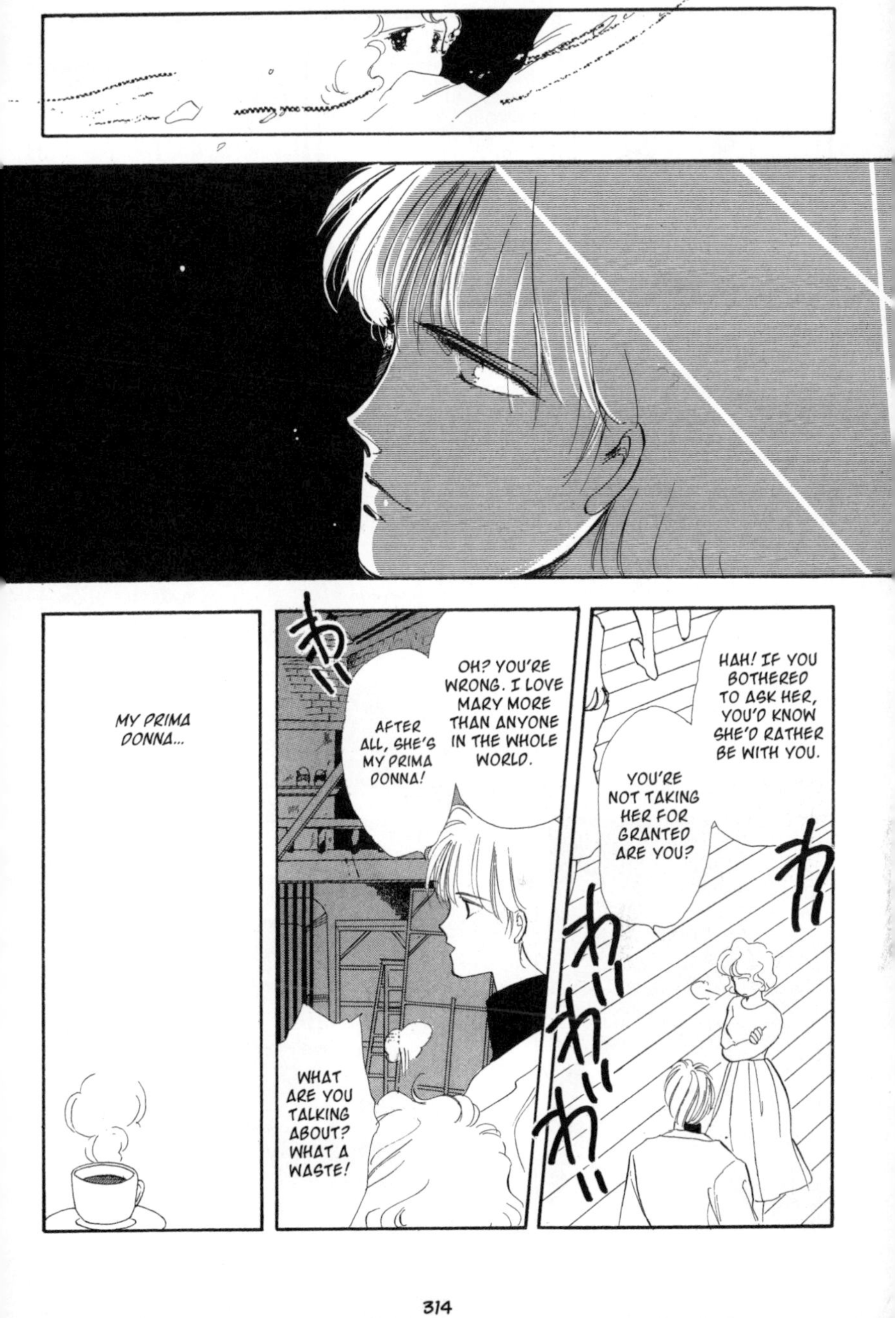
HAH! IF YOU BOTHERED TO ASK HER, YOU'D KNOW SHE'D RATHER BE WITH YOU.
YOU'RE NOT TAKING HER FOR GRANTED ARE YOU?
OH? YOU'RE WRONG. I LOVE MARY MORE THAN ANYONE IN THE WHOLE WORLD.
AFTER ALL, SHE'S MY PRIMA DONNA!
WHAT ARE YOU TALKING ABOUT? WHAT A WASTE!
MY PRIMA DONNA...

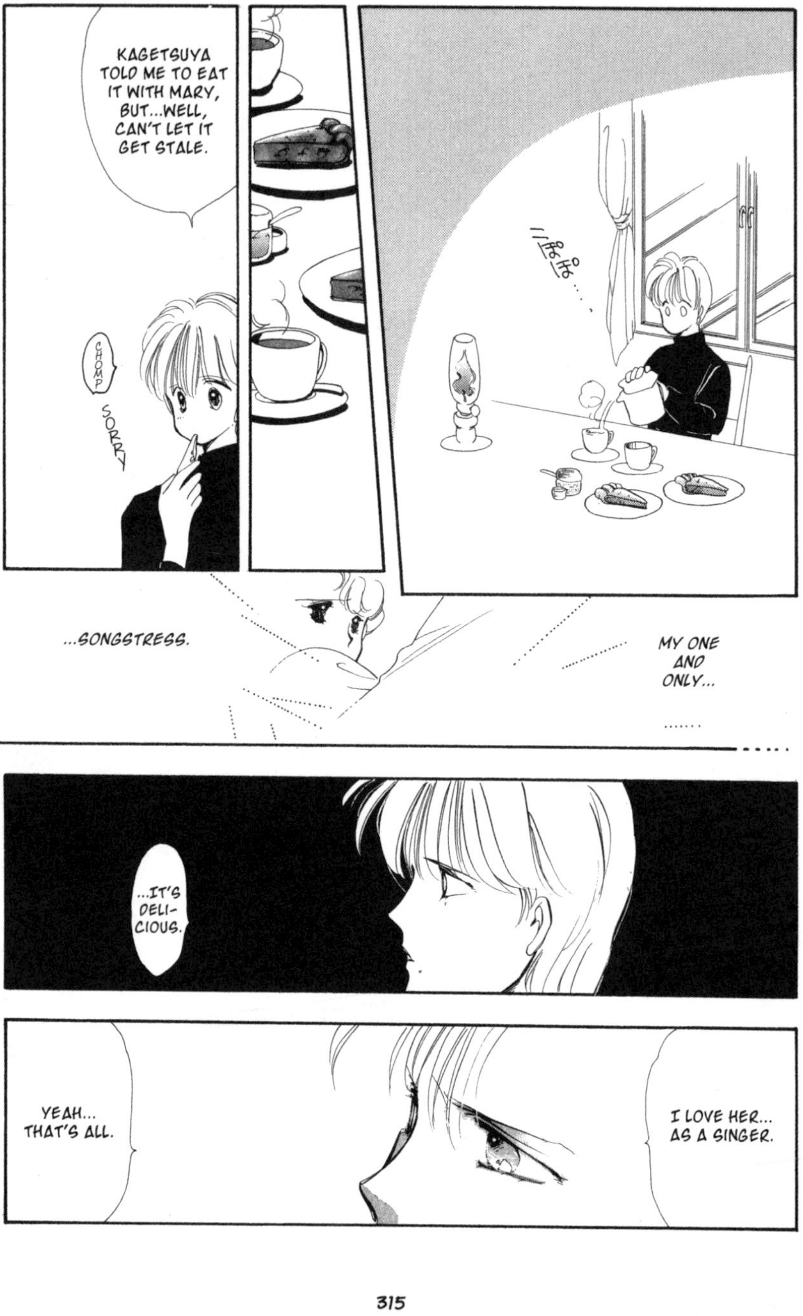
こぽぽ……
KAGETSUYA TOLD ME TO EAT IT WITH MARY, BUT...WELL, CAN'T LET IT GET STALE.
CHOMP
SORRY
MY ONE AND ONLY...
......
...SONGSTRESS.
...IT'S DELICIOUS.
I LOVE HER... AS A SINGER.
YEAH... THAT'S ALL.

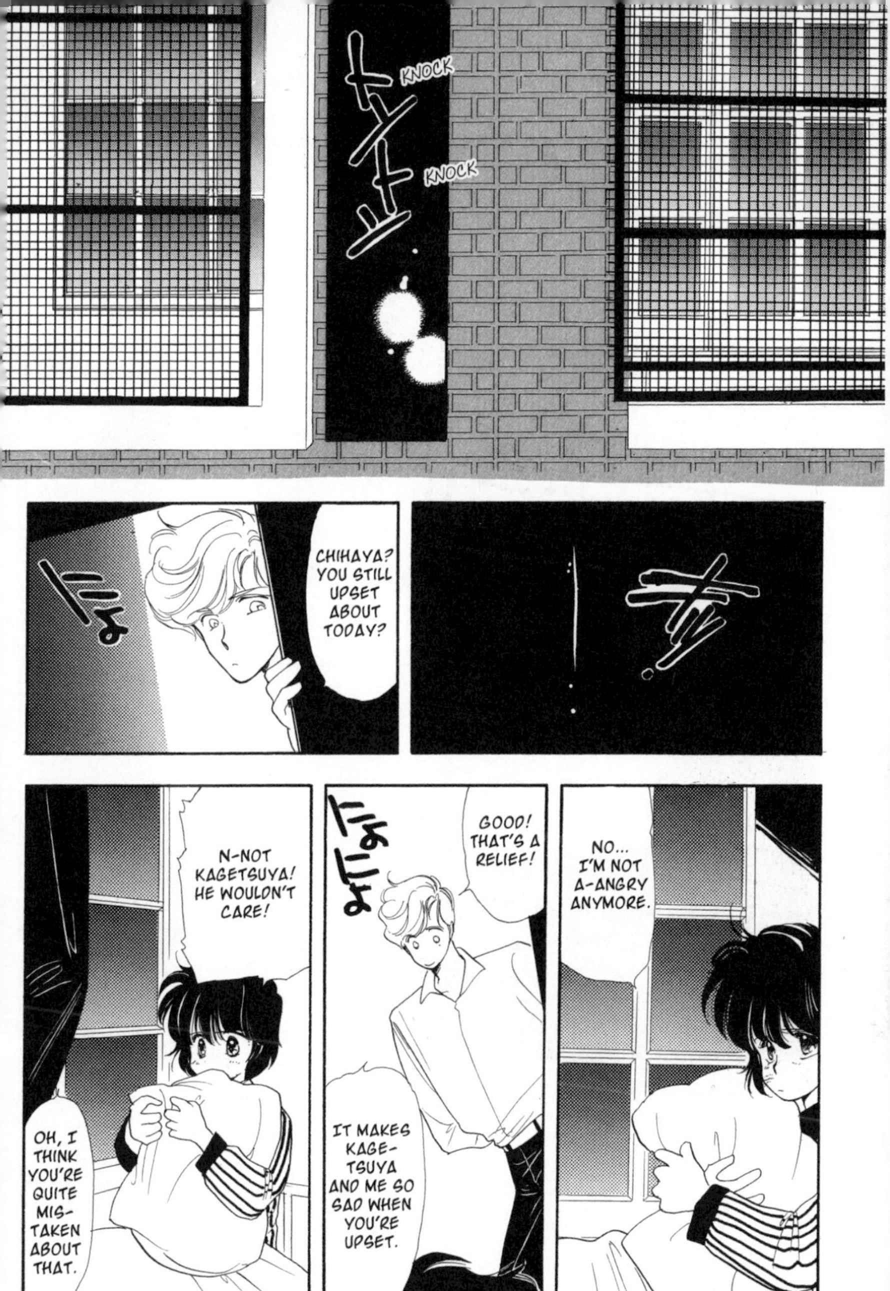
KNOCK
KNOCK
CHIHAYA? YOU STILL UPSET ABOUT TODAY?
NO... I'M NOT A-ANGRY ANYMORE.
GOOD! THAT'S A RELIEF!
IT MAKES KAGE-TSUYA AND ME SO SAD WHEN YOU'RE UPSET.
N-NOT KAGETSUYA! HE WOULDN'T CARE!
OH, I THINK YOU'RE QUITE MIS-TAKEN ABOUT THAT.

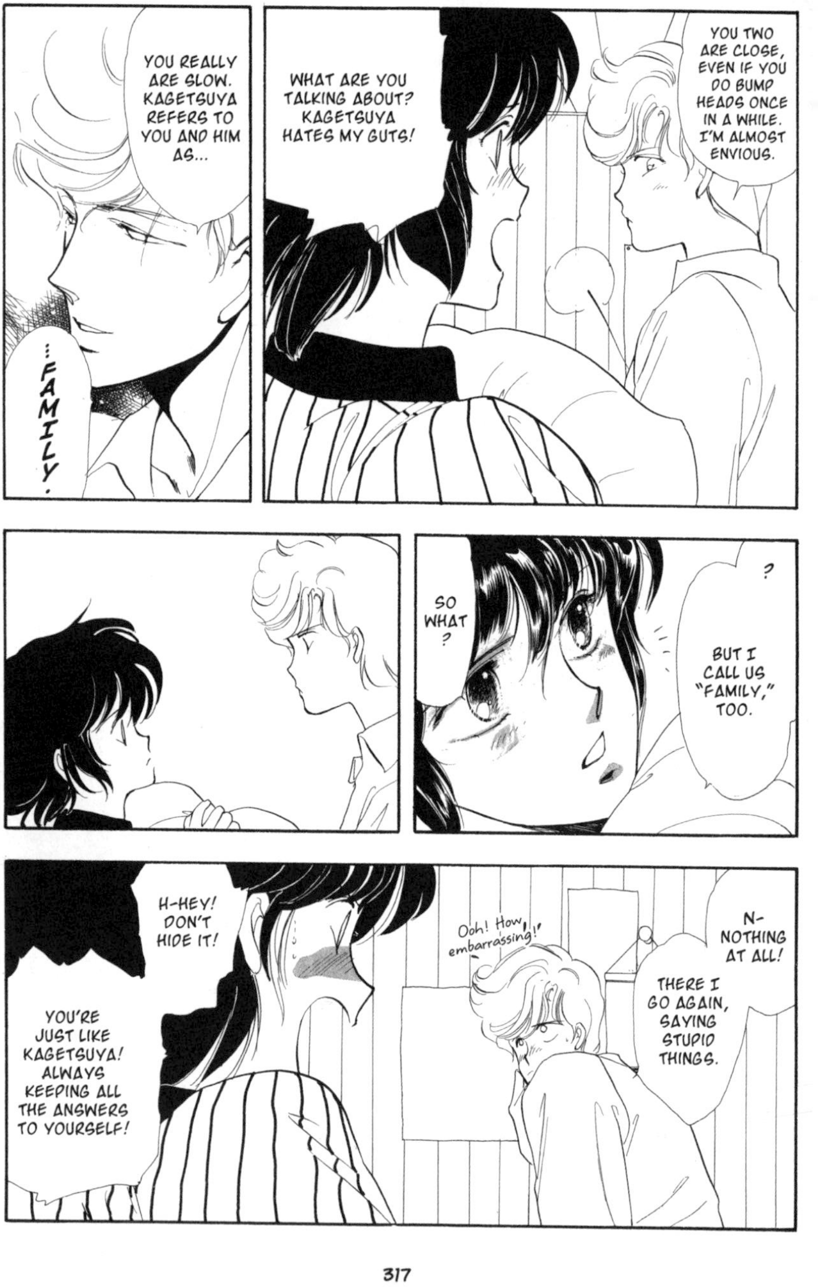
YOU TWO ARE CLOSE, EVEN IF YOU DO BUMP HEADS ONCE IN A WHILE. I'M ALMOST ENVIOUS.
WHAT ARE YOU TALKING ABOUT? KAGETSUYA HATES MY GUTS!
YOU REALLY ARE SLOW. KAGETSUYA REFERS TO YOU AND HIM AS...
...FAMILY.
?
BUT I CALL US "FAMILY," TOO.
SO WHAT?
N- NOTHING AT ALL!
THERE I GO AGAIN, SAYING STUPID THINGS.
Ooh! How embarrassing!
H-HEY! DON'T HIDE IT!
YOU'RE JUST LIKE KAGETSUYA! ALWAYS KEEPING ALL THE ANSWERS TO YOURSELF!

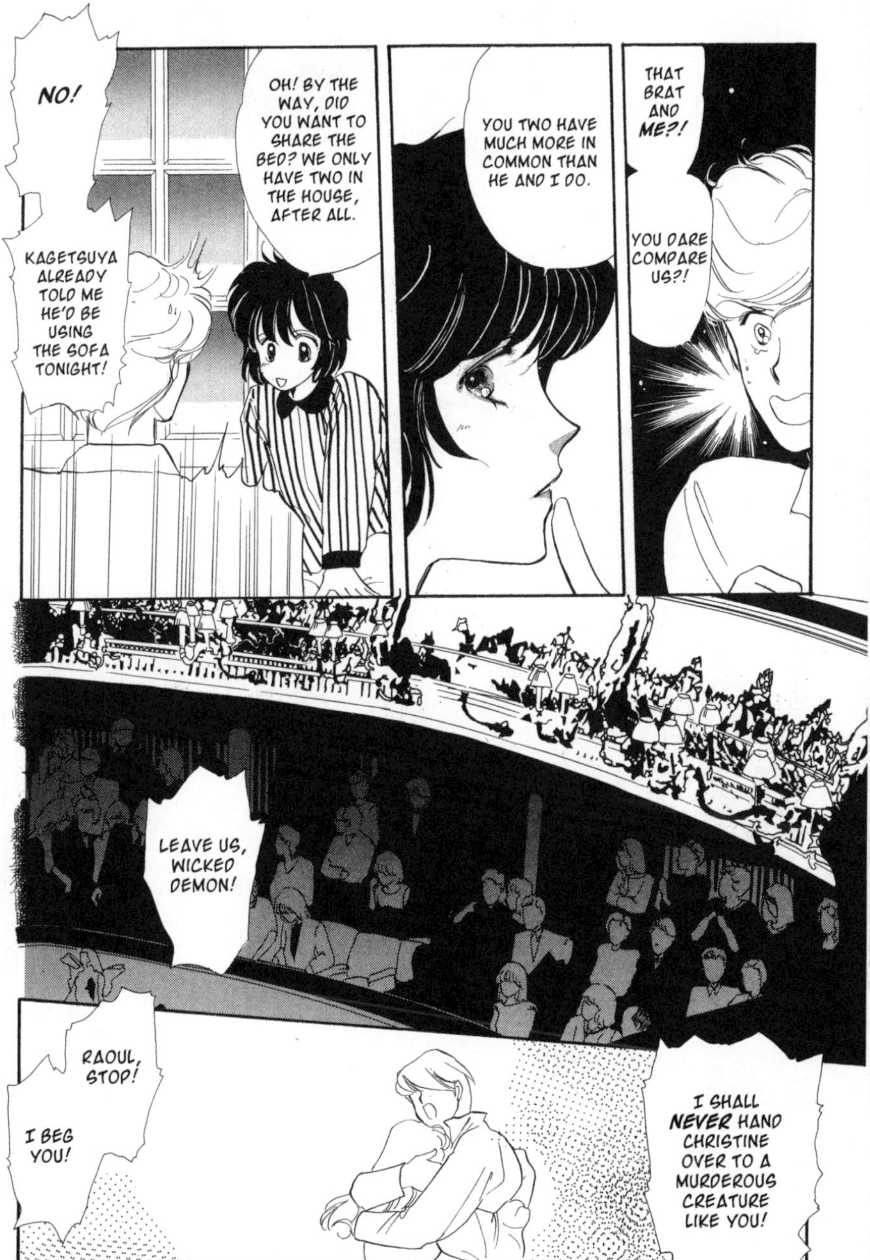
THAT BRAT AND *ME?!*
YOU DARE COMPARE US?!
YOU TWO HAVE MUCH MORE IN COMMON THAN HE AND I DO.
OH! BY THE WAY, DID YOU WANT TO SHARE THE BED? WE ONLY HAVE TWO IN THE HOUSE, AFTER ALL.
NO!
KAGETSUYA ALREADY TOLD ME HE'D BE USING THE SOFA TONIGHT!
LEAVE US, WICKED DEMON!
I SHALL ***NEVER*** HAND CHRISTINE OVER TO A MURDEROUS CREATURE LIKE YOU!
RAOUL, STOP!
I BEG YOU!

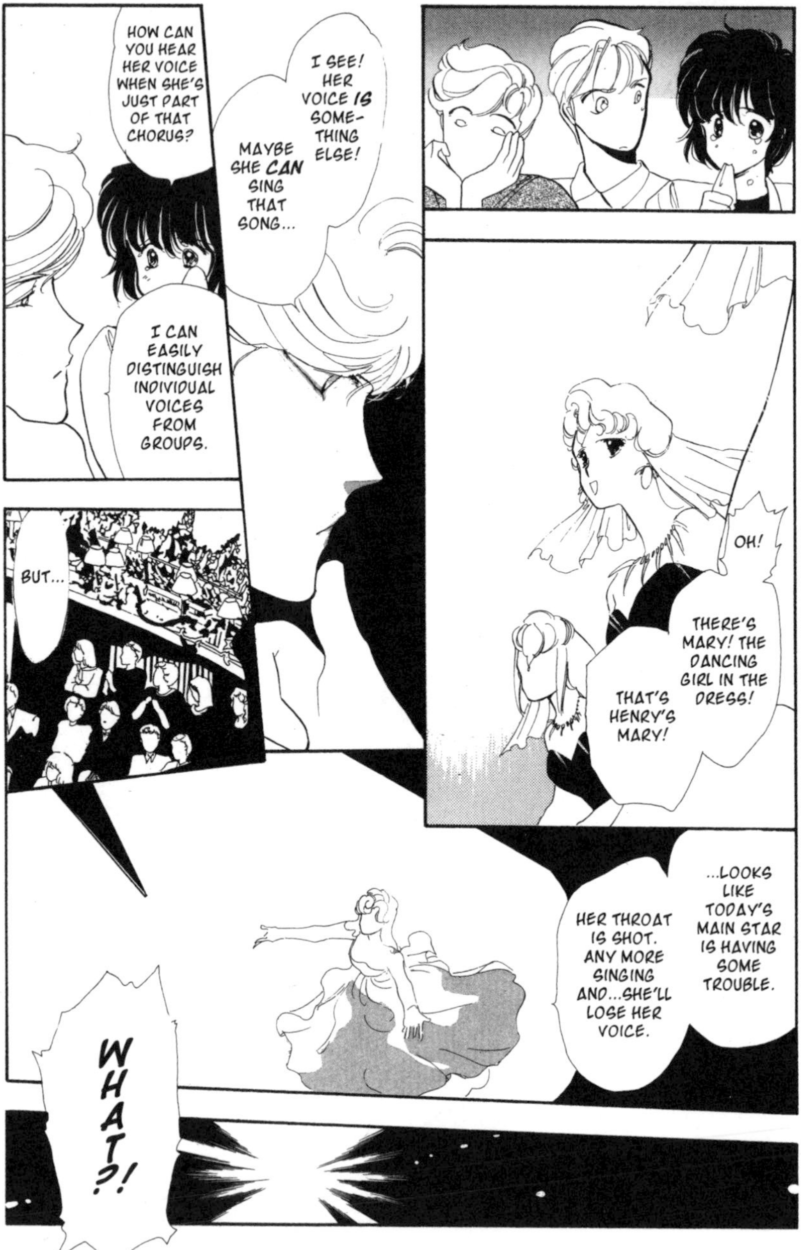
HOW CAN YOU HEAR HER VOICE WHEN SHE'S JUST PART OF THAT CHORUS?
I CAN EASILY DISTINGUISH INDIVIDUAL VOICES FROM GROUPS.
I SEE! HER VOICE IS SOMETHING ELSE!
MAYBE SHE CAN SING THAT SONG...
OH!
THERE'S MARY! THE DANCING GIRL IN THE DRESS!
THAT'S HENRY'S MARY!
BUT...
...LOOKS LIKE TODAY'S MAIN STAR IS HAVING SOME TROUBLE.
HER THROAT IS SHOT. ANY MORE SINGING AND...SHE'LL LOSE HER VOICE.
WHAT?!

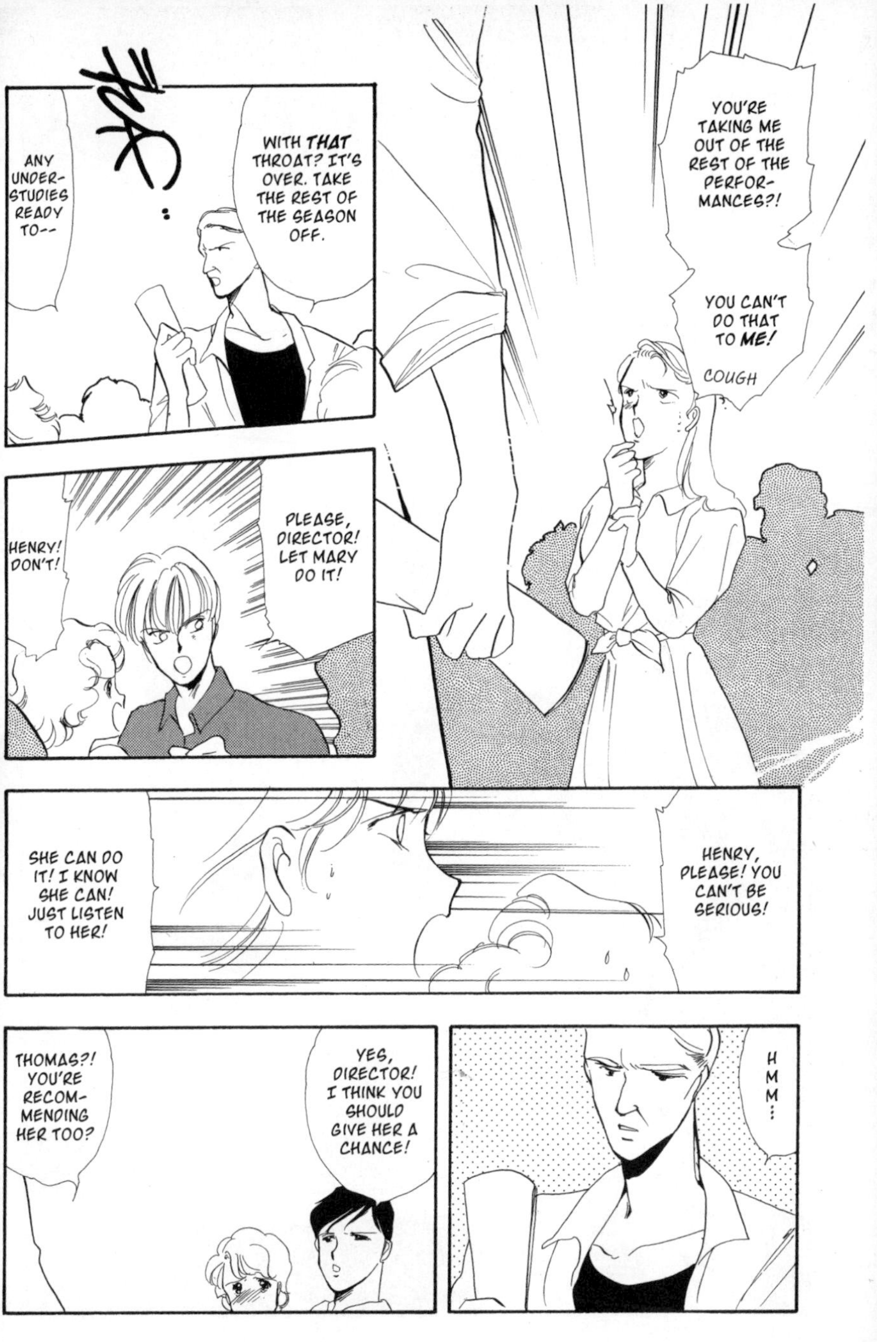
YOU'RE TAKING ME OUT OF THE REST OF THE PERFORMANCES?!
YOU CAN'T DO THAT TO **ME!**
COUGH
WITH **THAT** THROAT? IT'S OVER. TAKE THE REST OF THE SEASON OFF.
ANY UNDERSTUDIES READY TO--
PLEASE, DIRECTOR! LET MARY DO IT!
HENRY! DON'T!
HENRY, PLEASE! YOU CAN'T BE SERIOUS!
SHE CAN DO IT! I KNOW SHE CAN! JUST LISTEN TO HER!
HMM...
YES, DIRECTOR! I THINK YOU SHOULD GIVE HER A CHANCE!
THOMAS?! YOU'RE RECOMMENDING HER TOO?

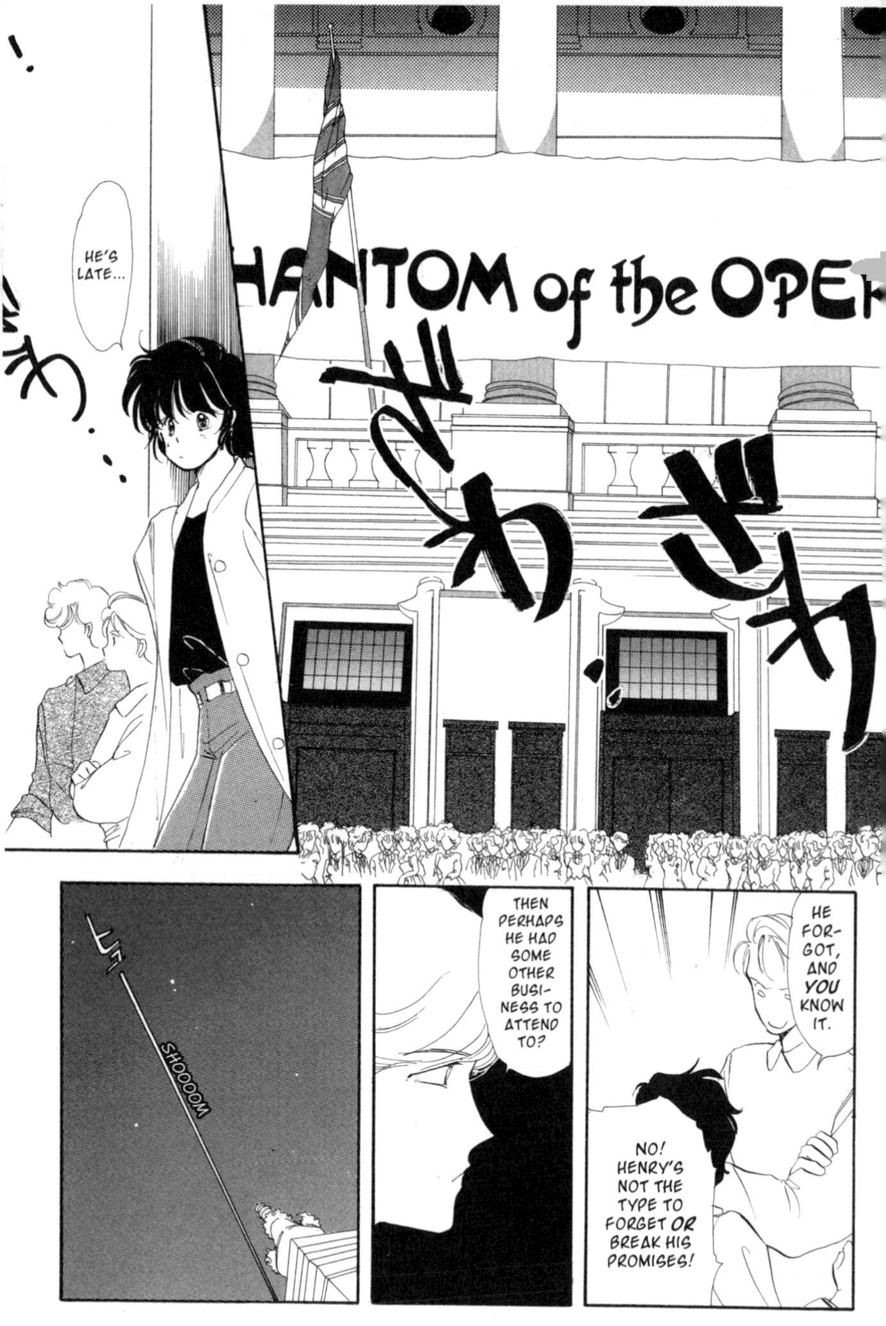
HANTOM of the OPER
HE'S LATE...
HE FOR-GOT, AND *YOU* KNOW IT.
NO! HENRY'S NOT THE TYPE TO FORGET *OR* BREAK HIS PROMISES!
THEN PERHAPS HE HAD SOME OTHER BUSI-NESS TO ATTEND TO?
SHOOOOM

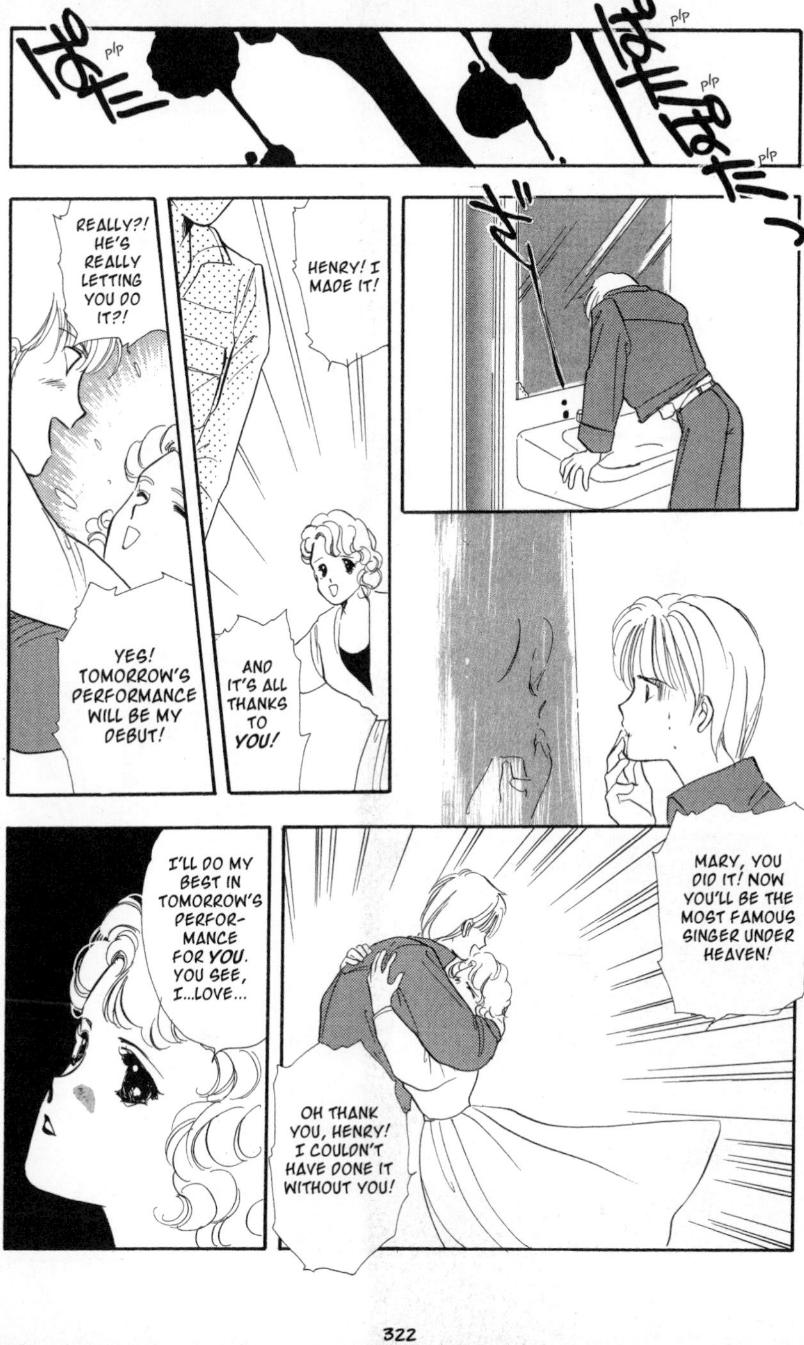
p/p
p/p
p/p
p/p
HENRY! I MADE IT!
AND IT'S ALL THANKS TO YOU!
REALLY?! HE'S REALLY LETTING YOU DO IT?!
YES! TOMORROW'S PERFORMANCE WILL BE MY DEBUT!
MARY, YOU DID IT! NOW YOU'LL BE THE MOST FAMOUS SINGER UNDER HEAVEN!
OH THANK YOU, HENRY! I COULDN'T HAVE DONE IT WITHOUT YOU!
I'LL DO MY BEST IN TOMORROW'S PERFORMANCE FOR YOU. YOU SEE, I...LOVE...

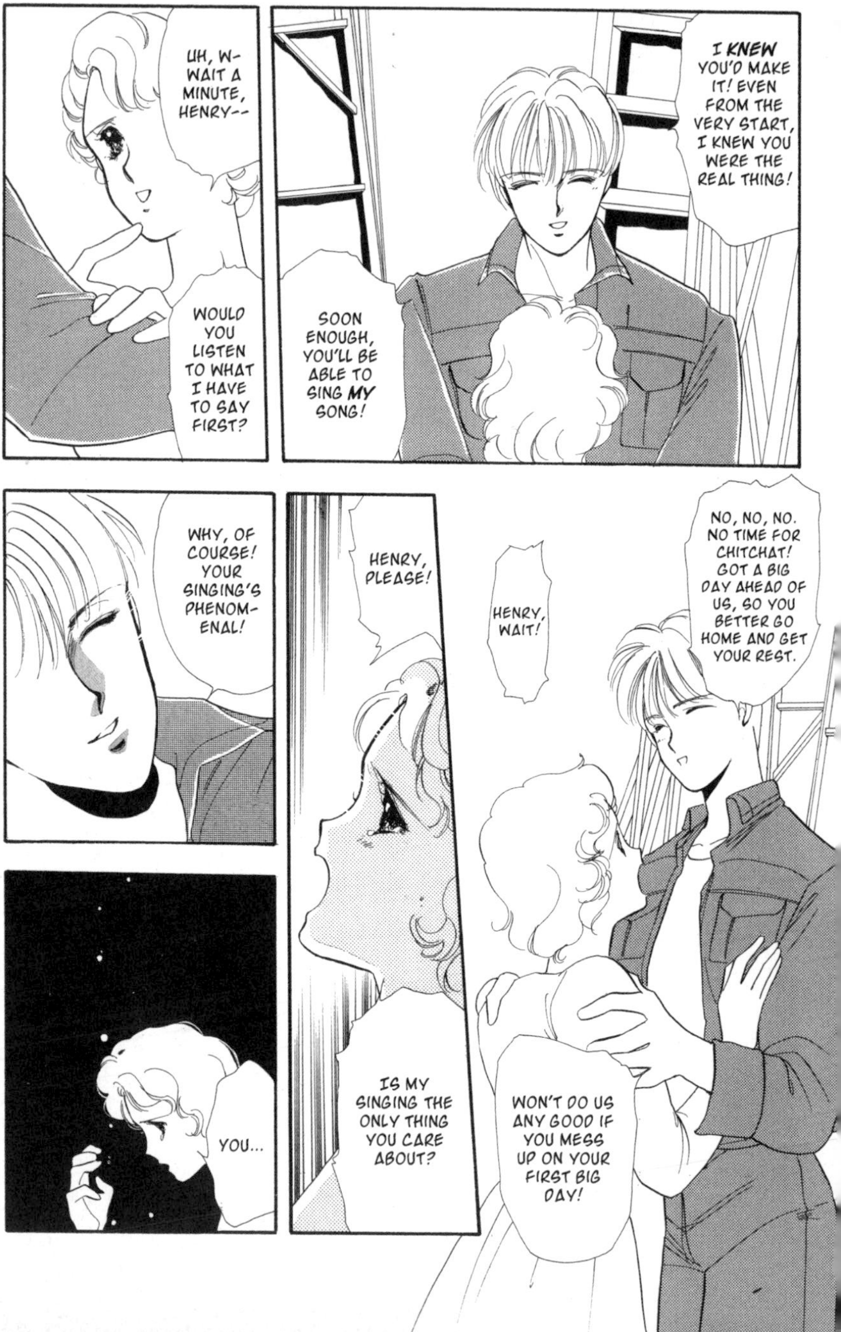
I KNEW YOU'D MAKE IT! EVEN FROM THE VERY START, I KNEW YOU WERE THE REAL THING!
SOON ENOUGH, YOU'LL BE ABLE TO SING MY SONG!
UH, W-WAIT A MINUTE, HENRY--
WOULD YOU LISTEN TO WHAT I HAVE TO SAY FIRST?
NO, NO, NO. NO TIME FOR CHITCHAT! GOT A BIG DAY AHEAD OF US, SO YOU BETTER GO HOME AND GET YOUR REST.
HENRY, WAIT!
WON'T DO US ANY GOOD IF YOU MESS UP ON YOUR FIRST BIG DAY!
HENRY, PLEASE!
IS MY SINGING THE ONLY THING YOU CARE ABOUT?
WHY, OF COURSE! YOUR SINGING'S PHENOMENAL!
YOU...

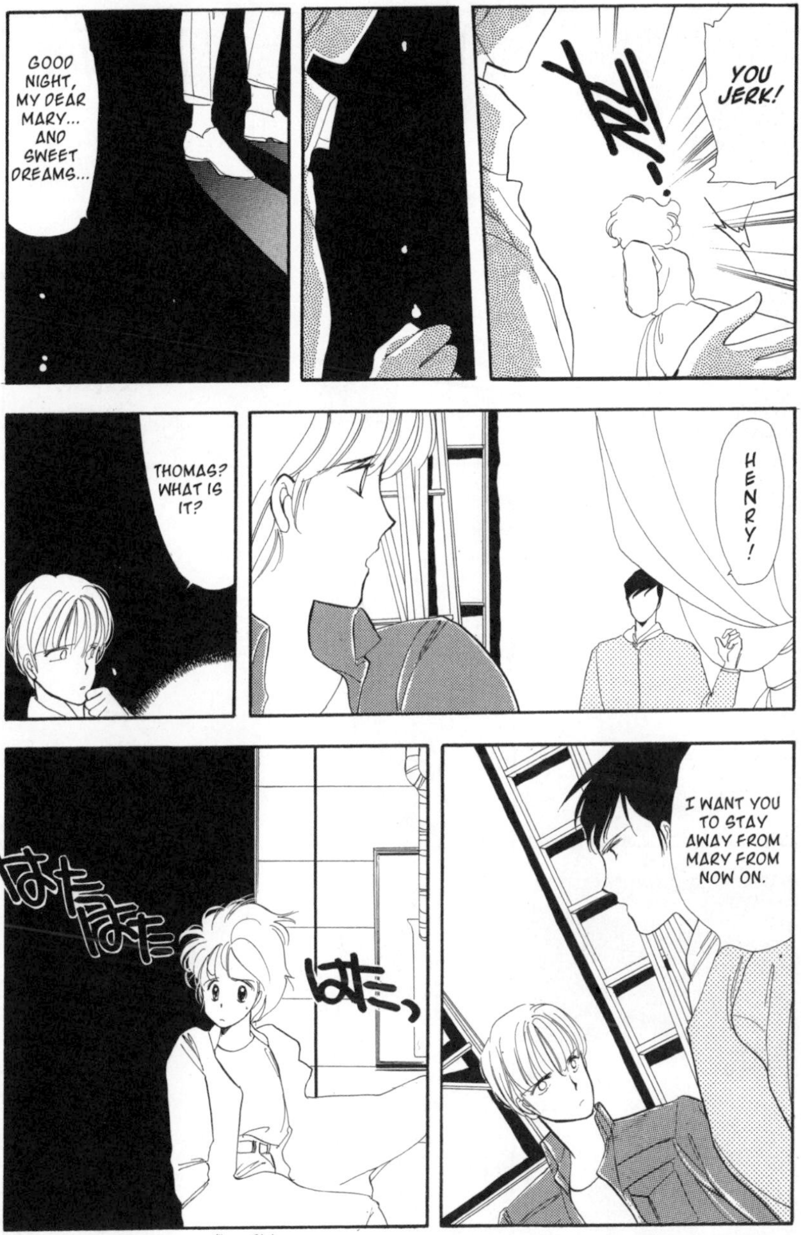
YOU JERK!
GOOD NIGHT, MY DEAR MARY... AND SWEET DREAMS...
HENRY!
THOMAS? WHAT IS IT?
I WANT YOU TO STAY AWAY FROM MARY FROM NOW ON.
はたはた
はたっ

This is Chihaya.

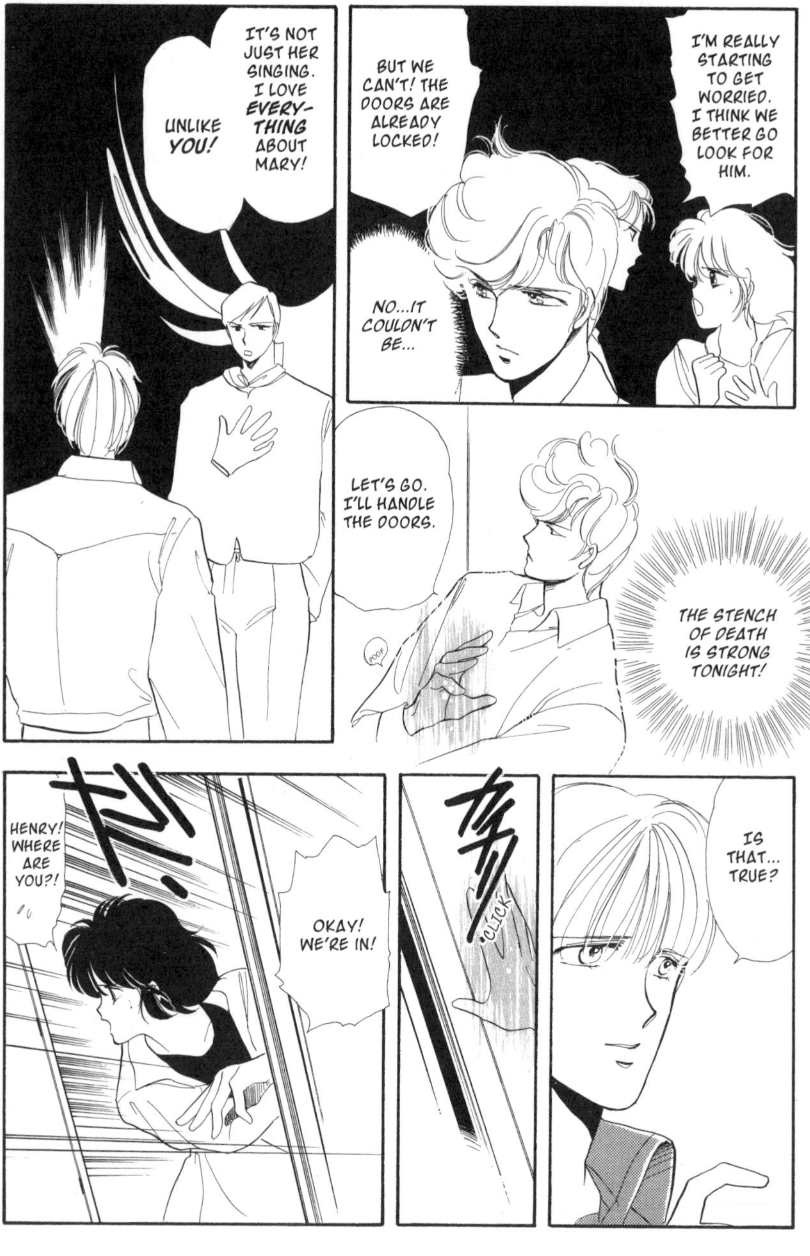
I'M REALLY STARTING TO GET WORRIED. I THINK WE BETTER GO LOOK FOR HIM.
BUT WE CAN'T! THE DOORS ARE ALREADY LOCKED!
NO...IT COULDN'T BE...
THE STENCH OF DEATH IS STRONG TONIGHT!
LET'S GO. I'LL HANDLE THE DOORS.
POOF
IT'S NOT JUST HER SINGING. I LOVE EVERYTHING ABOUT MARY!
UNLIKE YOU!
IS THAT... TRUE?
CLICK
OKAY! WE'RE IN!
HENRY! WHERE ARE YOU?!

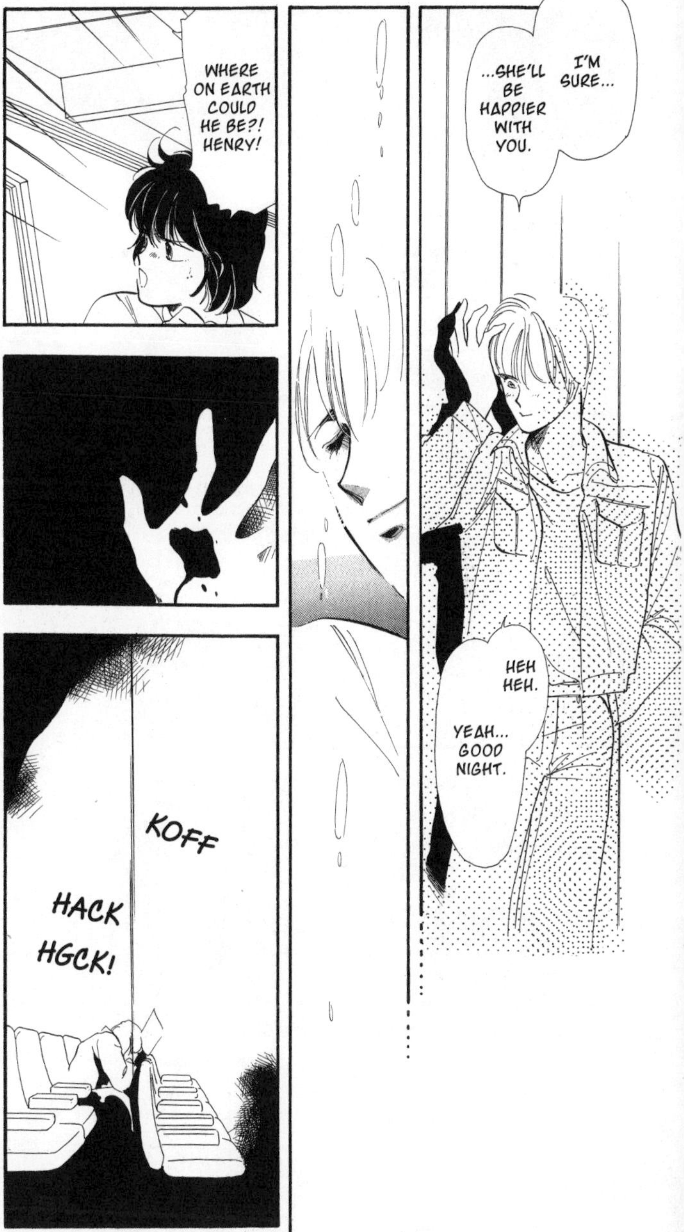
I'M SURE...
...SHE'LL BE HAPPIER WITH YOU.
HEH HEH.
YEAH... GOOD NIGHT.
WHERE ON EARTH COULD HE BE?! HENRY!
KOFF
HACK
HGCK!

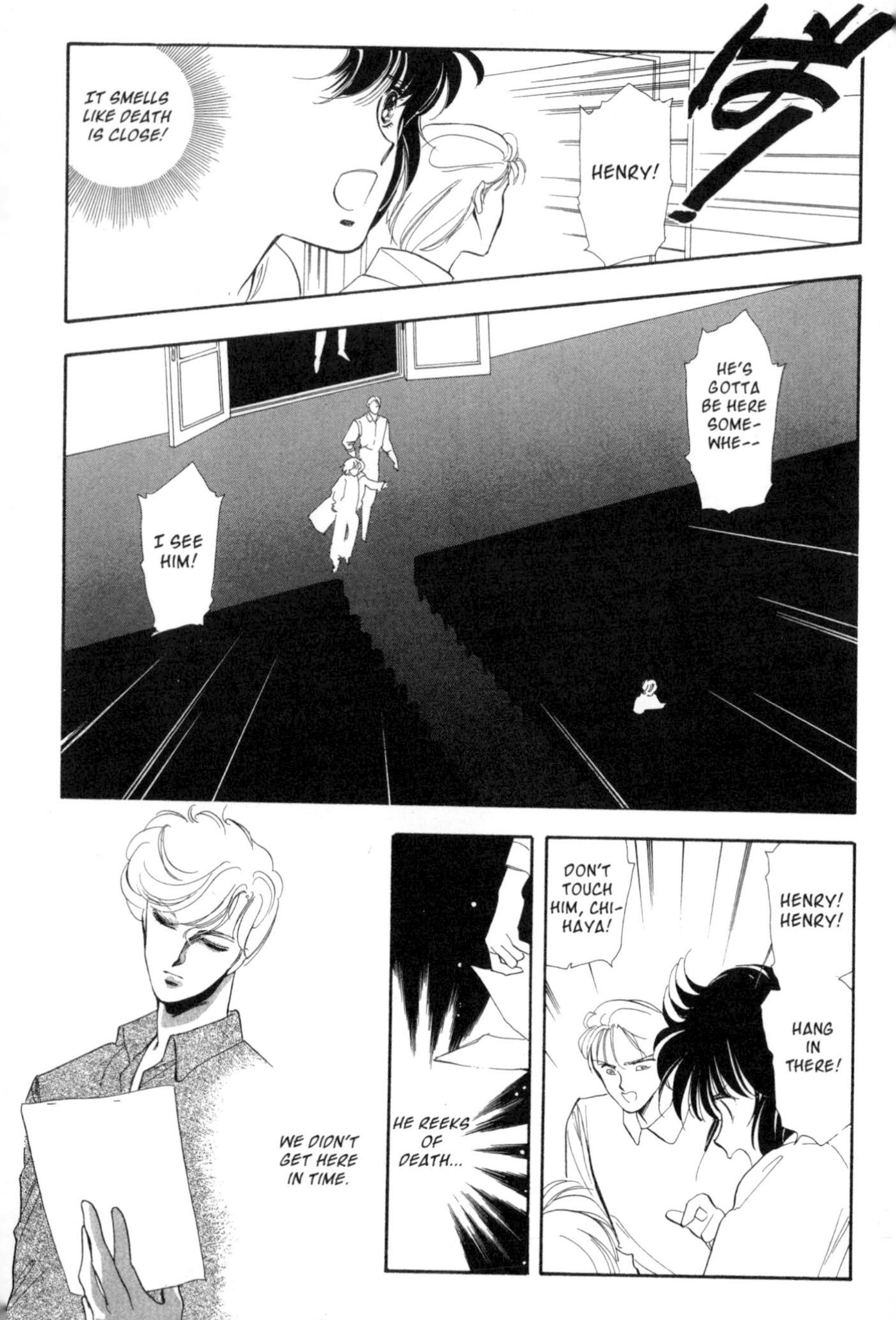
HENRY!
IT SMELLS LIKE DEATH IS CLOSE!
HE'S GOTTA BE HERE SOME-WHE--
I SEE HIM!
HENRY! HENRY!
DON'T TOUCH HIM, CHI-HAYA!
HANG IN THERE!
HE REEKS OF DEATH...
WE DIDN'T GET HERE IN TIME.

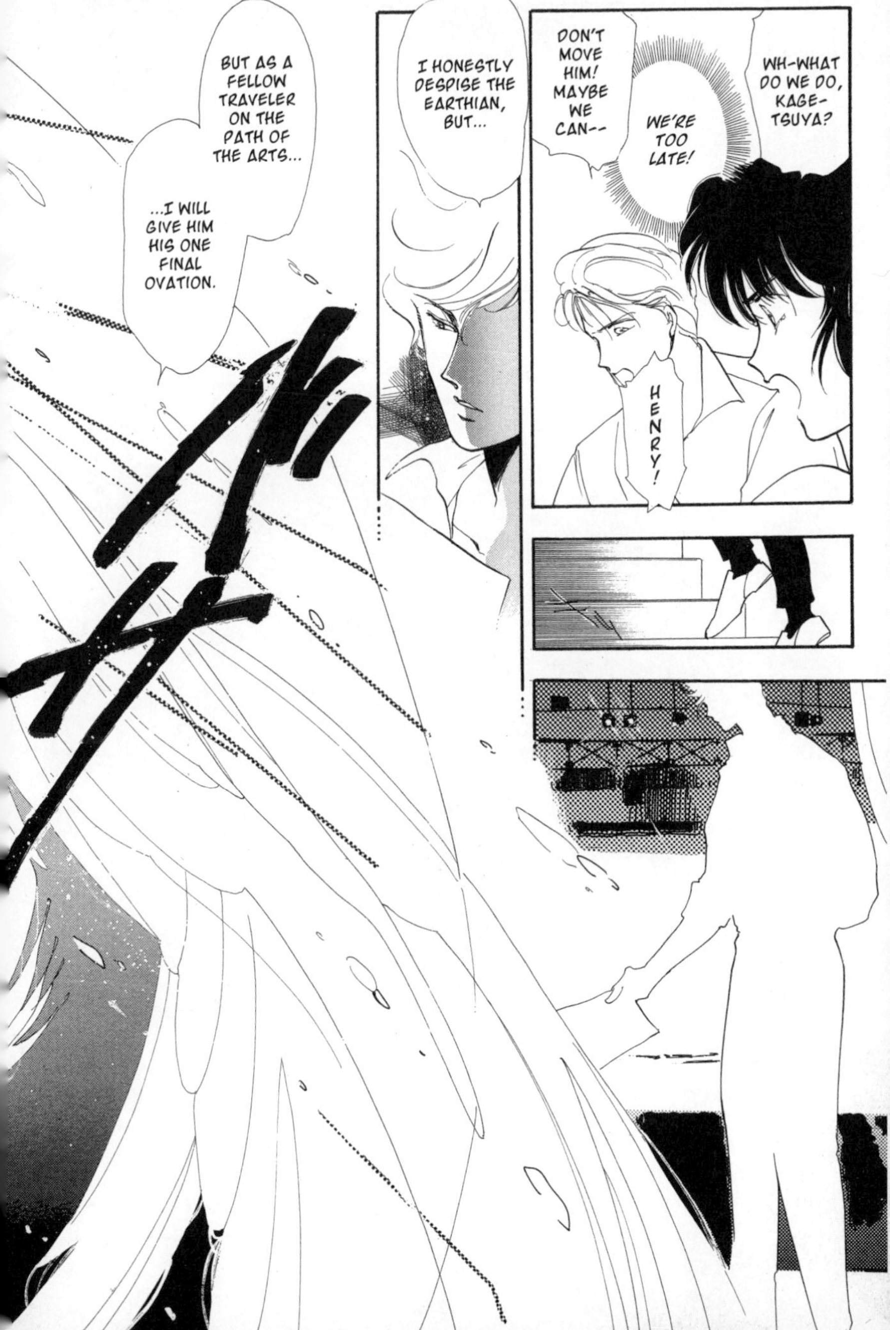
WH-WHAT DO WE DO, KAGE-TSUYA?
DON'T MOVE HIM! MAYBE WE CAN--
WE'RE TOO LATE!
HENRY!
I HONESTLY DESPISE THE EARTHIAN, BUT...
BUT AS A FELLOW TRAVELER ON THE PATH OF THE ARTS...
...I WILL GIVE HIM HIS ONE FINAL OVATION.

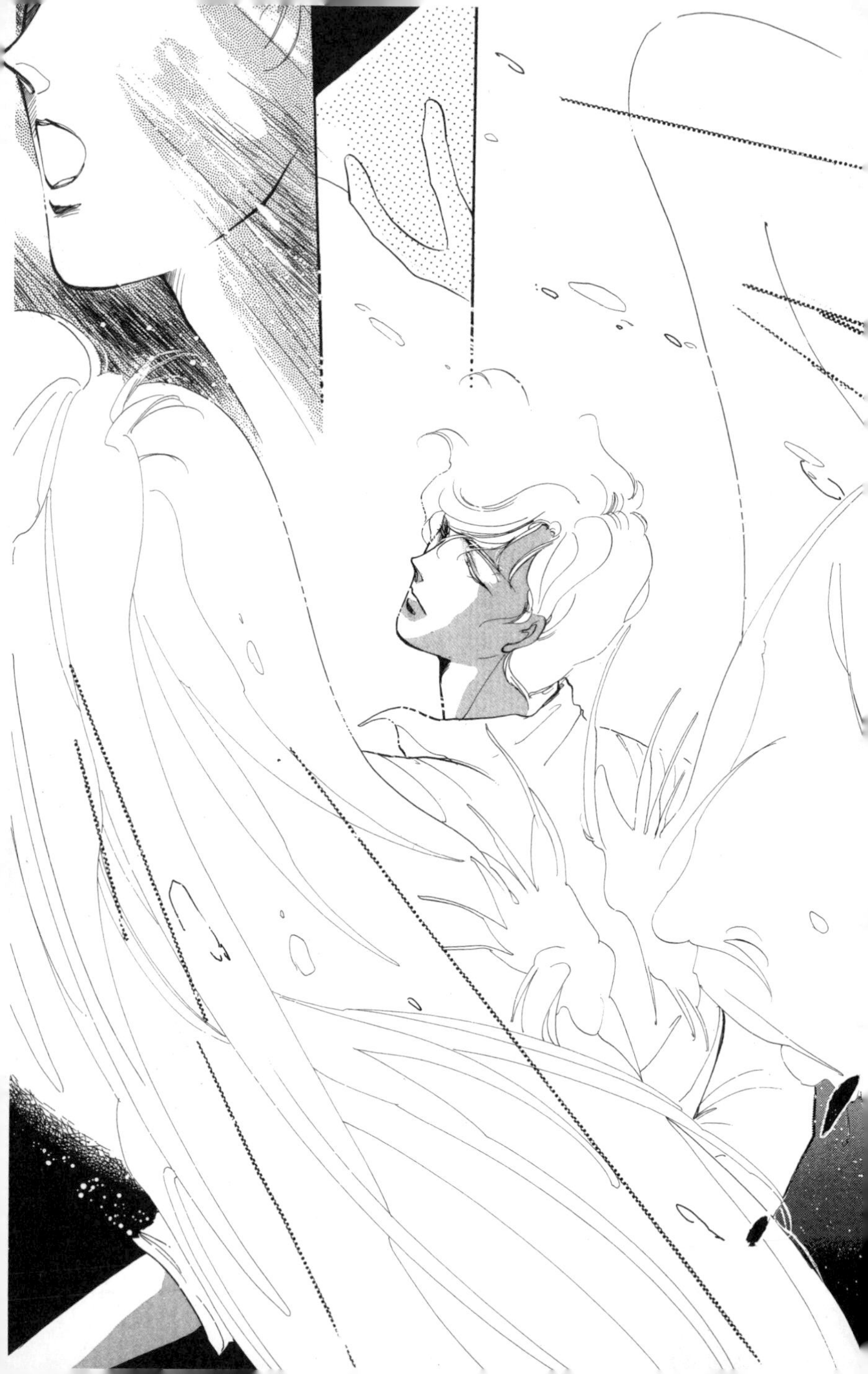

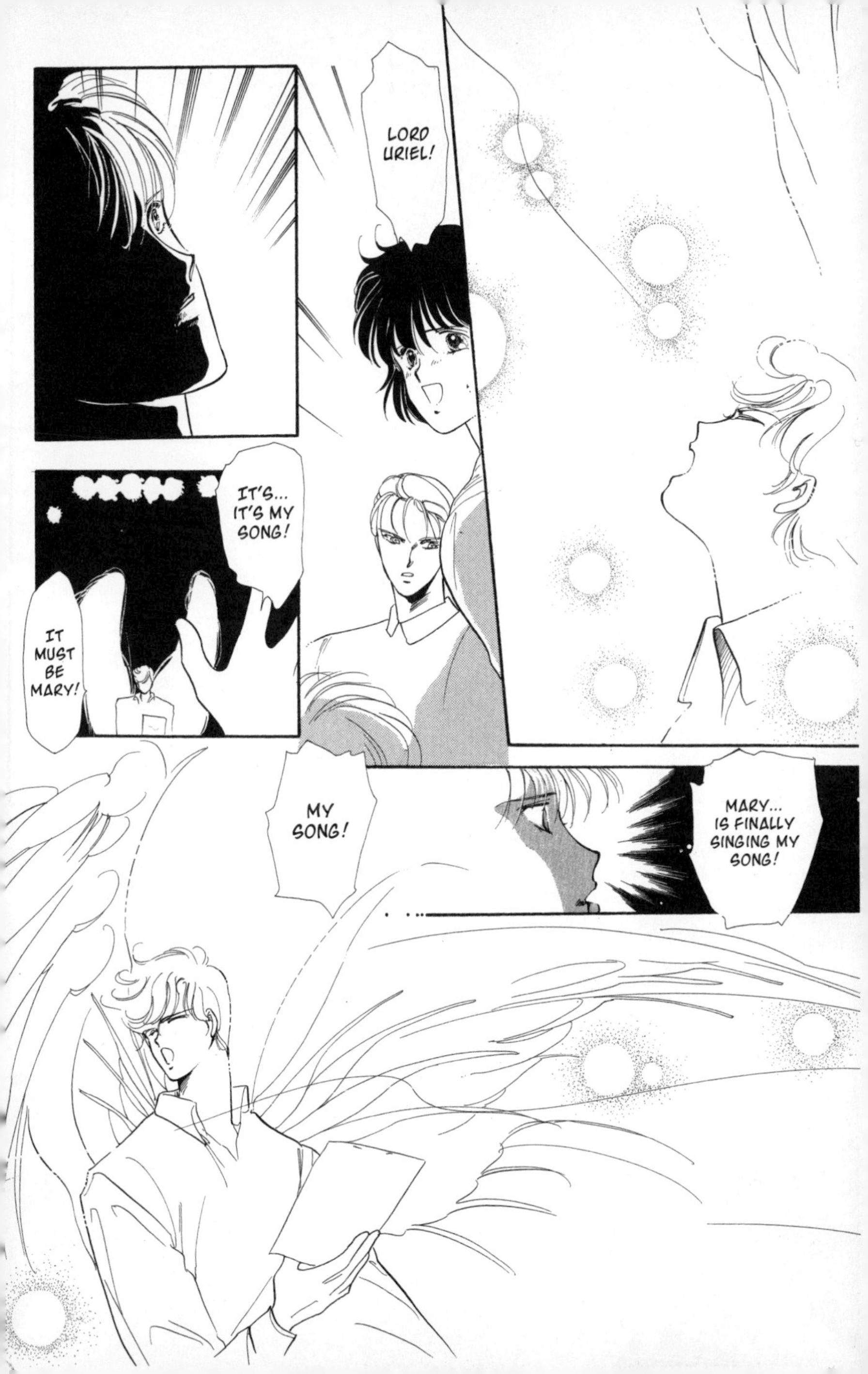
LORD URIEL!
IT'S... IT'S MY SONG!
IT MUST BE MARY!
MARY... IS FINALLY SINGING MY SONG!
MY SONG!

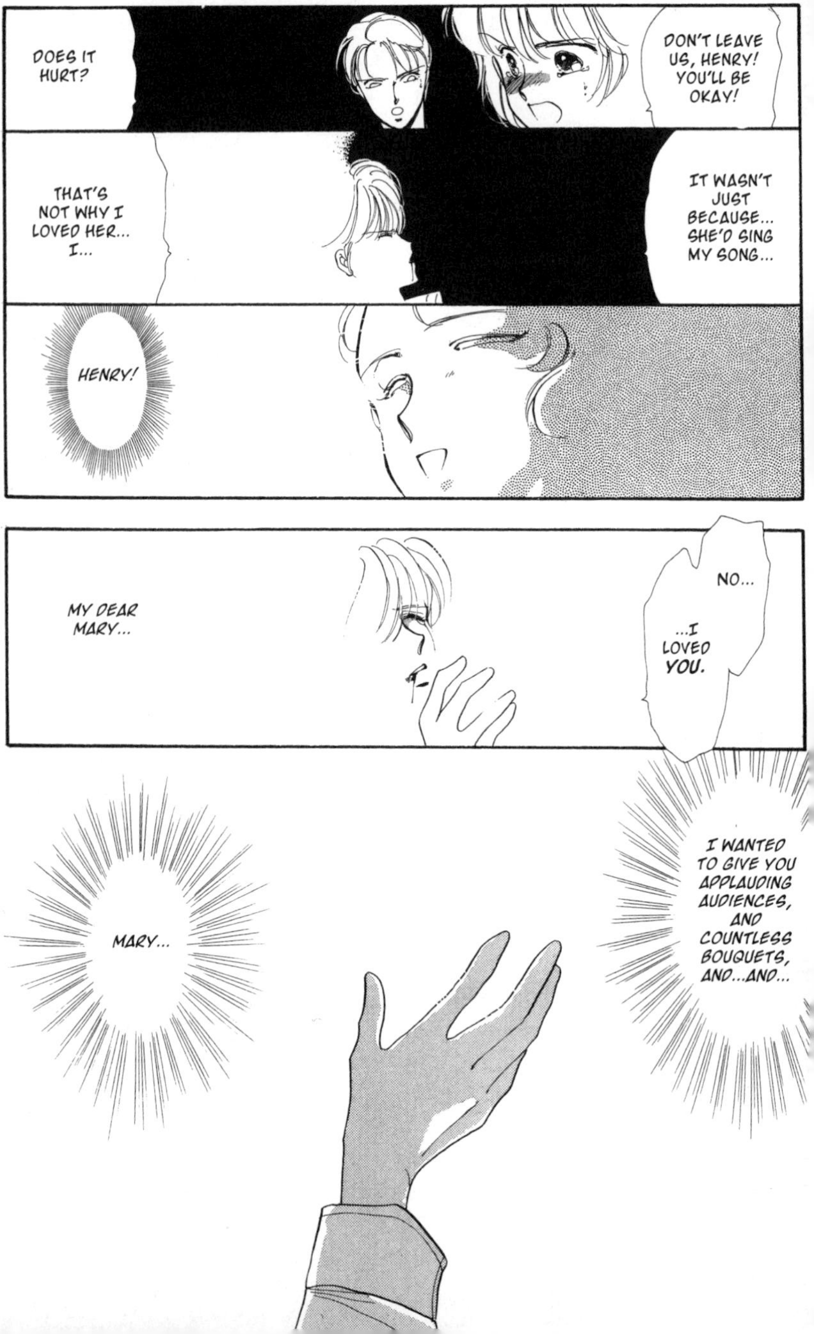
DON'T LEAVE US, HENRY! YOU'LL BE OKAY!
DOES IT HURT?
IT WASN'T JUST BECAUSE... SHE'D SING MY SONG...
THAT'S NOT WHY I LOVED HER... I...
HENRY!
NO...
...I LOVED **YOU.**
MY DEAR MARY...
I WANTED TO GIVE YOU APPLAUDING AUDIENCES, AND COUNTLESS BOUQUETS, AND...AND...
MARY...

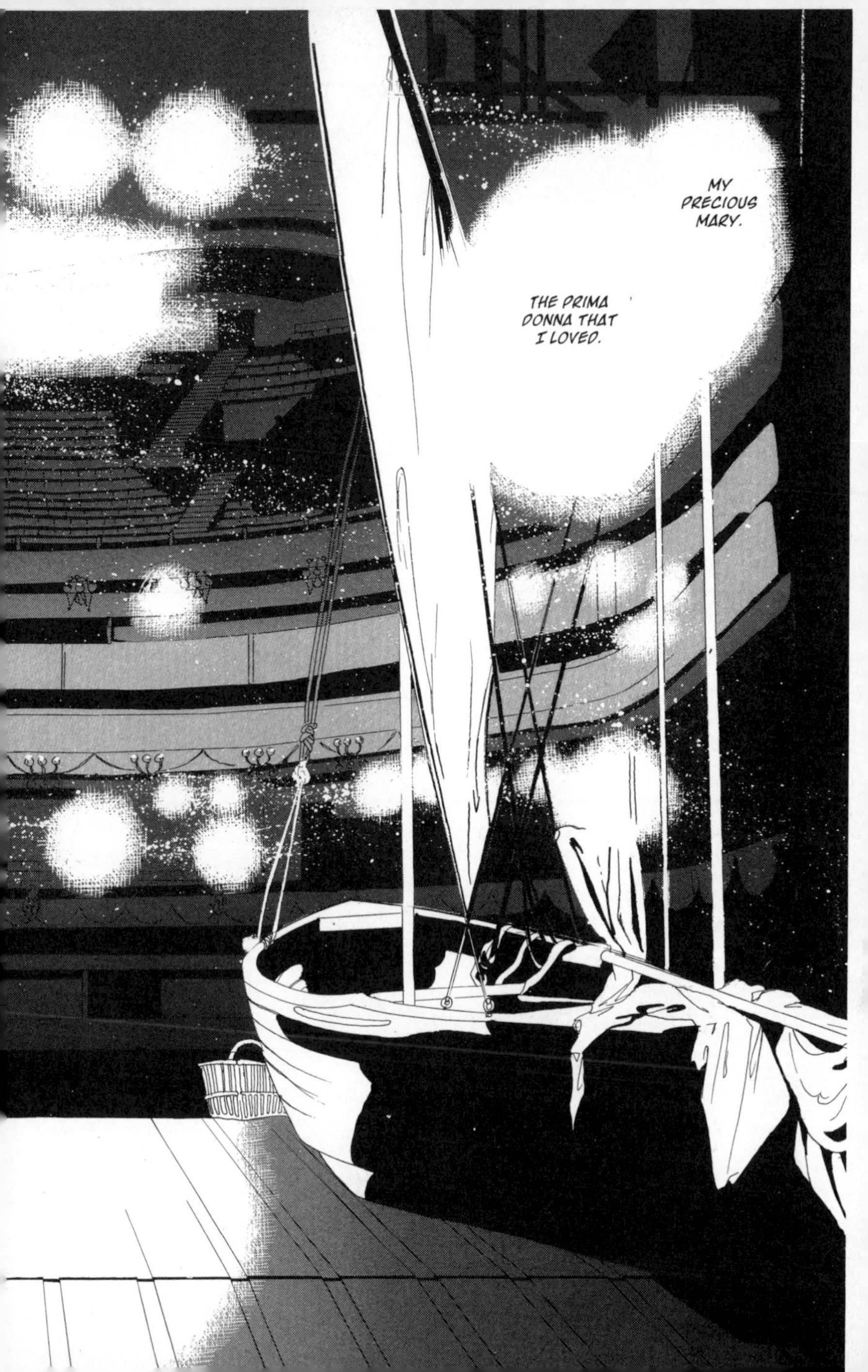
MY PRECIOUS MARY.
THE PRIMA DONNA THAT I LOVED.

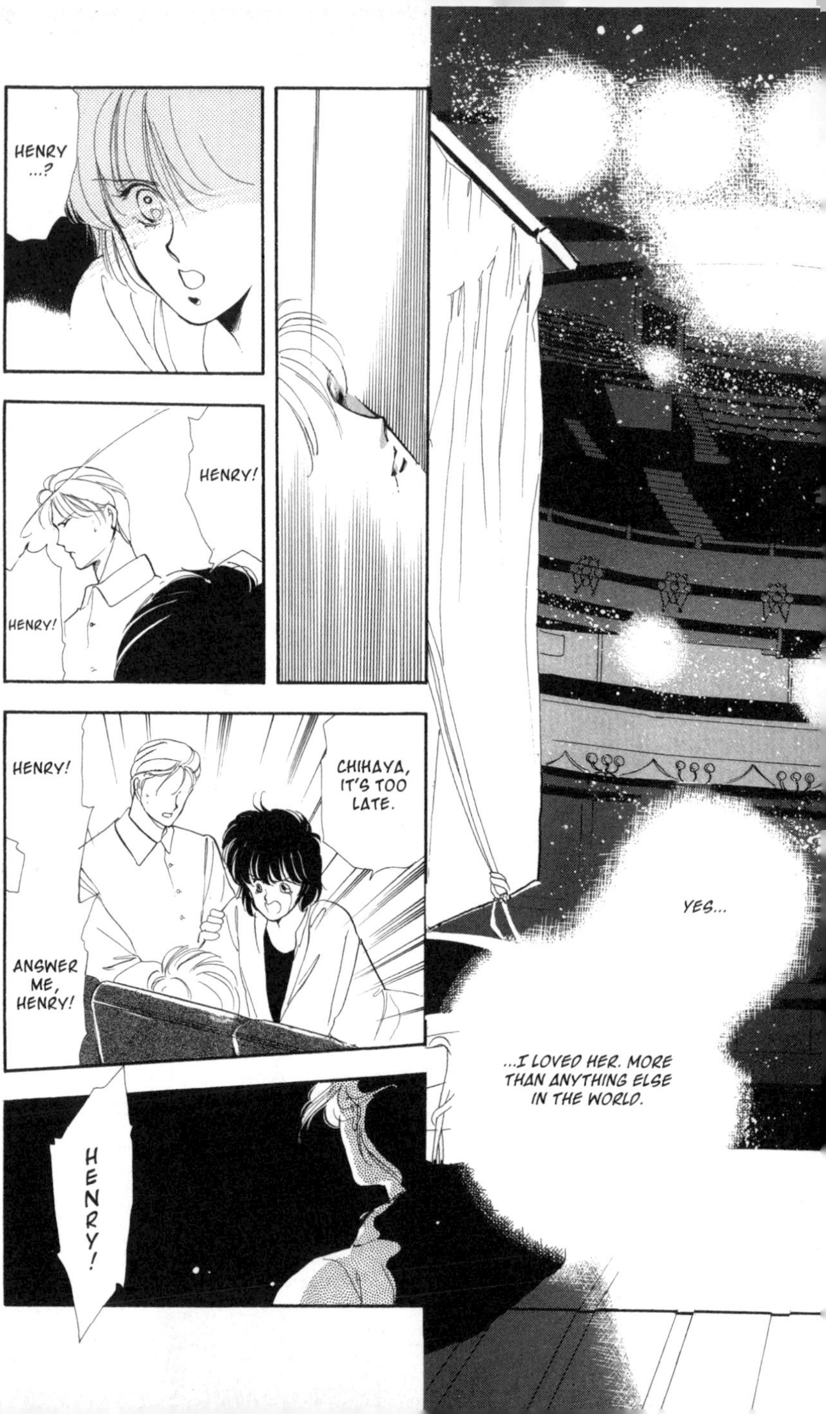
YES...
...I LOVED HER. MORE THAN ANYTHING ELSE IN THE WORLD.
HENRY ...?
HENRY!
HENRY!
CHIHAYA, IT'S TOO LATE.
HENRY!
ANSWER ME, HENRY!
HENRY!

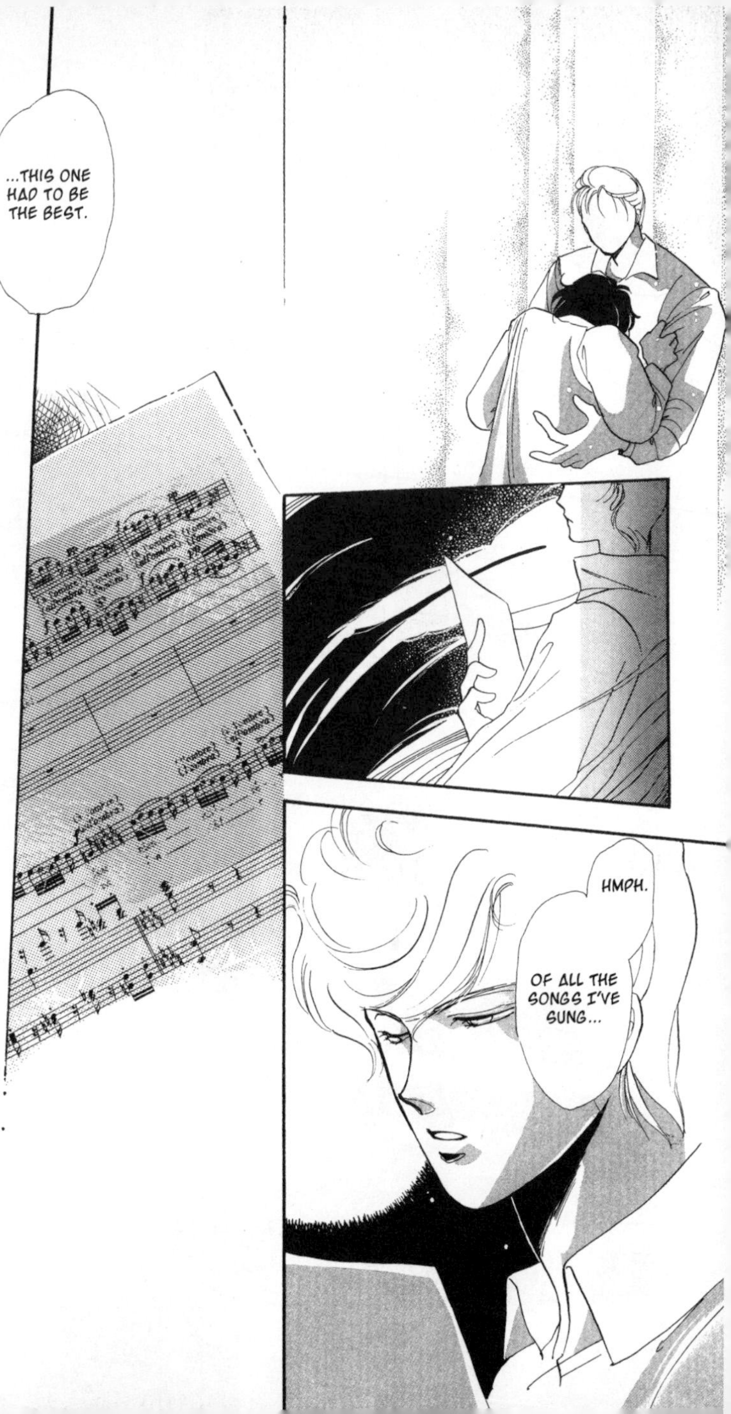
HMPH.
OF ALL THE SONGS I'VE SUNG...
...THIS ONE HAD TO BE THE BEST.

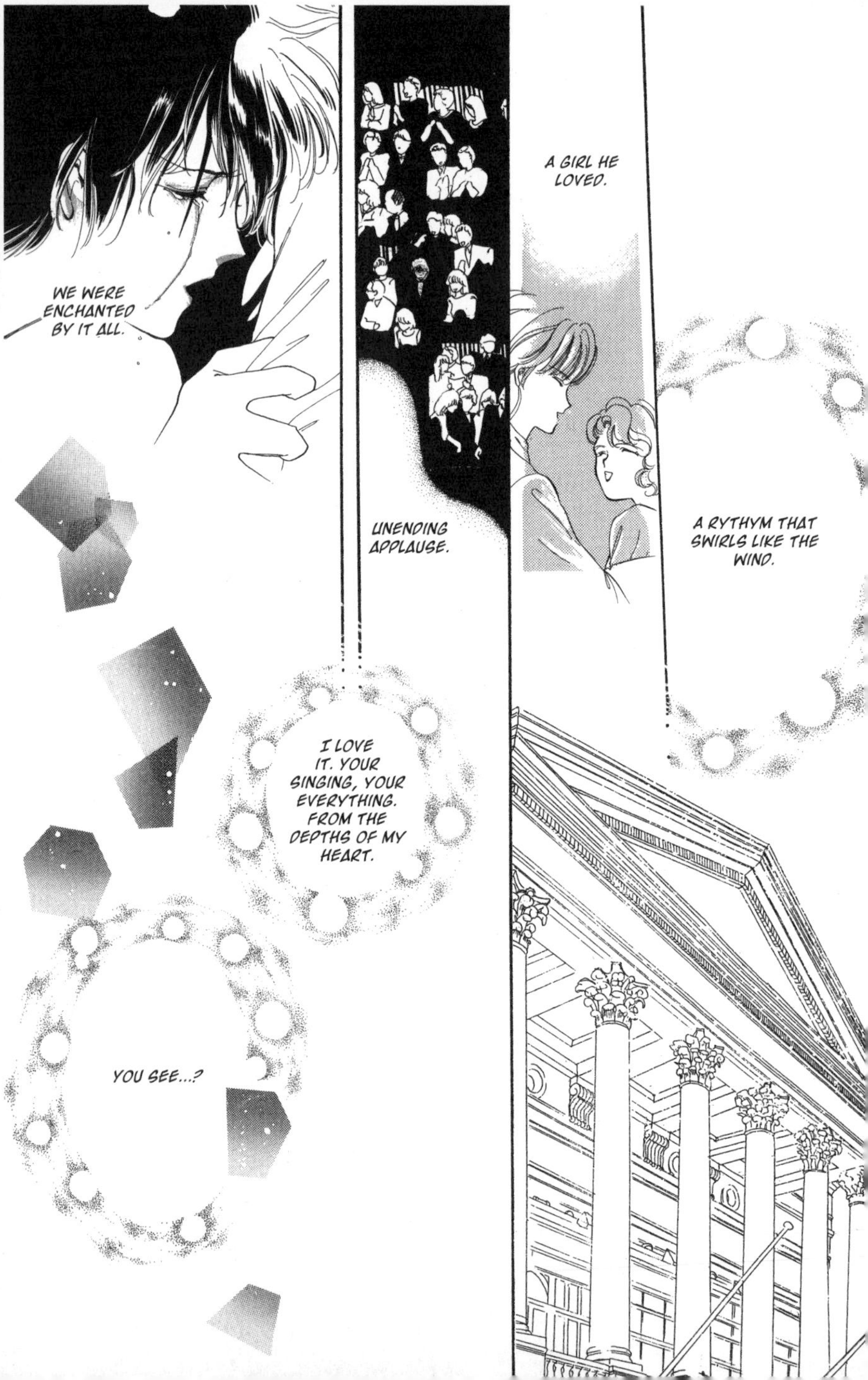
A GIRL HE LOVED.
A RYTHYM THAT SWIRLS LIKE THE WIND.
UNENDING APPLAUSE.
I LOVE IT. YOUR SINGING, YOUR EVERYTHING. FROM THE DEPTHS OF MY HEART.
WE WERE ENCHANTED BY IT ALL.
YOU SEE...?

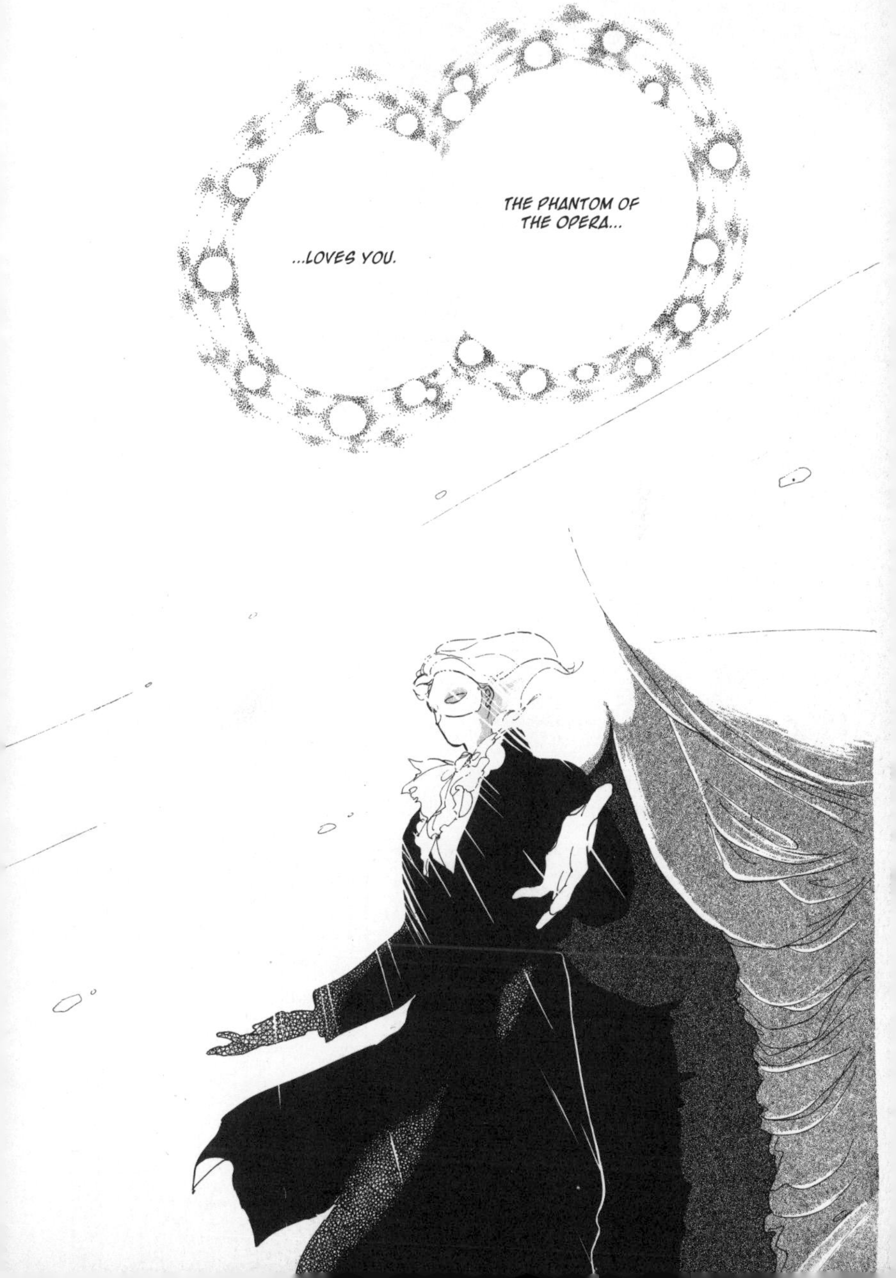
THE PHANTOM OF THE OPERA...
...LOVES YOU.

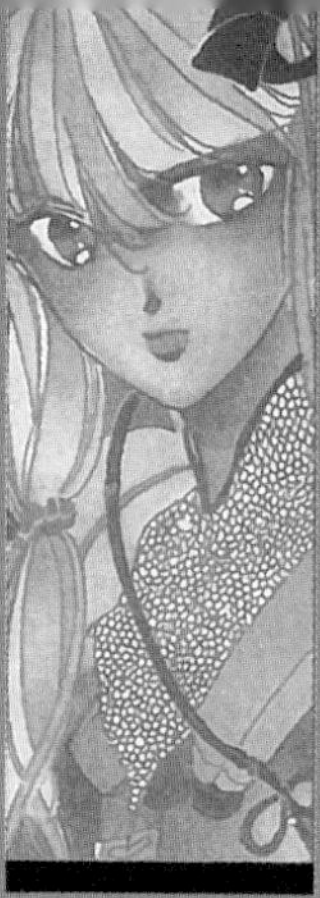

ARMED ANGELS ATTACK

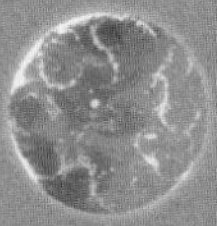

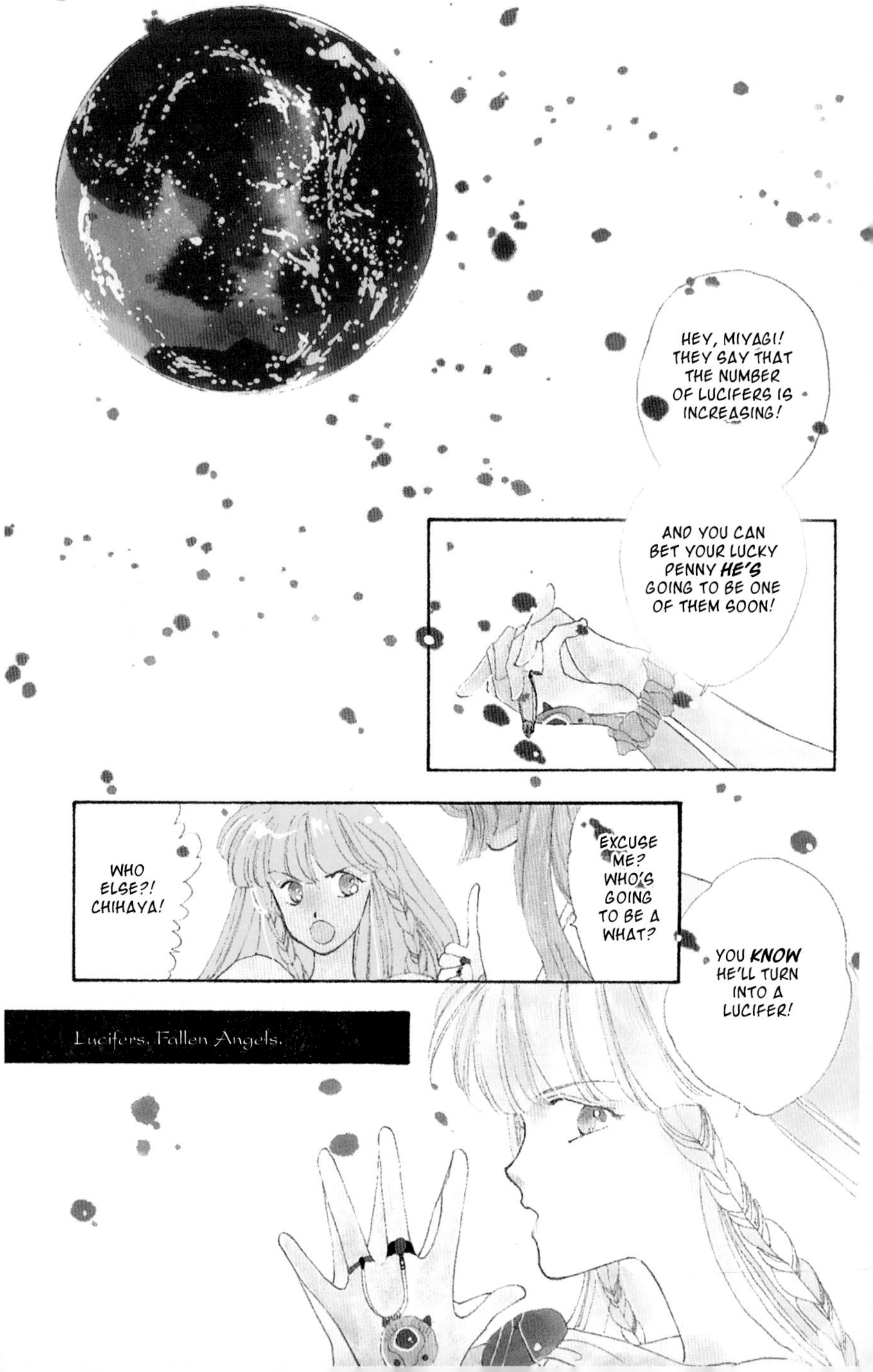
HEY, MIYAGI! THEY SAY THAT THE NUMBER OF LUCIFERS IS INCREASING!
AND YOU CAN BET YOUR LUCKY PENNY **HE'S** GOING TO BE ONE OF THEM SOON!
EXCUSE ME? WHO'S GOING TO BE A WHAT?
WHO ELSE?! CHIHAYA!
YOU **KNOW** HE'LL TURN INTO A LUCIFER!
Lucifers. Fallen Angels.

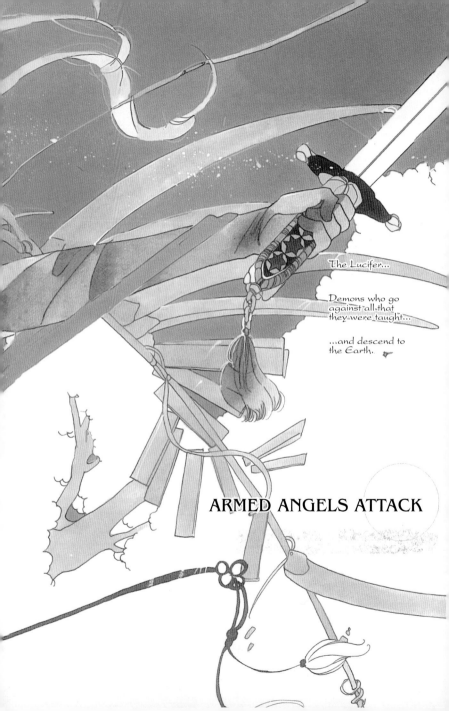

The Lucifer...

Demons who go against all that they were taught...

...and descend to the Earth.

ARMED ANGELS ATTACK

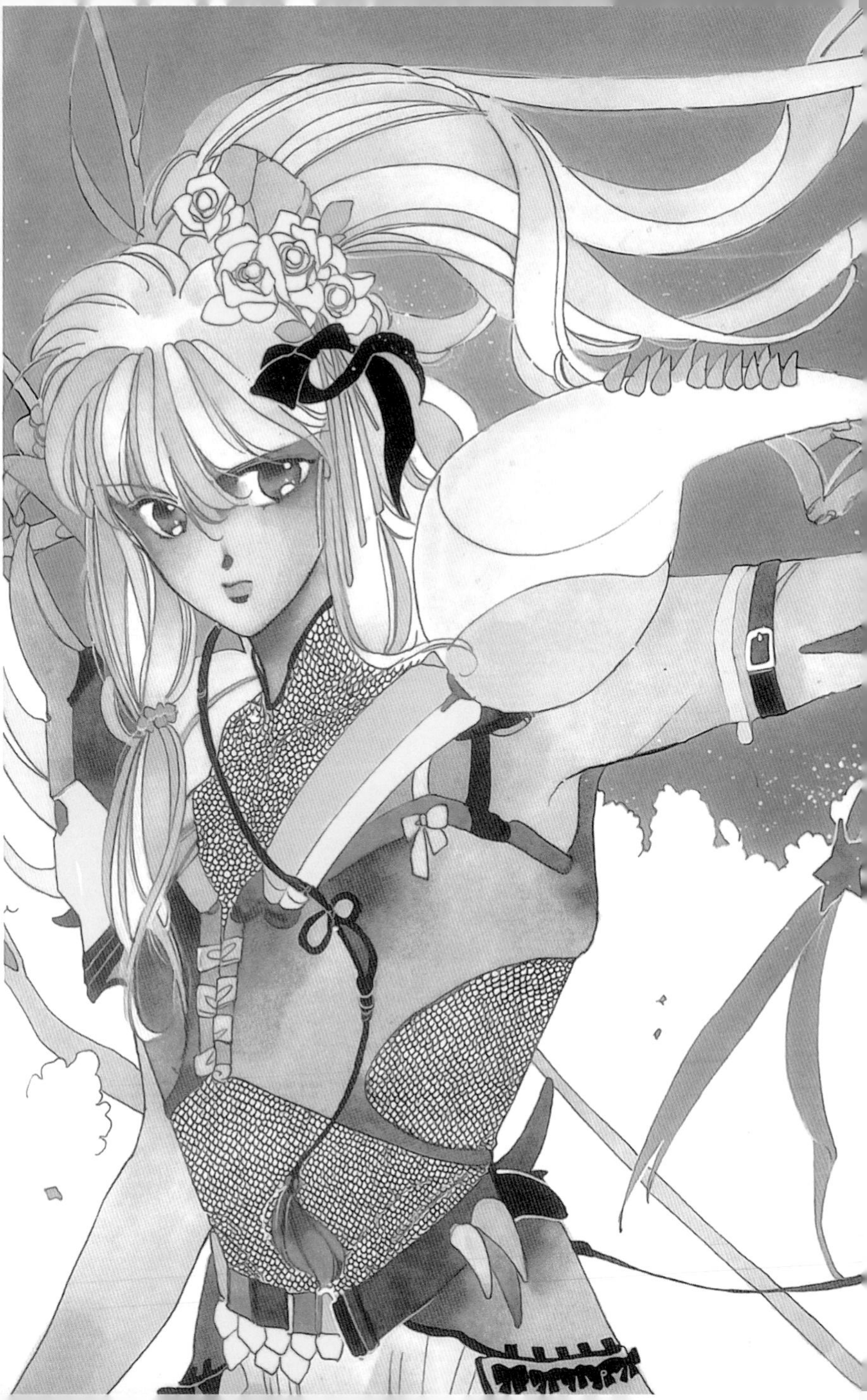

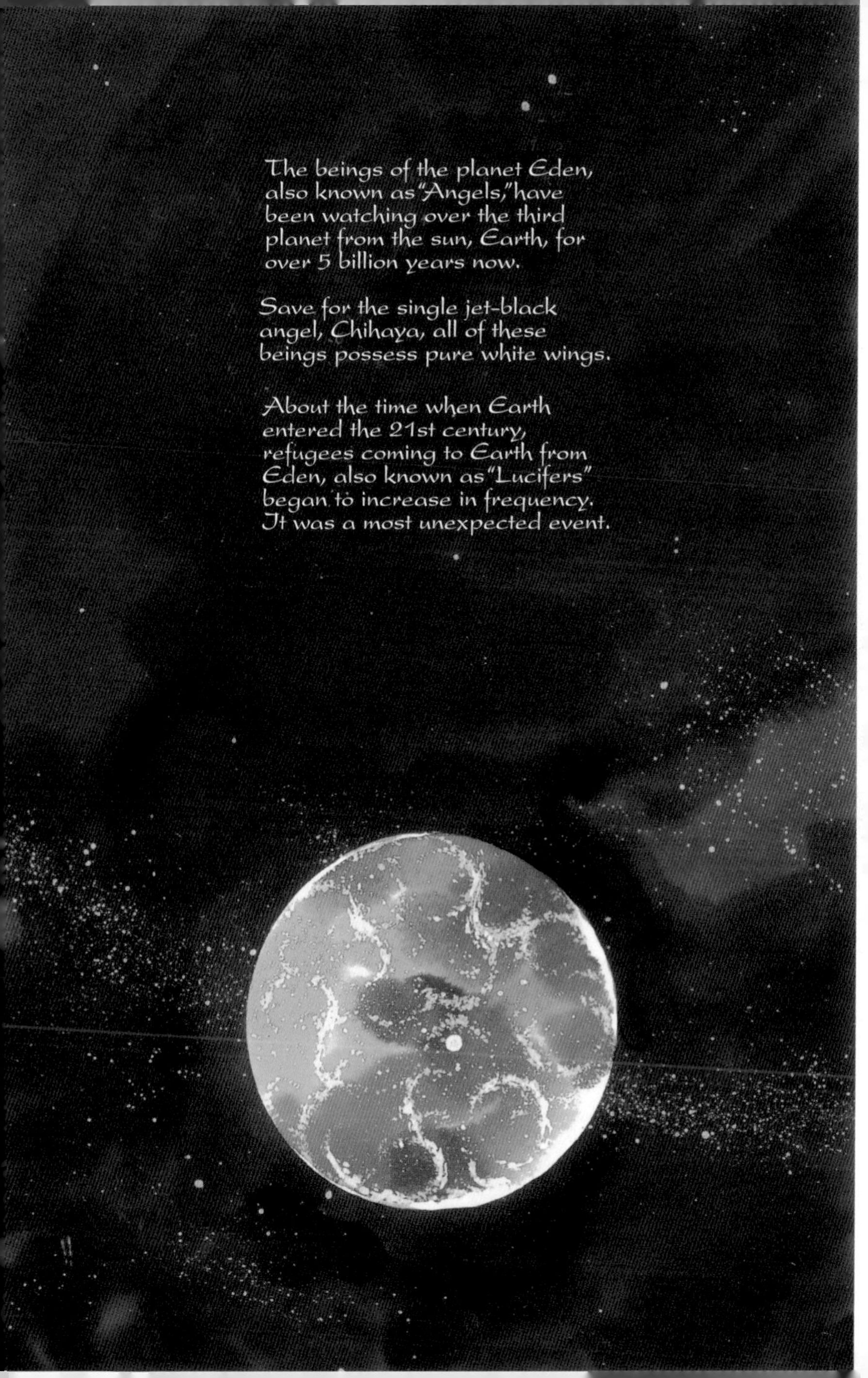
The beings of the planet Eden, also known as "Angels," have been watching over the third planet from the sun, Earth, for over 5 billion years now.
Save for the single jet-black angel, Chihaya, all of these beings possess pure white wings.
About the time when Earth entered the 21st century, refugees coming to Earth from Eden, also known as "Lucifers" began to increase in frequency. It was a most unexpected event.

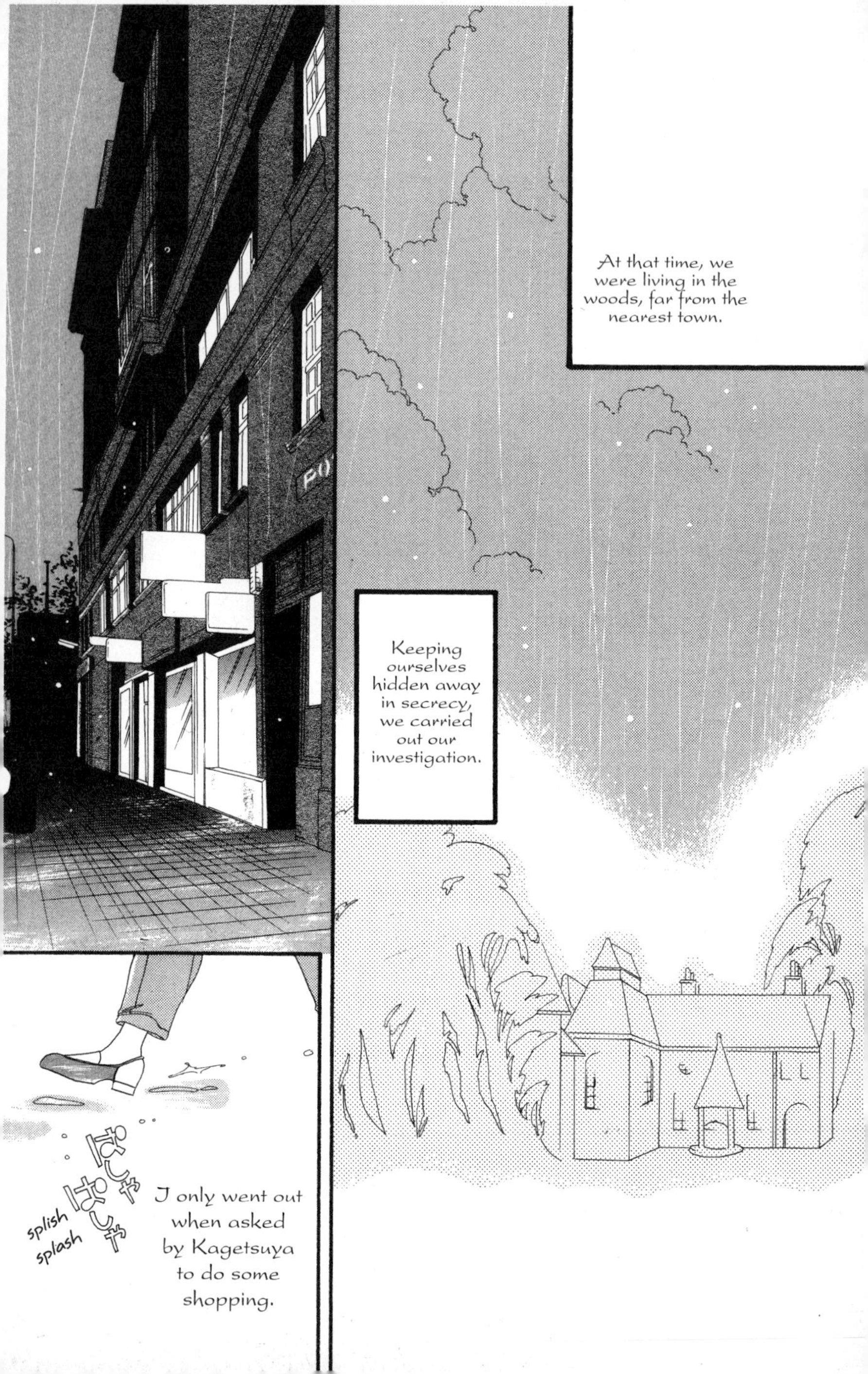
At that time, we were living in the woods, far from the nearest town.
Keeping ourselves hidden away in secrecy, we carried out our investigation.
ぱしゃぱしゃ
splish splash
I only went out when asked by Kagetsuya to do some shopping.

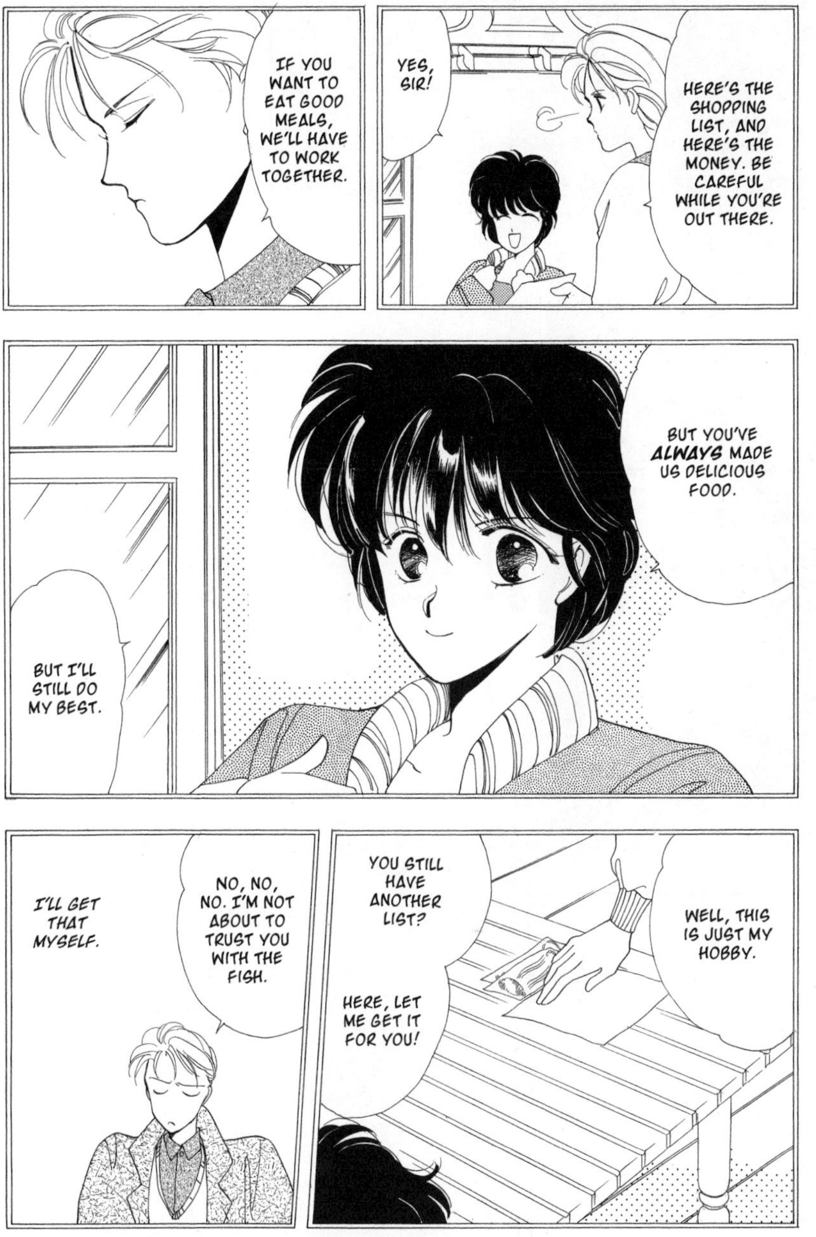
HERE'S THE SHOPPING LIST, AND HERE'S THE MONEY. BE CAREFUL WHILE YOU'RE OUT THERE.
YES, SIR!
IF YOU WANT TO EAT GOOD MEALS, WE'LL HAVE TO WORK TOGETHER.
BUT YOU'VE ALWAYS MADE US DELICIOUS FOOD.
BUT I'LL STILL DO MY BEST.
WELL, THIS IS JUST MY HOBBY.
YOU STILL HAVE ANOTHER LIST?
HERE, LET ME GET IT FOR YOU!
NO, NO, NO. I'M NOT ABOUT TO TRUST YOU WITH THE FISH.
I'LL GET THAT MYSELF.

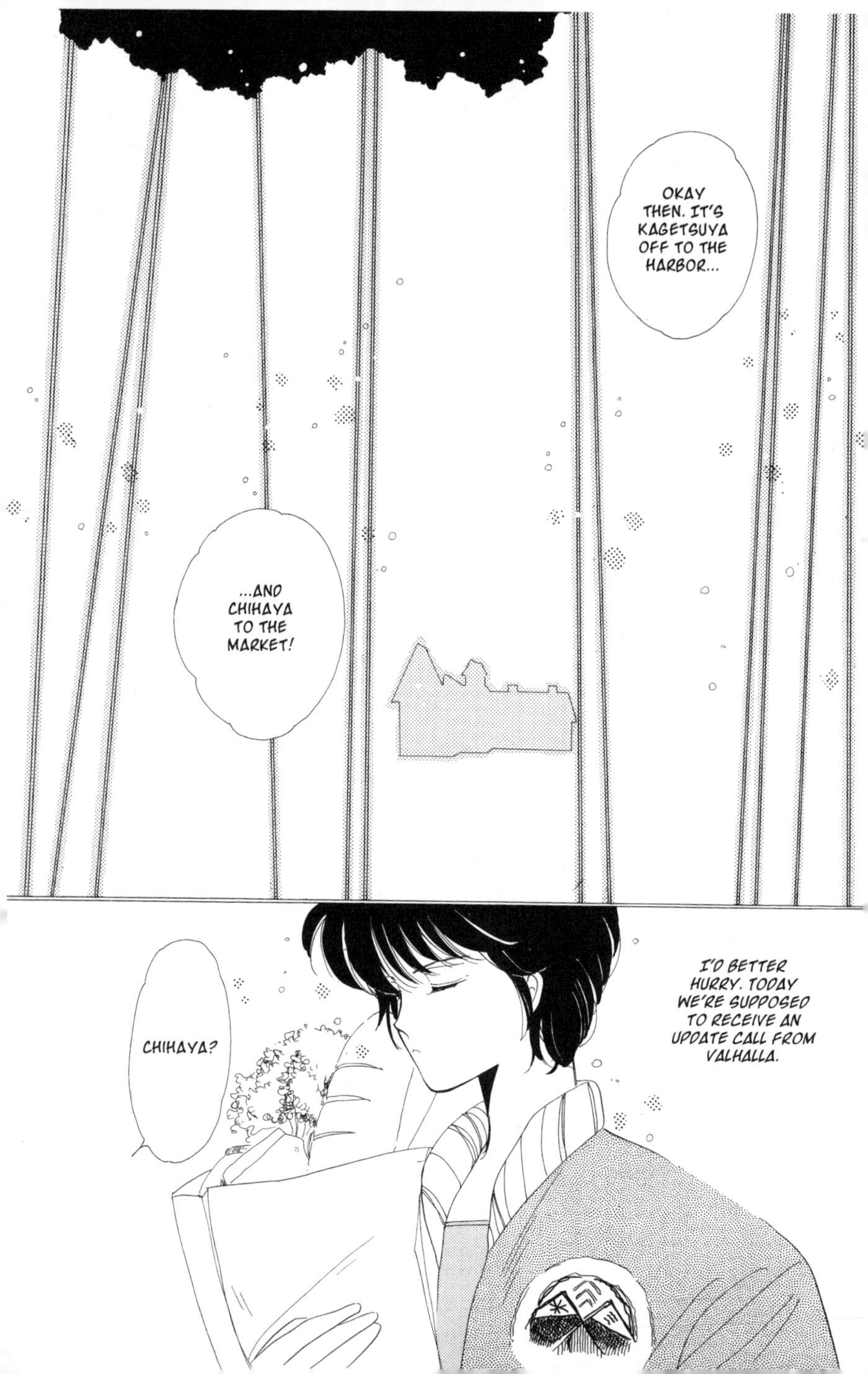
OKAY THEN. IT'S KAGETSUYA OFF TO THE HARBOR...
...AND CHIHAYA TO THE MARKET!
I'D BETTER HURRY. TODAY WE'RE SUPPOSED TO RECEIVE AN UPDATE CALL FROM VALHALLA.
CHIHAYA?

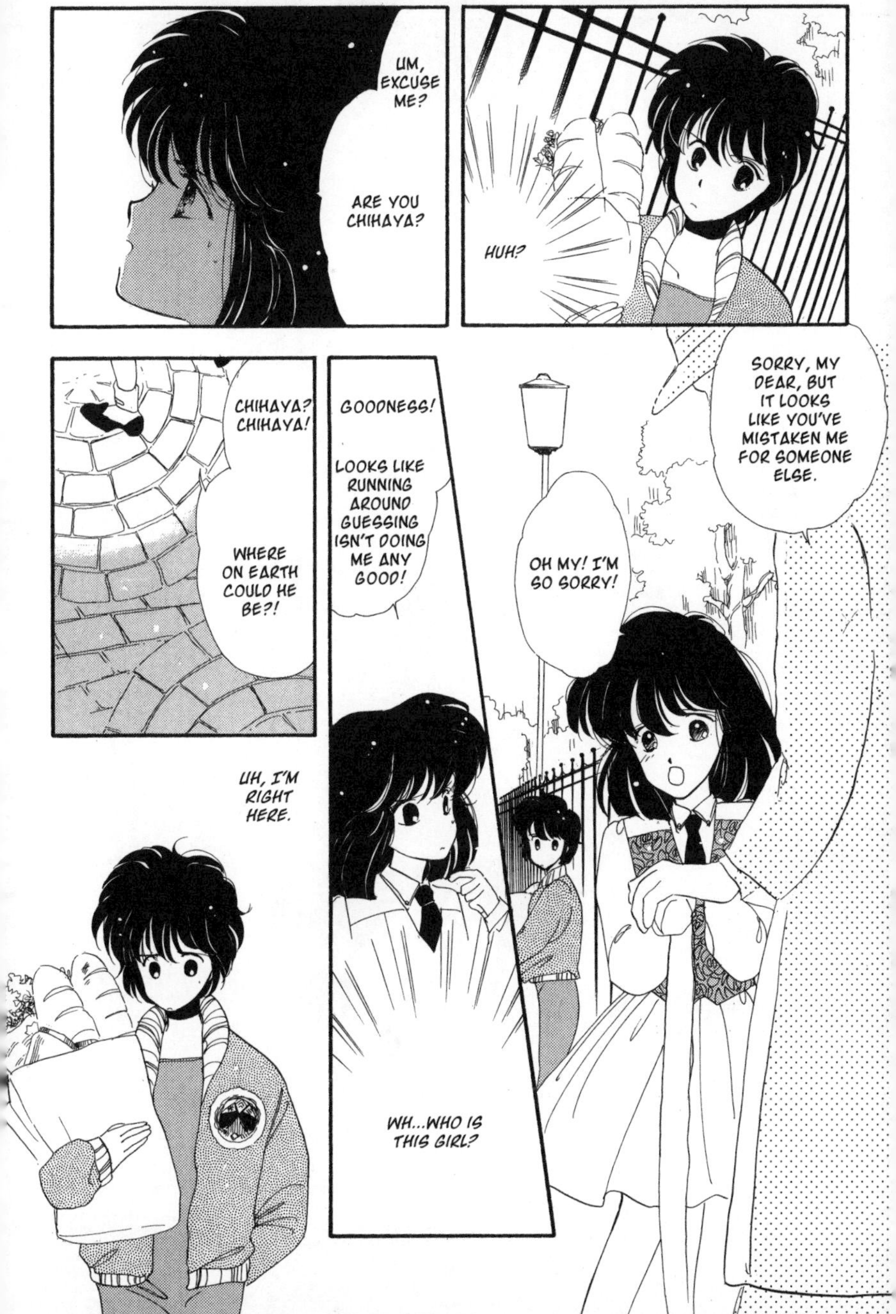
HUH?
UM, EXCUSE ME?
ARE YOU CHIHAYA?
SORRY, MY DEAR, BUT IT LOOKS LIKE YOU'VE MISTAKEN ME FOR SOMEONE ELSE.
OH MY! I'M SO SORRY!
GOODNESS!
LOOKS LIKE RUNNING AROUND GUESSING ISN'T DOING ME ANY GOOD!
WH...WHO IS THIS GIRL?
CHIHAYA? CHIHAYA!
WHERE ON EARTH COULD HE BE?!
UH, I'M RIGHT HERE.

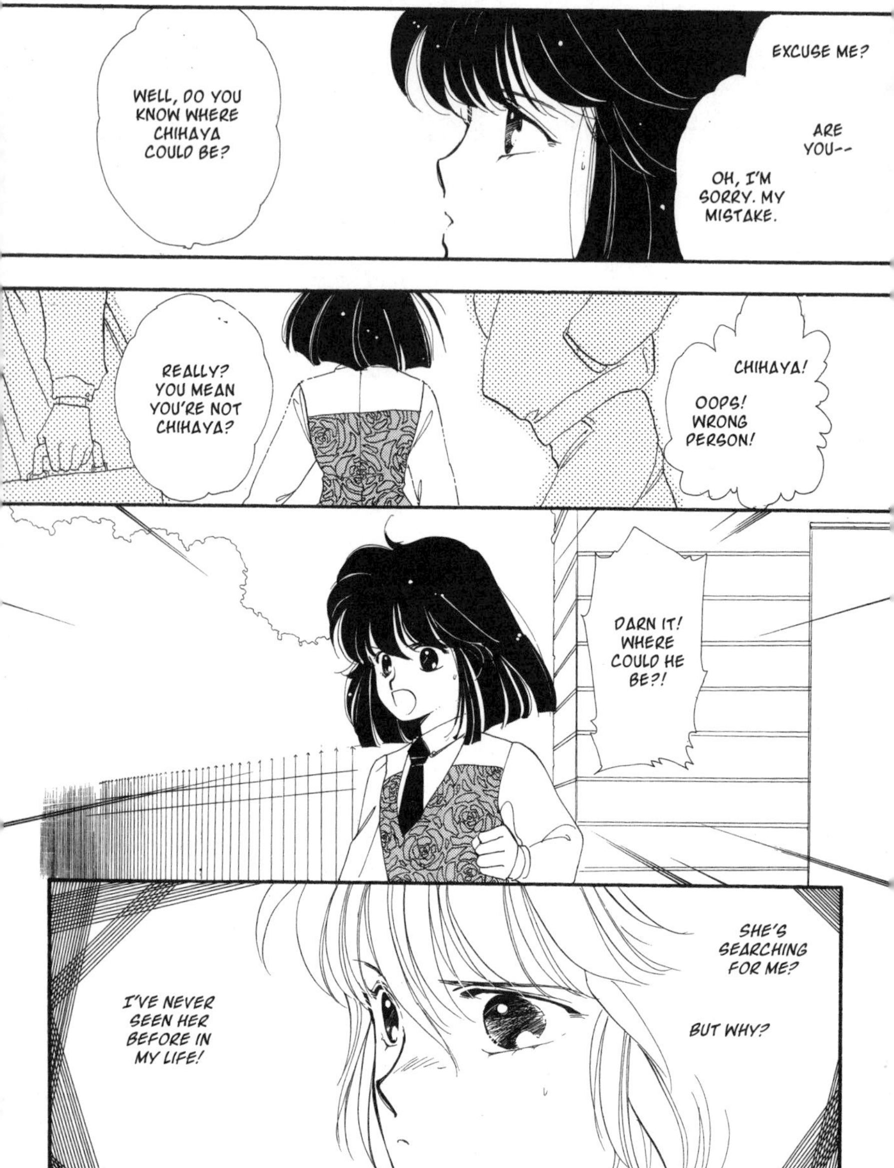
EXCUSE ME?
ARE YOU--
OH, I'M SORRY. MY MISTAKE.
WELL, DO YOU KNOW WHERE CHIHAYA COULD BE?
CHIHAYA!
OOPS! WRONG PERSON!
REALLY? YOU MEAN YOU'RE NOT CHIHAYA?
DARN IT! WHERE COULD HE BE?!
SHE'S SEARCHING FOR ME?
BUT WHY?
I'VE NEVER SEEN HER BEFORE IN MY LIFE!

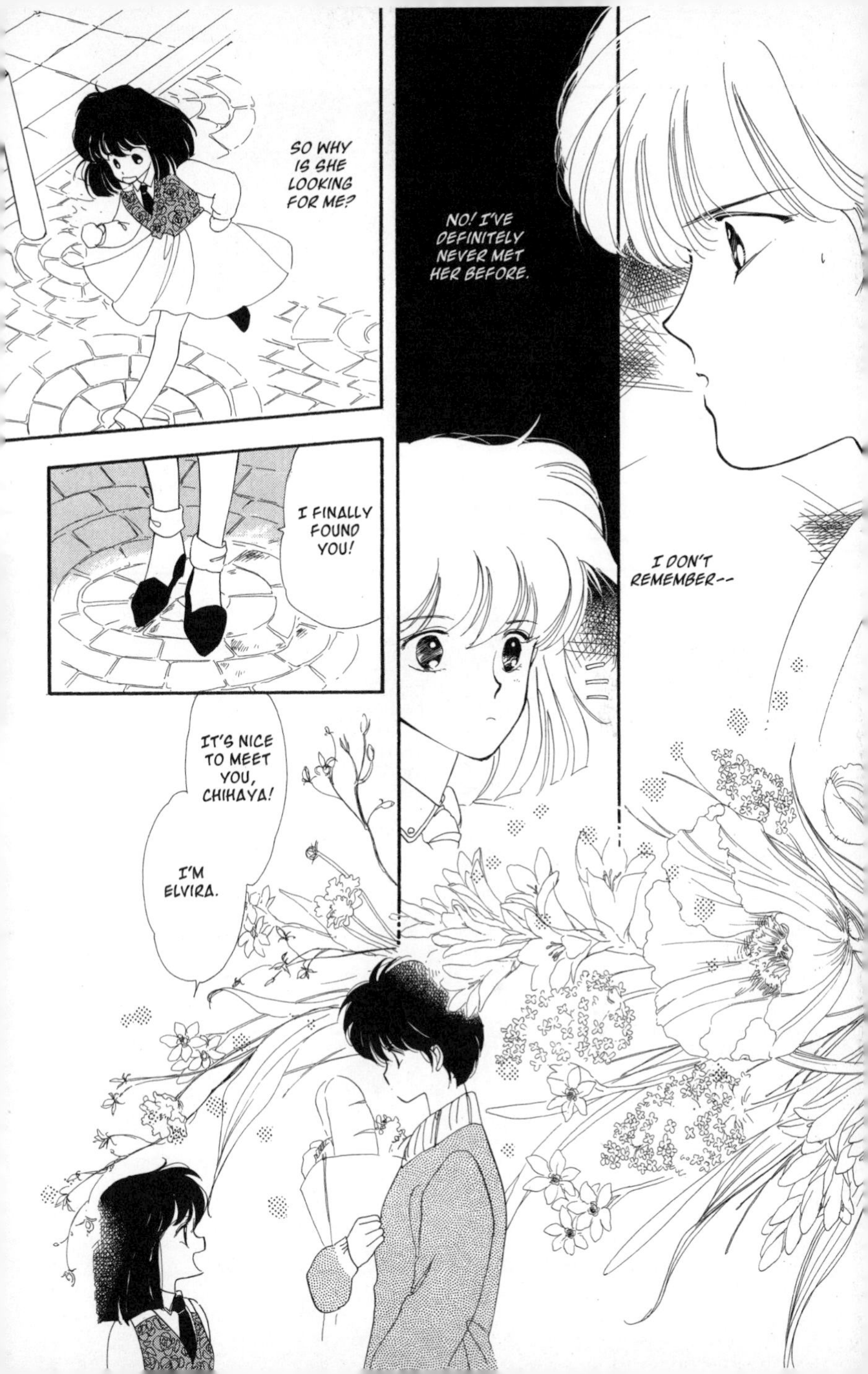
NO! I'VE DEFINITELY NEVER MET HER BEFORE.
I DON'T REMEMBER--
SO WHY IS SHE LOOKING FOR ME?
I FINALLY FOUND YOU!
IT'S NICE TO MEET YOU, CHIHAYA!
I'M ELVIRA.

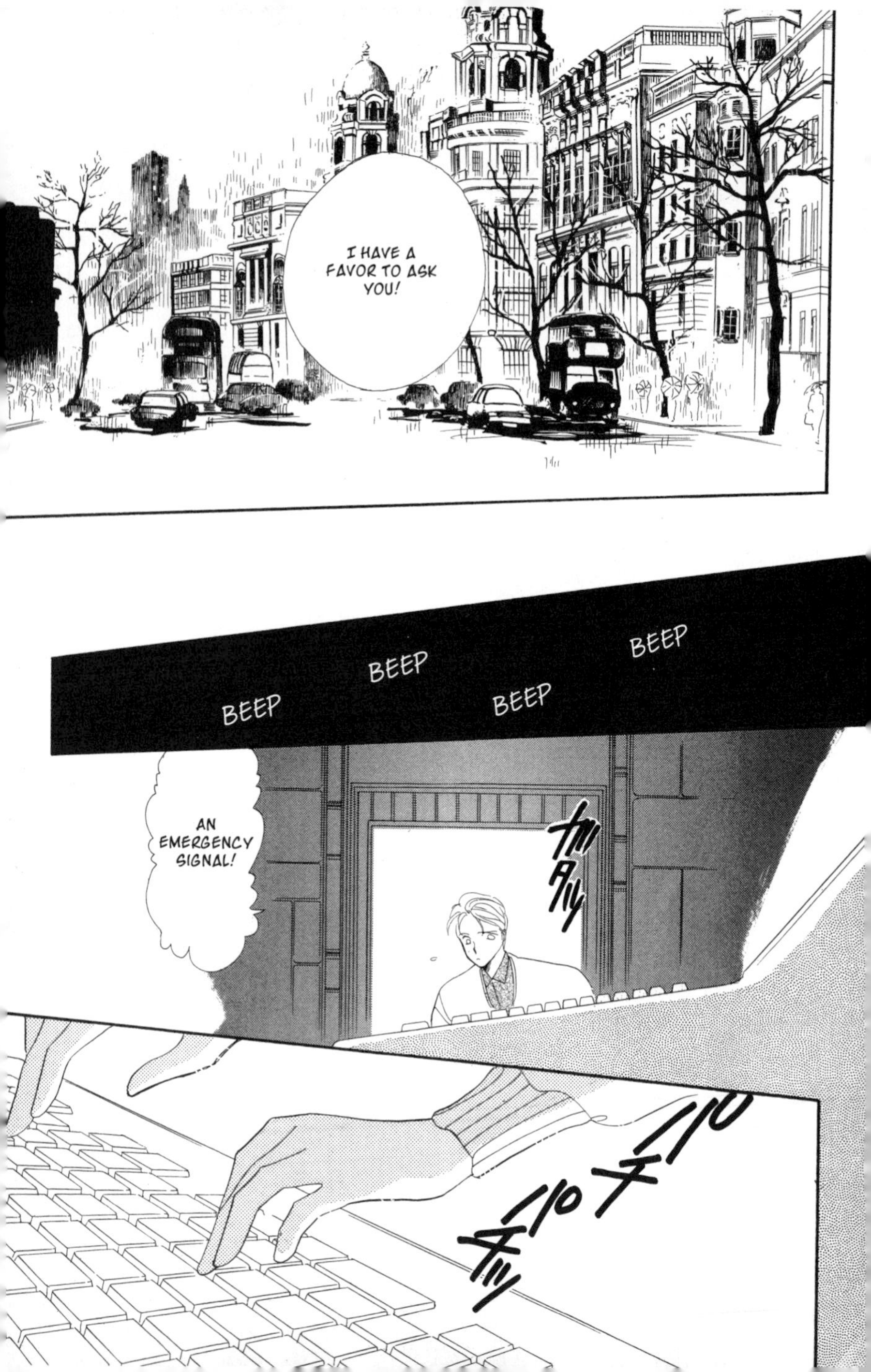
I HAVE A FAVOR TO ASK YOU!
BEEP
BEEP
BEEP
BEEP
AN EMERGENCY SIGNAL!

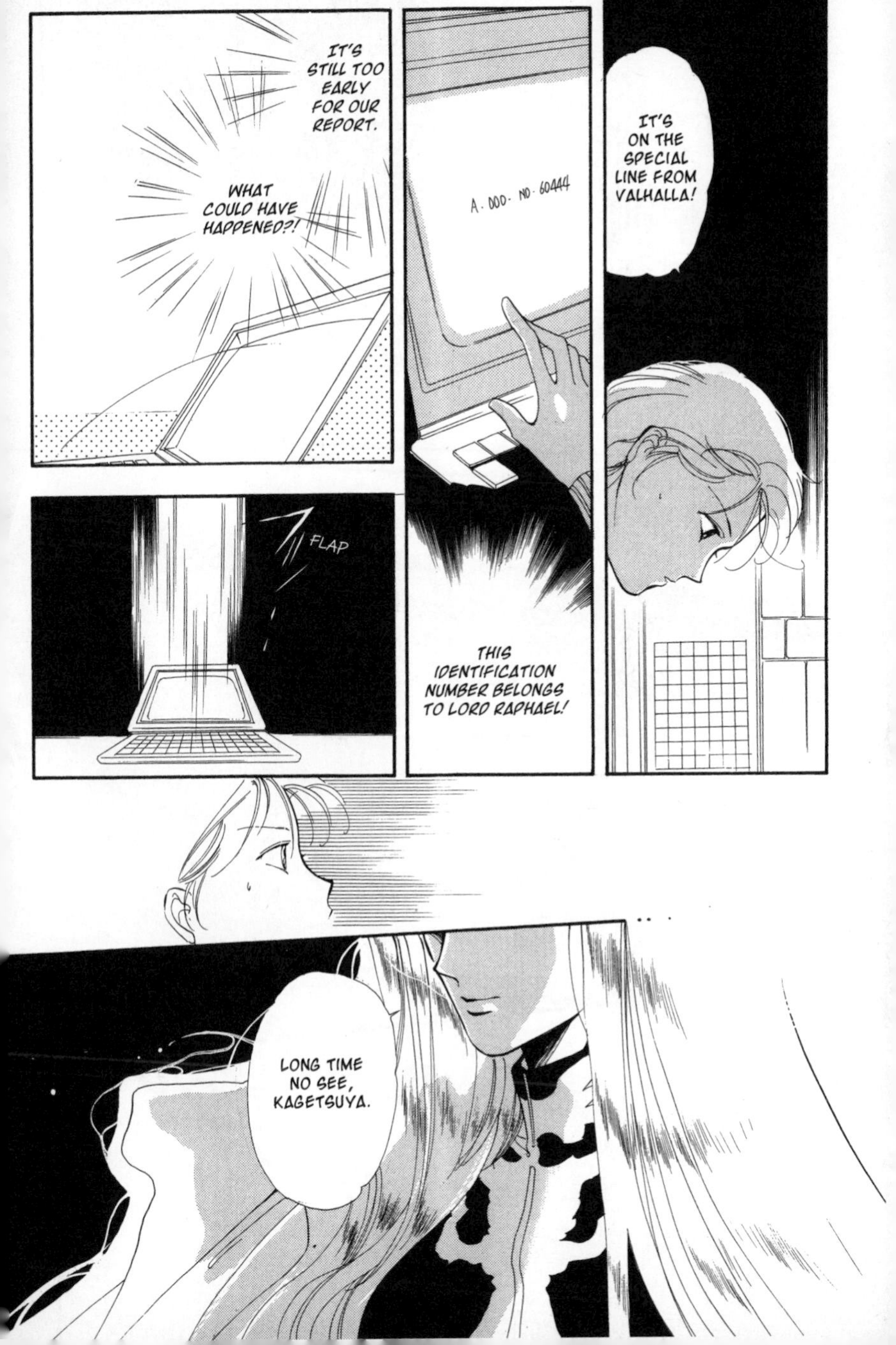
IT'S ON THE SPECIAL LINE FROM VALHALLA!
A.000-NO-60444
THIS IDENTIFICATION NUMBER BELONGS TO LORD RAPHAEL!
IT'S STILL TOO EARLY FOR OUR REPORT.
WHAT COULD HAVE HAPPENED?!
FLAP
...
LONG TIME NO SEE, KAGETSUYA.

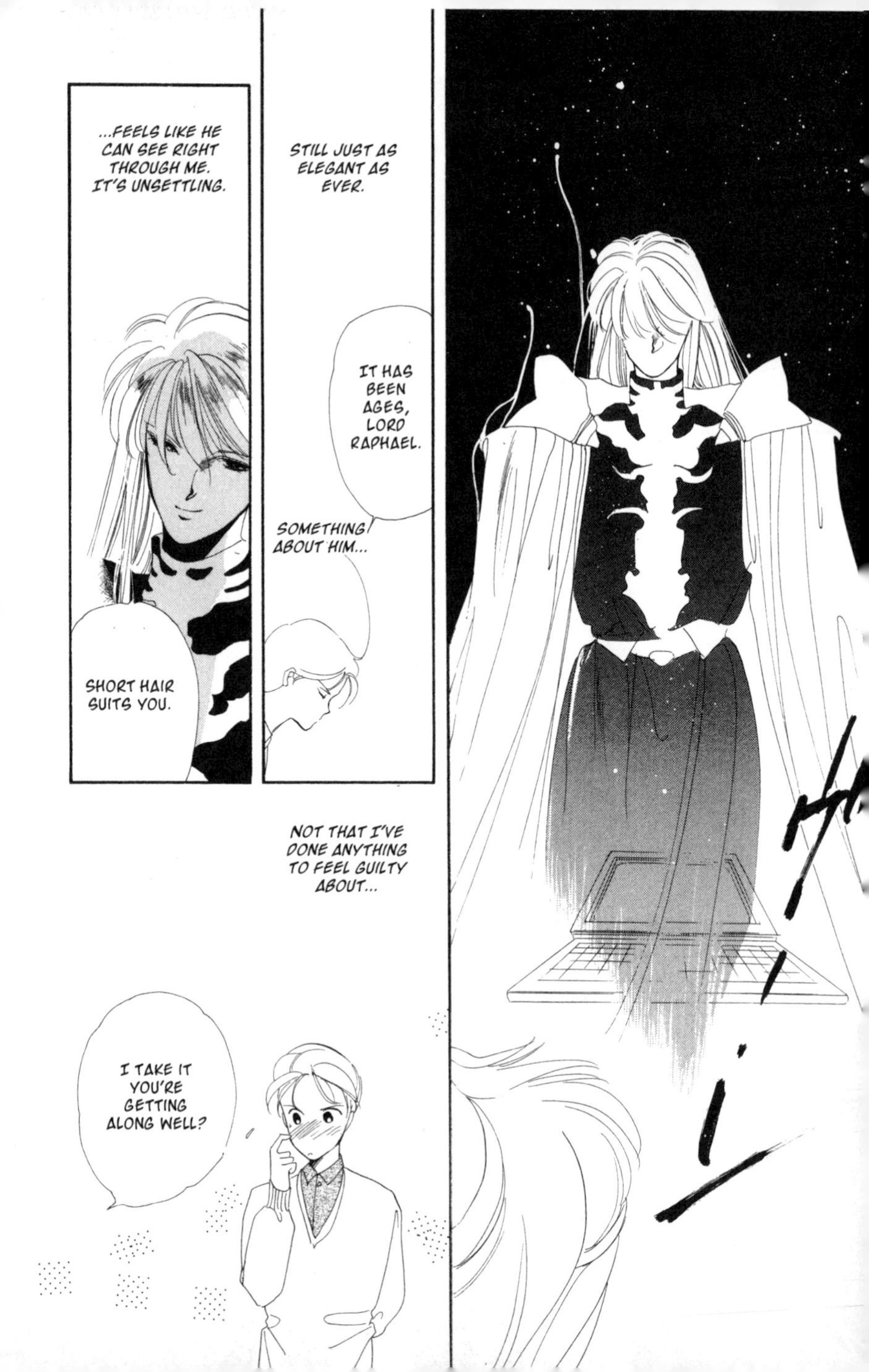
STILL JUST AS ELEGANT AS EVER.
IT HAS BEEN AGES, LORD RAPHAEL.
SOMETHING ABOUT HIM...
...FEELS LIKE HE CAN SEE RIGHT THROUGH ME. IT'S UNSETTLING.
SHORT HAIR SUITS YOU.
NOT THAT I'VE DONE ANYTHING TO FEEL GUILTY ABOUT...
I TAKE IT YOU'RE GETTING ALONG WELL?

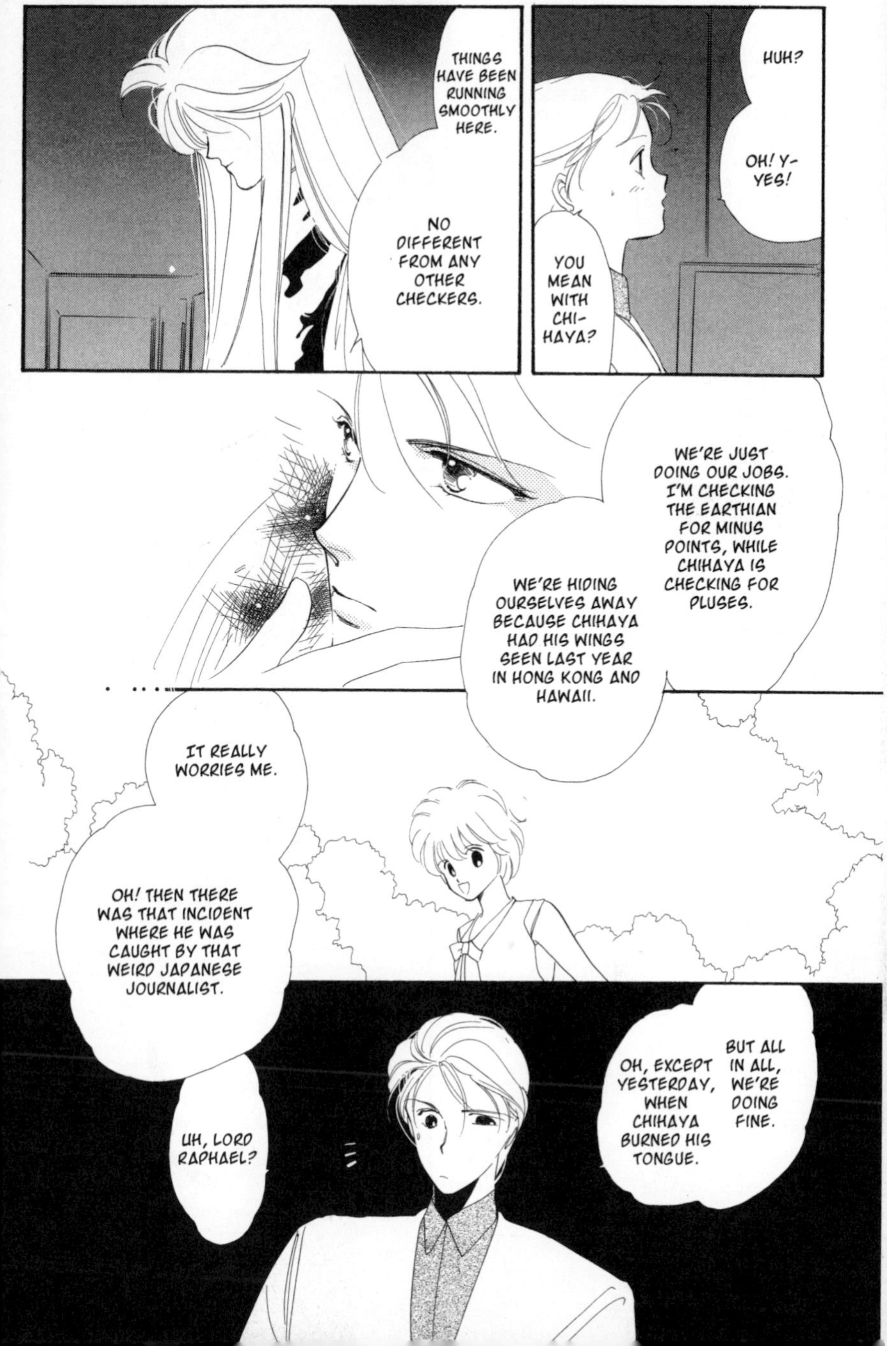
HUH?
OH! Y-YES!
YOU MEAN WITH CHI-HAYA?
THINGS HAVE BEEN RUNNING SMOOTHLY HERE.
NO DIFFERENT FROM ANY OTHER CHECKERS.
WE'RE JUST DOING OUR JOBS. I'M CHECKING THE EARTHIAN FOR MINUS POINTS, WHILE CHIHAYA IS CHECKING FOR PLUSES.
WE'RE HIDING OURSELVES AWAY BECAUSE CHIHAYA HAD HIS WINGS SEEN LAST YEAR IN HONG KONG AND HAWAII.
. ...
IT REALLY WORRIES ME.
OH! THEN THERE WAS THAT INCIDENT WHERE HE WAS CAUGHT BY THAT WEIRD JAPANESE JOURNALIST.
BUT ALL IN ALL, WE'RE DOING FINE.
OH, EXCEPT YESTERDAY, WHEN CHIHAYA BURNED HIS TONGUE.
UH, LORD RAPHAEL?

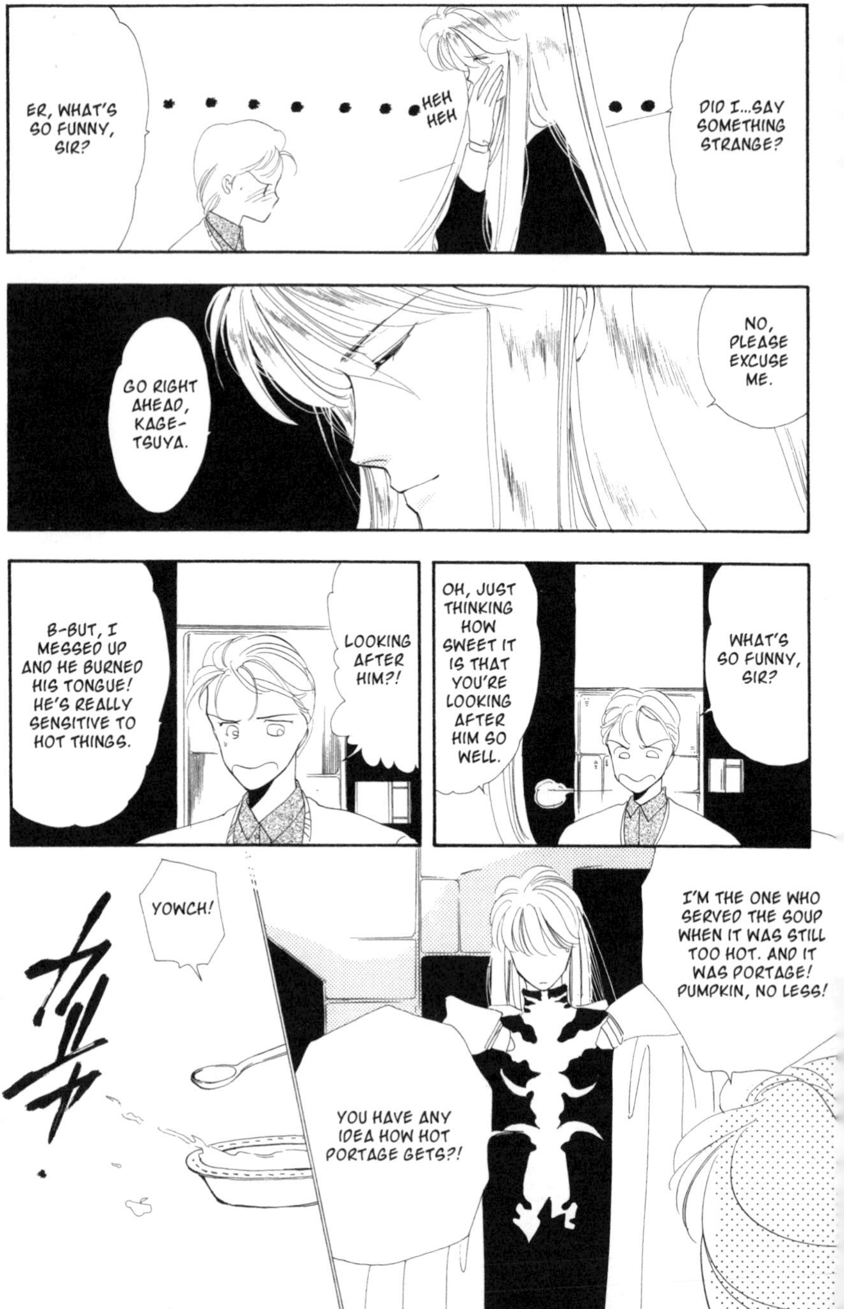
DID I...SAY SOMETHING STRANGE?
• •
HEH HEH
• • • • • • •
ER, WHAT'S SO FUNNY, SIR?
NO, PLEASE EXCUSE ME.
GO RIGHT AHEAD, KAGE-TSUYA.
WHAT'S SO FUNNY, SIR?
OH, JUST THINKING HOW SWEET IT IS THAT YOU'RE LOOKING AFTER HIM SO WELL.
LOOKING AFTER HIM?!
B-BUT, I MESSED UP AND HE BURNED HIS TONGUE! HE'S REALLY SENSITIVE TO HOT THINGS.
I'M THE ONE WHO SERVED THE SOUP WHEN IT WAS STILL TOO HOT. AND IT WAS PORTAGE! PUMPKIN, NO LESS!
YOU HAVE ANY IDEA HOW HOT PORTAGE GETS?!
YOWCH!

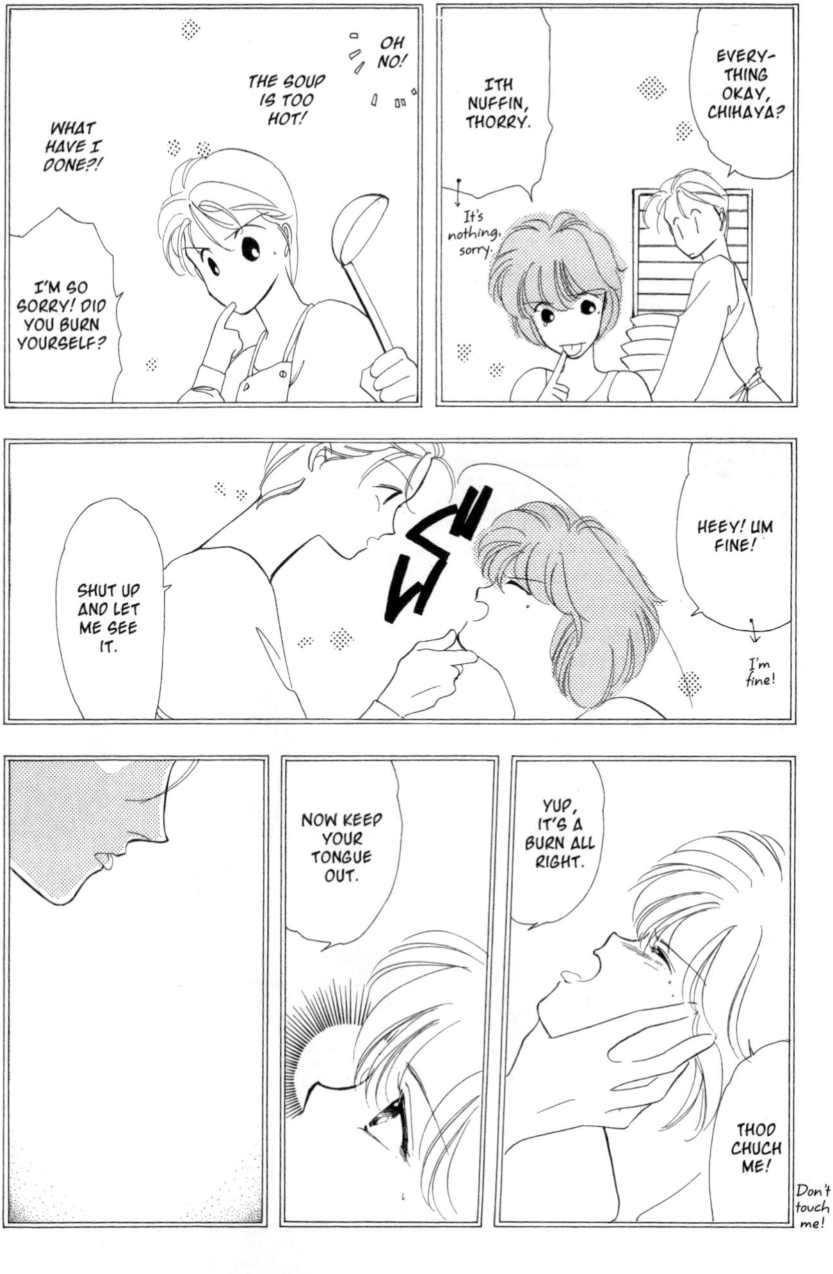
EVERY-THING OKAY, CHIHAYA?
ITH NUFFIN, THORRY.
It's nothing, sorry.
OH NO!
THE SOUP IS TOO HOT!
WHAT HAVE I DONE?!
I'M SO SORRY! DID YOU BURN YOURSELF?
HEEY! UM FINE!
I'm fine!
SHUT UP AND LET ME SEE IT.
YUP, IT'S A BURN ALL RIGHT.
THOO CHUCH ME!
Don't touch me!
NOW KEEP YOUR TONGUE OUT.

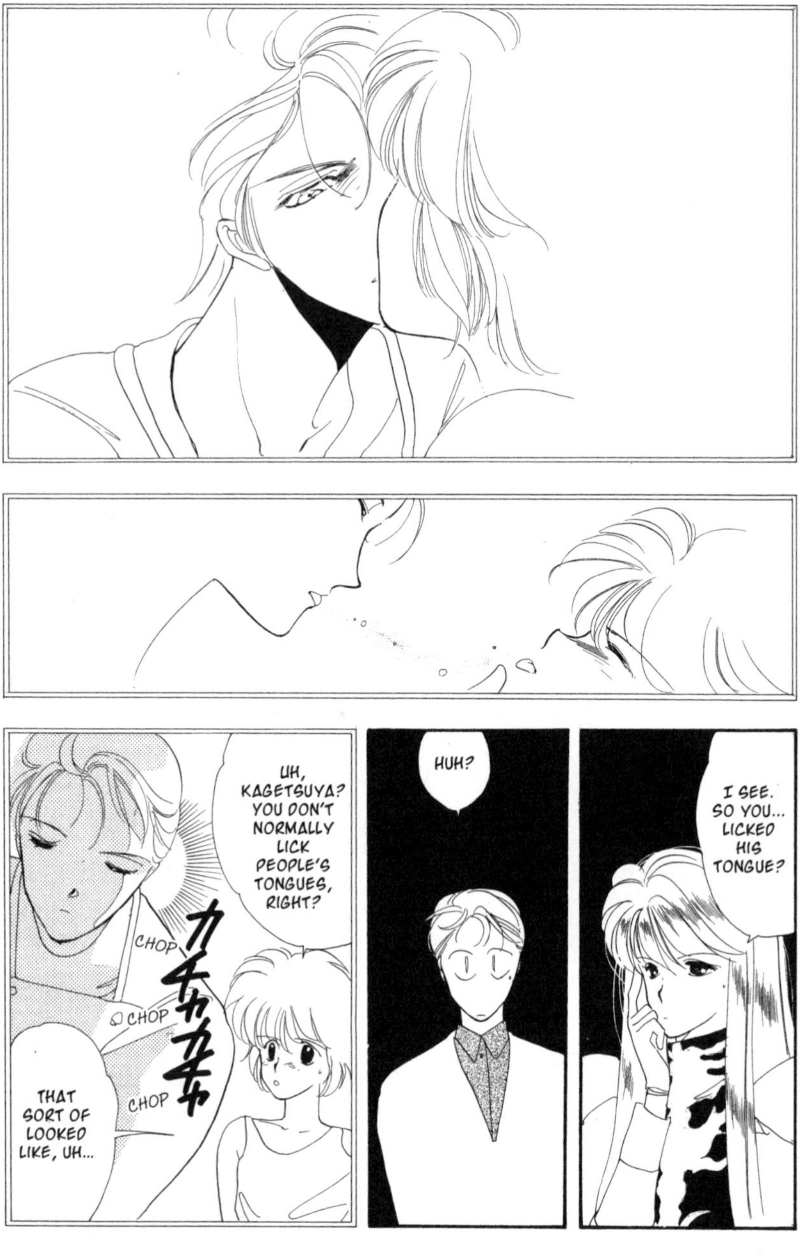
I SEE. SO YOU... LICKED HIS TONGUE?
HUH?
UH, KAGETSUYA? YOU DON'T NORMALLY LICK PEOPLE'S TONGUES, RIGHT?
CHOP
CHOP
CHOP
THAT SORT OF LOOKED LIKE, UH...

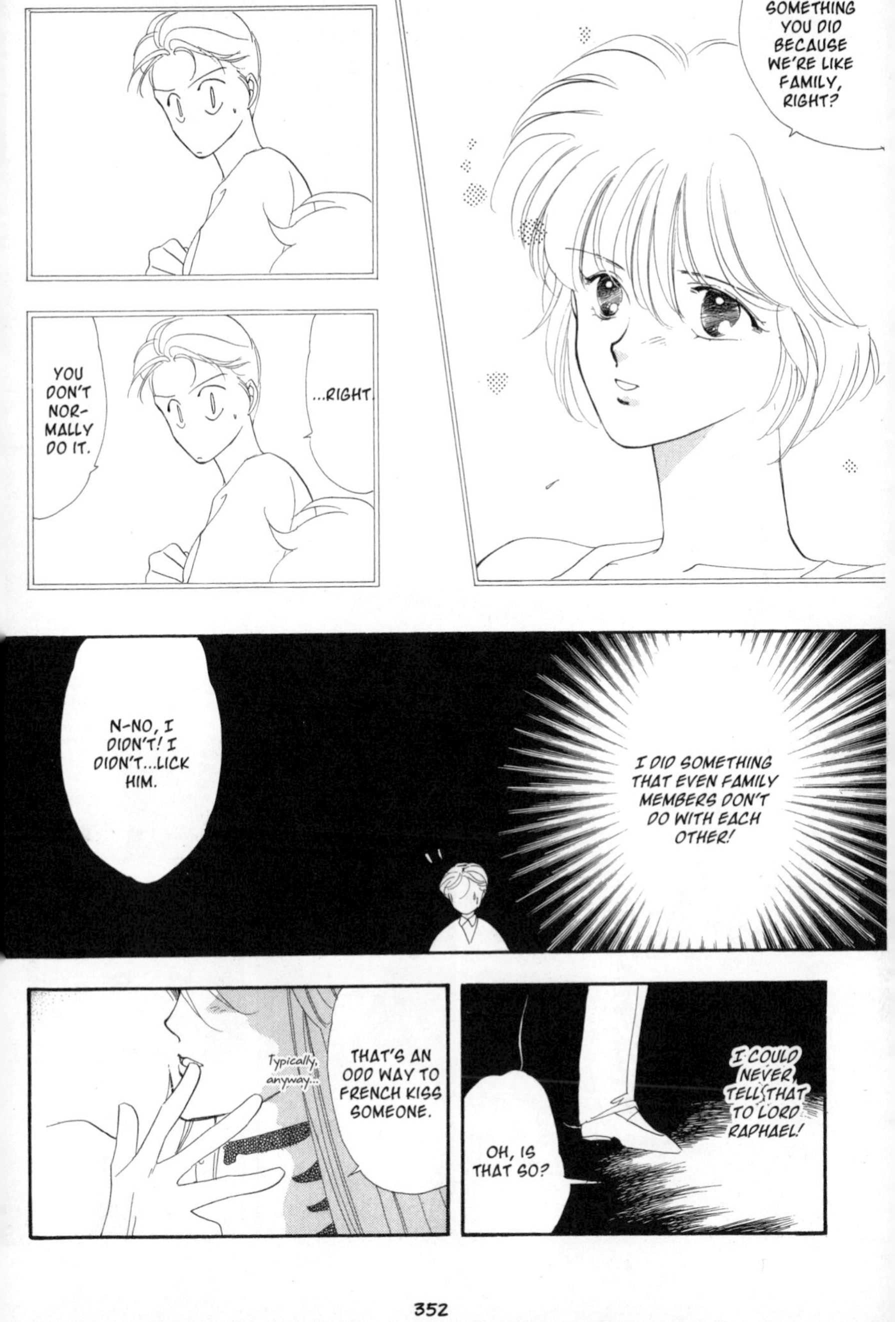
IT'S SOMETHING YOU DID BECAUSE WE'RE LIKE FAMILY, RIGHT?
...RIGHT.
YOU DON'T NOR-MALLY DO IT.
I DID SOMETHING THAT EVEN FAMILY MEMBERS DON'T DO WITH EACH OTHER!
N-NO, I DIDN'T! I DIDN'T...LICK HIM.
I COULD NEVER TELL THAT TO LORD RAPHAEL!
OH, IS THAT SO?
THAT'S AN ODD WAY TO FRENCH KISS SOMEONE.
Typically, anyway...

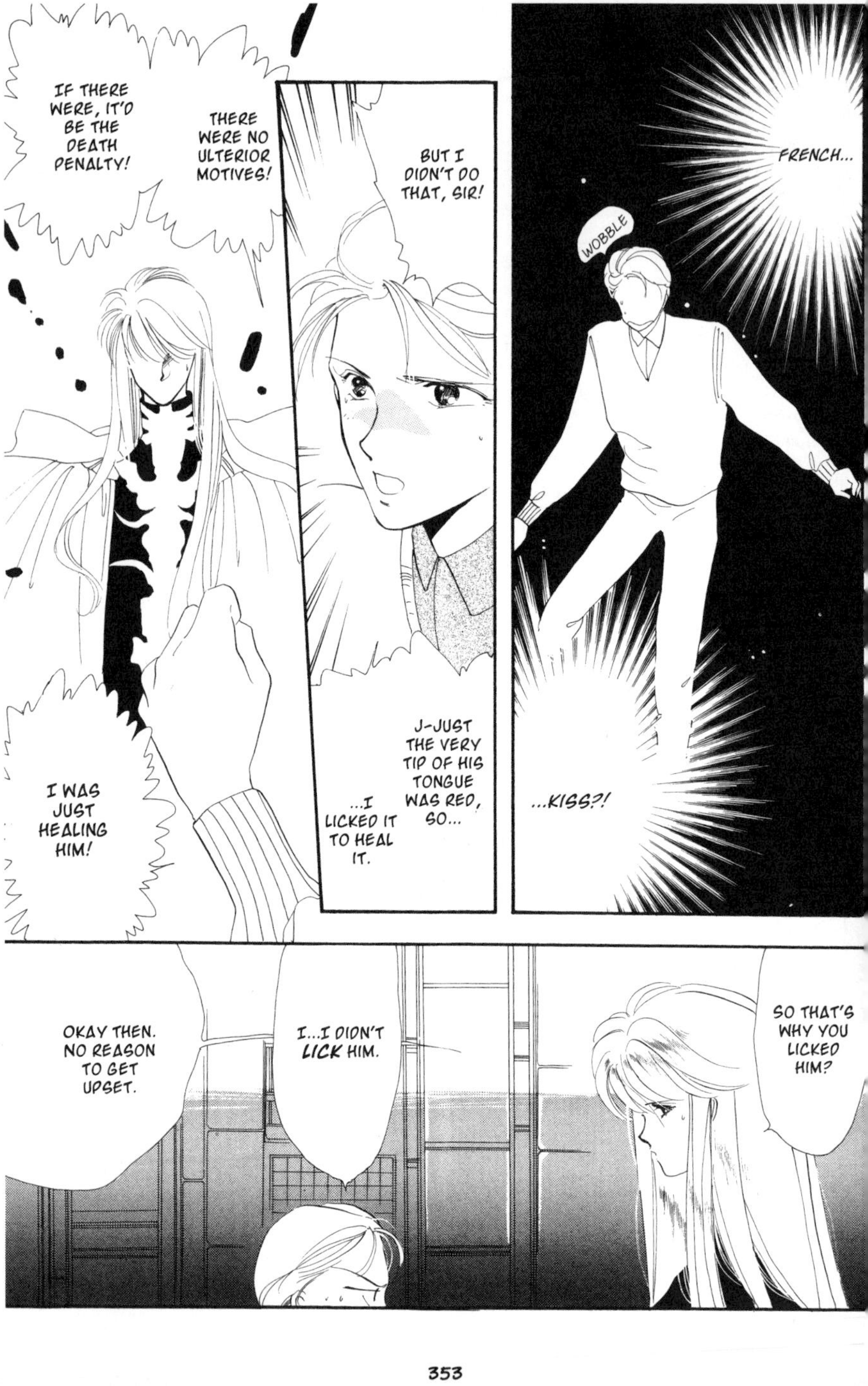
FRENCH...
WOBBLE
...KISS?!
BUT I DIDN'T DO THAT, SIR!
J-JUST THE VERY TIP OF HIS TONGUE WAS RED, SO...
...I LICKED IT TO HEAL IT.
THERE WERE NO ULTERIOR MOTIVES!
IF THERE WERE, IT'D BE THE DEATH PENALTY!
I WAS JUST HEALING HIM!
SO THAT'S WHY YOU LICKED HIM?
I...I DIDN'T *LICK* HIM.
OKAY THEN. NO REASON TO GET UPSET.

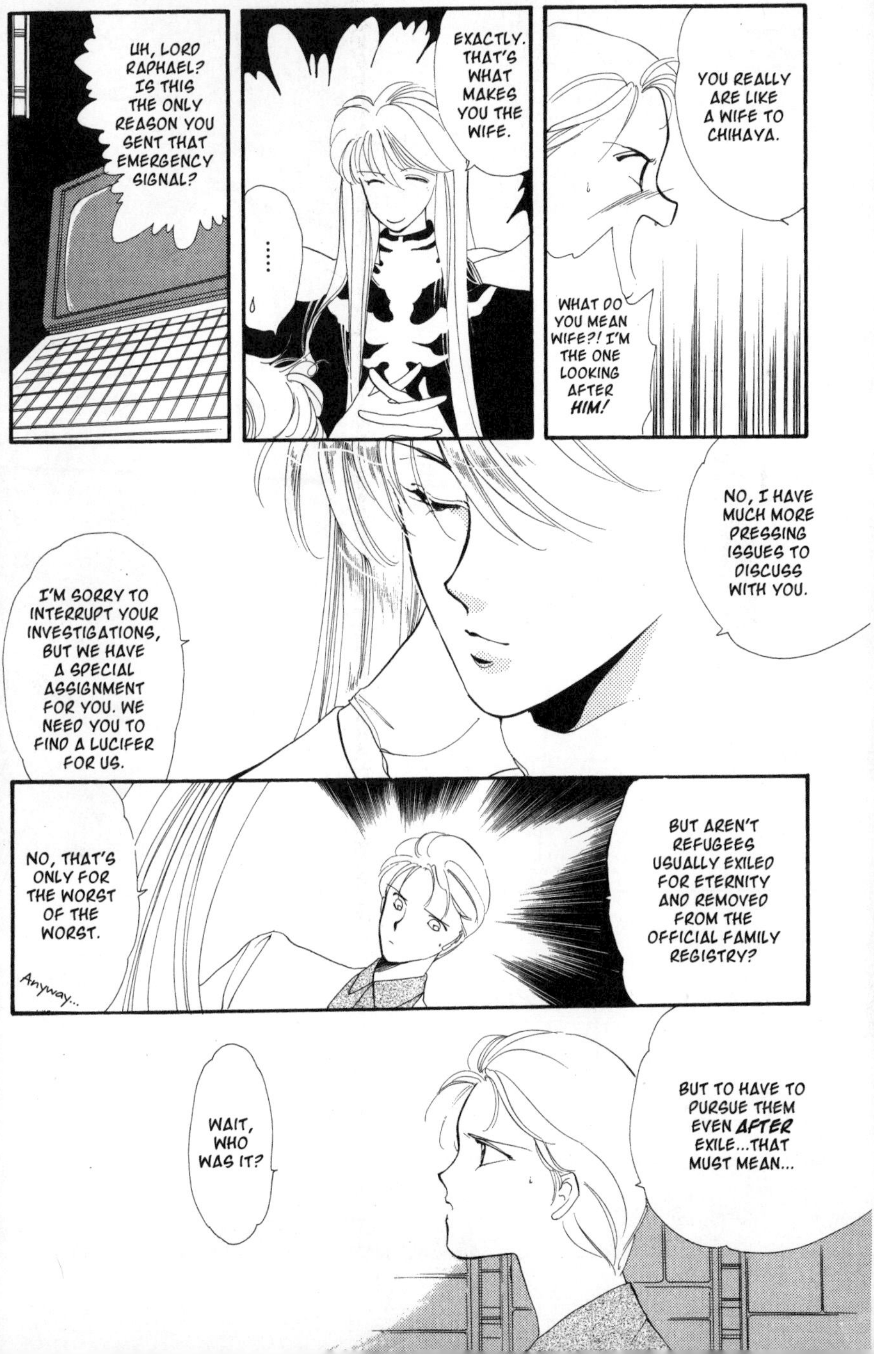
YOU REALLY ARE LIKE A WIFE TO CHIHAYA.
WHAT DO YOU MEAN WIFE?! I'M THE ONE LOOKING AFTER *HIM!*
EXACTLY. THAT'S WHAT MAKES YOU THE WIFE.
……
UH, LORD RAPHAEL? IS THIS THE ONLY REASON YOU SENT THAT EMERGENCY SIGNAL?
NO, I HAVE MUCH MORE PRESSING ISSUES TO DISCUSS WITH YOU.
I'M SORRY TO INTERRUPT YOUR INVESTIGATIONS, BUT WE HAVE A SPECIAL ASSIGNMENT FOR YOU. WE NEED YOU TO FIND A LUCIFER FOR US.
BUT AREN'T REFUGEES USUALLY EXILED FOR ETERNITY AND REMOVED FROM THE OFFICIAL FAMILY REGISTRY?
NO, THAT'S ONLY FOR THE WORST OF THE WORST.
Anyway...
BUT TO HAVE TO PURSUE THEM EVEN ***AFTER*** EXILE...THAT MUST MEAN...
WAIT, WHO WAS IT?

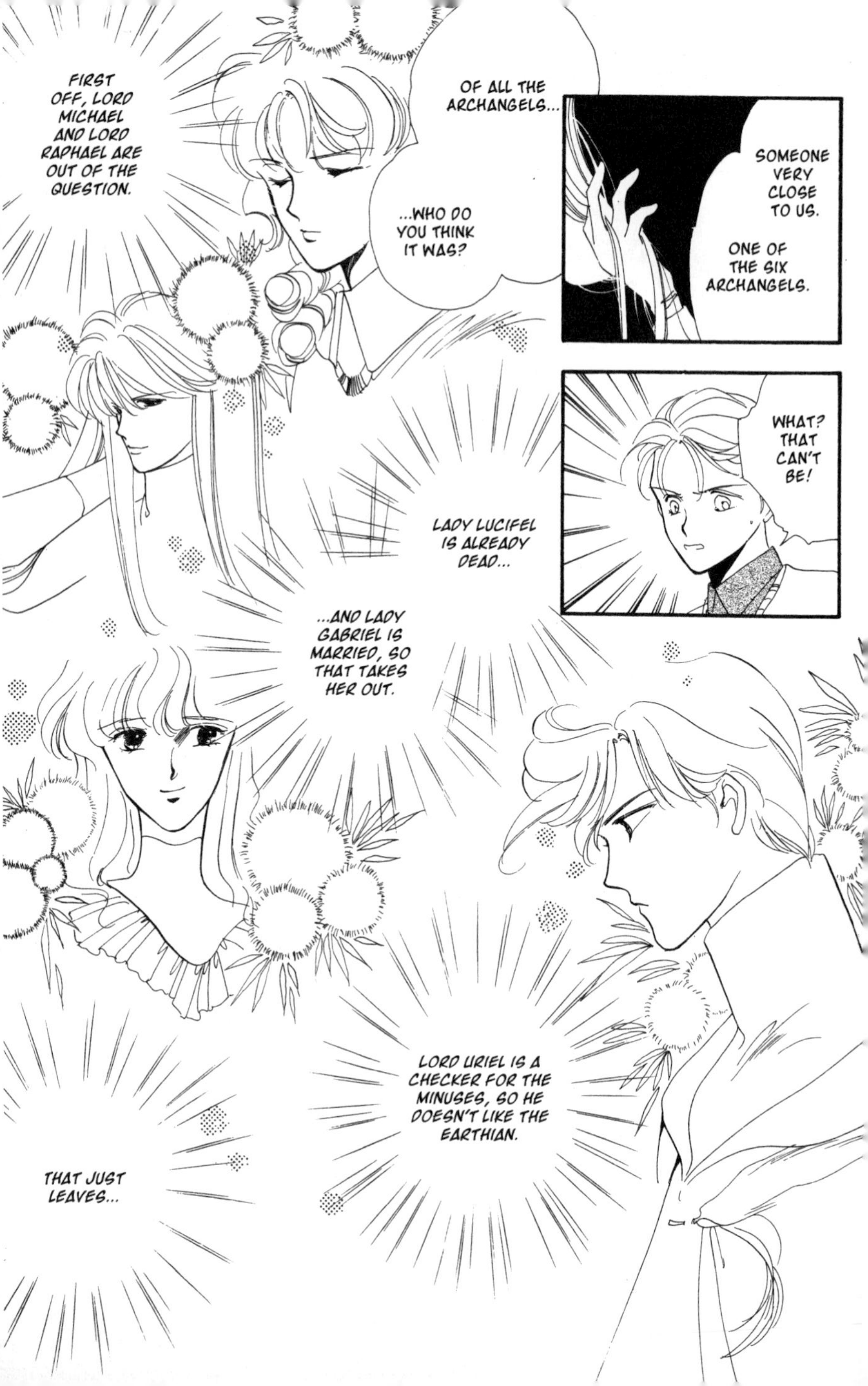
SOMEONE VERY CLOSE TO US.
ONE OF THE SIX ARCHANGELS.
OF ALL THE ARCHANGELS...
...WHO DO YOU THINK IT WAS?
WHAT? THAT CAN'T BE!
FIRST OFF, LORD MICHAEL AND LORD RAPHAEL ARE OUT OF THE QUESTION.
LADY LUCIFEL IS ALREADY DEAD...
...AND LADY GABRIEL IS MARRIED, SO THAT TAKES HER OUT.
LORD URIEL IS A CHECKER FOR THE MINUSES, SO HE DOESN'T LIKE THE EARTHIAN.
THAT JUST LEAVES...

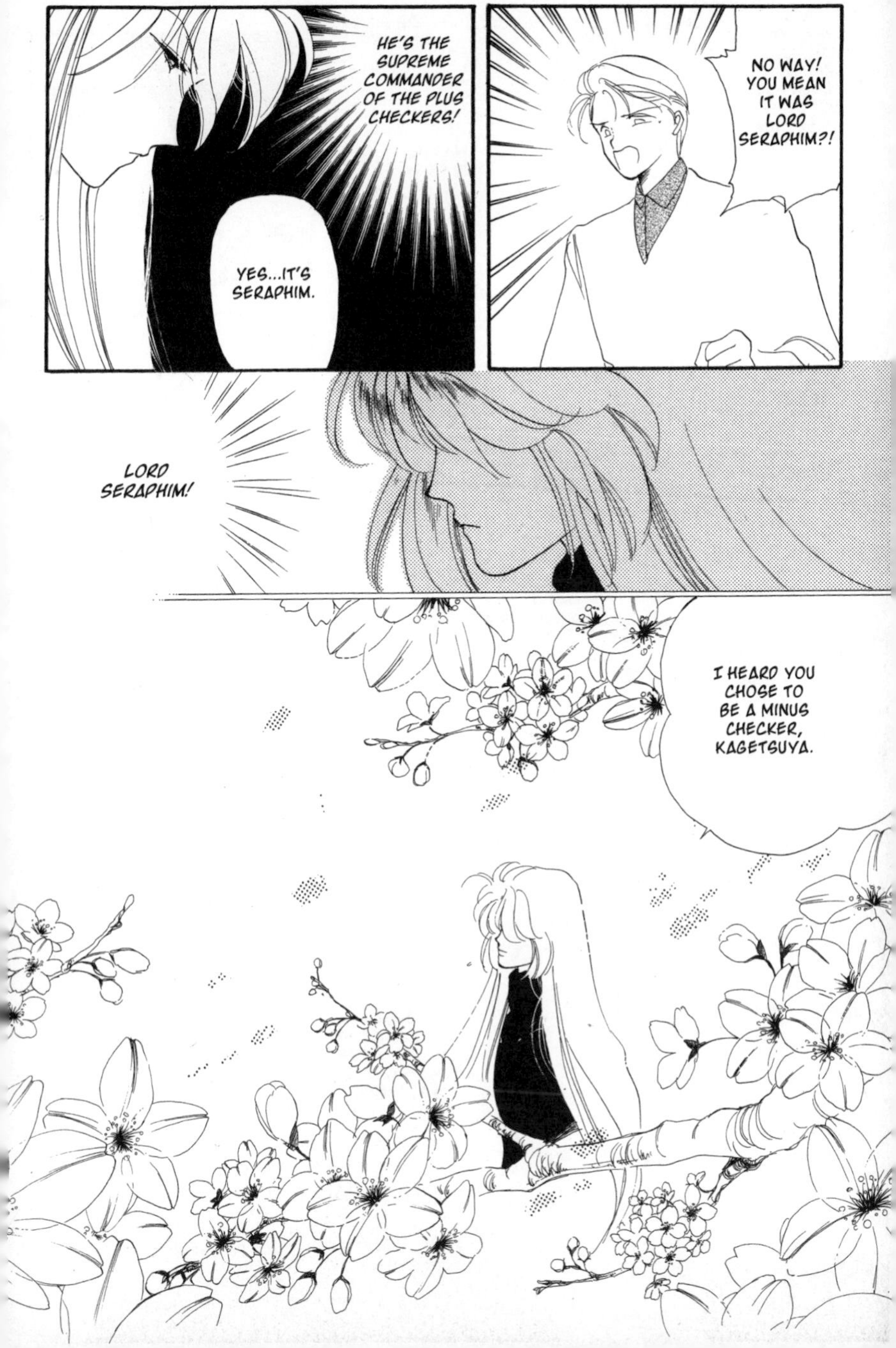
NO WAY! YOU MEAN IT WAS LORD SERAPHIM?!
HE'S THE SUPREME COMMANDER OF THE PLUS CHECKERS!
YES...IT'S SERAPHIM.
LORD SERAPHIM!
I HEARD YOU CHOSE TO BE A MINUS CHECKER, KAGETSUYA.

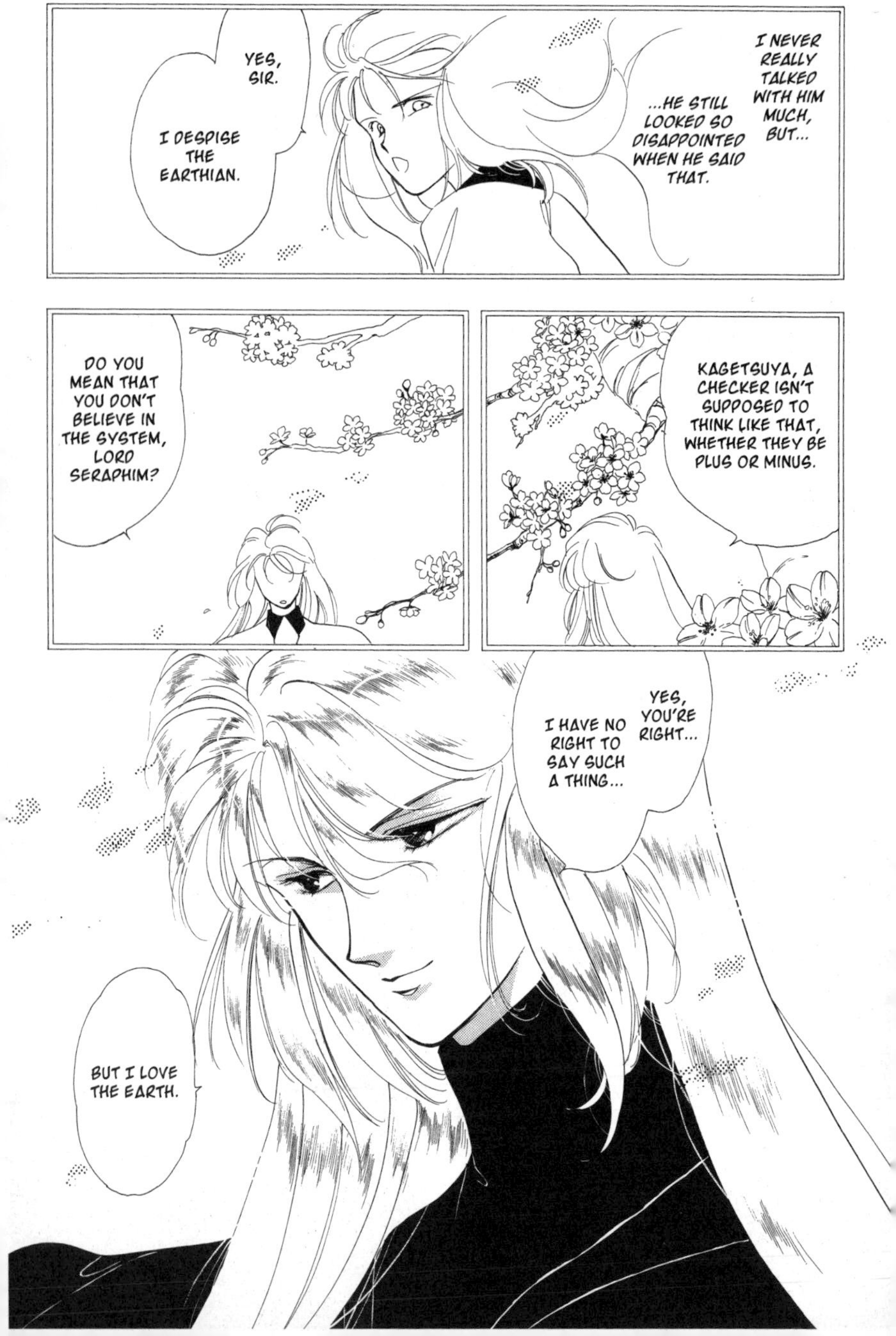
I NEVER REALLY TALKED WITH HIM MUCH, BUT...
...HE STILL LOOKED SO DISAPPOINTED WHEN HE SAID THAT.
YES, SIR.
I DESPISE THE EARTHIAN.
KAGETSUYA, A CHECKER ISN'T SUPPOSED TO THINK LIKE THAT, WHETHER THEY BE PLUS OR MINUS.
DO YOU MEAN THAT YOU DON'T BELIEVE IN THE SYSTEM, LORD SERAPHIM?
YES, YOU'RE RIGHT...
I HAVE NO RIGHT TO SAY SUCH A THING...
BUT I LOVE THE EARTH.

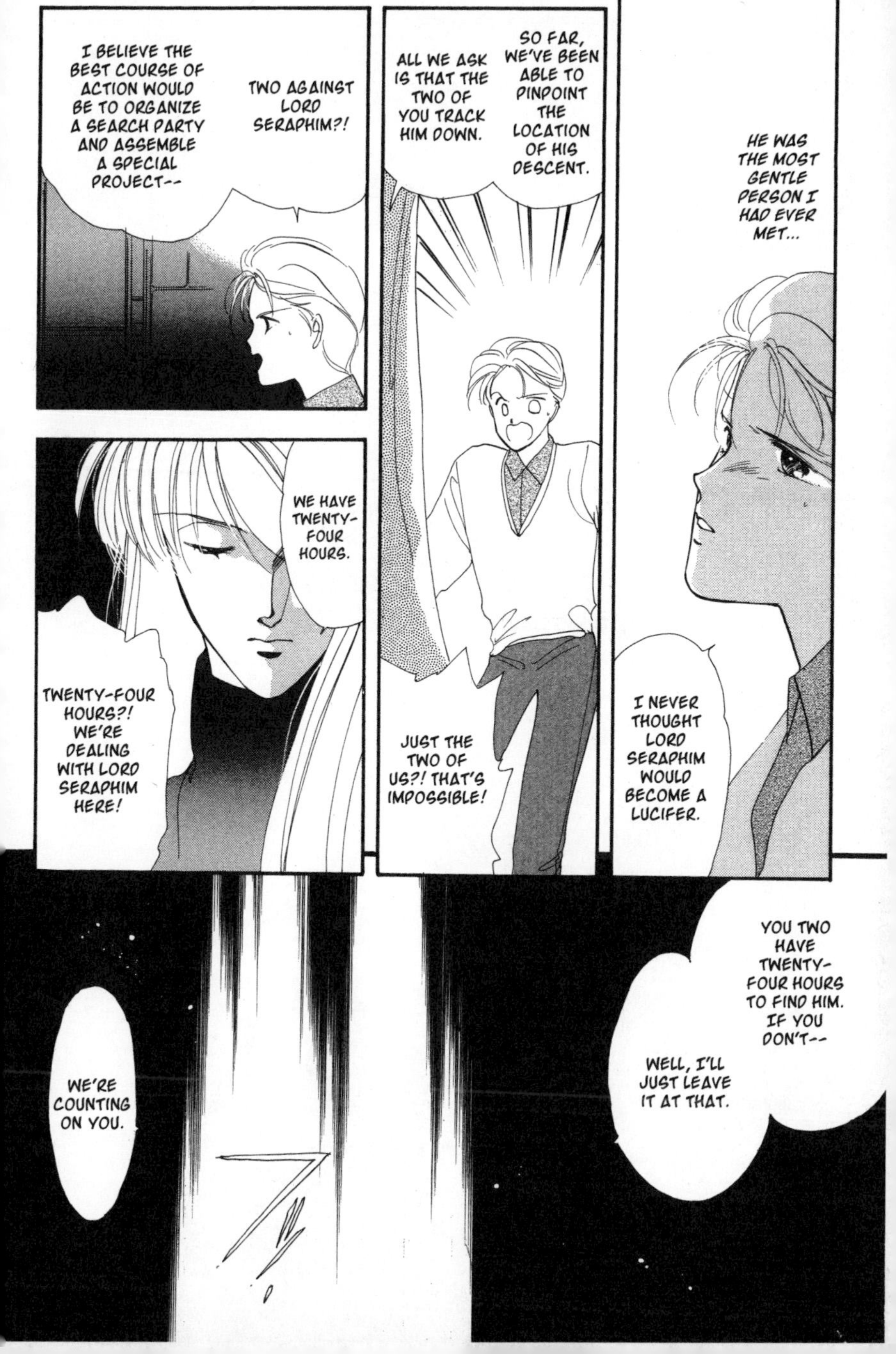
HE WAS THE MOST GENTLE PERSON I HAD EVER MET...
I NEVER THOUGHT LORD SERAPHIM WOULD BECOME A LUCIFER.
SO FAR, WE'VE BEEN ABLE TO PINPOINT THE LOCATION OF HIS DESCENT.
ALL WE ASK IS THAT THE TWO OF YOU TRACK HIM DOWN.
JUST THE TWO OF US?! THAT'S IMPOSSIBLE!
TWO AGAINST LORD SERAPHIM?!
I BELIEVE THE BEST COURSE OF ACTION WOULD BE TO ORGANIZE A SEARCH PARTY AND ASSEMBLE A SPECIAL PROJECT--
WE HAVE TWENTY-FOUR HOURS.
TWENTY-FOUR HOURS?! WE'RE DEALING WITH LORD SERAPHIM HERE!
YOU TWO HAVE TWENTY-FOUR HOURS TO FIND HIM. IF YOU DON'T--
WELL, I'LL JUST LEAVE IT AT THAT.
WE'RE COUNTING ON YOU.

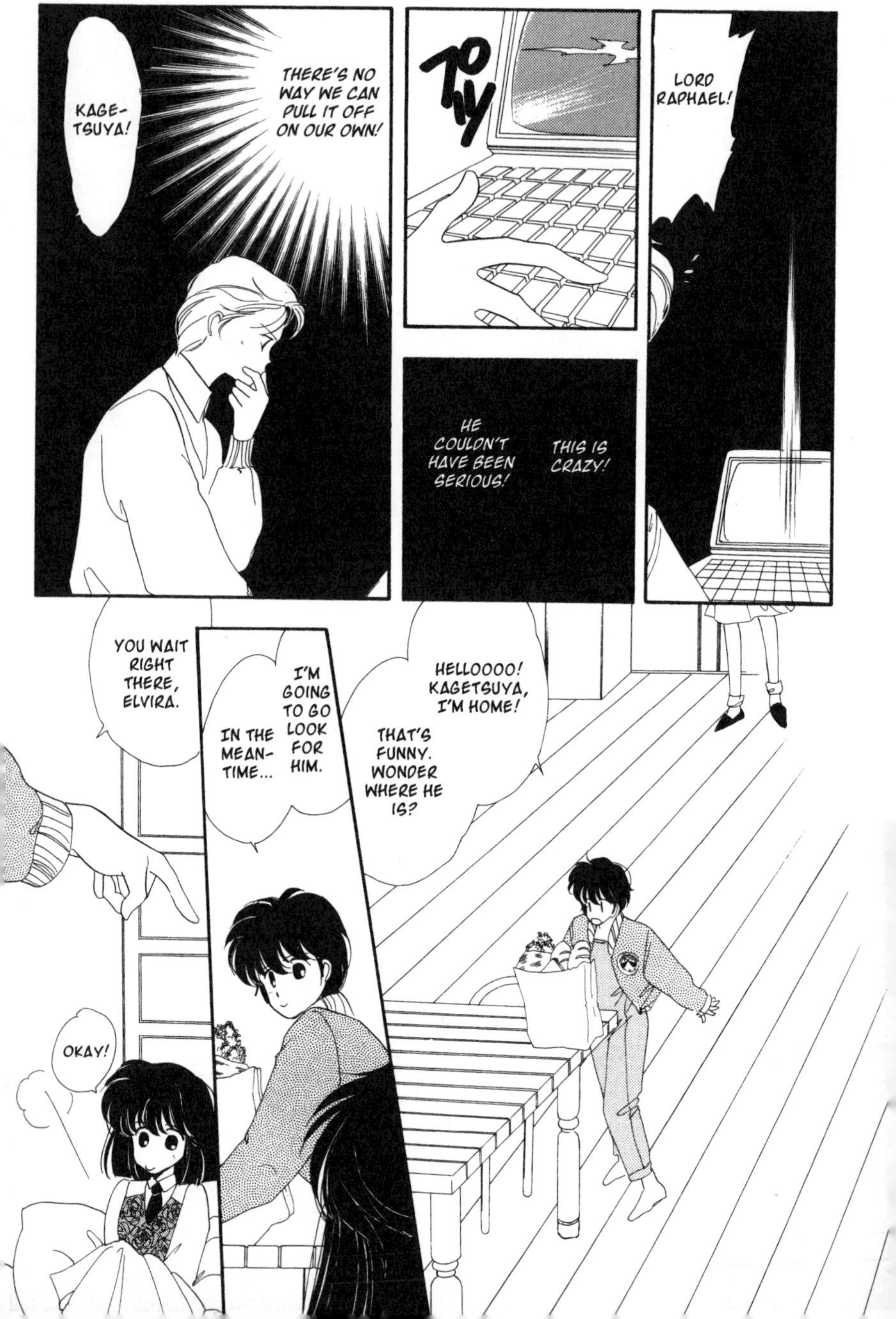
LORD RAPHAEL!
THIS IS CRAZY!
HE COULDN'T HAVE BEEN SERIOUS!
THERE'S NO WAY WE CAN PULL IT OFF ON OUR OWN!
KAGE-TSUYA!
HELLOOOO! KAGETSUYA, I'M HOME!
THAT'S FUNNY. WONDER WHERE HE IS?
I'M GOING TO GO LOOK FOR HIM.
IN THE MEAN-TIME...
YOU WAIT RIGHT THERE, ELVIRA.
OKAY!

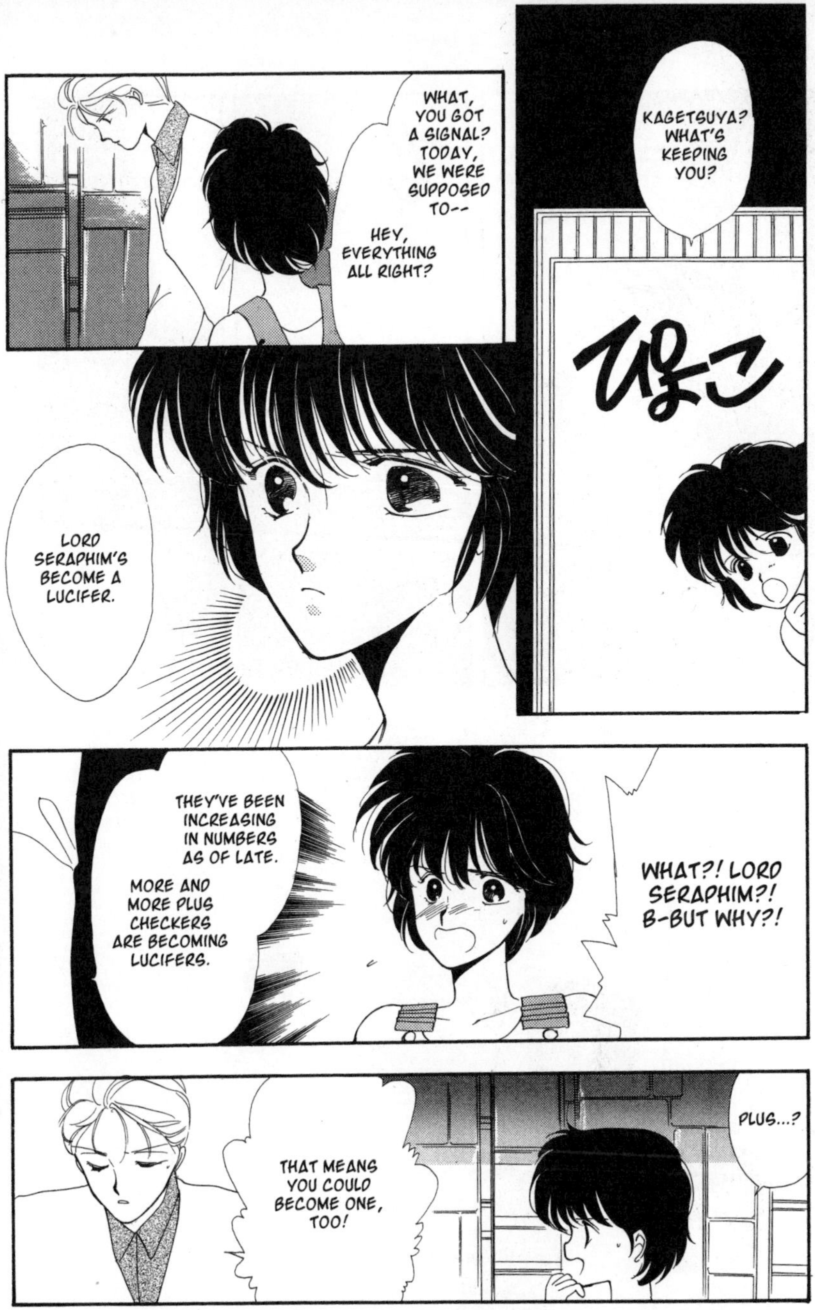
KAGETSUYA? WHAT'S KEEPING YOU?
ひよこ
WHAT, YOU GOT A SIGNAL? TODAY, WE WERE SUPPOSED TO--
HEY, EVERYTHING ALL RIGHT?
LORD SERAPHIM'S BECOME A LUCIFER.
WHAT?! LORD SERAPHIM?! B-BUT WHY?!
THEY'VE BEEN INCREASING IN NUMBERS AS OF LATE.
MORE AND MORE PLUS CHECKERS ARE BECOMING LUCIFERS.
PLUS...?
THAT MEANS YOU COULD BECOME ONE, TOO!

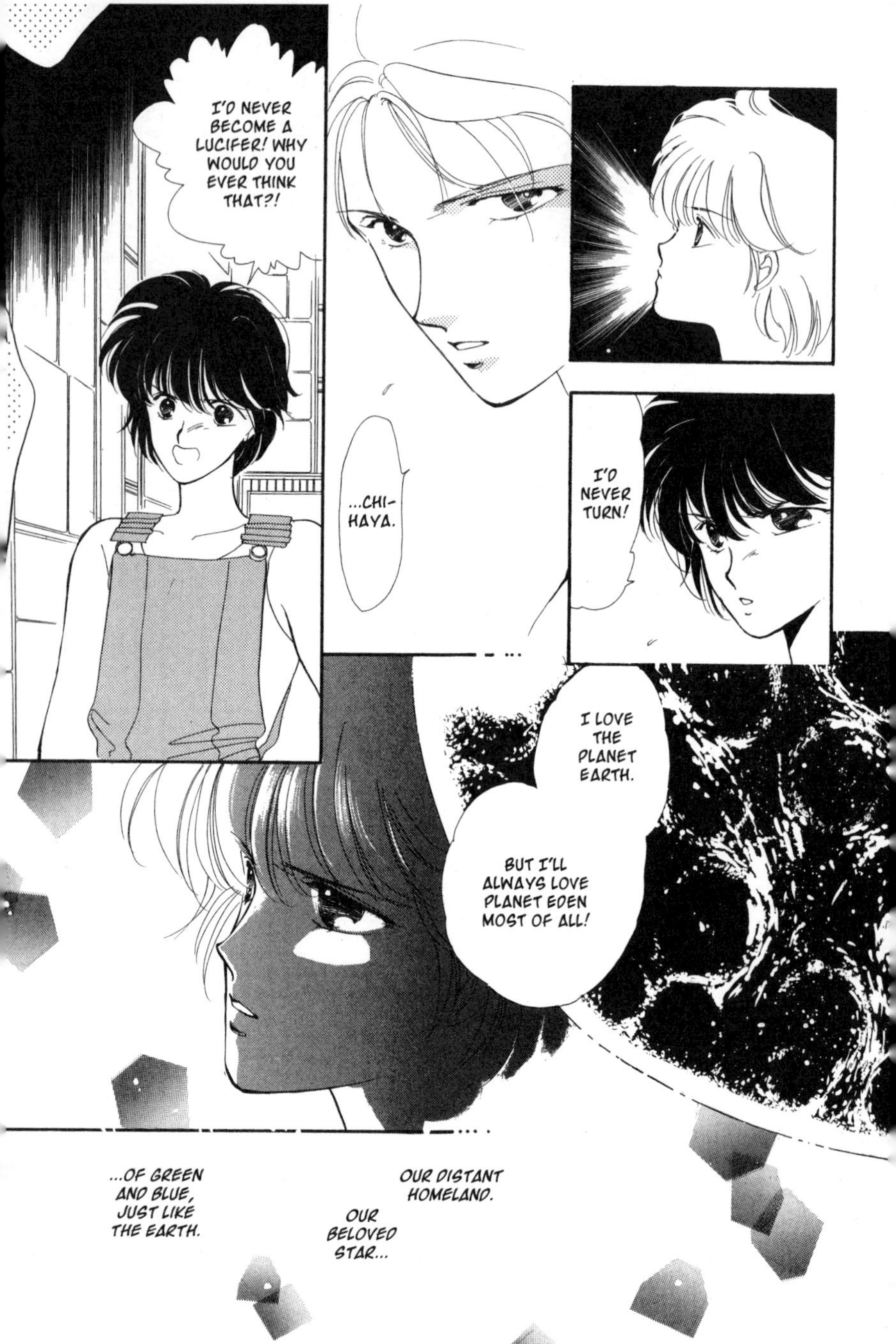
I'D NEVER TURN!
...CHI-HAYA.
I'D NEVER BECOME A LUCIFER! WHY WOULD YOU EVER THINK THAT?!
I LOVE THE PLANET EARTH.
BUT I'LL ALWAYS LOVE PLANET EDEN MOST OF ALL!
OUR DISTANT HOMELAND.
OUR BELOVED STAR...
...OF GREEN AND BLUE, JUST LIKE THE EARTH.

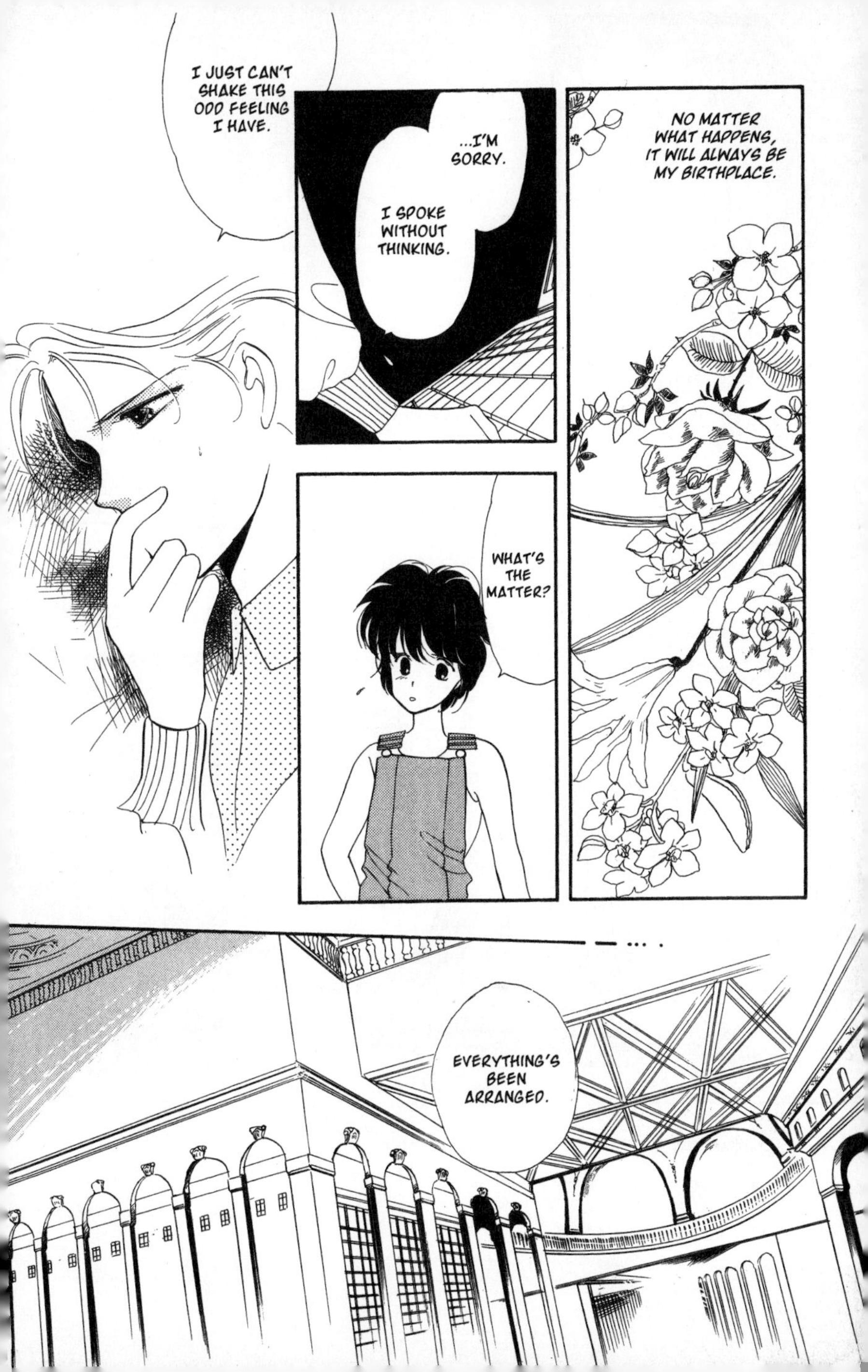
NO MATTER WHAT HAPPENS, IT WILL ALWAYS BE MY BIRTHPLACE.
...I'M SORRY.
I SPOKE WITHOUT THINKING.
WHAT'S THE MATTER?
I JUST CAN'T SHAKE THIS ODD FEELING I HAVE.
EVERYTHING'S BEEN ARRANGED.

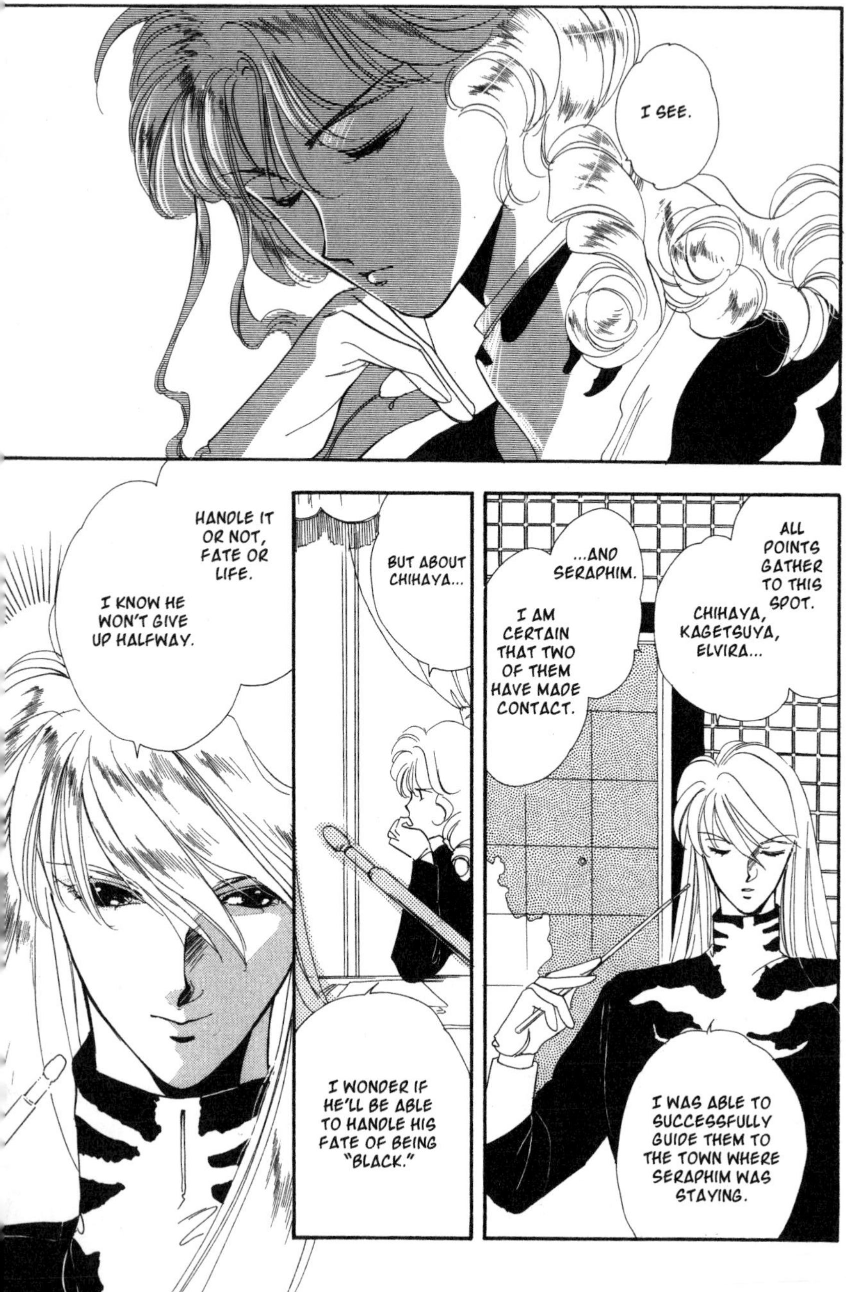
I SEE.
ALL POINTS GATHER TO THIS SPOT.
CHIHAYA, KAGETSUYA, ELVIRA...
...AND SERAPHIM.
I AM CERTAIN THAT TWO OF THEM HAVE MADE CONTACT.
I WAS ABLE TO SUCCESSFULLY GUIDE THEM TO THE TOWN WHERE SERAPHIM WAS STAYING.
BUT ABOUT CHIHAYA...
I WONDER IF HE'LL BE ABLE TO HANDLE HIS FATE OF BEING "BLACK."
HANDLE IT OR NOT, FATE OR LIFE.
I KNOW HE WON'T GIVE UP HALFWAY.

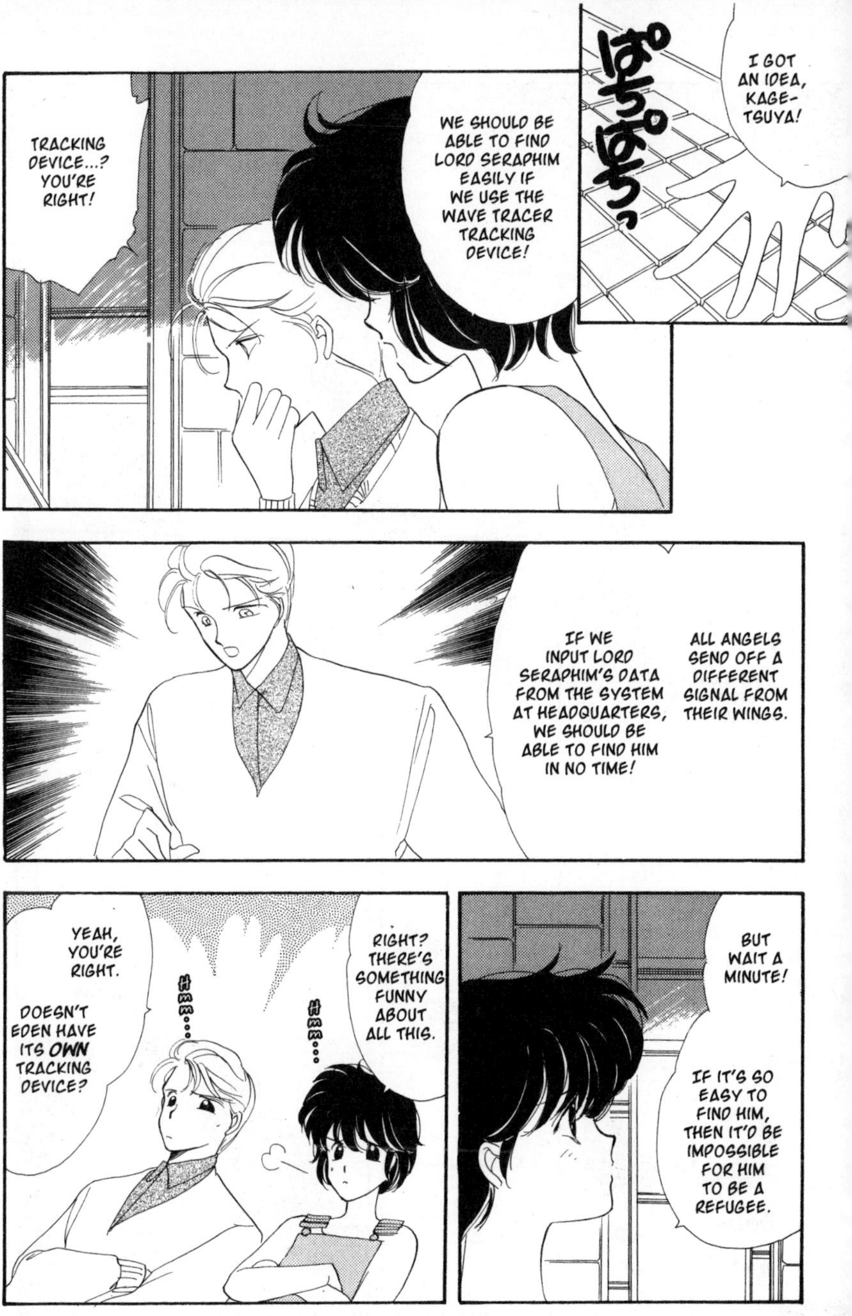
ぽちぽちっ
I GOT AN IDEA, KAGE-TSUYA!
WE SHOULD BE ABLE TO FIND LORD SERAPHIM EASILY IF WE USE THE WAVE TRACER TRACKING DEVICE!
TRACKING DEVICE...? YOU'RE RIGHT!
ALL ANGELS SEND OFF A DIFFERENT SIGNAL FROM THEIR WINGS.
IF WE INPUT LORD SERAPHIM'S DATA FROM THE SYSTEM AT HEADQUARTERS, WE SHOULD BE ABLE TO FIND HIM IN NO TIME!
BUT WAIT A MINUTE!
IF IT'S SO EASY TO FIND HIM, THEN IT'D BE IMPOSSIBLE FOR HIM TO BE A REFUGEE.
RIGHT? THERE'S SOMETHING FUNNY ABOUT ALL THIS.
Hmm...
Hmm...
YEAH, YOU'RE RIGHT.
DOESN'T EDEN HAVE ITS *OWN* TRACKING DEVICE?

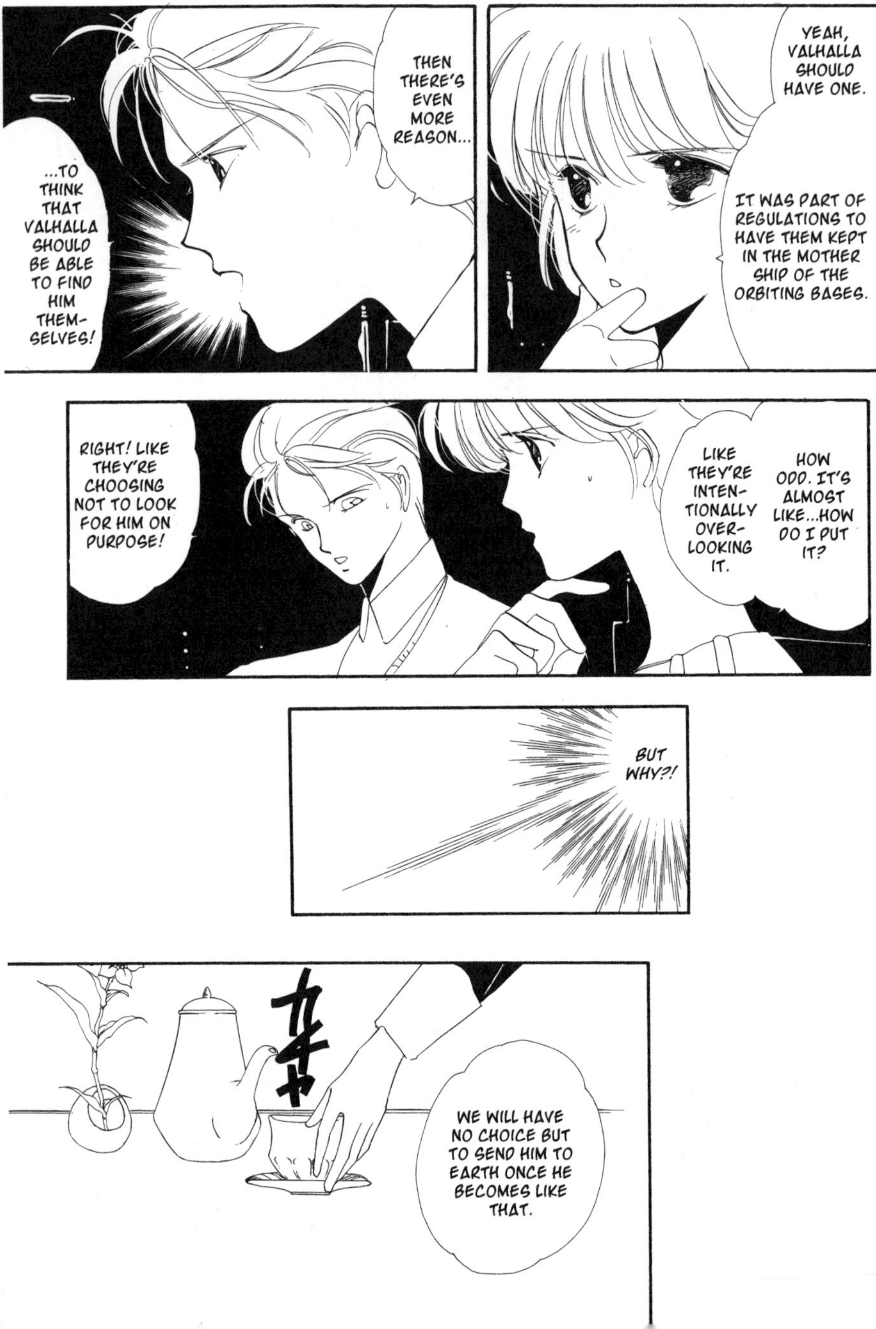
YEAH, VALHALLA SHOULD HAVE ONE.
IT WAS PART OF REGULATIONS TO HAVE THEM KEPT IN THE MOTHER SHIP OF THE ORBITING BASES.
THEN THERE'S EVEN MORE REASON...
...TO THINK THAT VALHALLA SHOULD BE ABLE TO FIND HIM THEM-SELVES!
HOW ODD. IT'S ALMOST LIKE...HOW DO I PUT IT?
LIKE THEY'RE INTEN-TIONALLY OVER-LOOKING IT.
RIGHT! LIKE THEY'RE CHOOSING NOT TO LOOK FOR HIM ON PURPOSE!
BUT WHY?!
カチャ
WE WILL HAVE NO CHOICE BUT TO SEND HIM TO EARTH ONCE HE BECOMES LIKE THAT.

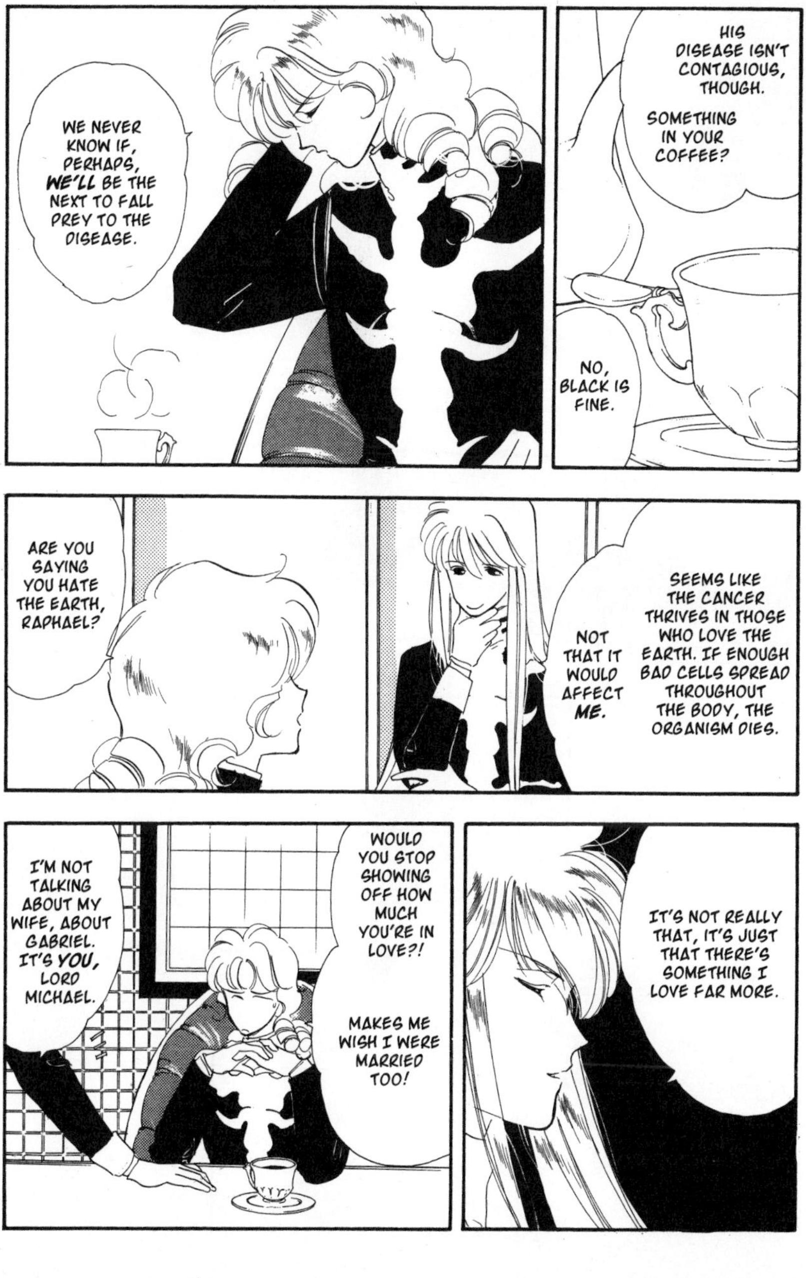
HIS DISEASE ISN'T CONTAGIOUS, THOUGH.
SOMETHING IN YOUR COFFEE?
NO, BLACK IS FINE.
WE NEVER KNOW IF, PERHAPS, **WE'LL** BE THE NEXT TO FALL PREY TO THE DISEASE.
SEEMS LIKE THE CANCER THRIVES IN THOSE WHO LOVE THE EARTH. IF ENOUGH BAD CELLS SPREAD THROUGHOUT THE BODY, THE ORGANISM DIES.
NOT THAT IT WOULD AFFECT **ME.**
ARE YOU SAYING YOU HATE THE EARTH, RAPHAEL?
IT'S NOT REALLY THAT, IT'S JUST THAT THERE'S SOMETHING I LOVE FAR MORE.
WOULD YOU STOP SHOWING OFF HOW MUCH YOU'RE IN LOVE?!
MAKES ME WISH I WERE MARRIED TOO!
I'M NOT TALKING ABOUT MY WIFE, ABOUT GABRIEL. IT'S **YOU,** LORD MICHAEL.

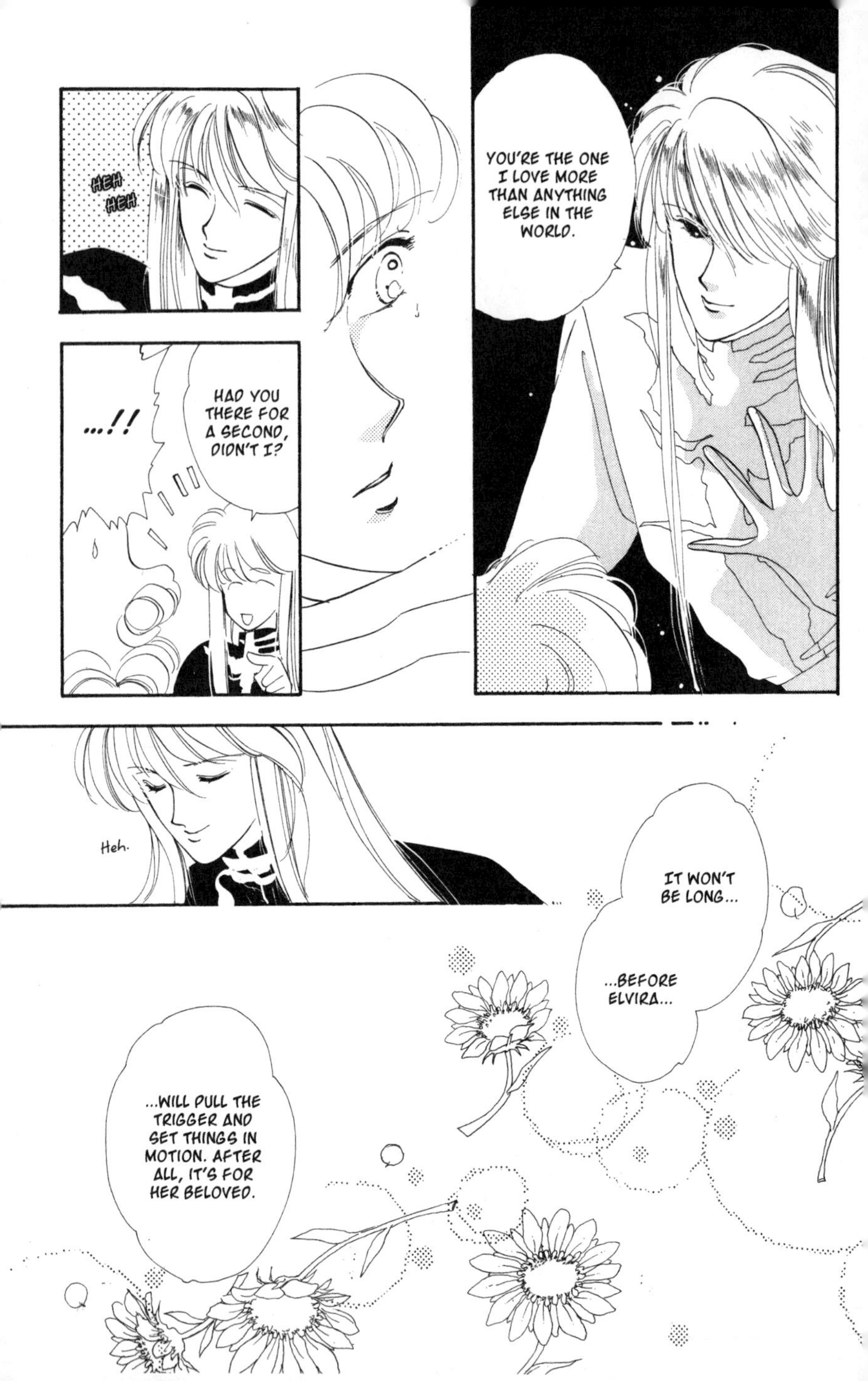
YOU'RE THE ONE I LOVE MORE THAN ANYTHING ELSE IN THE WORLD.
HEH HEH
HAD YOU THERE FOR A SECOND, DIDN'T I?
...!!
Heh.
IT WON'T BE LONG...
...BEFORE ELVIRA...
...WILL PULL THE TRIGGER AND SET THINGS IN MOTION. AFTER ALL, IT'S FOR HER BELOVED.

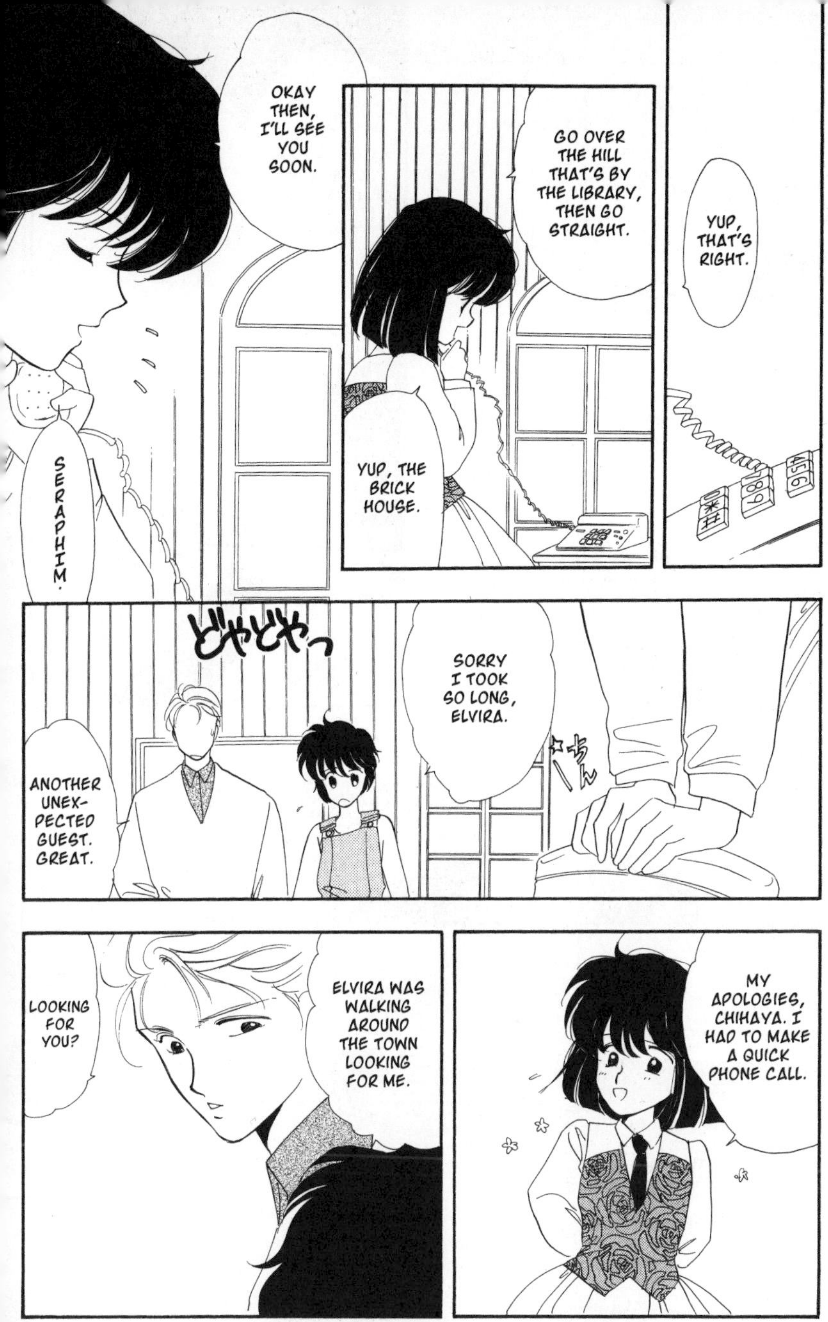
YUP, THAT'S RIGHT.
GO OVER THE HILL THAT'S BY THE LIBRARY, THEN GO STRAIGHT.
YUP, THE BRICK HOUSE.
OKAY THEN, I'LL SEE YOU SOON.
SERAPHIM.
ちん
SORRY I TOOK SO LONG, ELVIRA.
どやどやっ
ANOTHER UNEXPECTED GUEST. GREAT.
MY APOLOGIES, CHIHAYA. I HAD TO MAKE A QUICK PHONE CALL.
ELVIRA WAS WALKING AROUND THE TOWN LOOKING FOR ME.
LOOKING FOR YOU?

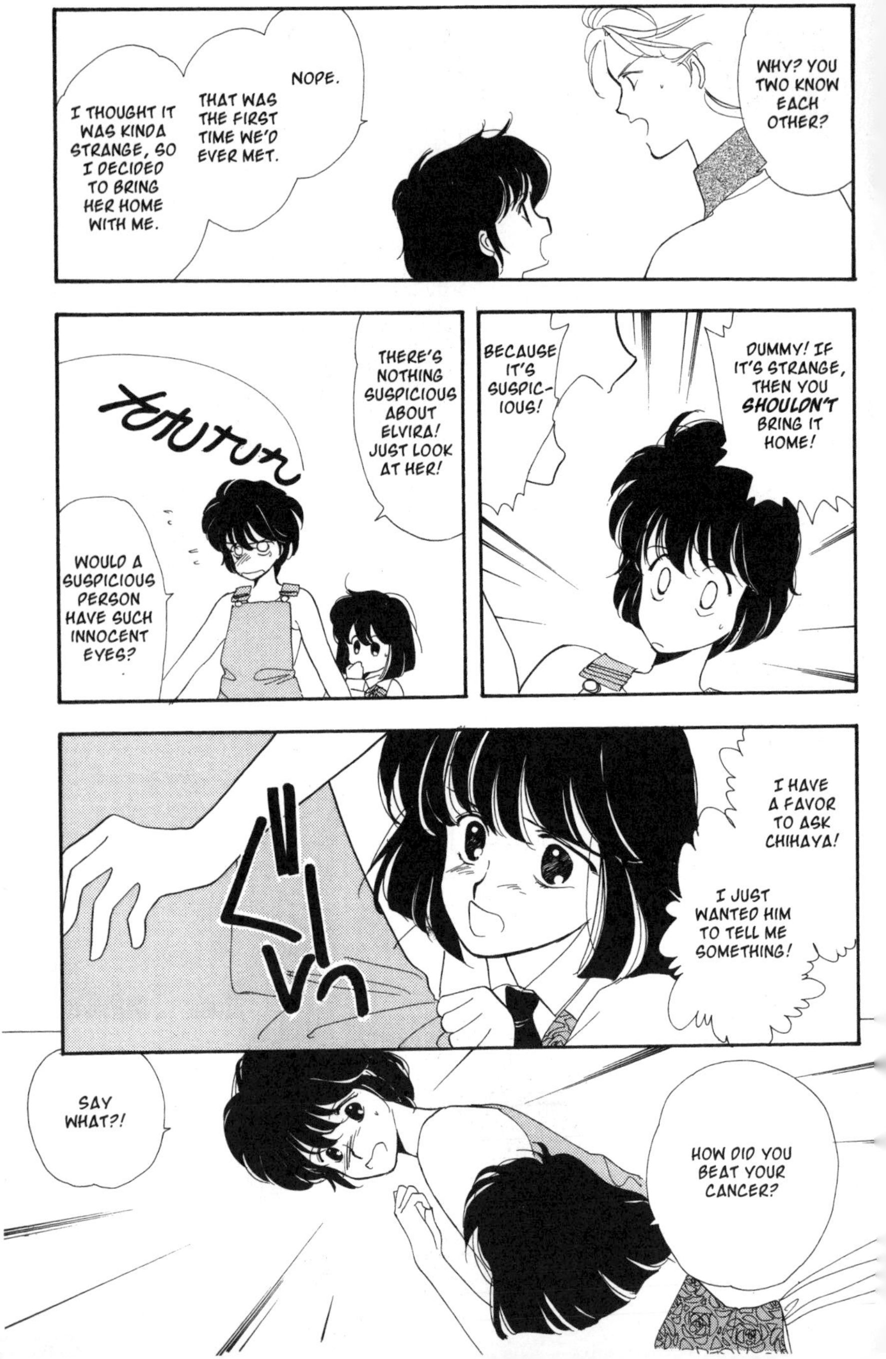
WHY? YOU TWO KNOW EACH OTHER?
NOPE.
THAT WAS THE FIRST TIME WE'D EVER MET.
I THOUGHT IT WAS KINDA STRANGE, SO I DECIDED TO BRING HER HOME WITH ME.
DUMMY! IF IT'S STRANGE, THEN YOU SHOULDN'T BRING IT HOME!
BECAUSE IT'S SUSPICIOUS!
THERE'S NOTHING SUSPICIOUS ABOUT ELVIRA! JUST LOOK AT HER!
WOULD A SUSPICIOUS PERSON HAVE SUCH INNOCENT EYES?
I HAVE A FAVOR TO ASK CHIHAYA!
I JUST WANTED HIM TO TELL ME SOMETHING!
HOW DID YOU BEAT YOUR CANCER?
SAY WHAT?!

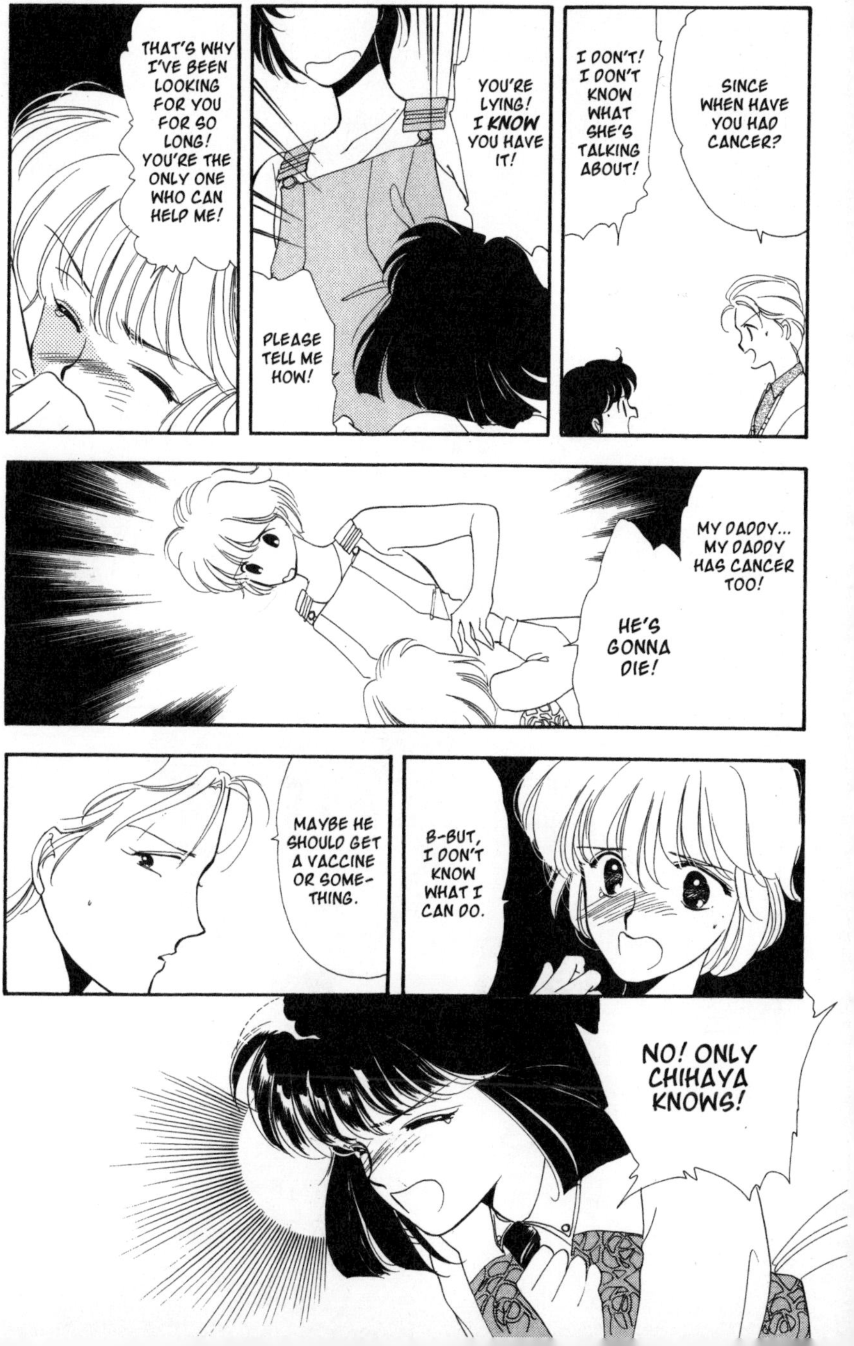
SINCE WHEN HAVE YOU HAD CANCER?
I DON'T! I DON'T KNOW WHAT SHE'S TALKING ABOUT!
YOU'RE LYING! I **KNOW** YOU HAVE IT!
PLEASE TELL ME HOW!
THAT'S WHY I'VE BEEN LOOKING FOR YOU FOR SO LONG! YOU'RE THE ONLY ONE WHO CAN HELP ME!
MY DADDY... MY DADDY HAS CANCER TOO!
HE'S GONNA DIE!
B-BUT, I DON'T KNOW WHAT I CAN DO.
MAYBE HE SHOULD GET A VACCINE OR SOME-THING.
NO! ONLY CHIHAYA KNOWS!

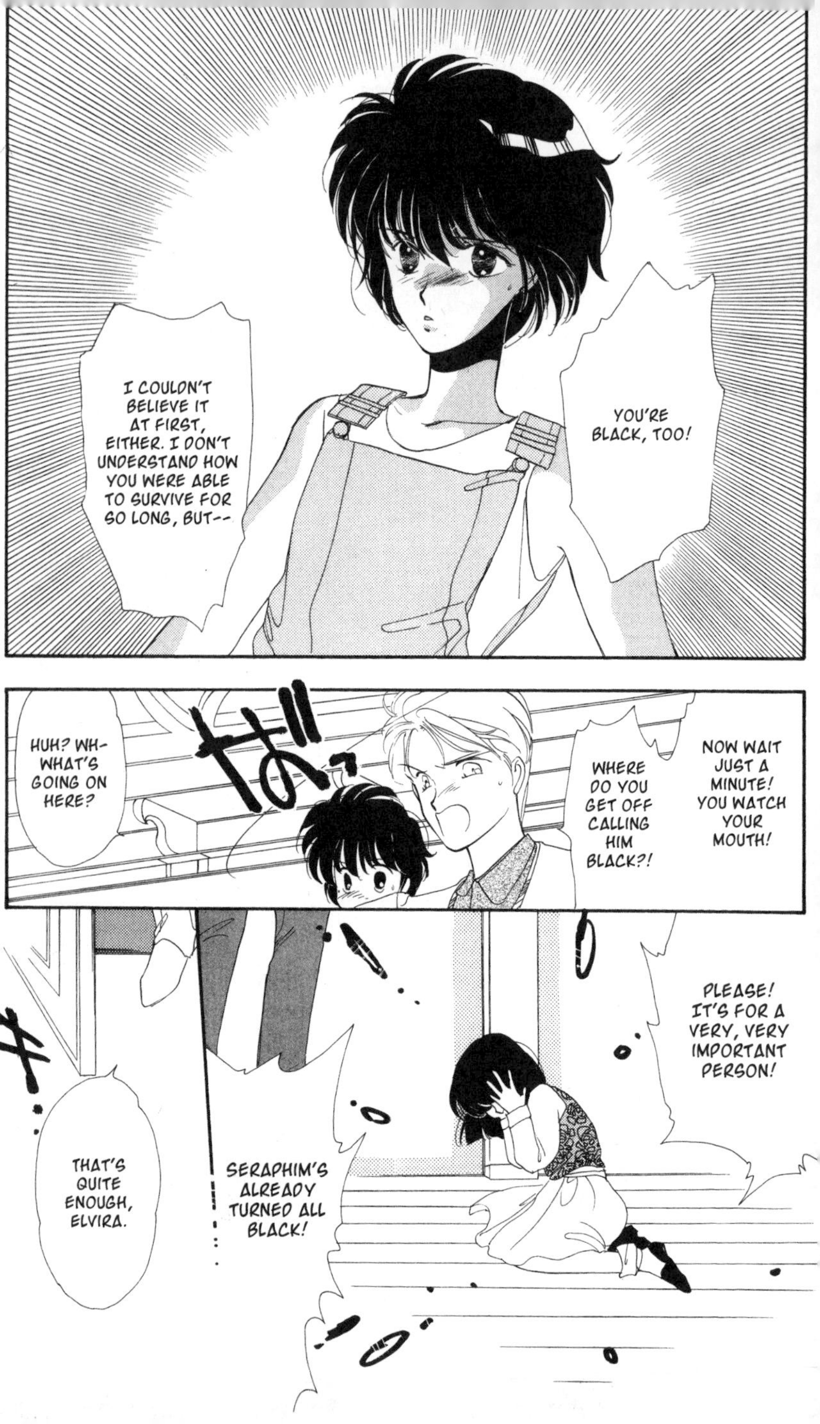
I COULDN'T BELIEVE IT AT FIRST, EITHER. I DON'T UNDERSTAND HOW YOU WERE ABLE TO SURVIVE FOR SO LONG, BUT--
YOU'RE BLACK, TOO!
NOW WAIT JUST A MINUTE! YOU WATCH YOUR MOUTH!
WHERE DO YOU GET OFF CALLING HIM BLACK?!
はっ
HUH? WH-WHAT'S GOING ON HERE?
PLEASE! IT'S FOR A VERY, VERY IMPORTANT PERSON!
SERAPHIM'S ALREADY TURNED ALL BLACK!
THAT'S QUITE ENOUGH, ELVIRA.

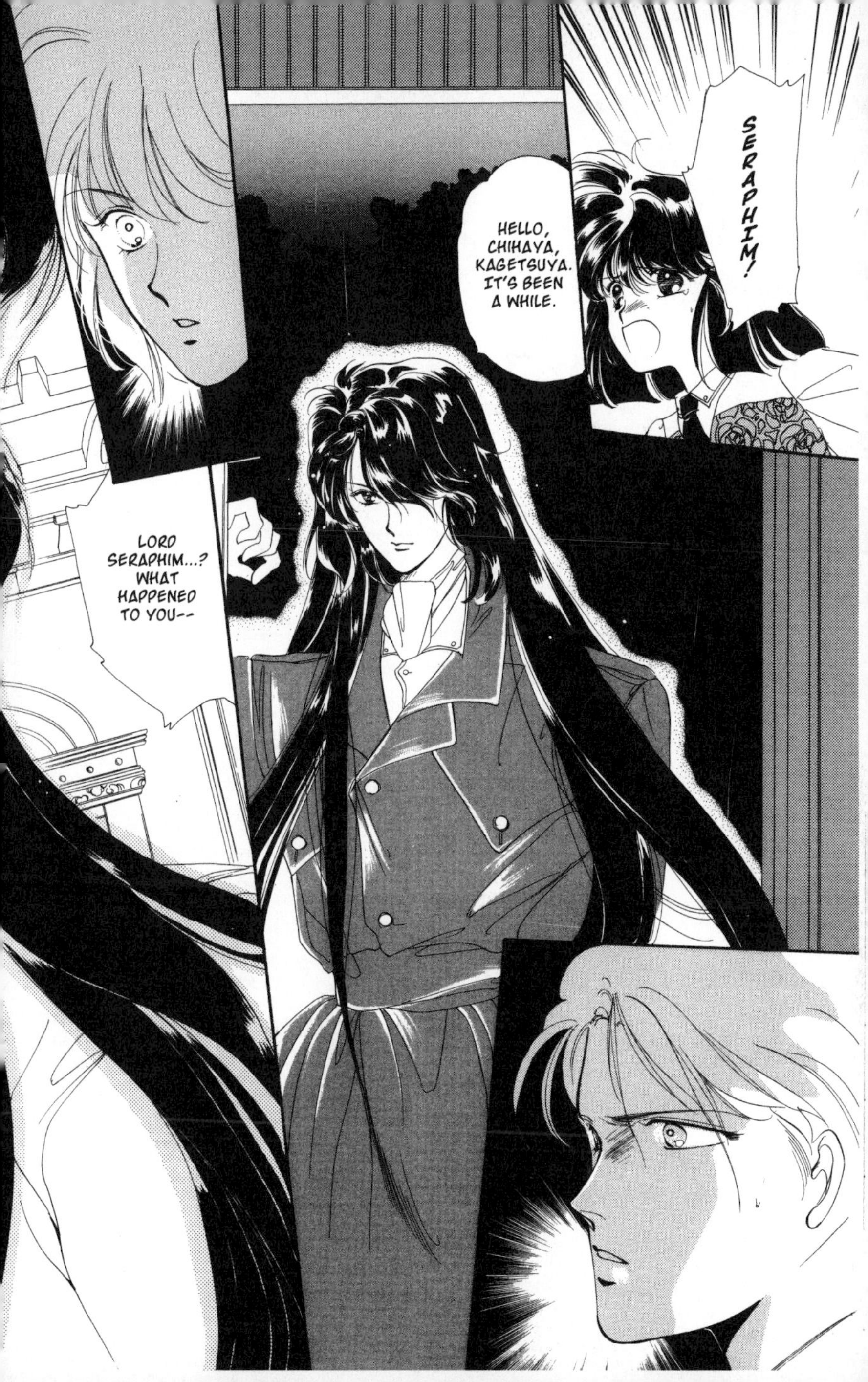
SERAPHIM!
HELLO, CHIHAYA, KAGETSUYA. IT'S BEEN A WHILE.
LORD SERAPHIM...? WHAT HAPPENED TO YOU--

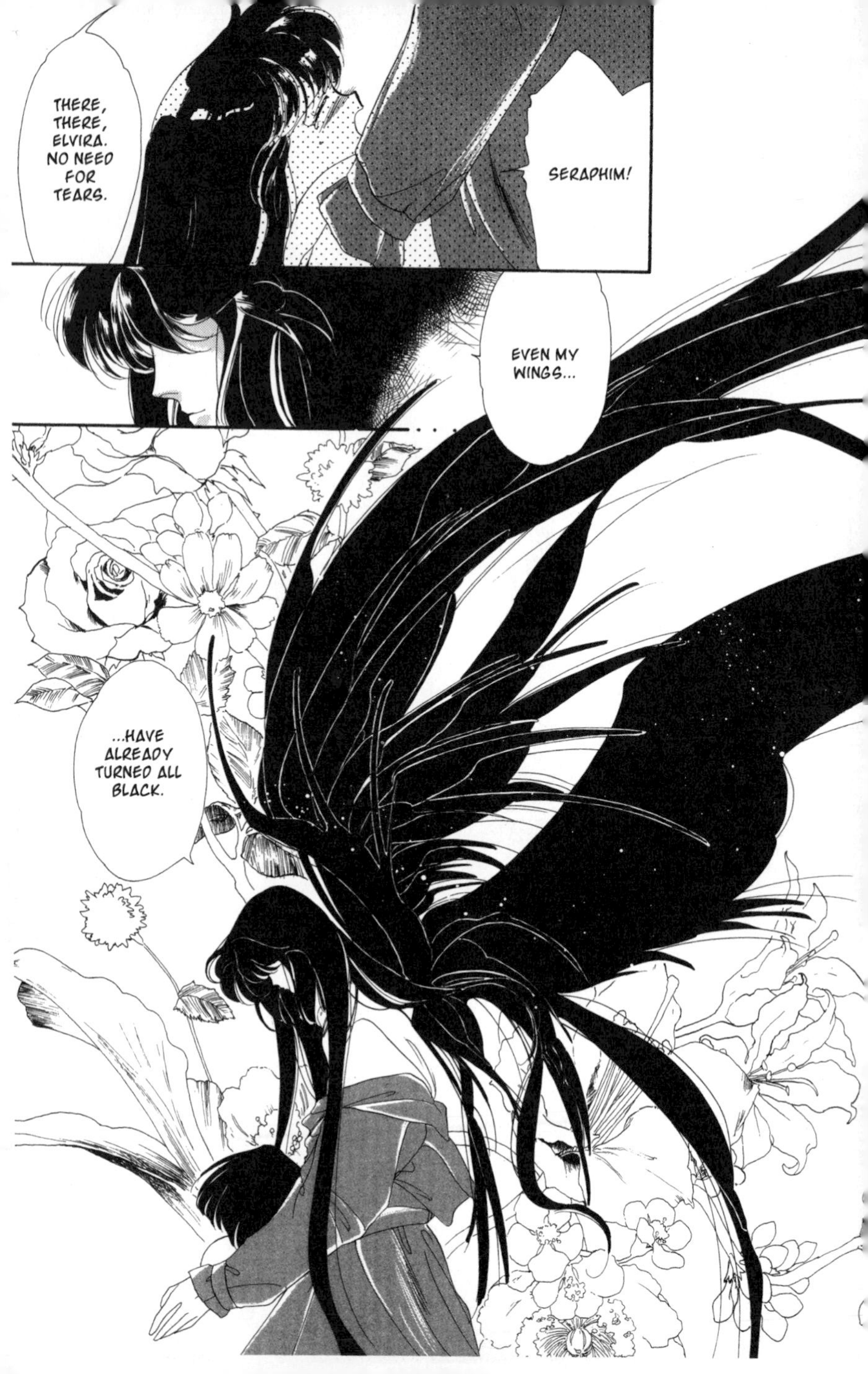
SERAPHIM!
THERE, THERE, ELVIRA. NO NEED FOR TEARS.
EVEN MY WINGS...
...HAVE ALREADY TURNED ALL BLACK.

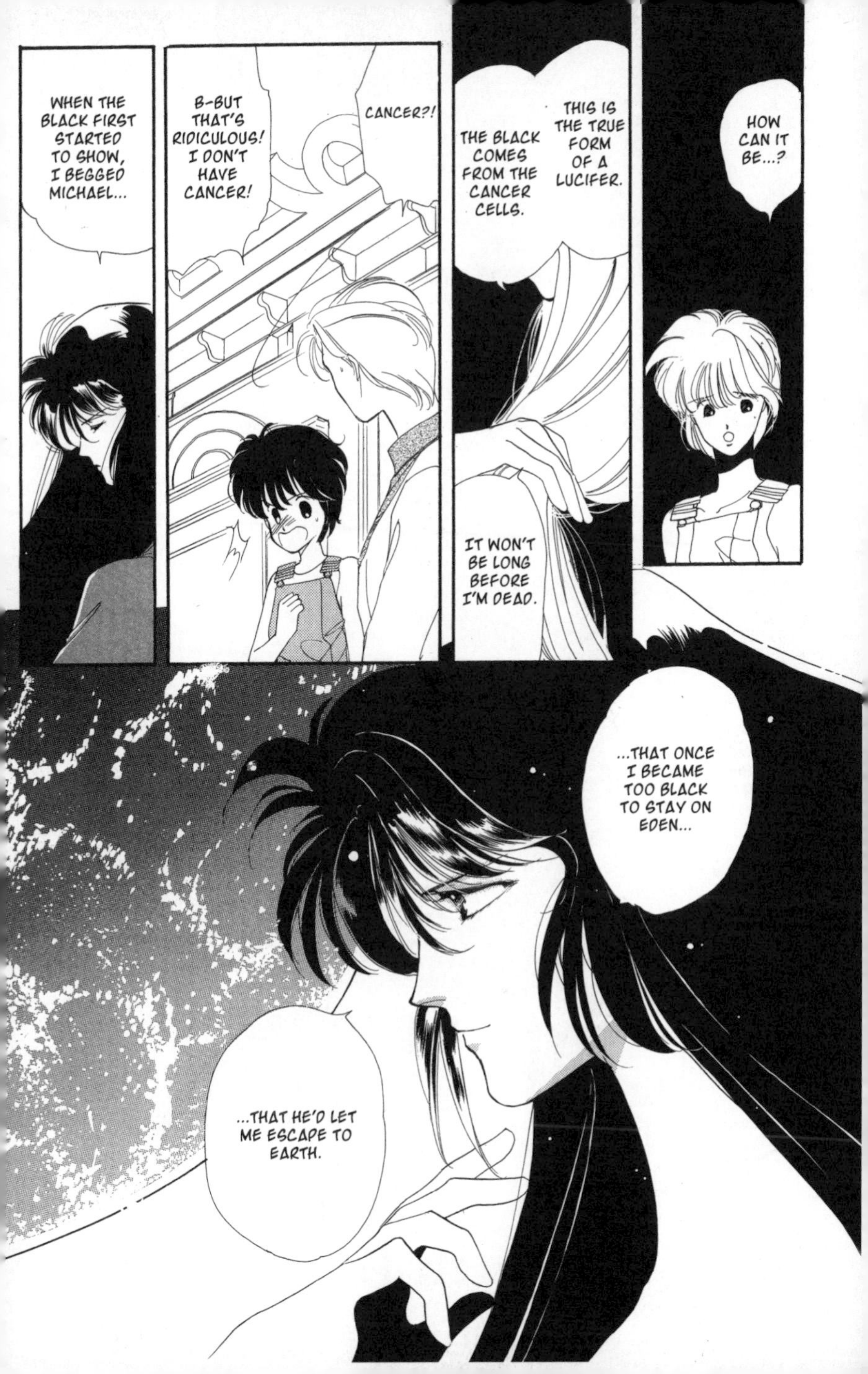
HOW CAN IT BE...?
THIS IS THE TRUE FORM OF A LUCIFER.
THE BLACK COMES FROM THE CANCER CELLS.
IT WON'T BE LONG BEFORE I'M DEAD.
CANCER?!
B-BUT THAT'S RIDICULOUS! I DON'T HAVE CANCER!
WHEN THE BLACK FIRST STARTED TO SHOW, I BEGGED MICHAEL...
...THAT ONCE I BECAME TOO BLACK TO STAY ON EDEN...
...THAT HE'D LET ME ESCAPE TO EARTH.

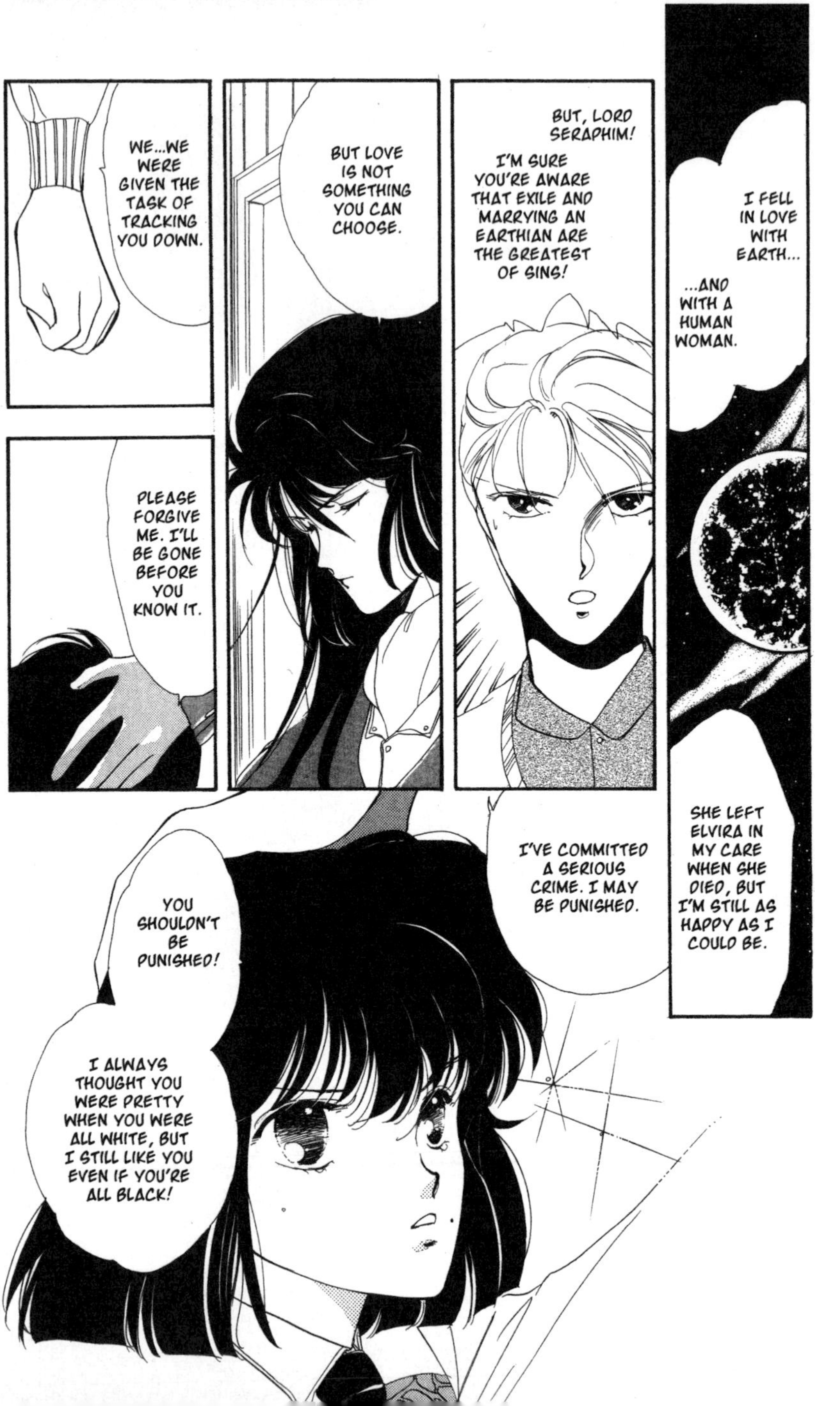
I FELL IN LOVE WITH EARTH...
...AND WITH A HUMAN WOMAN.
SHE LEFT ELVIRA IN MY CARE WHEN SHE DIED, BUT I'M STILL AS HAPPY AS I COULD BE.
BUT, LORD SERAPHIM!
I'M SURE YOU'RE AWARE THAT EXILE AND MARRYING AN EARTHIAN ARE THE GREATEST OF SINS!
BUT LOVE IS NOT SOMETHING YOU CAN CHOOSE.
WE...WE WERE GIVEN THE TASK OF TRACKING YOU DOWN.
PLEASE FORGIVE ME. I'LL BE GONE BEFORE YOU KNOW IT.
I'VE COMMITTED A SERIOUS CRIME. I MAY BE PUNISHED.
YOU SHOULDN'T BE PUNISHED!
I ALWAYS THOUGHT YOU WERE PRETTY WHEN YOU WERE ALL WHITE, BUT I STILL LIKE YOU EVEN IF YOU'RE ALL BLACK!

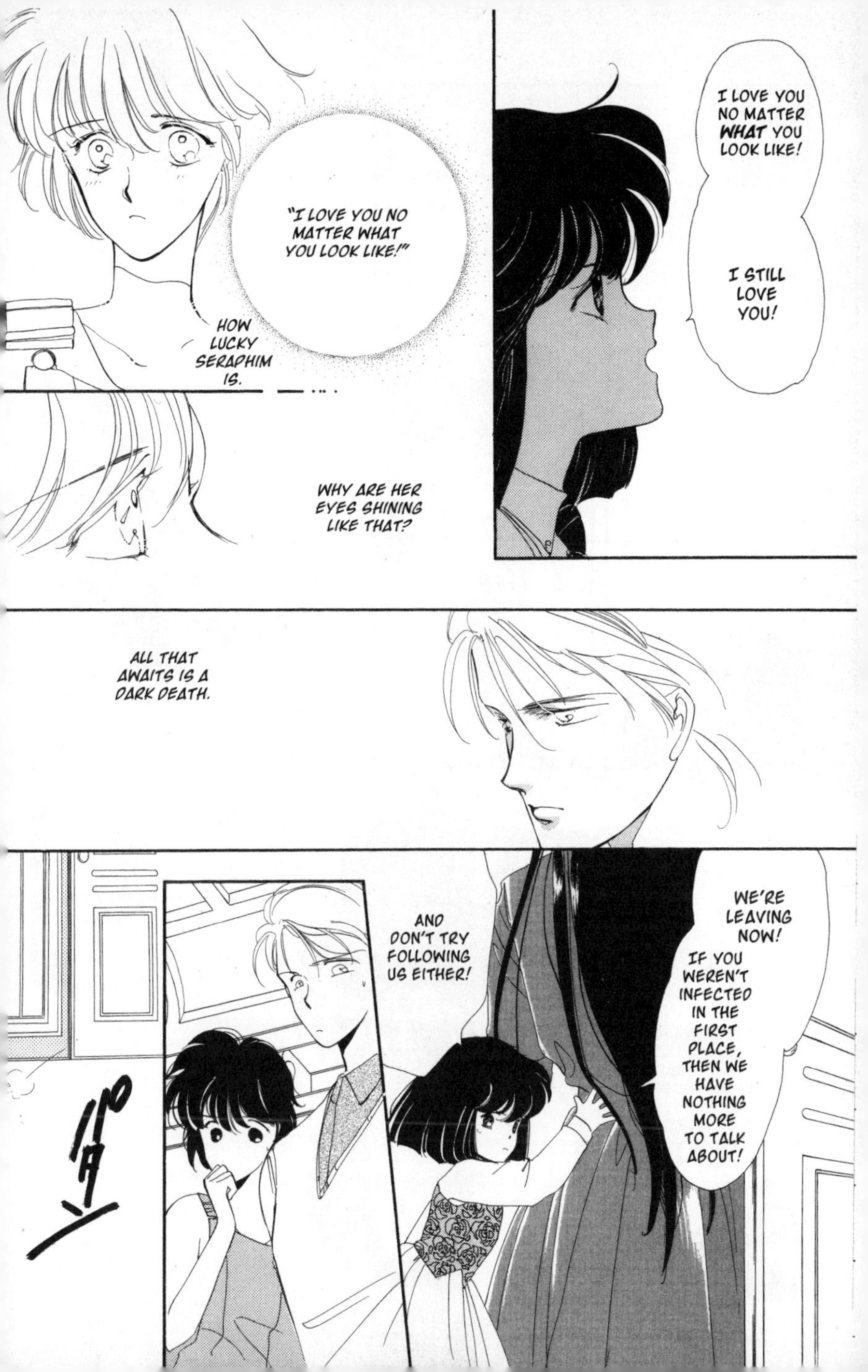
I LOVE YOU NO MATTER WHAT YOU LOOK LIKE!
I STILL LOVE YOU!
"I LOVE YOU NO MATTER WHAT YOU LOOK LIKE!"
HOW LUCKY SERAPHIM IS.
— ...
WHY ARE HER EYES SHINING LIKE THAT?
ALL THAT AWAITS IS A DARK DEATH.
WE'RE LEAVING NOW!
IF YOU WEREN'T INFECTED IN THE FIRST PLACE, THEN WE HAVE NOTHING MORE TO TALK ABOUT!
AND DON'T TRY FOLLOWING US EITHER!

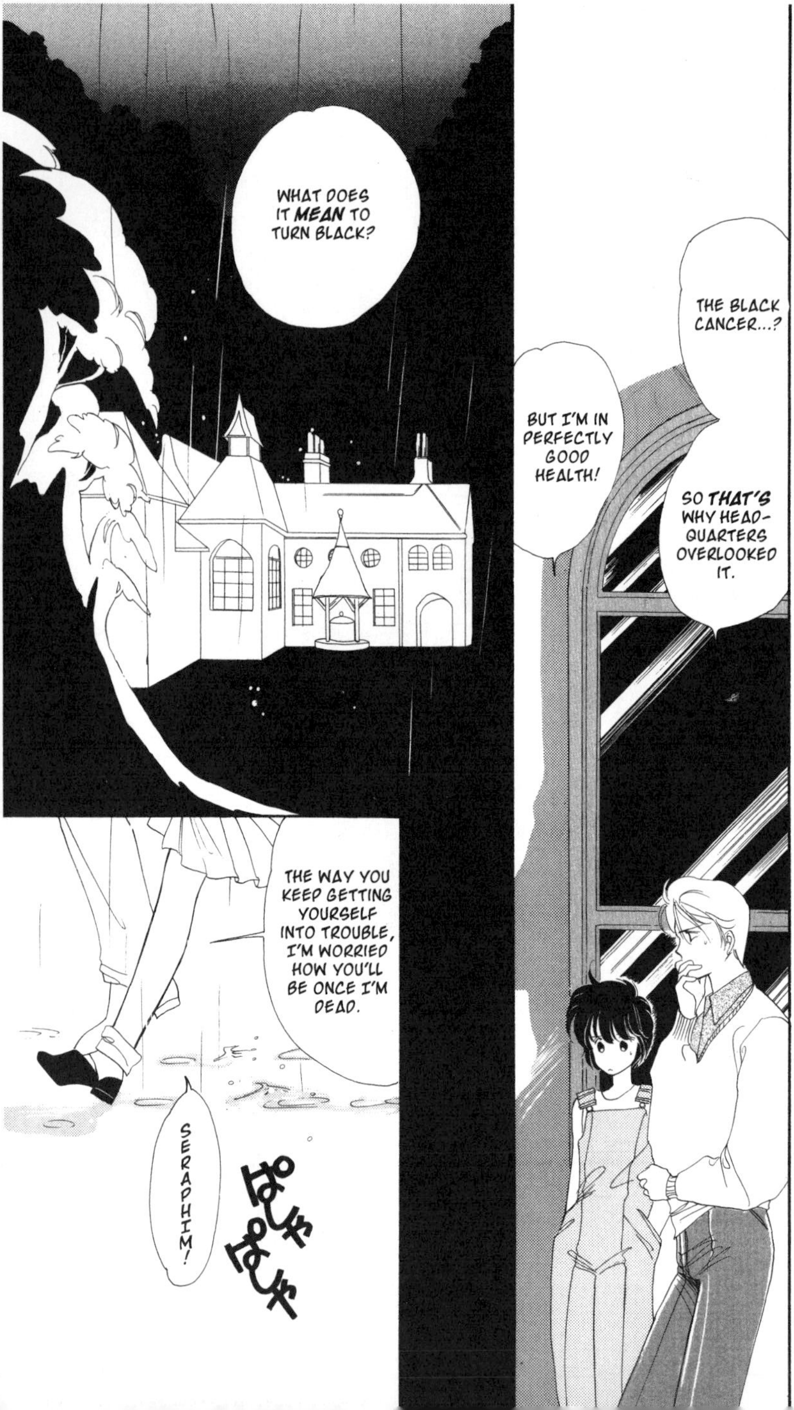
THE BLACK CANCER...?
BUT I'M IN PERFECTLY GOOD HEALTH!
SO THAT'S WHY HEAD-QUARTERS OVERLOOKED IT.
WHAT DOES IT MEAN TO TURN BLACK?
THE WAY YOU KEEP GETTING YOURSELF INTO TROUBLE, I'M WORRIED HOW YOU'LL BE ONCE I'M DEAD.
SERAPHIM!
ぱしゃ ぱしゃ

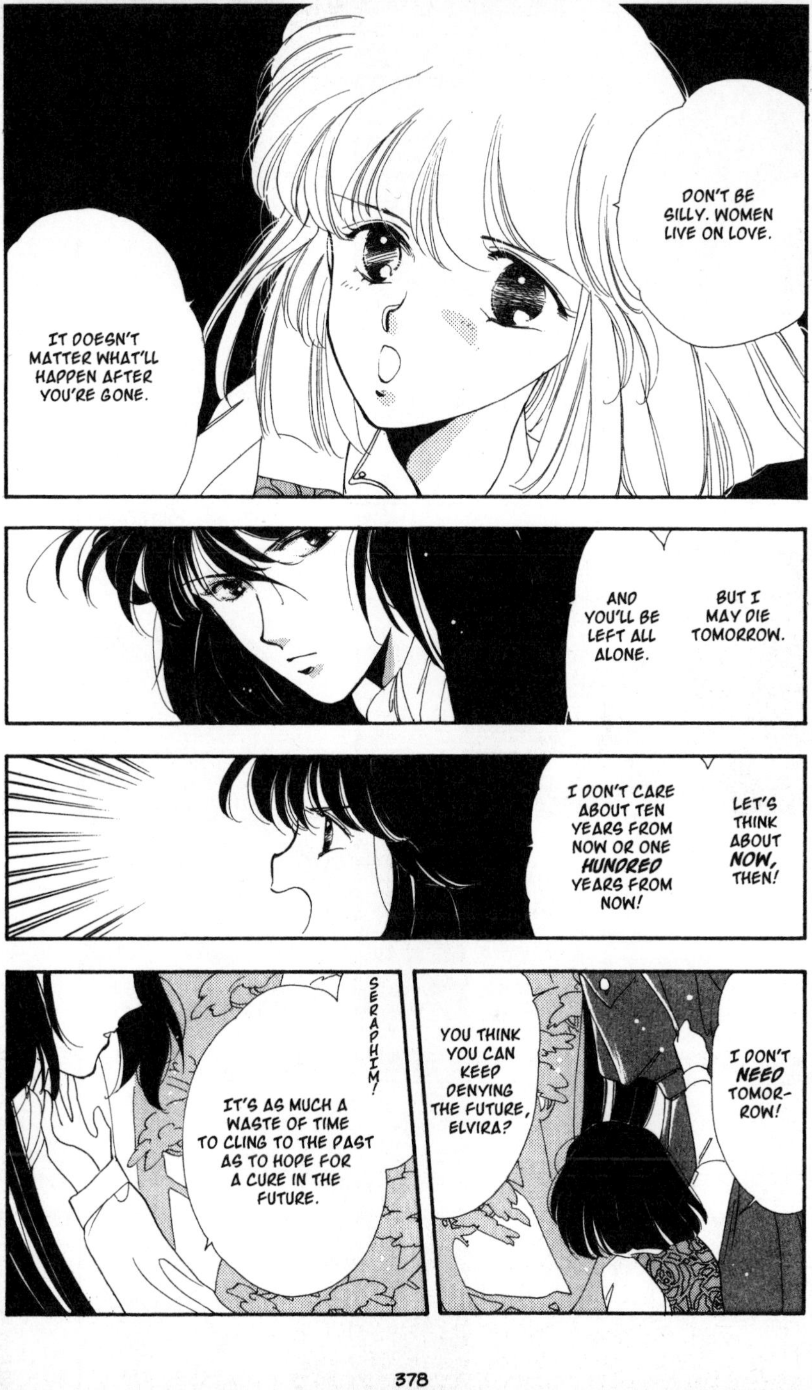
DON'T BE SILLY. WOMEN LIVE ON LOVE.
IT DOESN'T MATTER WHAT'LL HAPPEN AFTER YOU'RE GONE.
BUT I MAY DIE TOMORROW.
AND YOU'LL BE LEFT ALL ALONE.
LET'S THINK ABOUT NOW, THEN!
I DON'T CARE ABOUT TEN YEARS FROM NOW OR ONE HUNDRED YEARS FROM NOW!
I DON'T NEED TOMORROW!
YOU THINK YOU CAN KEEP DENYING THE FUTURE, ELVIRA?
SERAPHIM!
IT'S AS MUCH A WASTE OF TIME TO CLING TO THE PAST AS TO HOPE FOR A CURE IN THE FUTURE.

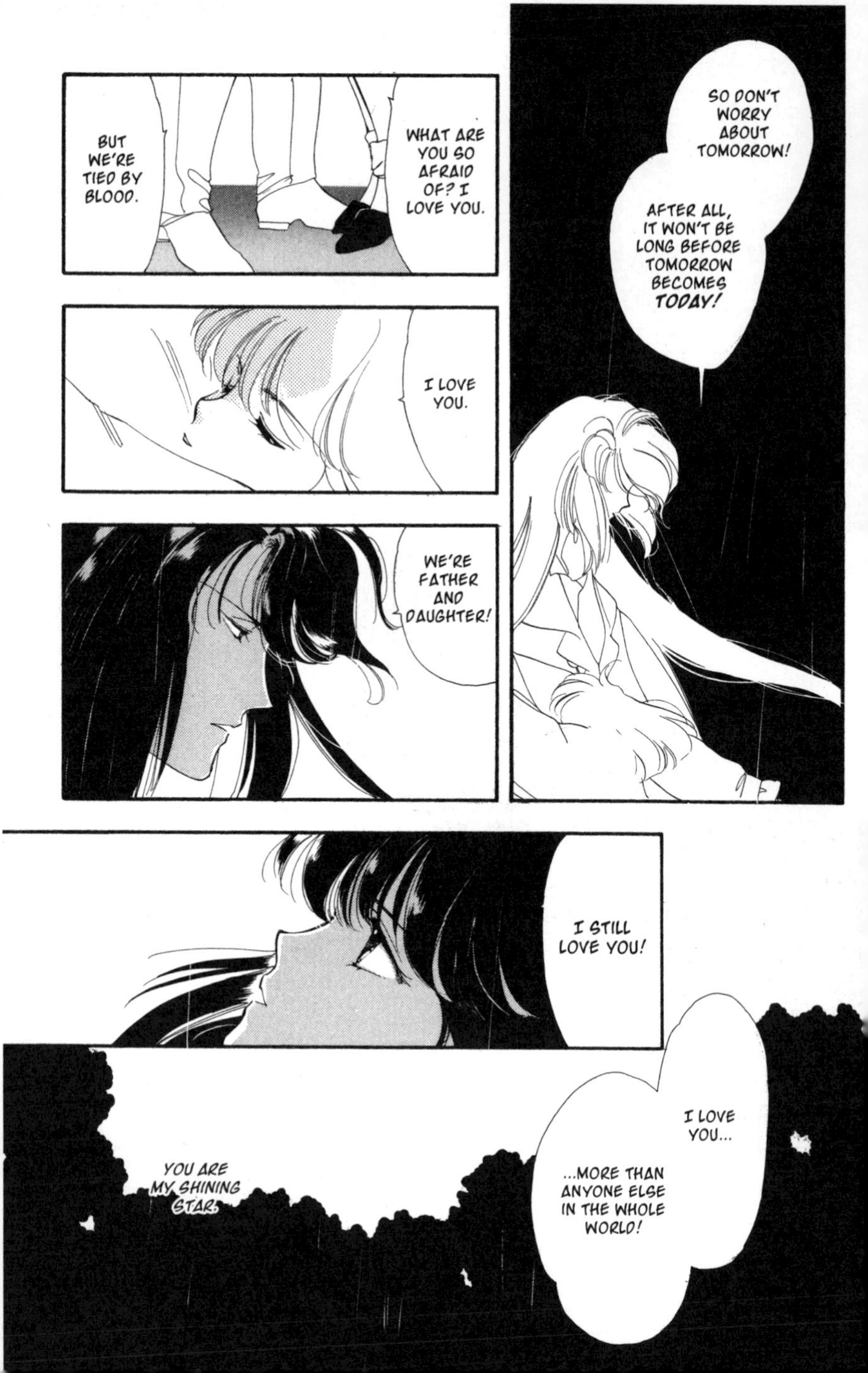
SO DON'T WORRY ABOUT TOMORROW!
AFTER ALL, IT WON'T BE LONG BEFORE TOMORROW BECOMES *TODAY!*
WHAT ARE YOU SO AFRAID OF? I LOVE YOU.
BUT WE'RE TIED BY BLOOD.
I LOVE YOU.
WE'RE FATHER AND DAUGHTER!
I STILL LOVE YOU!
I LOVE YOU...
...MORE THAN ANYONE ELSE IN THE WHOLE WORLD!
YOU ARE MY SHINING STAR.

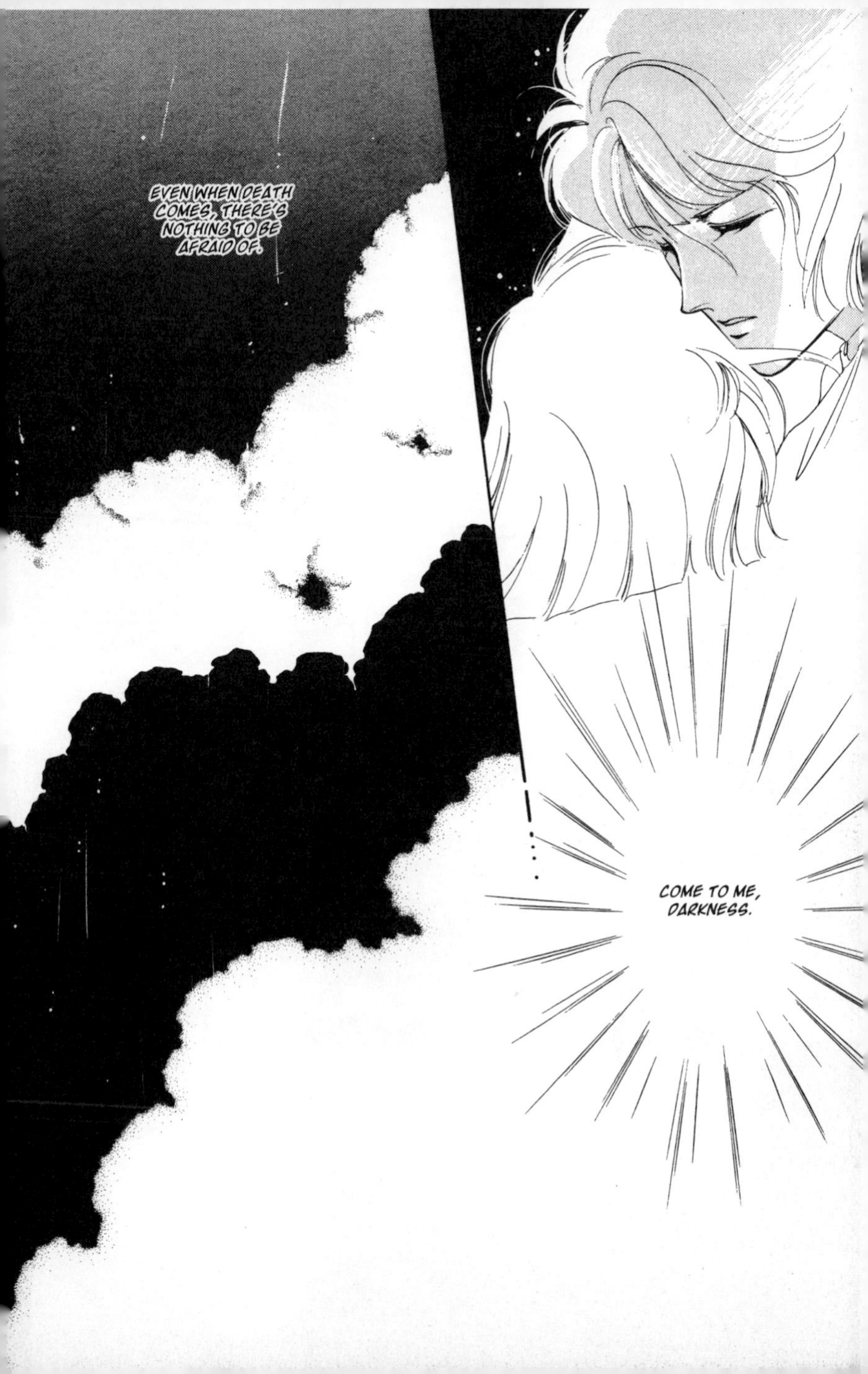
COME TO ME, DARKNESS.
EVEN WHEN DEATH COMES, THERE'S NOTHING TO BE AFRAID OF.

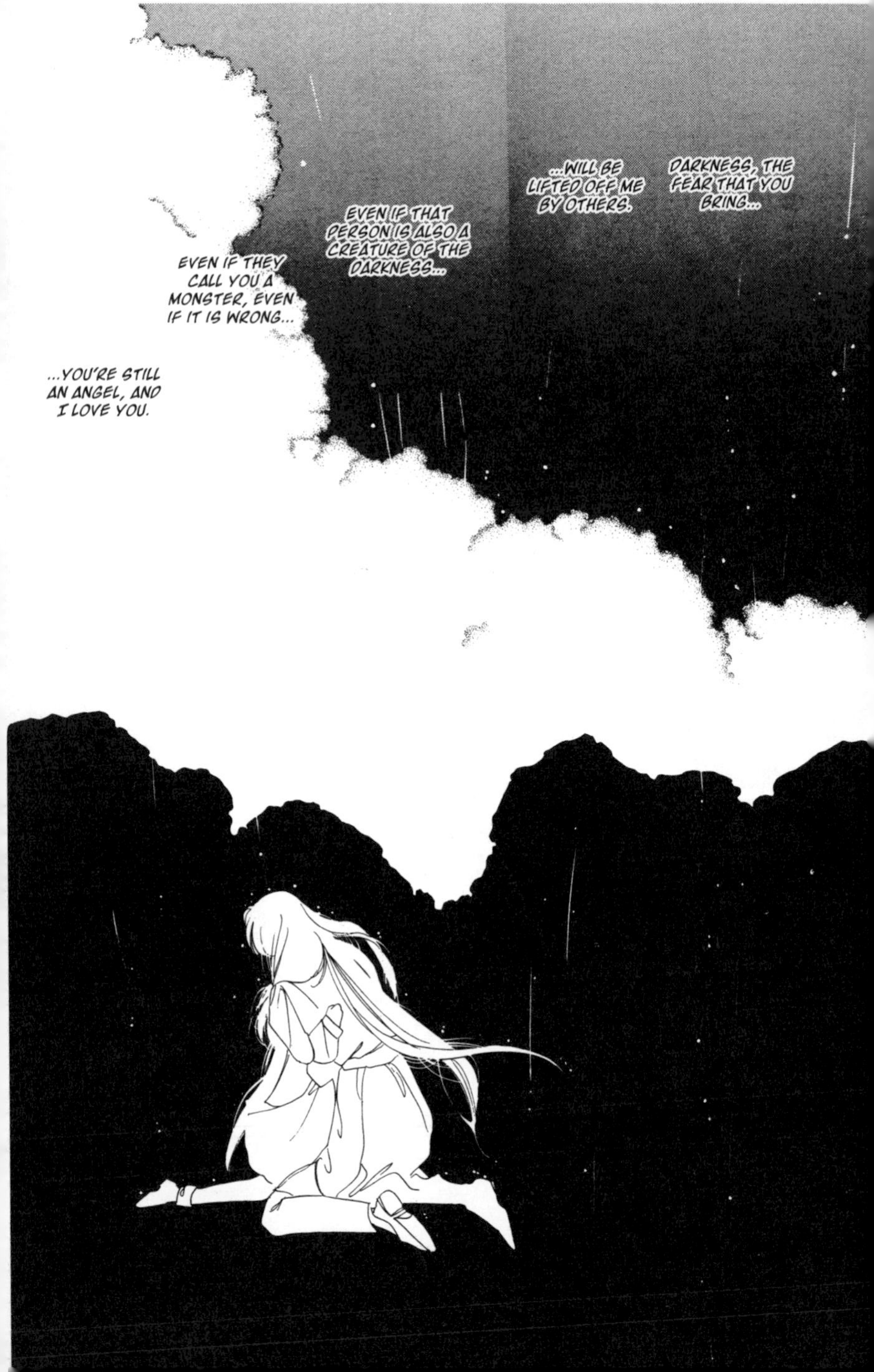
DARKNESS, THE FEAR THAT YOU BRING...
...WILL BE LIFTED OFF ME BY OTHERS.
EVEN IF THAT PERSON IS ALSO A CREATURE OF THE DARKNESS...
EVEN IF THEY CALL YOU A MONSTER, EVEN IF IT IS WRONG...
...YOU'RE STILL AN ANGEL, AND I LOVE YOU.

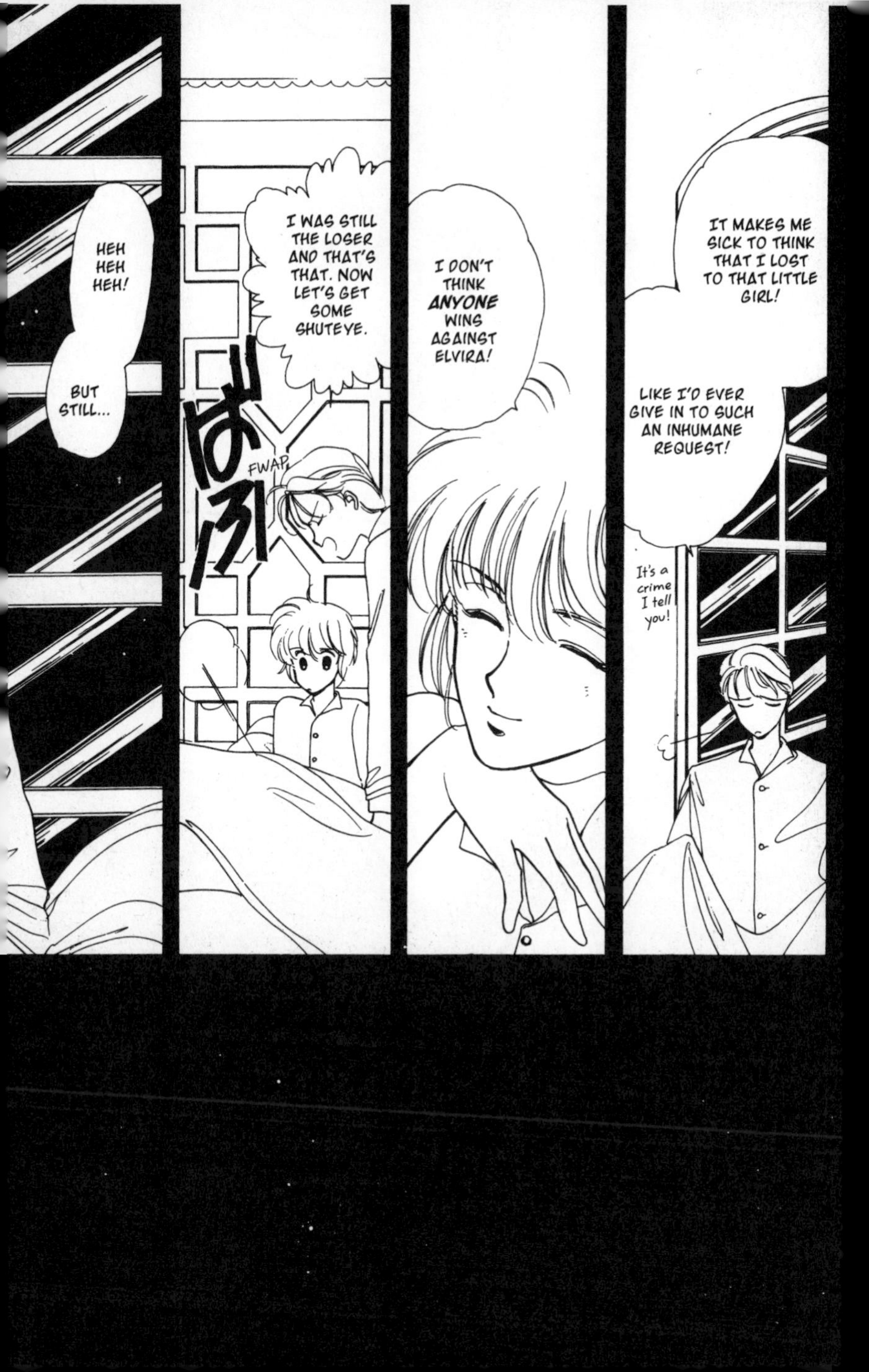
IT MAKES ME SICK TO THINK THAT I LOST TO THAT LITTLE GIRL!
LIKE I'D EVER GIVE IN TO SUCH AN INHUMANE REQUEST!
It's a crime I tell you!
I DON'T THINK **ANYONE** WINS AGAINST ELVIRA!
I WAS STILL THE LOSER AND THAT'S THAT. NOW LET'S GET SOME SHUTEYE.
FWAP
HEH HEH HEH!
BUT STILL...

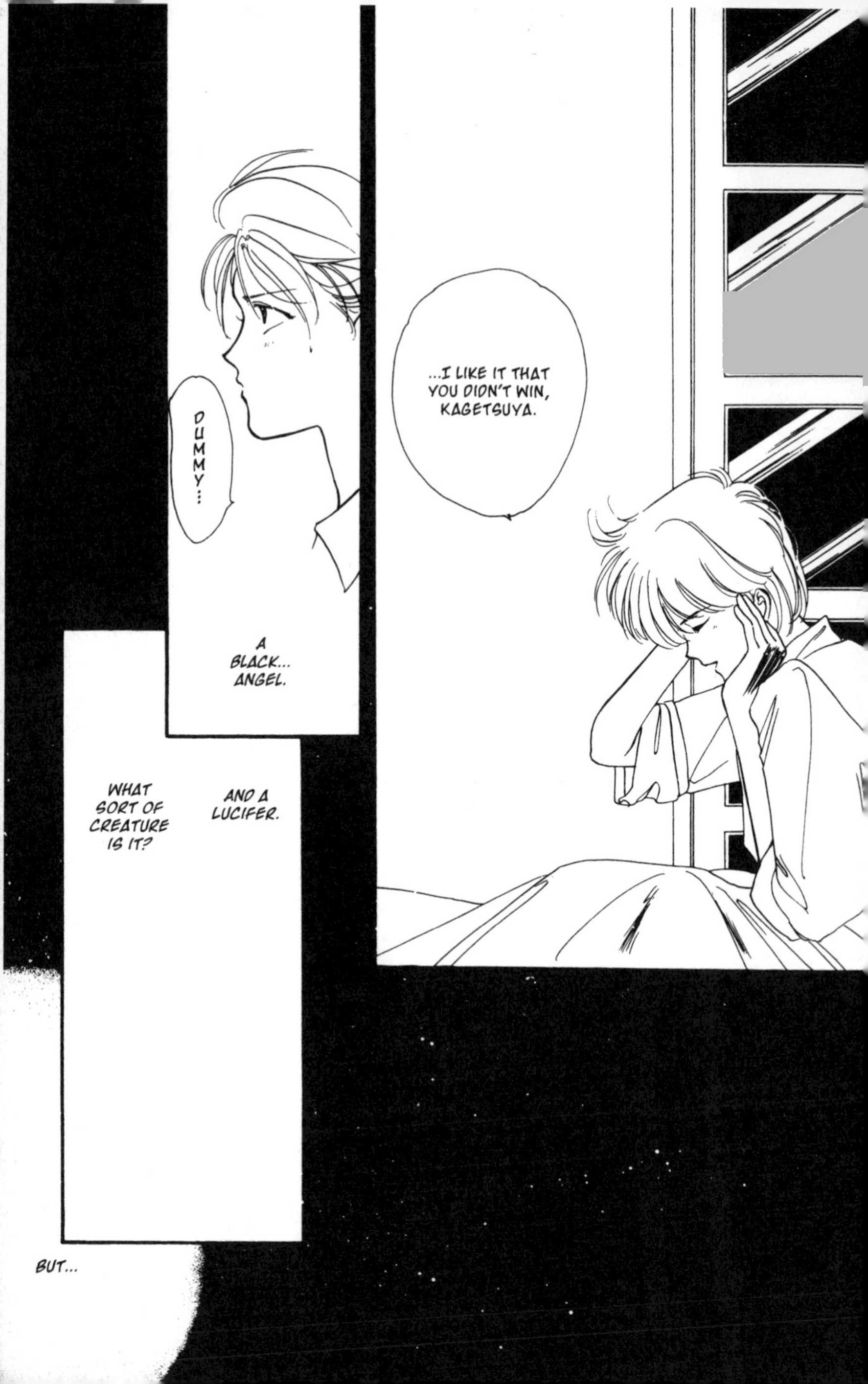
...I LIKE IT THAT YOU DIDN'T WIN, KAGETSUYA.
DUMMY...
A BLACK... ANGEL.
AND A LUCIFER.
WHAT SORT OF CREATURE IS IT?
BUT...

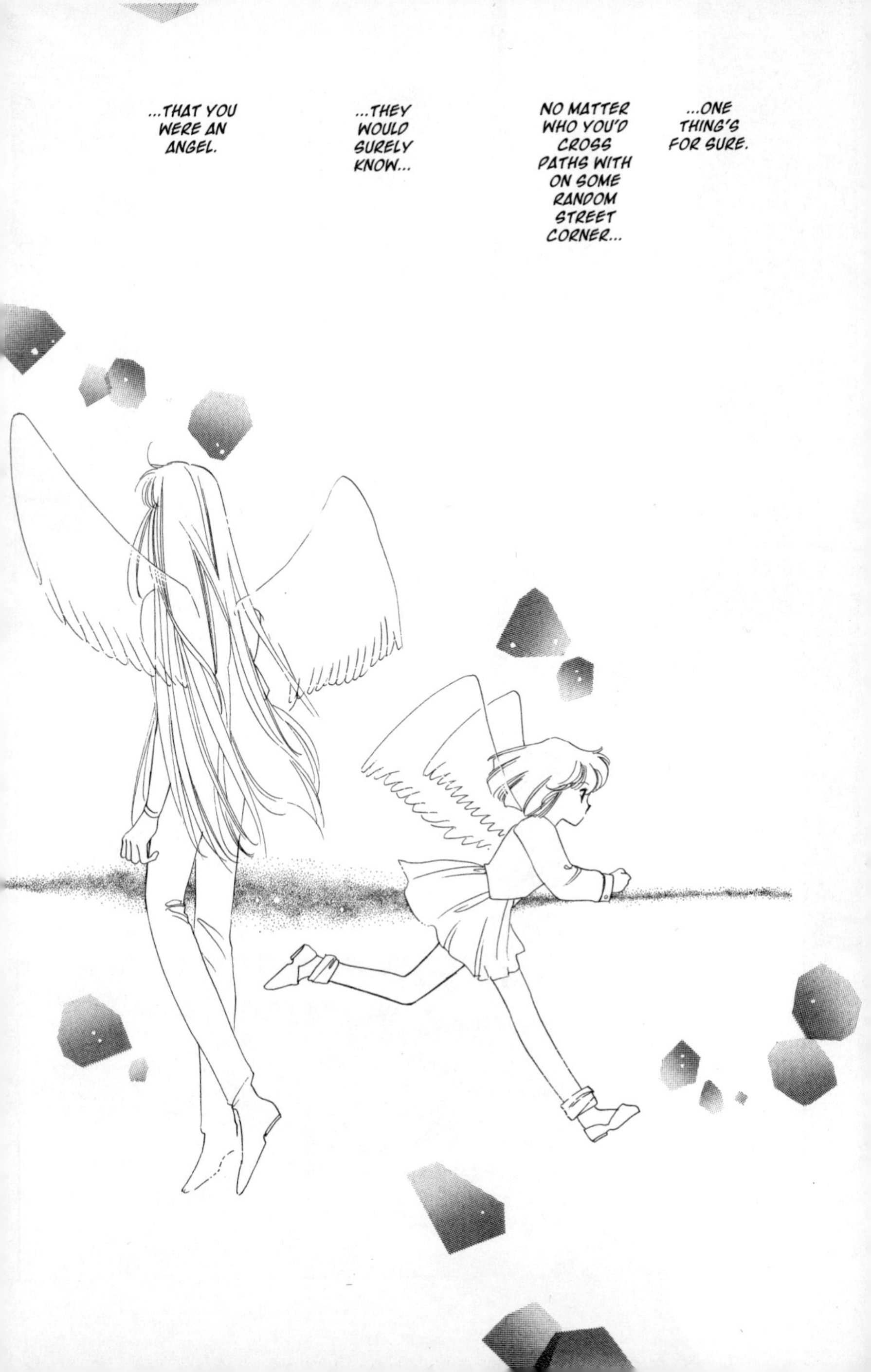
...ONE THING'S FOR SURE.
NO MATTER WHO YOU'D CROSS PATHS WITH ON SOME RANDOM STREET CORNER...
...THEY WOULD SURELY KNOW...
...THAT YOU WERE AN ANGEL.

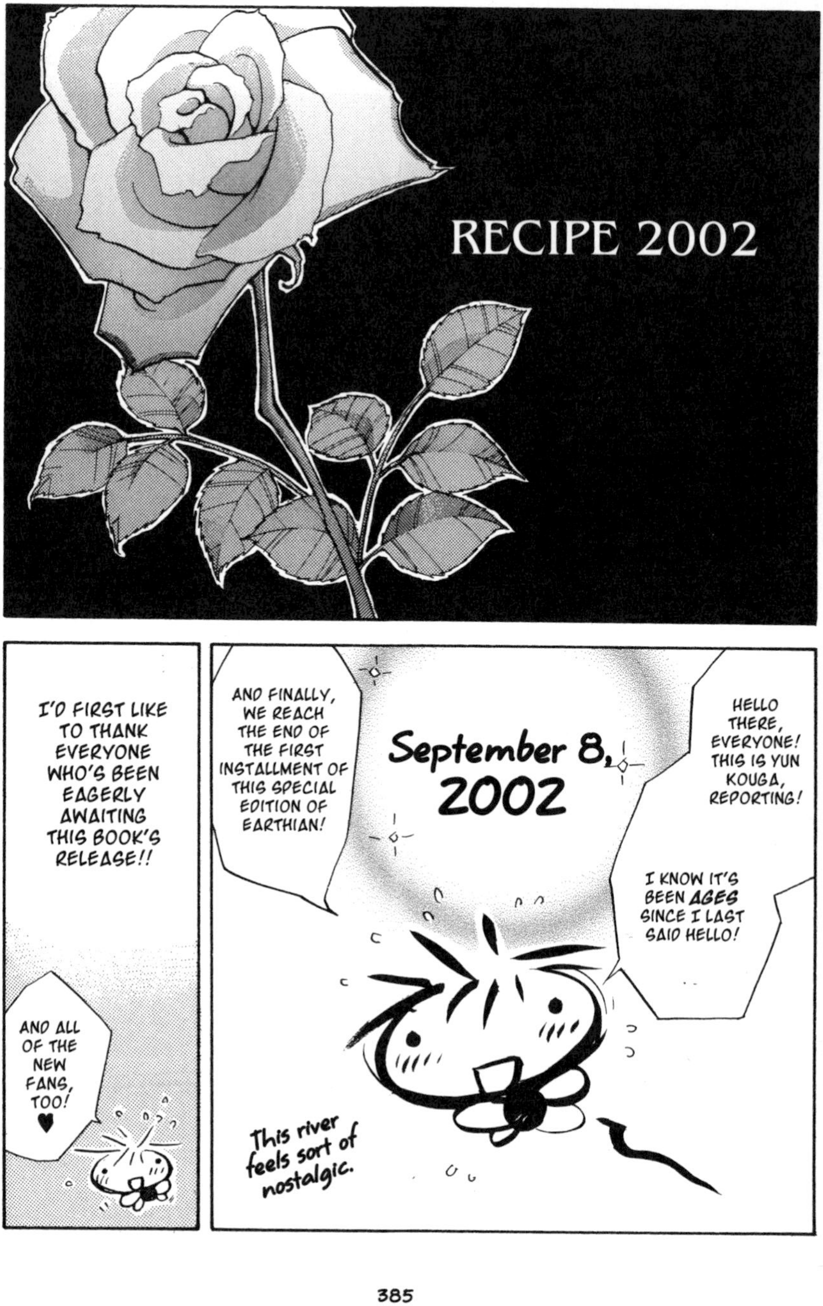
RECIPE 2002
HELLO THERE, EVERYONE! THIS IS YUN KOUGA, REPORTING!
September 8, 2002
AND FINALLY, WE REACH THE END OF THE FIRST INSTALLMENT OF THIS SPECIAL EDITION OF EARTHIAN!
I KNOW IT'S BEEN AGES SINCE I LAST SAID HELLO!
This river feels sort of nostalgic.
I'D FIRST LIKE TO THANK EVERYONE WHO'S BEEN EAGERLY AWAITING THIS BOOK'S RELEASE!!
AND ALL OF THE NEW FANS, TOO! ♥

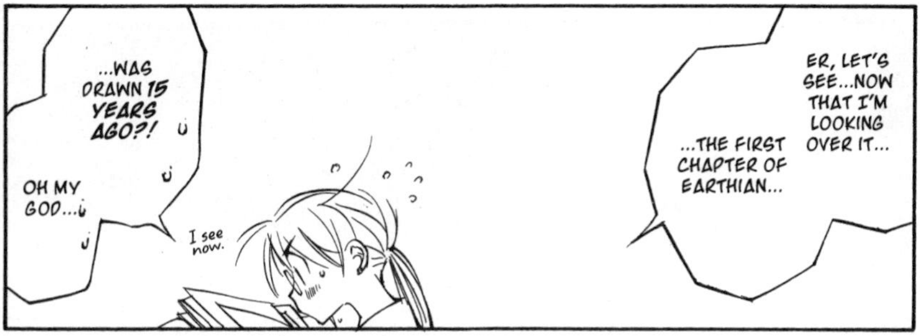
ER, LET'S SEE...NOW THAT I'M LOOKING OVER IT...
...THE FIRST CHAPTER OF EARTHIAN...
...WAS DRAWN 15 YEARS AGO?!
I see now.
OH MY GOD...

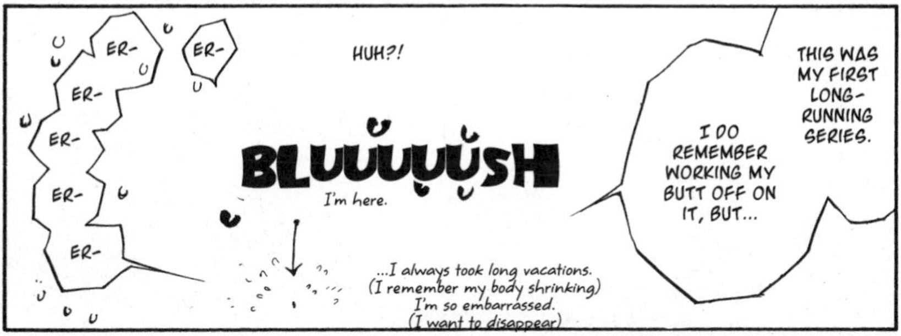
THIS WAS MY FIRST LONG-RUNNING SERIES.
I DO REMEMBER WORKING MY BUTT OFF ON IT, BUT...
HUH?!
BLUUUUUSH
I'm here.
...I always took long vacations. (I remember my body shrinking) I'm so embarrassed. (I want to disappear)
ER-
ER-
ER-
ER-
ER-
ER-

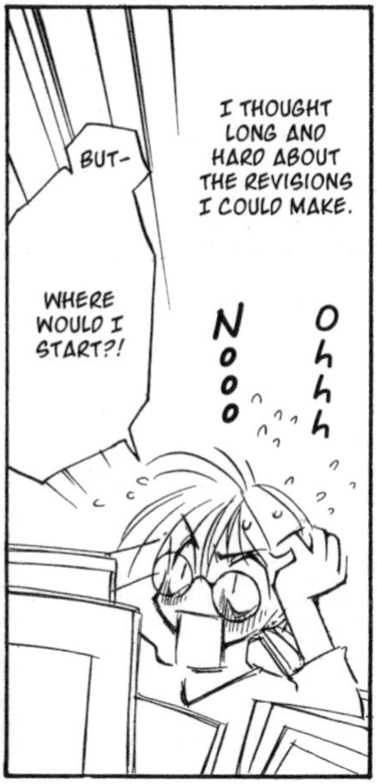
I THOUGHT LONG AND HARD ABOUT THE REVISIONS I COULD MAKE.
BUT-
Ohhh
Nooo
WHERE WOULD I START?!

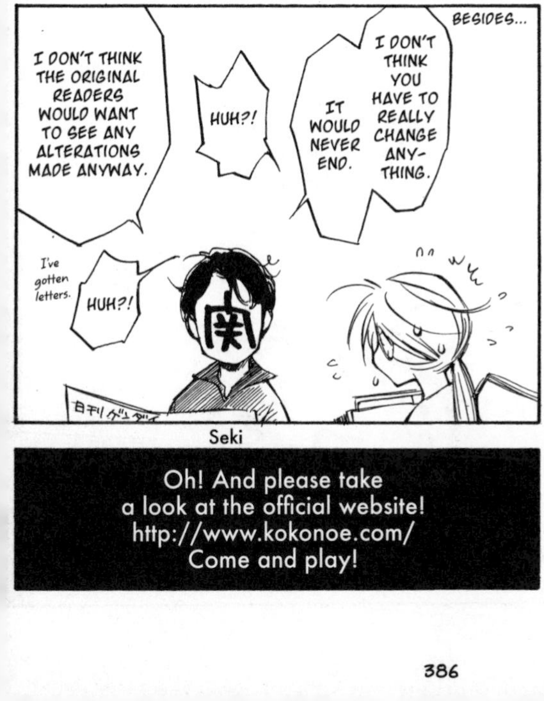
BESIDES...
I DON'T THINK YOU HAVE TO REALLY CHANGE ANYTHING.
IT WOULD NEVER END.
HUH?!
I DON'T THINK THE ORIGINAL READERS WOULD WANT TO SEE ANY ALTERATIONS MADE ANYWAY.
HUH?!
I've gotten letters.

Seki

Oh! And please take a look at the official website!
http://www.kokonoe.com/
Come and play!

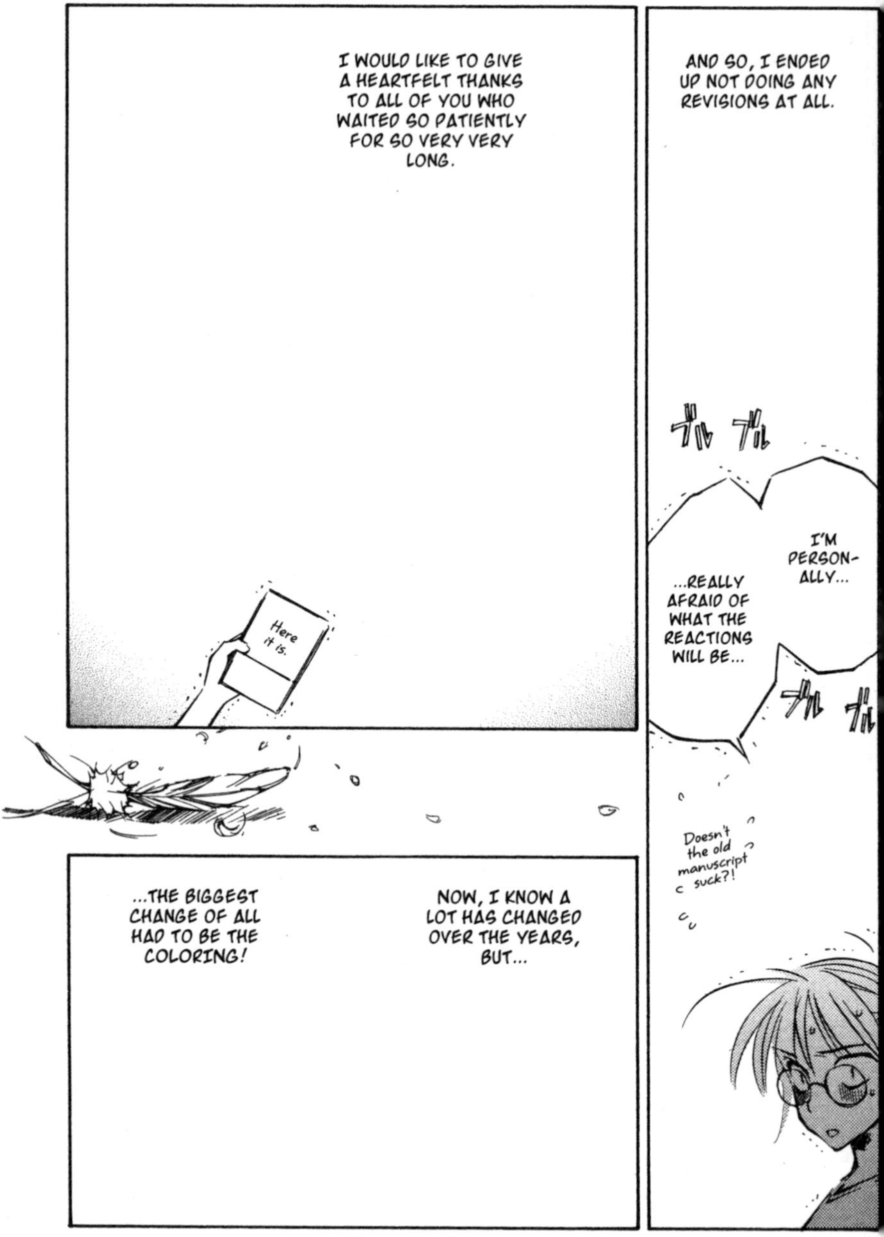
AND SO, I ENDED UP NOT DOING ANY REVISIONS AT ALL.
ブル ブル
I'M PERSON-ALLY...
...REALLY AFRAID OF WHAT THE REACTIONS WILL BE...
ブル ブル
Doesn't the old manuscript suck?!
I WOULD LIKE TO GIVE A HEARTFELT THANKS TO ALL OF YOU WHO WAITED SO PATIENTLY FOR SO VERY VERY LONG.
Here it is.
NOW, I KNOW A LOT HAS CHANGED OVER THE YEARS, BUT...
...THE BIGGEST CHANGE OF ALL HAD TO BE THE COLORING!

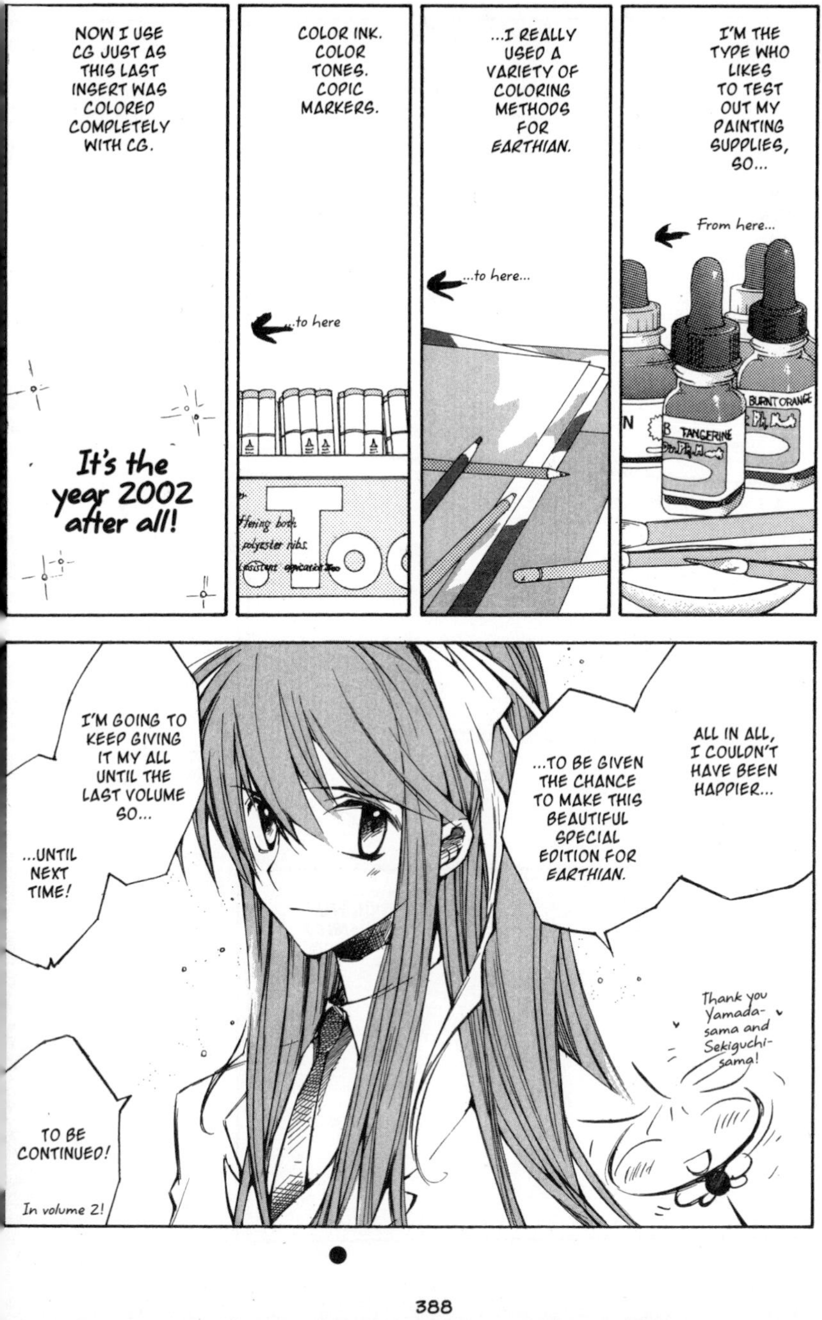
I'M THE TYPE WHO LIKES TO TEST OUT MY PAINTING SUPPLIES, SO...
From here...
BURNT ORANGE
TANGERINE
...I REALLY USED A VARIETY OF COLORING METHODS FOR EARTHIAN.
...to here...
COLOR INK. COLOR TONES. COPIC MARKERS.
...to here
NOW I USE CG JUST AS THIS LAST INSERT WAS COLORED COMPLETELY WITH CG.
It's the year 2002 after all!
ALL IN ALL, I COULDN'T HAVE BEEN HAPPIER...
...TO BE GIVEN THE CHANCE TO MAKE THIS BEAUTIFUL SPECIAL EDITION FOR EARTHIAN.
Thank you Yamada-sama and Sekiguchi-sama!
I'M GOING TO KEEP GIVING IT MY ALL UNTIL THE LAST VOLUME SO...
...UNTIL NEXT TIME!
TO BE CONTINUED!
In volume 2!

In the Next Volume of

As Chihaya and Kagetsuya continue to investigate the mystery behind the Black Cancer, they discover a disk of information left behind by Seraphim and a secret about the possible future of the Angels! Meanwhile, the increasingly close relationship between the pair has come under scrutiny by Valhalla, and they are ordered to split up. Kagetsuya winds up with a new partner, and Chihaya is left to decide just what it is he really wants. A working vacation to a sweltering rain forest may leave the pair a little hotter than they expected--and even the ever-practical Kagetsuya might not be entirely sure of his desires anymore!

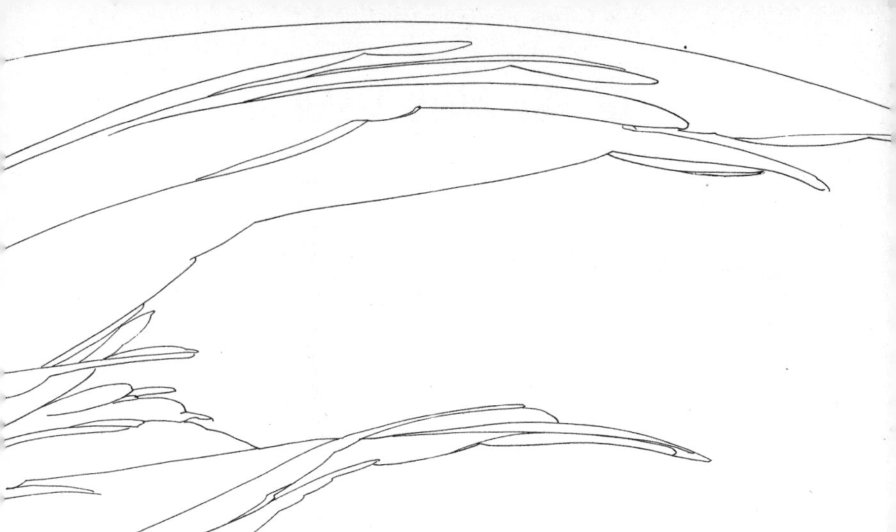

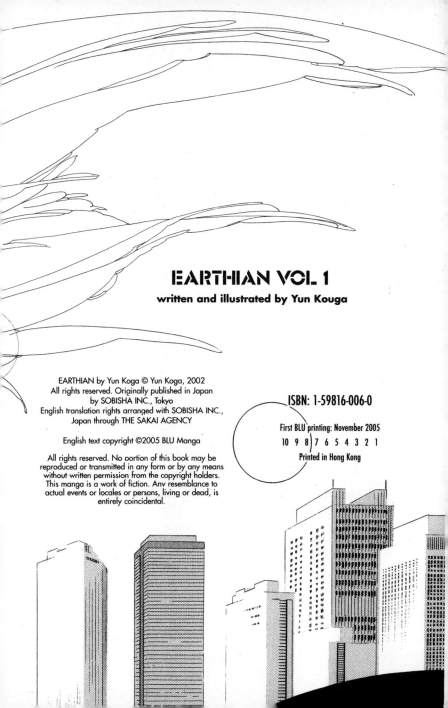

EARTHIAN VOL 1

written and illustrated by Yun Kouga

ISBN: 1-59816-006-0

First BLU printing: November 2005

10 9 8 7 6 5 4 3 2 1

Printed in Hong Kong

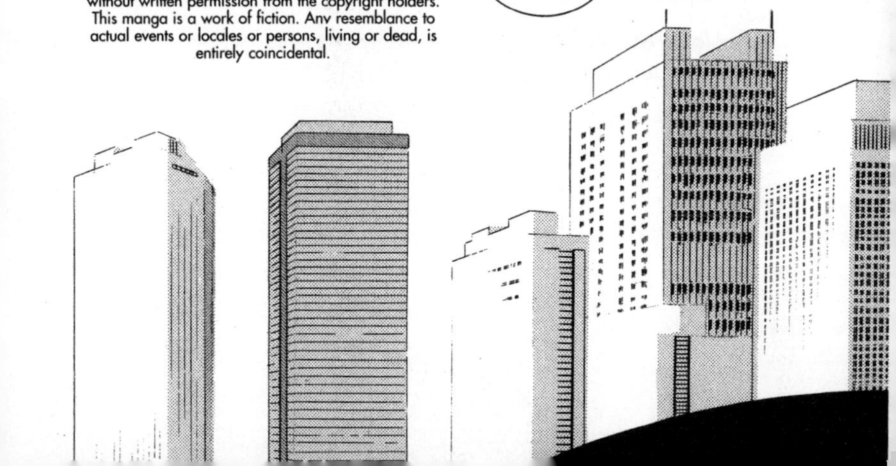

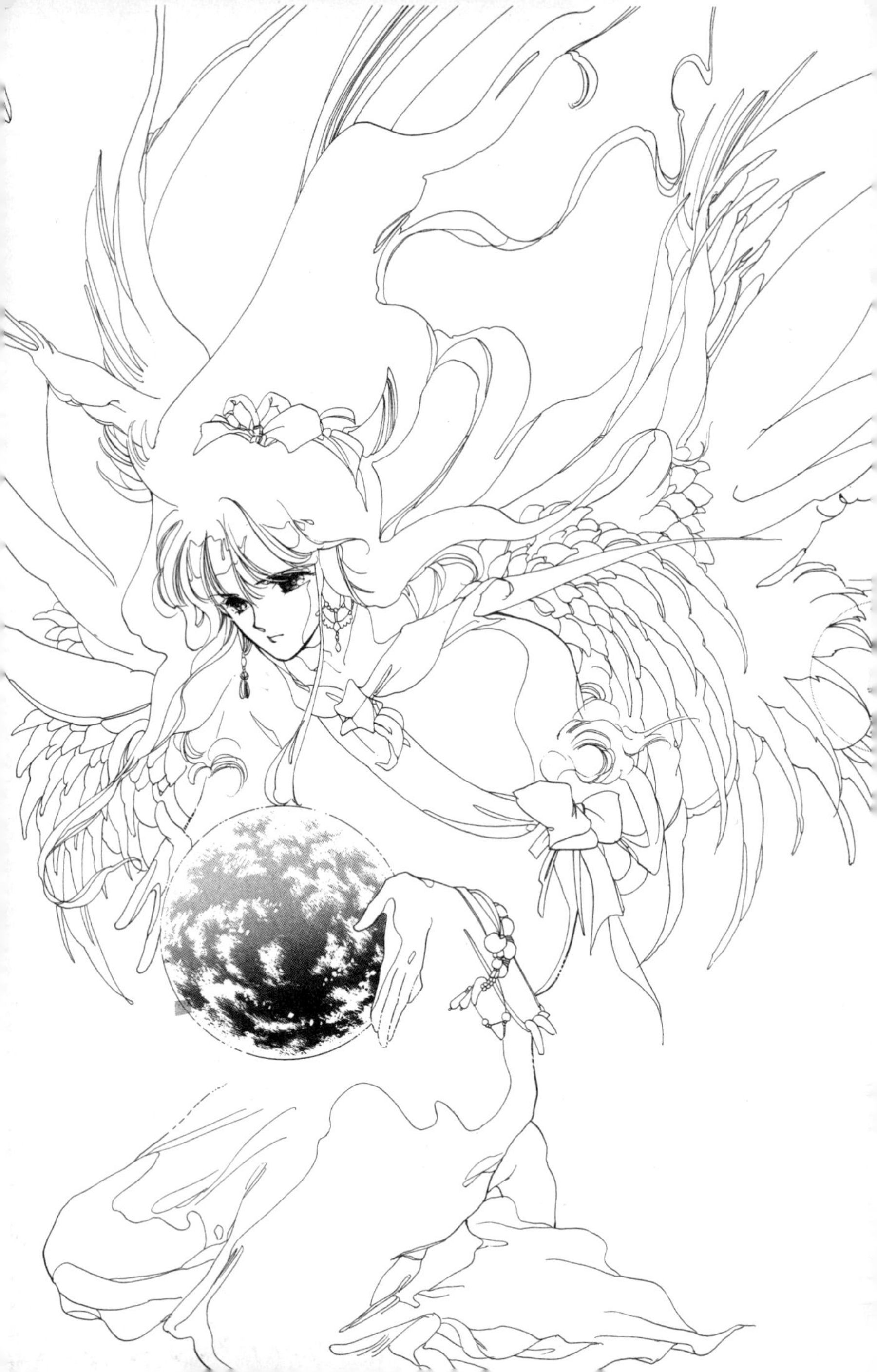

W9-CTQ-019

stop

blu manga are published in the original japanese format

go to the other side and begin reading